O9-CFU-546

658.4   K 3

PASADENA CITY COLLEGE
LIBRARY
PASADENA, CALIFORNIA

ORGANIZATION AND MANAGEMENT

A SYSTEMS APPROACH

McGRAW-HILL SERIES IN MANAGEMENT

KEITH DAVIS, CONSULTING EDITOR

McGRAW-HILL BOOK COMPANY

NEW YORK
ST. LOUIS
SAN FRANCISCO
DÜSSELDORF
JOHANNESBURG
KUALA LUMPUR
LONDON
MEXICO
MONTREAL
NEW DELHI
PANAMA
RIO de JANEIRO
SINGAPORE
SYDNEY
TORONTO

ORGANIZATION AND MANAGEMENT

A SYSTEMS APPROACH

SECOND EDITION

FREMONT E. KAST

JAMES E. ROSENZWEIG

GRADUATE SCHOOL OF BUSINESS ADMINISTRATION
UNIVERSITY OF WASHINGTON

ORGANIZATION AND MANAGEMENT: A SYSTEMS APPROACH

Copyright © 1970, 1974 by McGraw-Hill, Inc. All rights reserved. Printed in the United States of America. No part of this publication may be reproduced, stored in a retrieval system, or transmitted, in any form or by any means, electronic, mechanical, photocopying, recording, or otherwise, without the prior written permission of the publisher.

1 2 3 4 5 6 7 8 9 0 MAMM 7 9 8 7 6 5 4 3

This book was set in Helvetica Light by Rocappi, Inc. The editors were Thomas H. Kothman and Claudia A. Hepburn; the designer was Joseph Gillians; and the production supervisor was Sally Ellyson. The drawings were done by John Cordes, J & R Technical Services, Inc. The printer and binder was The Maple Press Company.

Library of Congress Cataloging in Publication Data

Kast, Fremont Ellsworth, date
Organization and management.

(McGraw-Hill series in management)
Bibliography: p.
1. Organization. 2. Management. I. Rosenzweig,
James Erwin, date   joint author. II. Title.
HD31.K33 1974   658.4   73-13550
ISBN 0-07-033350-5

To our families
and friends

WITHDRAWN

750064

WITHDRAWN

CONTENTS

PREFACE

Man is an activist. He has created and destroyed civilizations. He has developed vast technological complexes. He has utilized natural resources in ingenious ways and in the process he has wreaked havoc with the ecosystem. He has even broken the umbilical cord from mother earth; he has gone to the moon and returned. Future generations may see him go to the planets and beyond. We are all amazed at (and probably failed to fully comprehend) the enormity of modern scientific and technological achievements. But a second thought causes us to recognize a major factor underlying these achievements—man's ability to develop *social organizations* for accomplishing his purposes. The development of these organizations and *effective management* of them is truly one of modern man's greatest achievements.

> It is worth reminding ourselves that management does not really exist. It is a word, an idea. Like science, like government, like engineering, management is an abstraction. But managers exist. And managers are not abstractions; they are men, they are human beings. Particular and special kinds of human beings. Individuals with a special function: to lead and move and bring out the latent capabilities—and dreams—of other human beings. . . . This I believe, and this my whole life's experience has taught me: the managerial life is the broadest, the most demanding, by all odds the most comprehensive and the most subtle of all human activities. And the most crucial.[1]

This book is about organizations and their management. It is an attempt to facilitate understanding of the managerial role in a complex and dynamic organizational society. The environment is obviously multidimensional and turbulent. And the number of variables seems infinite. However, we can identify several related and interdependent trends of importance in the twentieth century: (1) advancement in science and

---

[1] David E. Lilienthal, *Management: A Humanist Art*, Columbia University Press, New York, 1967, p. 18.

technology, (2) development of complex social organizations, and (3) an increase in the degree of education, knowledge, and specialization of human participants in society.

Complex organizations are the primary means for carrying out scientific and technological endeavors. Increasing specialization of knowledge requires organization and, at the same time, makes more effective organization possible. These three trends are paramount in determining the degree of advancement in society. Of particular importance is the educational system which underlies each of the trends identified. Industrial and social advancement in all cultures is based on the educational system, which facilitates knowledge and skill development for human participants.

The most obvious differences between advanced and developing societies appear to be in the physical manifestations of technology. However, there is an increasing awareness that the abilities in organization and management are equally, if not more, important.

Organization theory is an eclectic body of knowledge, reflecting the diversity of the environment and the many internal forces involved. All types of complex systems—businesses, hospitals, schools, public agencies, and military units—reflect the need for knowledgeable and skillful managers.

During the first part of the twentieth century there developed many specific concepts about organizations and many principles of management. These have been modified substantially by recent developments in the behavioral and quantitative sciences. The modern view, and the one which we will utilize throughout this book, is the systems approach. We will view the organization as a subsystem of its environmental suprasystem. It has five primary subsystems: (1) goals and values, (2) technology, (3) structure, (4) psychosocial, and (5) managerial.

Major changes in all fields of science occur with the development of new conceptual schemes or "paradigms." These new paradigms do not just represent a step-by-step advancement in "normal" science (the science generally accepted and practiced) but rather a revolutionary change in the way the scientific field is perceived by the practitioneers. New paradigms frequently are rejected by the scientific community. (At first they may seem crude and limited—offering very little more than older paradigms.) They frequently lack the apparent sophistication of the older paradigms which they ultimately replace. They do not display the clarity and certainty of older paradigms which have been refined through years of research and writing. But, a new paradigm does provide for a "new start" and opens up new directions which were not possible under the old. "We must recognize how very limited in both scope and precision a paradigm can be at the time of its first appearance. Paradigms gain their status because they are more successful than their competitors in solving a few problems that the group of practitioners has come to recognize as acute. To be more successful is not, however, to be either completely successful with a single problem or notably successful with any large number."[2]

---

[2] Thomas S. Kuhn, *The Structure of Scientific Revolutions*, University of Chicago Press, Chicago, 1962, p. 23.

Systems theory does provide a new paradigm for the study of social organizations and their management. At this stage it is obviously crude and lacking in precision. In some ways it may not be much better than older paradigms which have been accepted and used for a long time (such as the management process approach). As ir. other fields of scientific endeavor, the new paradigm must be applied, clarified, elaborated, and made more precise. But, it does provide a fundamentally different view of the reality of social organizations and can serve as the basis for major advancements in our field.

We think the systems approach facilitates understanding the important forces affecting organizations as well as the development of a comprehensive body of knowledge concerning their internal atmosphere and external environment. This body of knowledge provides the foundation for management practice. Our primary concern is helping managers (and potential managers) understand the increasing complexity of their organizational context rather than holding out false hopes of success in terms of simplistic models and how-to-do-it techniques.

In this edition we have tried to use the new systems paradigm more completely. We have revised major sections of the book to more effectively reflect this approach, deleted some of the more traditional materials, and added several new parts and chapters.

In the new Part 3: "Environment, Boundaries, and Goals," we have tried to look more specifically at the ways in which the environmental suprasystem affects the organization. We discuss the nature of the boundaries between organizations and their environment and have dealt more explicitly with goals and values.

We have added a new Part 7: "Comparative Analysis and Contingency Views," which focuses on the systems paradigm as a means to compare and understand organizations. We also show how the systems approach has provided a basic framework for contingency views of organizations and their management—the attempt to understand patterns of relationships and configurations of subsystems.

Organizations are open systems in interaction with their environment and are continually changing. Because of the inevitability of change and the importance of organization renewal via a planned change process, we have included a new chapter, "Organizational Change."

This book is not meant to be the "last word." Rather, we hope that it is an integrated view of organization theory and management practice at a point in time. The field is evolving and dynamic; any book is somewhat out of date before publication.

We wish to thank our students and colleagues in the Department of Management and Organization, University of Washington, who have questioned many of our ideas— lending both support and criticism. In academia, an active, intellectually stimulating environment is essential for research and writing. Our colleagues helped provide this. It is quite likely that many ideas, which we think are original, were first suggested by our professional colleagues. We are particularly indebted to Prof. Richard A. Johnson, who collaborated with us on an earlier book and helped develop many ideas concerning the systems approach. Numerous organizations and managers have provided us with illustrative material. We are particularly grateful to the Boeing Company and to the central administration at the University of Washington.

We appreciate the resources made available by the Graduate School of Business Administration. Excellent typing, clerical, administrative, and artistic support was provided by Nona Pedersen, Margaret Trudo, Sandra Goodman, and Jean Frank.

Fremont E. Kast

James E. Rosenzweig

ORGANIZATION AND MANAGEMENT

A SYSTEMS APPROACH

Wherever I have studied human affairs, I have carefully labored not to mock, lament nor condemn, but only to understand.

Spinoza

Where there is much desire to learn, there of necessity will be much arguing, many opinions; for opinion in good men is but knowledge in the making.

Milton

What "must be done" is usually closely related to what is believed to be the "nature of things"; however, beliefs about "what is" are often disguised assumptions of "what ought to be."

Clyde Kluckhohn

The dissenting opinions of one generation become the prevailing interpretation of the next.

Burton Hendrick

In one way or another, we are forced to deal with complexities, with "wholes" or "systems," in all fields of knowledge. This implies a basic re-orientation in scientific thinking.

Ludwig von Bertalanffy

PART 1

CONCEPTUAL FOUNDATIONS

Part 1 is designed to set the stage for the entire book. It establishes a framework within which the other seven parts can be integrated.

In Chapter 1, the pervasiveness of organization and management is stressed. The eclectic nature of organization theory is emphasized, indicating the role played by various disciplines. Organization theory is described as the foundation for management practice. Key concepts which recur throughout the book are introduced. And, finally, the plan of the book is set forth by parts and chapters.

Chapter 2 traces management values over many centuries. The impact of contemporary cultural or societal values on management thought is emphasized. The evolution of Western culture and value systems has had an important influence on managerial attitudes. Of particular concern are the developments since the industrial revolution and the seemingly accelerating changes in the twentieth century. Contemporary society, with its pluralistic values, provides an exceedingly complex and dynamic setting for organizations and managers.

1
THE SETTING OF
ORGANIZATION AND MANAGEMENT

Man is a social animal with a propensity for organizing and managing his affairs. He does so in an increasingly complex and dynamic environment. Many disciplines are contributing to an eclectic body of knowledge—organization theory—which, coupled with experience, is the foundation for management practice. In this chapter the setting of organization and management will be introduced via the following topics:

Man: A Social Animal
Pervasiveness of Organization and Management
Newness of Relevant Disciplines
Nature of Organization Theory and Management
Increasing Complexity of Organizations
Key Concepts
Outline of Book

MAN: A SOCIAL ANIMAL

Man is a social animal. This statement seems universally acceptable, yet it is deceptively simple. Moreover, it contains a number of implications which are fundamental to the development of an integrated body of knowledge concerning organization and management.

More specifically, man is a biped primate mammal (Homo sapiens) anatomically related to the great apes but distinguished especially by notable development of the brain that provides him with the capacity for articulate speech and abstract reasoning.

Man is an organizing animal. His perceptions are organized into a meaningful whole. This is the universal characteristic of the cognitive, or thinking, process. The term *social* implies that men tend to develop cooperative and interdependent relationships.

Behavior is goal-oriented. Thus it is important to understand the basic objectives of men in society in order to attain a clear understanding of behavior. Two diametrically opposed views of the innate nature of man have been presented throughout history: (1) that man is basically aggressive and competitive (evil) and (2) that man is basically good-natured and cooperative (good). [1] Undoubtedly this polar approach is an oversimplification, but it serves as an example of the diverse frames of reference for studying behavior. As in most such debates, reality lies somewhere in the middle. For example, in discussing the genesis of man Robert Ardrey stresses "the development of a dual code of behavior—amity for the social partner, hostility for the territorial neighbor." [2]

This dual behavior pattern is quite evident in society. Children compete with brothers or sisters for parental attention or specific family resources and yet cooperate in many endeavors. They may cooperate in competition with other neighborhood children, for example. Companies compete in a given industry and yet cooperate in associations for particular purposes, often to compete with other industries or to fight unions or governmental regulation. Individuals compete for a position on an athletic team but cooperate with other team members in competition against opponents. Thus it is apparent that competition and cooperation are both pervasive and fundamental aspects of man's behavior patterns.

Goal-oriented behavior, cognitive processes, cooperation, and conflict are only a few of the fundamental and pertinent issues in the study of man the social animal. These are part of the total system within which man organizes and manages his affairs.

PERVASIVENESS OF ORGANIZATION AND MANAGEMENT

The tendency to organize or cooperate in interdependent relationships is inherent in man's nature. Although conflict within families and clans is evident, the group provides a means of protection and hence survival. Organized activity today ranges on a continuum from informal, ad hoc groups to formal, highly structured organizations. Military activities and religious affairs were among the first to become formally organized. Elaborate systems were developed and by and large have persisted, with modifications, to the present. Business and government are other spheres of activity which have developed formal organizations geared to task accomplishment. Man engages in many voluntary organizations in his leisure time—some recreational, some philanthropic, and some of a crusading nature.

Many different definitions of organization have been set forth by scholars, depending on their background and point of view with respect to what is relevant and/or

---

[1] Henry P. Knowles and Borje O. Saxberg, "Human Relations and the Nature of Man," *Harvard Business Review,* March–April 1967, pp. 22ff.; Robert Ardrey, *African Genesis,* Dale Publishing Company, Inc., New York, 1963; and Alexander Alland, Jr., *The Human Imperative,* Columbia University Press, New York, 1972.
[2] Ardrey, op. cit., p. 19.

important. Certain fundamental or essential elements are apparent in these definitions. As stated previously, behavior is goal-oriented. Therefore it should follow that organization behavior is directed toward objectives which are more or less understood by members of the group. The organization uses knowledge and techniques in the accomplishment of its tasks. Organization implies structuring and integrating activities, that is, people working or cooperating together in interdependent relationships. The notion of interrelatedness suggests a social system. Therefore we can say that *organizations* are: (1) *goal-oriented,* people with a purpose; (2) *psychosocial systems,* people working in groups; (3) *technological systems,* people using knowledge and techniques; and (4) *an integration of structured activities,* people working together.

Although organization implies integration and coordination of individual or subgroup activities, some conflict is inevitable. It may be overt; often it is covert. It may be functional or dysfunctional, depending on whether it leads to effective and/or efficient organization performance. Moreover, short-run ineffectiveness and/or inefficiency may lead to superior results in the long run. Management's task is the integration of diverse—sometimes cooperative, sometimes conflictive—elements into a total organizational endeavor.

Management involves the coordination of human and material resources toward objective accomplishment. We often speak of individuals managing their affairs, but the usual connotation suggests group effort. Four basic elements can be identified: (1) *toward objectives,* (2) *through people,* (3) *via techniques,* and (4) *in an organization.* Typical definitions suggest that management is a process of planning, organizing, and controlling activities. Some increase the number of subprocesses to include assembling resources and motivating; others reduce the scheme to include only planning and implementation. Still others cover the entire process with the concept of decision making, suggesting that decisions are made in establishing objectives, in planning programs or projects to accomplish those objectives, in dividing the work and establishing structural relationships, and in controlling the activity in question. This requires a broad connotation for the decision-making process and is one alternative approach to the study of management.

Management is the primary force within organizations which coordinates the activities of the subsystems and relates them to the environment. The study of management is relatively new in our society, stemming primarily from the growth in size and complexity of business and other large-scale organizations since the industrial revolution.

The emergence of management as an essential, a distinct and a leading institution is a pivotal event in social history. Rarely, if ever, has a new basic institution, a new leading group, emerged as fast as has management since the turn of this century. Rarely in human history has a new institution proven indispensable so quickly; and even less often has a new institution arrived with so little opposition, so little disturbance, so little controversy. . . . Management, which is the organ of society specifically charged with making resources productive, that is, with the responsibility for organized economic advance, therefore reflects the basic spirit of the modern age. It is in fact indispensable—and this explains why, once begotten, it grew so fast and with so little opposition. [3]

Managers are needed to convert the disorganized resources of men, machines, material, money, time, and space into a useful and effective enterprise. Essentially, management is the process whereby these unrelated resources are integrated into a total *system for objective accomplishment*. A manager gets things done by working with people and physical resources in order to accomplish the objectives of the system. He coordinates and integrates the activities and work of others. To accomplish this task, the manager should be analytical while recognizing relationships and the need to synthesize.

A recurring question is the distinction between the terms *management* and *administration*. "Administration" often has had the connotation of governmental or other nonprofit organizations, whereas "management" has been relegated to business enterprises. However, there is considerable overlap in usage. YMCAs have boards of managers, for example. The military has program managers with overall responsibility for mission accomplishment. On the other hand, many colleges of business administration have management departments. We will use the terms interchangeably and tend toward the use of the term management regardless of whether the specific example involves business organizations, hospitals, philanthropic institutions, or government bureaus. On this basis, management is a most pervasive activity. According to Hertz, "the single ubiquitous mind-driven activity of mankind is management." [4] We are all involved in management—of ourselves, of our economic and social activities, and of society as a whole.

Individuals and organizations make adaptive decisions continually in order to remain in a dynamic equilibrium with their environment. Information flow is essential for the decision-making process. It involves knowledge of the past, estimates of the future, and timely feedback concerning current activity. Management's task is implementing this information-decision system to coordinate effort and maintain a dynamic equilibrium.

With organization and management as pervasive as they are and have been for centuries, we might naturally assume a well-defined body of knowledge which provides a framework for research, teaching, and practice. There is a body of knowledge, but it is not particularly well defined, and currently it appears to be evolving rapidly. A number of conditions have hampered the development of a well-defined body of knowledge—particularly the increasing complexity within organizations and the dynamic nature of their environment. This increasing complexity makes the managerial task exceedingly difficult in most instances. Before lamenting the seeming lack of progress in organiza-

---

[3] Peter F. Drucker, *The Practice of Management*, Harper & Row, Publishers, Incorporated, New York, 1954, pp. 3–4.
[4] David B. Hertz, "The Unity of Science and Management," *Management Science*, April 1965, p. B–89.

tion theory, it might be well to consider the state of knowledge in general. Explicit consideration of the relative newness of relevant disciplines can be rather startling.

NEWNESS OF RELEVANT DISCIPLINES

"If the age of the universe is taken as one day, mankind has existed only for the last ten seconds."[5] Human civilization, or the development of man as we tend to think of him, has been in progress for approximately 10,000 years. Anthropologists seem to disagree with regard to the actual point of emergence, with estimates ranging between 200,000 and 1,000,000 years ago. Recorded history, however, relates primarily to the period designated as "human civilization."

For example, Sédillot begins his discussion of the ancient world by considering the civilization of the Nile at approximately 5000 B.C.[6] He prefaces this beginning point with some discussion of prehistoric man and his development as a hunter, herdsman, farmer, and eventually a town dweller. In this historical framework man has developed for approximately 7,000 years. Organizations and management have been important and fundamental elements in society and have been affected by progress on many fronts during this period. Science and technology have received considerable attention throughout the centuries, but even in this regard, the last 300 years have been the most important.

Philosophical considerations, particularly moral and ethical systems, have had an impact on society in general and on organization and management in particular. But the concern of philosophers was seldom focused on practical considerations such as organizing and managing specific endeavors. Scientific disciplines have emerged as separate and distinct bodies of knowledge as man's search for enlightenment has continued. However, the entire social science field, behavioral science in particular, has been relatively slow in developing.[7] Anthropology, sociology, and psychology are products of the last 100 years. Economics and political science emerged somewhat earlier as specific disciplines. Organization theory and/or management practice did not receive concerted attention until the twentieth century.

Within this historical context, a well-developed body of knowledge may be too much to ask of this fledgling discipline. Yet significant strides have been made, and a body of knowledge has been developing which in turn has been useful in managing organizations of diverse characteristics and objectives.

NATURE OF ORGANIZATION THEORY AND MANAGEMENT

What do we mean by the phrase "management and organization theory"? Is it one body of knowledge, a group of interrelated and consistent principles? Or, are there two separate bodies of knowledge—(1) organization theory, and (2) management theory?

---

[5] Victor F. Weisskopf, *Knowledge and Wonder*, Doubleday & Company, Inc., Garden City, N.Y., 1966, p. 56.
[6] René Sédillot, *The History of the World*, Harcourt, Brace & World, Inc., New York, 1951.
[7] Kenneth E. Boulding, *The Impact of the Social Sciences*, Rutgers University Press, New Brunswick, N.J., 1966.

The literature that has developed around these concepts is somewhat ambiguous with regard to these questions. Numerous books or articles can be found with "management theory," "organization theory," or "management and organization theory" in the title. And they tend to treat the same subjects. There may be different emphasis on the various terms or concepts involved. However, there are essential elements or common threads evident throughout the literature.

We think it may be useful to distinguish these concepts in order to provide a useful framework for research, teaching, and practice. We suggest that organization theory is the body of knowledge, including hypotheses and propositions, stemming from a definable field of study which can be termed *organization science*. [8] The study of organizations is an applied science because the resulting knowledge is relevant to problem solving or decision making in ongoing enterprises or institutions. "Describing it thus implies two things: one, that there is a formulated body of method and basic knowledge; two, that there is a special group of problems to which this corpus of methods and knowledge applies with observable results." [9]

Because of the pervasiveness of organizations, the related theory and scientific study are extremely broad-based. It is an eclectic theory, a total system comprised of many subsystems of relevant disciplines such as parts of sociology, psychology, anthropology, economics, political science, philosophy, and mathematics (see Figure 1.1). Not all these above mentioned disciplines are applicable to the same degree; only a small subpart of a particular subject-matter area may be relevant. During the twentieth century, however, society's organizations have received increasing attention, and the study of organizations has evolved as an important, visible, and definable field.

As indicated in Figure 1.1, contributions to organization theory come from many sources. Deductive and inductive research in a variety of disciplines provides a theoretical base of propositions which are useful for understanding organizations and for managing them. Experience gained in management practice is also an important input to organization theory. In short, Figure 1.1 illustrates how the art of management is based on a body of knowledge generated by practical experience *and* scientific research concerning organizations.

Management's task is one of integrating and coordinating organizational resources (men, material, money, time, and space, for example) toward the accomplishment of objectives as effectively and efficiently as possible. The importance of the translation of theory into practice in the real world is emphasized by Storer: "It is the application of scientific knowledge in engineering and other forms of technology that has brought such spectacular changes in the material contexts of our lives over the past century, and it has been the 'popularizers' rather than the scientists themselves who have facilitated the impact of scientific findings upon our basic values and our view of the world." [10]

Organization theory, itself, stems from an applied science which draws upon the

[8] "Organizationology" might be appropiate if the term were less cumbersome.
[9] Marshall A. Robinson, "The Science of Organizations: A Pediatric Note," *Management International Review*, 1966, no. 4, p. 3.
[10] Norman W. Storer, *The Social System of Science*, Holt, Rinehart and Winston, Inc., New York, 1966, p. 1.

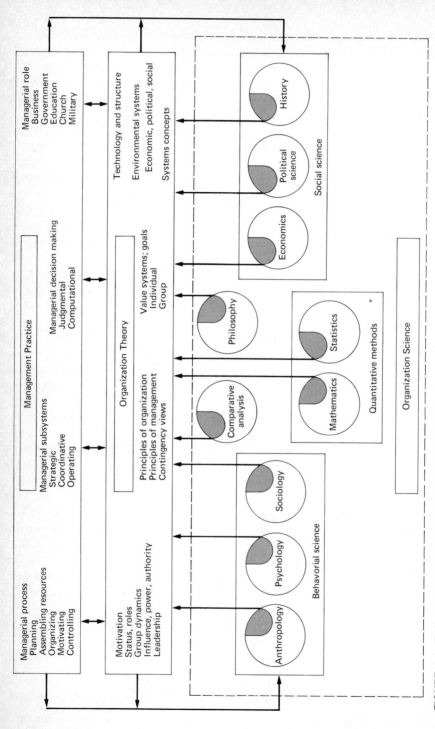

FIGURE 1.1 THE FOUNDATIONS OF ORGANIZATION THEORY AND MANAGEMENT PRACTICE

basic disciplines and their relatively more abstract theories only as they are relevant to organizations found in society. Management technology stems from organization theory and is even more applied in the sense that it focuses on the practice of management in ongoing organizations. With this view of the relationship between organization theory and management in mind, let us turn to a more specific discussion of the requirements of an organization science.

Requirements of an Organization Science

Organization science, like any particular field of study, has subject matter in some specific segment of reality, and in addition, research in the field is carried out in a specific manner which has been designated as "scientific." Thus propositions stemming from work in organization science must (1) be relevant to organizations and (2) possess scientific quality. [11]

The pervasiveness of organizations and management argues for considerable latitude with regard to the organizations studied and the scientific methods used. Moreover, the value systems of researchers, teachers, and practitioners are quite diverse, and hence the determination of relevance and scientific method may vary considerably. On the other hand, the concerted effort toward the development of organization theory during the mid-twentieth century has resulted in useful dialogue, cross-fertilization, and mutual understanding among participants. While no well-defined consensus has yet appeared, there are consistent threads of inquiry and agreement with regard to the general scope of organization theory. Although not exhaustive, Figure 1.1 indicates many of the key concepts and areas of interest.

The scientific quality of propositions is important in establishing the soundness of any body of knowledge. Relevance is not enough. Research must be carried on in a careful, systematic, objective manner in order that the research findings be credible. Inductive research must be carried on in a "public" manner so that resulting theories may be cross-checked and verified via concurrent or subsequent research. The source of deductive conclusions (propositions) must be evaluated in order to ascertain the knowledge and experience of the contributor.

Early management concepts came from practitioners. Texts were often the distillation of experience in ongoing enterprises. Such contributions are important and valuable additions to the body of knowledge comprising organization theory. We need continued observation and conceptualization from astute practicing managers. Meanwhile, scientist-scholars have become more and more involved in research related to organizations but carried on in the context of basic disciplines. Other scholars have been engaged in integrating findings from basic disciplines and translating the results into meaningful concepts or propositions.

Integration of the body of knowledge comes from two directions. Those primarily

---

[11] Paul Hanly Furfey, "Sociological Science and the Problem of Values," in Llewellyn Gross (ed.), *Symposium on Sociological Theory*, Harper & Row, Publishers, Incorporated, New York, 1959, p. 511.

engaged in studying organizations and management have looked toward the basic disciplines for new insight. Simultaneously, those engaged in the work of basic disciplines have become increasingly aware of the pervasiveness of organizations in society and have begun to concentrate attention on relevant problems. Industrial psychology and industrial sociology are two subfields which give evidence of this trend.

Two Kinds of Knowledge

What kind of body of knowledge do we have in mind for organization theory? Adler describes two kinds of knowledge—(1) in the high or strong sense and (2) in the moderate sense. [12] Knowledge in the strong sense lies beyond the challenge of skeptical doubt and is final, that is, beyond the possibility of revision in the course of time. This connotation of knowledge is unrealized so far and probably is an unrealistic ideal for any discipline. Yet philosophers and scientists, for centuries, have sought to establish systems which could meet such criteria. Often, the proponent was "certain" that he had the ultimate system and that "everything" fell neatly into place.

There have been many references to the exact versus the inexact sciences. However, as new findings continue to come in on all fronts in man's search for knowledge, we find that exactness is a relative concept. Some disciplines are relatively more exact than others, and all knowledge developed to date remains open to further refinement. Increasingly, propositions are stated in terms of probabilities, which vary between 0 and 1, depending on the discipline and the particular proposition in question. In short, the concept of knowledge in the high or strong sense can be ruled out for science in general and organization science in particular.

What are the characteristics of knowledge in a more moderate sense? "The properties of knowledge in this moderate sense are that it consists of propositions which are (1) testable by reference to evidence, (2) subject to rational criticism, and either (3) corrigible or rectifiable or (4) falsifiable." [13] This framework is much more amenable to the study of organizations. These properties connote the probabilistic nature of propositions in organization theory. They imply an evolving body of knowledge which is adjusted as new evidence is developed or as new concepts emerge from astute criticism. Refinements are made continually in the theory, and there is always the chance that some propositions may be eliminated altogether if they prove to be false on the basis of new findings. Taken together, these properties indicate that a body of knowledge can be described as "responsible, reliable, well-founded, reasonable opinion." [14]

The term *opinion* is used to emphasize that there is no knowledge in the high sense, that is, the final irrefutable truth. On the contrary, knowledge is opinion based on objective, well-founded inductive and deductive reasoning. Obviously some opinions have better bases than others. There are tentative hypotheses and there are laws.

---

[12] Mortimer J. Adler, *The Conditions of Philosophy*, Dell Publishing Co., Inc., New York, 1965, pp. 21–31.
[13] Ibid., p. 28.
[14] Ibid., p. 29.

Unfortunately the word "opinion" has an everyday or common use which connotes the lack of foundation, even bias or prejudice. Actually, the foundation for opinion can vary along a continuum. Some is well founded; some is not.

An Intellectually Respectable Discipline

It seems to us that organization theory meets the criteria for a body of knowledge in the moderate sense set forth above. If so, the study of organization is apparently a legitimate scientific endeavor. Unfortunately, however, society has often attached a gradation of goodness or legitimacy along the continuum of exactness. Research, teaching, and practice which stem from so-called "exact sciences" have been regarded as relatively more worthwhile endeavors than those based on the less exact sciences. In some cases the question of the newness of relevant disciplines has affected attitudes. Those activities based on new and emerging disciplines have sometimes been considered less worthy as measured by some societal consensus.

The struggle for "a place in the sun" goes on in academic institutions and in society as a whole. The tremendous emphasis on science and engineering in the immediate post-*Sputnik I* era is an indication of the relative merit assigned to occupations by society in general. This trend has been ameliorated somewhat since then; yet the newer, so-called "inexact" or "soft" sciences and their derivative occupations have a continual struggle for relative legitimacy. This problem is of particular import for organization theory and the practice of management.

The study of organizations and their management is an intellectually respectable discipline. Organization theory sets forth propositions which are testable. It is also conducted as a public enterprise with many contributors. Everyone has theories concerning individual and organizational behavior—at least implicit if not explicit. Research and the resulting literature have increased at an accelerating rate and will continue to do so. Research is conducted by scholars from many disciplines; indeed, the same organization is often studied from several points of view. The results are compared at separate points in time, for organizations in various cultures, and for different types of institutions within a given culture. All this activity has made the study of organizations one of the most visible and public enterprises in society.

Organization science has questions of its own which set it apart as a relatively autonomous discipline. That is, it is concerned with questions that other disciplines are not. Obviously many questions cross discipline boundaries with perhaps some variation in emphasis. Some of the topics of particular interest to organization students are:

1 Goals and value systems
2 The use of technology and knowledge in organizations
3 The structuring of organizations
4 The relationship between formal and informal structure
5 Differentiation and integration of activities

    6 Motivation of organizational participants
    7 Group dynamics in organizations
    8 Status and role systems in organizations
    9 Power, authority, and influence in organizations
    10 Managerial processes in organizations
    11 Information-decision systems in organizations
    12 Stability and innovation in organizations
    13 Organizational boundaries and domains
    14 Interface between organizations

In studying organizations time should be devoted to introspection. For those engaged in the field of study (possibly all of the time for some and some of the time for all), some effort should be devoted to thinking about the discipline itself, its growth and evolution. Researchers, teachers, and practitioners should be aware of the body of knowledge that now exists and is developing. In addition, they should be concerned about new directions of inquiry. In other words, what should organization science encompass, and what should be its thrust? These questions provide a framework within which the field of study develops.

There is the danger at times that a scientific discipline may begin to exist for its own sake and emphasize esoteric concepts. It is true that there is a gradation from applied to pure research. However, there is no absolutely "pure" research. In the long run everything is applied; hence, a discipline must keep in touch with the real world. In an evolving body of knowledge such as organization theory, there are many tentative conclusions and propositions. However, the real world cannot wait for the ultimate body of knowledge (there is none!). Practicing managers in business firms, hospitals, and government agencies continue to operate on a day-to-day basis. Therefore, they must use whatever theory is available. Practitioners must be included in the search for new knowledge because they control access to an essential ingredient—organizational data. Mutual understanding among managers, teachers, and researchers will facilitate the development of a relevant body of knowledge.

An Emerging Discipline

Organization theory is relatively new and evolving. Its subject matter is extremely complex and fraught with compounding variables stemming from the nature of man and his intricate relationships with his fellow men. While many give lip service to the interdisciplinary nature of organization science, the satisfactory mingling of the separate disciplines is certainly not an accomplished fact. There is much evidence of integration, yet many difficulties remain. Robinson describes the problem as follows:

> The significant task ahead is that the mix of organizational science, its constituent scientific elements, must now be masterfully and tactfully drawn to-

gether. And this may not be easy. Economists fret and chafe over the weak, unquantifiable sociological variables that spoil the rigor and symmetry of their models. The psychologists are outraged when the subtleties of motivational influences are belittled. Hard core disciplinarians are simply not easily persuaded of the significance of integrating their special knowledge with that of a different scientific specialist, however much they may grumble about the need for improvement in the other's field. Consequently, one of the essential steps that must be followed in the recipe for our new organization science is coaxing the necessary ingredients to blend wholesomely with one another. Without this process, even the right ingredients will not produce the desired outcome. One will dominate the others, and the flavor of some will be lost altogether. [15]

This is an exciting challenge. Development of a body of knowledge and a scientific discipline relevant to organizations is an extremely important endeavor in the overall societal system. Providing the scientific basis for management technology involves us in man's most pervasive activity. Man is a social animal who tends to organize. He manages organizational activity toward objective accomplishment. The astute development of organization theory can have a tremendous impact on society. Because of the pervasiveness and importance of organizations, even slight improvements in effectiveness and efficiency can have far-reaching consequences.

INCREASING COMPLEXITY OF ORGANIZATIONS

Organizations have become increasingly complex over time. The trend begins with the evolution of organisms, of which man is the most complex example.

There is a characteristic trend in this development—the units are bound to become more and more complicated. They lose the simple features they had at the beginning of life's history. Most changes are steps toward higher differentiation, toward change of nucleic acids which produce more proteins with more specialized tasks. Hence from the moment when units exist that can form replicas of themselves, a development toward more and more complicated units is bound to start. Better adaptation to external conditions leads almost always to more complicated units. [16]

Haskins describes this phenomenon by saying: "Paleontological research has yielded dramatic evidence that in the evolutionary development of living matter there has been an unmistakable broad trend from the simple to the complex. Both the variety of life on

---

[15] Robinson, op. cit., p. 5.
[16] Weisskopf, op. cit., p. 251.

earth and the intricacy of its organization reflect and emphasize this trend." [17] The essential element in this trend is that of specialization. It allows organisms a means of dividing up the work in performing each subpart more effectively and efficiently. However, specialization requires integration of activities in pursuit of identified goals. It is a process of analysis and synthesis; that is, it breaks up the task into parts according to specialized activities and integrates those activities toward objective accomplishment. The tendency to integrate is a ''companion feature'' of specialization. Haskins states: ''What may be called a drive to integration is another great feature of the social continent which deeply affects organic and social evolution. It is the tendency both of organisms and of certain kinds of societies, evolving under the pressure of natural selection, to become more and more close-knit entities, and of their parts to become increasingly specialized and dependent upon the whole.'' [18]

These same trends are evident in organizations. More specialization requires increasingly sophisticated methods of coordination and integration. Tendencies toward both cooperation and conflict are evident among organizational participants. The question of individualism versus conformism is relevant and important. In short, many forces are at work in organizations—some divisive, some cohesive, all somewhat confounding. These factors have led to increasing complexity within organizations and hence have made the job of management more and more difficult.

Size of Organizations

For small face-to-face groups in a rather stable environment, the job of management is relatively straightforward. Once a particular approach is found effective, it can be applied indefinitely with likely success. As groups grow in size, face-to-face relationships become impossible; the number of interrelationships among organizational participants increases dramatically; and managers cannot hope to maintain personal contact throughout the organization.

Trends toward increased organizational size are not likely to taper off. The population continues to grow. Thus sheer numbers of people will provide a complex environment for society and its subunits. Boulding suggests, for example, ''At present rates of population expansion, it will take only a little over 300 years for the whole land area of the world to become a single city. It takes only 700 or 800 years before we have standing room only over the whole face of the planet.'' [19] The trend from a sparse, rural population to urban concentrations has been in effect for many centuries. Crises of many kinds—housing, crime, transit, air pollution—are evident in large metropolitan areas. What if the earth were one giant megalopolis? While the 700- to 800-year time span involved may seem unimportant to us today, it is certainly an extremely short

[17] Caryl P. Haskins, *Of Societies and Men,* The Viking Press, Inc., New York, 1960, p. 15.
[18] Ibid., p. 30.
[19] Kenneth E. Boulding, *The Meaning of the 20th Century,* Harper & Row, Publishers, Incorporated, New York, 1965, pp. 124–125.

period of time compared to the history of mankind. It indicates the accelerating nature of environmental developments which pose organizational and managerial problems.

Science and Technology

Another development which evidences an accelerating trend is that of scientific knowledge and its implication for society in the form of technological developments. Again, we might gain perspective by referring to developments throughout the evolution of mankind. If man's time on earth is taken as 240,000 years and if we imagine that those years take place in one hour, he spent fifty-five minutes of that time in Paleolithic (Old Stone Age) culture.

> Five minutes ago, he embarked upon the neolithic culture, the cultivation of plants, the domestication of animals, the making of pottery, weaving, and the use of the bow and arrow; 3½ minutes ago he began the working of copper; 2½ minutes ago he began to mold bronze; 2 minutes ago he learned to smelt iron; ¼ of a minute ago he learned printing; 5 seconds ago the Industrial Revolution began; 3⅓ seconds ago he learned to apply electricity; and the time he has had the automobile is less than the interval between the ticks of a watch, i.e., less than one second. [20]

With the industrial revolution representing only five seconds of an imaginary hourglass, the accelerating nature of technology is apparent. And concerted effort toward organization theory and principles of management is a post-industrial revolution phenomenon. Think of the developments since the automobile was introduced—"less than one second ago." Television, jet airplane travel, birth control pills, and space exploration are examples of science and technology proceeding at an accelerating pace. One recalls the phrase, "If it works it is obsolete."

Developments in science and technology have magnified trends toward specialization. Scientists, researchers, technicians, and other "knowledge workers" are becoming increasingly prevalent in organizations. Integration of their efforts toward organizational accomplishment can be difficult. There may be differences in value systems between scientists and managers. The former may be concerned with the effectiveness of a product or process (i.e., striving for perfection), while the manager may be more interested in efficiency (i.e., cost as related to effectiveness).

Scientific and technological progress have proceeded and are proceeding on a variety of fronts, thus adding to the complexity. Automated information processes are being developed along with automated production processes. Advances in both areas have definite impacts on organizations and hence are important managerial considerations.

---

[20] Wilson D. Wallis, as cited in Charles R. Walker, *Modern Technology and Civilization*, McGraw-Hill Book Company, New York, 1962, p. 10.

Other Considerations

Science and technology are only a part of the picture. The general increase in the education of participants provides a more sophisticated atmosphere in organizations. People are becoming less tractable and more prone to "think for themselves." This trend is also accelerating and provides another confounding variable for management.

An increasing governmental role is another consideration. Organizations must keep tuned to governmental propensities for regulatory action in many areas of interest. The most obvious are economic and defense matters, but the spectrum of influence widens over time. Trends in all the areas of governmental concern—federal, state, and local—provide meaningful background for managerial decision making in organizations.

Findings in the behavioral science disciplines—anthropology, psychology, and sociology—are also coming forth at increasing rates. Although not very old as scientific disciplines go, developments in these areas have been rapid and are accelerating. More and more attention is being devoted to cultural anthropology, industrial psychology, and industrial sociology—topics which are of particular concern to organization theory and management. At this stage there is no clear-cut, well-defined body of knowledge or set of propositions to guide managerial behavior. However, concepts are evolving, and progress is being made. But managers must practice their art while the knowledge underlying it is still developing. This is analogous to the physician who continues to practice while research and development continues in medicine.

Coupled with developments in the sciences (natural, social, and behavioral) is progress in the philosophy of management. In a sense all of us are philosophers because we hold views concerning what *is* or happens in the world as well as what men *ought* to do or seek. Some development can proceed prescriptively via common sense, experience, and reflection. It is more likely, however, that a combination of the experiential approach and inputs from scientific research will round out an individual's philosophy of management.

Acceleration of Confounding Variables

"The hallmark of public administration in this decade is change—swift, incessant, fundamental change."[21] The only thing constant is change. The dynamic interplay of forces in the environment of organizations is evident. Similarly, within organizations the atmosphere is becoming much more complex from the point of view of management. Thus it becomes increasingly important to understand the trends and developments taking place. The pace of change is likely to increase. Therefore managers must better understand the behavior of individuals and organizations in order to be able to predict and ultimately coordinate effort toward objectives. The aim of this book is to contribute to this understanding.

---

[21] Brochure describing the focus of the American Society for Public Administration's 1967 National Conference.

KEY CONCEPTS

One approach to solving complex problems is to assume away much of the complexity and then solve a much simpler problem. Theoretically the interim step provides insight into how the more complex problem might be solved. Many introductory texts treat problem solving in this way. However, unless students pursue the subject in later courses, they are left with an oversimplified view of the real world, one which may be more dysfunctional than functional. "A little knowledge is a dangerous thing." We hope to avoid that problem in this book.

Our general purpose will be to understand the increasingly complex nature of organizations in a dynamic environment and the attendant difficult problem-solving task of managers. We may use abstractions and models from time to time but in all cases hope to link them adequately to the real world. Our primary purpose is to recognize and understand the dynamic complexity rather than to simplify the real world in order to develop straightforward cookbook approaches.

Eclectic Approach

Organization theory is eclectic in nature. That is, many disciplines provide bits and pieces which go to make up the total body of knowledge. Its researchers and teachers are distillers and translators of knowledge from basic disciplines. There is a need to integrate the findings from industrial engineering, mathematics, the social sciences, and the behavioral sciences. This process can lead to conceptual developments which provide useful frames of reference for additional research, teaching, and practice.

We are interested in both descriptive findings and normative considerations. There is a great need for empirical research concerning organizations and management. At times there seems to be a tendency in the behavioral sciences toward conducting experimental research in unrealistic settings as a way of emulating the physical sciences. It might be more useful to emulate the zoologists and biologists, whose observation of what *is and happens* in the real world has occupied a considerable amount of time and attention. There is a need to understand clearly how individuals and organizations behave in a variety of circumstances. Once we have a more complete understanding of what *is,* we can begin to consider normative propositions of what managers *ought to do or seek.* Such an approach facilitates the development of conceptual schemes which will provide useful frames of reference for managers in organizations.

Comparative Approach

We are concerned in this book with a wide variety of organizations or institutions and are interested in those propositions which have broad applicability—in business, governmental, medical, educational, religious, military, philanthropic, voluntary, and other types of organizations. Also of interest is diversity, not only in type of institution but in size as well. For the most part, organization theory and management principles have been developed within the context of large organizations. Consideration will be given to the applicability of findings to small- and medium-sized organizations as well.

Although we have not emphasized it to the same degree as institutional comparisons, we will be interested in management and organization theory as it applies across cultures. What findings hold in Japan as well as in the United States or Great Britain? Indeed, are there differences between findings in New Orleans and Seattle? Unless otherwise stated, the material presented will refer primarily to developments in the United States, since (1) most of the research has been carried out in this environment and (2) this is the scope of our familiarity.

Systems Approach

A *system* is an *organized, unitary whole composed of two or more interdependent parts, components, or subsystems and delineated by identifiable boundaries from its environmental suprasystem.* Systems theory provides one major conceptual scheme of significance to organization theory and management: an approach to analysis and synthesis in a complex and dynamic environment. It considers interrelationships among subsystems as well as interactions between the system and its suprasystem, and also provides a means of understanding synergistic aspects. [22] This conceptual scheme allows us to consider organizations—individuals, small-group dynamics, and large-group phenomena—all within the constraints of an external environmental system. In this context we define an organization as:

1 A *subsystem of its broader environment,* and
2 *Goal-oriented*—people with a purpose; including
3 A *technical subsystem*—people using knowledge, techniques, equipment, and facilities;
4 A *structural subsystem*—people working together on integrated activities;
5 A *psychosocial subsystem*—people in social relationships; and coordinated by
6 A *managerial subsystem*—planning and controlling the overall endeavor.

This conceptual model provides the framework for the book. The supra- and subsystems identified will be discussed in detail as a means of understanding organizations and their management.

Contingency View

Throughout the book we will stress the relationship of organization theory and management practice in specific situations. The contingency view depends on a body of knowledge and research endeavors that focus on interrelationships among key vari-

---

[22] Synergy: The whole is greater than (or at least different from) the sum of its parts.

ables and subsystems in organizations. It also emphasizes the role of the manager as a diagnostician, pragmatist, and artist. In terms of the model set forth above we can say that:

> The contingency view of organizations and their management suggests that an organization is a system composed of subsystems and delineated by identifiable boundaries from its environmental suprasystem. The contingency view seeks to understand the interrelationships within and among subsystems as well as between the organization and its environment and to define patterns of relationships or configurations of variables. It emphasizes the multivariate nature of organizations and attempts to understand how organizations operate under varying conditions and in specific circumstances. Contingency views are ultimately directed toward suggesting organizational designs and managerial actions most appropriate for specific situations. [23]

The essence of this view is that there is *no one best way* and that there is a middle ground between "universal principles" and "it all depends." This approach recognizes the complexity involved in managing modern organizations but uses patterns of relationships and/or configurations of subsystems in order to facilitate improved practice.

Structure and Process

Another thread in the book will be the comparison and contrast of structure and process. Much attention in organization theory has been devoted to structural aspects—specialization, hierarchy, span of control, and other similar concepts. These are important considerations in the study of organizations. At the same time, it is necessary to consider organizational processes—how goals are established, how means are developed to accomplish them, and how the system is measured in order to control progress toward objectives. An integral part of this approach is understanding decision-making processes at all levels in the organization. What sort of decisions do individual members make? How do managers make decisions in structuring organizations and in guiding organizational processes toward objectives?

Effectiveness and Efficiency

Another important conceptual theme throughout the study of organization and management is that of effectiveness versus efficiency. In all organizations the question of effectiveness is paramount. Does the organization accomplish or approach the goal established? In business firms, measuring the degree of achievement is possible and

---

[23] Fremont E. Kast and James E. Rosenzweig, *Contingency Views of Organization and Management*, Science Research Associates, Inc., Palo Alto, Calif., 1973, p. ix.

sometimes straightforward, but in other types of organizations it is not so obvious. An even more difficult problem is measuring efficiency. Even if the system is effective, we are concerned with the most efficient use of human and material resources. For business organizations an absolute measure is survival. But there may be considerable variation in efficiency among surviving firms. In governmental and other similar institutions efficient use of resources within budgetary constraints is a valid consideration for management. Thus our treatment of organization and management will be concerned with criteria of both effectiveness and efficiency.

OUTLINE OF BOOK

Part 1 presents conceptual foundations for studying organization and management. In this chapter we have emphasized the pervasiveness of organization and management, shown the relationship of management practice to organization theory, indicated the newness and evolving nature of organization science, and stressed its increasingly complex and dynamic environment. Chapter 2 is concerned with the evolution of value systems over time and with their impact upon management thinking. This is a key step in the development of later materials because value systems and ideologies provide a basis for the development of management and organization concepts.

Part 2 traces the evolution of organization theory and management practice with particular reference to the twentieth century. The traditional concepts involved in scientific management, bureaucracy, and administrative management are set forth. The behavioral and management science contributions are then discussed, and their impact upon the evolving theory is evaluated. In Chapter 5, systems concepts are presented as a framework for modern theory, stressing the usefulness of this approach in the study of complex organizations. This chapter sets forth the view of the organization as an open system interacting with its environment and then establishes the primary subsystems of the organizations as goals and values, technical, structural, psychosocial, and managerial. This provides a framework for the remainder of the book.

Part 3 includes coverage of the environmental suprasystem of organizations—both general and specific. The concept of boundaries delineating organizations is important because it helps focus analysis on reasonably well-defined systems. The subject of organizational goal setting (in an environmental context) is also covered in Part 3.

Part 4 looks at the technical and structural subsystems. The impact of rapidly changing technology upon modern organizations is discussed, and the relationship of the technical system to the other subsystems is evaluated. The ways in which the organization establishes a formal structuring of relationships in order to accomplish its purposes are then discussed.

Part 5 is concerned with the psychosocial systems within the organization. Attention is given to individual behavior in organizations and to the various influences affecting motivation. Status and role systems are presented as inevitable phenomena in social groups. The discussion then turns to group dynamics and its role in organization improvement. The concept of an influence system is set forth and related to power and authority. Finally, the impact of leadership styles on the psychosocial system is discussed.

Part 6 considers the managerial system within complex organizations with emphasis upon decision making as the most pervasive activity. Information-decision systems are discussed in terms of their role in the planning and control functions. As a background for considering decision-making processes and specific management tasks, the concept of open and closed systems is explored in detail. Typical management science techniques are discussed in terms of their usefulness in relatively closed systems and computational decision making. Behavioral aspects of decision making (value and ethical considerations, for example) are considered as they relate to open-system models of organizations. The functions of planning and control are viewed as means for coordinating organizational activities.

In Part 7 we reemphasize systems concepts, highlight contingency views of organization theory and management practice, and set forth a model for comparative analysis across institutions and cultures. The framework provides the means to analyze two of society's basic organizations—the hospital and the university.

Part 8 includes a consideration of organization change and renewal, emphasizing the delicate and necessary balance between stability/continuity and adaptation/innovation. Organization and management in the future are previewed in Chapter 23. With the eclectic nature of organization theory in mind, we set forth some notions about trends and developments in organizations and the role of management in the future.

QUESTIONS AND PROBLEMS

1 Define organization. Why are organizations so pervasive?
2 Define management. Do you agree that management is the "single ubiquitous mind-driven activity of mankind"? Why or why not?
3 Illustrate the continuum of organizations ranging from small, informal groups to large, complex institutions (such as General Motors, a university, or a large hospital). What common characteristics can you cite?
4 Compare and contrast organization science, organization theory, and management practice.
5 Is management an art or a science? Why?
6 Discuss (a) the eclectic nature of organization theory and (b) the relative newness of some of the relevant underlying disciplines.
7 Screen current periodicals in the behavioral and social sciences (such as *American Sociological Review, American Economic Review, Journal of Personality and Social Psychology,* and *American Behavioral Scientist*), and list the various articles which relate to organization theory and management practice.
8 How does the study of organizations measure up as a scientific endeavor?
  a What criteria can be used?
  b What is your evaluation of progress to date?
  c What is your prognosis for the future?
9 Discuss the tentativeness of knowledge about organizations.

10 What basic trends have led to increasing complexity within organizations as well as in their external environment? What impact does this increasing complexity have on organization theory and management practice?

11 Consider a particular organizational type, such as a business corporation, university, or hospital, and discuss the forces which have led to greater internal and environmental complexity for that institution.

PERSPECTIVES ON
MANAGEMENT VALUES

The modern manager operates in a dynamic system with rapidly changing technologies and in an increasingly complex environment. The development of organization theory and management practice is strongly influenced by these forces. Concepts and actions are affected by value systems determined not only from within the organization but by the sociocultural norms of the broader society as well. It is necessary to understand the evolution of values in order to comprehend some of the underlying forces which have affected the development of management thought. This chapter considers the influences of sociocultural values on managerial concepts and practices, beginning with a brief discussion of the historical evolution of the capitalistic ethic and the transformation to modern industrialism. Closely related to values is the question of professionalism of management. The following topics provide the framework for the chapter:

> Influence of Sociocultural Values
> Evolutionary Nature of Values
> Historical Evolution of Capitalistic Ethic
> Transformation of Capitalistic Ethic
> Current Business Ideologies
> Professionalization of Management
> Social Control over Business Activity
> Influence of Changing Values on Management Concepts

INFLUENCE OF SOCIOCULTURAL VALUES

The organization can be thought of as a subsystem of the broader sociocultural environment in which it operates . "It seemed appropriate to define an organization as a social system which is organized for the attainment of a particular type of goal; the attainment of that goal is at the same time the performance of a type of function on behalf of a more inclusive system, the society." [1] The ideologies of the business enterprise are therefore strongly influenced by the norms and values of the broader society. [2] In this sense the values of the organization legitimatize its existence and activities in the broader social system. Our fundamental thesis is that values are a primary basis for guiding decision making and other actions and therefore set the basic framework for the development of organization theory and management practice.

Values and ideologies are closely related. "We conceive of values as normative propositions, held by individual human beings of what human beings *ought* to desire, e.g., the desirable. They are supported by internalized sanctions and functions as (a) imperatives in judging how one's social world ought to be structured and operated, and (b) standards for evaluating and rationalizing the propriety of individual and social choices." [3] This approach emphasizes that values are normative standards by which human beings are influenced in their choice of actions. The primary function of values in terms of managerial behavior is that they serve as determinants and guidelines for decision making and action.

Ideologies are "the aggregate of the ideas, beliefs, and modes of thinking characteristic of a group, such as a nation, class, caste, profession or occupation, religious sect, political party, etc. These ideologies are conditioned and determined by the geographical and climatic situation, habitual activities, and cultural environment of their respective groups. They are not necessarily mutually exclusive and may overlap." [4] These definitions suggest that values are individually held and that ideologies emphasize group ideas, beliefs, and modes of thinking; however, we will use them interchangeably to represent both individual and group beliefs.

Ideologies and values set the social role which individuals fulfill in their society. According to the concept of "role theory" the individual attempts to operate within the expectations of the broader social group and also internalizes the values and norms which the group explicitly or implicitly prescribes for him. Thus the role prescribed for the manager is reinforced by his own internal motivation to fulfill it effectively. His role in contemporary society has evolved substantially from that prescribed earlier under traditional capitalism.

We should not look at the issue of values as a one-way street. While the broad sociocultural system does influence the values of the manager, business organizations also have affected social norms. Ours has been characterized as a "business society" in which the ideology of the large corporate enterprise sets the dominant theme for the

---

[1] Talcott Parsons, "Suggestions for a Sociological Approach to the Theory of Organizations—II," *Administrative Science Quarterly*, September 1956, p. 238.

[2] Parsons emphasizes this point. "The main point of reference for analyzing the structure of any social system is its value pattern. This defines the basic orientation of the system (in the present case, the organization) to the situation in which it operates; hence it guides the activities of participant individuals." Talcott Parsons, "Suggestions for a Sociological Approach to the Theory of Organizations—I," *Administrative Science Quarterly*, June 1956, p. 67.

[3] Philip E. Jacob and James J. Flink, with the collaboration of Hedvah L. Shuchman, "Values and Their Function in Decision-Making," Supplement no. 9 to *The American Behavioral Scientist*, May 1962, p. 22.

[4] H. P. Fairchild (ed.), *Dictionary of Sociology*, Philosophical Library, Inc., New York, 1944, p. 149.

total system. The beliefs of businessmen have always exerted a strong influence in the United States. Some suggest that this influence is even stronger today than in the past. The modern business organization is the primary mechanism for the transformation of accelerating technology into products and services. Furthermore, it is a dominant force in receiving inputs from the environment, in the transformation of these inputs, and in the distribution of output back to society. In performing this role, it has a major influence.

There is a dynamic interplay between the organization and society. For example, the business firm is a subunit of the economic system, and its operations depend upon its role in the overall system. "Society makes use of the business firm as an instrument. This is only another way of stating that private operations are public assets, to be used in accordance with social goals. Their privacy is protected only because it derives from the culture's value set and is looked on as itself contributing to social ends."[5] In response to meeting these social goals, the firm in a private enterprise system is granted substantial autonomy in carrying out its functions. It has substantial latitude in utilizing the resources in its environment to accomplish its own goals. "Its high degree of autonomy permits it to treat society itself—the system of which it is a part—as a field of exploitation for its own ends."[6] This same characteristic is true of other organizations such as hospitals and school systems. They utilize resources provided by the environment and are granted a degree of autonomy to accomplish their goals, but they are constrained by the requirement of meeting the needs of the broader societal system.

EVOLUTIONARY NATURE OF VALUES

The social ethic evolves over time and with changing circumstances. Business values also are subject to evolutionary changes. It is important to recognize these transformations. However, it is equally important to realize that in modern society many different value subsystems have become intertwined.

> We have reached a stage in our civilization where many different strands of ethical tradition have been woven together. Imbedded in the culture which conditions us and our relationships, and imbedded also in us as civilized, educated persons, are several distinctive ethical patterns. These sets of moral attitudes are contradictory enough to be competitive—both in their institutional forms and in their personal aspects. Instead of having an impossible ideal confronting a practical necessity, we have such a diverse inheritance of ethical ways that no matter which one we choose, the others are, at least to some degree, betrayed."[7]

---

[5] Neil W. Chamberlain, *Enterprise and Environment: The Firm in Time and Place*, McGraw-Hill Book Company, New York, 1968, p. 139.

[6] Ibid., p. 141.

[7] Samuel H. Miller, "The Tangle of Ethics," *Harvard Business Review*, January–February 1960, p. 59. He suggests that a few strands of this complex ethical system are: (1) The Hebraic culture, based on the Ten Commandments, with emphasis on the group in total "covenant." (2) The Christian system, based on the Beatitudes, with emphasis on redemption of the individual born into the Kingdom. (3) The medieval way of life, based on penance, with emphasis on the future life. (4) The Renaissance culture, based on the individual and his freedom. (5) The industrial revolution, based on the technical application of science to production and distribution. (6) The scientific approach, based on the empirical method and the reign of law.

Values, viewed in this way, often provide contradictory and unclear guidelines for managerial behavior. Consider the problem of the automobile manufacturers in the establishment of safety features for their products. One system of ethics would suggest that the manufacturer has a direct social responsibility to ensure that his automobile be as safe as possible. Another would suggest that he has a responsibility to provide the customer with what is demanded in terms of the market factors only. Adhering to one set of values could contradict the other.

Thus, our ethical heritages will often result in a conflicting basis for practical decision making by the business manager. How did modern society develop such complexity in its value systems? In the next sections we will look at the historical evolution of the classical capitalistic ethic and its transformation to contemporary capitalism with specific references to the current problems of responsibility.

HISTORICAL EVOLUTION OF CAPITALISTIC ETHIC

The capitalistic ideology has not been the norm or standard ethic throughout Western history. In fact, for much of recorded history this ideology was unacceptable. Yet exchange and commercial activities are as old as the recorded history of mankind. The books of the Old Testament, for example, are filled with examples of commercial activities and with laws and regulations for their governance. Archaeologists have discovered many artifacts which indicate commercial activities that were often subject to rather elaborate and sophisticated rules and codes of ethics. For example, the Code of Hammurabi, approximately 2000 B.C., was set forth by the Babylonian ruler and provided guidelines for merchants and peddlers. [8]

Commerce in ancient Greece flourished in spite of the ideal of self-sufficiency with emphasis upon an economic base of agriculture and animal husbandry which provided ideological constraints against commercial activities. The Greek philosophers generally looked down upon commercial activities as necessary but distasteful. The Roman view regarding commercial activities was patterned after the Grecian ideology and thus was tolerant of commerce and trade but relegated these activities to a low calling. Although the Roman aristocracy entered into agreements with business in return for the provision of money for more noble conquests, there was a general and persistent mistrust of the merchant. Thus both Grecian and Roman ideology shared a disdain for businessmen but were pragmatic enough to recognize that these activities were necessary in order to accomplish the broader purposes of the empires.

The Medieval Period

The medieval age has been characterized as a period of stagnation and lack of economic and social development. It was dominated by the two primary social organizations of the time, the feudal system and the Catholic Church. The feudal system with its

---

[8] Edward C. Bursk, Donald T. Clark, and Ralph W. Hidy, "The Oldest Business Code: Nearly 4000 Years Ago," *The World of Business*, vol. I, Simon and Schuster, Inc., New York, 1962, pp. 9–10.

closed structure and specific definition of role for the lord and for the peasant-serf dominated the economic life of Western Europe. The church provided the ideology and set forth the value system for the whole society. The primary concern of all was the salvation of the soul. The religious concept suggested that man was only on earth for a brief period of time in which he must prepare himself for eternity and salvation. The church was the dominant institution which prevailed over the feudal community and national boundaries. Its influence was great in all areas of human activity.

In the early phases of the Middle Ages, in particular, the dominant church ideology held business and commercial activities in disdain and set forth strict rules and limitations. Usury was a sin, and trade itself was of dubious purity. Church doctrine reflected a hostility toward the businessman and commercial activity. However, there was an important transition in church views of business activities during the latter part of the medieval period, coincident with growing commercialism. The Italian city-states had a resurgence of trade within the Mediterranean area. There was growing commerce between local communities and an increase in the number of craftsmen under the guild system. The modification of the church views regarding commercial activities is seen in the pronouncements of St. Thomas Aquinas in the middle of the thirteenth century. Although he continued to hold that trade was degrading and a necessary evil, he saw that the growing commercialism of the time did have a social role. He set forth the concept of a just price and rationalized profit margins acquired in the process of trade as a wage for the labor of the trader. His view that there was a just price which might be determined by the market was a major concession to the merchants' activities. Although there continued to be constraints against usury, the church relaxed prohibitions against interest charges.

In spite of these relaxations in church regulations concerning business activities, the dominant view during the medieval period was that trade and commerce were tolerated as necessary evils. Many business practices were not within the realm of the accepted ethic. Tawney describes the medieval period and its view of business activities as follows:

> At every turn, therefore, there are limits, restrictions, warnings against allowing economic interests to interfere with serious affairs. It is right for man to seek such wealth as is necessary for a livelihood in his station. To seek more is not enterprise, but avarice, and avarice is a deadly sin. Trade is legitimate; the different resources of different countries show that it was intended by Providence. But it is a dangerous business. A man must be sure that he carries it on for the public benefit, and that the profits which he takes are no more than the wages of his labor. Private property is a necessary institution, at least in a fallen world; men work more and dispute less when goods are private than when they are common. But it is to be tolerated as a concession to human frailty, not applauded as desirable in itself. [9]

---

[9] R. H. Tawney, *Religion and the Rise of Capitalism,* Mentor Books, New American Library of World Literature, New York, 1954, p. 35.

This negative view of business which predominated during the medieval times still persists in many present-day cultures and among certain groups in the United States. It remains a part of modern ideology about business.

Rise of Capitalistic Ethic

It should be emphasized that the capitalistic creed did not appear suddenly in full bloom in Western society. Rather, it developed as an evolutionary process which had its roots in the changing views of the church regarding commercial activities during the latter part of the Middle Ages. By the beginning of the sixteenth century, many of the constraints of the medieval period were being broken down. The urbanization of the population and the development of communities and nations stimulated the growth of commerce and trade. The growing overseas trade of such nations as England, France, Holland, Portugal, and Spain further stimulated commercial activities.

A number of historians consider the changes in religious values and attitudes as an important basis for the development of the capitalistic ethic. Several consider Judaism as the primary force in the development of the capitalistic system. Sombart, for example, suggests that the Jewish religion did not invoke the same restrictions against commerce and the accumulation of wealth that were evident in the Christian faith. The Jews in Europe were restrained from owning land and from participating in many other activities and therefore turned to trade and commerce as alternatives. The basic Judaic values of self-control, hard work, sobriety, thrift, and abidance by religious laws and teachings were conducive to economic development and were compatible with the growing capitalism.

> Jewish ethics required a place apart, so far as their influence on the modern spirit goes, for yet another reason. They received form and shape at a time when Christianity moved in such different channels. While Christianity was yet held in bonds by the Essene ideal of poverty, Judaism did not reject the riches; while the former was filled with Pauline and Augustinian spirit of love, the latter preached a rabid and extremist nationalism. Thus all those ethical regulations that were favourable to the development of the capitalist spirit were influential in Judaism a thousand years longer than in Christianity. . . . We have called the Jews the Father of Free Trade and therefore of capitalism. They were prepared for this role by the free-trading spirit of their commercial and industrial law. [10]

Other writers, most notably Max Weber, emphasized that the changes in the religious ethic resulting from the Reformation and the Protestant movement provided an

---

[10] Werner Sombart, *The Quintessence of Capitalism,* trans. and ed. by M. Epstein, T. Fisher Unwin, London, 1915, pp. 265-266.

ethical and hence economic climate which was highly favorable to the progress of capitalism. [11] Weber suggested that the growing Protestantism in England, Scotland, the Netherlands, and later in New England was the primary reason why these countries were the first to undergo industrial development. Others have indicated that the new spirit of individualism encouraged by humanism and Protestantism were dominant forces in the evolving capitalism. Eells and Walton summarize the role of the Reformation leaders in the development of this new ethic as follows:

> Luther's emphasis on individual enterprise, on biblical interpretation, and on the importance of work was reinforced and expanded by Calvin, who placed frugality, thrift, and industry—virtues dear to those earlier businessmen—high in his schema of values. Furthermore, by focusing on the notion that worldly success and prosperity might be construed as signs of God's approval for the elect, Calvin provided a religious incentive that harmonized effectively with the spread of the profit motive in Western society. [12]

Thus the tenets of Calvinism provided the basic framework for the encouragement of capitalism and set the stage for the development of the Protestant ethic. In the new world, puritanism continued the stress on the virtues of hard work, sobriety, and an accumulation of worldly goods as a sign of being in God's grace. Weber saw in the pronouncements of Benjamin Franklin the essence of the Protestant ethic. He said that all Franklin's moral attitudes were colored by strong utilitarianism. "Honesty is useful, because it assures credit; so are punctuality, industry, frugality, and that is the reason they are virtues." [13] Weber cited Franklin's view that the accumulation of wealth was a sign of God's grace. "If we thus ask, *why* should 'money be made out of men,' Benjamin Franklin himself, although he was a colourless deist, answers in his autobiography with a quotation from the Bible, which his strict Calvinistic father drummed into him again and again in his youth: 'Seest thou a man diligent in his business? He shall stand before kings.' (Prov. xxii. 29)." [14]

Adam Smith and the Triumph of Laissez Faire

At the time of the American Revolution the capitalist ethic was well entrenched in the Netherlands, England, and in the American Colonies. Although the philosophy of mercantilism had dominated the economic scene during the sixteenth and seventeenth centuries, by the mid-1700s it was breaking down. Under the mercantilistic concept the

---

[11] For a more complete development of this thesis, see Max Weber, *The Protestant Ethic and the Spirit of Capitalism,* trans. by Talcott Parsons, Charles Scribner's Sons, New York, 1958.
[12] Richard Eells and Clarence Walton, *Conceptual Foundations of Business,* Richard D. Irwin, Inc., Homewood, Ill., 1961, pp. 29-30.
[13] Weber, op. cit., p. 52.
[14] Ibid., p. 53.

individual was subordinate to the state, and economic and business activities were dedicated to the support of the power of the state. The acquisition of wealth was the important economic mission of the nation, and all economic activities were dedicated to this goal.

In 1776 with the publication of Adam Smith's *An Inquiry into the Nature and Causes of the Wealth of Nations,* the capitalistic ethic received its grand theory. His view set the theoretical background for the growing capitalistic ethic which has dominated economic thought in Western Europe and America since that time. Smith argued for economic freedoms on the premise that by maximizing his self-interests, each individual would benefit the total society. The "invisible hand" of the market and competition would restrain the self-interest of individuals, thus ensuring maximization of social benefits. The beauty of the Smithonian theory was that it allowed each individual to consider only his own interests and to maximize his own profit and wealth and yet automatically to make the best possible allocation of resources for the broad social benefit. The control mechanism was the competition of the marketplace which was automatic and needed neither state nor any other external control to ensure its effective operation.

Smith emphasized that any governmental interference with commercial activities would tend to upset the natural balance, and he championed the laissez faire concept of letting business alone to work out the allocation of resources within the constraints of the marketplace. This ideology fit admirably the technological and industrial developments of the time and provided a perfect justification for the growth of the industrialist. "Smith's theory of capitalism, reinforced and somewhat modified by Bentham and Ricardo, formed the philosophy of the Industrial Revolution and is still widely held in the Western world. It produces a wonderful world of full employment, lowest possible prices and costs, maximum efficiency, and progress and freedom. This dream is clearly seen in many of the pronouncements made by American business leaders today." [15]

Embracing Science and Technology

The Protestant ethic and the emerging spirit of capitalism were favorable to the growing emphasis upon scientific investigation and technological applications in Western societies. There are many common values in the Protestant ethic, capitalism, and science and technology: emphasis upon rationality, empiricism, a utilitarian mentality, the view of man's need to utilize the resources of nature for his own betterment here on earth and for the glory of God, and the importance placed upon knowledge and literacy. These movements converged during the seventeenth and eighteenth centuries to provide the basis for industrial societies. Merton suggests that "Puritanism and the scientific temper are in most salient agreement, for the combination of *rationalism and empiricism* which

---

[15] Joseph W. McGuire, *Business and Society,* McGraw-Hill Book Company, New York, 1963, pp. 59–60.

is so pronounced in the Puritan ethic forms the essence of the spirit of modern science.'' [16]

The Protestant ethic provided the ideology for both capitalism and the advancement of science. Capitalism encouraged the utilization of scientific knowledge for technical applications. The emergence of a market system organized around the principle of private property provided the institutional means for the accumulation of resources necessary to translate the growing scientific knowledge into an industrial technology. [17]

These three forces were associated with another, perhaps even more fundamental, trend. Each of them—the Protestant ethic, the emergence of capitalism, and the development of science and technology—required a fundamental change in the education of people. They depended upon a better-educated citizenry, at least among the elites, and this led to an expansion of general and specialized education, particularly in the scientific and technical fields.

Social Darwinism and the Survival of the Fittest

In 1858 Charles Darwin published his classic *Origin of the Species,* in which he set forth the theory of evolution of biological organisms from lower to higher forms of life. He emphasized that in the evolutionary process the organism adapted itself successfully to its environment and that it was in a continual process of struggle. This concept of ''survival of the fittest'' was extended from the biological organism to the broader social order by Herbert Spencer in the latter part of the nineteenth century. Social Darwinism suggested that the most capable and resourceful of people would rise to the top of the social hierarchy and that this was the natural order of things. Under Social Darwinism it was only natural that there would be poor and rich classes, and any attempt to upset this hierarchical order was considered unnatural and against the best interest of society. Social Darwinism clearly reinforced the Protestant ethic and Adam Smith's concept of laissez faire. It provided the basic ideology for the businessman in the late nineteenth century and helped justify the accumulation of resources and their use for self-interest.

Thus, these ideological strands converged during the latter part of the nineteenth century to provide the high point of the classical capitalistic ethic. But even at that time there were dissenters from this ideology. Perhaps the most famous dissenter was Karl Marx, who wrote *The Communist Manifesto* with Frederick Engels in 1848 and *Das Kapital* in 1867. Marx and Engels saw the evolving capitalistic system as a primary threat to the social structure and recommended revolutionary remedies. The industrialists and capitalists were breaking down the established social order. They said, ''The *bourgeoisie,*

---

[16] Robert K. Merton, ''Puritanism, Pietism and Science,'' in *Social Theory and Social Structure,* rev. ed., The Free Press of Glencoe, New York, 1957, p. 579.
[17] See Robert L. Heilbroner, ''Do Machines Make History?'' *Technology and Culture,* July 1967, pp. 335–345; and Lewis Mumford, *Technics and Civilization,* Harcourt, Brace and Company, New York, 1934, pp. 26–27.

wherever it got the upper hand, put an end to all feudal, patriarchal, idyllic relations, pitilessly tore asunder the motley feudal ties that bound man to his 'natural superiors,' and left remaining no other bond between man and man than naked self-interest and callous cash payments.'' [18] Marx called for a proletarian revolution to break the capitalistic order and to establish communism. However, there were many other dissenters in the nineteenth century who advocated not revolution but rather evolutionary reforms in the capitalistic ideology.

TRANSFORMATION OF CAPITALISTIC ETHIC

Prior to the Civil War, agriculture and small business enterprises dominated the American scene. Although there had been rapid developments in fledgling industries, trade, and transportation facilities in the early part of the nineteenth century, it was not until after the Civil War that large-scale industrial developments took place. The industrial revolution, with its emphasis on the technology of production, utilization of machinery, and the factory system, required the collective organization of men and resources. This was the era of the industrial capitalist who accumulated and utilized vast resources in shaping the new world. The development of the corporate form of business provided the means for the accumulation of the capital necessary for the operations of the industrial empire. Carnegie, Gould, Morgan, Vanderbilt, Cook, Hill, and others became the popular heroes of the day and were the champions of Industrial Darwinism.

The evolving Protestant ethic, the competitive model of Adam Smith, and Social Darwinism provided the ideological support for industrial capitalism. This period, from the end of the Civil War until 1890, can be considered as the apex in the evolution of the traditional capitalistic ethic. In American society the basic ideological heritages and values merged with the expanding technology and opportunities of the industrial revolution to achieve the high point of a militant and frequently unremitting capitalistic ethic. Even though the growing concentration of power and monopolization of industry created a real situation totally different from that envisioned in Adam Smith's pure, competitive model, the ideology of individualism and laissez faire continued to dominate business thinking.

Many of the captains of industry at this time engaged in highly unethical practices as measured by today's standards. [19] However, these actions should not be viewed only in terms of today's ideologies. They should also be considered prevailing norms of that period. Industrialists were the popular heroes of the day and had substantial popular support for their activities. However, toward the end of the nineteenth century many dissenters pointed to the antisocial consequences of the prevailing Industrial Darwinism.

---

[18] Cited in Tawney, op. cit., p. 223.
[19] For a discussion of business practices during this period, see Keith Davis and Robert L. Blomstrom, *Business and Its Environment,* McGraw-Hill Book Company, New York, 1966, pp. 64–72.

Emerging Government Regulations

During much of the early part of the nineteenth century governmental actions were highly favorable to the development of industry and commerce. Tariff laws which protected the emerging manufacturing interest were passed. The Supreme Court held that the private corporate form was legal, and this decision set the stage for the later development of huge corporate enterprises. The government provided vast sums of money and land for the development of the railroad transportation system. During the period from the formation of the United States to the 1880s, governmental actions, particularly those of the federal government, were quite favorable to the business system. McGuire says:

> During the traditional phase, then, the Federal government attempted to en-
> courage business activities with a minimum of regulation and intervention. The
> government minted money, established a patent office, collected taxes, de-
> fended our nation, and even gave pensions to veterans of the Revolutionary
> War and the War of 1812. Government's task in these years, it was thought by
> many politicians and businessmen, was to aid business enterprise in accord
> with the best principles of mercantilism, and still leave business free to grow
> and develop without restraint, as set forth in the doctrine of *laissez faire*. The
> tradition thus grew that businessmen in the United States could do what so few
> people were able to do—have their cake and eat it too. [20]

The federal government provided the basic social structure and environment for the dynamic growth of the business system during these formative years.

The antisocial actions of many industrialists in the late 1800s created substantial public dissatisfaction with the business system. The development of huge corporations and trusts—and the evident monopolistic powers which they maintained—led various forces within the society to demand some form of regulation or control. They suggested that the unfettered application of the laissez faire concept (built upon Adam Smith's pure, competitive model) might not be effective in a system of oligopoly and monopoly. Thus the period between 1880 and World War I saw the beginning of regulation and control of American business in a variety of ways. The Grange movement—a combination of farmers, local communities, and state legislatures—represented a popular uprising against the monopolistic powers of the big railroads. This movement resulted in the passage of many state acts to regulate the railroads and finally led to the enactment of the Interstate Commerce Act in 1887. Although in the early phases this act was ineffectively enforced, it did set the stage for the broader regulation of business activities by the federal government.

---

[20] McGuire, op. cit., p. 78.

The Sherman Antitrust Act was passed in 1890. Although this act was very general and its interpretation was left to the courts, it did set the groundwork for the view that the government should regulate business in the public interest. Actually the Sherman Antitrust Act did not represent a major philosophical deviation from the laissez faire ethic of Adam Smith. The primary purpose of this act was to restrict monopolistic practices and to roll back the business system to that of the competitive model. This, however, was impossible in view of the changing industrial structure, and the government continued to pass laws to regulate business practices directly. The Pure Food and Drug Act was passed in 1906, and the Clayton Act and the Federal Trade Commission Act were enacted in 1914. Thus, during this period the basic framework for governmental regulation of certain aspects of business activities was established.

Rise of Labor Movements

Although there are incidents of organized labor activities in America dating back to the seventeenth century, labor unions did not become effective as a countervailing power to the industrialists until the latter part of the nineteenth century. During the early phases of the industrial revolution many legal restraints were placed upon collective actions of work groups. Essentially, the courts held that unions were conspiracies in restraint of trade. Although there are numerous examples of small-scale unions during this period, the impact of organized labor was localized and not substantial. However after the Civil War, with the growth of complex industrial organizations, the labor movement received added impetus.

The Knights of Labor was organized in 1869 and remained a secret society until 1879, when it began open activities. It was opened to all workers, and a coalition with agrarian groups was formed to advocate major social reform which was viewed as necessary because of the antisocial practices of industrialists. Because the Knights were a loosely formed coalition of widely divergent interest groups, showed a lack of concern with immediate problems, and exhibited radical fervor, there was a decline in the movement. Membership, which rose spectacularly to 700,000 in 1886, dropped to only 75,000 in 1893.

The American Federation of Labor (AFL), established in 1886, set the pattern for the American labor movement. Under the pragmatic leadership of Samuel Gompers it adopted a policy of operating within the capitalistic framework but with a view to gaining a greater share of the benefits of the economic system for labor. Although it did accept the capitalistic ideology, the AFL became a strong countervailing power against the large corporations and, in effect, did have a part in modifying and transforming this ideology.

Radical unions such as the Socialist Labor Party and the Industrial Workers of the World (IWW) developed between 1895 and 1920. The IWW or "Wobblies" gathered workers into militant industrial unions with the purpose of overthrowing the capitalistic system. Although this movement passed from the American scene after World War I, it represented a violent reaction to the dominant Industrial Darwinism of the period.

The Great Depression and the Keynesian Revolution

The decade of the 1920s was the high point for American business and the industrial system with predictions of endless prosperity. But the 1930s brought a low point for the esteem of the businessman and the greatest challenge to the capitalistic ideology. The Great Depression, beginning with the stock market crash of 1929 and continuing with a massive economic collapse, threatened the very framework of our economic and social system. Widespread unemployment and the collapse of the market challenged the roots of the classical capitalistic ideology, and business was the scapegoat.

In classical economic theory, depressions, while accepted as inevitable, were considered to be short-term periods of adjustment which represented only minor dislocation in utilization of resources. Under this model full employment and utilization of resources would be established at a new equilibrium. This, however, did not happen during the Great Depression. It extended with minor modifications from 1929 until the World War II stimulus to industrial activity caused the turn. The Depression, furthermore, cast grave doubts upon some of the basic tenets of the Protestant ethic—individualism, self-determinism, and the value of hard work and thrift. The individual was not totally responsible for his own fate. Many forces operating in a complex industrial society could not be coped with by the individual—man was affected by events far beyond his control.

Although the Depression itself was evidence of the breakdown of the economic system and the classical capitalistic ethic, it took economist John Maynard Keynes in *The General Theory of Employment, Interest, and Money* in 1936 to provide the theoretical explanation. The Keynesian view challenged the classical economic theory and the capitalistic ethic. Perhaps this explains why Keynes and his followers suffered the derision of the business communities for so long a period. Few people liked to have their basic ideology questioned, especially by a foreign professor. Keynes challenged a basic tenet of the Protestant ethic by saying that savings withheld from consumption could lead to dislocation and underutilization of economic resources. Even more important, the Keynesian thesis questioned the foundation of the classical economic doctrine of laissez faire, whereby the market mechanism and price system would automatically adjust to an equilibrium point for full utilization of resources and employment. The classical doctrine was a beautiful model of an automatically adjusting closed system. No interference or external force was necessary in order to ensure optimal allocation and full utilization of economic resources—and this to the broad social benefit. A wonderful ideology, unique in its simplicity! Keynes explained the Depression by suggesting that equilibrium could be reached in spite of a large number of involuntarily unemployed people and other nonutilized resources. He emphasized consumption rather than savings as the way to achieve full utilization of resources. Without a self-adjusting system operating at full employment of both people and other resources, it was necessary under this thesis to have an external force provide the balancing mechanism—this force was the government.

Although Keynes's theory was received with substantial hostility from the business community and still remains suspect in many circles, there is little doubt that the inescapable reality of the Great Depression and the persuasiveness of his views had a significant influence on the transformation of the capitalistic ethic.

Human Relations and the Behavioral Revolution

In the early part of the twentieth century the followers of scientific management looked at the business organization from a highly mechanistic view and saw the worker as a rational, profit-maximizing element of the system. Scientific management influenced many of the ideas regarding the management of organizations.

The human relations movement starting in the late 1920s evolved a different view of the employee. It saw the organization as a social system with members strongly influenced by intragroup relationships and with the individual motivated by a complex hierarchy of needs. Although the human relationists recognized the importance of economic needs, they emphasized social needs as basic for motivation of organizational participants. The importance of the human relations movement to developing managerial ideology will be discussed in more detail in Chapter 4. It is sufficient to point out here that these efforts were the forerunners of industrial humanism.[21]

The human relations movement in industry was not isolated from underlying developments in behavioral science. The theory and research in the behavioral sciences—psychology, sociology, and anthropology—had a profound influence upon the basic view of man in the organization and in society and thus had a major effect in the transformation of the capitalistic ethic and managerial ideology.

World War II and Continued Preparedness

World War II required the massive interjection of the government into all phases of economic activity in our society in order to accumulate and manage the resources necessary for the war effort. Although most of these controls were relaxed after the war, the vestiges of this intervention remained. In 1946, a predominantly Republican Congress passed the Fair Employment Act of 1946, which established the policy that the federal government had prime responsibility for the maintenance of full employment and full utilization of economic resources. What a major transformation from the hostility toward Keynesian theory just ten years earlier! Although the United States did demobilize immediately after the end of the war, this period was short-lived, and by 1948 we were again in a state of continued preparedness. The cold war and the hot Korean and

---

[21] For a discussion of industrial humanism, see William G. Scott, "Technology and Organization Government: A Speculative Inquiry into the Functionality of Management Creeds," *Academy of Management Journal*, September 1968, pp. 301–313.

Vietnam Wars have caused our society to remain in a partial state of mobilization with a huge allocation of economic resources for "defense" efforts. During the past twenty years nearly 10 percent of our gross national product has been allocated to defense, an expenditure of hundreds of billions of dollars. Furthermore, the government has made other massive expenditures in such areas as the Atomic Energy Commission and the National Aeronautic and Space Administration programs. In fiscal year 1973, expenditures for defense, atomic energy, and space research and technology were over $85 billion, approximately 8 percent of our gross national product.

What has been the impact upon the capitalistic ideology of this continued high level of government expenditures? These expenditures do not operate according to the market mechanism assumed in the competitive model. Of even greater importance, these funds have gone predominantly to the advanced technology industries and have stimulated the development of large-scale, complex organizations to deal with military and space programs. The managerial concepts which are developing in these advanced technology industries are significantly different from those in a more typical production organization. Furthermore, with the continued high level of expenditures by the government, the business community has come to more readily accept the government's role as a partner rather than a combatant. Increasingly, businessmen have been working with or through governmental agencies, and this process has influenced managerial ideology.

Technological and Social Change

Since the end of World War II, we have seen profound technological and social change. The necessity for dealing with technological change within the complex organization has influenced the prevailing business ideology. The introduction of scientists, professionals, and other highly trained specialists into the organization has affected managerial concepts and approaches. Furthermore, major social changes outside the business system have also had an impact upon the ideology. The civil rights movement, to mention one of many social forces, has given the business community good reasons for considering its own responsibilities in dealing with broad social challenges. The growing social awareness and activism of university students have also profoundly jolted the manager into reconsidering his own values. [22] Figure 2.1 illustrates the long-term evolution and transformation of the capitalistic ethic.

This period since World War II has been one of major technological and social change which has challenged the traditional ideology and raised major questions for the manager. What is the dominant business ideology today? What role should business play in society, and what is the impact of the changing ideology upon managerial concepts and practices? These questions will be discussed in the following sections.

---

[22] Samuel A. Culbert and James M. Elden, "An Anatomy of Activism for Executives," *Harvard Business Review*, November–December 1970, pp. 131–142.

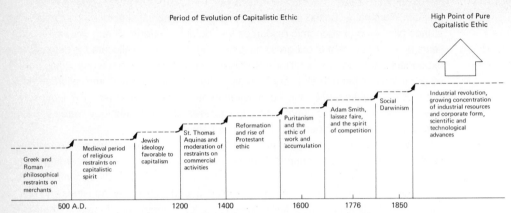

FIGURE 2.1 EVOLUTION AND TRANSFORMATION OF CAPITALISTIC ETHIC. The primary forces contributing to the rise and transformation of the capitalistic ethic are shown. The time periods are not to exact scale, and many of these forces influenced development for longer periods than could be indicated in this simplified model.

CURRENT BUSINESS IDEOLOGIES

It is impossible to define a single current dominant business ideology. Ours is a society of ethical pluralism, and the business manager as an element of this society is caught in the middle of conflicting values. Pluralism has been a dominant characteristic of the American social scene.

> The great genius of the American pattern of society has always been its pluralism—its capacity to accommodate, in the peace of one society, the manifold private motives and energies which are generated by the social life. The society is one; the centers of initiative for its acts are many. Such a distributive pattern of power is inherently precarious, for it depends on the preservation of balance between the claims of the society and the claims of the centers of initiative which appear within it. [23]

Although there are many threads to this ethical pluralism, the major conflict appears to be between the Calvinistic or Protestant ethic and the Judeo-Christian ethic. Farmer suggests that the Calvinist ethic was the theme dominating American life from 1620 to 1930 but that the Judeo-Christian ethic, although much older and going back several thousand years, has come into prominence in the United States since 1930. [24]

---

[23] John F. A. Taylor, "Is the Corporation above the Law?" *Harvard Business Review*, March–April 1965, p. 128.
[24] Richard N. Farmer, "The Ethical Dilemma of American Capitalism," *California Management Review*, Summer 1964, pp. 47–58.

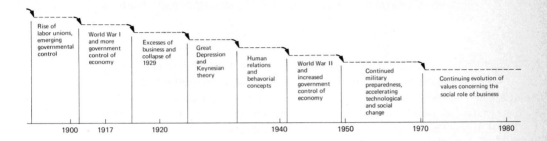

Period of Transformation in Capitalistic Ethic

The Calvinistic ethic supports the view that laissez faire and the profit maximization ideology are the basis upon which business operates and places primary emphasis on production efficiency and the role of the business organization as a creator of goods and services. The Judeo-Christian ethic, on the other hand, suggests that the business enterprise has a broader social responsibility and should not be solely concerned with profit maximization. Farmer sees this as a major dilemma for American society. "The dilemma is that both groups are essentially correct. The Calvinist ethic is correct in economic terms, and this can be demonstrated historically. The Judeo-Christian ethic is correct in personal terms, and it requires little imagination to project the ethic to the national scene. But there is little economic content in this ethic." [25]

One of the major contributions to this dilemma has been the traditional ideology, stemming from the laissez faire concept and reinforced by traditional economics, that the only objective of the business enterprise is profit maximization. The dominant economic theory of the firm takes as its basic premise that the business manager operates as a profit maximizer and that the competitive market operates to ensure social welfare. Elbing and Elbing make this point clear:

> In this moral model, the *arbiter* of the social and moral value of economic goods is the marketplace. Thus, it is not necessary to be concerned with the social value of goods since the office of the marketplace is to perform this function. The fact that a commodity is not purchased or cannot compete in the marketplace is held as evidence that it is not a social good. The marketplace being the arbiter of social values, the morality of business and businessmen is primarily taken care of in the very production of goods and services which

[25] Ibid., p. 57.

society chooses as valuable. That a business competes successfully is prima facie evidence of the social value of that business over its less successful competitors. In such a broad formulation of the value issue, value problems need not be matters of direct concern for business, since its primary moral function is fulfilled in successful competition in a marketplace which arbitrates values. [26]

A more recent view is that the business does not act as an individual profit maximizer but rather that the organization has a number of interest groups such as customers, suppliers, stockholders, employees, unions, and various government agencies. Under this view the business organization consists of a number of sometimes cooperating but frequently conflicting groups who make demands upon its resources. The business manager operating in this dynamic coalition must seek to satisfy the interests of these various groups in order to retain their cooperation and participation in organizational activities. "The objectives of big business, then, are conceived of here as varied rather than monolithic and as shaped by interactions of many participants in flexible coalition rather than being only profits to owners. To go on, the goals of organization arrived at in a coalition manner take a 'satisficing' rather than maximizing form." [27]

This view holds that profits are certainly one of the prime goals of the business enterprise and are vital to the long-range viability of the organization. However, it suggests that there are many additional goals of the various participants in the organization which have to be satisfied. This obviously makes the role of the businessman more ambiguous and strained than the profit maximization model. But is this not a realistic view? The objectives and motives of managers are social as well as economic in origin and are set by the broad culture. It is unrealistic to expect that the manager can isolate himself from this climate. He is intricately interwoven with the environment and should recognize that he will influence and be influenced by the broader social system.

Above all, the value system of contemporary capitalism is pragmatic, and increasingly the businessman is recognizing that he operates not only in an economic but in a total social environment. He should not be discouraged by the frequent ideological dilemmas which face him and by the various and often seemingly impossible demands made upon him by different groups. We reject monolithic authority in American society and have traditionally valued pluralistic expressions and conflicting views. "The coexistence of Puritanism, Hamiltonianism, Keynesism, and the welfare state is one of the marvels of our still more or less capitalistic economy. The American melting pot, which works imperfectly with ethnic groups, doesn't do much better with ideas or ideologies.

---

[26] Alvar O. Elbing, Jr., and Carol J. Elbing, *The Value Issue of Business*, McGraw-Hill Book Company, New York, 1967, pp. 56-57.
[27] Harold L. Johnson, "Alternative Views of Big Business Goals and Purposes," *The Annals of the American Academy of Political and Social Science*, September 1962, p. 3.

But in the survival and clash of opposing ideas may be found the explanation of much of the dynamism of American life—as well as of the abiding disorder and incompleteness of the American experiment." [28]

PROFESSIONALIZATION OF MANAGEMENT

Concurrent with the rise of our industrial society and the large-scale, complex organization has been the development of professionalism as a means for delineation of role specialization. [29] There is a close relationship between the issue of managerial ideology and roles and the concept of professionalism.

The Concept of Professionalism

It is virtually impossible to get any authoritative agreement upon the definition of a professional. The ministry, law, and medicine have been considered to be the original professions. Increasingly other occupational groups are classifying themselves as professions and are assuming some of the characteristics. However, even the traditional professional groups fall short of an "ideal" professional model in some respects. It is probably useful to describe professionalism in terms of a continuum with the ideal type of profession at one end and unorganized occupational categories, or nonprofessions, at the other end, rather than as a unique set of characteristics from which we can measure an occupational group on an all-or-nothing basis. "Professionalization is a process, then, that may affect any occupation to a greater of lesser degree." [30]

Using this continuum, we may describe the essential elements in an ideal profession as follows:

1 Professions have a systematic body of theory. Skill is achieved through a lengthy process of training. The skills that characterize a profession flow from and are supported by information which has been organized into an internally consistent system, called a *body of knowledge*. Preparation for a profession must be an intellectual as well as a practical experience.

---

[28] *Business Week*, Apr. 15, 1967, p. 196.
[29] Parsons sees the development of professionalism as a vitally important force in our society, equal in importance to the development of capitalism and the business economy. He says,
> Comparative study of the social structures of the most important civilizations shows that the professions occupy a position of importance in our society which is, in any comparable degree of development, unique in history. . . . It seems evident that many of the most important features of our society are to a considerable extent dependent on the smooth functioning of the professions. Both the pursuit and the application of science and liberal learning are predominantly carried out in a professional context. Their results have become so closely interwoven in the fabric of modern society that it is difficult to imagine how it could get along without basic structural changes if they were seriously impaired.

Talcott Parsons, "The Professions and Social Structure," *Essays in Sociological Theory*, rev. ed., The Free Press of Glencoe, New York, 1964, p. 34.
[30] Howard M. Vollmer and Donald L. Mills (eds.), *Professionalization*, Prentice-Hall, Inc., Englewood Cliffs, N.J., 1966, p. 2.

2 The professional has an authority based upon superior knowledge which is recognized by his clientele. This authority is highly specialized and is related only to the professional's sphere of competence.

3 There is a broad social sanction and approval of the exercise of this authority. The community sanctions the exercise of this authority within certain spheres by conferring upon professionals certain powers and privileges. Control over entry into the profession, licensing procedures, and the confidentiality of communications between the professional and the client are examples of these.

4 There is a code of ethics regulating relations of professional persons with clients and with colleagues such as the Hippocratic oath of the medical profession. Thus self-discipline is utilized as a basis of social control.

5 There is a culture sustained by organizations. A professional is a member of many formal and informal groups. The interactions of social roles required by these groups generate a social configuration unique to the profession, a professional culture. [31]

Is Management a Profession?

If we use this ideal model of professionalism, it is difficult to classify modern management as a profession. It has not developed these five elements to the extent of the traditional professional groups. Nevertheless, if we view the concept of professionalism on a continuum, it is apparent that the trend over the past several decades has been toward greater compliance with these elements of professionalism. While we may agree with Donham that "business is not a profession," "business cannot be a profession," and that "business should not attempt to 'pass' as a profession," there has been a movement along the continuum toward professionalism of management. [32] There is a growing body of systematic knowledge concerning the management and administration of complex organizations; the authority role of the manager has been legitimatized in our culture; this role has the sanction of the community; there is a growing number of professional management associations, particularly in the various specialized aspects of business; and finally there is a nucleus of the development of self-control.

Technical Competence as a Basis of Professionalism

Parsons suggests that the distinction between professionals and business management based upon the "self-interest" motives of the businessman and the "altruistic" motives of the professionals has been overemphasized. He states that the central focus of the

---

[31] Ibid., pp. 9–19.
[32] Paul Donham, "Is Management a Profession?" *Harvard Business Review,* September–October 1962, p. 66.

professional role lies in the technical competence of the professional and the recognition of this by society. [33] Certainly, the management of complex business organizations requires a high level of technical competence, and this role has been accepted by society. A distinction may be made between the professional manager who has achieved his position as a result of his competence in the performance of this function as compared to the manager who achieves his position because of parental background, ownership, or other traditional methods of managerial selection. The fact that we do not classify management as an ideal type of profession does not diminish the importance of the managerial function. Indeed, it is our view that management of social organizations is one of the most vital and important functions in society.

Although business management is not currently a profession as measured against the ideal model, the trend is in this direction. This is important when considering the question of the role of management because one of the primary attributes of professionalism is self-control rather than pure self-interest.

SOCIAL CONTROL OVER BUSINESS ACTIVITY

Figure 2.2 is a conceptual diagram showing several forms of social control over business and their changing relationships from the latter part of the nineteenth century until the present. Three primary forms of social control are (1) competition in the marketplace, where the control is exerted primarily through the market mechanisms, (2) governmental regulation wherein control is exerted directly by federal, state, and local governments, and (3) self-control, the growing professionalism of management.

The American business ideology has been transformed over the past century from one of total reliance upon the classical capitalistic ideology and laissez faire to one which accepts the proper role of governmental regulations and control and also gives recognition to the importance of the social responsibilities of the corporate enterprise. It is obvious that it would be impossible to quantify these various forms of social control. It is important to place as much reliance as possible upon the competitive mechanism because it provides the decentralized and automatic adjustment necessary for a viable economy and society. Nevertheless, it is not a perfect mechanism and must be balanced by judicious use of government regulation and by acceptance of self-control.

Business has increasingly come to accept the legitimate role of government regulation. In fact it has actually sought governmental intervention in such areas as tariffs, resale price maintenance legislation, and protection for small business.

> In a society of ever-mounting complexity, a reconstructed framework that guides and limits business activities is required. Beneath the superficial vestiges of business-government antipathy lies a not too well-hidden reliance by

---

[33] Parsons, ''The Professions and Social Structure,'' pp. 34–49.

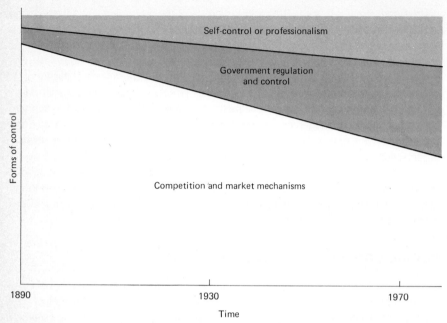

Self-control or professionalism

Government regulation and control

Competition and market mechanisms

Forms of control

1890   1930   1970

Time

FIGURE 2.2   FORMS OF SOCIAL CONTROL OVER BUSINESS

business upon government, for businessmen are well aware that the federal government is the one institution that can establish the rules and procedures which bring order to our modern business world. Businessmen are aware of the great necessity for order in their affairs, for business is future oriented, and only through order and rules can environmental uncertainty be reduced in a rapidly changing society. In their search for order businessmen have recognized—discreetly to be sure—the limitations of our traditional system and are groping toward new parameters and a fresh perspective for business behavior. [34]

The growing professionalization of business management has fostered a concept of social responsibility, which is becoming one of the accepted norms of business behavior. There certainly is not complete harmony between the three primary elements of social control mentioned at the beginning of this section. They are not always complementary but, rather, are often in conflict when specific issues are considered. But this conflict is the very essence of our pluralistic American society, and it should be recognized that each of these types of social control has a legitimate role.

---

[34] Joseph W. McGuire, "How Much Freedom Does Business Really Want?" *Business Horizons,* Summer 1965, p. 74.

INFLUENCE OF CHANGING VALUES ON MANAGEMENT CONCEPTS

There have been significant changes in the capitalistic ideology and in society's views of the legitimate role of the manager and the corporation. Heilbroner summarizes this change:

> In the concept of a new capitalism, distinguished by its sense of professional responsibility, characterized by large-scale technological units, imbued with a concern for human values, and aware of the legitimacy of labor and government as centers of economic powers, we have an expression, however incomplete, of what capitalism means that is markedly different from what it meant to the late nineteenth—or early twentieth—century big businessman and considerably different from the lingering conservative depiction today. [35]

It is essential to recognize, particularly as a frame of reference for the next three chapters, that organization theory and management practice have been strongly influenced by a changing society and the evolving ideology. Frederick Taylor's scientific management cannot be considered as an isolated force but should be viewed in the light of the industrial and social situation within which it developed. The writings of Elton Mayo and the human relationists reflect a substantial evolution in management ideology.

The motivation and action orientation of the practicing manager are determined by his value system. His own personality and the environmental forces which operate within his frame of reference provide the motivational stimuli. [36] A commonality of ideology is the basis for legitimatizing the organization as a social system. The managerial concepts that guide the actions of the participants are the primary "unseen" networks which hold the organization together and make it a functioning entity. They are prime determinants of management practices. Above all, it should be emphasized that the modern business executive is not guided by a universal or monistic ethic. Rather, he is guided by contemporary ethical pluralism, which provides general guidelines for decision making but never specific answers.

SUMMARY

Management concepts and practices are influenced by the ideologies of the broader society. Values are normative standards which influence human beings in their social roles and choice of actions. Values are subject to evolutionary change, and the modern manager is faced with a number of ethical norms which are often in conflict.

---

[35] Robert L. Heilbroner, "The View from the Top," in Earl F. Cheit (ed.), *The Business Establishment,* John Wiley & Sons, Inc., New York, 1964, p. 30.
[36] R. J. Monsen, B. O. Saxberg, and R. A. Sutermeister, "The Modern Manager: What Makes Him Run?" *Business Horizons,* Fall 1966, pp. 23-24.

The capitalistic ideology has not been the norm or standard ethic throughout history. In ancient Greece and Rome, and throughout much of the medieval period, commercial activities were tolerated as necessary evils. The rise of the capitalistic ethic has been associated with changing religious views. Some historians consider Judaism as the primary force in the development of the capitalistic system. Others suggest that the changes in the religious ethic resulting from the Reformation and the Protestant movement provided a climate which was highly favorable to capitalism.

Adam Smith provided the capitalistic ethic with its grand theory. He argued for economic freedoms on the premise that by maximizing his self-interests, each individual would benefit the total society. In the latter part of the nineteenth century, the Protestant ethic and Smith's economic theory were reinforced by Social Darwinism, which suggested that the most capable and resourceful of people would rise to the top of the social order. The Protestant ethic and the emerging spirit of capitalism were favorable to the growing emphasis on scientific investigation and technological applications.

There were, however, dissenters from the capitalistic ideology. Marx and Engels saw the capitalistic system as a primary threat to the social structure and recommended revolutionary remedies. Other forces, such as emerging government regulation and labor unions, helped transform the classical capitalistic ethic.

The Great Depression of the 1930s brought a low point to the esteem for business and the greatest challenge to the capitalistic ideology. In 1936 Keynes provided the theoretical explanation for the breakdown. His thesis questioned whether the market mechanism and price system would automatically adjust to an equilibrium point for full utilization of resources and employment. He called for governmental action to restore employment and to prevent depressions.

It is impossible to define a single, current business ideology. Ours is a society of ethical pluralism, and the manager is caught in the middle of conflicting values. There is a major conflict between the Protestant and the Judeo-Christian ethics. Above all, the value system of contemporary capitalism is pragmatic. There is increasing evidence of the business community's willingness to recognize the social consequences of the changes which it has created and to participate in finding some means for moderating any adverse effects. Furthermore, it has shown a greater tolerance for accepting the roles of other institutions, such as the government and unions, in dealing with social problems.

There is a close relationship between the role of management and the concept of professionalism. Although management is not a profession as measured against the "ideal" model, the trend is in that direction. Organization theory and management practice have been strongly influenced by a changing society and its evolving ideologies.

QUESTIONS AND PROBLEMS

1 Why is our society characterized by "ethical pluralism"? Discuss the various components of our ethical system.

2 Discuss the various forces which led to the high point of the pure capitalistic ethic in the latter part of the nineteenth century. What contributed to the transformation of this ethic during the twentieth century? What will be the major changes in the future?

3 How were the values under the Protestant ethic and the norms of science and technology similar? Is this relationship still true today?

4 Discuss the basic distinctions between the Protestant and Judeo-Christian ethics. What are the implications of these differences for managers?

5 How have the rise of labor unions and the growing governmental regulations affected the value systems of businessmen?

6 Review current periodicals such as *Business Week, Fortune,* and *Wall Street Journal* for current situations involving the question of the role of business in society.

7 What is your evaluation of the view that big business seeks to satisfy a number of objectives imposed by different groups rather than to maximize a single profit objective?

8 Discuss the concept that professionalism is a form of social control which modifies self-interest in favor of social interest.

9 Using Figure 2.2 as a point of reference, discuss the past and future trends in relative importance of these three forms of social control over business.

*Knowledge about what man has been and is can
protect the future.*
Margaret Mead

*Here and elsewhere we shall not obtain the best
insight into things until we actually see them growing
from the beginning.*
Aristotle

*Because we live in a time of great change, and because
our philosophy of optimism makes us expectant
of and receptive to change, we may easily overlook a
deeply important aspect of historic development.
This is its quality of inertia. It is a quality which is
manifest not only in resistance to change—
although that is one of its more important aspects—
but in the viscosity which is imparted to history
because people tend to repeat and continue their ways
of life as long as it is possible for them to do so.*
Robert L. Heilbroner

*Open-system theory is . . . a framework, a
meta-theory, a model in the broadest sense of that
overused term. Open-system theory is an approach
and a conceptual language for understanding and
describing many kinds and levels of phenomena. It is
used to describe and explain the behavior of living
organisms and combinations of organisms, but it
is applicable to any dynamic, recurring process, any
patterned sequence of events.*
Daniel Katz and Robert Kahn

*The rung of a ladder was never meant to rest
upon, but only to hold a man's foot long enough to
enable him to put the other somewhat higher.*
Thomas Huxley

PART 2
EVOLUTION OF ORGANIZATION
AND MANAGEMENT THEORY

The attempts to codify organization and management knowledge as a separate and identifiable field of study are relatively recent. It has been only during the twentieth century that attempts have been made to develop a general theory. The contributors to this development represent a heterogeneous group of practitioners as well as academic generalists and specialists. Much of the early management thought came from practicing executives and administrators who recorded their observations and experiences and set them forth as general guidelines for others. Scientific management, with its engineering approach and emphasis upon observation and measurement, provided another source of knowledge. On the academic side, sociologists, influenced by Max Weber's bureaucratic model, have made contributions to the theory. Economists with their microeconomic theory set forth a limited and closed model of organization, but one which has had an influence. Finally, there has been a growing trend toward using scientific research in the study of organizations and management practices.

Many new developments have increased our understanding of organization theory and management practice. These developments can be broadly categorized as two types: (1) the behavioral sciences, which emphasize the psychosocial aspects of organization and management, and (2) the management sciences, which emphasize quantification, mathematical models, and applications of computer technology.

In this part, we will look at the evolution of organization and management concepts in three stages: (1) the traditional views, (2) the behavioral and management science revolutions, and (3) the development of the modern or systems approach. In Chapter 3 we review traditional organization and management concepts with a discussion of the primary contributors, the key ideas, and the limitations. In Chapter 4 we consider the behavioral and management science revolutions and their impact upon organization theory and management practice. In Chapter 5 we set forth the modern or systems approach, which is the basis for the development of current organization theory and management practice and which sets the stage for the remainder of the book.

TRADITIONAL ORGANIZATION AND MANAGEMENT CONCEPTS

While we are primarily concerned with modern organization theory and management practice, there is value in looking at the traditional views and in tracing their development. Modern concepts are not completely distinct and unrelated; they evolved from earlier views. Moreover, many current management practices are influenced and guided, either consciously or subconsciously, by these traditional concepts. There are many ways to classify the components of traditional theory, and it is impossible to give credit to all the contributors. This chapter is not an exhaustive treatise, but it does provide the overall framework necessary for later consideration of current organization theory and management practice. The following topics are discussed:

> Setting of Traditional Theory
> Scientific Management
> Administrative Management Theory
> Bureaucratic Model
> Microeconomics: Theory of the Firm
> Public Administration
> Major Assumptions of Traditional Theory
> Critique of Traditional View

SETTING OF TRADITIONAL THEORY

A systematic body of knowledge concerning organization and management is a product of the late nineteenth and of the twentieth centuries. However, there is a rich heritage of ideas from the past. Throughout recorded history, men have pondered the problems of human organizations and the administration of governments, churches, armies, empires, and other complex social groups. "The nature of this achievement may be inferred from the remaining records concerning these organizations. But this belongs to the history of administration, not of administrative thought." [1]

The beginnings of a systematic body of knowledge are closely associated with the industrial revolution and the rise of large-scale economic enterprises which required the development of new organizational forms and management practices. John Mee says:

> There is evidence to support the proposition that management thought in the United States was initiated and influenced by the economic, social, political, and technological forces in the environment during the last portion of the nineteenth century. A relationship still exists between the cumulative forces in the environment of our organized society and the nature of management philosophy applied to business and industrial enterprises.
>
> There seemed to be little interest in management thought or philosophy in the United States until the political and economic climate provided a fertile field for the seeds of management thought to germinate and develop. Management thought followed closely in the wake of the political and economic philosophies of our nation. [2]

Even after the start of large-scale commercial and industrial enterprises, the development of management thought was relatively slow. [3] We read of the capitalistic ideology of the dynamic industrialists of the latter part of the nineteenth century such as Carnegie, Rockefeller, and Cook but little about their management philosophies. During this period management style was very individualistic and depended more upon the unique personality of the industrialist than upon any well-defined body of knowledge. Jenks suggests this highly individualistic nature of management practices:

> Problems of organization and the use of the labor force were solved *ad hoc,* empirically for each establishment. Knowledge about the solutions was transmitted by observation or word of mouth and had to be rediscovered by most new firms. This type of thinking probably predominated in American and British business concerns at the beginning of the twentieth century. Here management was an uncertain mixture of the traditional with the arbitrary or capricious—a personal autocracy of varying degrees of benevolence—an emanation of the personality of the owner-manager. [4]

---

[1] Bertram M. Gross, *The Managing of Organizations,* The Free Press of Glencoe, New York, 1964, vol. I, p. 91.
[2] John F. Mee, *Management Thought in a Dynamic Economy,* New York University Press, New York, 1963, pp. xvi–xvii.
[3] There were some practitioners who did set forth their management philosophies during the early part of the nineteenth century. Most notable were the contributions of Andrew Ure and Charles Babbage. See Andrew Ure, *The Philosophy of Manufacturers,* Charles Knight, London, 1835; and Charles Babbage, *On the Economy of Machinery and Manufacturers,* Charles Knight, London, 1832.
[4] Leland H. Jenks, "Early Phases of the Management Movement," *Administrative Science Quarterly,* December 1960, p. 424.

It was not until the scientific management movement, the writings of Max Weber on bureaucracy, and the early administrative management theorists that there developed a systematic body of knowledge related to the management of complex business and other organizations.

SCIENTIFIC MANAGEMENT

The scientific management movement was given its initial impetus under the driving force of Frederick W. Taylor (1856–1915) in the latter part of the nineteenth and early part of the twentieth centuries. Taylor was stimulated in his early thinking by a number of predecessors, particularly the American industrialist and engineer Henry R. Towne.

Taylor's views were strongly influenced by the Protestant ethic of the time. He emphasized the value of hard work, economic rationality, individualism, and the view that each man had a role to play in society. "Taylor's Puritan frame of reference—compounded with a touch of Quaker concern for responsible service and Unitarian rationalism—thus goes a long way toward explaining his attitudes towards individuals, groups and systems."[5] Taylor and the scientific management movement were a product of the Protestant ethic of the latter part of the nineteenth century and the key concepts of this early theory reflect that ideology.

Taylor did not develop a broad, general theory of management. He was pragmatically oriented with an empirical, engineering, and mechanistic emphasis that focused primarily upon increasing worker efficiency. In his earlier writings he referred to his ideas as "task management." It was not until 1910 that the term *scientific management* was coined by Louis Brandeis in a statement before the Interstate Commerce Commission. The primary emphasis of scientific management was on planning, standardizing, and improving human effort at the operative level in order to maximize output with minimum input.

Taylor's ideas came from his actual work experiences at the Midvale Steel Company, Bethlehem Steel Company, and as a consultant to many industrial firms. Early in his career he became interested in improving work efficiency and methods and in ascertaining scientifically the "one best way" of doing each task. By this means increases in productivity could be achieved, and both employer and employee would benefit. "By maximizing the productive efficiency of each worker, scientific management would also maximize the earnings of workers and employers. Hence, all conflict between capital and labor would be resolved by the findings of science."[6]

Basic Approaches of Scientific Management

Taylor thought that work could be analyzed scientifically and that it was management's responsibility to provide the specific guidelines for worker performance. This led to the development of the one best method of doing the task, standardization of this method

---

[5] J. Boddewyn, "Frederick Winslow Taylor Revisited," *Academy of Management Journal,* August 1961, p. 104.
[6] Reinhard Bendix, *Work and Authority in Industry,* John Wiley & Sons, Inc., New York, 1956, pp. 274–275.

(usually through time and motion studies), selection of workers best suited to performing the specific tasks, and training them in the most efficient method for performing the work. It was an engineering approach and viewed the worker as an adjunct to the machine. The assumption was that workmen would be motivated by greater economic rewards which would come from the increasing productivity. "It is no single element, but rather this whole combination, that constitutes scientific management, which may be summarized as: Science, not rule of thumb. Harmony, not discord. Cooperation, not individualism. Maximum output, in place of restricted output. The development of each man to his greatest efficiency and prosperity." [7]

Role of Management

Under Taylor's philosophy the role of management changed significantly from that of the past. His emphasis was on making management a science rather than an individualistic approach based upon rule of thumb. He set forth the new duties of management as follows: (1) Develop a science for each element of a man's work, which replaces the old rule-of-thumb method. (2) Scientifically select and then train, teach, and develop the workman, whereas in the past he chose his own work and trained himself as best he could. (3) Cooperate with the men so as to ensure that all the work would be done in accordance with scientific principles. (4) Divide responsibility between management and workmen. Management takes over all functions for which they are better fitted than the workmen. [8]

Scientific management had a direct impact upon the worker's relationship to his task. It removed the worker's discretion in the planning, organizing, and controlling of his own task performance. If the worker did exactly as he was told by the management specialist, he would gain through increased productivity and greater monetary rewards.

Scientific management required that management plan, organize, and control task performance. It demanded a new, more systematic approach to the processes of management. Taylor stated that although there was some resistance on the part of the workers to the scientific approach, the primary resistance came from management itself, which was required to give up the old rule-of-thumb methods in favor of scientific approaches. This strong role for management was emphasized by Taylor:

> It is only through *enforced* standardization of methods, *enforced* adoption of the best implements and working conditions, and *enforced* cooperation that this faster work can be assured. And the duty of enforcing the adoption of standards and of enforcing this cooperation rests with the *management* alone. ... The *management* must also recognize the broad fact that workmen will not submit to this more rigid standardization and will not work extra hard, unless they receive extra pay for doing it. [9]

---

[7] Frederick Winslow Taylor, "The Principles of Scientific Management," *Scientific Management,* Harper & Row, Publishers, Incorporated, New York, 1947, p. 140.
[8] Ibid., pp. 36–37.
[9] Ibid., p. 83.

Followers of Scientific Management

Taylor had a major impact upon management practices for the next several decades. Even today the basic principles which he set forth are a key part of our management thought, particularly in factory and industrial operations. Taylor and his associates, Henry Gantt, Frank and Lillian Gilbreth, Harrington Emerson, Horace Hathaway, and Sanford Thompson, spread the gospel of scientific management through countless speeches, articles and books. [10] Scientific management became a "movement" with wide application and many spokesmen. This system had a major impact upon industrial practice, not only in the United States but in Europe as well. It not only affected the task performance at the worker level, but also created many changes in industrial organization structures. Before scientific management, such departments as industrial engineering, personnel, maintenance, and quality control were nonexistent.

Opposition to Scientific Management

It is little wonder that Taylor and his followers were not without opposition and critics because the new approach involved a complete overhauling of traditional managerial practices. Many managers resisted Taylor's approach because they opposed his substitution of the scientific method and techniques for their own judgment and discretion. "Taylor had questioned their good judgment and superior ability which had been the subject of public celebration for many years. Hence, many employers regarded his methods as an unwarranted interference with managerial prerogatives." [11]

Taylor anticipated that management would oppose his new approach. However, he may have been naïve in thinking that his views were compatible with the interests of workers. Resentment over many of the practices and techniques grew. Workers resisted time study procedures and standardization of every aspect of their performance. In their view they were being treated like machines and were required to operate according to mechanistic rather than humanistic principles. They resisted Taylor's incentive systems, which required that they perform at a high level continuously. They objected to the distribution of the "savings" which had resulted from the adoption of scientific management because an overwhelming proportion seemed to go to the company rather than to themselves. However, it was the leaders of organized labor who provided the greatest resistance. Although Taylor professed not to be an opponent of the union movement, a reading of his testimony before a special committee of the U.S. House of Representatives in 1912 suggests that he really did not believe unions were necessary and that he thought effective cooperation between employer and employees could exist without them. One senses that Taylor is suggesting that unions were only necessary when management did not do its job effectively, that is, by adopting the principles of scientific management. Union leaders saw Taylor's scientific management as a challenge to their role and to the growth of the union movement.

---

[10] For a discussion of how the early proponents of scientific management disseminated their views and findings in the various engineering, mechanical, management, and industrial journals, see Jenks, op. cit., pp. 421–447.
[11] Bendix, op. cit., p. 280.

In spite of these criticisms, the principles of scientific management spread rapidly throughout American industry. Pragmatically they worked to increase the efficiency of industrial operations, and the resistance could be brushed aside in the drive for greater productivity. However, there was a growing philosophical confrontation with Taylor's ideas from many sources. It was stated that scientific management treated workers like cogs in a well-oiled machine and that the system destroyed humanistic practices in industry. This remains the primary criticism today. [12] When we recognize the time setting in which Taylor and his followers were experimenting and writing about their management views, it is inconceivable that they could have the same views on "industrial humanism" that may exist today. Taylor was a product of his environment. He was strongly influenced by the Protestant ethic of his time and the rationalism of economic theory and engineering practices. Within this framework he made major contributions to management thought, contributions which are applied widely throughout industry today.

Scientific Management and Organization Theory

Taylor and his followers were not organizational theorists but were practitioners who operated at the shop level and who were concerned with efficient worker performance. However, Taylor did have a number of implicit concepts concerning management and organization which were important in the development of a general theory. He provided many of the ideas for the conceptual framework later adopted by administrative management theorists, including clear delineation of authority and responsibility, separation of planning from operations, the functional organization, the use of standards in control, the development of incentive systems for workers, the principle of management by exception, and task specialization. Many of the concepts from scientific management were similar to those in Max Weber's bureaucratic model. This was particularly true of Taylor's view that management itself should be governed by rational rules and procedures. He said, "I have tried to point out that the old-fashioned dictator does not exist under scientific management. The man at the head of the business under scientific management is governed by rules and laws which have been developed through hundreds of experiments just as much as the workman is, and the standards which have been developed are equitable." [13]

ADMINISTRATIVE MANAGEMENT THEORY

Scientific management was concerned with optimizing effort at the shop or operative level and thus was a micro approach. In contrast, there developed a body of knowledge during the first half of the twentieth century whose primary emphasis was on establish-

---

[12] J. Boddewyn suggests that many criticisms of Taylor for his lack of consideration for the well-being of the worker and work group are unjustified and are a result of taking his views out of context. He suggests that Taylor was concerned with justice for the workers and that one of his primary considerations was the well-being of the work group. Boddewyn, op. cit., pp. 100-107.

[13] Frederick Winslow Taylor, "Testimony before the Special House Committee," *Scientific Management*, p. 189.

ing broad administrative principles applicable to higher organizational levels. The emphasis was on the development of macro concepts. March and Simon refer to this body of knowledge as ''administrative management theory.'' [14] Other writers call it the traditional or classical theory of management. It focuses on formal organization structure and the delineation of the basic processes of general management.

Henri Fayol: Early Management Theorist

Fayol, a leading French industrialist, was one of the earliest exponents of a general theory of management. He has been described as the father of management theory. His observations, based upon experiences as a top manager, were first published in 1916 as *Administration Industrielle et Générale.* This work was not translated into English until 1929 and was not widely available in the United States until 1949. [15]

Despite the fact that Fayol's writings did not receive wide dissemination until years after the original publication, his concepts have had a profound impact. He defined administration in terms of five primary elements: planning, organization, command, coordination, and control. These five elements of administration have become the foundation for considering the basic processes or functions of management. Fayol and his followers advocated the idea that management was a universal function which could be defined in terms of the various processes which the manager performed. He emphasized that the managerial processes and the principles which he developed were applicable not only to business but to governmental, military, religious, and other organizations. Fayol developed a comprehensive list of principles to provide guidelines for the manager. In introducing these principles he said:

> The soundness and good working order of the body corporate depend on a certain number of conditions termed indiscriminately principles, laws, rules. For preference I shall adopt the term principles whilst dissociating it from any suggestion of rigidity, for there is nothing rigid or absolute in management affairs, it is all a question of proportion. Seldom do we have to apply the same principle twice in identical conditions; allowance must be made for different changing circumstances. [16]

Fayol's fourteen principles were:

1 Division of Work. The principle of specialization of labor in order to concentrate activities for more efficiency.
2 Authority and Responsibility. Authority is the right to give orders and the power to exact obedience.

---

[14] James G. March and Herbert A. Simon, *Organizations,* John Wiley & Sons, Inc., New York, 1958, p. 22.
[15] This translation was Henri Fayol, *General and Industrial Management,* trans, by Constance Storrs, Sir Issac Pitman & Sons, Ltd., London, 1949.
[16] Ibid., p. 19.

3 Discipline. Discipline is absolutely essential for the smooth running of business, and without discipline no enterprise could prosper.

4 Unity of Command. An employee should receive orders from one superior only.

5 Unity of Direction. One head and one plan for a group of activities having the same objectives.

6 Subordination of individual interests to general interests. The interest of one employee or a group should not prevail over that of the organization.

7 Remuneration of Personnel. Compensation should be fair and, as far as possible, afford satisfaction both to personnel and the firm.

8 Centralization. Centralization is essential to the organization and is a natural consequence of organizing.

9 Scalar Chain. The scalar chain is the chain of superiors ranging from the ultimate authority to the lowest rank.

10 Order. The organization should provide an orderly place for every individual. A place for everyone and everyone in his place.

11 Equity. Equity and a sense of justice pervades the organization.

12 Stability of Tenure of Personnel. Time is needed for the employee to adapt to his work and to perform it effectively.

13 Initiative. At all levels of the organizational ladder zeal and energy are augmented by initiative.

14 Esprit de corps. This principle emphasized the need for teamwork and the maintenance of interpersonal relationships. [17]

Although there have been modifications by later administrative management theorists, Fayol's fourteen principles provided the basic foundation for this school of thought. However, it should be emphasized that he recognized that these were neither absolute nor rigid. "Principles are flexible and capable of adaptation to every need; it is a matter of knowing how to make use of them, which is a difficult art requiring intelligence, experience, decision and proportion." [18] He suggested that there was no limit to the number of administrative principles and that new principles whose worth was determined by experience would evolve.

Other Administrative Management Theorists

During the 1920s and 1930s a number of other writers, primarily those actively engaged in management or consulting practices, set forth their views, following the pattern established by Fayol. Luther Gulick and Lyndall Urwick, in particular, carried on Fayol's work in the development of principles based upon wide experience in industry and government. In 1937 they cooperated in editing *Papers on the Science of Administra-*

---

[17] Ibid., pp. 19–42.
[18] Ibid., p. 19.

tion. [19] In these papers and other writings they popularized such principles as (1) fitting people to the organization structure; (2) recognizing one top executive as the source of authority; (3) adhering to unity of command; (4) using special and general staffs; (5) departmentalizing by purpose, process, persons, and place; (6) delegating and utilizing the exception principle; (7) making responsibility commensurate with authority; and (8) considering appropriate spans of control.

Another major contributor to the development of management thought during this period was Mary Parker Follett. Although she was a contemporary of the other administrative management theorists and set forth certain general principles as guidelines for practice, her approach was significantly different. She brought to her writings and speeches a vast knowledge of governmental and business administration. She presented many lectures and wrote articles which taken together established a philosophy of management. [20] She was unique in emphasizing the psychological and sociological aspects of management. She viewed management as a social process and the organization as a social system. Her ideas in such areas as the acceptance of authority, the importance of lateral coordination, the integration of organizational participants, and the necessity for a change in a dynamic administrative process differed substantially from those of other writers. In many ways her ideas can be viewed as a link between the classical administrative management theorists and the behavioral scientists (see Chapter 4).

In the United States the most important contribution to the development of administrative management theory came from two General Motors executives, James D. Mooney and Alan C. Reiley. [21] The principles which Mooney and Reiley set forth had a major impact upon management practice in the United States. They not only drew upon their experiences as business executives but also utilized a historical evaluation of governmental agencies, the Roman Catholic Church, and military organizations as a basis for their views. Their ideas were developed around four major principles: (1) the coordinative principle, which provided for a unity of action in the pursuit of a common objective, (2) the scalar principle, which emphasized the hierarchical organizational form and authority, (3) the functional principle, which organized tasks into departmental units, and (4) the staff principle, which recognized the role of line management in the exercise of authority but provided a staff to give advice and information. Their ideas were related to the development of a pyramidal organizational structure with a clear delineation of authority, specialization of tasks, coordination of activities, and utilization of staff specialists. Application of their concepts led to the establishment of formal organizational charts, position descriptions, and organizational manuals.

---

[19] Luther Gulick and Lyndall Urwick (eds.), *Papers on the Science of Administration,* Institute of Public Administration, Columbia University, New York, 1937.

[20] H. C. Metcalf and Lyndall Urwick (eds.), *Dynamic Administration: The Collected Papers of Mary Parker Follett,* Harper & Row, Publishers, Incorporated, New York, 1941.

[21] James D. Mooney and Alan C. Reiley, *Onward Industry,* Harper & Row, Publishers, Incorporated, New York, 1931.

The Management Process School

The basic ideas of the administrative management theorists are the antecedents of what has been termed the *management process school.*

> This school analyzes the management process, establishes a conceptual framework for it, identifies its principles, and builds a theory of management from them. It regards management as a universal process, regardless of the type or level of enterprise, although recognizing that obviously the environment of managing differs widely between enterprises and levels. It looks upon management theory as a way of organizing experience so that practice can be improved through research, empirical testing of principles, and proper teaching of fundamentals. [22]

The basic approach of this school is to look at the processes of management—planning, organizing, assembling resources, motivating, and controlling—and to set forth certain fundamental principles. It is dedicated to the view that the knowledge concerning management practices can be set forth as a cohesive and coherent body of thought and that generalizations concerning good management practices can be transmitted.

Contribution of Administrative Management Theorists

Although there have been serious questions raised regarding the appropriateness of the approach and principles of the administrative management theorists, many of the concepts from this school are currently applied in organizations. The pyramidal form, the scalar principle, the concept of unity of command, the exception principle, the delegation of authority, limited span of control, and departmentalization principles are currently being applied in the design of many organizations. Although the administrative management theorists have been criticized for their rigid approach with little recognition of human and sociological factors, their ideas still have applicability in the structuring of organizations and in providing general guidelines.

Many current management authors retain as their basic framework the classical approach and have integrated recent developments from the behavioral and management sciences into their views. They utilize the classical viewpoint as a first approximation in their development of organization and management concepts and then make substantial modifications based upon recent empirical research and theory.

Even though, throughout this book, we make substantial modifications to the rigid structure of the administrative management theorists, we recognize that they provided

---

[22] Harold Koontz and Cyril O'Donnell, *Principles of Management,* 4th ed., McGraw-Hill Book Company, New York, 1968, p. 36.

an important link in the development of modern theory. One of their most fundamental contributions was the emphasis on management as a distinct field which should be observed, studied, and improved and which is therefore an important scientific and academic endeavor.

BUREAUCRATIC MODEL

The third major pillar in the development of classical organization concepts was provided by Max Weber's bureaucratic model. Although Weber's views had a profound effect upon sociologists and political scientists, it has only been in recent years that his concepts have been utilized by students of business management.

He was one of the founders of modern sociology and was a significant contributor to economic, social, and administrative thought. Writing during the first part of the twentieth century, he was contemporary with the scientific management movement and the early phases of administrative management thought. However, he not only studied the administration of the single organization but was also interested in the broad economic and political structure of society. His ideas concerning the bureaucratic organization were only a part of a total social theory. In his various writings he traced the changes in religious views, discussed their impact upon the growth of capitalism, and examined the effect of industrialization upon organization structure. His discussions of the bureaucratic mechanism were a natural evolution from broader considerations of historical and social factors which led to the development of complex organizations.

The term *bureaucracy* as developed by Weber and his followers is not used in the popularized, emotionally charged sense of red tape and inefficiency. The bureaucratic model possesses certain structural characteristics and norms which are used in every complex organization. The concept of bureaucracy used herein connotes neither good nor bad in terms of performance but, rather, refers to certain characteristics of organizational design. Weber viewed bureaucracy as the most efficient form, that which could be used most effectively for complex organizations—business, government, military, for example—arising out of the needs of modern society.

The view of rational-legal authority was basic to Weber's concept of bureaucracy. It is the right to exercise authority based on position. "In the case of legal authority, obedience is owed to the legally established impersonal order. It extends to the persons exercising the authority of office under it only by virtue of the formal legality of their commands and only within the scope of the authority of the office." [23] Rational-legal authority is based upon position within the organization, and when it evolves into an organized administrative staff, it takes the form of a "bureaucratic structure." Within this structure each member of the administrative staff occupies a position with a specific delineation of power, compensation is in the form of a fixed salary, the various positions

---

[23] Max Weber, *The Theory of Social and Economic Organization*, trans. by A. M. Henderson and Talcott Parsons, The Free Press of Glencoe, New York, 1964, p. 328. This is a translation of Part One of Weber's *Wirtschaft und Gesellschaft* (Economics and Society), which was unfinished at his death in 1920.

are organized in a hierarchy of authority, fitness for office is determined by technical competence, and the organization is governed by rules and regulations. Weber suggests that the bureaucratic form is the most efficient instrument of large-scale administration which has ever been developed and that modern industrial societies are heavily dependent upon its effective use. He says:

> Experience tends universally to show that the purely bureaucratic type of administrative organization—that is, the monocratic variety of bureaucracy—is, from a purely technical point of view, capable of attaining the highest degree of efficiency and is in this sense formally the most rational known means of carrying out imperative control over human beings. It is superior to any other form in precision, in stability, in the stringency of its discipline, and in its reliability. It thus makes possible a particularly high degree of calculability of results for the heads of the organization and for those acting in relation to it. It is finally superior both in intensive efficiency and in the scope of its operations, and is formally capable of application to all kinds of administrative tasks.
>
> The development of the modern form of the organization of corporate groups in all fields is nothing less than identical with the development and continual spread of bureaucratic administration. This is true of church and state, of armies, political parties, economic enterprises, organizations to promote all kinds of causes, private associations, clubs, and many others. Its development is, to take the most striking case, the most crucial phenomenon of the modern Western state. . . . The whole pattern of everyday life is cut to fit this framework. For bureaucratic administration is, other things being equal, always, from a formal, technical point of view, the most rational type. For the needs of mass administration today, it is completely indispensable. The choice is only that between bureaucracy and dilletantism in the field of administration. [24]

Thus Weber saw the bureaucratic form as emerging from the needs of the environment and as the most effective means for the administration of large, complex organizations in an industrial society. [25]

Dimensions of Bureaucracy

The bureaucratic model has served as a point of departure for many writers, particularly sociologists and political scientists. Recently, a number of social scientists have suggested that bureaucracy is a condition that exists along a continuum rather than being

---

[24] Ibid., p. 337.
[25] For a discussion of the conditions within a society which provides the framework for the development of bureaucratic organizations, see S. N. Eisenstadt, "Bureaucracy, Bureaucratization, and Debureaucratization," *Administrative Science Quarterly*, December 1959, pp. 302–320.

in an absolute sense either present or absent. Hall, for example, suggests that the degree of bureaucratization can be determined by measuring the following six dimensions: (1) a division of labor based upon functional specialization, (2) a well-defined hierarchy of authority, (3) a system of rules covering the rights and duties of positional incumbents, (4) a system of procedures for dealing with work situations, (5) impersonality of interpersonal relations, and (6) promotion and selection for employment based upon technical competence. [26]

In the "ideal" type of bureaucracy all these dimensions would exist to a high degree, whereas in a less bureaucratic organization they would be present to a smaller degree.

Appraisal of large-scale, complex organizations suggests that these dimensions are always present in varying degrees. Bureaucracy is consistent with the general framework of the formal organization structure established by administrative management theorists such as Fayol, Mooney, and Reiley. Weber and his bureaucratic model have provided the theoretical framework and the point of departure for much of the current theory and empirical research on complex organizations.

Research and Modification of Bureaucratic Model

Students of bureaucracy have analyzed Weber's ideal model to determine both its functional and dysfunctional consequences. Merton, Selznick, Gouldner, and others have critically evaluated the bureaucratic form and have suggested that while it may describe an ideal type in terms of formal relationships, it does not take into account consequences dysfunctional to organizational effectiveness. Their studies indicate that the bureaucratic organization is influenced by behavioral factors which Weber did not consider. Merton says that one consequence of bureaucratic structuring on the behavior of organizational participants is disruption in goal achievement. [27] He suggests that the bureaucratic form affects its members' personalities and encourages rigid adherence to rules and regulations for their own sake which may displace the primary goals of the organization.

Selznick suggests modifications in Weber's bureaucratic model. In particular, he emphasizes the delegation of authority and the maintenance of an organization as an adaptive, cooperative system. [28]

Gouldner engaged in empirical research to test the appropriateness of the bureaucratic dimensions and suggested major modifications in Weber's concepts. He was concerned with the consequences of bureaucratic rules on the maintenance of organizational structure and effectiveness. He suggests that bureaucratic mechanisms de-

[26] Richard H. Hall, "The Concept of Bureaucracy: An Empirical Assessment," *American Journal of Sociology,* July 1963, p. 33.

[27] Robert K. Merton, "Bureaucratic Structure and Personality," in *Social Theory and Social Structure,* rev. ed., The Free Press of Glencoe, New York, 1957, pp. 195–206.

[28] Philip Selznick, *TVA and the Grass Roots,* University of California Press, Berkeley, Calif., 1949.

velop certain forms of autocratic leadership and control which may have dysfunctional consequences for the organization. [29]

The modern view is to utilize the Weberian bureaucratic model as a point of departure but also to recognize the limitations and dysfunctional consequences of this highly structured approach. At the risk of oversimplification, the prevailing view suggests that (1) the bureaucratic form is most appropriate for routine organizational activities where productivity is the major objective and that (2) this form is not appropriate for the highly flexible organization which faces many nonroutine activities where creativity and innovation are important. Litwak says: "In short, where organizations deal with non-uniform events, a model of bureaucracy may be more efficient which differs in degree from Weber's in at least six characteristics: horizontal patterns of authority, minimal specialization, mixture of decisions on policy and on administration, little a priori limitation of duty and privileges to a given office, personal rather than impersonal relations, and a minimum of general rules." [30] Many modern writers stress the view that the Weberian bureaucratic form is not appropriate for the innovative organization and further emphasize that in a dynamic society the innovative, creative organization is becoming the rule rather than the exception.

Weber's model was highly mechanistic, and as March and Simon observe, he had more in common with the administrative management theorists such as Fayol than with later writers who conducted empirical studies using the bureaucratic model. [31]

MICROECONOMICS: THEORY OF THE FIRM

The value system of classical economics and the "ideal competitive model" strongly influenced managerial thought and action and provided a rationale for the operation of the business firm within society. Economic theory is also related to organizational theory, particularly in regard to the assumptions about entrepreneurial behavior. It was a basic premise of classical economics that the role of the business manager in a competitive economy was primarily one of adaptation to market forces. The economic theory of the firm was an outgrowth of the broader, more inclusive macroeconomic theory and accepted its premises.

A Normative Theory

Microeconomics is a normative theory in that it attempts to prescribe what the businessman should do in order to maximize profits given a set of simplifying assumptions. It does not describe how managers or firms actually operate.

The economist's view of the firm is not a theory of organization because it treats the firm as a single person. "The economic theory of the firm assumes a single decision

---

[29] Alvin W. Gouldner, *Patterns of Industrial Bureaucracy,* The Free Press of Glencoe, New York, 1954.
[30] Eugene Litwak, "Models of Bureaucracy Which Permit Conflict," *American Journal of Sociology,* September 1961, p. 179.
[31] March and Simon, op. cit., p. 36.

maker who maximizes profit under environmental constraints."[32] While this approach certainly does not describe the complex business organization of today, economists suggest that viewing the firm in this way provides a simplifying assumption which does not basically limit the model's predictive utility.

Other Simplifying Assumptions of Microeconomics

The basic assumption of the firm acting as a single entrepreneur to maximize one goal (profits) was basic to the classical microeconomic view under ideal competitive situations. Modification of this competitive model and considerations of other types of market structures have not changed this basic assumption. Both the theories of monopolistic competition and oligopoly have taken the basic theory of the firm as given and changed the market assumptions. Even in situations of monopoly the assumption is that the entrepreneur is aware of the total environmental situation and acts to maximize the economic profits.

> The concept of the firm to the economist is in reality the concept of the entrepreneurial role, which is treated as though it were the firm for purposes of theoretical analysis. The entrepreneur, as a person or persons, is generally only a figure lurking in the shadow of his actions, although it is his transformation functions that are studied. The person of the entrepreneur is seen only through his actions, which are fatalistically guided by his rational incentive function, which in turn is apparently predetermined (although this is not clear) by technical, biological, or institutional forces rarely examined by economists.[33]

In addition to the basic assumption of the firm acting as an individual entrepreneur with the goal of profit maximization, there are additional simplifying assumptions from the economic theory of the firm such as:

> **1** The firm has a goal (or goals) toward which it strives.
> **2** It moves toward its objectives in a "rational" manner.
> **3** The firm's function is to transform economic inputs into outputs.
> **4** The environment in which the firm operates is given.
> **5** The theory concentrates particularly upon changes in the price and quantities of inputs and outputs.[34]

---

[32] Julian Feldman and Herschel E. Kanter, "Organizational Decision Making," in James G. March (ed.), *Handbook of Organizations*, Rand McNally & Company, Chicago, 1965, p. 629.
[33] Joseph W. McGuire, *Theories of Business Behavior*, © 1964, p. 19. Reprinted by permission of Prentice-Hall, Inc., Englewood Cliffs, N.J.
[34] Ibid., p. 47.

From the viewpoint of the management and organization theorists, it is difficult to accept these simplifying assumptions of the business organization. Furthermore, it is difficult for the astute observer to accept some of the premises relating to the economic environment. [35]

Modifications in the Theory of the Firm

To suggest that there have not been criticisms regarding the theory of the firm from economists themselves would do a disservice to the profession. Many critics have suggested that these limiting assumptions not only present an unreal picture of actual business organizations but, even more pertinent, may restrict the predictive value of the theory. There appear to be at least two major difficulties with the traditional theory of the firm. First, the motivational and rationality assumptions of the theory are unrealistic. There is a question as to whether profit maximization is the single goal of the complex organization. Second, as Cyert and March say, "The 'firm' of the theory of the firm has few of the characteristics we have come to identify with actual business firms. It has no complex organization, no problems of control, no standard operating procedures, no budget, no controller, no aspiring 'middle management'. To some economists it has seemed implausible that a theory of an organization can ignore the fact that it is one." [36]

Within the past several decades there have been a number of economists who have attempted to release the theory of the firm from some of the confining simplifications. Papandreou, for example, emphasized the necessity for looking at the firm as an organization rather than as an entrepreneur. He sees the firm as being influenced by internal and external forces which may modify the traditional view. [37] A number of economists have engaged in empirical research to test the validity of the assumptions of the theory of the firm. Baumol's studies, for example, suggest that firms seek to maximize sales subject to a profit constraint. [38]

Many economists are recognizing that while the theory of the firm may be appropriate as a normative model for limited purposes, it has been severely abused by utilizing it as a descriptive model of actual organizational and managerial behavior. [39] The most important recent work in modifying this view was by Cyert and March in which they developed a theory of the firm considering behavioral factors. "We believe that, in

---

[35] Cyert and March say, "In a modern market society, economic decisions on price, output, product lines, product mix, resource allocation, and other standard economic variables are made not by individual entrepreneurs but by a complex of private and public institutions. Many of these decisions are made within the large, multifunctional, and complicated organizations called firms. These are simple facts. They may not be facts with which economic theory should concern itself, but the disparity between the process by which business decisions appear to be made by complex organizations in the real world and the way in which they are explained by economic theory has provided material for several decades of debate." Richard M. Cyert and James G. March, *A Behavioral Theory of the Firm*, © 1963, p. 4. Reprinted by permission of Prentice-Hall, Inc., Englewood Cliffs, N.J.

[36] Ibid., p. 8.

[37] Andreas G. Papandreou, "Some Basic Problems in the Theory of the Firm," in Bernard F. Haley (ed.), *A Survey of Contemporary Economics*, Richard D. Irwin, Inc., Homewood, Ill., 1952, vol. 2, pp. 183-219.

[38] William J. Baumol, *Business Behavior, Value and Growth*, The Macmillan Company, New York, 1959.

[39] For a discussion of this point, see Fritz Machlup, "Theories of the Firm: Marginalist, Behavioral, Managerial," *The American Economic Review*, March 1967, pp. 1-33.

order to understand contemporary economic decision making, we need to supplement the study of market factors with an examination of the internal operations of the firm— to study the effects of organizational structure and conventional practice on the development of goals, the formation of expectations, and the execution of choices." [40] Their views represent a major modification to the traditional theory of the firm by integrating recent empirical research and findings from the behavioral sciences with economic theory.

In summary, classical economic theory of the firm made little contribution to organization theory. In fact, acceptance of such premises actually precluded the need for organization theory. The simplifying assumptions, while they may have been useful in predicting certain economic aspects of the organization's behavior, certainly were unrealistic in the light of real-world organizations. The current trend is one of questioning this view, engaging in empirical research to determine the validity of the assumptions, and integrating knowledge from other behavioral sciences into the field.

PUBLIC ADMINISTRATION

There is a close relationship between traditional management theory as applied to business and the development of concepts of public administration. Max Weber, in establishing his bureaucratic model, drew upon his observations of public agencies. In the early part of the twentieth century there was continual cross-fertilization between the fields of business and public administration. Public administration was influenced by "scientific management" and the attempts to develop principles of administration. Writers in public administration emphasized the need for increased effectiveness and efficiency in government through improving managerial practices. One of the early leaders in advocating improved administrative practices in government was Woodrow Wilson. [41]

A dominant concept of early writers in public administration was the need for separation between policy making and administration. The policy-making function established the ends or objectives to be achieved and was assumed to be determined by legislative enactment or executive order. The implementation of decisions was the province of the administrative arm of the government. Emphasis was placed upon the development of a non-political civil service system for the administration of the policy decisions of the legislative branch. Consideration was also given to the development of efficient organizations through better financial and personnel management, more effective planning and control, and other administrative techniques. In these areas such writers as Gulick and Urwick had a major influence on public administration as well as business management.

In recent years a number of writers on public administration have challenged the traditional view of the separation of policy making and administration. Peabody and

[40] Cyert and March, op. cit., p. 1.
[41] Woodrow Wilson, "The Study of Administration," *Political Science Quarterly*, June 1887, pp. 197–222.

Rourke suggest this transformation. "This simplified model of decision-making and administration based on a clear-cut separation of policy and administration has long dominated the literature in this area, but since World War II it has increasingly been regarded as an inadequate point of departure for the study of decision-making in public bureaucracies." [42] Many other traditional principles of public administration established in the earlier part of the twentieth century have been challenged. Increasingly, public administration has been concerned with such factors as informal organization, special-interest groups, authority and power, conflict, decision-making processes, and communications. Such writers as Dahl and Lindblom, Gore, and Simon have made significant contributions to developing new approaches in public administration. [43]

In the past two decades writers with a primary interest in public administration have contributed to the development of organization theory. For example, based upon research and observations of public agencies, Blau and Scott have developed many concepts which contribute substantially to the understanding of all types of formal organizations. [44] The bodies of knowledge or theories relevant to business and public organizations have merged. [45] Current emphasis is on the development of concepts concerning all types of formal organizations, rather than on highly specialized theories for individual types.

MAJOR ASSUMPTIONS OF TRADITIONAL THEORY

So far we have reviewed some of the most significant twentieth-century contributions to traditional theory—scientific management, the bureaucratic model, administrative management theory, the microeconomic theory of the firm, and public administration. Although these contributions come from a wide variety of sources based on different experiences and observations, there are certain common threads and similarities.

The basic premise of a rational economic man (complete knowledge and maximizing behavior) was integrated by the classical management writers into their views of the organization. Through specialization in a well-defined hierarchical relationship, work could be organized so as to accomplish the goals of the organization most efficiently. The organization was viewed as a mechanistic system which was planned and controlled by the legitimate authority of management.

The primary emphasis was upon increasing efficiency through structuring and controlling the human participants. People were assumed to be motivated primarily by economic incentives. It was necessary to specialize tasks and to provide detailed

[42] Robert L. Peabody and Francis E. Rourke, "Public Bureaucracies," in March, op. cit., p. 805.
[43] Robert A. Dahl and Charles E. Lindblom, *Politics, Economics, and Welfare,* Harper & Row, Publishers, Incorporated, New York, 1953; William J. Gore, *Administrative Decision-making,* John Wiley & Sons, Inc., New York, 1964; and Herbert A. Simon, *Administrative Behavior,* 2d ed., The Macmillan Company, New York, 1959.
[44] Peter M. Blau and W. Richard Scott, *Formal Organizations,* Chandler Publishing Company, San Francisco, 1962.
[45] For a discussion of the similarities in the evolution of organization theory and political theory, see Herbert Kaufman, "Organization Theory and Political Theory," *The American Political Science Review,* March 1964, pp. 5–14.

instructions and controls. In order to ensure cooperation in meeting organizational goals the participants had to be closely supervised. Management was the primary integrative force and the formal hierarchy was the mechanism for achieving coordination. [46]

The classical management theory thus evolved into the development of concepts such as the pyramidal structure, unity of command, span of control, management by exception, specialization by function, line-staff dichotomy and other generalized "principles of management" which were appropriate for all organizations.

CRITIQUE OF TRADITIONAL VIEW

One of the major criticisms of the classical theory is that it employed closed-system assumptions about organizations which were unrealistic. [47] It was a model which failed to consider many of the environmental influences upon the organization as well as many important internal aspects. Simplifying assumptions were made in order to reduce uncertainty, a process which often led to an incomplete view of actual organizational situations.

Another major criticism of the classical view concerns its unrealistic assumption concerning human behavior. Many of the "principles" derived from the traditionalists have been questioned as being truisms or plain common sense and so general that they lack specific guidelines for application. It has been suggested that many of these concepts actually are internally contradictory. Simon cites, for example, that the principle of specialization is frequently in conflict with the principle of unity of command. [48]

Victor A. Thompson questions the basic premise of authority related to the classical hierarchical structure. He sees a major conflict between the institution of hierarchy based upon position within the organization and the growing importance of technological specialization with its authority of knowledge. [49] Numerous other current writers suggest the necessity for modifying the basic hierarchical structuring of complex organizations.

Another criticism of the classical concepts is that they were written by practitioners in management and were based only upon personal experience and limited observation. The principles have not stood the test of rigorous empirical research using scientific methods.

A primary focus of dissent concerns the view of man in the organization. Thus, March and Simon describe the classical theory as the "machine model." [50] Bennis

---

[46] For a discussion of the underlying assumptions of the classical school, see Joseph L. Massie, "Management Theory," in March, op. cit., pp. 405–418.

[47] James D. Thompson, *Organizations in Action*, McGraw-Hill Book Company, New York, 1967, p. 6.

[48] Herbert A. Simon, *Administrative Behavior*, 2d ed., The Macmillan Company, New York, 1959, pp. 21–26. These views are amplified in March and Simon, op. cit., pp. 12–33.

[49] Victor A. Thompson, "Hierarchy, Specialization, and Organizational Conflict," *Administrative Science Quarterly*, March 1961, pp. 485–521.

[50] March and Simon, op. cit., p. 36.

suggests that the focus of the classical theory is on "organizations without people."[51] However, it may be unfair to criticize the classical theorists too strongly for their restricted view of the nature of man in organizations. Their primary emphasis was upon structuring the organization, formalizing relationships, and setting forth useful principles.

In Chapter 4 we will look at some of the modifications made in the classical theory primarily by behavioral and management scientists. However, we should recognize that the classical concepts still represent an important, although not a total, part of management thinking. Many managers are being guided by these traditional principles (even though they may not be conscious of this heritage). Many of the ideas and concepts coming from the traditional school are useful as an initial or first approximation. The student of organization and management should not accept the classical views without critical evaluation. On the other hand, he should not reject them outright. Current management thought has a heritage from many sources and the traditional theory provides an important linkage. In the next two chapters we build upon these traditional views toward a modern theory of organization and management.

SUMMARY

A systematic body of knowledge concerning organization and management is relatively new. It is closely associated with the industrial revolution and the rise of large-scale enterprises which required the development of new organizational forms and management practices. Traditional organization and management theory is based upon contributions from a number of sources, including scientific management, administrative management theorists, the bureaucratic model, microeconomics, and public administration.

The primary emphasis of scientific management was on planning, standardizing, and improving the efficiency of human work. It viewed management as a science rather than an individualistic approach based upon rule of thumb.

During the first half of the twentieth century there developed a body of knowledge termed "administrative management theory." Henri Fayol was one of the earliest exponents of a general theory of administration. Other writers, primarily those actively engaged in management or consulting practices, set forth their views following the pattern established by him. The pyramidal form, scalar principle, unity of command, exception principle, authority delegation, span of control, and departmentalization concepts were set forth by this group.

Another thread in classical organization theory was provided by Max Weber and his bureaucratic model. He viewed bureaucracy as the most efficient form for complex

---

[51] Warren G. Bennis, "Leadership Theory and Administrative Behavior," *Administrative Science Quarterly,* December 1959, pp. 259–301.

organizations. His model included such dimensions as well-defined hierarchy of authority, division of labor based upon functional specialization, a system of rules, impersonality of interpersonal relationships, a system of work procedures, and placement based upon technical competence.

Economic theory is also related to organization theory and entrepreneurial behavior. It was a basic premise of classical economics that the role of the business manager in a competitive economy was primarily one of adapting to market forces. Microeconomics is a normative theory and attempts to prescribe what businessmen should do in order to maximize profits given a set of simplifying assumptions.

In the early part of the twentieth century there was a continual cross-fertilization between the field of business and public administration. Public administration was influenced by scientific management and the early administrative management theorists. In the past two decades writers with a primary interest in public administration have made contributions to organization theory which are applicable to all types of large-scale, complex organizations.

Traditional management theory operated under certain assumptions such as that of the rational economic man. Management should plan, direct, and control the activities of the work group. Authority had its source at the top of a hierarchy and was delegated downward. Principles were established to guide managerial practices.

Classical theory has been criticized for employing closed-system assumptions about the organization which are unrealistic. It fails to consider many of the environmental and internal influences. It makes unrealistic assumptions about human behavior. The principles of management have been criticized as being too vague and contradictory.

In spite of these criticisms, the classical concepts represent an important, although limited, part of organization theory. Many of them are still utilized in organizations and can serve as an initial or first approximation. They serve as the foundation for more modern views of organization theory and management practice.

QUESTIONS AND PROBLEMS

1 Discuss the relationship between the Protestant ethic and scientific management.
2 Why would management resist scientific management principles? Why would workers and unions react adversely to this movement?
3 Why was the theory of bureaucracy established at a time in history which saw a tremendous increase in the number and size of organizations? How did this theory differ from the ''old'' order?
4 Select any large-scale organization and evaluate the degree to which it adheres to bureaucratic concepts.
5 Relate the development of a body of knowledge concerning organizations to the trend toward professionalism in management.
6 Investigate a business or other large organization to see whether any of the principles from the administrative management theorists are being applied.

7 Give your evaluation of the view of management and organizations contained in classical economic theory. Does this fit "real world" organizations? Why or why not?

8 Do you think business organizations and public agencies should have similar organization and management concepts?

9 Evaluate the major contributions and deficiencies of traditional organization theory.

10 Discuss the view that traditional organization theory emphasized "organizations without people."

11 What assumptions concerning the "nature of man" are represented by the traditional theory?

4
THE BEHAVIORAL AND MANAGEMENT
SCIENCE REVOLUTIONS

Many forces have affected the evolution of organization theory and management practice. New knowledge has come from conceptualization and empirical research in a number of related disciplines—psychology, economics, sociology, anthropology, political science, mathematics and statistics, and industrial engineering, for example. It is difficult to summarize the scientific research being carried on in many fields. However, two broad categories emerge as fundamental: (1) the behavioral sciences, which emphasize the psychosocial system and the human aspects of administration, and (2) the management sciences, which emphasize quantification, mathematical models, and the application of computer technology. The contributions from these two areas have had a profound influence. They will be used as the basic framework for our discussion of the following specific topics:

> Forces Contributing to Change
> Revolution in Two Directions
> The Behavioral Sciences
> The Management Sciences
> Divergence and Convergence in Theory and Practice

FORCES CONTRIBUTING TO CHANGE

Many forces both within organizations and in the external environment have stimulated change in theory and practice. The growth in size of organizations has been unparalleled. In addition to growth, there has been an increase in complexity. For example, in the early part of the twentieth century business firms typically concentrated on a limited line of products. By the middle of the twentieth century many large firms had heterogeneous operations. Diversity has come about in several ways. Companies have grown through diversification into new fields. The development of large-scale conglomerates and multinational corporations has accelerated. These trends have fostered increased complexity in the business organization. Other types of organizations have undergone similar growth in size and complexity—hospitals, schools, and government agencies, for example.

Specialization within the organization has increased. At the worker level it resulted from mechanization and the scientific management movement. The use of management specialists increased during the first part of the twentieth century—the personnel expert, the quality control technician, the industrial engineer, the market researcher, and a number of others. With increased specialization, the problems of integrating people into organizational effort multiplied and required new management concepts.

Another characteristic of modern organizations is the diversity of objectives of various participants and subgroups. To speak of an enterprise as having one single goal does not give recognition to the fact that it is a social institution.

Technological change has forced many adaptations. Mechanization and assembly line production plus more recent trends in automation, computers, and information technology are all factors which have altered traditional relationships between man and machine. Modern organizations must draw upon the specialized scientific and technical knowledge of many highly trained participants, and must provide the mechanism for the coordination of their efforts and informational inputs. Galbraith sees technology as fundamentally altering organizations. "The requirements of technology and planning have greatly increased the need of the industrial enterprise for specialized talent and for its organization." [1] He calls the new corporate organization the "technostructure" which includes all participants who bring specialized knowledge, talent, or experience to group decision making and who collectively are the guiding intelligence of the organization.

Much has been written of the human consequences of the sociotechnical changes brought on by advancing industrialization. One of the earliest and most pessimistic forecasts was made at the turn of the century by the sociologist Emil Durkheim. [2] He believed that the rapid industrialization had broken down the *solidaire* within social groups. Family and community relationships were destroyed, and the individual was unable to replace these with new satisfactory social interactions. In this country, Mayo said: "This is a clear statement of the issue the civilized world is facing now, a rapid industrial, mechanical, physiochemical advance, so rapid that it has been destructive of all the historic social and personal relationships." [3] More recently it has been suggested that the work organization is an important substitute for the traditional systems

---

[1] John Kenneth Galbraith, *The New Industrial State,* Houghton Mifflin Company, Boston, 1967, p. 57.
[2] Emil Durkheim, *Le Suicide,* Librairie Félix Alcan, Paris, 1930.
[3] Elton Mayo, *The Social Problems of an Industrial Civilization,* Harvard Graduate School of Business Administration, Boston, 1945, p. 8.

of social interaction and psychological attachments which people had in older societies. Levinson says: "Affiliation with an organization in which a person works seems to have become a major device for coping with the problems resulting from these economic, social, and psychological changes. . . . In a man's movement from one neighborhood or community to another, the work organization is his thread of continuity and may well become a psychological anchor point for him." [4]

There were many other changes in the sociocultural environment which affected organizations and management. Increased general educational levels provided people with more intellectual skills and required new inducements to secure effective participation. The rising aspiration levels for satisfaction of economic and other needs were important factors. Increasing collective actions through union membership, particularly during the 1930s, forced managerial modifications. Our society is becoming increasingly aware of ecological and environmental issues. The impact of all organizations on their environment is a major social concern.

These changes during the twentieth century have led to an evolution in organization theory and management practice. Traditional theory was based upon the environmental and organizational characteristics of the industrial revolution. It has been modified by new intellectual inputs to meet the needs of a modern industrial society.

REVOLUTION IN TWO DIRECTIONS

Much of the development in modern theory can be attributed to interdisciplinary contributions. Organizations and management have become focal points for research. This field is relatively new and there is no single well-defined community of scholars and practitioners. Researchers, working in such diverse fields as biology, mathematics, animal psychology, logic, and philosophy, have made indirect contributions to organization theory and management. Other fields that have contributed more directly are sociology, anthropology, economics, psychology, political science, and history, as well as closely related fields such as public administration, management science, and industrial psychology or sociology. While these contributions have added greatly to our knowledge and understanding, the wide diversity of assumptions, models, and research findings has increased the problem of understanding and integration for the student.

The traditional school suggested a rather clear-cut concept of the process of management and provided definitive principles as guidelines to action. In so doing it provided a relatively restricted model which excluded many variables from consideration. Basically the revolution resulted in the opening up of the traditional views to many intervening and confounding variables which have become increasingly important in organization theory.

---

[4] Harry Levinson, "Reciprocation: The Relationship between Man and Organization," *Administrative Science Quarterly*, March 1965, p. 373.

The two primary sources of new ideas have been the behavioral and management sciences. Management science can be considered as a basic extension of scientific management but with modification. It is concerned with the organization primarily as an *economic-technical* system. This approach has developed since the end of World War II with contributions from economics, engineering, mathematics, and statistics. The primary emphasis of this school is in the establishment of normative models of managerial and organizational behavior for maximizing efficiency. This view focuses on the manager as a decision maker and uses systematic analysis and quantitative techniques to optimize performance toward certain objectives. The growing sophistication and development of techniques in mathematics, statistics, economics, and engineering, together with advancing computer technology, have provided the primary tools for analyzing complex problems.

The second major segment of the revolution came from the behavioral sciences. In their study of organizations the behavioral scientists emphasize the *psychosocial system* with primary consideration of the human components. They are concerned with studying organizations in the real world and less interested in establishing normative models. Using an open-system approach, they have considered many variables which were excluded from the closed-system models. Whereas traditional management concepts were concerned with structure and task, the emphasis of the behavioral scientists is on human factors and the way the people behave in actual organizations. The behavioral school is interested in empirical research to verify theories of organizational behavior. Typically they have a "humanistic" view which differs substantially from the mechanistic orientation of the traditionalists and management scientists. "In contrast to other approaches, the behavioral view centers more on the people, their interactions and cooperation. It emphasizes, more than the traditional approach, the development of insights and understanding based on empirical investigation." [5]

These two approaches, behavioral and management sciences, have made such important contributions to organization theory and management practice that they should be considered in detail.

THE BEHAVIORAL SCIENCES

The behavioral sciences are relatively recent academic and intellectual disciplines. Much of the work in psychology, sociology, and anthropology is a product of this century, particularly the empirical research. They have provided new insights into human behavior over the whole spectrum of man's activities. Obviously in this section we cannot consider the whole body of knowledge developed in the behavioral sciences. Therefore we will concentrate on those areas which are pertinent to organization theory and managerial practices.

---

[5] Paul J. Gordon, "Transcend the Current Debate on Administrative Theory," *Academy of Management Journal,* December 1963, p. 295.

Definition of the Behavioral Sciences

Berelson and Steiner distinguish the behavioral sciences—psychology, sociology, and anthropology—from the social sciences as follows:

> In our usage here, we do not equate the behavioral sciences with the social sciences. The latter term is usually understood to cover six disciplines: anthropology, economics, history, political science, psychology, and sociology. By the behavioral sciences we mean the disciplines of anthropology, psychology, and sociology—minus and plus: *Minus* such specialized sectors as physiological psychology, archeology, technical linguistics, and most of physical anthropology; *Plus* social geography, some psychiatry, and the behavioral parts of economics, political science, and law. In short, we are concerned here with the scientific research that deals directly with human behavior. [6]

To be classified as a behavioral science a field of study must satisfy at least two basic criteria: (1) it must deal with human behavior and (2) it must use a "scientific" approach. "The scientific aim is to establish generalizations about human behavior that are supported by empirical evidence collected in an impersonal and objective way. . . . The ultimate end is to understand, explain, and predict human behavior in the same sense in which scientists understand, explain, and predict the behavior of physical forces or biological factors or closer to home, the behavior of goods and prices in the economic market." [7] Many research efforts and conceptualizations from the behavioral sciences have contributed to organization theory and management practice, beginning with the pioneer human relationists.

Pioneer Human Relationists

The human relations movement in industry began with the research of Elton Mayo and his associates in a series of studies carried out at the Hawthorne Plant of the Western Electric Company between 1927 and 1932. [8] The background of the Hawthorne experiments provides an interesting picture of the transition from scientific management to the early human relations movement. Employees had been considered as mechanistic elements in the productive system. Industrial engineers and psychologists made many

---

[6] Bernard Berelson and Gary A. Steiner, *Human Behavior: An Inventory of Scientific Findings*, Harcourt, Brace & World, Inc., New York, 1964, pp. 10–11.

[7] Bernard Berelson (ed.), *The Behavioral Sciences Today*, Basic Books, Inc., Publishers, New York, 1963, p. 3.

[8] The research in the Hawthorne experiments has been described in detail in a number of books and reports. For example, Elton Mayo, *The Human Problems of an Industrial Civilization*, The Macmillan Company, New York, 1933; T. N. Whitehead, *The Industrial Worker*, Harvard University Press, Cambridge, Mass., 1938, vol. II; F. J. Roethlisberger and W. J. Dickson, *Management and the Worker*, Harvard University Press, Cambridge, Mass., 1939.

investigations of the relationship of work environment to productivity. Studies on fatigue, rest periods, and physical surroundings were prevalent during the early part of the twentieth century.

The stimulus for the Hawthorne experiments resulted from earlier studies which were based upon the scientific management tradition. At the Hawthorne Plant, the Western Electric Company, in collaboration with the National Research Council, initiated a study to determine the relationship between the intensity of illumination and the efficiency of workers as measured by output. Although good research methods were used, including control groups, the experiment failed to show any simple relationship between intensity of illumination and rate of output. In fact, when the engineers reversed the experiment and reduced the illumination in the experimental room, instead of output declining as predicted, it actually increased. This experiment suggested that variables other than physical conditions might be affecting output. Psychological and sociological factors might have an important bearing not only upon worker motivation and attitude but upon output as well. At this point Elton Mayo and his Harvard colleagues, F. J. Roethlisberger and T. N. Whitehead, were called in by the company to help establish more rigid controls for experimental purposes and to isolate these intervening variables.

The basic studies by Mayo and his group took place over a five-year period and covered three phases: (1) the relay assembly test room experiment, (2) the interviewing program, and (3) the bank wiring observation room. The relay assembly test room experiment involved the prolonged observation of six girls making telephone assemblies. A series of studies was undertaken to determine the effects on output of working conditions, length of working day, frequency and length of rest periods, and other factors relating to the physical environment. As these studies continued, it was found that regardless of variations in these conditions, production increased. Even more astounding, production continued to increase even after the girls were returned to the original conditions with longer working days, without rest pauses, and with poor surroundings. Mayo and his group hypothesized that the increased production was a result of changed social situations of the workers, modifications in their motivation and satisfactions, and differing patterns of supervision.

This experiment provided a break from the tradition of scientific management and industrial psychology which had held that illumination, work conditions, rest periods, fatigue, and other physical and physiological variables combined with strong monetary incentives were the primary factors influencing output and productivity. Social and psychological factors were now seen as being of major importance in determining worker satisfaction and productivity.[9]

This led to the second stage of the Hawthorne studies, in which over 21,000 people were interviewed during a three-year period. It was initially started as directed interviewing but moved toward nondirective, in-depth interviewing. Although this phase

---

[9] Roethlisberger and Dickson, op. cit., pp.185–186.

of the program did not lead to a quantifiable result, it did indicate the importance of human and social factors in the total work situation. Some generalizations from this program were:

1 A complaint is not necessarily an objective recital of facts; it is a symptom of personal disturbance the cause of which may be deep seated.

2 Objects, persons, and events are carriers of social meanings. They become related to employee satisfaction or dissatisfaction only as the employee comes to view them from his *personal situation.*

3 The personal situation of the worker is a configuration of relationships composed of a personal reference involving sentiments, desires, and interests of that person and a social reference constituting the person's social past and his present interpersonal relations.

4 The position or status of the worker in the company is a reference from which the worker assigns meaning and value to the events, objects, and features of his environment, such as hours of work, wages, etc.

5 The social organization of the company represents a system of values from which the worker derives satisfactions or dissatisfactions according to his conception of his social status and the expected social rewards.

6 The social demands of the worker are influenced by social experiences in groups both inside and outside the work plant. [10]

The third and final phase of the research program consisted of a study to observe and record group behavior of workers. The bank wiring observation room study was an intensive observation of a small work group of fourteen male operators for a period of six months. [11] The informal work group established production and output norms which were often in conflict with those set forth by management. In spite of the fact that the workers were paid on a group piecework incentive plan, each worker restricted output, thereby reducing possible earnings. The work group determined the output of individual workers, indicating that production was more determined by social rather than aptitude and physiological factors. The work group established many other types of social norms in addition to output standards. These norms set forth various roles for individual workers and supervisory personnel.

The bank wiring room observations indicated the strength of the informal social organization which was based upon sentiments and feelings, status roles, and social interactions which were often far removed from the formal organizational policies and procedures.

---

[10] Delbert C. Miller and William H. Form, *Industrial Sociology*, Harper & Row, Publishers, Incorporated, New York, 1951, p. 58.
[11] The interpretations and conclusions are set forth in detail in Roethlisberger and Dickson, op. cit., chaps. 22 and 23.

Contributions of Early Human Relationists

The Hawthorne studies provided scientific verification for the changing view of many students of industrial organizations. The early human relationists brought to the forefront the concept of the organization as a social system encompassing individuals, informal groups, and intergroup relationships as well as formal structure. In effect, this view put the human element back into the organization—the aspect which the traditionalists had minimized.

The early human relationists had two primary orientations. The first was a basic concern for man in the organization. Scott calls this ideological approach *industrial humanism*. "Basic to the philosophy of industrial humanism is the design of the work environment to provide for the restoration of man's dignity." [12] Mayo emphasized the necessity for reevaluating the traditional hypothesis of economic theory which considered society to be made up of individuals who were trying to maximize self-interest. He called for modifications in the industrial system to give greater recognition to human values. [13]

The second major emphasis of the human relationists was the utilization of the research methods of the behavioral sciences in studying organizational behavior. The Hawthorne studies continue to be important examples of behavioral research in industry and set the foundation for later investigations.

Mayo, Roethlisberger, Whitehead, and other early human relationists developed many concepts about human behavior in organizations such as:

1 The business organization is a social system as well as a technical-economic system. This social system defines individual roles and establishes norms which may be at variation with those of the formal organization.

2 The individual is not only motivated by economic incentives, but is motivated by diverse social and psychological factors. His behavior is affected by feelings, sentiments, and attitudes.

3 The informal work group became a dominant unit of consideration. The group has an important role in determining the attitudes and performance of individual workers.

4 Leadership patterns based upon the formal structure and authority of position in the organization under the traditional view should be modified substantially in order to consider psychosocial factors. The human relationists emphasized "democratic" rather than "authoritarian" leadership patterns.

5 The human relations school generally associated worker satisfaction with productivity and emphasized that increasing satisfaction would lead to increased effectiveness.

---

[12] William G. Scott, *Organization Theory*, Richard D. Irwin, Inc., Homewood, Ill., 1967, p. 43.
[13] Elton Mayo, *The Social Problems of an Industrial Civilization*, and Elton Mayo, *The Human Problems of an Industrial Civilization*.

6 It is important to develop effective communication channels between the various levels in the hierarchy that allow the exchange of information. Thus "participation" became an important approach of the human relations movement.

7 Management requires effective social skills as well as technical skills.

8 Participants can be motivated in the organization by fulfilling certain social-psychological needs.

In spite of the fact that the human relations school had a major impact upon management thought, there has been substantial dissent. Few research programs have been so thoroughly criticized or reinforced. They continue to be the subject of intense debate. [14]

As the traditional management writers overemphasized the technical and structural aspects, the human relationists overemphasized the psychosocial aspects. They have been criticized for viewing human relations in a closed system and for not considering economic, political, and other environmental forces. One of the major neglects of the early human relationists was inadequate consideration of the role of unions in the industrial society. The impression from many of Mayo's writings is that he thought unions were rather unnecessary if management was performing its functions effectively. This coincides with another criticism that Mayo was authoritarian and really was bent upon the maintenance of the hierarchical structure but with the manager giving greater consideration to human factors in order to maintain the traditional system. In spite of these criticisms there is little doubt that the early human relationists had an impact upon management practices. [15]

Other Behavioral Transitionalists

Mayo, Roethlisberger, and other early human relationists were by no means the only behavioral scientists who contributed to the new developments in organization theory. Actually several intellectual currents prior to the Hawthorne studies supported the changing views. The writings of Freud and his followers concerning subconscious motivation, frustration of needs, and the importance of attitudes and sentiments upon behavior had an impact upon the human relationists. Pareto's work in general sociology provided the theoretical framework for the Hawthorne research. As Scott says, "A comparative analysis of Pareto's general sociology and the major works of the Hawthorne human relationists reveals striking similarities in the theoretical systems. . . . The concepts of the social system, logical and nonlogical behavior, equilibrium, the func-

---

[14] For example, see Alex Carey, "The Hawthorne Studies: A Radical Criticism," *American Sociological Review.* June 1967, pp. 403–416.

[15] Many have suggested that the human relationists had more of an impact upon managerial ideology than upon actual practices. For example, Reinhard Bendix says, "My conclusion will be that Mayo's ideological synthesis has found only limited acceptance in managerial *practice,* but that its contribution to managerial *ideology* has been pervasive." *Work and Authority in Industry,* John Wiley & Sons, Inc., New York, 1956, p. 319.

tions of language, and the circulation of the elite are the essential features of the theoretical scheme of Pareto and the human relationists." [16]

During the 1930s and 1940s others provided important behavioral insights for organization theory and management practice. Carl Rogers and his client-centered therapy and sociometric studies by Moreno were important landmarks. Rogers used a neo-Freudian approach to counseling therapy, clinical methods, and nondirective interviewing techniques. [17] Moreno, in his studies of interpersonal relations, developed sociometric techniques which received wide interest. [18] Kurt Lewin and his followers contributed to group dynamics and emphasized field theory. Much of the current work in individual behavioral change through group dynamics (Alcoholics Anonymous, Weight Watchers, sensitivity training, etc.) and the action-research approach to organization development is based on his pioneering efforts and concepts. Concepts of organizational behavior have been strongly influenced by the theory of motivation advanced by Maslow. [19] His hierarchy directed the emphasis away from the satisfaction of basic economic and survival needs toward higher-level social, esteem, and self-actualization needs. These are but a few of the earlier behavioral scientists who contributed to the "body of knowledge" concerning human behavior, social interactions, and interpersonal relations in organizations.

In addition there were a number of management writers who had a definite behavioral orientation. As indicated previously, one of the earliest writers with a psychological-sociological orientation was Mary Parker Follett. Writing at the time of classical management theorists, her ideas represented a substantial departure. She viewed management as a social process and developed many ideas which have been supported by behavioral research.

One of the most profound and insightful treatises on organization and management was written by Chester Barnard, based upon his many years of experience as president of the New Jersey Bell Telephone Company. Barnard can be called a transitionalist between traditional management theory and the evolving behavioral concepts. He stressed the psychosocial aspects of organization and management rather than economic and technical aspects. He developed a broad conceptual model based upon practical experience and a wide intellectual contact with economics, sociology, psychology, philosophy, and many other fields. He was among the first to consider the organization as a social system. "It is the central hypothesis of this book that the most useful concept for the analysis of experience of coöperative systems is embodied in the definition of a formal organization as a *system of consciously coördinated activities or forces of two or more persons.*" [20]

Barnard set forth many concepts similar to the developing views of the behavioral

[16] Scott, op. cit., p. 38. Scott provides a detailed evaluation of the similarities in the theoretical systems of Pareto and the Hawthorne human relationists on pp. 40-41.
[17] Carl P. Rogers, *Counseling and Psychotherapy,* Houghton Mifflin Company, Boston, 1942.
[18] J. L. Moreno, *Who Shall Survive?* Beacon House, Inc., Beacon, N.Y., 1953.
[19] A. H. Maslow, *Motivation and Personality,* Harper & Row, Publishers, Incorporated, New York, 1954.
[20] Chester I. Barnard, *The Function of the Executive,* Harvard University Press, Cambridge, Mass., 1938, p. 73.

scientists. The existence of the organization depends upon the maintenance of an equilibrium between the contributions and the satisfactions of the organizational participants. Psychosocial rewards as well as material inducements should be provided. Informal organizations and their relationships to the formal structure should be considered. His "acceptance" theory of authority differed substantially from the legitimate positional authority of Max Weber and the management traditionalists. Authority depends basically upon the willingness of the subordinate to comply rather than upon the position of the superior. He emphasized the role of communication in maintaining the organization as a cooperative system and stressed social and psychological factors in his discussion of the environment of the decision-making process.

Many other behavioral scientists and management writers with a behavioral orientation made significant contributions during the 1950s and 1960s. It would be impossible to discuss all of these individually; many of their findings and views will be interwoven into the discussion in the following chapters.

There has been a growing interest on the part of behavioral scientists in studying business organizations. Business schools have attracted behavioral scientists to their faculties and have encouraged interactions with other university departments. The Ford Foundation, among others, provided substantial support to stimulate interdisciplinary approaches in business schools. Many studies using behavioral research methods have been undertaken in such areas as leadership, motivation, intergroup relationships, communication, and control. Also, broad conceptual models for understanding complex organizations have been developed. Throughout this book we will integrate research findings and concepts from the behavioral sciences into the specific topical discussion. However, it is important to emphasize two trends—change agents and power equalization.

Behavioral Scientists as Change Agents

In our society there is a growing interest and concern for social as well as technological change. During the twentieth century we have moved away from the concept of nonintervention in social affairs which stemmed from the "natural law" and "invisible hand" ideology of the laissez faire doctrine of automatic adjustment. Today in a large number of our activities we are becoming concerned with the methods used in planning and controlling the forces of change. "Human interventions designed to shape and modify the institutionalized behaviors of men are now familiar features of our social landscape." [21] Increasingly, we are not only studying the social system but are actively engaged in shaping its course.

Behavioral scientists interested in the study of organization and management are not just neutral observers and describers but are taking an active interest in changing the system. "In short, behavioral scientists are not only *interpreting* the world in different

---

[21] Warren G. Bennis, Kenneth D. Benne, and Robert Chin (eds.), *The Planning of Change*, 2d ed., Holt, Rinehart, and Winston, Inc., New York, 1969, p. 30.

ways; some intend to *change* it."[22] This new role as a change agent presents many dilemmas in terms of professional versus organizational identification for the behavioral scientists. It also brings to the forefront basic questions of value systems.[23] There frequently develops an "understanding gap" between the perspective of the behavioral scientist and his psychosocial orientation and the manager who must also consider economic-technical factors. However, the trend is evident and will have a continuing important impact.

Power Equalization Emphasis of the Behavioral Scientists

The writings of many of the behavioral scientists emphasize the value of more democratic, less authoritarian, less hierarchically structured organizations than proposed in the traditional view which attempted to structure human behavior. Shepard refers to a "coercion-compromise" system which relies heavily upon internal systems of command, on authority and obedience, and upon bureaucratic relations for governing the actions of participants.[24] He sees many adverse consequences of this approach. By comparison most behavioral scientists advocate a "collaboration-consensus" or "power equalization" system. Leavitt describes this as follows:

> Besides the belief that one changes people first, these power-equalization approaches also place major emphasis on other aspects of the human phenomena of organizations. They are, for example, centrally concerned with affect; with morale, sensitivity, psychological security. Secondly, they value evolutionary, internally generated change in individuals, groups, and organizations over externally planned or implemented change. Thirdly, they place much value on human growth and fulfillment as well as upon task accomplishment; and they often have stretched the degree of causal connection between the two. Finally, of course, the power-equalization approaches, in their early stages at least, shared a normative belief that power in organizations should be more equally distributed than in most existent "authoritarian" hierarchies. Operationally, this belief was made manifest in a variety of ways: in encouraging independent decision making, decentralization, more open communication, and participation.[25]

Many modern behavioral scientists advocate a democratic, participative approach. The concepts will be discussed in detail in Part 5: The Psychosocial System.

---

[22] Warren G. Bennis, "New Role for Behavioral Science," *Administrative Science Quarterly*, September 1963, p. 127.
[23] B. F. Skinner, *Beyond Freedom and Dignity*, Alfred A. Knopf, Inc., New York, 1971.
[24] Herbert A. Shepard, "Changing Interpersonal and Intergroup Relationships in Organizations," in James G. March (ed.), *Handbook of Organizations*, Rand McNally & Company, Chicago, 1965, p. 1130.
[25] Harold J. Leavitt, "Applied Organizational Change in Industry: Structural, Technological and Humanistic Approaches," March, op. cit., p. 1154.

At this stage we will merely introduce them briefly. Likert suggests an "interaction-influence" system which uses the concept of supportive relationships between members in the organization as a central theme. He advocates the development of effective working groups linked to other such groups in a large organizational system.[26] McGregor also followed this theme by emphasizing the desirability of replacing the authoritarian Theory X by the more democratic-participative Theory Y.[27] Argyris reflects still more support for this view. He focuses upon the need for the organization to provide an "authentic" relationship for its participants. In his view the traditional organization restricts human growth and self-fulfillment.[28] Maslow has extended his theory of motivation to emphasize the importance of providing an organization environment in which the individual can achieve maximum "self-actualization."[29] Bennis is perhaps even more outspoken when he says "democracy is inevitable." In his view the traditional concepts of Weber's bureaucracy and the administrative management theorists are inappropriate for modern organizations.

> [The bureaucratic] form of organization is becoming less and less effective. . . . it is hopelessly out of joint with contemporary realities, and. . . . new shapes, patterns, and models—currently recessive—are emerging which promise drastic changes in the conduct of the corporation and in managerial practices in general. So within the next twenty-five to fifty years, we should all be witness to, and participate in, the end of bureaucracy and the rise of new social systems better able to cope with the twentieth-century demands.[30]

Bennis advocates that behavioral scientists should be actively engaged in changing the traditional bureaucratic form toward more democratic social systems.

We have presented a few of the views of current behavioral scientists, with varying academic specialties, who have a general humanistic orientation toward organization and management. They emphasize human values and, consequently, tend to depreciate economic and technical considerations, which may be overriding in some situations. Their views have profoundly influenced organization theory and management practices. In the future they will be active as "change agents" through direct participation in organizational activities.

---

[26] Rensis Likert, *New Patterns of Management*, McGraw-Hill Book Company, New York, 1961. See also: Rensis Likert, *The Human Organization*, McGraw-Hill Book Company, New York, 1967.

[27] Douglas McGregor, *The Human Side of Enterprise*, McGraw-Hill Book Company, New York, 1960. In a later book, McGregor amplified this view as follows:"Management must seek to create conditions (an organizational environment) such that members of the organization at all levels can best achieve their own goals by directing their efforts toward the goals of the organization." *The Professional Manager*, ed. by Warren G. Bennis and Caroline McGregor, McGraw-Hill Book Company, New York, 1967, p. 13.

[28] Chris Argyris, *Integrating the Individual and the Organization*, John Wiley & Sons, Inc., New York, 1964.

[29] Abraham Maslow, *Toward a Psychology of Being*, D. Van Nostrand Company, Inc., Princeton, N.J., 1962.

[30] Warren G. Bennis, *Changing Organizations*, McGraw-Hill Book Company, New York, 1966, p. 4.

THE MANAGEMENT SCIENCES

A second major revolution came about through the application of quantitative methods to decision making. This is a post-World War II development and has generally been termed *operations research* or *management science.* In many ways the approach is a descendant from the scientific management movement with the addition of more so-phisticated (primarily mathematical) methods, computer technology, and an orientation toward broader problems. It adopts the *scientific method* as a framework for problem solving with emphasis on objective rather than subjective judgment. Like Taylor, the current management scientists are dedicated to the utilization of scientific approaches for the solution of management problems and emphasize a normative approach to provide the manager with optimal decisions. It prescribes how the manager should decide, give certain assumptions of economic-technical rationality and the objectives to be achieved.

In order to develop an approach which emphasizes optimal managerial decision making, certain assumptions about organizations and participant behavior have been made by the operations researchers or management scientists. These assumptions often differ from those made by behavioral scientists. This difference may be basic to the background disciplines which have become interested in these two approaches. As indicated previously, the behavioral scientists were drawn primarily from the social sciences with a psychosocial orientation. In contrast, most of the contributors to man-agement science come from mathematics, statistics, engineering, and economics and have an economic-technical orientation. It is normal, therefore, that these two ap-proaches take different views and operate under varying assumptions.

Definition and Nature of Management Science

It is difficult to define this area and even to select an appropriate label. It has been called management science, operations research, or quantitative analysis, and is also related to industrial engineering and mathematical economics. We have selected a convenient title, management sciences, recognizing that there are differences of opinion. It is useful to look at the various fields in order to determine the broad boundaries and areas covered. Miller and Starr define operations research simply as *applied decision theory.* "Operations research uses any scientific, mathematical, or logical means to attempt to cope with the problems that confront the executive when he tries to achieve a thorough-going rationality in dealing with his decision problems." [31] They emphasize that opera-tions research is directed toward solving actual problems facing the executive. It is not theoretically oriented, it is directed to problem solving and application. The Operations

---

[31] David W. Miller and Martin K. Starr, *Executive Decisions and Operations Research,* Prentice-Hall, Inc., Engle-wood Cliffs, N.J., 1960, p. 104.

Research Society of America, Committee on Professional Standards, provides a similar definition: "Operations research is an experimental and applied science devoted to observing, understanding, and predicting the behavior of purposeful man-machine systems; and operations-research workers are actively engaged in applying this knowledge to practical problems in business, government, and society." [32]

The term "management science" received its initial impetus with the establishment of The Institute of Management Sciences (TIMS) in 1953 with the objective "To identify, extend, and unify scientific knowledge that contributes to the understanding and practice of management." Although there have been numerous attempts made to distinguish between operations research and management science, it is difficult to make any clear-cut distinction. Several have suggested that the term management science is broader in that it encompasses within its sphere such fields as mathematical economics and behavioral sciences and also has a close relationship with engineering and the physical sciences.

Others have suggested that operations research is operationally oriented while management science is directed toward establishment of broad theory. "Although operations research and management science are now closely related, they are quite different but complementary in their purposes. Operations research represents the problem-solving objective; management science the development of general scientific knowledge. Nevertheless, much of our understanding of management science came through operations research, as well as industrial engineering and econometrics." [33] Although this may be a sound theoretical separation, in practice it is difficult to see a distinction between people who call themselves management scientists or operations researchers. A look at recent issues of *Management Science* and *Operations Research*, the two major publications in this area, suggests that there is a good deal of similarity and that the authors of articles do not make a distinction between these terms. In fact many authors use the designation MS/OR (Management Science/Operations Research) to designate the profession. [34] Simon summarizes his views as to the relationships between scientific management, operations research, and management science as follows:

> Except in matters of degree (e.g., the operations researchers tend to use rather high-powered mathematics) it is not clear that operations research embodies any philosophy different from that of scientific management. Charles Babbage and Frederick Taylor will have to be made, retroactively,

---

[32] "Guidelines for the Practice of Operations Research," *Operations Research*, September 1971, p. 1138.
[33] Gifford H. Symonds, "The Institute of Management Sciences: Progress Report," *Management Science*, January 1957, p. 126.
[34] See, for example, William H. Gruber and John S. Niles, "Problems in the Utilization of Management Science/Operations Research: A State of the Art Survey," *Interfaces*, November 1971, pp. 12–19.

charter members of the operations research societies. . . .No meaningful line can be drawn any more to demarcate operations research from scientific management or scientific management from management science. [35]

There is a close relationship between management science and industrial engineering. They are interested in many of the same problems and frequently use similar techniques. Industrial engineering often uses concepts and models developed by management science for direct applications. [36]

In recent years MS/OR also has been influenced by mathematical economists. Subjects such as marginal analysis, maximization, demand theory, equilibrium analysis, input-output analysis, and utility theory have been included in the management sciences. Baumol suggests that a basic hallmark of the economic theorist's approach to the analysis of business problems is the concept of optimization. "The approach of optimality analysis is to take these alternatives into account and to ask which of these possible sets of decisions will come *closest* to meeting the businessman's objectives, i.e., which decisions will be best or *optimal*." [37] He says that the operations researcher also attempts to use optimality as the normative criterion for managerial decision making but from a different viewpoint. The economist's focus is on theory development, while the operations researcher is concerned with practical application. However, there is substantial cross-fertilization between the fields.

Other disciplines have contributed to the development of the management sciences. Mathematics and statistics have provided many analytical tools; evolving computer technology has facilitated the utilization of sophisticated quantitative methods. Although MS/OR is a rather loose conglomeration of interests and approaches, there are key concepts which permeate the field:

1 Emphasis upon scientific method
2 Systematic approach to problem solving
3 Mathematical model building
4 Quantification and utilization of mathematical and statistical procedures
5 Concern with economic-technical rather than psychosocial aspects
6 Utilization of electronic computers as tools
7 Emphasis on total systems approach
8 Seeking optimal decisions under closed-system assumptions
9 Orientation to normative rather than descriptive models

---

[35] Herbert A. Simon, *The Shape of Automation: For Men and Management*, Harper & Row, Publishers Incorporated, New York, 1965, pp. 68-69.
[36] Norman N. Barish, "Operations Research and Industrial Engineering: The Applied Science and Its Engineering," *Operations Research*, May-June 1963, p. 391.
[37] William J. Baumol, *Economic Theory and Operations Analysis*, Prentice-Hall, Inc., Englewood Cliffs, N.J., 1961, p. 4.

While most of the management scientists tend to emphasize economic-technical aspects of organizations, this distinction is not absolute. Within the Institute of Management Sciences there are a number of behaviorally oriented people. However, a review of the articles published in *Management Science* suggests that they are a minority.

Early Operations Research Approaches

As indicated, operations research (OR) and management science are descendants from the scientific management movement. However, there was a definite break between generations. Operations research as currently conceived is an outgrowth of World War II efforts in which scientists with a wide variety of skills were called upon to assist in solving military problems. The first use of organized operations research groups occurred in England in 1940. One of the projects was a study of the application of the newly developed radar systems. The group studied the radar-interceptor defense systems as an integrated man-machine system in order to develop optimal utilization of available resources. The effectiveness of the British air defense during the Battle of Britain was increased dramatically as a result of these efforts. In Great Britain OR teams were established for each of the three military services and were used extensively. In the United States the military services also adopted the operations research approach to deal with such problems as deploying merchant marine convoys to minimize losses from enemy submarines, improving methods of search for submarines, and achieving greater accuracy in aerial bombing.

The success of these efforts set the foundation for the future development of operations research teams with applications to nonmilitary problems. However, it was not until the early 1950s that OR caught on in American industry. During this developmental period there were a wide variety of approaches, and it was not until the late 1950s that the field began to stabilize. Writing in 1957, Churchman, Ackoff, and Arnoff said: "Ten years ago it would have been difficult to get an operations researcher to describe a procedure for conducting OR. Today it is difficult to keep one from doing it. Each practitioner's version of OR's method (if recorded) would differ in some respect. But there would also be a great deal in common."[38] For example, there seems to be a consensus with regard to the following major phases of an OR project:

1 Formulating the problem.
2 Constructing a mathematical model to represent the system under study.
3 Deriving a solution from the model.
4 Testing the model and the solution derived from it.
5 Establishing controls over the situation.
6 Putting the solution to work: Implementation.[39]

---

[38] C. West Churchman, Russell L. Ackoff, and E. Leonard Arnoff, *Introduction to Operations Research,* John Wiley & Sons, Inc., New York, 1957, pp. 12–13.
[39] Ibid.

The early philosophy of operations research was directed toward total system optimality and toward interdisciplinary effort in order to ensure that all significant factors in the problem were given consideration. This theoretical approach was never achieved in practice. In looking at the results from OR projects, it is evident that many were not interdisciplinary team efforts, nor did they ensure total system optimality. It appears that the trend has moved more toward the development of techniques and toward problem solving at the subsystem level with a narrower interdisciplinary team than was envisioned by early operations researchers.

Of significance in the management science approach was the introduction of many scientists to actual military and business decision-making problems where they could apply their specialized knowledge and skills. Under scientific management it was the practicing manager and the industrial engineer who applied scientific methods to problem solving at the task level. In operations research many scientists with backgrounds in mathematics, physics, statistics, economics, and the other disciplines are contributing their knowledge to managerial problem solving.

Current Developments in Management Science

Information concerning management science techniques has been disseminated broadly. Until the 1950s approaches such as linear programming, game theory, queuing theory, statistical decision theory, systems analysis, simulation, Monte Carlo techniques, and other similar analytical tools were relatively unknown. Today they have not only become commonplace in business and industry but also are a basic part of the curriculum in professional schools such as business and engineering.

This rapid growth in the management sciences is reflected by the substantial increase in the number of practitioners in the field. One indication is the membership growth of the two related professional societies. In the early 1950s, both the Operations Research Society of America and the Institute of Management Sciences were formed with less than 100 members each. Today, each of these societies has thousands of members who have diverse academic backgrounds and are associated with many different organizations—universities, business firms, the military, and other government agencies, for example. Research studies indicate that most of these MS/OR practitioners have academic training in mathematics and statistics, engineering, and economics. Many more people engaged in industrial operations research have training in the technical disciplines than in the social sciences or humanities.

There has also been a dramatic growth in MS/OR applications in governmental organizations, particularly in national defense and space activities. Many of the new approaches, such as systems analysis, cost-effectiveness analysis, network analysis, and planning-programming-budgeting systems, have a management science orientation. In military and space programs the term *systems analysis* is used to describe an integrative decision-making process using MS/OR approaches. [40]

---

[40] E. S. Quade (ed.), *Analysis for Military Decisions*, The Rand Corporation, Santa Monica, Calif., 1964, p. 4.

Systems analysis can be thought of as an extension of the operations research utilized during World War II. During this early phase, operations research was concerned with tactical problems. In contrast, systems analysis also deals with longer-range strategic problems. It makes use of quantitative approaches but also involves nonquantifiable inputs. Hitch suggests its broad, integrative nature by stating, "Systems analysis at the national level, therefore, involves a continuous cycle of defining military objectives, designing alternative systems to achieve those objectives, evaluating these alternatives in terms of their effectiveness and cost, questioning the objectives and the other assumptions underlining the analysis, opening new alternatives, and establishing new military objectives." [41]

MS/OR has made a major contribution toward the development and implementation of planning-programming-budgeting systems (PPBS) used extensively in federal as well as numerous state and local government agencies. Systems analysis, input-output analysis, and cost-effectiveness analysis are basic ingredients of PPBS.

On the industry level, management science typically has not been directed toward strategic problems but has been concerned primarily with tactical decisions. For the most part, management scientists have not been engaged in problem solving for those types of "ill-structured" problems which are the concern of top management and which generally have not been amenable to precise mathematical and statistical approaches. They have emphasized lower- to middle-level problems where quantification is possible. Heany suggests that management scientists have been drifting toward the lower-level organizational problems which are well structured and where the techniques of mathematical analysis can be applied. He suggests that many practitioners have equated management science with applied mathematics and that there is a gap between "managers" on the one hand and "management scientists" on the other. [42]

The way is open, however, for management scientists to deal more effectively with ill-structured problems. Development in computer technology and programming over the past two decades has provided new resources. In the early development of the computer, the primary concern was the automation of many routine data processing activities. The next step was the utilization of the computer and management science approaches for programming lower-level well-structured problems such as inventory control, production control, and allocation problems. With computer and programming developments there are greater opportunities to move to higher-level decision problems. Simulation approaches, for example, can be used for ill-structured problems. The recent developments in programming for "heuristic decision making" open new vistas for the management scientist. Greater emphasis on heuristic problem solving will move the management scientist away from concentration upon statistical and mathematical techniques and will require the integration of knowledge from the behavioral sciences.

---

[41] Charles J. Hitch, "A Planning-Programming-Budgeting System," in Fremont E. Kast and James E. Rosenzweig (eds.), *Science, Technology, and Management*, McGraw-Hill Book Company, New York, 1963, p. 64.
[42] Donald F. Heany, "Is TIMS Talking to Itself?" *Management Science*, December 1965, p. B-146.

Role of the Management Scientist

In many ways the role of the management scientist and his relationship to the operating manager are similar to those of the behavioral scientist. In the early stages the management scientist was content with the development of an optimal decision which he presented to management for implementation. He was often most interested in the development of sophisticated, quantitative models and computer programming for these models and felt that his task was performed once his recommendations were presented. As a result of a communications gap, the manager often did not understand the basis of the recommendations, and therefore many OR reports became the last folder in a dusty file. Gruber and Niles summarize the problems involved in the utilization of MS/OR in practice:

1 Operations researchers do not emphasize enough human factors, since these factors are hard to model mathematically.
2 The task of explaining and convincing the customer should unconsciously shape the formulation and solution of the problem.
3 Management science must become involved in management as a total process.
4 Management quite often lacks the confidence to use the result that the operations research group has produced.
5 The inertia of management slows down implementation.
6 Operations research people should realize that management operates in a real-time, crisis environment. [43]

Management scientists have become increasingly concerned about the implementation of their recommendations and thus are having to deal with the organization as a social as well as an economic-technical system. They have begun to recognize the need for *both quality and acceptance of* solutions in organizational problem solving. The management scientist, like the behavioral scientist, has become an agent of change in organizations. Often he develops new concepts and ideas which challenge traditional management approaches. Increasingly, he recognizes that if he is to carry out his role in applied problem solving, he cannot only be concerned with the development of esoteric, highly technical, and refined mathematical models but also must be actively engaged in the communication and implementation of his findings. [44] Furthermore, many management scientists are becoming disenchanted with applying their techniques to the lower-level problems and are interested in strategic decision-making problems of the organization.

---

[43] Gruber and Niles, op. cit., p. 13.
[44] Herbert Halbrecht, et al., "Through a Glass Darkly," *Interfaces,* August 1972, pp. 1-17.

DIVERGENCE AND CONVERGENCE IN THEORY AND PRACTICE

The behavioral and management science revolutions have done much to modify traditional organization theory and management practice. Ideally, these two approaches would converge with the traditional one to provide a unified and clearly delineated modern theory. This has not happened. There are many reasons for this lack of integration—a basic difference in values and ideologies, varying academic disciplines, and a conflict between descriptive and normative theory. This latter dichotomy is an important difference. The normative approach has been used primarily in economics and the management sciences. "Economists and operations research analysts are interested in things as they should be: they observe organizations and their environments in order to develop analytical models which will enable the organization to make more rational decisions. Their essential motivation may be to prove that they are smarter than managers." [45] On the other hand, most psychologists, sociologists, and other behavioral scientists question the economic-technical assumptions of human behavior and are concerned with describing the way people and organizations actually behave.

As many more disciplines have become interested in organization and management, researchers have brought into consideration their own traditional preoccupation with certain selective subject matters. [46] Instead of developing a more simplified, less complex organization theory, the tendency has been in quite the opposite direction—toward greater complexity and consideration of more variables. The development of a "general theory" is becoming even more difficult.

There is currently much controversy over which approach—the traditional, behavioral science, or management science—is best. The arguments are often meaningless. "These three approaches are complementary rather than competitive; each occupies a different part of the broad field of organizational studies, with overlapping boundaries." [47] Much of the controversy stems from the "understanding gap" among the various fields. We have discussed the gap between behavioral scientists and managers and between management scientists and managers. In reality it is a three-way separation—behavioral scientist—management scientist—manager. Both behavioral and management scientists become impatient when managers do not seem to understand them or immediately recognize the value of their findings. Managers in turn are

---

[45] William R. Dill, "Desegregation or Integration? Comments about Contemporary Research on Organizations," in W. W. Cooper, H. J. Leavitt, and M. W. Shelly, II (eds.), *New Perspectives in Organization Research*, John Wiley & Sons, Inc., New York, 1964, p. 47.

[46] Stogdill emphasizes these differences.

> Students of organization are at present confronted with a situation in which numerous fragments of theory are presented as complete theories. It is often difficult to find any overlap between two different systems of variables. The systems developed by business organization theorists, behavioral scientists, and operations researchers are likely to consist of widely different variables. Each developer is likely to insist that his system includes the variables that are really important to a theory of organization. The value systems and theoretical allegiances of different schools of thought tend to make each distrustful of the concepts and problems regarded as important by the others.

Ralph M. Stogdill, "Dimensions of Organization Theory," in James D. Thompson (ed.), *Approaches to Organizational Design*, University of Pittsburgh Press, Pittsburgh, Pa., 1966, p. 3.

[47] Kenneth E. Boulding, "Evidences for an Administrative Science," *Administrative Science Quarterly*, June 1958, p. 4.

frequently suspicious of untried theories and recommendations which do not seem to fit the reality of their own organizations. These attitudes are a reflection of long-standing and deep-seated problems arising out of the general backgrounds of the different cultures. [48] These differences are a mirror of the basic conflicts between the scientific and nonscientific cultures as discussed by C. P. Snow. [49] The cultural differences of behavioral scientists, management scientists, and members of management impose serious problems for communication and understanding. Value systems vary and are deep-seated; specialists are interested in different aspects of the organization and of society and emphasize the utility of different endeavors. It is essential that we recognize diverse contributions and do not refer to the efforts of other groups as inferior. All are valuable. All three have important contributions to make to understanding organizations and improving management practice.

Some Approaches toward Convergence

In spite of the fact that many contributions to management and organization theory by the behavioral and management sciences have been polarized and divergent rather than convergent, there have been attempts at integration. For example, March and Simon and their colleagues were among the first to take a broad interdisciplinary approach. Their overriding emphasis has been in looking at decision-making processes in organizations from an open-system viewpoint. Several economists such as Margolis and Baumol have challenged traditional normative economics and have integrated behavioral concepts into their views. [50] Current work on computer simulation of human behavior represents a merging of various interests in decision-making processes. [51]

Students are faced with highly fragmented and diverse inputs concerning organizational theory and management practice. They are often required to take various courses which emphasize the traditional, or behavioral, or management science approaches. The integration of these separate approaches is left to the student. Yet there is a bright side; the diversity can provide a stimulating and exciting educational program.

The student should welcome these diverse contributions to his area of study and should not seek a simplified, clear-cut body of knowledge. The subject matter is complex and dynamic, and the body of knowledge is continually evolving. Many disciplines can make contributions. Organizations are complex systems made up of psychological, sociological, technological, and economic elements which in themselves require inten-

---

[48] For a discussion of these different cultures, see James E. Rosenzweig, "Managers and Management Scientists (Two Cultures)," *Business Horizons,* Fall 1967, pp. 79-86.
[49] C. P. Snow, *The Two Cultures and the Scientific Revolution,* Cambridge University Press, New York, 1959.
[50] Julius Margolis, "The Analysis of the Firm: Rationalism, Conventionalism, and Behaviorism," *The Journal of Business,* July 1958, pp. 187-199; and William J. Baumol, *Business Behavior, Value and Growth,* The Macmillan Company, New York, 1959.
[51] Edward A. Feigenbaum and Julian Feldman (eds.), *Computers and Thought,* McGraw-Hill Book Company, New York, 1963; John M. Dutton and William N. Starbuck, *Computer Simulation of Human Behavior,* John Wiley & Sons, Inc., New York, 1971; and James R. Emshoff, *Analysis of Behavioral Systems,* The Macmillan Company, New York, 1971.

sive investigation. The suggestion that we wrap it all up nicely in one bundle and tie it together with a ribbon of simplified theory is unrealistic. The student of organizations and the practicing manager should recognize and accept contributions from diverse fields. Attempts to freeze this field of study to a restricted view would reduce our flexibility and opportunity for continued investigation.

Future progress is tied closely with developments in the disciplines underlying organization and management theory. "The progress of management theory today is inextricably interwoven with techniques of observation and experiment, with sociology, psychology, and economics, and with the sharp tools of mathematics. In this respect, there is no more confusion than exists in other areas of scientific endeavor that has its observational techniques, its bodies of general theory, and its tools of analysis. Confusion, by another name, is progress to which we have not yet become accustomed."[52]

This is the excitement of the study of organization theory and management practice. It has become an important field of study for students in schools of business administration, public administration, hospital administration, and other areas where professional managers are being trained, but it is also becoming an exciting laboratory for many other academic disciplines.

Figure 4.1 illustrates the evolution of organization and management theory. After discussing the diverse contributions to the relevant body of knowledge and indicating that there has not been a convergence into one unified theory, we are seemingly left without a logical framework for the development of this book. We do, however, see one overriding concept that does provide a basis of integration—the *systems approach*. In every segment contributing to the development of organization theory and management practice, there has been a trend toward the use of system concepts. As discussed in the following chapter, they provide a framework for the remainder of this book.

SUMMARY

Many forces have modified traditional organization and management theory. The two broad strands of change are the behavioral sciences, which emphasize the psychosocial system and the human aspects of administration, and the management sciences, which emphasize the economic-technical system and quantification, mathematical models, and the application of computer technology.

The behavioral sciences use an open-systems approach and consider many variables which were excluded from the traditional models. The behavioral approach has been developed primarily by psychologists, sociologists, and anthropologists who are interested in empirical investigation to verify their concepts. They have a humanistic orientation which differs from the traditional school and also from the management science approach.

---

[52] Herbert A. Simon, "Approaching the Theory of Management," in Harold Koontz (ed.), *Toward a Unified Theory of Management*, McGraw-Hill Book Company, New York, 1964, p. 82.

TRADITIONAL THEORY	MODIFICATIONS	EMERGING VIEW—SYSTEMS APPROACH
Scientific Management (Efficient task performance) Bureaucratic Model (Authority and structure) Administrative Management theory (Universal management principles)	Behavioral Sciences (Psychological, sociological, and cultural issues) Management Sciences (Economic-technical rationality)	Views an organization as: (1) a subsystem of its broader environment, and (2) goal-oriented; including (3) a technical subsystem, (4) a structural subsystem, (5) a psychosocial subsystem; and coordinated by (6) a managerial subsystem.
1900	1930s 1960s	1970s

FIGURE 4.1 EVOLUTION OF ORGANIZATION AND MANAGEMENT THEORY

Management science can be considered as a basic extension of scientific management, with modifications. It is concerned with the organization primarily as an economic-technical system. This movement has flourished since the end of World War II, with major contributions from economics, engineering, mathematics, and statistics. The increasing sophistication of quantitative techniques, together with advancing computer technology, has provided the basic tools for this approach.

The newer approaches have utilized knowledge from a wide variety of disciplines and have provided new informational inputs for organization theory and management practice. The behavioral scientists and the management scientists have frequently become change agents in organizations by advocating approaches and practices which differ from traditional ways of operating. Conflicts and a "communications gap" frequently develop between these scientists and managers.

A fully integrated body of knowledge called organization and management theory has not emerged. With the great diversity of disciplinary inputs the theory has tended toward divergence rather than convergence. Each school of thought has emphasized the aspects of the organization which it considers most important. This tendency to view organization and management from a subsystems view is reinforced by the type of academic training of the various theorists.

This diversity should not be considered undesirable. Rather, it is an indication of the active intellectual interest in the study of organizations and their management. Students should welcome these diverse contributions. Organizations are complex systems made up of psychological, sociological, technical, and economic elements which require intensive investigation. The view which is emerging as a basis for modern theory is the *systems approach.*

QUESTIONS AND PROBLEMS

1 Why have researchers become more interested in the study of organizations and their management?

2 What are the major distinctions between the management science and the behavioral science approaches?

3 Look at recent issues of *Management Science* and *Administrative Science Quarterly.* What are the major differences in emphasis between these two periodicals? How do you explain these differences?

4 How did the approach and findings of the pioneer human relationists differ from scientific management?

5 What is your evaluation of the eight concepts about organizational behavior listed on pages 81–82?

6 Do you see any difficulty for behavioral and management scientists as change agents in organizations in maintaining scientific objectivity? Why or why not?

7 How are scientific management and management science related?

8 Discuss the various disciplines that are contributing to the development of manage-

ment science. (An appraisal of authors and articles in recent issues of *Management Science* and *Operations Research* will help in answering this question.)

9 Why has effort in operations research been primarily directed toward tactical rather than strategic decisions?

10 Discuss the gap between management scientists and managers.

11 Evaluate the probabilities of (1) divergence and (2) convergence in organization theory.

5

THE MODERN VIEW:
A SYSTEMS APPROACH

Organization theory and management practice have undergone substantial changes in recent years. Traditional theory has been modified and enriched by informational inputs from the management and behavioral sciences. These research and conceptual endeavors have, at times, led to divergent findings. During the past decade, however, an approach has emerged which can serve as a basis of convergence—the systems approach, which facilitates unification in many fields of knowledge. It has been used in the physical, biological, and social sciences as a broad frame of reference. It can also be used as a framework for the integration of a modern organization theory. General systems theory, its pervasiveness, its relationship to organization theory, and its potential usefulness are discussed in this chapter via the following topics:

General Systems Theory
Pervasiveness of Systems Theory
Systems Approach and Organization Theory
Organization as an Open System
An Integrated Systems View of Organizations
Other Properties of Organizational Systems
Managerial Systems
Systems Concepts for Organization and Management

GENERAL SYSTEMS THEORY

Over the past two decades the development of general systems theory has provided a basis for the integration of scientific knowledge across a broad spectrum. [1] We have defined a *system* as *an organized, unitary whole composed of two or more interdependent parts, components, or subsystems and delineated by identifiable boundaries from its environmental suprasystem.* The term *system* covers a broad spectrum of our physical, biological, and social world. In the universe there are galaxial systems, geophysical systems, and molecular systems. In biology we speak of the organism as a system of mutually dependent parts, each of which includes many subsystems. The human body is a complex organism including, among others, a skeletal system, a circulatory system, and a nervous system. We come into daily contact with such phenomena as transportation systems, communication systems, and economic systems.

In considering the various types of systems in our universe, Kenneth Boulding provides a useful classification of systems which sets forth a hierarchy of levels as follows:

1 The first level is that of static structure. It might be called the level of *frameworks;* for example, the anatomy of the universe.
2 The next level is that of the simple dynamic system with predetermined, necessary motions. This might be called the level of *clockworks.*
3 The control mechanism or cybernetic system, which might be nicknamed the level of the *thermostat.* The system is self-regulating in maintaining equilibrium.
4 The fourth level is that of the "open system," or self-maintaining structure. This is the level at which life begins to differentiate from not-life: it might be called the level of the *cell.*
5 The next level might be called the genetic-societal level; it is typified by the *plant,* and it dominates the empirical world of the botanist.
6 The *animal* system level is characterized by increased mobility, teleological behavior, and self-awareness.
7 The next level is the *human* level, that is, of the individual human being considered as a system with self-awareness and the ability to utilize language and symbolism.
8 The *social system* or systems of human organization constitute the next level, with the consideration of the content and meaning of messages, the nature and dimensions of value systems, the transcription of images into historical record, the subtle symbolizations of art, music, and poetry, and the complex gamut of human emotion.

---

[1] The name "general systems theory" and many of the basic concepts were set forth by the biologist Ludwig von Bertalanffy. For a general discussion of his views, see "The Theory of Open Systems in Physics and Biology," *Science,* Jan. 13, 1950, pp. 23-29; and *General System Theory,* George Braziller, Inc., New York, 1968.

9 *Transcendental systems* complete the classification of levels. These are the ultimates and absolutes and the inescapable unknowables, and they also exhibit systematic structure and relationship. [2]

The first three levels in this hierarchy can be classified as physical or mechanical systems and provide the basis of knowledge in the physical sciences such as physics and astronomy. The fourth, fifth, and sixth levels are concerned with biological systems and are the interest of biologists, botanists, and zoologists. The last three levels are involved with human and social systems and are the concern of the social sciences as well as the arts, humanities, and religion.

General systems theory provides a basis for understanding and integrating knowledge from a wide variety of highly specialized fields. In the past, traditional knowledge has been along well-defined subject matter lines. Bertalanffy suggests that the various fields of modern science have had a continual evolution toward a parallelism of ideas. This parallelism provides an opportunity to formulate and develop principles which hold for systems in general. "In modern science, dynamic interaction is the basic problem in all fields, and its general principles will have to be formulated in General System Theory." [3] General systems theory provides the broad macro view from which we may look at all types of systems. "So has arisen systems theory—the attempt to develop scientific principles to aid us in our struggles with dynamic systems with highly interacting parts." [4]

Bertalanffy made another major contribution in setting forth a distinction between closed systems and open systems. Physical and mechanical systems can be considered as closed in relationship to their environment. Thus, the first three levels in Boulding's hierarchy are closed systems. On the other hand, biological and social systems are not closed but are in constant interaction with their environment. This view of biological and social phenomena as open systems has profound importance for the social sciences and organization theory. Traditional theory assumed the organization to be a closed system, whereas the modern approach considers it an open system in interaction with its environment. While the development of general systems theory has provided an overall conceptual view for dealing with all types of phenomena—physical, biological, and social—there have been many additional threads in intellectual development which have contributed to the development of the systems approach.

---

[2] Kenneth E. Boulding, "General Systems Theory: The Skeleton of Science," *Management Science,* April 1956, pp. 197–208.

[3] Ludwig von Bertalanffy, *Problems of Life,* John Wiley & Sons, Inc., New York, 1952, p. 201. On page 176 he stresses this view: "If we survey the various fields of modern science, we notice a dramatic and amazing evolution. Similar conceptions and principles have arisen in quite different realms, although this parallelism of ideas is the result of independent developments, and the workers in the individual fields are hardly aware of the common trend. Thus, the principles of wholeness, of organization, and of the dynamic conception of reality become apparent in all fields of science."

[4] W. Ross Ashby in Mihajlo D. Mesarovic (ed.), *Views on General Systems Theory,* John Wiley & Sons, Inc., New York, 1964, p. 166.

PERVASIVENESS OF SYSTEMS THEORY

In complex societies with rapid expansion of knowledge, the various scientific fields become highly differentiated and specialized. In many scientific fields, the concentration over the past several decades has been on analytical, fact-finding, and experimental approaches in highly specific areas. This has been useful in helping to develop knowledge and to understand the details of specific but limited subjects. At some stage, however, there should be a period of synthesis, reconciliation, and integration, so that the analytical and fact-finding elements are unified into broader, multidimensional theories. [5] There is evidence that every field of human knowledge passes alternately through phases of analysis and fact finding to periods of synthesis and integration. Recently systems theory has provided this framework in many fields—physical, biological, and social. Even more important, it provides a basis for communication between scientists in the various disciplinary areas—a problem of immense importance with the high degree of specialization of knowledge. [6]

Ackoff suggests this movement into the Systems Age as follows:

> World War II marked the end of an era of Western culture that began with the Renaissance, the Machine Age, and the beginning of a new era, the Systems Age.
>
> In the Machine Age man sought to take the world apart, to analyze its contents and our experiences of them down to ultimate indivisible parts: atoms, chemical elements, cells, instincts, elementary perception, and so on. These elements were taken to be related by causal laws, laws which made the world behave like a machine. This mechanistic concept of the world left no place in science for the study of free will, goal seeking, and purposes. . . .
>
> With World War II we began to shift into the Systems Age. A system is a whole that cannot be taken apart without loss of its essential characteristics, and hence it must be studied as a whole. Now, instead of explaining a whole in terms of its parts, parts began to be explained in terms of the whole. [7]

The application of systems thinking has been of particular relevance to the social sciences. There is a close relationship between general systems theory and the devel-

---

[5] Eddington suggests that attention has been focused more and more on overall systems as frames of reference for analytical work in various areas. This synthesizing process "marked a reaction from the view that everything to which science need pay attention is discovered by microscopic dissection of objects. It provided an alternative standpoint in which the centre of interest is shifted from the entities reached by the customary analysis (atoms, electric potentials, etc.) to qualities possessed by the system as a whole, which cannot be split up and located— a little here and a little bit there." Sir Arthur Eddington, *The Nature of the Physical World*, The University of Michigan Press, Ann Arbor, Mich., 1958, pp. 103–104.

[6] For an overview of the integrative possibilities of the systems approach, see Walter Buckley (ed.), *Modern Systems Research for the Behavioral Scientist*, Aldine Publishing Company, Chicago, 1968.

[7] Russell L. Ackoff, "A Note on Systems Science," *Interfaces*, August 1972, p. 40.

opment of functionalism in the social sciences. [8] Although there are several connotations of the word "functionalism," its basic emphasis is upon systems of relationships and the integration of parts and subsystems into a functional whole. [9] Functionalism attempts to look at social systems in terms of structures, processes, and functions and attempts to understand the relationship between these components. It emphasizes that each element of a culture or social institution has a function in the broader system.

Functionalism, under the influence of the earlier works of A. R. Radcliffe-Brown and Bronislaw Malinowski, has become the framework for modern anthropology. [10] They pioneered the view that social customs, patterns of behavior, and institutions do not exist independently but must be considered in relationship to the total culture. All aspects of social life form a related whole, and society can best be understood as an interconnected system. Thus each social action, such as a marriage ceremony or the punishment of a crime, has a function in the culture as a whole and contributes to the maintenance of the social structure.

In sociology, Talcott Parsons led in the adoption of functionalism and the general systems viewpoint. [11] Although Parsons acknowledges his debt to Pareto for the concept of systems in scientific theory, it is Parsons himself who has fully utilized the open-systems approach for the study of social structures. [12] He not only developed a broad social system framework but also related his ideas to the organization. Many of his concepts relating to the structure and processes of social systems will be used later in this book.

In the field of psychology, the systems approach has achieved prominence. The various types of behaviorism in psychological theory have given way to the holism of gestalt psychology and field theory. The very word *gestalt* is German for configuration or pattern. [13] "The Gestaltists early adopted the concept of system, which is more than the sum of its components, and which determines the activity of these components." [14] Kurt Lewin was among the first to apply the tenets of gestalt psychology to the field of individual personality. He found that purely psychological explanations of personality were inadequate and that sociocultural forces had to be taken into account. He viewed

---

[8] Don Martindale, *Functionalism in the Social Sciences*, Monograph 5, American Academy of Political and Social Science, February 1965, pp. viii-ix.

[9] Robert K. Merton discusses various connotations of the word *function* in *Social Theory and Social Structure*, rev. ed., The Free Press of Glencoe, New York, 1957, pp. 20-25.

[10] A. R. Radcliffe-Brown, *Structure and Function in Primitive Society*, Cohen & West, London, 1952; and Bronislaw Malinowski, *A Scientific Theory of Culture*, Oxford University Press, New York, 1960.

[11] Talcott Parsons uses the systems approach in much of his writings. His *The Social System*, The Free Press of Glencoe, New York, 1951, presents a comprehensive treatise on his views.

[12] For a view of Pareto's works, see Lawrence J. Henderson, *Pareto's General Sociology*, Harvard University Press, Cambridge, Mass., 1935.

[13] "A *gestalt* is an organized entity or whole in which the parts, though distinguishable, are interdependent; they have certain characteristics produced by their inclusion in the whole, and the whole has some characteristics belonging to none of the parts. The gestalt thus constitutes a 'unit segregated from its surroundings,' behaving according to certain laws of energy distribution. It is found throughout human behaviour as well as in physiological and physical events and is thus a fundamental aspect of scientific data." Julius Gould and William L. Kolb (eds.), *A Dictionary of the Social Sciences*, The Free Press of Glencoe, New York, 1964, p. 287.

[14] Ian Whitaker, "The Nature and Value of Functionalism in Sociology," in *Functionalism in the Social Sciences*, Monograph 5, American Academy of Political and Social Science, February 1965, pp. 137-138.

personality as a dynamic system, influenced by the individual's environment. Harry Stack Sullivan, in his *Interpersonal Theory of Psychiatry,* went even further in relating personality to the sociocultural system. He viewed the foundation of personality as an extension and elaboration of social relationships. A further extension of psychology to give greater consideration to broader interpersonal and social systems is seen in the rapidly expanding field of social psychology. [15]

Modern economics has increasingly used the systems approach. Equilibrium concepts are fundamental in economic thought, and the very basis of this type of analysis is consideration of subsystems of a total system. Economics is moving away from static equilibrium models appropriate to closed systems toward dynamic equilibrium considerations appropriate to open systems. Leontief and his followers in industrial input-output analysis utilize the systems approach. "Considered from the point of view of the input-output scheme any national economy can be described as a system of mutually interrelated industries or—if one prefers a more abstract term—interdependent economic activities. The interrelation actually consists in the more or less steady streams of goods and services which directly or indirectly link all the sectors of the economy to each other." [16]

The very foundation of the discipline of cybernetics is based upon a systems approach. [17] It is primarily concerned with communication and information flow in complex systems. Although cybernetics has been applied primarily to mechanistic engineering problems, its model of feedback, control, and regulation has a great deal of applicability for biological and social systems as well.

Even more recently, our society has become increasingly concerned over the pollution and deterioration of the natural environment. Traditionally, we viewed the environment and natural resources as available for man's utilization and exploitation. We had a mechanistic, piecemeal, and suboptimal view of the ecosystem. Each act of man against nature was viewed separately. The accumulation of individual actions might lead to drastic environmental deterioration, but this was not understood. More recently, it is being recognized that man's relationship to his environment must be viewed from a systems approach. Commoner says:

The First Law of Ecology: Everything is Connected to Everything Else. It reflects the existence of the elaborate network of interconnections in the ecosphere: among different living organisms, and between populations, species, and individual organisms and their physico-chemical surroundings. [18]

---

[15] Daniel Katz and Robert L. Kahn, *The Social Psychology of Organizations,* John Wiley & Sons, Inc., New York, 1966, is an example of the movement of social psychology into broader systems of analysis.
[16] Wassily Leontief et al., *Studies in the Structure of the American Economy,* Oxford University Press, New York, 1953, p. 8.
[17] Norbert Wiener, *Cybernetics,* John Wiley & Sons, Inc., New York, 1948.
[18] Barry Commoner, *The Closing Circle,* Alfred A. Knopf, Inc., New York, 1971, p. 33.

Another similar point of view permeating many of the social and physical sciences is the concept of holism, which is closely related to functionalism and the systems approach. Holism is the view that all systems—physical, biological, and social—are composed of interrelated subsystems. The whole is not just the sum of the parts, but the system itself can be explained only as a totality. Holism is the opposite of elementarism, which views the total as the sum of its individual parts. The holistic view is basic to the systems approach. In traditional organization theory, as well as in many of the sciences, the subsystems have been studied separately, with the view to later putting the parts together into the whole. The systems approach emphasizes that this is not possible and that the starting point has to be with the total system.

The foregoing discussion has attempted to show how the systems approach and associate views have become the operating framework for many physical and social sciences. We agree with Chin, who says:

> Psychologists, sociologists, anthropologists, economists, and political scientists have been "discovering" and using the system model. In so doing, they find intimations of an exhilarating "unity" of science, because the system models used by biological and physical scientists seem to be exactly similar. Thus, the system model is regarded by some system theorists as universally applicable to physical and social events, and to human relationships in small or large units. [19]

It is important for the student of organization and management to recognize that the developing body of knowledge and applications of the systems approach to complex organizations is but a part of the broad trend in many of the physical and social sciences and that this field is part of a pervasive stream of thought. Furthermore, understanding that organization theory can be put in the context of general systems theory allows for a growing community of interest and understanding with widely diverse disciplines. We will now look more closely at the direct relationship between the systems approach and organization theory.

SYSTEMS APPROACH AND ORGANIZATION THEORY

Traditional organization theory used a highly structured, closed-system approach. Modern theory has moved toward the open-system approach. "The distinctive qualities of modern organization theory are its conceptual-analytical base, its reliance on empirical research data, and, above all, its synthesizing, integrating nature. These qualities are

---

[19] Robert Chin, "The Utility of System Models and Developmental Models for Practitioners," in Warren G. Bennis, Kenneth D. Benne, and Robert Chin (eds.), *The Planning of Change*, 2d ed., Holt, Rinehart, and Winston, Inc., New York, 1969, p. 299.

framed in a philosophy which accepts the premise that the only meaningful way to study organization is as a system." [20]

Chester Barnard was one of the first management writers to utilize the systems approach. [21] Herbert Simon and his associates viewed the organization as a complex system of decision-making processes. Simon has ranged widely in seeking new disciplinary knowledge to integrate into his organization theories. However, the one broad consistency in both his research and his writings has been the utilization of the systems approach. "The term 'systems' is being used more and more to refer to methods of scientific analysis that are particularly adapted to the unraveling of complexity." [22] He not only emphasizes this approach for the behavioral view of organizations but also stresses its importance in management science.

The systems approach has been advocated by a number of other writers in management science. Churchman and his associates were among the earliest to emphasize this view. "The comprehensiveness of O. R.'s aim is an example of a 'systems' approach, since 'system' implies an interconnected complex of functionally related components. Thus a business organization is a social or man-machine system." [23] Although the systems approach has been adopted and utilized in management science, the models typically used are closed in the sense that they consider only certain variables and exclude from consideration those not subject to quantification.

The sociologist George Homans uses systems concepts as a basis for his empirical research on social groups. He developed a model of social systems which can serve as an appropriate basis for small groups and also for larger organizations. [24] In his view, an organization is comprised of an external environmental system and an internal system of relationships which are mutually interdependent. There are three elements in a social system. *Activities* are the tasks which people perform. *Interactions* occur between people in the performance of these tasks, and *sentiments* develop between people. These elements are mutually interdependent.

Philip Selznick utilizes structural functional analysis and the systems approach in his studies of organizations. The institutional leader is concerned with the adaptation of the organization to its external systems. The organization is a dynamic system, constantly changing and adapting to internal and external pressures, and is in a continual process of evolution. The organization is a formal system influenced by the internal social structure and subject to the pressure of an institutional environment. "Cooperative systems are constituted of individuals interacting as wholes in relation to a formal system of coordination. The concrete structure is therefore a resultant of the reciprocal

[20] William G. Scott and Terence R. Mitchell, *Organization Theory*, rev. ed., Richard D. Irwin, Inc., Homewood, Ill., 1972, p. 55.
[21] Chester I. Barnard, *The Functions of the Executive*, Harvard University Press, Cambridge, Mass., 1938.
[22] Herbert A. Simon, "Approaching the Theory of Management," in Harold Koontz (ed.), *Toward a Unified Theory of Management*, McGraw-Hill Book Company, New York, 1964, pp. 82–83.
[23] C. West Churchman, Russell L. Ackoff, and E. Leonard Arnoff, *Introduction to Operations Research*, John Wiley & Sons, Inc., New York, 1957, p. 7.
[24] George C. Homans, *The Human Group*, Harcourt, Brace & World, Inc., New York, 1950.

influences of the formal and informal aspects of organization. Furthermore, this structure is itself a totality, an adaptive 'organism' reacting to influences upon it from an external environment." [25] Selznick used this systems frame of reference for empirical research on governmental agencies and other complex organizations.

The systems approach has also been used in other countries. Miller points out that Alexander Bogdanov, the Russian philosopher, developed a theory of tektology or universal organization science in 1912 which foreshadowed general systems theory and used many of the same concepts as modern systems theorists. [26] The group of social scientists associated with Tavistock Institute of Human Relations in London is one of the strongest proponents of the open-systems approach. As a result of a number of research studies in the mining, textile, and manufacturing industries in England and other countries, this group developed the concept of the sociotechnical system. [27] They also stressed that the organization is an open system in interaction with its environment.

The systems approach has also been adopted by social psychologists as a basis for studying organizations. Using open-systems theory as a general conceptual scheme, Katz and Kahn present a comprehensive theory of organization. [28] They suggest that the psychological approach has generally ignored or has not dealt effectively with the facts of structure and social organization, and they use systems concepts to develop an integrated model.

There are numerous examples of the utilization of the systems approach at operational levels. For example, the trend toward automation involves implementation of these ideas. Automation suggests a self-contained system with inputs, outputs, and a mechanism of control. Automated production systems for processing of materials are becoming increasingly important in many industries. Another phase which has been automated is information flow. With the introduction of large-scale, electronic data processing equipment, information processing systems have been developed for many applications. Physical distribution systems have received increasing attention. The concepts of logistics, or material management, have been used to emphasize the flow of materials through distribution channels.

The systems approach has been utilized as a basis of organization for many of our advanced defense and space programs. Program management is geared to changing managerial requirements in research, development, procurement, and utilization. With the new, complex programs such as ballistic missiles and advanced space programs it became impossible to think of individual segments or parts of the program as separate

---

[25] Philip Selznick, "Foundations of the Theory of Organization," *American Sociological Review*, February 1948, pp. 25-35.

[26] Robert F. Miller, "The New Science of Administration in the USSR," *Administrative Science Quarterly*, September 1971, pp. 249-250.

[27] F. E. Emery and E. L. Trist, "Socio-technical Systems," in C. West Churchman and Michael Verhulst (eds.), *Management Sciences: Models and Techniques*, Pergamon Press, New York, 1960, vol. 2, pp. 83-97; and A. K. Rice, *The Enterprise and Its Environment*, Tavistock Publications, London, 1963.

[28] Katz and Kahn, op. cit.

entities, and it was necessary to move to a broader systems approach. [29] In many other types of governmental projects, which require the integration of many agencies and activities—transportation problems, pollution control, and urban renewal, for example—the systems approach is being used.

The development of the planning-programming-budgeting systems (PPBS) represents one of the most important and comprehensive examples of the application of the systems approach to the management of complex organizations. Essentially, PPBS is a systematic approach which attempts to establish goals, develop programs for their accomplishment, consider the costs and benefits of various alternative approaches, and utilize a budgetary process which reflects program activities over the long run. PPBS was first developed by the federal government and is currently being used by numerous state and local government agencies.

These examples of the increasing trend in adapting the systems approach to modern organization theory and management practice are by no means exhaustive; they merely illustrate current developments. However, they are sufficient to indicate that increasing attention is being given to the study of organizations as complex systems. This modern view treats the organization as a system of mutually dependent parts and variables, which is part of the whole system of society. Modern organization theory and general systems theory are closely related. Many systems concepts taken from the investigation of other types of physical, biological, and social systems are meaningful to the study of organizations.

ORGANIZATION AS AN OPEN SYSTEM

Systems can be considered in two ways: (1) closed or (2) open and in interaction with their environments. This distinction, although not absolute, is important in organization theory. Closed-system thinking stems primarily from the physical sciences and is applicable to mechanistic systems. Many of the earlier concepts in the social sciences and in organization theory were closed-system views because they considered the system under study as self-contained and deterministic. Traditional management theories were primarily closed-system views concentrating only upon the internal operation of the organization and adopting highly rationalistic approaches taken from physical science models. The organization was considered as sufficiently independent so that its problems could be analyzed in terms of internal structure, tasks, and formal relationships— without reference to the external environment.

A characteristic of all closed systems is that they have an inherent tendency to move toward a static equilibrium and entropy. Entropy is a term which originated in thermodynamics and is applicable to all physical systems. It is the tendency for any

---

[29] For a discussion of the evolution of this approach in military and space programs, see Fremont E. Kast and James E. Rosenzweig, "Organizations and Management of Space Programs," in Frederick I. Ordway, III (ed.), *Advances in Space Science and Technology*, Academic Press, Inc., New York, 1965, vol. 7, pp. 273–364.

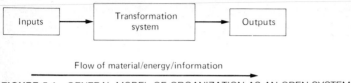

Flow of material/energy/information

FIGURE 5.1 GENERAL MODEL OF ORGANIZATION AS AN OPEN SYSTEM

closed system to move toward a chaotic or random state in which there is no further potential for energy transformation or work. "The disorder, disorganization, lack of patterning, or randomness of organization of a system is known as its *entropy*." [30] A closed system tends to increase in entropy over time, to move toward greater disorder and randomness.

Biological and social systems do not fall within this classification. The open-system view recognizes that the biological or social system is in a dynamic relationship with its environment and receives various inputs, transforms these inputs in some way, and exports outputs. The receipt of inputs in the form of material, energy, and information allows the open system to offset the process of entropy. These systems are open not only in relation to their environment but also in relation to themselves, or "internally" in that interactions between components affect the system as a whole. The open system adapts to its environment by changing the structure and processes of its internal components. [31]

The organization can be considered in terms of a general open-system model, as in Figure 5.1. The open system is in continual interaction with its environment and achieves a "steady state" or dynamic equilibrium while still retaining the capacity for work or energy transformation. The survival of the system, in effect, would not be possible without continuous inflow, transformation, and outflow. In the biological or social system this is a continuous recycling process. The system must receive sufficient input of resources to maintain its operations and also to export the transformed resources to the environment in sufficient quantity to continue the cycle.

For example, the business organization receives inputs from the society in the form of people, materials, money, and information; it transforms these into outputs of products, services, and rewards to the organizational members sufficiently large to maintain their participation. For the business enterprise, money and the market provide a mechanism for recycling of resources between the firm and its environment. The same kind of analysis can be made for all types of social organizations. Open-system views provide the basis for the development of a more comprehensive organization theory.

Although we will use the open system perspective throughout this book we should recognize that the concept of open/closed is a matter of degree. In an absolute sense, all systems are open or closed depending upon the point of reference. Thus, all systems

---

[30] James G. Miller, "Living Systems: Basic Concepts," *Behavioral Science*, July 1965, p. 195.
[31] Walter Buckley, "Society as a Complex Adaptive System," in Buckley, op. cit., pp. 490-491.

are "closed" in some degree from external forces. The system's boundaries always prevent *some* environmental factors from impacting upon the system; it provides for selective inputs. We will discuss this issue of degrees of openness and closedness more completely in Chapter 6.

AN INTEGRATED SYSTEMS VIEW OF ORGANIZATIONS

We view the organization as an open, sociotechnical system composed of a number of subsystems, as illustrated in Figure 5.2. It receives inputs of energy, information, and materials from the environment, transforms these, and returns outputs to the environment. Under this view an organization is not simply a technical or a social system. Rather, it is the structuring and integrating of human activities around various technologies. The technologies affect the types of inputs into the organization, the nature of the transformation processes, and the outputs from the system. However, the social system determines the effectiveness and efficiency of the utilization of the technology.

The internal organization can be viewed as composed of several major subsystems. The organizational *goals and values* are one of the more important of these subsystems. The organization takes many of its values from the broader sociocultural environment. A basic premise is that the organization as a subsystem of the society must accomplish certain goals which are determined by the broader system. The organization performs a function for society, and if it is to be successful in receiving inputs, it must conform to social requirements.

The *technical* subsystem refers to the knowledge required for the performance of tasks, including the techniques used in the transformation of inputs into outputs. It is determined by the task requirements of the organization and varies depending upon the particular activities. The technology for manufacturing automobiles differs significantly from that used in an oil refinery or an electronics company. Similarly, the task requirements and technology in a hospital are different from those in a university. The technical subsystem is shaped by the specialization of knowledge and skills required, the types of machinery and equipment involved, and the layout of facilities. The technology affects the organization's structure as well as its psychosocial subsystem.

Every organization has a *psychosocial* subsystem which is composed of individuals and groups in interaction. It consists of individual behavior and motivation, status and role relationships, group dynamics, and influence systems. It is also affected by sentiments, values, attitudes, expectations, and aspirations of the people in the organization. Obviously, this psychosocial subsystem is affected by external environmental forces as well as by the tasks, technology, and structure of the internal organization. These forces set the "organizational climate" within which the human participants perform their roles and activities. We would therefore expect psychosocial systems to differ significantly among various organizations. Certainly the climate for the "man on the assembly line" is different from that of the scientists in the laboratory or the doctor in the hospital.

Structure involves the ways in which the tasks of the organization are divided (differentiation) and coordinated (integration). In the formal sense, structure is set forth by the organization charts, by position and job descriptions, and by rules and procedures. It is also concerned with patterns of authority, communication, and work flow. The organization's structure provides for formalization of relationships between the technical and the psychosocial subsystems. However, it should be emphasized that this linkage is by no means complete and that many interactions and relationships occur between the technical and psychosocial subsystems which bypass the formal structure.

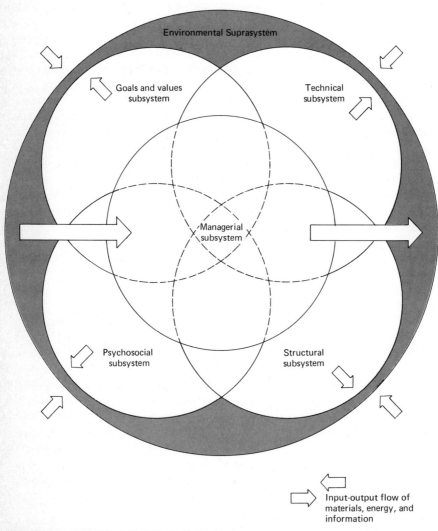

FIGURE 5.2 THE ORGANIZATIONAL SYSTEM

The *managerial* subsystem spans the entire organization by relating the organization to its environment, setting the goals, developing comprehensive, strategic, and operational plans, designing the structure, and establishing control processes.

Figure 5.2 provides one way for viewing the organization. The goals and values, as well as the technical, structural, psychosocial, and managerial subsystems, are shown as integral parts of the overall organization. This figure is an aid to understanding the evolution of organization theory. Traditional management theory emphasized the structural and managerial subsystems and was concerned with developing principles. The human relationists and behavioral scientists emphasized the psychosocial subsystem and focused their attention on motivation, group dynamics, and other related factors. The management science school emphasized the technical subsystem and methods for quantifying decision-making and control processes. Thus each approach to organization and management has tended to emphasize particular subsystems, with little recognition of the importance of the others. The modern approach views the organization as an open, sociotechnical system and considers *all* the primary subsystems *and* their interactions.

OTHER PROPERTIES OF ORGANIZATIONAL SYSTEMS

The systems approach emphasizes that an organization has a number of interacting subsystems and can only be considered in a holistic or synergistic framework. A number of other characteristics of organizational systems can be identified.

Contrived Systems

Social organizations are not natural like mechanical or biological systems; they are contrived. They have structure, but the structure of events rather than of physical components, and it cannot be separated from the processes of the system. The fact that social organizations are contrived by human beings suggests that they can be established for an infinite variety of objectives and do not follow the same life-cycle pattern of birth, maturity, and death as biological systems. Katz and Kahn say:

> Social structures are essentially contrived systems. They are made of men and are imperfect systems. They can come apart at the seams overnight, but they can also outlast by centuries the biological organisms which originally created them. The cement which holds them together is essentially psychological rather than biological. Social systems are anchored in the attitudes, perceptions, beliefs, motivations, habits, and expectations of human beings. [32]

Recognizing that the social organization is a contrived system cautions us against making an exact analogy between it and physical or biological systems.

---

[32] Katz and Kahn, op. cit., p. 33.

Boundaries

The view of the organization as an open sociotechnical system suggests that there are boundaries which separate it from the environment. The concept of boundaries helps us understand the distinction between open and closed systems. The closed system has rigid, impenetrable boundaries, whereas the open system has permeable boundaries between itself and a broader supersystem. "Boundaries are the demarcation lines or regions for the definition of appropriate system activity, for admission of members into the system, and for other imports into the system. The boundary constitutes a barrier for many types of interaction between people on the inside and people on the outside, but it includes some facilitating device for the particular types of transactions necessary for organizational functioning." [33]

The boundaries set the "domain" of the organization's activities. In a physical, mechanical, or biological system the boundaries can be identified. In a social organization, the boundaries are not easily definable and are determined primarily by the functions and activities of the organization. It is characterized by rather vaguely formed, highly permeable boundaries. Frequently, in the study of social organizations, where to draw the boundaries is a matter of convenience and strategy. Thus, in the study of a small work group, we may artificially establish the boundary to include only the activities of the immediate group and may consider interactions with other groups as outside these boundaries. Or, we might set our boundaries to include an entire department, division, company, industry, or total economic system. The boundaries of a social organization are often quite flexible and changeable over time, depending upon its activities and functions.

One of the key functions within any organization is that of boundary regulation between systems. A primary role of management is serving as a linking pin or boundary agent between the various subsystems to ensure integration and cooperation. [34] Furthermore, an important managerial function is that of serving as boundary agent between the organization and environmental systems.

The concept of *interface* is useful in understanding boundary relationships. An interface may be defined as the area of contact between one system and another. Thus, the business organization has many interfaces with other systems: suppliers of materials, the local community, prospective employees, unions, customers, and state, local, and federal governmental agencies. There are many transactional processes across systems boundaries at the interface involving the transfer of energy, materials, people, money, and information.

---

[33] Ibid., pp. 60–61.
[34] This point is made by Rensis Likert in *New Patterns of Management,* McGraw-Hill Book Company, New York, 1961. In his interaction-influence system, he recommends the overlapping-group form of organization in which a "linking-pin function" is performed to integrate activities of the various subsystems in the organization.

Hierarchy of Systems

In general, all systems—physical, biological, and social—can be considered in a hierarchical sense. A system is composed of subsystems of a lower order and is also part of a suprasystem. Thus, there is a hierarchy of the components in the system. Large organizations are almost universally hierarchical in structure. People are organized into groups; groups are organized into departments; departments are organized into divisions; divisions are organized into companies; and companies are part of an industry and economy. Many general systems writers have concluded that this hierarchical relationship is paramount in all types of systems. "Hierarchical subdivision is not a characteristic that is peculiar to human organizations. It is common to virtually all complex systems of which we have knowledge. [There are] strong reasons for believing that almost any system of sufficient complexity would have to have the rooms-within-rooms structure that we observe in actual human organizations. The reasons for hierarchy go far beyond the need for unity of command or other considerations relating to authority." [35]

The hierarchical structure is not only related to levels but is based upon the need for more inclusive clustering or combination of subsystems into a broader system, in order to coordinate activities and processes. In complex organizations there is a hierarchy of processes as well as structure.

Negative Entropy

Closed physical systems are subject to the force of entropy which increases until eventually the entire system stops. The tendency toward maximum entropy is a movement to disorder, complete lack of resource transformation, and death. In a closed system, the change in entropy must always be positive. However, in the open biological or social system, entropy can be arrested and may even be transformed to negative entropy—a process of more complete organization and ability to transform resources. This is possible because in open systems the resources (material, energy, and information) utilized to arrest the entropy process are imported from the external environment. "Living systems, maintaining themselves in a steady state, can avoid the increase of entropy, and may even develop towards states of increased order and organization." [36] Obviously, for the biological system, this process of negative entropy is never perfect. The organism lives and grows for a period of time but is subject to deterioration and death. The contrived, or social, organization which can continue to import new human components and other resources in order to continue its functioning may be capable

---

[35] Herbert A. Simon, *The New Science of Management Decision*, Harper & Row, Publishers, Incorporated, New York, 1960, pp. 40-42.
[36] Ludwig von Bertalanffy, "General System Theory," in *General Systems*, Yearbook of the Society for the Advancement of General Systems Theory, vol. I, 1956, p. 4.

of indefinitely offsetting the entropy process. However, the only way in which the organization can offset entropy is by continually importing material, energy, and information in one form or another, transforming them, and redistributing resources to the environment.

The Steady State or Dynamic Equilibrium

The concept of *steady state* is closely related to that of negative entropy. A closed system must eventually attain an equilibrium state with maximum entropy—death or disorganization. An open system, however, may attain a state where the system remains in dynamic equilibrium through the continuous inflow of material, energy, and information. This is called a steady state. This relationship between negative entropy and the steady state for living organisms and social systems is suggested by Emery and Trist.

> In contradistinction to physical objects, any living entity survives by importing into itself certain types of material from its environment, transforming these in accordance with its own system characteristics, and exporting other types back into the environment. By this process the organism obtains the additional energy that renders it "negentropic"; it becomes capable of attaining stability in a time-independent steady state—a necessary condition of adaptability to environmental variance. [37]

The steady state for the open system, as contrasted to the closed system subject to entropy, occurs while the system can still maintain its functions and perform effectively. Under this concept, an organization is able to adapt to changes in its environment and to maintain a continual steady state. An analogy can be seen in a biological system. The human body is able to maintain a steady state of body temperature in spite of wide variations in the environmental temperature. Obviously, there are limits to the degree to which the biological organism or the social organization can maintain a steady state in response to environmental changes. Massive environmental changes may be so great that it is impossible for the system to adapt. The organism dies, or the social organization is disbanded.

The steady state has an additional meaning; within the organizational system, the various subsystems have achieved a balance of relationships and forces which allows the total system to perform effectively. In biological organisms, the term *homeostasis* is applied to the organism's steady state. For social organizations, it is not an absolute steady state but rather a dynamic or moving equilibrium, one of continual adjustment to environmental and internal forces. The social organization will attempt to accumulate a certain "slack" of resources which helps it to maintain its equilibrium and to mitigate some of the possible variations in the inflow and environmental requirements.

---

[37] F. E. Emery and E. L. Trist, "The Causal Texture of Organizational Environments," *Human Relations*, February 1965, p. 21.

Feedback Mechanisms

The concept of feedback is important in understanding how a system maintains a dynamic equilibrium. Through the process of feedback, the system continually receives information from its environment which helps it adjust.

The concept of feedback has been used in looking at a number of biological phenomena. The maintenance of homeostasis, or the balance in a living organism, depends on a continual feedback of information to that organism from its environment. For example, the cooling of the blood from a drop in external temperatures stimulates certain centers in the brain which activate heat-producing mechanisms of the body, and the organism's temperature is monitored back to the center so that temperature is maintained at a steady level. Man uses principles of feedback in many of his physical activities. For example, in riding a bicycle, he receives feedback in regard to direction and balance which causes him to take corrective actions. Feedback can be both positive and negative, although for our purposes the most important consideration is that of negative feedback. Negative feedback is informational input which indicates that the system is deviating from a prescribed course and should readjust to a new steady state. Feedback is of vital importance in the complex organization which must continually receive informational inputs from its environment. Management is involved in interpreting and correcting for this information feedback. This is a vital part of the organizational control function and will be discussed in detail in Chapter 18.

Adaptive and Maintenance Mechanisms

Systems must have two mechanisms which are often in conflict. First, in order to maintain an equilibrium, they must have maintenance mechanisms which ensure that the various subsystems are in balance and that the total system is in accord with its environment. The forces for maintenance are conservative and attempt to prevent the system from changing so rapidly that the various subsystems and total system become out of balance. Second, adaptive mechanisms are necessary in order to provide a *dynamic* equilibrium, one which is changing over time. Therefore, the system must have adaptive mechanisms which allow it to respond to changing internal and external requirements.

Some forces within the social organization are geared to the maintenance of the system, and other forces and subsystems are geared to adaptation. These counteracting forces will often create tensions, stresses, and conflicts which are natural and should not be considered as totally dysfunctional. [38] Katz and Kahn describe the importance of maintenance and adaptive mechanisms for social organizations.

---

[38] Robert Chin says, "The presence of tensions, stresses or strains, and conflict within the system often are reacted to by people in the system as if they were shameful and must be done away with. Tension reduction, relief of stress and strain, and conflict resolution become the working goals of practitioners but sometimes at the price of overlooking the possibility of increasing tensions and conflict in order to facilitate creativity, innovation, and social change." Chin, op. cit., p. 204.

If the system is to survive, *maintenance substructures* must be elaborated to hold the walls of the social maze in place. Even these would not suffice to insure organizational survival, however. The organization exists in a changing and demanding environment, and it must adapt constantly to the changing environmental demands. *Adaptive structures* develop in organizations to generate appropriate responses to external conditions. [39]

Growth through Internal Elaboration

In the closed system subject to the laws of physics, the system moves toward entropy and disorganization. In contrast, open systems appear to have the opposite tendency and move in the direction of greater differentiation and a higher level of organization. Bertalanffy points to the continual elaborations of biological organisms: "In organic development and evolution, a transition toward states of higher order and differentiation seems to occur. The tendency toward increasing complication has been indicated as a primary characteristic of the living, as opposed to inanimate, nature." [40]

This same process appears to hold true for most social systems. There is a tendency for them to elaborate their activities and to reach higher levels of differentiation and organization. An examination of certain attributes of complex organizations may help explain this tendency. Complex social organizations are made up of many subsystems, some of which have excess capacity or resources which create a continual pressure toward growth. Furthermore, social organizations will often try to encompass within their boundaries additional activities in order to limit uncertainties and to ensure their survival. The business organization may use vertical integration in order to ensure a continual source of raw materials. The pattern of conglomerate diversification and mergers by many corporations in the United States is another indication of this process. In many cases, these mergers result from product innovation and technological breakthroughs which provide opportunities for the organization to extend its boundaries into new areas. Or it may be attributed to an imbalance of managerial and technical skills which are seeking outlets for their activities and creativity. An indication of this elaboration has been the expansion of many of our large corporations into international activities, significantly increasing the boundaries of their operations.

There is also a tendency for complex organizations to achieve greater differentiation and specialization among internal subsystems. The increased number of specialized departments and activities in complex business organizations is readily apparent. The great proliferation of departments, courses, and subject matter in universities is another example of differentiation and elaboration.

Equifinality of Open Systems

In physical systems there is a direct cause-and-effect relationship between the initial conditions and the final state. Biological and social systems operate differently. The concept of *equifinality* says that final results may be achieved with different initial

---

[39] Katz and Kahn, op. cit., p. 39.
[40] Ludwig von Bertalanffy, "The Theory of Open Systems in Physics and Biology," *Science,* Jan. 13, 1950, p. 26.

conditions and in different ways. This view suggests that the social organization can accomplish its objectives with varying inputs and with varying internal activities. Thus, the social system is not restrained by the simple cause-and-effect relationship of closed systems.

The equifinality of social systems has major importance for the management of complex organizations. The closed-system cause-and-effect relationship adopted from the physical sciences would suggest that there is *one best way* to achieve a given objective. The concept of equifinality suggests that the manager can utilize a varying bundle of inputs into the organization, can transform these in a variety of ways, and can achieve satisfactory output. Extending this view further suggests that the management function is not necessarily one of seeking a rigid optimal solution but rather one of having available a variety of satisfactory alternatives.

The foregoing are a few of the characteristics of open systems.[41] To the student who is initially exposed to some of these concepts, they may seem complicated. Much of our educational experience emphasizes closed-system approaches—mathematics and the physical sciences, for example. The open-system view, with the properties set forth in the previous sections, is pertinent for organization theory.

MANAGERIAL SYSTEMS

The managerial system spans the entire organization by directing the technology, organizing people and other resources, and relating the organization to its environment. Our view is similar to that expressed by Churchman:

> This last component, which determines the overall objectives and relates the subsystem standards to the overall, can be called the ''management subsystem.'' It is the subsystem that thinks about the overall plan and implements its thinking.[42]

One approach to the study of management focuses attention on the fundamental administrative processes—planning, organizing, and controlling—which are essential if an organization is to meet its primary goals and objectives. These basic managerial processes are required for any type of organization—business, government, education—where human and physical resources are combined to achieve certain objectives. Furthermore, these processes are necessary regardless of the specialized area of management—production, distribution, finance, or facilitating activities.

Another way to help understand the managerial task is to look within organizations at various levels or subsystems. The model shown in Figure 5.3 is an extension of the

---

[41] For a further discussion of systems characteristics see: Russell L. Ackoff, ''Towards a System of Systems Concepts,'' *Management Science*, July 1971, pp. 661–671; and F. Kenneth Berrien, *General and Social Systems*, Rutgers University Press, New Brunswick, N.J., 1968.
[42] C. West Churchman, *The Systems Approach*, Dell Publishing Co., Inc., New York, 1968, p. 8.

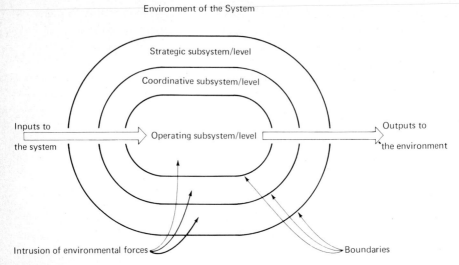

Environment of the System

Strategic subsystem/level

Coordinative subsystem/level

Inputs to the system

Operating subsystem/level

Outputs to the environment

Intrusion of environmental forces

Boundaries

FIGURE 5.3 THE ORGANIZATION AS A COMPOSITE OF STRATEGIC, COORDINATIVE, AND OPERATING SUBSYSTEMS/LEVELS

work of Parsons, Petit, and Thompson. [43] There are basic differences in the orientation of the managerial system at these different levels. The operating subsystem is concerned primarily with economic-technical rationality and tries to create certainty by "closing the technical core" to many variables. Thompson says, "Under norms of rationality, organizations seek to seal off their core technologies from environmental influences. Since complete closure is impossible, they seek to buffer environmental influences by surrounding their technical cores with input and output components." [44] The closed-system view is applicable to the "technical core" or operating subsystem of the organization.

By contrast, at the strategic level the organization faces the greatest degree of uncertainty in terms of inputs from its environment over which it has little or no control. Therefore, management at this level should have an open-system view and concentrate on adaptive and/or innovative strategies. The coordinative manager operates between the operating and the strategic levels and serves to mediate and coordinate the two. This level transforms the uncertainty of the environment into the economic-technical rationality necessary for input into the operating subsystem.

In many organizations these roles are separated theoretically. For example, in the university, the board of regents is thought of as fulfilling the strategic role, whereas the

---

[43] Talcott Parsons, *Structure and Process in Modern Societies*, The Free Press, New York, 1960, pp. 60–96; Thomas A. Petit, "A Behavioral Theory of Management," *Academy of Management Journal*, December 1967, pp. 341–350; and James D. Thompson, *Organizations in Action*, McGraw-Hill Book Company, New York, 1967.
[44] James D. Thompson, op. cit., p. 24.

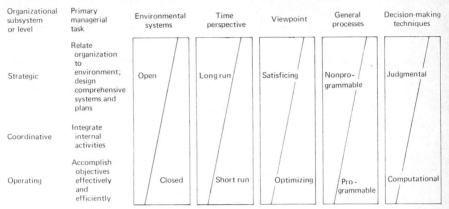

Organizational subsystem or level	Primary managerial task	Environmental systems	Time perspective	Viewpoint	General processes	Decision-making techniques
Strategic	Relate organization to environment; design comprehensive systems and plans	Open	Long run	Satisficing	Nonpro-grammable	Judgmental
Coordinative	Integrate internal activities					
Operating	Accomplish objectives effectively and efficiently	Closed	Short run	Optimizing	Pro-grammable	Computational

FIGURE 5.4 THE MANAGERIAL TASK: STRATEGIC, COORDINATIVE, AND OPERATING SUB-SYSTEMS

president, deans, and department heads are involved with coordinative aspects. The professors, under this concept, perform the operating functions. In a hospital, the board of trustees performs the strategic role, the hospital administrator's staff is involved with coordinative aspects, while the doctors, nurses, and other specialists perform the "operating" functions. Theoretically, in the business organization the board of directors relates the institution to its environment, upper and middle management deal with coordinative aspects, and other employees perform the operating tasks. However, this distinction is not clear-cut in any of these organizations. For example, the president of a corporation usually has both strategic and coordinative roles.

Figure 5.4 illustrates in more detail the differences in managerial tasks at the various levels in organizations. The smaller the organization, the more likely that the various aspects of the managerial task will be carried out by one individual. Obviously, for a proprietorship, the owner-manager is involved in all the activities set forth in Figure 5.4. He must define his task in relation to his environment, plan his activities over the short and long run, and then carry them out in order to achieve his objectives.

In larger, more complex organizations it is more likely that these subsystems are separable and identifiable. Top management is involved in relating the organization to its environment—identifying a niche which it must fill in order to survive and grow. Strategy formulation also involves designing comprehensive systems and plans. A systems philosophy is useful in conceptualizing the long-run nature of the organization and assembling the appropriate resources for achieving desired goals. The environmental system is relatively open; general processes are typically nonprogrammable; and the viewpoint is essentially one of satisficing—finding workable solutions to complex, ill-structured, novel problems. Decision making is largely judgmental and cogitative—reasoned evaluation of all relevant inputs to the problem-solving process.

In the operating subsystem the primary task is accomplishing stated objectives effectively and efficiently. It is here that the organization "does its thing"—producing bicycles or toothpaste, providing health care or fire protection. The environmental system is relatively closed and general processes can be programmed, for example, standard operating procedures or computer programs. Systems analysis provides a framework for a short-run, optimizing outlook and computational decision making through the use of quantitative techniques.

In the coordinative subsystem—ranging between the strategic and operating activities—the primary concern is integrating internal activities which have been specialized by function and/or level. Middle management is involved in translating comprehensive plans into operational plans and procedures. It is involved in interpreting the results of the operating system and in focusing existing resources in appropriate directions. Systems management facilitates coordination of several functions, projects, or programs within an overall organization. A pragmatic point of view is essential in integrating short- and long-run considerations. Compromise is often necessary in decision making at this level in order to achieve a practical or utilitarian outcome via analysis and synthesis of problems.

The terms used in the various dimensions shown in Figure 5.4 are illustrative of general tendencies, i.e., most likely activities or approaches. It is not to say that judgment is not important in the operating system or that computational techniques are never used in developing comprehensive plans. However, the terms do provide a basic flavor of the managerial task in three relatively distinct organizational subsystems. Nor does this mean that the different managerial subsystems can operate independently. Quite the contrary, they are interdependent. For example, the strategic subsystem must perform effectively if the organization is to receive the necessary inputs for the operating subsystem. Also, the operating subsystem must produce outputs efficiently to ensure that the organization receives environmental support.

Role of Manager

The view of the organization as an open system suggests a substantially different role for management from that which it played in traditional theory. "A profound change in the way management is perceived has been produced by the advent of the so-called systems revolution." [45] In the traditional theory, the emphasis was upon economic-technical rationality. This closed-system view was appropriate for the operating level but not for the coordinative and strategic levels. The human relations emphasis did bring into focus the psychosocial subsystem but neglected the technical, structural, and environmental aspects. The management science approach adopted a closed-system view, focusing on the techniques of managerial decision making.

The view of an open sociotechnical system creates a more difficult role for management. It must deal with uncertainties and ambiguities and, above all, must be

---

[45] John A. Beckett, *Management Dynamics*, McGraw-Hill Book Company, New York, 1971, p. 13.

concerned with adapting the organization to new and changing requirements. Management is a process which spans and links the various subsystems of the organization.

The systems view suggests that management faces situations which are dynamic, inherently uncertain, and frequently ambiguous. Management is not in full control of all the factors of production, as suggested by traditional theory. It is strongly restrained by many environmental and internal (technological, structural, and psychosocial) forces. Sayles outlines the role of management under the systems approach:

> A systems concept emphasizes that managerial assignments do not have these neat, clearly defined boundaries; rather, the modern manager is placed in a network of mutually dependent relationships. . . .The one enduring objective is the effort to build and maintain a predictable, reciprocating system of relationships, the behavioral patterns of which stay within reasonable physical limits. But this is seeking a moving equilibrium, since the parameters of the system (the division of labor and the controls) are evolving and changing. Thus the manager endeavors to introduce regularity in a world that will never allow him to achieve the ideal. . . .Only managers who can deal with uncertainty, with ambiguity, and with battles that are never won but only fought well can hope to succeed. [46]

One of the most pervasive functions of management at all levels is decision making. Figure 5.4 indicates that the decision-making strategy differs in various organizational subsystems. In the operating subsystem, closed-system approaches are appropriate. However, at the coordinative and strategic levels, open-system decision-making approaches are necessary. We will consider managerial information-decision systems in detail in Part 6.

SYSTEMS CONCEPTS FOR ORGANIZATION AND MANAGEMENT

The foregoing sections provide the basis for the remainder of this book. These basic concepts will be discussed and illustrated in the following six parts:

Environment, Boundaries, and Goals
Technology and Structure
The Psychosocial System
The Managerial System
Comparative Analysis and Contingency Views
Organizational Change and the Future

---

[46] Leonard Sayles, *Managerial Behavior*, McGraw-Hill Book Company, New York, 1964, pp. 258–259.

This framework will be used as a basis for the development of modern organization theory and management practice. We will begin with a discussion of the environmental suprasystem and its impact upon the organization. Next we will look at organizational goals. This will set the stage for the discussion of technology and an appraisal of its effects on the organization structure as well as on the psychosocial system. Structural relationships will then be considered in detail. The components of the psychosocial system are analyzed in depth. The managerial system is then reviewed, with emphasis on information flow, decision making, and the key functions of planning and controlling the activities of the organization. In effect we will follow an orderly process of looking in more detail at each of the major subsystems of the organization as shown in Figure 5.2.

We recognize that this concentrated attention to subsystems is not really keeping the spirit and philosophy of the systems approach. However, it is necessary to look at the major subsystems in more detail before we can return to a more integrated, systems viewpoint. In Chapter 19, "Comparative Analysis and Contingency Views," we will return to a more explicit consideration of patterns of relationships and configurations among the various subsystems. We will then apply this integrated systems viewpoint as a framework for comparative analysis in our discussion of hospitals and universities.

SUMMARY

The systems approach provides an integrative framework for modern organization theory and management practice. General systems theory includes concepts for integrating knowledge in the physical, biological, and social sciences.

There is a close relationship between general systems theory and the development of functionalism in the social sciences. Functionalism emphasizes integration of parts and subsystems into a functional whole. It has been used as a primary frame of reference in anthropology and sociology. In the field of psychology, the systems concept has achieved prominence. Modern economics also uses this approach, particularly in dynamic equilibrium analysis and input-output studies. The discipline of cybernetics is founded on the systems approach, focusing on communication and information flow in complex systems. Although it has been applied primarily to mechanistic systems, its model of feedback, control, and regulation has applicability for social systems as well.

The systems approach is directly related to organization theory. Traditional theory used closed-system thinking. Modern theory has moved toward considering the organization as an open system interacting with its environment. In contrast to the closed or mechanical system, the open system is not subject to the process of entropy—it can maintain a dynamic equilibrium by importing material, energy, and information from its environment.

The organization can be viewed as an open system in interaction with its environment and composed of five primary components—goals and values, and technical, structural, psychosocial, and managerial subsystems.

There are several key characteristics of organizational systems. They are not natural, like physical or biological systems, but are *contrived*. There are *boundaries* which separate the organization from its environment. In general, a system is composed of subsystems of a lower order and is also part of a suprasystem; there is a *hierarchy* of systems. In open biological or social systems, entropy can be arrested and may even be transformed to *negative entropy*—a process of more complete organization. The concept of *steady state* is closely related to that of negative entropy. The organization is able to adapt to changes in its environment and to maintain a continual dynamic equilibrium.

The concept of *feedback* is important in understanding how a system maintains a steady state. Through the process of feedback, it continually receives information from its environment which helps it to adjust. A system must have both *adaptive and maintenance mechanisms*. The forces for maintenance are conservative and attempt to prevent the system from changing so rapidly that the various subsystems become out of balance. In contrast, adaptive mechanisms are necessary in order to provide for change. Open systems display *growth through internal elaboration*. They tend to move in the direction of greater differentiation and to a higher level of organization. Finally, open systems have the characteristic of *equifinality*—objectives may be achieved with varying inputs and in different ways.

There are three subsystems levels in the managerial system of complex organizations: operating, coordinative, and strategic. The *operating* subsystem is involved with actual task performance. The *strategic* level relates the activities of the organization to its environment. The *coordinative* subsystem serves to integrate activities vertically (strategic and operating) and horizontally (among different functions at the same level). The view of the organization as a sociotechnical system creates a different role for the manager. He must integrate and balance the various subsystems and their activities in the environmental setting.

QUESTIONS AND PROBLEMS

1 Define systems. Can you describe systems that fit each level of Boulding's hierarchy?
2 Compare and contrast mechanistic and biological or social systems.
3 Differentiate open and closed systems. Which model is more appropriate for business and for government organizations? Why?
4 Why might modern organization theory be considered as a special element of general systems theory?
5 Relate a specific organization to the subsystems in Figure 5.2.
6 How can automation, electronic data processing, and network analysis (PERT, for example) be considered applications of the systems approach?
7 Why can an organization be considered as a contrived system which operates under the concept of equifinality?

8 Why is it necessary for organizations to have both maintenance and adaptive mechanisms?

9 Relate the concept of ''growth through internal elaboration'' to a specific type of organization such as a business or university.

10 Discuss the major differences between the operating, coordinative, and strategic subsystems in the managerial system.

11 How does the systems approach affect management practices?

12 How would you use the systems approach to describe these types of organizations?

    a a business

    b a hospital

    c a university

Contemporary society, whether observed globally, nationally, or locally, is realistically characterized as "the chaotic society."

Philip M. Hauser

Primitive randomness evolves into organized complexity. This is true for the beginnings of life and, before that, in the chemical evolution of the universe. It is equally true of our social evolution.

F. Kenneth Berrien

Ecological survival does not mean the abandonment of technology. Rather, it requires that technology be derived from a scientific analysis that is appropriate to the natural world on which technology intrudes.

Barry Commoner

For all men are polluters—and all living Americans are big polluters. The greedy and the ungreedy alike befoul the air with automobile exhaust fumes, the humble 1960 jalopy contributing somewhat more poison than the arrogant 1970 Cadillac.

Max Ways

An obvious characteristic of modern society is ever increasing interdependency; little can be changed without affecting a wide array of institutions, and many new developments depend upon close, collaborative, and integrated activities that criss-cross organizational boundaries and the dividing line between the public and private sectors.

Leonard R. Sayles and Margaret K. Chandler

When a man does not know what harbor he is making for, no wind is the right wind.

Seneca

PART 3

ENVIRONMENT, BOUNDARIES, AND GOALS

Every organization is a subsystem of an environment which provides resource inputs and utilizes the organization's outputs. Each society has certain fundamental characteristics, such as values, people, and resources, which greatly affect the nature of its organizations and their management. The social organization has a loosely defined boundary which separates it from its environmental suprasystem. However, organizations are open systems and this boundary is permeable to a variety of inputs and outputs. The environment in modern societies is becoming increasingly turbulent and organizations must continually adapt.

Organizational values and goals are not determined in isolation but, rather, through interactions with the environmental suprasystem. In this part we will begin to use the systems model developed in Chapter 5 to consider in depth the environmental suprasystem, the boundaries between organizations and their environment, and the goals and values subsystem.

Chapter 6, Environmental Suprasystem, looks in detail at the nature of the environmental system and how it affects organizations. Both the general environment for all organizations and the specific task environment for each individual organization will be considered. As an illustration of these relationships, we will look at the interface between business organizations and society.

In Chapter 7 we turn to a consideration of Organizational Goals. Goals are considered from three perspectives—environmental constraints, system goals, and goals of individual participants. The role of management in setting goals and developing programs for their accomplishment is discussed. The problems of measuring the organization's performance in achieving its goals are also considered.

ENVIRONMENTAL SUPRASYSTEM

Organizations are subsystems of a broader suprasystem—the environment. They have identifiable but permeable boundaries which separate them from their environment. They receive inputs across these boundaries, transform them, and return outputs. As society becomes more and more complex and dynamic, organizations need to devote increasing attention to environmental forces. This chapter will look at the interrelationships between organizations and their external suprasystem and will consider more specifically the impact of societal forces on business organizations. The following topics are discussed:

> Environment, Boundaries, and Organizations
> The Societal (General) Environment
> The Specific (Task) Environment
> More Complex and Uncertain Environments
> Society's View of Business
> Social Responsibilities of Business
> Environmental Improvement

ENVIRONMENT, BOUNDARIES, AND ORGANIZATIONS

In Chapter 5 we suggested that any social organization is a subsystem of its broader environment. Organizations have boundaries which delineate them from some broader suprasystem, and they receive inputs, transform them in some way, and return outputs to their environment. This open-system view suggests the need for a more complete understanding of the interactions between organizations and their environments.

In organization theory and management practice there is a growing awareness of environmental forces.

> It is generally accepted that the total situation (including constraints and contingencies) existing in the relevant environment must be incorporated into organization theory if it is to be of value in an increasingly turbulent era. No longer will it be possible to assume a "frictionless" stable environment for most firms and to proceed to look for rational answers to technical and organizational problems within the boundaries of the firm. . . .In short, environmental turbulence, cultural variables, and the relevant task environment have an unquestioned but inadequately assessed impact on organizational performance. [1]

More explicit understanding of environmental impacts upon organizations is important for the organization theorist, and it is significant for the practicing manager. Certain principles of organization and/or management may be appropriate for uniform operations in a relatively stable environment. A mass-production organization such as an automobile assembly line might operate most efficiently under a rather rigid hierarchy with precise planning and control and routinization of activities. This approach would also be appropriate for a routine service organization such as the post office. In contrast, other organizations, operating in an uncertain environment and with nonroutine technology, may perform most efficiently under a very different set of principles. A research and development laboratory or a university graduate program, for example, would have a very different environment and would be characterized by a flexible structure, nonroutine activities, and adaptive planning and control processes.

It is therefore essential in applying the systems approach to the study of organizations and their management to start with the environmental suprasystem rather than with any internal subsystem. "The first step should always be to go to the next higher level of systems organization, to study the dependence of the system in question upon the supersystem of which it is a part, for the supersystem sets the limits of variance of behavior of the dependent system." [2]

Open-System View

The organization is an open system which exchanges information, energy, and materials with its environment. For example, the business organization receives inputs of money, people, and other resources; transforms these through its production pro-

---

[1] Winston Oberg, as reported in Anant R. Negandhi (ed.), *Environmental Settings in Organizational Functioning*, Comparative Administration Research Institute, Kent State University, Kent, Ohio, 1970, p. 121.
[2] Daniel Katz and Robert L. Kahn, *The Social Psychology of Organizations*, John Wiley & Sons, Inc., New York, 1966, p. 58.

cesses; and exports products or services. The university receives inputs of students and financial and other resources, transforms them, and exports educated graduates and new knowledge. In this view organizations are dependent for their survival and efficiency upon an exchange of goods and services with their environment. [3]

This open-system view makes the study of organizations much more difficult than a closed-system perspective. It is simpler to study any organization as a closed system, to concentrate upon internal operations, and to dismiss environmental influences. But this can lead to erroneous conclusions.

One point needs clarification. When speaking of organizations as open systems we should qualify this by saying "relatively" open systems. In fact, most biological organisms and social organizations are "partially open" and "partially closed." Open and closed are a matter of degree. For example, human beings are certainly an open biological system and receive many inputs from their environment. However, we cannot receive all possible inputs and are therefore not totally open. For example, we can hear sounds only within a narrow range. We can see only a narrow spectrum of light rays. Thus we are severely limited as to the nature and type of inputs which we receive from our environment. Conversely, we have only a limited range of behavioral outputs. The social organization is also "selectively" open to inputs. The organization cannot respond to all possible environmental influences; it must be selective in the inputs it receives, the transformations it performs, and the outputs it produces. In effect it must establish a "domain" for its activities and boundaries which separate it from its external environment. [4]

Organizational Boundaries

All systems have boundaries which separate them from their environmental suprasystem. The concept of boundaries helps one understand the distinction between open and closed systems. The relatively closed system has rigid, impenetrable boundaries; whereas the open system has permeable boundaries between itself and a broader suprasystem. Boundaries are relatively easily defined in physical and biological systems—they are visible. For example, we can define the physical boundaries of the human body very precisely. However, what happens when we depart from a purely physical description of the boundaries of the human being? How can we describe the sociological and psychological boundaries of human behavior? We must begin to define the boundary between the human and his society in terms of activities or processes rather than physical structures.

This point is even more important when considering social systems such as organizations. They do not have any precise physical boundaries. What are the boundaries of the U.S. Army, General Motors, the Teamsters, or the corner service station? Organizations have no clearly observable boundaries and are open to many inputs and

---

[3] David Silverman, *The Theory of Organizations*, Basic Books, Inc., Publishers, New York, 1971, p. 35.
[4] James D. Thompson, *Organizations in Action*, McGraw-Hill Book Company, New York, 1967, pp. 25–38.

outputs. Generally, those activities which are necessary for the organization's transformation process define its boundary.

There are important differences among organizations concerning the degree of permeability. For example, the inner circle of a crime syndicate would generally have very closed, impenetrable boundaries where people would be screened thoroughly; entering and leaving the system might be very difficult (often in a concrete block in the East River). Institutions such as maximum security prisons and some mental hospitals also tend to have tight boundaries. The Communist Party in the United States and other revolutionary groups tend to be closed. In contrast, the boundaries of many other organizations are very permeable. It is not very difficult to become a member of the PTA (in fact, it is difficult *to not* become a member). The Republican and Democratic parties have few constraints on membership.

The fact that organizations are social institutions composed of people contributes to openness and boundary permeability. People are continually moving back and forth between the environment and the organization. Few of us spend a large part of our time in a single organization. We have other activities and roles. As Perrow suggests:

> The organization is not the total world of the individual; it is not a society. People must fulfill other social roles; besides, society has shaped them in ways which affect their ability to perform organizational tasks. A man has a marital status, ethnic identification, religious affiliations, a distinctive personality, friends, to name only a few. . . . Daily, people come contaminated into the organization. [5]

In spite of the fact that boundaries of social organizations are somewhat open and permeable, they do provide a filtering function. Organizational boundaries screen the inputs and outputs. In this sense, the boundaries are barriers to the flow of energy, material, and information. This is a vital function of boundaries because it would be impossible for any organization to deal with *all possible* inputs. Frequently, the boundaries serve to homogenize the inputs so that the organization can deal with them more effectively. For example, elementary schools set forth certain age requirements for entry into the first grade, thus standardizing inputs. Universities generally require graduation from high school with a certain grade point and course prerequisites. The business organization sets up requirements for employment, again homogenizing the human inputs. And it typically sets forth raw material specifications to standardize material inputs.

Boundaries also filter the outputs of the organization. The organization cannot perform an infinite variety of transformation functions but must restrict itself to certain activities. It therefore can return only certain specific outputs to its environment. The Red

---

[5] From *Organizational Analysis: A Sociological View* by Charles Perrow. Copyright 1970 by Wadsworth Publishing Company, Inc. Reprinted by permission of the publisher, Brooks/Cole Publishing Company, Monterey, California.

Cross requires trainees to pass certain tests before they are certified as lifeguards. The manufacturing company develops quality controls which standardize product outputs. However, it is difficult to be precise about the nature of all outputs. For example, there may be various indirect outputs which are not readily delineated in the input-transformation-output model. As a by-product of its production processes, the manufacturing plant may output waste products which pollute the environment. Even more subtly, a highly autocratic and coercive organization with little regard for human participants may "output" a great deal of human dissatisfaction.

Furthermore, as we indicated in Chapter 5, there may be internal boundaries or filtering processes which standardize inputs and outputs to the various operating subsystems. For example, in the university various courses (the operating subsystems) frequently have prerequisites which standardize the inputs. Thus, the strategic and coordinative subsystems "buffer" the operating subsystems of the organization from environmental influences. (See Figure 5.3.)

Organizational boundaries perform another vital function. They provide a degree of autonomy and independence for the organization from intrusion of environmental influences. For example, in our society the "private enterprise" system provides substantial autonomy for the business organization. This system allows the individual firm a great deal of discretion in conducting its internal operations as long as it meets broad social goals.[6]

This view can also be transferred to the public sector. The individual organization, such as a school system, must have a certain amount of independence from environmental intrusions in order to carry out its transformation functions efficiently. The filtering function of the organizational boundary is important in maintaining this autonomy.

Boundary-spanning Components

Environmental forces have a direct impact on the way the organization structures its activities. When the environment is dynamic and heterogeneous it is usually necessary to establish functional departments within the organization to deal with a specific set of environmental inputs or outputs. In business enterprises many specialized departments have a boundary-spanning function. Purchasing is concerned with receiving material inputs; personnel departments recruit and select employees; market research departments obtain information from the environment. On the output side, sales departments represent the major boundary-spanning component. Public relations departments are concerned with feeding informational outputs to the environment which will enhance the reputation and prestige of the organization.

Generally speaking, the more heterogeneous and dynamic the environment, the more complex and differentiated the internal structuring of the organization. We see many examples of this. As environmentalists and other groups have become more vociferous and influential, companies have responded by establishing new environmen-

---

[6] Neil W. Chamberlain, *Enterprise and Environment*, McGraw-Hill Book Company, New York, 1968, p. 139.

tal or ecology departments to deal with these specific groups. Many staff departments in organizations are established as boundary-spanning components.

> One way to view staff positions is to consider them contact points with the environment—the personnel man recruits, hires, fires, and judges the labor market; the accountant deals with the intake and outflow of money; R and D units survey technical developments; marketing forecasts the demand and product changes. [7]

These boundary-spanning positions are often stressful. For example, the sales department may have continual conflicts in responding to the needs of customers while recognizing the requirements for efficient production. The university football coach may have difficulty in responding to the internal system requirements of players, other students, and faculty as well as to those of the alumni and general public.

THE SOCIETAL (GENERAL) ENVIRONMENT

In the broadest sense, the environment is everything external to the organization's boundaries. However, it may be useful to think of the environment in two ways: (1) the societal (general) environment which affects all organizations in a given society and (2) the specific (task) environment which affects the individual organization more directly. [8]

Many forces at the societal, general, or macro environmental level influence organizations. Frequently we take these conditions as given with little recognition of the ways they affect the internal operations of organizations.

> In the United States we take for granted a whole set of cultural conditions which permit the efficient functioning of complex organizations—such as literacy, authority relations, and an emphasis upon achievement as a basis of judging people rather than characteristics ascribed at birth. But it is a mistake to take these conditions for granted, for they explain a good deal about our society and its organizations. [9]

There are so many forces in the general environment which affect organizations that they are difficult to classify and describe. Various authors have suggested a number of major environmental characteristics which affect all organizations. [10] (See Figure 6.1.)

---

[7] Perrow, op. cit., p. 55.
[8] Richard H. Hall, *Organizations: Structure and Process,* Prentice-Hall, Inc., Englewood Cliffs, N.J., 1972, pp. 297–324.
[9] Perrow, op. cit., p. 94.
[10] See, for example, Hall, op. cit., pp. 298–306; Richard N. Farmer and Barry M. Richman, *Comparative Management and Economic Progress,* Cedarwood Publishing Company, Bloomington, Ind., 1970, pp. 25–31; Anant R. Negandhi (ed.), *Environmental Settings in Organizational Functioning,* Comparative Administration Research Institute, Kent State University, Kent, Ohio, 1970; and Billy J. Hodge and Herbert J. Johnson, *Management and Organizational Behavior,* John Wiley & Sons, Inc., 1970, pp. 65–83.

FIGURE 6.1 GENERAL ENVIRONMENTAL CHARACTERISTICS FOR ORGANIZATIONS

Cultural. Including the historical background, ideologies, values, and norms of the society. Views on authority relationships, leadership patterns, interpersonal relationships, rationalism, science, and technology define the nature of social institutions.

Technological. The level of scientific and technological advancement in society. Including the physical base (plant, equipment, facilities) and the knowledge base of technology. Degree to which the scientific and technological community is able to develop new knowledge and apply it.

Educational. The general literacy level of the population. The degree of sophistication and specialization in the educational system. The proportion of the people with a high level of professional and/or specialized training.

Political. The general political climate of society. The degree of concentration of political power. The nature of political organization (degrees of decentralization, diversity of functions, etc.). The political party system.

Legal. Constitutional considerations, nature of legal system, jurisdictions of various governmental units. Specific laws concerning formation, taxation, and control of organizations.

Natural Resource. The nature, quantity, and availability of natural resources, including climatic and other conditions.

Demographic. The nature of human resources available to the society; their number, distribution, age, and sex. Concentration or urbanization of population is a characteristic of industrialized societies.

Sociological. Class structure and mobility. Definition of social roles. Nature of the social organization and development of social institutions.

Economic. General economic framework, including the type of economic organization—private versus public ownership; the centralization or decentralization of economic planning; the banking system; and fiscal policies. The level of the investment in physical resources and consumption characteristics.

These characteristics set the framework for businesses, unions, governmental agencies, and all other organizations and have a homogenizing effect. For example, although most of our large state universities do operate in different specific environments (the individual state), they have many similar characteristics. Professors and students find that the Universities of Minnesota, Washington, and California have many more similarities than differences. City governments throughout the United States have similar structures and processes. Public school systems in New Jersey and Oregon have many similarities. These general environmental characteristics have an important effect in determining the resources available for inputs, the specific mission, the most appropriate transformation processes, and the acceptability of organizational outputs.

Climate for Growth

The environmental characteristics set forth in Figure 6.1 are generally favorable to the growth of diverse, complex social organizations. Stinchcombe suggests that the key societal conditions favorable to this process are (*a*) general literacy and specialized advanced schooling; (*b*) urbanization; (*c*) a money economy; (*d*) political change; (*e*) the density of social life, including especially an already rich organizational life. [11] This

---

[11] Arthur L. Stinchcombe, "Social Structure and Organizations," in James G. March (ed.), *Handbook of Organizations*, Rand McNally & Company, Chicago, 1965, p. 150.

model suggests that a society with many complex, diverse organizations will find it easier to create new organizations and new organizational forms. Reflecting back over the past century we can see this process working in our society. The development of the corporate form, conglomerates, multinational businesses, multiversities, labor unions, complex hospital systems, and governmental organizations such as the Tennessee Valley Authority, the Atomic Energy Commission, and the National Aeronautics and Space Administration are examples. There is every evidence that this process is continuing, with more organizations being spawned and nurtured to meet social needs. At the same time, many organizations do not survive the changing conditions and go out of existence.

There is another aspect of the view that general environmental conditions are favorable to the growth and development of organizations. "An organizationally dense society is one in which the change process is both rapid and intense. . . . In a society in which a wide variety of organizations and organizational forms exists, as in the contemporary United States, social change is also a constant condition." [12] Thus, there is a circular effect between society and organizations. A society with certain environmental characteristics provides a climate favorable to the growth of organizations and new organizations form. In turn, an "organizationally rich" society creates conditions of continual social change.

THE SPECIFIC (TASK) ENVIRONMENT

The individual organization, while operating in the general environmental setting set forth above, may not be directly influenced by nor can it respond to all of these forces. The *task environment* is defined as the more specific forces which are relevant to the decision-making and transformation processes of the individual organization. [13] The general environment is the same for all organizations in a given society. The task environment is different for each organization.

The distinction between the general environment and the task environment is not always clear-cut and is continually changing. Forces in the general environment are continually "breaking through" into the task environment of the specific organization. "Even beyond the task environment there are environmental factors and phenomena which may affect the organization (and be affected by it.) Clearly, the environment is a continuum in which relevance is a matter of degree." [14] For example, universities have traditionally been able to maintain barriers to external forces (the ivory tower) and have restricted their task environment to a limited range of factors. Increasingly, forces from the general environment, such as international conflicts, political activities, minority

---

12 Hall, op. cit., p. 326.
13 William R. Dill, "Environment as an Influence on Managerial Autonomy," *Administrative Science Quarterly,* March 1958, pp. 409-443.
14 Hans B. Thorelli, "Organization Theory: An Ecological View," *Academy of Management Proceedings,* Washington, D.C., 1967, p. 69.

FIGURE 6.2 RELEVANT COMPONENTS OF THE TASK ENVIRONMENT FOR A TYPICAL INDUS-
TRIAL FIRM

Customer Component
    Distributors of product or service
    Actual users of product or service

Suppliers Component
    New materials suppliers
    Equipment suppliers
    Product parts suppliers
    Labor supply

Competitor Component
    Competitors for suppliers
    Competitors for customers

Socio-political Component
    Government regulatory control over the industry
    Public political attitude towards industry and its particular product
    Relationship with trade unions with jurisdiction in the organization

Technological Component
    Meeting new technological requirements of own industry and related industries in production
    of product or service
    Improving and developing new products by implementing new technological advances in the
    industry

SOURCE: Robert B. Duncan, ''Characteristics of Organizational Environments and Perceived Environmental Uncertainty,'' *Administrative Science Quarterly,* September 1972, p. 315.

rights movements, and women's lib, have become relevant forces in their task environment. Business organizations have had to consider many broader social conditions,
such as civil rights movements and environmental pollution, as being within their relevant task environment. The major components in the task environment for the typical
business organization are shown in Figure 6.2.

    Figure 6.3 shows the relationship between the general and task environments and
the organizational system for an industrial firm. The figure also shows the strategic,
coordinative, and operating subsystems of the organization. The strategic subsystem is
a primary boundary-spanning component of the organization and buffers the inputs into
the coordinative and operating subsystems. The operating subsystem or technical core
must receive and transmit filtered (standardized and homogenized) inputs and outputs
in order to perform the transformation functions effectively. Conceptually, there are a
series of permeable boundaries, moving from the general environment to the operating
subsystem, which serve to filter both inputs and outputs.

MORE COMPLEX AND UNCERTAIN ENVIRONMENTS

There is increasing evidence that the environment is becoming more dynamic and
uncertain in our society. A close look at the general environmental characteristics
shown in Figure 6.3 suggests that each involves an accelerating rate of change. Technological conditions are changing rapidly; major cultural and social changes are under

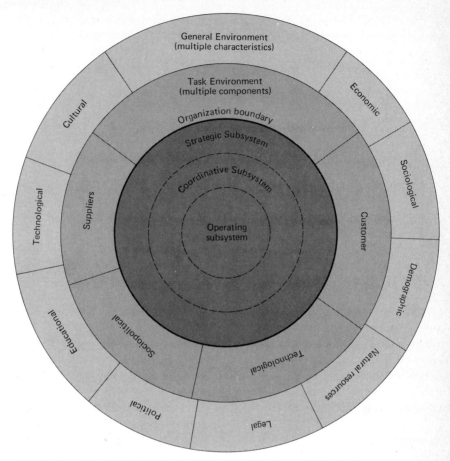

FIGURE 6.3   RELATIONSHIP OF GENERAL AND TASK ENVIRONMENTS TO THE ORGANIZATIONAL SYSTEM

way; and so on. "A main problem in the study of organizational change is that the environmental contexts in which organizations exist are themselves changing, at an increasing rate, and towards increasing complexity." [15] Emery and Trist suggest that the environments of organizations are moving from "placid, randomized" to "turbulent fields." Many writers, such as Alvin Toffler in *Future Shock,* suggest the increasing turbulence in modern societies.

The acceleration of change in our time is, itself, an elemental force. This accelerative thrust has personal and psychological, as well as sociological

---

[15] F. E. Emery and E. L. Trist, "The Causal Texture of Organizational Environments," *Human Relations,* February 1965, p. 21.

consequences. . . . *Future Shock* is a time phenomenon, a product of the greatly accelerated rate of change in society. It arises from the superimposition of a new culture on an old one. It is culture shock in one's own society. [16]

Terreberry agrees that environments are becoming more uncertain and suggests a further elaboration. Organizational change is increasingly externally induced; organizational adaptation is a function of the ability to learn and perform according to changes in the environment. [17]

Organizations of the future will be even more subject to external forces and must be prepared to adapt. This is evident from current experiences. Automobile companies are hearing more directly not only from customers concerning safety and performance, but also from "environmentalists" concerning air pollution. The hospital is being called upon to expand its boundaries and to deal with the total medical care needs of people in the community. On all fronts, organizations are facing a more heterogeneous and uncertain suprasystem.

This growing environmental turbulence creates many problems for organizations. We have suggested that organizations attempt to reduce or minimize environmental uncertainties in a number of ways, such as routinization of inputs and outputs. In a placid environment this process is not difficult. The organization need only respond to a limited number of inputs which are relatively static over time. It can develop specific policies, rules, and regulations to deal with routine events. It can operate with a rigid structure, clearly defined hierarchy, and specific roles for all participants. In effect it can become a highly structured bureaucracy and can operate effectively and efficiently *as long as the environment remains placid.* However, in a turbulent environment this form is not viable. The organization must develop a more adaptive-responsive system. Old principles of organization and management, geared to a placid environment, are no longer appropriate. Buckley suggests this difference:

> Complex adaptive systems are open systems in intimate interchange with an environment characterized by a great deal of shifting variety ("booming, buzzing confusion") and its constraints (its structure of causal interrelations). The concept of equilibrium developed for closed physical systems is quite inappropriate and usually inapplicable to such a dynamic situation. Rather, a characteristic resultant is the elaboration of organization in the direction of the less probable and the less inherently stable. [18]

A word of caution. We should not get carried away in overemphasizing environmental turbulence. All organizations are not (nor will they be) operating in a dynamic

---

[16] Alvin Toffler, *Future Shock,* Random House, Inc., New York, 1971, pp. 2 and 11.
[17] Shirley Terreberry, "The Evolution of Organizational Environments," *Administrative Science Quarterly,* March 1968, pp. 590–613.
[18] Walter Buckley (ed.), *Modern Systems Research for the Behavioral Scientist,* Aldine Publishing Company, Chicago, 1968, p. 509.

setting. Some organizations, and some components and functions within organizations, are able to establish boundaries for their activities which allow them to operate within a more placid environment. We do not see a demise of the more routinized, structured organization in all fields. Throughout this book we stress the importance of a systems approach which considers the task environment as one of the key forces affecting the organization and its management. Task environments will be significantly different; therefore, the most appropriate structures and processes should vary among organizations.

Interorganizational Relationships

In modern societies, the environment itself is increasingly composed of other organizations. In developing societies the environment is characterized by informal, social institutions. In an organizationally rich society, the environment of any one organization is composed of many other organizations.

> When the environment becomes turbulent, however, its constituents are a multitude of other formal organizations. Increasingly, an organization's markets consist of other organizations; suppliers of material, labor, and capital are increasingly organized, and regulatory groups are more numerous and powerful. [19]

The development of a comprehensive theory of interorganizational relations is still in its infancy. [20] In the past, management and organization theory has concentrated on the individual organization and has been primarily concerned with internal relationships. Classical economic theory provides an idealized model of interrelationships between organizations—the free marketplace. In this view, the marketplace and the pricing mechanism determine the relationships between firms. However, in a complex society of many organizations, we need to develop new means for interorganizational integration.

> Organizational study has a long way to go before it will do justice to the crucial question of the organization of organizations. The importance of this problem should not be underestimated. Modern society is composed more and more of larger and larger organizations. Society has long recognized that it cannot leave economic interaction to the free play of market forces because this might not lead these organizations to pursue a course that will bring the greatest happiness to the greatest number. The same holds for interaction among

[19] Terreberry, op. cit., p. 600.
[20] William M. Evan, "The Organization-Set: Toward a Theory of Interorganizational Relations," in James D. Thompson (ed.), *Approaches to Organizational Design,* University of Pittsburgh Press, Pittsburgh, 1966, pp. 175–191.

organizations that do not pursue economic goals, and for the non-economic interactions of economic organizations. Modern society has found it necessary to build more and more instruments to regulate this interaction to encourage increase not only in the effectiveness and satisfaction within each one but also of the relations among them. [21]

There has been an increase in the development of new organizational forms which integrate the activities of existing complex organizations. For example, the construction of giant hydroelectric dams requires the combined efforts of several large construction companies, as does the construction of the Alaskan pipeline. Space exploration requires the integration of numerous governmental agencies and private contractors. The development of multistate port authorities, regionwide waste disposal programs, and area transportation systems all require new interorganizational arrangements. Many of the major social and environmental problems facing our society cannot be dealt with by an individual organization. They require the combined efforts of many complex organizations, often both public and private.

Over the past century we have learned a great deal about the design and management of complex organizations. This knowledge will serve as the foundation for understanding and dealing with interorganizational relationships. Many of the concepts which we will discuss in later sections of this book are important for these issues. In looking at interorganizational relationships we are expanding the boundaries of the system under consideration to include many organizations (rather than one).

Learning-Adapting Systems

Organizations operating in a dynamic environment must change their internal structure and processes to deal with these external forces. This provides a fundamental challenge to organization theory. In the past theory, emphasis has been placed upon standardization and routinization of activities through structure, rules and procedures, and programmed processes. A turbulent environment requires new cómcepts. The older theory was based on the premise of stability. Contending with the absence of stability will be a major future problem. Schon suggests this for programs dealing with national social problems.

We will forever be dealing with programs which cannot be once-and-for-all solutions to the problems they are designed to attack. We are living with a loss of the stable state. As a consequence, virtually no established institution feels adequate to the problems it now confronts. [22]

---

[21] Amitai Etzioni, *Modern Organizations*, Prentice-Hall, Inc., Englewood Cliffs, N.J., 1964, pp. 112–113.
[22] Donald A. Schon, "Implementing Programs of Social and Technological Change," *Technology Review*, February 1971, pp. 48.

In a changing environment, the organization must be a learning-adapting system which considers change as the natural state rather than as a temporary aberration. [23]

New Means of Conflict Resolution

One of the consequences of environmental turbulence and the increase in number and types of organizations is more interorganizational conflict. Increasingly, social conflict is taking the form of one organization against another, corporation versus labor union, business versus organized consumer groups, environmentalist groups versus public utilities, and "establishment" versus "anti-establishment" groups.

Organization and management theory has dealt with conflicts that occur within the organization. Concepts such as bargaining, influencing, and use of authority help the organization resolve internal conflict. However, we have not developed effective means for interorganizational conflict resolution within society.

> To achieve these goals we must manage conflict so that parochial views are expanded to a higher and more balanced plane. It is in the interest of business and other institutions, as well as society generally, that we develop new "societal bargaining tables" that can turn conflicting views of these new crises into a truly integrated awareness of the wider implications of debated issues. [24.]

We need new social mechanisms which provide the means for reduction and resolution of conflict between organizations. The current system of competition and legal means of conflict resolution appear to be inflexible and inadequate. We need to design new means for collaboration. Many of the concepts which organizations utilize to confront and deal with internal conflict may be appropriate for dealing with interorganizational conflict. Approaches such as team building, program management, participative management, legitimized bargaining, and integrated planning may provide the foundation for handling interorganizational conflicts.

In the following section we will try to bring some of the foregoing discussion of the impact of environmental forces on organizations into sharper focus by considering more specifically the relationships between business and society.

SOCIETY'S VIEW OF BUSINESS

The esteem in which society has held commercial activities has undergone significant fluctuations. In the medieval period commercial activities were viewed as a necessary evil. This view was gradually transformed, so that businessmen were held in high

---

[23] Mervyn L. Cadwallader, "The Cybernetic Analysis of Change in Complex Social Organizations," in Buckley, op. cit., p. 438.
[24] Hazel Henderson, "Toward Managing Social Conflict," *Harvard Business Review,* May–June 1971, p. 83.

regard, particularly during the second half of the nineteenth century. During the twentieth century there have been many fluctuations and variations. The regard for business reached a zenith during the 1920s but declined to a very low ebb during the Depression of the 1930s.

Public opinion surveys taken during the mid-1960s suggested a high degree of public acceptance. [25] People regarded business favorably for its accomplishments in providing goods and services, for building up the economy, for providing jobs and good wages. However, there were indications of some misgivings. People were satisfied with the economic output and functioning of the business system but there was a growing concern about the social consequences of business activities.

Recent public opinion surveys indicate more societal disenchantment with the performance of business:

> Since the mid-1960s, Americans have been turning sour on America—on its dreams, its promises, its leaders. Every major poll of public opinion has shown that. Now, in increasing numbers, Americans are focusing their new, European-style cynicism on the profits, prices, and policies of the country's largest corporations and on the workings of the entire economy. [26]

This skepticism is not directed exclusively at business organizations. There is evidence of a loss of public confidence in the performance of most institutions: business, government, education, courts, labor unions, religion, and the scientific community. Although we cannot begin to assess all the reasons for this growing suspicion of "the establishment" or "the system," the previous discussions suggest some of the possible roots of the problem. During periods of increasing environmental turbulence, it is very difficult for established organizations to respond and adapt. Organizations, by their very nature, routinize and standardize their operations and screen environmental inputs in order to operate effectively. In a sense, they are "conservative" and resistors of change. This also represents a source of strength because they provide stability.

Organizations have great difficulty in responding to all of the demands posed by society, many of which are not well articulated and are often in conflict with each other. This is occurring not only for private corporations, but for public agencies as well. For example, in our community there are many contradictory pressures upon the municipally owned Seattle City Light. Customers demand more and improved electrical service. At the same time, ecology groups are strongly resisting the construction of new hydroelectric facilities which may have a deleterious effect upon the natural environment. The apparently simple answer of moving to fuel-fired generation of power or

---

[25] See, for example, "What Americans Really Think of Business," *Newsweek*, May 2, 1966, pp. 84–90. This nationwide survey was conducted by Louis Harris and Associates.
[26] "America's Growing Antibusiness Mood," *Business Week*, June 17, 1972, p. 100.

atomic power raises a number of other issues. These means of power generation also may create major environmental pollution. Electric utilities, both public and private, throughout the United States are facing confrontation with these divergent and conflicting forces within the community.

Frequently, social demands outrun the ability of organizations to respond. In many cases we view social progress as too slow, not because improvements are not being made, but because aspirations outrun our ability to perform.

> At any given moment the public must have in mind some criteria, however imprecise, of what constitutes a satisfactory performance by business. The public keeps raising its standards—as, in an achieving society, it should. Trouble develops because the public is not aware of how rapidly it raises its standards. Because it believes its standards are unchanging, it tends to perceive business performance as moving backward. [27]

Society's view of what is adequate performance for the business sector appears to be undergoing significant changes in recent years. In a Statement on National Policy, the Committee for Economic Development suggested these changes:

> Business functions by public consent, and its basic purpose is to serve constructively the needs of society—to the satisfaction of society.
>
> Historically, business has discharged this obligation mainly by supplying the needs and wants of people for goods and services, by providing jobs and purchasing power, and by producing most of the wealth of the nation. This has been what American society required of business, and business on the whole has done its job remarkably well. . . .
>
> Notwithstanding these accomplishments, the expectations of American society have now begun to rise at a faster pace than the nation's economic and social performance. . . .
>
> There is now a pervasive feeling in the country that the social order somehow has gotten out of balance, and that greater affluence amid a deteriorating environment and community life does not make much sense.
>
> The discontinuity between what we have accomplished as producers and consumers and what we want in the way of a good society has engendered strong social pressures to close the gap—to improve the way the overall American system is working so that a better quality of life can be achieved for the entire citizenry within a well-functioning community. [28]

---

[27] Max Ways, "Business Needs to Do a Better Job of Explaining Itself," *Fortune,* September 1972, pp. 86.
[28] *Social Responsibilities of Business Corporations,* A Statement by the Research and Policy Committee, Committee for Economic Development, New York, June 1971, pp. 11-13.

Society appears to be changing the "rules of the game" for business organizations. No longer will effectiveness be measured exclusively in terms of economic performance. For example, there is a growing interest in the development of national social indicators and a program of social system accounting. [29] Development of such a system of social accounts will help in evaluating the performance of agencies and organizations in the accomplishment of goals. Increasingly, society is demanding that business organizations be responsive to and help alleviate many of the broader social problems, such as poverty, urban blight, and environmental deterioration. These questions raise some major issues concerning the social responsibilities of business and how managers should respond.

SOCIAL RESPONSIBILITIES OF BUSINESS

The modern business corporation has become a major source of power and influence on the American scene. Over the past 100 years the corporation has become not only our most important economic institution but also a major force for social change. "The great corporation is the dominant non-governmental institution of modern American life. The university, the labor union, the church, the charitable foundation, the professional association—other potential institutional centers—are all, in comparison, both peripheral and derivative." [30]

Although the business sector is often viewed as politically conservative, in many ways it is one of the more radical forces in society. The corporation has become the predominant device for the transformation of science and technology into economically useful goods and services. In performing this economic role the corporation has created vast social changes. [31]

It would be misleading to suggest that business' view concerning its social role has undergone changes only in recent years. However, there does appear to be an accelerated trend to consider social responsibilities in an ever broadening context. [32]

A report on social responsibilities of business by the Committee for Economic Development suggests the following expectations of society regarding business.

The fact is that the public wants business to contribute a good deal more to achieving the goals of a good society. Its expectations of business have

---

[29] Raymond A. Bauer, *Social Indicators,* the M.I.T. Press, Cambridge, Mass., 1966; U.S. Department of Health, Education, and Welfare, *Toward a Social Report,* Government Printing Office, Washington, D.C., 1969; and Michael Springer, "Social Indicators, Reports, and Accounts: Toward the Management of Society," *The Annals of the American Academy of Political and Social Science,* March 1970, pp. 1-13.

[30] Abram Chayes, "The Modern Corporation and the Rule of Law," in Edward S. Mason (ed.), *The Corporation in Modern Society,* Harvard University Press, Cambridge, Mass., 1959, p. 27.

[31] Alvar O. Elbing, Jr., and Carol J. Elbing, *The Value Issue of Business,* McGraw-Hill Book Company, New York, 1967, pp. 77-80.

[32] Morrell Heald, *The Social Responsibilities of Business: Company and Community, 1900-1960,* The Press of Case Western Reserve University, Cleveland, 1970.

broadened into what may be described as three concentric circles of responsibility.

The *inner circle* includes the clear-cut basic responsibilities for the efficient execution of the economic function—products, jobs, and economic growth.

The *intermediate circle* encompasses responsibility to exercise this economic function with a sensitive awareness of changing social values and priorities: for example, with respect to environmental conservation; hiring and relations with employees; and more rigorous expectations of customers for information, fair treatment, and protection from injury.

The *outer circle* outlines newly emerging and still amorphous responsibilities that business should assume to become more broadly involved in actively improving the social environment. Society is beginning to turn to corporations for help with major social problems such as poverty and urban blight. [33]

The public at large and many businessmen, particularly in larger corporations, are prepared to accept the social responsibilities indicated in the first two circles. However, when it comes to business responsibilities for solving broader social problems, the issues become very blurred. Even the largest corporation can deal with only a limited range of activities and cannot respond to all social needs. Which broad social problems does it assume responsibility for? It must be selective, but what are the criteria for decision making?

Although there are no easy solutions to this question of the extent of business responsibility, we can identify some broad guidelines. Where the corporation is clearly involved in the creation of social problems, such as air and water pollution, it should participate with other agencies in finding ways to ameliorate these harmful effects. On the other hand, some adverse consequences of economic activities are beyond the control of individual corporations. For example, product breakthroughs may make individual firms or entire industries obsolete. The social consequences of the resulting unemployment may be devastating to an entire community. Yet, the company involved may be unable to cope with the situation.

Business is directly, but not exclusively, involved in social problems such as urban renewal, civil rights movements, and environmental improvement. These massive and complex domestic tasks require cooperative efforts on the part of business and government. Increasingly, business has been joining with other agencies—particularly federal, state, and local governmental units—in attempting to meet these problems. While we might not expect business managers to take the total responsibility upon themselves to deal with these broader social problems, they should not close their eyes to the need for social change and should not resist programs which are directed toward social

---

[33] Committee for Economic Development, op. cit., p. 15.

improvement. Active cooperation with governmental agencies in dealing with social issues is one of the emerging responsibilities of business.

The scope of business' social responsibilities is contingent upon the size and power of the corporation. For the small business, there may be only the expectation of operating legally and fairly and being a good citizen in the local community. For the large corporations, with their massive size and power, society has much greater expectations.

> The great growth of corporations in size, market power, and impact on society has naturally brought with it a commensurate growth in responsibilities; in a democratic society, power sooner or later begets equivalent accountability. [34]

There have been many recent pressures for businesses, particularly large corporations, to develop more precise means of measuring their "social accountability." A number of large corporations have initiated a *corporate social audit.* They "are looking into ways of measuring their performance in activities that affect the society around them or at least assess the true costs of such programs." [35] The social audit would be directed toward spelling out more precisely those areas where the corporation contributes to social betterment which do not normally appear in traditional financial statements. What has the company done about pollution control? Consumer protection? Community development? It should be emphasized that the concept and practical application of the corporate social audit are still in their infancy. There are many difficulties and controversies involved. "If normal financial accounting causes debate, as it does today, the corporate social audit is sure to cause even more." [36] So far the primary emphasis has been on measuring the actual costs to the corporation of dealing with social issues. Little has been done to measure benefits. However, in spite of the difficulties in application, the concept of the corporate social audit is important. It is a first step in making the business organization more directly accountable for its performance in social endeavors.

Over the past three decades there has been evidence of the business community's willingness to recognize the social effects of the changes which it has created and to participate in finding some means for ameliorating the adverse consequences. Furthermore, it has shown a better understanding of the role of various levels of government in dealing with social problems.

---

[34] Ibid., p. 21.
[35] "The First Attempts at a Corporate 'Social Audit,'" *Business Week*, Sept. 23, 1972, p. 88. For a more comprehensive discussion, see Raymond A. Bauer and Dan H. Fenn, Jr., *The Corporate Social Audit*, The Russell Sage Foundation, New York, 1972.
[36] Ibid., pp. 88.

ENVIRONMENTAL IMPROVEMENT

There is a deep and growing concern today over the deterioration of the natural environment. Water and air pollution, accumulation of solid wastes, and numerous cases of poisoning of humans, other animals, and plant life are clearly evident. Organizations, particularly business corporations, have a high stake in these environmental issues.

> American business, since it organizes and channels a high proportion of the total action of this society, has been and still is deeply implicated in depredations against the environment. Any way out of the present mess will have to rely heavily upon business for resources, for innovations, and for leadership. The political and social ground rules within which business is conducted will have to be drastically amended. Important corrections will have to be made in the terms of economic calculations that now skew business decisions in destructive directions. In short, business, along with all other major functions of society, will have to change if Americans are to achieve a better environment. [37]

Why is there a growing concern over environmental issues? The first answer is obvious—the evidence of pollution is overwhelming. But there has also been a gradual change in attitudes and views concerning the ecosystem. Traditionally, we viewed nature as available for man's exploitation; resources were to be used for his betterment. Science and technology accelerated this process. Resources—trees, animals, minerals, agricultural land, water, and air—were plentiful and considered "expendable." Greater realization of the important balance between man and nature required an overall systems view.

"It is quite clear that life on this planet depends on a delicate ecological balance among many forms of life at all levels of complexity. Each organism contributes to and takes from its surroundings in such a way that an overall equilibrium is maintained. Upset this equilibrium at any point and monumental consequences ensue. Each organism, and each group of diverse organisms, must somehow achieve an environment that all find at least reasonably congenial if it is to survive. Only today, and slowly, is man coming to recognize that this great imperative of nature applies as much to him as to the creatures from whose study he has gained this knowledge. We can no longer blindly change the world about us, ignoring the consequences of change, without threatening our own survival as a species." [38]

---

[37] Max Ways, "How to Think about the Environment," *Fortune*, February 1970, p. 99.
[38] Harold M. Proshansky, William H. Ittelson, and Leanne G. Rivlin (eds.), *Environmental Psychology: Man and His Physical Setting*, Holt, Rinehart and Winston, Inc., New York, 1970, pp. 1 and 2.

Many traditional economic and social views prevent us from taking a systems view of the physical and social environment. Individuals and organizations are granted substantial autonomy to utilize natural resources to maximize their own satisfactions. Technology also deals with specialized problems and is generally applied from a very narrow perspective. "This same fault lies behind every ecological failure of modern technology: attention to a single facet of what in nature is a complex whole." [39] We have established organizations and developed concepts which tend to deal with the environment in a fragmented, piecemeal way rather than as a unitary whole. "Here we come to the root cause of our abuse of the environment: *in modern society the principle of fragmentation, outrunning the principle of unity, is producing a higher and higher degree of disorder and disutility.*" [40]

The root cause of environmental depredation is not to be found in the "bad" behavior of any one group—businesses, government, or consumers. We noted with interest that students were borrowing the family car to *drive to* the Bay Bridge in San Francisco for a sit-in to stop traffic and call attention to pollution from automobiles. We are all polluters, and the higher the standard of living we develop, the more adverse consequences to the ecological system. This obviously raises major questions about economic, materialistic, and social progress, as well as other issues. [41]

In a private enterprise system one of the major problems is dealing with the side effects of advancing technology and the operations of the individual organization. In performing its transformation functions, the business organization must pay the costs of inputs into its transformation processes. It receives payments from customers for goods and services produced. However, there may be other outputs of the organization—such as polluted air or water. These social costs have to be paid for by someone. [42]

Before getting carried away with the implications that the private enterprise system is the root cause of environmental deterioration, we should look at the evidence. Every industrialized society is facing problems of environmental deterioration, regardless of its political or economic-political system. The United States, Russia, Sweden, and Japan—all with different economic and political systems—are facing similar environmental problems. Radioactive fallout from atomic tests are just as much a pollutant from communist China as from the capitalistic United States. Thus, it is not just a matter of the particular political or economic system but, more fundamentally, man's whole relationship with his environment. There is growing evidence that man's traditional demands for greater industrialization, a higher standard of living, and more resource utilization have a disastrous effect upon the environment, regardless which political system he is under.

---

[39] Barry Commoner, *The Closing Circle,* Alfred A. Knopf, Inc., New York, 1971, pp. 182–183.
[40] Max Ways, "How to Think about the Environment," op. cit., pp. 159–160.
[41] Allen U. Kneese, "Economic Responsibility for the By-products of Production," *The Annals of the American Academy of Political and Social Science,* May 1970, pp. 56–62.
[42] John C. Narver, "Rational Management Response to External Effects," *Academy of Management Journal,* March 1971, pp. 99–115.

Meeting environmental issues will require many reevaluations of our concepts and priorities. We already see these changes emerging. It is likely that many of the social costs will be cranked back into the internal costing and pricing system for the firm. This is happening when automobile users have to bear a greater proportion of costs of pollution control. It is estimated that meeting the federal emission control standards will add approximately $300 to the cost of each 1976 automobile. Producers of paper will incur higher costs for pollution control which ultimately must be passed on to the consumers of paper products. There are obviously many legal, political, and administrative problems in allocating these costs of maintaining the environment. For example, it may be possible for a pulp and paper producer to locate in a region which has lower pollution control requirements, thus gaining a cost advantage over other producers. Or, we may even "export" polluting industries to other countries which will bear the consequences. It is obvious that new ground rules, concepts, and organizational arrangements will be necessary in order to safeguard the environment. [43]

Just as the growth of large-scale organizations required the development of administrative and organizational skills necessary to deal with the integration of these complexities, so we see the need for the social role of an "environmental administrator" who will integrate the activities of various organizations and individuals with an emphasis upon environmental protection and improvement.

> U.S. society is going to need tens of thousands of "integrators," men who can handle environmental material from several natural sciences in combination with material from several of the social sciences. These men will utilize very high technologies, such as computers and space satellites, to diagnose and cure the side effects of other technologies. Tomorrow's integrators, moreover, must be able to deal with broad questions of human value, purpose, and law that lie beyond (and between) the sciences. The universities that produced the specialists who taught us how to take the world apart will now have to train the men who will take the lead in putting it together again. [44]

A number of spokesmen see the growing concern over environmental issues not only as a challenge to business, but also as an opportunity.

> Environmental improvement *can* become a dynamic, profitable series of markets for industry—markets that will pay for themselves in the end and represent important additions to GNP. Such a breakthrough will not happen automatically, it demands a high level of government-business understanding and leadership. [45]

---

[43] Lynton K. Caldwell, "Authority and Responsibility for Environmental Administration," *The Annals of the American Academy of Political and Social Science,* May 1970, pp. 107-115.
[44] Max Ways, "How to Think about the Environment," op. cit., p. 166.
[45] James Brian Quinn, "Next Big Industry: Environmental Improvement," *Harvard Business Review,* September-October 1971, p. 120.

New ideologies, administrative arrangements, and management skills will be necessary to utilize existing organizational resources, both public and private, to deal with environmental problems. We have had some limited experience in massive programs, such as the Manned Space Flight Program and metropolitan transportation systems (e.g., the Bay Area Rapid Transit System [BART] in the San Francisco area), which provide beginning concepts. These programs will expand in the future.

While these challenges seem monumental, we should not be too pessimistic. Our growing sophistication in designing and managing organizations to meet our needs provides the basic foundation of values, knowledge, and skills to cope with these problems creatively. [46]

SUMMARY

There is a need for more complete understanding of the interrelationships between organizations and their environments. Every organization is dependent upon its broader suprasystem for inputs of resources and for acceptance of its outputs. It is therefore essential in applying the systems approach to the study of organizations and their management to start with the environmental suprasystem rather than with any internal subsystem.

The open-system view suggests that organizations are separated from their environment by a permeable boundary which filters inputs and outputs. Boundaries provide a degree of autonomy and independence for organizations from intrusion of external influences. Organizations utilize boundary-spanning components such as sales and purchasing departments to deal with specific sets of environmental inputs or outputs. These boundary-spanning positions are often stressful and subject to conflicting pressures.

It is useful to think of the environment in two ways: (1) the societal *(general)* environment, which affects all organizations in a given society, and (2) the specific *(task)* environment, which affects the individual organization more directly. In our society the setting has been favorable to growth in number and diversity of organizations. The environment is becoming more dynamic and uncertain, thus creating many problems for organizations. An organization operating in a dynamic situation must become a learning-adapting system which considers change as a natural state.

Society's view of business has undergone significant modifications. In recent years the public image of business has become tarnished. People are satisfied with the economic performance of the business system, but there is a concern over the social consequences of economic activities. This skepticism is not directed exclusively at business organizations; there is evidence of a loss of public confidence in the performance of most institutions—the "establishment" in general. One of the root causes of

---

[46] Leonard R. Sayles and Margaret K. Chandler, *Managing Large Systems: Organizations for the Future*, Harper & Row, Publishers, Incorporated, New York, 1971.

this disenchantment is the acceleration of societal change and the difficulties of timely organizational adjustments.

The question of the social responsibilities of business is a matter of growing concern. Traditionally, the role of business was limited to efficient production of goods and services. Increasingly, this role has expanded to include broader social consequences of business activities.

One of the most important issues facing our society is the deterioration of the natural environment. Traditional economic and technological views caused us to deal with the environment in a fragmented, piecemeal way rather than as a unitary whole. No one is specifically to blame—we are all contributors to environmental depredation. Meeting environmental issues will require reevaluations of our concepts and priorities. Over the past decade we have witnessed the emergence of many new approaches to dealing with environmental issues. New organizational arrangements and managerial skills will be important in dealing with these problems.

QUESTIONS AND PROBLEMS

1 What is meant by organizational boundaries? Define the boundaries for a specific organization. How permeable are these boundaries?
2 What is meant by boundary-spanning component? Why are these roles stressful?
3 Select a specific organization and list those forces in the *general* and *task* environments which affect it.
4 Do you agree that our general environmental characteristics have been conducive to the development of new organizational forms? Speculate on the possible types of organizations that will emerge in the future.
5 Investigate a specific organization and describe it in terms of the model presented in Figure 6.3.
6 Why are there ambivalent feelings toward business? What are your own attitudes about business?
7 Do you see any evidence of businessmen accepting greater social responsibilities? Document your answer with examples.
8 Why is it necessary to adopt a total system view when dealing with environmental issues? Briefly describe examples of where a subsystem approach has led to environmental depredation.
9 Who should deal with environmental issues? What is the role of the business community?

ORGANIZATIONAL GOALS

Formal organizations are contrived social systems designed to accomplish specific purposes. The basic values which underlie goal setting and decision making are a fundamental part of the organizational system. The organization performs some function for society in order to receive resource inputs. And it satisfies certain needs of internal participants in order to maintain their continuing support. The organization also has system goals which it strives to achieve. Therefore, goals should be considered from three perspectives—social goals imposed on the organization, system goals, and participant goals. The discussion in this chapter will be structured around the following topics:

> The Issue of Values
> What Are Goals?
> Environmental Determinants of Organizational Goals
> Organizational System Goals
> Individual Participant Goals
> The Role of Management in Goal Setting and Implementation
> Measuring Organizational Performance

THE ISSUE OF VALUES

We have indicated that goals and values are one of the integral subsystems of every organization. Values are normative views held by individual human beings (consciously or subconsciously) of what is good and desirable. They provide standards by which people are influenced in their choice of actions. Social values reflect a system of shared beliefs which serve as norms for human conduct.

> In the course of social interaction common notions arise as to how people should act and interact and what objectives are worthy of attainment. First, common values crystalize, values that govern the goals for which men strive— their ideals and their ideas of what is desirable—such as our belief in democracy or the importance financial success assumes in our thinking. Second, social norms develop—that is, common expectations concerning how people ought to behave—and social sanctions are used to discourage violations of these norms. . . .
>
> If values define the ends of human conduct, norms distinguish behavior that is a legitimate means for achieving these ends from behavior that is illegitimate. [1]

In our society we place a high value on "winning" in competitive sports but we also have social norms which prescribe how a "winner" or "loser" should behave. We get upset when one of our sports heroes (or *our* opponent) is an "arrogant winner" or a "poor loser."

Organizations appear to hold certain values, but defining them precisely and showing how they influence decision making is difficult. However, there are several broad generalizations. Organizations depend on a minimum level of shared values among internal participants and the external society for their very existence. Deeply ingrained cultural values provide a measure of cohesiveness. Values such as "individual human dignity," "individual property rights," "everyone should work for a living," and "acceptance of legitimate authority" provide a foundation without which organizations could not exist. Every human participant brings a certain "set of values" to the organization. Value inputs also come from a wide variety of external sources—customers, competitors, suppliers, and other elements of the organization's task environment. Therefore, in dealing with values issues we should consider at least five levels:

> *Individual values.* Those values which the individual holds which affect his actions.
>
> *Group values.* Those values which small, informal and formal groups hold which affect the behavior of individuals and also the actions of the organization.
>
> *Organizational values.* Those values which are held by the organization which represent a composite of individual, group, total organizational, and cultural inputs.

---

[1] Copyright © 1962 by Chandler Publishing Company. Reprinted from *Formal Organizations: A Comparative Approach* by Peter M. Blau and W. Richard Scott by permission of Chandler Publishing Company, an Intext publisher.

Values of constituents of the task environment. Values which are held by those in direct contact with the organization—customers, suppliers, competitors, governmental agencies, etc.

Cultural values. Values of the total society.

Depending on specific issues, we might want to consider values from one, several, or all these perspectives. In discussing the goals and values subsystem we are most concerned with those values which directly affect the internal operations and actions of the organization. But in an open system complete closure is not possible and interactions with the environment are inevitable. This is particularly true with value issues.

Because value issues affect so many levels—the culture, task environment, organization, group, and individual—we will not try to cover them directly in this chapter, but will deal with them in the context of discussions of the environmental suprasystem and organizational subsystems. In Chapters 2 and 6 we have already dealt extensively with the evolution of management values as well as cultural values. In later chapters we will consider organizational, group, and individual values and how they affect decision making and behavior. We will try to consider value issues "where they count" rather than in the abstract. The remainder of this chapter will focus on organizational goals.

WHAT ARE GOALS?

Simply stated, goals represent the desired future conditions which the organization strives to achieve. In this sense, goals include missions, purposes, objectives, targets, quotas, and deadlines. However, the concept of a "goal" has acquired a variety of meanings depending upon the perspective of the writer. It is sometimes used to legitimize and justify the role of the organization in society (the goal of General Motors is to make automobiles for people to use), or to provide a motive for the organization's activity (General Motors' goal is to make a profit). A goal may also be a specific accomplishment, such as manufacturing 15,000 automobiles during a given time period. In another sense goals may be considered as the set of constraints which the organization must satisfy, i.e., profit for the stockholders, meeting government demands for "safe" automobiles, pacifying the environmentalists, and providing customer satisfaction. [2]

One of the major problems in the analysis of organizational goals is the distinction between official goals and actual operational goals. Official goals are often stated in broad, ambiguous terms to justify the activities of the organization. For example, the official goals of a mental institution may be to treat mental illness. However, the operational goals are those actually pursued. The mental hospital may provide little in the way of treatment and be geared to custodial care of patients.

---

[2] Herbert A. Simon, "On the Concept of Organizational Goal," *Administrative Science Quarterly*, June 1964, pp. 1-22.

> The type of goals most relevant to understanding organizational behavior are not the official goals, but those that are embedded in major operating policies and the daily decisions of the personnel. . . . These goals will be shaped by the particular problems or tasks an organization must emphasize, since these tasks determine the characteristics of those who will dominate the organization. [3]

The goals of an organization have an important influence on its interactions with the environmental suprasystem and on the other subsystems. The efforts to achieve goals affect the ability of the organization to receive resource inputs from the broader society and thus legitimize its existence. Goals focus the attention of participants upon actions which are organizationally relevant. They provide the standards for measurement of success. They help determine the technologies required and also set the basis for specialization of effort, authority patterns, communication and decision networks, and other structural relationships. The nature of the goals affects the basic character of the organization. Perrow says:

> They reflect more readily the uniqueness of organizations and the role of specific influences within the more general technological and structural categories. For goals are the product of a variety of influences, some of them enduring and some fairly transient. To enumerate some of these influences: the personality of top executives, the history of the organization, its community environment, the norms and values of the other organizations with which it deals (e.g., the "mentality of the steel industry"), the technology and structure of the organization, and ultimately the cultural setting. [4]

Management is directly involved with organizational goals. Chief executives generally establish the broad institutional goals which help relate the organization to its environment. Management then translates these broad goals into operational objectives and provides means of control to measure the extent of accomplishment. It must continually deal with goal conflicts and find a means of satisfying the interests of many internal and external individuals and groups.

Do Organizations Have Goals?

We have defined organizations as goal-seeking systems. This personalization of the organization—attributing individual human qualities to a social system—is reflected in much of the thinking about organizational goals. Perhaps the origins of this view stem

---

[3] Charles Perrow, "The Analysis of Goals in Complex Organizations," *American Sociological Review,* December 1961, p. 854.
[4] From *Organizational Analysis: A Sociological View* by Charles Perrow. Copyright 1970 by Wadsworth Publishing Company, Inc. Reprinted by permission of the publisher, Brooks/Cole Publishing Company, Monterey, California.

from classical economic theory of the firm, which considered the organization as a single entrepreneur—the goals of the firm and those of the entrepreneur are identical. Similarly in public agencies, the classical approach assumed that goals were determined by legislative action and that the primary function of the agency was action planning and implementation. However, in reality there are many organization participants—stockholders, boards of directors, executives, and other employees—whose individual goals affect the activities of the organization. The goal structure of organizations is much more complex than that postulated by traditional economic and administrative theory. But we are left with a dilemma. If we do not accept the entrepreneurial goal as the organization goal, what is the organization goal? Cyert and March set forth this problem as follows:

1 People (i.e., individuals) have goals; collectivities of people do not.
2 To define a theory of organizational decision making, we seem to need something analogous—at the organization level—to individual goals at the individual level. [5]

They also suggest a solution to this problem by conceptualizing the organization as a coalition of many participants.

> In a business organization the coalition members include managers, workers, stockholders, suppliers, customers, lawyers, tax collectors, regulatory agencies, etc. In the governmental organization the members include administrators, workers, appointive officials, elective officials, legislators, judges, clientele, interest group leaders, etc. In the voluntary charitable organization there are paid functionaries, volunteers, donors, donees, etc. [6]

These organizational members have different and frequently conflicting goals. The actual goals of the organization result from a continuous bargaining-learning process. Therefore, organizations do have multiple goals. These goals are frequently not officially stated and are often in conflict. There may be inconsistencies and ambiguities. The goal set of the organization is continually changing as a result of this learning-adapting process.

We need to look more closely at the forces influencing organizational goal setting. In order to do so we will consider goals from three primary perspectives: (1) the environmental level—the constraints imposed on the organization by society; (2) the

---

[5] Richard M. Cyert and James G. March, *A Behavioral Theory of the Firm*, Prentice-Hall, Inc., Englewood Cliffs, N.J., 1963, p. 26.
[6] Ibid., p. 27.

organizational level—the goals of the organization as a system; and (3) the individual level—the goals of organizational participants. Typically there are goal conflicts among these three levels. However, there must also be a minimum degree of goal compatibility if the organization is to survive.

ENVIRONMENTAL DETERMINANTS OF ORGANIZATIONAL GOALS

The general and the task environments both have an important impact upon organizational goals. As indicated in Chapter 6, the organization can survive only by meeting certain goals imposed by the society which legitimizes its activities. It is an instrument used in the accomplishment of society's goals. Responding to environmental forces leads to continual modification and elaboration in the goal set of the organization. [7]

Thompson and McEwen suggest that the impact of the environment upon organizational goal setting is influenced by the nature of the interaction: (1) competition, (2) bargaining, (3) co-optation, and (4) coalition. [8]

The *competitive* relationship exists where two organizations are competing for the support of a third party. This is illustrated by business firms which compete for material resources, labor inputs, and customers. Government agencies compete for tax dollars; universities compete for students and faculty; and hospitals compete for patients.

Bargaining involves direct negotiations between organizations. Collective bargaining is a prime example where management bargains directly with the labor union. In a bargaining situation, each party must modify its own goals in response to the needs of the other party. The business may want to minimize labor costs, whereas the labor union wants to maximize the earnings of employees. To reach agreement, both often modify their goals.

Co-optation involves a more complicated process. "Co-optation has been defined as the process of absorbing new elements into the leadership or policy-determining structure of an organization as a means of averting threats to its stability or existence." [9] For example, the business organization has on its board of directors representatives of banks or other financial institutions. Doctors are frequently members of the board of trustees of hospitals. University administrators have traditionally shared authority with the faculty. Increasingly, students are being included on university committees. Representatives of environmentalist groups are appointed to governmental committees. By giving the "outsider" a position of responsibility the organization makes him more aware of its problems and hopes to create common understanding. But co-optation also has an important influence upon the goals of the organization itself. "Co-optation further

---

[7] Stanley E. Seashore and Ephraim Yuchtman, "Factorial Analysis of Organizational Performance," *Administrative Science Quarterly*, December 1967, p. 393.

[8] James D. Thompson and William J. McEwen, "Organizational Goals and Environment: Goal-Setting as an Interaction Process," *American Sociological Review*, February 1958, pp. 23-31.

[9] Ibid., p. 27.

limits the opportunity for one organization to choose its goals arbitrarily or unilaterally.'' [10]

   Coalition between organizations requires an ever further modification of the goals. ''The term coalition refers to a combination of two or more organizations for a common purpose. Coalition appears to be the ultimate or extreme form of environmental conditioning of organizational goals.'' [11] Coalition is, of course, an important aspect of the political process. Another example is where a number of cities and communities develop common transportation facilities or waste disposal systems. Coalition suggests that each organization modify its goals to accommodate those of other parties.

   Competition, bargaining, co-optation, and coalition are means whereby the organization adapts to forces in its environment. This adapting process frequently modifies the organization's own goals and also requires adjustments in the means for their accomplishment.

ORGANIZATIONAL SYSTEM GOALS

Organizational system goals pertain to the purposes and desired conditions which the organization seeks as a distinct entity. Self-perpetuation, stability of operations, a high rate of return, growth, satisfaction of participants, enhancement of position in field, technological leadership, and innovation are examples of system goals.

   It was suggested earlier that organizations have multiple goals rather than a single goal, and that this goal set is determined in response to both external and internal forces. Organizations, like other open systems, display the characteristic of equifinality—they generally have alternative means for the accomplishment of system objectives. [12] The organization has substantial discretion concerning the goals which it attempts to satisfy and also alternatives within its transformation functions as to the means for their accomplishment. However, it must operate within the constraints imposed by environmental forces and the need to maintain the contributions of internal participants.

Nature of Organizational Goals

Wide variations in activities make it difficult to delineate any goal set appropriate for all organizations. In business organizations there is a growing trend toward more explicitly defining the multiple goals necessary for effective and efficient long-term operations. Peter Drucker was among the first to emphasize the importance of ''managing by objectives.'' He suggested that the enterprise's emphasis upon short-term profits alone could lead to adverse long-run consequences. ''Objectives are needed in every area where performance and results directly and vitally affect the survival and prosperity of the business.'' [13] He advocated that the business set objectives in the following eight

---

[10] Ibid., p. 28.
[11] Ibid., p. 28.
[12] Daniel Katz and Robert L. Kahn, *The Social Psychology of Organizations*, John Wiley & Sons, Inc., New York, 1966, pp. 26–27.
[13] Peter F. Drucker, *The Practice of Management*, Harper & Brothers, Publishers, New York, 1954, p. 63.

FIGURE 7.1 MAJOR CATEGORIES OF ORGANIZATIONAL GOALS

Satisfaction of interests. Organizations exist to satisfy the interests (or needs, desires, or wants) of various people, both members and outsiders. These interests are multiple, hard to identify, and overlapping. The satisfaction (or dissatisfaction) of these interests may vary by its intensity and by the location and number of people involved. This category of purposes is close to what is often referred to as *welfare, utility, benefit,* or *payoff.*

Output of services or goods. The output of an organization is composed of those products which it makes available for use by clients. These products may consist of services (tangible or nontangible) or goods. The quality and quantity of any product may sometimes be expressed in monetary as well as physical units. From the viewpoint of the organization as a whole, the output of any unit or individual is an intermediate or partial product rather than an end product.

Efficiency or profitability. When available inputs are perceived as scarce, attention is directed toward making efficient use of inputs relative to output. Since there are many ways of calculating input and output and of relating the two, there are many varieties of input-output objectives. Some of them are referred to as "efficiency" or "productivity." "Profitability" is applicable whenever output as well as input may be expressed in monetary terms.

Investment in organizational viability. In a minimal sense viability means the survival of an organization, without which no other purposes are feasible. In a fuller sense it refers to an organization's growth. In either sense viability requires the diversion of inputs from the production of output and their investment in physical, human and organizational assets.

Mobilization of resources. In order to produce services or goods and to invest in viability, an organization must mobilize resources that may be used as inputs. Because of the difficulties of obtaining scarce resources from the environment, "mobilization logic" may differ from "use logic."

Observance of codes. Codes include both the formal and informal rules developed by the organization and its various units and the prescribed behaviors imposed upon the organization by law, morality and professional ethics. These codes may be expressed in terms of what is expected or what is prohibited. In either case, code observance purposes are usually expressed in terms of tolerated margins of deviation.

Rationality. Rationality here refers to action patterns regarded as satisfactory in terms of desirability, feasibility, and consistency. *Technical* rationality involves use of the best methods developed by science and technology. *Administrative* rationality involves the use of the best methods of governing organizations.

SOURCE: Bertram M. Gross, *Organizations and Their Managing,* The Free Press, New York, 1968, pp. 273-274.

areas: (1) market standing, (2) innovation, (3) productivity, (4) physical and financial resources, (5) profitability, (6) manager performance and development, (7) worker performance and attitude, and (8) public responsibility.

While this listing of important system goals is appropriate for most business organizations, it is not readily transferable to other organizational types. Gross provides a more generalized model suitable for all organizations. He suggests that the following goal set is appropriate for any organization.

The performance of any organization or unit thereof consists of activities to (1) satisfy the varying interests of people and groups by (2) producing outputs of services or goods, (3) making efficient use of inputs relative to outputs, (4) investing in the system, (5) acquiring resources, and (6) doing all these things in a manner that conforms with various codes of behavior and (7) varying conceptions of technical and administrative rationality. [14]

A further elaboration of this list of organizational goals is shown in Figure 7.1. This listing recognizes that every organization has multiple goals. Because of obvious difficulties in developing measures of effectiveness in meeting these broad goals, it is necessary to translate them into more specific operational goals which can be measured.

This listing also emphasizes that the organizational goal set is not the same as the goals of any one group of participants, such as the board of directors or trustees, top executives, or other employees. Rather, they are the goals of the organization as a collectivity of all of these and other groups which define the primary characteristics and activities of the organization as a system.

Greater emphasis upon the delineation of system goals can be useful for the organization. They provide a sense of direction and purpose which are essential to long-run effectiveness. They help the organization identify the various interest groups and how they place constraints on and contribute to organizational activities. They provide the basis for the entire planning process, both strategic and operational. They can help in motivating participants toward goal accomplishment. They provide the broad standards against which the organization can measure its performance. There is increasing evidence that more explicit attention to the establishment of goals does lead to more effective performance and realization of goals. This is true for individuals as well as for organizations.

The Process of Goal Setting

While the above discussion suggests the nature of organizational goals, it does not provide much insight into the goal-setting process. It was suggested earlier that organizations are learning, adapting systems which have multiple goals. This view is in contrast to that of the organization as a mechanistic, single-goal-maximizing system. Cyert and March provide a comprehensive view of the goal-setting process. [15] They view goal setting primarily as a political process. Goals are formulated as a result of bargaining among the various interest groups. Thus, stockholders require profits, employees want wages and favorable working conditions, managers desire power and prestige, and customers demand quality products. The membership of participating groups and their power change over time; therefore, the goals of the organization are

[14] Bertram M. Gross, "What Are Your Organization's Objectives?" *Human Relations,* August 1965, p. 198.
[15] Richard M. Cyert and James G. March, op. cit. Their book is a comprehensive extension and elaboration based on a number of writings in the field such as Chester I. Barnard, *The Functions of the Executive,* Harvard University Press, Cambridge, Mass., 1938; Herbert A. Simon, *Administrative Behavior* (2d ed.), The Macmillan Company, New York, 1959; and James G. March and Herbert A. Simon, *Organizations,* John Wiley & Sons, Inc., New York, 1958. For an extension of these views see E. Eugene Carter, "The Behavioral Theory of the Firm and Top-Level Corporate Decision," *Administrative Science Quarterly,* December 1971, pp. 413–429.

continually shifting to reflect these changes. Because the demands of the various participating groups are frequently in conflict, it is rarely possible to maximize the goals of any one individual or group. Rather, the organization seeks to "satisfy" the goals of all participants in order to maintain their participation.

Goals are also continually being modified because of changing aspiration levels. The business which has achieved its sales quota within a given year will usually adjust its aspirations upward. Lack of success will cause the organization to seek alternative means or, if this is unsuccessful, to adjust the goal downward.

Means-Ends Chain

We have suggested that overall goal statements are usually very general. They are not operational because there are no accepted criteria for determining how particular programs or activities contribute to these goals. It is necessary to translate these broad statements of purpose into operational objectives. [16]

In analyzing goals it is also necessary to decide how they are to be accomplished—the *means* of attainment. In the organization, the relationship between means and ends is hierarchical. Goals established at one level requires certain means for their accomplishment. These means then become the subgoals for the next level, and more specific operational objectives are developed as we move down the hierarchy. A fire department has the primary goal of reducing fire losses. The means for attaining this end are prevention and extinguishing fires. These means then become the goals of the next level in the organization and lead to the creation of two functions—fire prevention and fire fighting. Typical means for accomplishing these goals might be specific programs for location of water hydrants, information to the public, and geographically decentralized fire stations.

The hierarchy of goals has important implications for organization structure. Generally, the division of labor and functional specialization within the organization are based on the means-ends chain. The business organization may have sales, finance, and production departments, each of which has specific subgoals related to its functional area.

Theoretically the rational organization would have perfect integration of the means-end chain within the hierarchy and through departmental specialization. Typically, however, it is impossible to attain perfect integration. There is usually competition between the organizational units as to the means for goal accomplishment. Personal values and biases influence the integration of the means-ends chain.

> It is also as true of organizational as of individual behavior that the means-end hierarchy is seldom an integrated, completely connected chain. Often the

---

[16] For further discussion of means and ends see Herbert A. Simon, *Administrative Behavior,* op. cit., pp. 62–66; James G. March and Herbert A. Simon, op. cit., pp. 190–193; Joseph A. Litterer, *The Analysis of Organizations,* John Wiley & Sons, Inc., New York, 1965, pp. 139–142; and R. W. Morell, *Management: Ends and Means,* Chandler Publishing Company, San Francisco, 1969, pp. 5–37.

connection between organization activities and ultimate objectives is obscure, or these ultimate objectives are incompletely formulated, or there are internal conflicts and contradictions among the ultimate objectives, or among the means selected to attain them. [17]

Goals at Different Levels

Through the means-ends chain general goals are translated into increasingly specific operational goals. Complex organizations have several administrative levels or subsystems with differing goals and activities.

The *strategic* level relates the activities of the organization to its environmental system. The goals at this level are broad and provide substantial flexibility as to the means for their attainment.

The *coordinative* subsystem translates the broad goals developed at the strategic level into more specific operational goals. The primary purposes of this subsystem are related to the coordination of activities between levels and between functions.

The *operating* subsystem is involved in actual task performance. The goals at this level are usually very specific, short-term, and measurable, such as sales and production goals.

As we move from the strategic to the operating levels, goals and the means for their accomplishment become more detailed. The organization attempts to reduce the uncertainty in its basic technical operations by setting forth specific goals and means of accomplishment. The coordinative subsystem performs a vital mediating function between the strategic and operating levels.

Interdepartmental Goal Conflict

In addition to greater specification of goals through the means-ends chain on a hierarchical basis, subgoals are established for different functional units within the organization. In a correctional institution there are certain subunits whose primary responsibility is confinement of inmates while other subunits have a primary goal of rehabilitation. In a business firm the sales department's goal may be increased sales, the production department's goal may be efficient production, and the research department's goal may be the development of new products.

Differentiation by function frequently leads to interdepartmental conflict. Maximizing the performance of one functional department may lead to sacrificing the goals of another department. Thus, maximizing the confinement goal in correctional institutions may create conflicts with other subunits which are seeking the rehabilitation goal. This is another reason why the goal structure of the organization is never perfectly rational. The actual goals of the organization are a result of the power interplay and negotiation among different organizational units and individuals.

---

[17] Simon, *Administrative Behavior*, p. 64.

Goal Displacement

Ascertaining effectiveness in meeting goals can be a difficult problem. When goals can be precisely stated, as frequently is the case at the operating level, measurement is relatively simple. However, with more general goals, the measurement becomes more difficult. For example, how do we measure effectiveness in meeting the university's goals of creation and dissemination of knowledge as well as public service? By number of graduates? By analysis of their lifetime earnings? By the volume of research publications? By the won/lost record of the football team?

One of the difficulties which organizations face is overemphasis of specific goals where quantification is possible and underemphasis of more abstract, less easily measured goals.

> Most organizations under pressure to be rational are eager to measure their efficiency. Curiously, the very effort—the desire to establish how we are doing and to find ways of improving if we are not doing as well as we ought to do— often has quite undesired effects from the point of view of the organizational goals. Frequent measuring can distort the organizational efforts because, as a rule, some aspects of its output are more measurable than the others. Frequent measuring tends to encourage over-production of highly measurable items and neglect of the less measurable ones. [18]

There are other forces which distort the goal structure of organizations. One of the more important is displacement of goals. Goal displacement stems from the need for the organization to differentiate activities and from the process of downward delegation of authority and responsibility.

> In order to accomplish their goals, organizations establish a set of procedures or means. In the course of following these procedures, however, the subordinates or members to whom authority and functions have been delegated often come to regard them as ends in themselves, rather than as means toward the achievement of organizations goals. As a result of this process, the actual activities of the organization become centered around the proper functioning of organization procedures, rather than upon the achievement of the initial goals. [19]

Through this process, the official goals of the organization are neglected in favor of goals associated with building or maintaining the organization. Many writers on organizations have noted this process. Michels, in his study of socialist parties and labor

---

[18] Amitai Etzioni, *Modern Organizations,* Prentice-Hall, Inc., Englewood Cliffs, N.J., 1964, p. 9.
[19] David L. Sills, ''Preserving Organizational Goals,'' in Oscar Grusky and George A. Miller (eds.), *The Sociology of Organizations,* The Free Press, New York, 1970, p. 227.

organizations in Europe, noted the displacement of the original goal of creating a democratic society by the goals of maintenance of the organization and the position of the leaders. The original means become the actual ends of organizational activity. He refers to the "Iron Law of Oligarchy," in which the leaders achieve an oligarchical power position and seek to maintain that position in order to direct and control the activities of the organization. This led to the subversion of the organization's original democratic goals. [20]

Merton says that goal displacement occurs because the bureaucratic organization affects participants' personalities and causes them to seek the security of rigid adherence to rules and regulations for their own sake. "Adherence to the rules, originally conceived as a means, becomes transformed into an end-in-itself; there occurs the familiar process of *displacement of goals* whereby an instrumental value becomes a terminal value." [21]

This problem is apparent in many social welfare agencies. For example, strict adherence to the rule of no welfare payments when there is an employable male in the household may create adverse family and social problems and defeat the overall goals of the agency.

This problem is not easily resolved. If organizational members are bound by rigid role prescriptions as well as rules and regulations to guide their activities, and strong sanctions are used to enforce adherence, goal displacement will occur. [22] This organization might work to more adequately develop the means-ends chains so that individual activities are related to ends. Attempts to translate the intangible, abstract goals into more meaningful, desired states of affairs can be helpful. One such approach, management by objectives, will be discussed in a later section of this chapter.

INDIVIDUAL PARTICIPANT GOALS

We turn now to the third level of analysis: the goals of individual participants and their relationship to organizational goals. Organizations are established to accomplish purposes which cannot be accomplished by individual action. It would be simple to assume that organizational goals and individual participant goals are complementary. This in effect was the assumption of classical economic theory and most traditional management theories. Employees were compensated through monetary and other inducements for their participation in meeting organizational goals, thus "presumably *assuring* that employees will adhere to the organization's goals except in exceptional, i.e., theoretically pathological, cases." [23] This simple assumption of compatibility failed to recognize many bases for conflict between organizational and individual goals. First, man is much more complex than the rational-economic man assumption. He has many needs and

---

[20] Robert Michels, *Political Parties,* The Free Press, New York, 1949.
[21] Robert K. Merton, *Social Theory and Social Structure,* rev. ed., The Free Press, New York, 1957, p. 199.
[22] For a discussion of goal displacement and related issues see: Michel Crozier, *The Bureaucratic Phenomenon,* The University of Chicago Press, 1964, Chicago, pp. 175–208.
[23] Peer Soelberg, "Structure of Individual Goals: Implications for Organizations Theory," in George Fisk (ed.), *The Psychology of Management Decision,* CWK Gleerup Publishers, Lund, Sweden, 1967, p. 16.

aspirations which are not easily met in purely economic terms. Second, the organization itself has a multiple and complex goal set.

The early human relationists saw the need for greater emphasis on human satisfaction as well as technical effectiveness. "An industrial organization may be regarded as performing two major functions, that of producing a product and that of creating and distributing satisfactions among the individual members of the organization."[24] Although they saw the need for creating greater human satisfaction, it was viewed as a *means* for obtaining better organizational effectiveness rather than as an *end* in itself. Increased satisfaction would lead to more effective organizational goal accomplishment.

There is a trend toward thinking of the *satisfaction of human participants* within organizations not only as a means for organizational effectiveness but also as an *end in itself.*

> We are not merely interested in the economic success or technological efficiency aspects of a system, but also, and more importantly, in its social efficiency aspects. . . . In general, social efficiency entails personal goal attainment on the part of the members at all levels in an organization, and this includes involvement, satisfaction, participation, and other variables associated with intrinsic motives and psychological rewards.[25]

We raise an even more critical issue when we question whether or not organizational goals and human needs are compatible. Many practices which are developed to increase organizational effectiveness may create human dissatisfactions. A high degree of task specialization may lead to technical efficiency but may also create employee boredom and apathy. A rigid authority structure may seem desirable from the organization's standpoint, but the humans may resist.

However, we should not overemphasize the possible conflicts between organizational goals and human satisfaction.

> Within limits, happiness heightens efficiency in organizations and, conversely, without efficient organizations much of our happiness is unthinkable. Without well-run organizations our standard of living, our level of culture, and our democratic life could not be maintained. Thus, to a degree, *organizational rationality and human happiness go hand in hand.* But a point is reached in every organization where happiness and efficiency cease to support each other. Not all work can be well paid or gratifying, and not all regulations and orders can be made acceptable. Here we face a true dilemma.[26]

---

[24] F. J. Roethlisberger and William J. Dickson, *Management and the Worker,* Harvard University Press, Cambridge, Mass., 1939, p. 552.
[25] Basil S. Georgopoulos, "An Open-System Theory Model for Organizational Research," in Anant R. Negandhi (ed.), *Modern Organizational Theory,* The Kent State University Press, Kent, Ohio, 1973, p. 104.
[26] Etzioni, op. cit., p. 2.

We are not going to assume either that (1) organizational and individual goals are compatible, or (2) that they are incompatible. To a major extent they are both. Without a minimum degree of compatibility, organizations could not exist. But total agreement is impossible and conflicts do exist.

Reciprocation between Individual and Organization

Frequently, a strong bond develops between the individual and the organization. There is a psychological contract which helps fulfill the goals of each.

> This process of fulfilling mutual expectations and satisfying mutual needs in the relationship between a man and his work organization was conceptualized as a process of *reciprocation*. Reciprocation is the process of carrying out a psychological contract between person and company or any other institution where one works. It is a complementary process in which the individual and the organization seem to become a part of each other. The person feels that he is part of the corporation or institution and, concurrently, that he is a symbol personifying the whole organization. [27]

In modern industrial society there has been a loosening of family, small social group, and other psychological ties—causing the work organization to become increasingly important to man. "In a man's movement from one neighborhood or community to another, the work organization is his thread of continuity and may well become a psychological anchor point for him." [28] This psychological contract is even stronger in other countries. In Japan, the employee and the work organization frequently make lifelong commitments to each other.

Several recent research studies suggest the extent of this reciprocation. Morse found that managers adapted to and found personal satisfaction in organizations with very different structures, interpersonal relations, and environmental forces. The organization which was appropriately designed to meet its task requirements and the demands of its environment provided important psychological rewards for members of the organization and led to a high sense of personal competency. [29] Porter and Lawler found that managers were motivated toward organizational goals when they perceived a high probability of rewards based upon performance and when they had an appropriate perception of their organizational role. When managers perceived inducements as rewards for good performance, they performed more effectively. High performers also reported significantly greater fulfillment and satisfaction. [30]

---

[27] Harry Levinson, *The Exceptional Executive*, Harvard University Press, Cambridge, Mass., 1968, p. 39.
[28] Harry Levinson, "Reciprocation: The Relationship between Man and Organization," *Administrative Science Quarterly*, March 1965, p. 393.
[29] John J. Morse, "Organizational Characteristics and Individual Motivation," in Jay W. Lorsch and Paul R. Lawrence (eds.), *Studies in Organization Design*, Richard D. Irwin, Inc., and The Dorsey Press, Homewood, Ill., 1970, pp. 84–100.
[30] Lyman W. Porter and Edward E. Lawler, III, *Managerial Attitudes and Performance*, Richard D. Irwin, Inc., and The Dorsey Press, Homewood, Ill., 1968.

The importance of reciprocation becomes apparent when the psychological contract is broken. When the aerospace industry suffered a severe downturn, organizations discharged many long-term employees, including managers and professionals. These employees had developed a high degree of loyalty and attachment to their organizations, and the results of the layoffs were devastating (both psychologically and economically). We might hypothesize that the stronger the bonds of reciprocation, the more severe the problems of adjustment for the individual when these bonds are severed. Many managers, engineers, scientists, and other professionals had great difficulty in accepting the fact of their dismissal. The importance of reciprocation might also explain the strong and unrelenting demand by most faculty members for maintaining the tenure system.

Internalization of Goals

Internalization occurs when the individual develops a personal commitment in meeting organizational goals. It is one of the most effective means of integration because it removes conflicts between organizational goals and individual motivation.

> In this way, through his subjection to organizationally determined goals, and through the gradual absorption of these goals into his own attitudes, the participant in organization acquires an "organization personality" rather distinct from his personality as an individual. The organization assigns to him a role; it specifies the particular values, facts, and alternatives upon which his decisions in the organization are to be based. [31]

While this internalization represents the ideal match between organizational goals and individual motivations, it is rarely fully achieved. Few participants make a full commitment toward meeting organizational goals. There may be conflicts between the organizational role and other roles which the individual tries to fulfill. This conflict is apparent for many participants, particularly scientists and other professionals. Traditionally, in professions such as medicine and law, activities were carried out in a nonorganizational context in close interpersonal relationship with clients. Early literature on professionalism focused on the pattern of behavior of these independent professionals and how this differed from that of bureaucrats or "organization men." This traditional view of independence and autonomy is no longer appropriate for most modern scientists-professionals. They are organization men affiliated with businesses, hospitals, governmental agencies, large law firms, and other complex institutions. "No profession has escaped the advancing tide of bureaucratization." [32]

Numerous studies of scientists-professionals in organizations suggest the prob-

---

[31] Simon, *Administrative Behavior*, op. cit., p. 198.
[32] Howard M. Vollmer and Donald L. Mills (eds.), *Professionalization*, Prentice-Hall, Inc., Englewood Cliffs, N.J., 1966, p. 264.

lems of role conflict and motivation. [33] These participants place high value on intellectual pursuits, specialized task performance, and autonomy. They have high need for achievement and self-actualization. These values may create many conflicts. The desire for autonomy runs counter to the organization's need for integration. The individual is more likely to internalize the goals of his profession rather than the goals of the organization. At best, he is likely to make only a "conditional commitment" to organization goals. The same limited commitment may also be true of other participants, such as the unionized employee. It is most likely that the "managerial elites" are the participants who develop the highest degree of internalization of organizational goals. This process is enhanced by bonus systems, profit sharing, and stock options.

The Continuing Dilemma

Many modern behavioral scientists see a continuing conflict between organizational goals and role requirements and individual satisfaction. In a sense it is unrealistic to expect perfect compatibility and optimal satisfaction of individual and organizational goals. The individual *must* give up some of his individual autonomy and self-expression to participate (and gain the advantages of membership) in the organization. This is as true of participation in the informal group or family as it is in the formal organization. Organization thus reduces personal autonomy in some spheres, but it also enhances opportunities for satisfaction in other areas. It is a trade-off that is never optimal for either the organization or the individual. For example, it could be argued that forced participation in our social security system reduces personal autonomy and individual discretion. However, it also increases independence and autonomy for the retiree.

THE ROLE OF MANAGEMENT IN GOAL SETTING AND IMPLEMENTATION

Management has a vital role in charting the organization's course. However, it is a mistake to suggest that the goals of management and the goals of the organization are one and the same. Certainly, management is one of the major elements in the coalition, but it is not the only element. Management's power is never absolute.

Monsen's studies of owner-controlled and manager-controlled firms in the same industries suggest that there are important differences in the actual operational goals of these firms. The owner-controlled firms had significantly higher rates of return on investment and lower dividend payouts than did manager-controlled firms within the same industry. It might be suggested that the owner-controlled firm is simply more efficient than the manager-controlled firm. Or (and from our viewpoint more logically)

---

[33] For example, see William Kornhauser; *Scientists in Industry: Conflict and Accommodation*, University of California Press, Berkeley, Calif., 1962; George A. Miller, "Professionals in Bureaucracy: Alienation among Industrial Scientists and Engineers," *American Sociological Review*, October 1967, pp. 755–768; and Gloria V. Engel, "Professional Autonomy and Bureaucratic Organization," *Administrative Science Quarterly*, March 1970, pp. 12–21.

it might be argued that they are responding to different goals. Monsen suggests this difference:

> The answer that seems most convincing is that two quite different motivational incentive systems are at work, emanating from the pursuit of different goals. It would seem that our business system is not generally structured to provide the same set of motivations or goals for both owners and managers. As a result, the behavior of our largest firms differs widely depending upon what group controls them. [34]

These findings are consistent with our previous discussion. The professional manager is responding to a different set of influences (including his own motivations) from those of the owner-manager. Because of these variations in actual (rather than publicized) goals, the organizations behave differently.

Management by Objectives (MBO)

Many approaches have been utilized to integrate individual and group goals with overall organizational goals. One of the most comprehensive is "management by objectives" (MBO). MBO attempts to structure this relationship by involving all levels of management in the goal-setting process. In these programs each manager works with his subordinates to establish goals and specific action plans for their accomplishment. Odiorne describes this approach as:

> The system of management by objectives can be described as a process whereby the superior and subordinate managers of an organization jointly identify its common goals, define each individual's major areas of responsibility in terms of the results expected of him and use these measures as guides for operating the unit and assessing the contributions of each of its members. [35]

Over the past two decades many organizations have adopted management by objectives programs. [36] Most of these programs started initially as managerial performance-appraisal procedures. However, many have advanced to a much broader approach encompassing long-range planning, a system of control, and a primary basis of integrating the goals of individual participants with the goals of the organization.

---

[34] R. Joseph Monsen, "Ownership and Management," *Business Horizons,* August 1969, p. 47.
[35] George S. Odiorne, *Management by Objectives,* Pitman Publishing Corporation, New York, 1965, pp. 55-56.
[36] For a discussion of the operations of a number of these company programs see: Walter S. Wikstrom, *Managing by—and With—Objectives,* Studies in Personnel Policy, no. 212, National Industrial Conference Board, Inc., New York, 1968.

Although management by objectives sounds deceptively simple, in practice organizations adopting this approach have had to spend considerable time in modifying managerial processes in order to make it effective. Figure 7.2 indicates the various stages in the introduction of an MBO program. Stage One is primarily a short-term performance-appraisal approach initiated by the Personnel Department. Stage Two reflects a more comprehensive approach and affects the entire managerial system of the organization. Stage Three is even longer-range (three to five years) and encompasses changes in other subsystems such as the structure. For example, successful MBO programs usually require basic changes in the nature of the management information system. It is obvious that an MBO program cannot be effectively established in a short time period. It usually takes the organization a number of years of learning to develop an effective program. Many of the companies report that learning to operate a

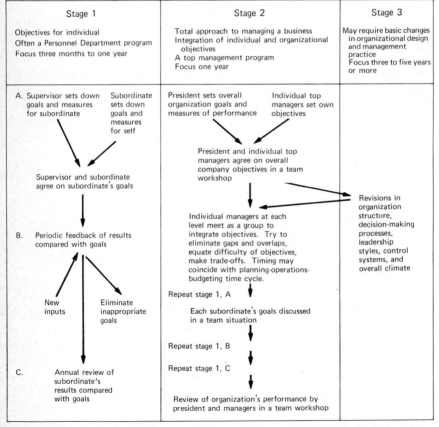

FIGURE 7.2 INTRODUCTION OF MANAGEMENT BY OBJECTIVES BY STAGES. (Source: Adapted from unpublished manuscript by Robert A. Sutermeister, Graduate School of Business Administration, University of Washington, Seattle, 1973.)

successful MBO program is a continuing process. In fact, one of the great advantages of such a program is that it does create a more effective learning-adapting system.

One of the major issues in any MBO program is whether objectives should be established from the top down or from the bottom up. There are advantages in either approach. The bottom-up approach maximizes the participation of lower-level personnel who are closer to the actual operations. However, the top-down approach has the advantage of providing clearer guidelines and parameters for lower-level participants in setting their own objectives. In most cases a compromise is best. ''Many companies have discovered that the process cannot be exclusively top-down or bottom-up if it is to be an effective way of managing the business. The communication and planning effort, they find, must go in both directions.'' [37] However, MBO programs are usually not effective when autocratically imposed from the top. Successful programs stress collaboration, cooperative effort, and team building.

Studies of specific MBO programs suggest that such programs do improve communications, increase mutual understanding, improve planning, create more positive attitudes toward the evaluation system, help in utilizing management abilities, and promote innovation. [38] However, there are also problems associated with these programs. Many organizational adjustments are necessary if it is to be successful. It requires long-term effort and is not a short-run panacea. Most programs include only managerial personnel and do not provide for other employees. It is often difficult to encompass the efforts of many staff groups within such a program. There is a tendency for managers to direct their efforts toward meeting only those objectives on which they are measured. Other, less quantifiable objectives may be short-changed. It is often difficult to set forth clearly definable objectives under conditions of rapid change or environmental turbulence. There are many difficulties in tying performance appraisal into the program. Finally, there may be problems in requiring objective accomplishment under uncertain and adverse conditions. Discussion with executives of companies which have established MBO programs indicates that they worked very well when environmental and market forces were favorable. However, during a business downturn, many managers thought they were held strictly accountable for accomplishment of objectives over which they had limited control. Many programs did not respond adequately to new environmental conditions, and, instead of being a basis for positive motivation, the programs became a source of major conflict.

In spite of these difficulties, management by objectives programs have been used successfully by a number of business organizations to integrate organizational and individual goals. The most successful programs appear to be those which emphasize a total systems approach to MBO and take into consideration its impact on all of the organization's subsystems. MBO seems to be catching on in other types of organizations. For example, within school systems similar types of programs, such as ''individual

---

[37] Ibid., p. 5.
[38] Stephen J. Carroll, Jr., and Henry L. Tosi, ''Goal Characteristics and Personality Factors in a Management-by-Objectives Program,'' *Administrative Science Quarterly*, September 1970, pp. 295–305.

growth contracts,'' have been advocated for goal setting and measuring of accomplishment of students, teachers, and administrators.

MEASURING ORGANIZATIONAL PERFORMANCE

There are many difficulties involved in measuring the performance of organizations. Organizations have a variety of goals and typically use multiple criteria in measuring performance. The business organization may evaluate its performance in terms of profits, return on investment, sales volume, market share, satisfaction of customers, well-being and development of employees, and a host of other measures. The university may measure its performance in terms of output of students, the stature of its alumni, the perceived quality of its faculty, the research output of the institution, and services provided to the community. It is impossible for the complex organization to set forth a single measure of performance for its multiple goals.

Performance measurements involve both *effectiveness* (the degree to which goals are accomplished) and *efficiency* (the use of resources in attaining goals). In most cases effectiveness and efficiency are related; however, the organization frequently needs to establish different ways of measuring them. Even if the organization is effective in accomplishing goals, it may not be efficient in the utilization of resources. Our nation was effective in reaching its goal of placing a man on the moon by 1970, but many have suggested that this required a very inefficient use of resources. Conversely, an organization could be efficient without being effective. A business might be efficient in the utilization of resources but not effective in reaching its sales goals because of a declining market, severe depression, or other forces. A college basketball coach might achieve near optimal efficiency by getting his players to perform beyond their ''capacity.'' However, if his tallest player is 5 feet 11 inches, the team may be very ineffective, as evidenced by a record of 0 wins and 25 losses.

Organizations need to evaluate performance is broad systems terms. The organization should establish measures of performance for all of its transformation processes—not just the financial and technical transactions. Performance in meeting the goals of the environmental suprasystem should be measured more accurately. It is desirable to establish measures of performance in each of the major subsystems—goal setting, effective utilization of technology, creation of an appropriate structure, meeting psychosocial needs, and developing the managerial system.

Measuring organizational performance is a vital concern of the managerial system. The managerial functions of planning and control are directly involved in establishing goals, developing plans for their accomplishment, setting up control processes, and measuring performance. These issues will be discussed more fully in Part 6.

SUMMARY

Goals and values are an integral subsystem of every organization. Values are normative views held by individual human beings of what is good and desirable. Social values reflect a system of shared beliefs which serve as norms for human conduct. The organization depends on a minimum level of shared values among internal participants and the external society for its very existence.

Goals can be considered from three primary perspectives: (1) the environmental level—the constraints imposed on the organization by society; (2) the organizational level—the goals of the organization as a system; and (3) the individual level—the goals of organizational participants. The general and the task environments both have an important impact upon organizational goals. Responding to environmental forces leads to continual modification and elaboration in the goal structure of the organization.

Organization system goals pertain to the purposes and desired conditions which the organization seeks as a distinct entity. Continuing existence, growth, profitability, and stability are examples of system goals. There is a trend toward more explicit definition of the multiple goals necessary for effective and efficient long-term operations. The means-ends chain is the mechanism whereby broad goals are translated into operational objectives. Moving from the strategic, through the coordinative, and to the operating level, goals and the means for their accomplishment become more specific, short-range, and measurable.

Goals of individual participants are frequently both compatible and in conflict with organizational goals. It is necessary to satisfy a certain level of participant needs in order to maintain their contributions. However, it is unrealistic to expect perfect compatibility and optimal satisfaction of individual and organizational goals. Some conflict is inevitable.

Management has a major role in the setting of operational goals and in providing resources for implementing action programs. Many approaches have been utilized to integrate individual and group goals with overall organizational goals. One of the most comprehensive is "management by objectives" (MBO). Research suggests that many MBO programs have been successful in better integrating individual and organizational goals; however, making the programs effective requires substantial long-term effort.

There are many difficulties involved in measuring the performance of organizations in meeting goals. Organizations have a variety of goals and typically use multiple criteria in measuring performance. It is necessary to establish measures of performance in meeting constraints of the environmental suprasystem and the goals of each of the major organizational subsystems.

QUESTIONS AND PROBLEMS

1 What are goals? Discuss the issue of whether or not organizations have goals.

2 What is meant by organization system goals? What is the distinction between "official" and operational goals? Select a specific organization and report on these differences.

3 How does the environmental suprasystem affect the goals of an organization?

4 Give examples of the interaction between an organization and its environment in terms of (a) competition, (b) bargaining, (c) co-optation, and (d) coalition.

5 What is meant by the means-ends chain? Give examples.

6 Why do organizations frequently have interdepartmental goal conflicts? Select a specific organization and report on these conflicts.

7 What is meant by goal displacement? Give examples.

8 Discuss the issue of the compatibility or conflict between individual and organizational goals. Relate this to your own goals and those of (*a*) the college or university you attend and/or (*b*) an organization in which you have worked.

9 What is meant by management by objectives (MBO)? Using your own experience, or the references and other library resources, report on a specific MBO program.

Rapid change has now left most Americans a little breathless. So complex are effects of changing technology that they have overtaken mankind as problems rather than as opportunities. If men are to utilize technology for the good life, they will have to find a substitute for time, which in the past permitted the human organism, and the community, to adjust to the pace of history.

Charles R. Walker

Technology and structure set relatively narrow limits on the boss's freedom to adopt various leadership styles—a production foreman just can't behave like a college dean.

George Strauss

A great many administrators and managers carry in their heads a pattern of the "ideal" organization. That pattern is the classic hierarchy, the family tree; one man at the top, with three below him, each of whom has three below him, and so on with fearful symmetry unto the seventh generation, by which stage there is a row of 729 junior managers and an urgent need for a very large triangular piece of paper.

Antony Jay

Structural relationships are not once and for all prescriptions but are "rules of the game" which are adaptable to changing situations and the changing desires of the participants.

Ogden H. Hall

PART 4

TECHNOLOGY AND STRUCTURE

The technologies of the organization are based on the knowledge, equipment, and other techniques which are used in task accomplishment. They affect the types of inputs into the organization and the output from the system. Every modern organization has been influenced by the rapid acceleration of technology in our society. The ways in which the organization adapts to the changing technology has a significant impact upon the other organizational subsystems.

The organization structure sets the formal framework for the ways in which tasks are accomplished. Structure is concerned with the differentiation of tasks into operating units and the pattern of established relationships among them. Organizations have both a formal (planned) and an informal structure. The formal structure is depicted by organization charts, position and job descriptions, and procedure manuals. The informal "structure" is determined by informal interactions between participants in the organization and is closely associated with the psychosocial system. It provides the integrative framework between the technological requirements and the psychosocial and managerial systems.

Chapter 8, Technology and Organization, is concerned with the impact of the technical systems on the organization—its structural, psychosocial, and managerial systems. Chapter 9, Organization Structure, considers the forces affecting formal organization, reviews traditional concepts, and investigates the elaboration of structure in complex organizations.

TECHNOLOGY AND ORGANIZATION

The organization is not simply a technical *or* a social system; it requires structuring and integrating human activities around various technologies. The technical system is determined by the task requirements of the organization and is shaped by the specialization of knowledge and skills required, the types of machinery and equipment involved, and the layout of facilities. In turn, the technical system has a major impact upon the organizational structure, human relationships, and the managerial system. Any change in the technical system affects these other organizational elements. The impact of technology on the organization—its goals, structure, psychosocial system, and managerial system—is the subject of this chapter. The following topics are discussed:

> Technology Defined
> Accelerating Technology
> Organizations: Creating and Applying Technology
> Classification of Technical Systems
> Impact of the Technical System
> Automation
> Automated Information-Decision Systems
> Man-Machine Systems Development

TECHNOLOGY DEFINED

The terms *technology* and *technological change* have many meanings ranging from specific to broad connotations. In the narrowest view, these terms are associated with *machine technology*, the mechanical means for production of goods and services and replacement of human effort. This mechanistic view emphasizes such visible manifestations of technology as the automated production line, television transmission and receiving equipment, electronic computer systems, and the vast complex system of boosters, capsules, launch pads, and monitoring equipment necessary for an Apollo flight to the moon. This emphasis upon physical artifacts as an indication of technology is associated with anthropological approaches for studying earlier or primitive societies. This view is understandable because the machine is the most obvious physical manifestation of technology. We can see it, watch it perform, and recognize our own inadequacies of comprehension of its design and capabilities. However, it is an oversimplification to associate the advancement of technology with the history of the machine. Machines are merely the physical artifacts of technology.

Technology as Knowledge

In the most general sense, technology refers to *knowledge* about the performance of certain tasks or activities. Jacques Ellul gives a broad connotation to technology or, as he calls it, technique. Technology is far more than the machine and refers to standardized means for attaining a predetermined objective or result. Thus, technology converts spontaneous and unreflective behavior into behavior that is deliberate and rationalized. "In our technological society, *technique* is the *totality of methods rationally arrived at and having absolute efficiency* (for a given stage of development) in *every* field of human activity." [1] Technology has come to dominate every field of human activity and is geared to the achievement of maximum efficiency in all human endeavors.

Walker points out that technology has both an *outer* and an *inner* aspect. "Modern technology may be perceived as an *environment* within which we live, made up of external and tangible things which we modify from time to time and which modify us. . . . Modern technology can also be viewed internally. In this sense it consists of skills of body and brain, of technical and administrative procedures, and of mental processes, both conscious and unconscious, some of them associated with value judgments which relate man's outer world to his inner one." [2]

By organizational technology we mean the technique used in the transformation of inputs into outputs. In accomplishing this transformation task, for example, the industrial concern utilizes both machine and other specialized technologies. The accountant may employ the computer in performing his task, but he also utilizes a technology based upon the knowledge of accounting procedures. Quite clearly, in this case as in many others, there is an interaction between the machine side of technology and specialized technique. When we talk about a change in the technology of the organization and its impact upon structure and human relationships, we are not confining the discussion to the impact of such mechanical devices as computers but are also considering changes in the nonmechanical technical system.

---

[1] Jacques Ellul, *The Technological Society,* trans. by John Wilkinson, © Alfred A. Knopf, Inc., New York, 1964, p. xxv.
[2] Charles R. Walker, *Modern Technology and Civilization,* McGraw-Hill Book Company, 1962, pp. 2–3.

ACCELERATING TECHNOLOGY

Science and technology have become pervasive forces in modern society. In the Western world since the beginning of the industrial revolution, technology and its parent, scientific research, have had a profound impact upon social structure and culture. The early industrial revolution was based primarily on the replacement of human energy with mechanical energy. During the twentieth century, mass-production and assembly line techniques have combined machinery and equipment into integrated operations. Automation is an extension of the process of integrating the mechanical means of production and also involves information feedback systems which replace human decision making in the control phase. Computer technology has facilitated the automation of both material and information flow.

In advanced societies, science and technology have been the handmaidens of industrialization. Together they are providing a new shape to the world. In particular, during the post-World War II period, these forces have brought about a growing discontinuity with the past. "Science and its lusty offspring Technology are more vigorous and dynamic than in any previous age or culture system. Put another way and perhaps more accurately, Science and Technology have given our age more of its unique characteristic and coloring than they have any other age. They have done so by altering nearly all the basic components which make up the life of modern man, and altering them in important ways." [3]

Certainly the changes wrought by science and technology are not limited to the United States and other industrialized countries. The developing and semi-industrialized countries of the world are gearing their national policies toward increasing industrialism and technical development. One of the manifestations of industrialism is a convergence in sociocultural systems. For example, there is an emphasis on education. A basic requirement of modern technology is a high level of literacy and specialized training. In the processes of accelerating industrialization and technological advancement, Russia has devoted substantial resources to provide the scientific and technical training necessary for this evolution. Although we may not recognize it, our processes of education show similarities to those in Russia. Both the United States and Russia have evolved systems of higher education, for example, which include a larger proportion of the college age group than other countries.

The effective utilization of technology requires the development of complex organizations which are quite similar, even in different cultures and economies and under different political ideologies. In fact, the goals of science and technology have frequently become the basis of comparison of different national societies. "So convinced have we become of the dependence of the total social, political, and economic order on technical development that national output of scientific discoveries and rate of technological advance have begun to appear as an ultimate criterion of culture, and different political and social systems are compared as facilitators of this kind of achievement." [4]

---

[3] Charles R. Walker (ed.), *Technology, Industry, and Man*, McGraw-Hill Book Company, New York, 1968, p. 9.
[4] Tom Burns and G. M. Stalker, *The Management of Innovation*, Tavistock Publications, London, 1961, p. 19.

Dangers of Technology

Many see imminent dangers to civilization due to the growing emphasis upon technology. They suggest that advancing technology has become an end in itself, and, unabated, will ultimately drive out humanistic and social considerations. Ellul is pessimistic about this development. "In fact, technique has taken substance, has become a reality in itself. It is no longer merely a means and an intermediary. It is an object in itself, an independent reality with which we must reckon." [5] He sees technology as the tyrant which will radically alter our entire sociocultural structure, negating individual autonomy and permeating all aspects and endeavors of mankind. The final result of this evolutionary process is one of total integration of man into the technical system.

> What yet remains of private life must be forced into line by invisible techniques, which are also implacable because they are derived from personal conviction. Reintegration involves man's covert spiritual activities as well as his overt actions. Amusements, friendships, art—*all* must be compelled toward the new integration, thanks to which there is to be no more social maladjustment or neurosis. Man is to be smoothed out, like a pair of pants under a steam iron. . . . With the final integration of the instinctive and the spiritual by means of these human techniques, the edifice of the technical society will be completed. [6]

We cannot, within the confines of this book, either dispute or confirm the pessimism of Ellul and others. Philosophically, however, we do not agree with the deterministic view of technology. Advancing science and technology will be primary forces for change and will most certainly contribute greatly to our "future shock." [7] Technology can be controlled by man, but not without some fundamental changes in values and goals. We agree with Mesthene, who suggests that advancing technology should not be viewed as an "unalloyed blessing for man and society" or an "unmitigated curse." Nor should it be considered as not worthy of special notice. "The heightened prominence of technology in our society faces us with the interrelated tasks of profiting from its opportunities and containing its dangers." [8]

The way in which we use technology in social organizations will be of prime importance. The technical system is one of the most important factors in the complex organization but by no means the only or overriding force. A corollary viewpoint is important. The interactions between the technical system and the psychosocial system in the organization will affect and can be a strong determinant of the relationship between technology and society.

---

[5] Ellul, op. cit., p. 63.
[6] Ibid., pp. 411 and 427.
[7] Alvin Toffler, *Future Shock*, Random House, Inc., New York, 1970.
[8] Emmanuel G. Mesthene, *Technological Change*, A Mentor Book, The New American Library, Inc., New York, 1970, p. 34.

ORGANIZATIONS: CREATING AND APPLYING TECHNOLOGY

A phenomenon of modern industrial society is the development of large-scale, complex organizations for the accomplishment of specific purposes. This relatively new development has been pervasive over the past century. Throughout most of man's history, his social institutions were primarily on an informal face-to-face basis. Up to medieval times, the feudal system provided the primary social system to which the individual belonged. The industrial revolution, with its demand for concentration of resources and greater scale, fostered larger economic and other organizational units. This condition is not restricted to Western cultures. As other countries pass through the phases of industrialization, they also find it necessary to evolve larger organizational units. It would appear that this trend toward more complex organization is basic in all human society and is moving in a massive wave through many cultures.

The development of large organizations is closely related to technological change. "Technical progress and organizational development are aspects of one and the same trend in human affairs. . . . Progress in power technology, in agriculture, in engineering, in chemicals, and the rest have proceeded—quite inevitably and necessarily—alongside developments in working organizations and in communications, and alongside the elaboration of social and political controls, financial and other economic mechanisms." [9]

It is difficult to determine which comes first—the social structure or the technology. Some would argue that developments in the social structure are a necessary prerequisite to advancing science and technology. Others suggest that developments in technology create the necessity for new social organizations. This is like the chicken and egg controversy, and we are content to consider them as codeterminant forces. It is, however, obvious that individuals and informal groups cannot accomplish certain results in small units. "Large-scale organizations have evolved to achieve goals which are beyond the capacities of the individual or the small group. They make possible the application of many and diverse skills and resources to complex systems of producing goods and services. Large-scale organizations, therefore, are particularly adapted to complicated *technologies,* that is, to those sets of man-machine activities which together produce a desired good or service." [10]

Our large-scale social organizations have become the primary creators and users of technology. They are, in effect, the social mechanism for the utilization of the developing knowledge from the sciences.

Technology in Industry

In the economic sector, large-scale organizations have become the primary mechanism for the creation and utilization of industrial technology. The term *technostructure* suggests the relationship between technology and organization structure. "The modern

---

[9] Burns and Stalker, op. cit., pp. 19–20.
[10] James D. Thompson and Frederick L. Bates, "Technology, Organization, and Administration," *Administrative Science Quarterly,* December 1957, p. 325.

large corporation is adapted to the needs of advanced technology and the large amounts of capital and comprehensive planning which this requires." [11]

Technology has not only transformed the structure and social and managerial systems but has fundamentally altered the goals of the industrial organization. "If the society sets high store by technological virtuosity and measures its success by its capacity for rapid technical advance, this will become a goal of the corporation and therewith of those who comprise it." [12] By adapting to and utilizing new technology, the corporation has developed the means for growth and diversification, and expanding its role in society. This movement toward technological virtuosity has been implemented by the growing number of highly trained scientists, professionals, and technical personnel in corporations who are aggressively seeking outlets for their creativity. This utilization of technology not only has an impact upon the goals and internal structure of the corporation but also has an important bearing upon its relationship with other institutions.

CLASSIFICATION OF TECHNICAL SYSTEMS

Many ways of classifying organizations have been proposed. For example, business firms are frequently classified in terms of industries. The Standard Industrial Classification system divides all manufacturing into twenty major groups with many subgroups. Other organizations are classified on the basis of primacy of functions which they perform: schools, hospitals, prisons, labor unions, and so forth.

While these bases may be appropriate in certain circumstances, there is an increasing tendency to classify organizations in terms of their technical system. "The perspective holds that technology is a better basis for comparing organizations than the several schemes which now exist." [13] In many ways, this view is more logical than other classifications. For example, the Standard Industrial Classification groups together the custom tailor and the highly mechanized or automated clothing factory. Two organizations, even though in the same industrial classification, may involve widely varying technologies and, consequently, different organization structures, as well as psychosocial and managerial systems.

Many recent authors have used technology as a basis for analysis of organizations. James D. Thompson says, "Those organizations with similar technological and environmental problems should exhibit similar behavior; patterns should appear. But if our thesis is fruitful, we should also find that patterned variations in problems posed by technologies and environments result in systematic differences in organizational action." [14]

We agree that a classification of organizations in terms of technology would be a

---

[11] John Kenneth Galbraith, *The New Industrial State,* Houghton Mifflin Company, Boston, 1967, p. 86.
[12] Ibid., p. 161.
[13] Charles Perrow, "A Framework for the Comparative Analysis of Organizations," *American Sociological Review,* April 1967, p. 195.
[14] James D. Thompson, *Organizations in Action,* McGraw-Hill Book Company, New York, 1967, pp. 1–2.

useful starting place for comparative organizational analysis. However, it is difficult to develop a simple classification which is satisfactory. For industrial organizations involved in the production of goods, the classification in terms of small batch, mass production, and continuous process provides a general technology continuum. However, it is appropriate primarily for industrial operations. It would be difficult to fit institutions such as hospitals and schools into this classification.

Thompson developed a scheme which is more appropriate for a wide variety of organizations. He classifies technologies in three ways.

> *Long-linked technology.* This type of technology involves serial interdependence between the various production units and is typified by the mass-production assembly line. The fully automated production line would be the final stage in the development of long-linked technology.
>
> *Mediating technology.* This technology involves the joining of clients, customers, or others who are otherwise independents. For example, the bank provides an interchange between depositors and borrowers. The telephone company and post office also provide a mediating or interchange function between various members of the society.
>
> *Intensive technology.* A variety of techniques is drawn upon in order to achieve a change in some object or to deal with a specific problem; it is a custom technology. This is the type utilized by the general hospital or the research and development laboratory. [15]

While these categories may be useful, we suggest a simplified approach based upon a continuum ranging from a uniform and relatively simple technology such as craft production to a nonuniform and complex technology such as that utilized by a research and development laboratory, university, or large-scale general hospital (see Figure 8.1). Many others have utilized similar classifications. [16] It is important to recognize that this continuum considers two primary dimensions. One deals with the degree of complexity of the technology required for task performance. The second emphasizes the degree of uniformity or nonuniformity of events, tasks, or decisions which the organization faces. Thus, there are a number of possible combinations along this continuum. At the left end of the continuum is the organization which has a very simple and uniform technology. At the other extreme is the organization which has a dynamic and complex technology, such as an aerospace company which is pushing the state of the art, a university, or a research and development laboratory. Obviously, within any complex organization,

---

[15] James D. Thompson, Ibid., pp. 15–19.
[16] Some of the writers who have adopted similar forms of classification are Perrow, op. cit., pp. 194–208; Eugene Litwak, "Models of Bureaucracy Which Permit Conflict," *American Journal of Sociology*, September 1961, pp. 177–184; James G. March and Herbert A. Simon, *Organizations*, John Wiley & Sons, Inc., New York, 1958; and Edward Harvey, "Technology and the Structure of Organizations," *American Sociological Review*, April 1968, pp. 247–259.

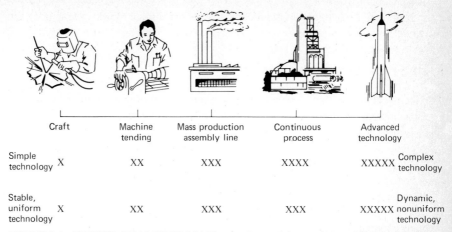

	Craft	Machine tending	Mass production assembly line	Continuous process	Advanced technology	
Simple technology	X	XX	XXX	XXXX	XXXXX	Complex technology
Stable, uniform technology	X	XX	XXX	XXX	XXXXX	Dynamic, nonuniform technology

FIGURE 8.1 TECHNOLOGY CONTINUUM. The simple-complex continuum relates to the degree of complexity of the technological system—both the mechanical and the knowledge aspects. Thus craft technology is the simplest form and the technology in atomic energy and space exploration is the most complex. The stable-dynamic dimension refers to the frequency of change in the technology. Here again, craft technology is the most stable. The most dynamic is found in industries such as aerospace and electronics.

there may be different departments which are at various positions along this continuum. In a hospital, for example, many functions are based upon uniform procedures and stable technology. However, at the other end of the spectrum, the hospital research activities and the diagnosis and treatment of many patients involve a dynamic and nonuniform technology.

There are evident difficulties in a complex organization with departments at various points on this technology continuum. One of the major problems facing the organization utilizing a mixed technology is that of developing "mechanisms of segregation," procedures by which the potentially contradictory social relationships of the differing subsystems are avoided by creating separate units which are coordinated via common organizational goals. The problem of the organization is more than just adapting to one technical component; it involves integrating and coordinating a number of significantly different technologies within the organizational system.

Although the illustrations in Figure 8.1 suggest industrial examples, it should be emphasized that this view of a technological continuum is appropriate for all types of organizations. Perrow, for example, has used a similar model to investigate the impact of technical systems in general hospitals, mental institutions, correctional institutions, and large corporations. [17] In every organization the goals, structure, psychosocial system, and managerial system are influenced by the location of the technical system on

---

[17] Charles Perrow, *Organizational Analysis: A Sociological View,* Wadsworth Publishing Company, Inc., Belmont, Calif., 1970.

this continuum. Any change in the technical system will have repercussions upon the other organizational systems.

IMPACT OF THE TECHNICAL SYSTEM

The technical system has received increasing attention in organization theory. In general, technology was neglected by traditional management theorists and human relationists alike. Weber's bureaucratic model and the administrative management principles were considered to be universalistic and applicable regardless of the specific technology. Although Taylor's scientific management did consider the techniques of task performance, concern was primarily with the operative level rather than the total technical system. The early human relationists frequently considered the technical system as given and constant; they focused their attention upon nontechnical factors such as informal group dynamics, types of supervision, and interpersonal relationships. The technological component of the organizational system was often considered a "closed" subsystem, which did not have any dynamic interaction with the other subsystems.

There have been some exceptions to this general neglect of technological factors. Dubin, for example, emphasizes the importance of technology and its impact upon the behavioral system.[18] Walker and his associates at Yale University also have made numerous studies on the impact of technology in the work organization.[19] These, however, were exceptions. For the most part, management theorists disregarded the technological factors and attempted to set forth prescriptions that would apply regardless of the technology. This lack of consideration of the technological system frequently led to unrealistic and idealistic generalizations.[20]

However, within the past decade the importance of the technological component in the organization has been stressed.

> In examining the influence of technology, we must again keep fixed in mind that technology and other system inputs are interdependently related. A useful way to begin our examination of technology, in fact, is to explore three basic ways in which technology influences behavior through its effects on other inputs. First, technology is a determinant of the human inputs required by an

---

[18] Robert Dubin, *The World of Work*, Prentice-Hall, Inc., Englewood Cliffs, N.J., 1958, pp. 62–65.

[19] See, for example, Charles R. Walker and Robert H. Guest, *The Man on the Assembly Line*, Harvard University Press, Cambridge, Mass., 1952; and Charles R. Walker, *Modern Technology and Civilization*.

[20] Perrow emphasizes this point:

> To call for decentralization, representative bureaucracies, collegial authority, or employee-centered, innovative or organic organizations—to mention only a few of the highly normative prescriptions that are being offered by social scientists today—is to call for a type of structure that can be realized only with a certain type of technology, unless we are willing to pay a high cost in terms of output. Given a routine technology, the much maligned Weberian bureaucracy probably constitutes the socially optimum form of organizational structure.

"A Framework for the Comparative Analysis of Organizations," op. cit., p. 204.

organization and, thus indirectly, of the predisposition of employees. Second, technology is a determinant of certain gross features of organizational structure and procedure. Third, technology is an immediate determinant of individual and group job designs and, therefore, indirectly a determinant of social structure and norms. [21]

The technical system is directly related to the environmental suprasystem and to the goals and values of the organization. As a subsystem of the society in which it exists, the organization utilizes the available technical knowledge in its transformation processes. However, new technology is also created by organizations and is made available as an output to society. Changing technology has had a profound impact on our entire social structure. "Changes in technology produce change in social institutions, and changes in institutions produce change in technology. In the enormously complex world of social interrelations we cannot say in any simple way that one change produces the other, only that they are enormously interrelated and both aspects of human life change together." [22]

The nature of the technical system also has an important impact on the goals and values of the organization. The value of striving for "technical rationality" is apparent in most organizations. The very goals which the organization attempts to accomplish are frequently determined by the available technology. We could not adopt the goal of "landing a man on the moon by 1970" without having the available technology. At the operating level in the organization, technology is one of the prime forces in determining the specific goals and the means for their accomplishment.

Impact upon Structure

A number of studies have focused specifically on the relationships between technology and organizational structure. Joan Woodward and her associates engaged in extensive research in 100 industrial firms in Great Britain. She divided the firms surveyed into three groups, based upon differences in technology. Twenty-four firms had unit or small-batch production, such as job-lot operations; thirty-one were classified as large-batch and mass production, such as assembly lines; and twenty-five were engaged in continuous process production, such as chemical and oil refineries. In addition, twelve firms were classified as combined systems. The transition from unit and small-batch to large-batch and mass production and then to continuous process production was one of increasing technological complexity.

There was a direct correlation between technology and structure. "Among the organizational characteristics showing a direct relationship with technical advance

[21] Paul R. Lawrence, "Technical Inputs," in John A. Seiler, *Systems Analysis in Organizational Behavior*, Richard D. Irwin, Inc., and The Dorsey Press, Homewood, Ill., 1967, p. 133.

[22] Kenneth E. Boulding, *The Meaning of the Twentieth Century*, Harper & Row, Publishers, Incorporated, New York, 1964, p. 9.

were: the length of the line of command; the span of control of the chief executive; the percentage of total turnover allocated to the payment of wages and salaries, and the ratios of managers to total personnel, of clerical and administrative staff to manual workers, of direct to indirect labour, and of graduate to non-graduate supervision in production departments."[23] The number of vertical levels of management in direct production departments increased with technical advance from unit production to continuous processing. The span of control of the chief executive (the number of people directly responsible to him) increased from a medium of four in unit production, to seven in large-batch and mass production, to ten in process production. Management by committee was more common in process industries than in the less complex systems. There was a direct link between a firm's technology and the relative size of its management group. The clerical and administrative personnel, including staff groups, were proportionately larger in the advanced companies.

The study also found a close relationship between successful performance and the organizational structure of companies within each industry. This finding is of key importance; there tended to be an optimal structure for each type of technology. "The fact that organizational characteristics, technology, and success were linked together in this way suggested that not only was the system of production an important variable in the determination of organizational structure, but also that one particular form of organization was the most appropriate to each system of production."[24] A replication of the Woodward study by Zwerman using fifty-six firms in the Minneapolis area generally corroborated her findings.[25]

A series of studies carried out by the Industrial Administration Research Unit of the University of Aston in England provided additional information concerning the impact of the technical system. In a study of forty-six diverse organizations they investigated the relationship between technology and structure. They classified technology into three components. *Operations technology* is the techniques used in the work-flow activities. *Materials technology* refers to the nature of the materials used in the transformation process. *Knowledge technology* refers to the characteristics of the knowledge used in the organization.

The Aston group found that operations technology did not have a major effect upon structural relationships except for those structural variables which were centered on the work-flow. They concluded:

> Operations technology is shown to affect only those structural variables immediately impinged on by the workflow. Thus the smaller the organization the

---

[23] Joan Woodward, *Industrial Organization: Theory and Practice,* Oxford University Press, Fair Lawn, N.J., 1965, p. 51. For a discussion of an extension of this research see: Joan Woodward, "Technology, Material Control, and Organizational Behavior," in Anant R. Negandhi and Joseph P. Schwitter (eds.), *Organizational Behavior Models,* The Comparative Administration Research Institute, Kent State University, Kent, Ohio, 1970, pp. 21-31.
[24] Ibid., pp. 69-70.
[25] William L. Zwerman, *New Perspectives on Organization Theory,* Greenwood Publishing Corporation, Westport, Conn., 1970.

more completely its structure is pervaded by the immediate effects of this technology; the larger the organization the more these effects are confined to variables such as the proportions employed in activities that are specifically linked with the workflow, and technology is not related to the wider administrative and hierarchical structure. [26]

More simply stated, the impact of the technical system upon structural variables is most apparent in what we have called the "operating subsystem or level." Technology is a prime determinant of the structure on the production line. It is also of major importance in a small organization such as an automobile repair shop. However, the operations technology would have a more limited impact upon the structure of the coordinative subsystem. At the strategic level it would have even less importance. These findings would fit in closely with our model as set forth in Figure 5.3. At the coordinative and strategic levels, factors other than operations technology are of major consequence to structure. Environmental influences are important in structuring the strategic level. [27] For example, the nature of the competitive environment would be very important in determining the structural variables within the advertising, market research, and public relations departments of a large industrial organization. The broad administrative structure of the conglomerate or the multinational corporation is influenced more by environmental forces than by technical considerations.

However, we should be reminded that the Aston study considered only "operations technology" and did not include materials and knowledge technology. It is likely that these two components of technology would have an impact upon structure at all levels. These various studies suggest that the relationships between technology and structure are complex. "Technology and structure are both multidimensional concepts that cannot be expected to be related in a simple manner." [28]

Impact upon Psychosocial System

Traditional management theory gave little consideration to the ways in which technology affected the psychosocial system. The technical system was considered as given and invariable, and the assumption was made that the people would adapt. Fortunately, human beings are adaptable and have responded to rapidly changing technologies. Technological progress in complex organizations over the past 100 years has required major adjustments on the part of social systems. The techniques of bureaucracy, scientific management, and mass production required fundamental changes. The newer innovations of automation—both in the factory and in the office—are currently having

---

[26] David J. Hickson, D. S. Pugh, and Diana C. Pheysey, "Operations Technology and Organization Structure: An Empirical Reappraisal," *Administrative Science Quarterly*, September 1969, p. 378.
[27] Jay Galbraith, "Environmental and Technological Determinants of Organizational Design," in Jay W. Lorsch and Paul R. Lawrence (eds.), *Studies in Organization Design*, Richard D. Irwin, Inc., and The Dorsey Press, Homewood, Ill., 1970, pp. 113–139.
[28] Lawrence B. Mohr, "Organizational Technology and Organizational Structure," *Administrative Science Quarterly*, December 1971, p. 444.

profound impacts; yet we have given little consideration to the relationship between technology and psychosocial systems. Haire states:

> Our industrial production layouts are built to utilize the production technique, the machine's characteristics, and the material's qualities to the utmost. The operator is considered the dependent variable. He is expected to (and fortunately does) bend and adjust. It is interesting to speculate on what might happen if we were to build a production line designed to maximize the human resources and motivations of the operators, and then consider the machines as dependent variables which must be built to conform to the requirements of a system designed to maximize the human's potentialities. [29]

Merton suggests that there are a number of ways in which technology affects the psychosocial system. [30] It affects the network of social relations among workers engaged in operations. There may be modifications in the size and composition of the immediate work group, in the range, character, and frequency of contact with fellow workers and with supervisors, in the status position of the worker in the organization, and in the extent of physical and social mobility. Technological change may create job insecurities and worker anxieties. Skills developed over a long period of time may become outmoded, vitally affecting the self-image and motivation of the worker. The high degree of specialization required in many mass-production operations may reduce the worker's task performance to one of great simplicity. Increased specialization of production leads inescapably to a greater need for predictability of work behavior and therefore for increased discipline in the work place. This is particularly true for mass-production and assembly-type operations.

More specifically, technology influences behavior through the specific design of each worker's task performance. It also has a collective effect on jobs throughout the organization and on the broader social relationships. With stable operations, the interdependence between the technical and the psychosocial systems often goes unnoticed. However, a major change in the technology component will often highlight this interdependence. Many of the most important studies showing the relationship between the technical system and the psychosocial system have been conducted during periods of change, when these relationships become more dramatic and observable.

Walker and his associates made several studies of the impact of technology on the social system. An intensive research program in an automotive assembly line plant provided important insights into the work environment of mass production and the impact of technology upon group relationships. "The character or type of work group is determined largely by technological requirements. In turn, the work group determines

---

[29] Mason Haire, *Psychology in Management*, 2d ed., McGraw-Hill Book Company, New York, 1964, pp. 6–7.
[30] Robert K. Merton, *Social Theory and Social Structure*, rev. ed., The Free Press of Glencoe, New York, 1957, pp. 563–565.

the kind of social relationship that is possible for its members." [31] Mass-production technology on an automobile assembly line affects the social organization in such matters as the size, function, and interactions of work groups; relationships with supervisors; wage structure; and the patterns of promotion and transfer.

Once the assembly line is established, it develops an "impersonal authority and control" over the workers and the social system. It sets forth the task of the workers, determines the materials and tools to be used, and sets the pace at which the work will be done. Even the foreman has limited control and is primarily concerned with keeping the assembly line moving. Walker also compared the social system on the automobile assembly line with that of a semiautomatic steel mill operation and found some rather significant variations due to the differing technologies.

In a study of several industries, Blauner also found important differentials in the psychosocial systems with different technologies. For example, alienation and dissatisfaction were greater on the assembly line than in craft and continuous process industries (such as chemicals and oil refining). These latter industries had a higher degree of worker motivation and satisfaction than those on the assembly line. [32]

In a study of 1491 Canadian workers in three different industries—printing, automobile, and oil—Fullan also found that integration and satisfaction were lowest among workers on the mass-production assembly line. [33] In recent contract negotiations between the United Auto Workers and the automobile companies one of the major issues has been the "dehumanizing" nature of the task on the production line. This is further evidence of the impact of technology upon the psychosocial system.

Members of the Tavistock Institute in England have engaged in a number of important research studies showing the relationship between technical and psychosocial systems. In the first of these studies, Trist and his associates investigated the effects of changing technology in the nationalized coal mines of Great Britain. [34] The traditional method of mining coal prior to World War I involved small groups working as independent teams. Each team was autonomous and established its own system of work with each worker performing a variety of tasks. These teams became the source of strong group identification.

Technological advances in coal mining and the emphasis upon larger-scale production led to modifications in the work situation and task performance. With the new technology and mechanical equipment for cutting and removing coal, the longwall method of production was adopted. Under this system, new work groups were formed, consisting of from forty to fifty men, and their activities were spread over a wide area, up to 200 yards. The task requirements under this system were specialized, and it was

---

[31] Walker and Guest, op. cit., p. 69.
[32] Robert Blauner, *Alienation and Freedom: The Factory Worker and His Industry*, The University of Chicago Press, Chicago, 1964, p. 182.
[33] Michael Fullan, "Industrial Technology and Worker Integration in the Organization," *American Sociological Review*, December 1970, pp. 1028–1039.
[34] E. L. Trist and K. W. Bamforth, "Some Social and Psychological Consequences of the Longwall Method of Coal-getting," *Human Relations*, February 1951, pp. 3–38.

impossible to develop close interpersonal relationships and group identifications. This new technology led to many dysfunctional consequences, including evidences of emotional strain and lack of group identification, with feelings of passivity and indifference. The productivity of the miners suffered. A program was developed to solve these problems. This evolved into the "composite longwall method" of production, which restored many of the social and group relationships that had been drastically changed by the conventional longwall method. Group members shared common pay and exchanged tasks and shifts according to rules which they established themselves. The groups again became self-regulating and autonomous to a large extent, and there was much higher morale and sense of identification. Productivity, attendance, safety, and general morale were substantially improved. [35]

Of key importance in these studies was the finding that change in a work organization determined only by engineering considerations can disrupt the social system to the extent that the new technology will not work effectively. Only after the psychosocial system was redesigned to alleviate difficulties created was the full potential of the new technical system achieved. These studies emphasized another vital factor. A given technical system does not automatically lead to one and only one social system. There may be alternatives in designing the social system which lead both to increased productivity and to more personal satisfaction. Another member of the Tavistock group, A. K. Rice, applied similar concepts to the organization of work groups in Indian textile mills. [36] Although the cultural setting was different, the social organization was redesigned deliberately to provide greater efficiency, quality, and individual satisfaction.

In the United States there have been an increasing number of studies of the social consequences of the newer technologies such as automation of material and information flow. One of the most conclusive of these studies was by Mann and his associates at the Institute for Social Research, University of Michigan. [37] This was a longitudinal study of the effects of a changeover to electronic data processing equipment in the Detroit Edison Company over a five-year period. It provided detailed information on a major technological change and on the problems of adjustment for the organization structure, as well as on the psychosocial and managerial systems. In adapting, management considered the psychosocial system within the constraints of the technological changes required.

> One of the most pressing problems during this period was the maintenance of a high level of group morale and individual job satisfaction. Every attempt was made to arrive at solutions that would be satisfactory to each individual. While the general policy of reassignment served as guidelines, many unique solu-

---

[35] F. E. Emery and E. L. Trist, "Socio-technical Systems," in C. West Churchman and Michael Verhulst (eds.), *Management Sciences: Models and Techniques,* Pergamon Press, New York, 1960, vol. 2, p. 90.
[36] A. K. Rice, *Productivity and Social Organization: The Ahmedabad Experiment,* Tavistock Publications, London, 1958.
[37] Floyd C. Mann and Lawrence K. Williams, "Observations on the Dynamics of a Change to Electronic Data-processing Equipment," *Administrative Science Quarterly,* September 1960, pp. 217–256.

tions had to be invented in individual cases. The old problem remained of devising a solution that would meet the employee's personal needs, the company objectives, and still be perceived as appropriate publicly. [38]

The changeover to electronic data processing accented formalization and demanded a more integrated work process with less autonomy for both individual employees and work groups in setting their work pace. The greater interdependence required by the new technology resulted in total system vulnerability and a need for more coordination. A breakdown in one phase of the work could stop the whole operation.

These studies are just a few of many which have investigated the impact of changing technology on the psychosocial system. Increasing evidence suggests that technological change should no longer be considered purely from the mechanistic-engineering viewpoint. Although the requirements of the technological components may set broad constraints, there are a wide variety of alternative ways of adapting so that human satisfaction can be maintained or even enhanced.

There is a growing movement to design jobs to provide more meaningful work and a higher level of individual need satisfaction. The term ''job enrichment'' identifies an approach in which the psychological and social, as well as the economic and technical, factors are considered. [39] This is fundamentally different from the traditional view of designing jobs based only upon technical and structural requirements and then ''fitting the person to the slot.'' Improved productivity through technological progress and greater participant satisfaction are not necessarily contradictory goals. Considering both factors as dynamic variables will lead to increased organizational effectiveness and efficiency.

Impact on Managerial System

In many ways, the impact of technology on the managerial system has been even more dramatic than on the other organizational subsystems. We marvel at the obvious technological advancements required to send men to the moon and return them safely. However, the managerial skills required to plan for and integrate all the diverse activities for successful mission accomplishment are equally important. [40] The improvements in management techniques in the United States have perhaps done more to revolutionize society than have scientific-engineering changes.

One of the major consequences of changing technology has been the increasing specialization of knowledge. The managerial system in most organizations includes

[38] Ibid., pp. 244–245.
[39] Harold M. F. Rush, *Job Design for Motivation*, The Conference Board, Inc., New York, 1971; and Richard E. Walten, ''How to Counter Alienation in the Plant,'' *Harvard Business Review*, November–December 1972, pp. 70–81.
[40] See Leonard R. Sayles and Margaret K. Chandler, *Managing Large Systems*, Harper & Row, Publishers, Incorporated, New York, 1971; and James E. Webb, *Space Age Management*, McGraw-Hill Book Company, New York, 1969.

many participants with specialized skills and training. Many highly trained specialists are in staff positions, and their number is growing: operations researchers, personnel staffs, engineers in research and development, communications experts, and industrial psychologists and sociologists. The modern managerial system is not comprised of a single individual who has overriding knowledge and power; it is composed of a complex team of trained specialists who are contributing their skills to the organization's performance. They are typically the "catalysts" who help the organization utilize and adapt to new technological developments.

Technology has had a primary impact not only on staff and functional personnel but also on middle and lower line managers. The role of the first-line supervisor has changed significantly; he is required to integrate activities across a broader spectrum. He is often the mediator between the requirements of the technical system and those of the psychosocial system. Supervisory requirements in terms of both technical and human relations skills are significantly increased as a result of the changing technology.

With accelerating technology, there has been a shift of emphasis for the managerial system. Under traditional management concepts, primary consideration was given to the differentiation or segmentation of activities into subsystems for task performance. Increasingly, with growing differentiation in complex organizations, problems of integration have been intensified. *Integration* is the process of achieving coordination of effort among the various subsystems in the accomplishment of the organization's goals.

Many research studies have considered the impact of changing technology upon managerial systems. One of the more comprehensive was conducted by Burns and Stalker in their investigation of English and Scottish firms. They examined a number of firms with a stable technology and environment which were attempting to move into the electronics field with its rapidly changing technology. "We hoped to be able to observe how management systems changed in accordance with changes in the technical and commercial tasks of the firm, especially the substantial changes in the rate of technical advance which new interests in electronics development and application would mean." [41] It was their hypothesis, substantiated by the research findings, that a different managerial system was appropriate for concerns involved in a stable technology and environment as compared with those adapting to rapidly changing technology. Managerial systems which were adapted to a stable technology were termed *mechanistic*. Such a system was characterized as having a rigidly prescribed organization structure. There were well-defined tasks, and the methods, duties, and powers attached to each functional role were determined precisely. The interactions within the management system tended to be vertical between superior and subordinate—a strong command hierarchy. "Management, often visualized as the complex hierarchy familiar in organization charts, operates a simple control system, with information flowing up through a succession of filters, and decisions and instructions flowing downwards through a succession of amplifiers." [42]

---

[41] Burns and Stalker, op. cit., p. 4.
[42] Ibid., p. 5.

By contrast, *organic* managerial systems are best adapted to conditions of rapidly changing technology and environment. They are suitable to unstable conditions when problems and requirements for action arise that cannot be broken down and distributed among specialized roles within a clearly defined hierarchy. The organic system is characterized by a relatively flexible structure. Continual adjustment and redefinition of individual tasks through interaction with others, a network rather than hierarchical control, emphasis upon lateral rather than vertical communications, and a wide dispersal of power and influence based upon technical expertise and knowledge rather than upon hierarchical position are characteristic of the organic system.

Burns and Stalker also emphasize the difficulties involved in making the transformation from the mechanistic to the organic system by the firms that were trying to move into the electronics industry. The unstructured and highly dynamic nature of the organic system often created anxiety and insecurity on the part of the managers who had been used to working in the structured, mechanistic system.

Burns and Stalker do not attempt to set up an idealized managerial system which would be appropriate for all types of technical and environmental situations. Just the opposite; they strongly emphasize that the most appropriate managerial system is dependent upon different kinds of technology and environmental circumstances.

The type of technology can have an important effect on managerial decision making. Organizations with stable, routine technologies tend to adopt computational decision-making approaches, whereas those with a dynamic, diffuse technology require more innovative, judgmental decision-making processes. [43] Organizations with a stable technology emphasize performance goals whereas organizations with a dynamic technology stress problem solving. [44]

The impact of technology upon managerial systems is by no means confined to industrial organizations. An interesting example is seen in changes in an organization which has been assumed to be the prototype of the structured bureaucracy—the military. The military has modified its traditional managerial system in order to adapt to changing technology. [45]

"The contemporary military establishment has for some time tended more and more to display characteristics typical of any large-scale nonmilitary bureaucracy. This is the result of technological change, which vastly increases the size of the military establishment, elaborates its interdependence with civilian society, and alters its internal social relations." [46] The rigid hierarchical structure of traditional military organization is not viable with a dynamic technology. Furthermore, the military, like other complex organizations, has become more dependent upon the skills and knowledge of special-

[43] Harvey, op. cit., pp. 257–259.

[44] Raymond G. Hunt, "Technology and Organization," *Academy of Management Journal*, September 1970, pp. 235–252.

[45] Adam Yarmolinsky, "Military Management in a Technological Society," in *The Military Establishment*, Harper & Row, Publishers, Incorporated, 1971, pp. 378–394.

[46] Morris Janowitz, "Changing Patterns of Organizational Authority: The Military Establishment," *Administrative Science Quarterly*, March 1959, p. 475.

ists. The technologies of modern warfare make it impossible to use the traditional types of authority which were appropriate with undifferentiated and unskilled participants.

In the past, military establishments frequently have resisted technological change. This resistance has to a large extent been eliminated through the routinization of innovation and modifications in the managerial system.

It is interesting to compare the movement from the mechanistic toward the organic managerial system in industry with concurrent trends in the military. As in industry, there is substantial resistance to the changing managerial system in the military. There are strong commitments to the traditional military hierarchical structure which make the transition to a less structured system more difficult. Furthermore, there are widely different functions within the military. Some of these functions—for example, the basic training of raw recruits—might best be performed with a mechanistic managerial system emphasizing a structured, authoritarian relationship. In contrast, the selection, development, and procurement of sophisticated weapon systems require the more flexible and innovative organic system. Investigation of many other types of complex organizations such as hospitals and educational institutions reveals that changing technology has an impact upon the appropriateness of various managerial systems.

AUTOMATION

Automation represents the current phase of a long-term trend toward greater complexity and sophistication of technical systems for the production of goods. In the early years of the industrial revolution the emphasis was on mechanization as a substitute for human or animal energy. The newer production technology utilizes devices that can perform increasingly complex sequences of operations with less and less human assistance. "The key to achieving this emphasis has been the development of mechanical substitutes not only for muscular energy but for other human faculties as well." [47]

The term *automation* has several connotations when applied to different industrial processes. It was originally coined to describe automatic work-feeding and material handling devices on production lines in the automobile industry. The term *Detroit automation* is used to specify this original usage of the term. This approach links together machine tools into a continuous production line by mechanical devices to load, unload, and transfer between machines or between stations in a single machine. It makes use of an integrated set of machines which permit materials to flow through various stages of manufacturing with a minimum of assistance in handling by human operators. There are many examples of Detroit automation in the automotive industry. It has also been satisfactorily applied in the metalworking industries and in the manufacturing of appliances, television sets, and many other mass-production items.

This type of automation is not a new development but rather a continuation of the long-term trend toward substitution of mechanical processes for human energy. The distinction between Detroit automation and previous mechanization is primarily a matter of degree. Traditional mechanization was suboptimal and piecemeal in its orientation,

---

[47] "Automation," *The Annals of the American Academy of Political and Social Science,* March 1962, p. viii.

whereas Detroit automation is based on a broader production-system approach. It is more than adopting a new production process for existing products. It may require, for example, a complete redesign of the product to complement the automated system. The automated production of television sets required the redesign of the chassis from handwired assembly to printed circuits and integrated electronic modular components.

Process automation has another connotation—the utilization of automatic devices for controlling continuous operations such as in chemical industries, oil refining, and metal-rolling mills. Process industries are those that handle bulk solids, liquids, or gases in some form, and modify these materials either by physical or chemical means to produce a finished product. Automation in process industries has been made possible by the development of computer programs which receive information, perform mathematical computations, make comparisons and evaluations, and provide output signals for control. It involves the integration of processing equipment with computers and replaces both human energy and many human decision-making and control functions.

Many examples of automation in the processing industries are significantly different from Detroit automation. Whereas Detroit automation is primarily an extension of the long-run processes of mechanization, *automation with feedback control* represents a revolutionary departure. The basic concept of feedback control is that part of the output of the system is measured continually in terms of the characteristic being controlled, and the process is modified to reduce any divergence or error. Prior to the 1940s control of production operations was relatively elementary, and usually human functions were included in the system. For example, in most chemical processing plants, open-loop feedback systems were used in which the human operator read instruments and made the necessary adjustments to control the process. In the newer processing systems, closed-loop feedback control is utilized, so that the human element is not required in the sequence, and the system is self-correcting. Systems with closed-loop feedback control can be termed *advanced automation,* as distinguished from Detroit automation.

> Feedback-control technology has added a new dimension to automation in that it permits design of control mechanisms which are electromechanical analogues of the human neuromuscular system. In fact, servomechanisms might well be thought of as mechanical muscles which are under control of sensing instruments and uniquely arranged circuitry that perform essentially the same functions as the human nerve system. [48]

Another application of automation has been termed *discontinuous automation.* One of the problems in most automated processes is that once established, they are fixed and inflexible. Discontinuous automation is illustrated by the development of numerically controlled machines which combine the advantages of quick setup and flexibility with automatic production. They are an example of a closed-sequence system which

---

[48] J. F. Reintjes, "The Intellectual Foundations of Automation," *The Annals of the American Academy of Political and Social Science,* March 1962, p. 6.

uses inputs of technical information in the form of a numerical code to instruct the producing machine to perform a complete work cycle. Commands that govern the machine's behavior are supplied on punched cards, magnetic tape, or paper tape and control the entire sequence of operations. Numerical control utilizes feedback to make corrections automatically during operations. A major advantage of discontinuous automation is its flexibility. It has current application in producing complex forms requiring close tolerances, such as in the aerospace industry. In the long run it can be applied in many mass-production industries which require the efficiency of automatic production but also flexibility in product design.

All these forms of automated technology have had an impact upon structure, psychosocial systems, and managerial systems. One effect has been to alter organization structure to provide more horizontal integration of activities. Automation reduces the ability of the organization to functionalize its activities and to maintain strict hierarchical relationships. It concentrates on the horizontal flow of materials through the entire organizational system.

There is a great deal of interest in the impact of automation on psychosocial systems. Studies suggest that it has had an effect upon such factors as the degree and types of skills required, social interaction, motivation and satisfaction, individual autonomy, and supervisory patterns. The issue is still in doubt as to whether automation has an overall positive or negative impact upon the psychosocial system. Several of the studies have indicated that it has had the effect of upgrading skill requirements, increasing autonomy, providing more opportunities for group interaction, and motivating employees through a feeling of participation. Other studies, however, come to opposite conclusions. These differing conclusions suggest that *automation* per se may not have a positive or negative impact. Rather, the effect is determined by how well the new technology is integrated with the psychosocial system.

The managerial system is frequently affected by automation. The advancing technology places new and different demands upon the managerial system, not only for technical skill but also in terms of the administrative and human relations skills required to integrate the various systems. Automation requires that the managerial system perform its functions of planning and controlling differently than would be appropriate for more traditional production. It reduces much of the slack in the managerial decision processes and requires more precise long-range planning.

AUTOMATED INFORMATION-DECISION SYSTEMS

Automation of material flow has meant some replacement of the decision-making and mental activities of man in the factory. In contrast, white-collar and managerial functions have remained humanized to a major extent. Although there have been typewriters, dictating machines, and other mechanical aids for these functions, much of the actual work has depended directly upon human skills. There has been a continual increase in the proportion of white-collar and managerial positions, whereas the proportion of those engaged in direct production—factory workers and farmers—actually has declined.

However, the same kinds of technical developments that led to automation in the factory promise an even more dramatic revolution in clerical operations. This involves two primary phases:

1 The use of automatic electronic equipment for the collection, processing, and comparison of data
2 The application of computers to aid directly in managerial decision-making processes

The most apparent impact is in the first phase, the use of electronic equipment for processing vast quantities of data. However, the second phase, the application of computers in decision making, will have the greatest impact in the future.

Automated information-decision processes will have a profound influence upon the psychosocial system in the organization, primarily upon clerical and white-collar employees. In many ways, the process of replacing clerical workers with data processing equipment is similar to that for workers in the factory. This technology not only replaces some workers but also restructures the jobs, functions, and roles of the remaining workers. The problem will be to motivate clerical personnel and to promote their identification with the organization. Numerous studies suggest that white-collar workers are even more resistant to technological change than blue-collar workers. If "the automated factory of the future will operate on the basis of programmed decisions produced in the automated office beside it," major changes will be required in the psychosocial system of the office. [49]

The trend toward automated information-decision systems will also affect structure. It will require more effective integration of operations across a broad spectrum of functions. It cannot be concerned only with the traditional vertical communication channels based upon the hierarchy but must also consider horizontal and diagonal relationships. [50] And—even more revolutionary—recent developments in data processing technology may affect system boundaries. Traditionally, information systems were developed on an intraorganizational basis—confined within the boundaries of the organization. The new data processing technology allows for the development of interorganization information systems which transcend the boundaries of the individual organization. This is possible through the establishment of computer networks with information flow across boundaries. The so-called "checkless society" of the future will depend upon the establishment of an elaborate system of information flow among many organizations and individuals.

Many early writers suggested that the impact of data processing technology would be to cause a recentralization of decision making in the organization. However,

---

[49] Herbert A. Simon, *The Shape of Automation for Men and Management,* Harper Torchbooks, Harper & Row, Publishers, Incorporated, New York, 1965, p. 76.
[50] Thomas L. Whisler, *Information Technology and Organizational Change,* Wadsworth Publishing Company, Inc., Belmont, Calif., 1970, pp. 63-66.

there is little evidence on the extent to which centralization has resulted. Others suggest that it is possible to decentralize operations by providing more complete information to managers at all levels. Instead of moving in one direction, it is likely that the new technology will provide for the centralization of some decisions and for the decentralization of others. The mix of types of decisions and the location of the decision makers will be altered.

There is, however, general agreement that the new information technique will affect the management system. The integrative effects of this technology, with its emphasis upon systematization, and the increased volume and accuracy of information can have an important impact upon management decision making. It is quite probable that many of the routine decision-making functions of technical management will be "automated." Programming of decision making in such areas as production and inventory control has already been accomplished in many organizations. With advances in automated information-flow technology, there is the possibility of using computers for nonprogrammed decision making. By *nonprogrammed decision making,* we mean those decisions which are new and unstructured and for which there are no set techniques. It is this type of decision making which is most important for the coordinative and strategic levels of management.

As more decision making becomes susceptible to programming, the basic management functions may be altered. Top management will have to deal with longer-range planning and will need a better perception of how the organization interacts with environmental systems. By programming his more routine, mechanical decisions, the manager will have more time available to deal with the highly variable factors of human motivation and participation. We agree with Ansoff, who says, "Paradoxically enough, the age of change and automation will call for increased management skills in human relations. In a climate of change, increasing importance will be placed on the manager's ability to communicate rapidly and intelligibly, gain acceptance for change and innovation, and motivate and lead people in new and varying directions." [51]

MAN-MACHINE SYSTEMS DEVELOPMENT

There is an increasing interest in the systematic application of psychological principles to the invention, design, development, and use of complex man-machine systems. Melton describes this as a theory of psychotechnology of man-machine systems and suggests that "it achieves integration of what has heretofore been variously called 'human engineering,' 'human factors engineering,' or 'engineering psychology' on the one hand and 'personnel psychology' or 'personnel and training research' on the other hand. This union comes easily and naturally once the concept of *system* is examined and once the full implications of the concept of the human being as a *component* of a man-machine system are recognized." [52] This detailed approach to the application of

---

[51] H. Igor Ansoff, "The Firm of the Future," *Harvard Business Review,* September-October 1965, p. 178.
[52] Arthur W. Melton, in Robert M. Gagné (ed.), *Psychological Principles in System Development,* Holt, Rinehart and Winston, Inc., New York, 1962, p. v.

psychological principles to man-machine systems has also been called *ergonomics*. It involves designing machines, tools, and work areas to better fit the physiological and psychological limitations of human beings.

This research on integrating human factors directly into complex technical and mechanical systems was stimulated by the Air Force and the National Aeronautics and Space Administration. For example, in the Apollo space capsule, it was necessary to consider the whole man-machine system and to integrate human capabilities and limitations with the physical equipment. The first stage is to determine the purpose, or

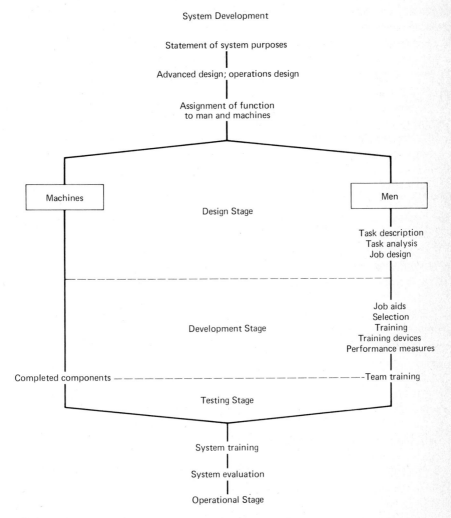

FIGURE 8.2   MAN-MACHINE SYSTEMS DEVELOPMENT [Robert M. Gagné (ed.), *Psychological Principles in System Development,* Holt, Rinehart and Winston, Inc., New York, 1962, p. 4]

mission, of the system and to develop an advanced operational design. From these, together with inputs about the current state of technological knowledge, decisions are made about components of the total system and the way in which they can be connected to fulfill the system's mission. This leads to the assignment of functions to men and machines. Figure 8.2 is a model of man-machine systems development.

Psychotechnology has important implications. The basic assumption is that man should be considered one of the major components of a complex man-machine system rather than merely a user of the system once it is developed. It denies that system development is purely an engineering problem—psychological and social problems must also be considered. "Any reasonably complex system requires a true interaction between man and the other parts of the system, which may be machines, other men, or combinations of these. Some way must therefore be found for thinking about the functions of machines and the functions of men within a framework which makes possible the relation of these two kinds of functions to common goals—that is, to system goals." [53]

This micro approach to man-machine system development has major implications for many advanced military and space programs, and this is where most of the current research is taking place. As a result of these studies, a great deal more will be learned about the interrelations between man and technology.

SUMMARY

Technology has two aspects—the physical manifestations such as machinery and equipment and the accumulated knowledge concerning the means to accomplish tasks. By organizational technology we mean the complex of techniques utilized in the transformation of the inputs of the system into outputs.

Science and technology have become a pervasive force in modern society, influencing all of man's activities and providing a new shape to the world. In modern industrial society large-scale complex organizations have become the primary means for utilizing technology.

Changing technology has an important effect upon organizational goals and values, structure, psychosocial systems, and management practice. For a stable technology, the mechanistic form is appropriate. However, with a changing, innovative technology, the flexible, organic system is most effective. The impact of changing technology is not only seen in the industrial firm but is also apparent in hospitals, universities, governmental agencies, and many other organizations.

The classification of organizations by type of technology is a useful starting place for comparative analysis. We have suggested the use of a relatively simple classification of technology in terms of stability and complexity. The technological system can be thought of as on a continuum ranging from a simple and stable technology to a highly complex and dynamic technology.

---

[53] Robert M. Gagné, "Human Functions in Systems," in ibid., p. 35.

Automation represents the current phase of a long-term trend toward greater complexity and sophistication of technical systems for the production of goods. *Detroit automation* makes use of an integrated set of machines which permits materials to flow through various stages of manufacturing with minimum assistance in handling by human operators. *Process automation* is the utilization of computer programs for controlling continuous operations such as oil refining.

The development of automated information-decision systems has had an effect upon the white-collar and managerial groups in many organizations. It has two phases: the use of automatic electronic equipment for the collection, processing, and comparison of data, and the application of computers to aid directly in the managerial decision-making process. The automation of production operations and information-decision systems affects the organization structure, as well as the psychosocial and managerial systems.

Throughout this chapter, we have emphasized that different technologies require different adaptations—there is no one best alternative. The effective organization must integrate technology with its other subsystems.

QUESTIONS AND PROBLEMS

1 Compare and contrast machine and knowledge technology.
2 How has technology shaped our sociocultural environment? How is advancing technology related to the growth of complex organizations?
3 Discuss the relationship between technology and organization structure. What are the basic structural differences between the firm with a routine, fixed technology and one with a dynamic, diffused technology?
4 Evaluate the impact of technology on the psychosocial system of organizations.
5 Consider your own work experience. How did the technology affect your job and your relationships with others in the organization?
6 How have managerial systems been affected by changing technology?
7 Discuss the distinctions between mechanistic and organic managerial systems.
8 What is the likely impact of automation on the various subsystems of organizations?
9 Prepare a list of man-machine systems (such as driver-automobile). Discuss the importance of man-machine system development.
10 How will new developments in automated information-decision systems affect organizational boundaries?

ORGANIZATION STRUCTURE

Structural relationships are fundamental considerations of organization theorists and practicing managers. The environmental suprasystem is an important determinant of structure, particularly at the strategic level. The technical system has an important effect upon the type of structure appropiate for task performance. In turn, the structure sets the framework for the psychosocial system and is inexorably interwoven with the managerial system. The primary emphasis, in this chapter, is on formal rather than on informal relationships. We are concerned with developing the concept of structure, investigating the variables affecting it, considering newer developments, such as horizontal relationships and program management, and examining the dynamics of structure in relationship to the other organizational subsystems. The following topics are discussed:

Definition of Structure
Traditional Concepts of Organization Structure
Differentiation of Organizational Activities
Integration of Organizational Activities
Elaboration of Structure
Horizontal and Diagonal Relationships
Program Management
An Example of Organization Structure
Dynamics of Organization Structure

DEFINITION OF STRUCTURE

The concept of organization structure is somewhat abstract and illusive. However, it is real and affects everyone in the organization. The student comes in contact with the structure of the university when he selects a major and then studies under the direction of a particular academic unit. When you walk into an unfamiliar bank the information clerk helps you find the "loan department" or the "new accounts department," depending on your needs. New employees in their first assignment are told, "You will be working under Smith in the Market Research Department." One of the more difficult things for the new employee to learn is the name and function of the various departments, the superior-subordinate relationships, and "who does what."

Very simply, structure may be considered as *the established pattern of relationships among the components or parts of the organization*. However, the structure of a social system is not visible in the same way as a biological or mechanical system. It cannot be seen but is inferred from the actual operations and behavior of the organization.

The distinction between *structure* and *process* in systems helps in understanding this concept. "The *structure* of a system is the arrangement of its subsystems and components in three-dimensional space at a given moment of time. . . . Process is dynamic change in the matter-energy or information of that system over time." [1]

In the biological system the structure of the organism may be studied separately from its processes. For example, the study of anatomy is basically the study of the structure of the organism. In contrast, physiology is concerned with the study of the functions of living organisms. In the study of a social system such as an organization, it is difficult if not impossible to make this clear-cut distinction. In fact, there are those who suggest that it is impossible to study the structure of the organization as separate from its processes. "A social system is a structuring of events or happenings rather than of physical parts and it therefore has no structure apart from its functioning." [2]

We agree that the structure of the organization cannot be looked at as completely separate from its functions; however, these are two separate phenomena. Taken together, the concepts of structure and process can be viewed as the static and dynamic features of the organization. In some systems the static aspects (the structure) are the most important for investigation; in others the dynamic aspects (the processes) are more important. Actually, structure and processes are correlative and not opposing aspects of the system. We will view the organization's structure as being the established pattern of relationships among the components in the organization. "Organization structure consists simply of those aspects of the pattern of behavior in the organization that are relatively stable and that change only slowly." [3]

In the complex organization, structure is set forth initially by the design of the major components or subsystems and then by the establishment of patterns of relation-

---

[1] James G. Miller, "Living Systems: Basic Concepts," *Behavioral Science*, July 1965, pp. 209-211.
[2] Daniel Katz and Robert L. Kahn, *The Social Psychology of Organizations*, John Wiley & Sons, Inc., New York, 1966, p. 31.
[3] James G. March and Herbert A. Simon, *Organizations*, John Wiley & Sons, Inc., New York, 1958, p. 170.

ship among these subsystems. It is this internal differentiation and patterning of relationships with some degree of permanency which is referred to as structure. The formal structure is frequently defined in terms of:

1 The pattern of formal relationships and duties—the organization chart plus job descriptions or position guides.
2 Formal rules, operating policies, work procedures, control procedures, compensation arrangements, and similar devices adopted by management to guide employee behavior (including that of executives) in certain ways, within the structure of formal relationships. [4]

Formal and Informal Organization

Formal organization is the planned structure and represents the deliberate attempt to establish patterned relationships among components which will meet the objectives effectively. The formal structure is typically the result of explicit decision making and is prescriptive in nature—a ''blueprint'' of the way activities should be accomplished. Typically it is represented by a printed chart and is set forth in organization manuals, position descriptions, and other formalized documents. Although the formal structure does not comprise the total organizational system, it is of major importance. It sets a general framework and delineates certain prescribed functions and the relationships between these activities.

Anyone who has participated in an organization recognizes that many interactions occur which are not prescribed by the formal structure. The *informal organization* refers to those aspects of the system that are not formally planned but arise spontaneously out of the activities and interactions of participants.

Informal relationships are vital for the effective functioning of the organization. Frequently groups develop spontaneous and informal means for dealing with important activities which contribute to overall performance. Often the formal organization is slow in responding to external forces such as technological changes, and informal relationships develop to deal with these new problems. Thus, the informal organization may be adaptive and serve to perform innovative functions which are not being adequately met by the formal structure. On the other hand, there are occasions in which the informal organization may operate to the detriment of goals—when work groups slow down or sabotage production, for example.

Traditional management theorists concentrated on the formal organization structure. The human relationists, in contrast, were concerned primarily with informal relationships. This diversity of interest led to the view that there is an actual separation between the formal and informal structures. However, they really are intermeshed.

---

[4] Ralph M. Hower and Jay W. Lorsch, ''Organizational Inputs,'' in John A. Seiler, *Systems Analysis in Organizational Behavior*, Richard D. Irwin, Inc., and The Dorsey Press, Homestead, Ill., 1967, p. 157.

It is impossible to understand the nature of a formal organization without investigating the networks of informal relations and the unofficial norms as well as the formal hierarchy of authority and the official body of rules, since the formally instituted and the informally emerging patterns are inextricably intertwined. The distinction between the formal and the informal aspects of organizational life is only an analytical one and should not be reified; there is only one actual organization. [5]

In this chapter we will discuss the formal structure and will consider the informal patterns and relationships in Part 5. We should keep continually in mind, however, that this cleavage is artificial. In the actual organization the informal and formal structures are so intertwined as to defy separation.

Authority and Organization Structure

There is a direct interrelationship between organization structure and the pattern of authority. In fact, many traditionalists made the underlying assumption that authority relationships were synonymous with the organization structure. Inasmuch as structure is concerned with the establishment of positions and the relationships between positions, it does provide the framework for authority relationships. However, the authority pattern is just one part of the total structure.

Authority refers to a relationship between the participants in the organization and is not an attribute of one individual. The authority structure provides the basis for assigning tasks to the various elements in the organization and for developing a control mechanism to ensure that these tasks are performed according to plan. It provides for the establishment of formalized influence transactions among the members of the organization.

The concept of authority is closely related to the idea of the legitimate exercise of the power of a position and depends on the willingness of subordinates to comply with certain directives of superiors. Obviously, the structure and the positioning of participants in a hierarchical arrangement facilitate the exercise of authority.

Organization Charts

A typical way of depicting the structure is through printed organization charts which specify the formal authority and communication networks of the organization. Figure 9.1 presents a simplified chart for a manufacturing company. The title of the position on the chart broadly identifies its activities, and its distance from the top indicates its relative status. The lines between positions are used to indicate the prescribed formal interactions. Most organization charts are hierarchical and emphasize relationships between

---

[5] Peter M. Blau and W. Richard Scott, *Formal Organizations: A Comparative Analysis*, Chandler Publishing Company, San Francisco, 1962, p. 6.

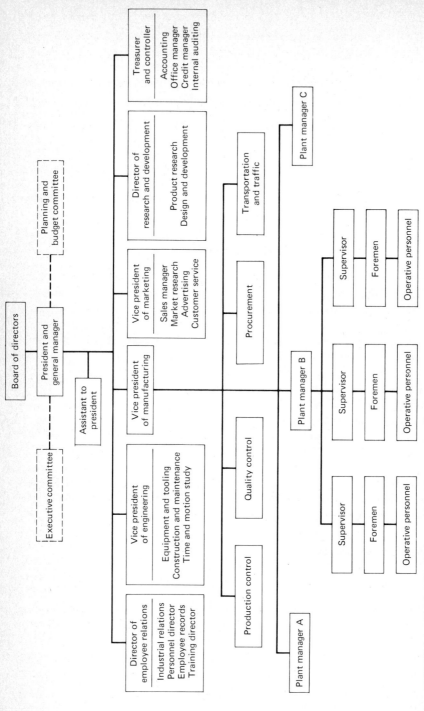

FIGURE 9.1 SIMPLIFIED ORGANIZATION CHART FOR A MANUFACTURING COMPANY

superiors and direct subordinates. They are frequently supplemented by position descriptions and organizational manuals which attempt to define the tasks of the various positions and the interactions between them more specifically.

The organization chart is usually a simplified, abstract model of the structure. It is not an exact representation of reality and therefore has limitations. It shows only a few of the relationships, even in the formal organization, and none of those in the informal organization. It does not, for example, indicate the degree of authority which a superior has over a subordinate. Does the superior have the right to hire and replace the occupant of a subordinate position? More importantly, it does not indicate the interactions between equals or the lateral relationships between people in different parts of the organization.

In spite of these limitations, the organization chart provides a useful starting point for the investigation of structure. Its inaccuracy generally lies in its simplicity and in its lack of consideration of many other important aspects of the structure. "It usually errs by not reflecting the nuances of relationships within the organization; it usually deals poorly with informal control and informal authority, usually underestimates the significance of personality variables in molding the actual system, and usually exaggerates the isomorphism between the authority system and the communication system." [6]

One problem of the organization chart is an inherent difficulty in trying to set forth in a simple, schematic two-dimensional plane the complex structural relationships existing in an organization. Conceptually, we would have a model closer to reality if we were able to utilize three-dimensional rather than two-dimensional charts. The requirement that the organization chart be confined to the printed page limits the development of schematic models.

TRADITIONAL CONCEPTS OF ORGANIZATION STRUCTURE

Traditional management theorists were primarily concerned with the design of efficient organization. They emphasized such concepts as objectivity, impersonality, and structural form. The organization structure was designed for the most efficient allocation and coordination of activities. The positions in the structure, not the people, had the authority and responsibility for getting tasks accomplished. The structure was emphasized as the most important and enduring characteristic of the organization. Many of the traditional concepts were based on experiences with stable organizations such as the military, church, and established public bureaucracies. Industrial organizations were concerned with developing a structure geared to stable production. They emphasized a rigid structure with well-defined relationships and clearly established lines of authority and communication. Let us consider some "principles" of organization.

---

[6] Richard M. Cyert and James G. March, *A Behavioral Theory of the Firm*, Prentice-Hall, Inc., Englewood Cliffs, N.J., 1963, p. 289.

Organizational Specialization and Division of Labor

A basic concept of traditional management theory is to divide work into specialized tasks and to organize them into distinct departments. Departmentalization with a natural division of labor is emphasized. It is desirable to determine the necessary activities for the accomplishment of overall organizational objectives and then to divide these activities on a logical basis into departments which perform the specialized functions. The organization structure is the primary means for achieving the technical and economic advantages of specialization and division of labor.

The Scalar Principle

The scalar principle states that authority and responsibility should flow in a direct line vertically from the highest level of the organization to the lowest level. It establishes the hierarchical structure of the organization. It refers to the vertical division of authority and responsibility and the assignment of various duties along the scalar chain. Primary emphasis is upon the superior-subordinate relationships. Most organization charts indicate that this principle is still used in designing the structure. The scalar principle is complementary to the concept of unity of command, in which each subordinate has only one superior.

Authority, Responsibility, and Accountability

In the classical view, the legitimatization of authority at a central source ensures that the superior "has the *right* to command someone else and that the subordinate person has the *duty* to obey the command. This is implied in the notion of official legitimacy, legal in nature rather than social and informal." [7] Authority is the right to invoke compliance by subordinates on the basis of formal position and control over rewards and sanctions. It is impersonal and goes with the position rather than the individual. Furthermore, authority and responsibility should be directly linked; that is, if a subordinate is granted the responsibility for carrying out an activity, he should also be given the necessary authority. Accountability is associated with the flow of authority and responsibility and is the obligation of the subordinate to carry out his responsibility and to exercise authority in terms of the established policies. This view of authority, responsibility, and accountability provides the framework for much of traditional management theory. It is the basis for legitimatizing organizational hierarchy and control systems and for establishing many other concepts such as span of control and line-staff relationships. Authority is the means for integrating the activities of participants toward objectives and provides the basis for centralized direction and control.

---

[7] John M. Pfiffner and Frank P. Sherwood, *Administrative Organization*, Prentice-Hall, Inc., Englewood Cliffs, N.J., 1960, p. 75.

Span of Control

The span of control, or span of supervision, relates to the number of subordinates which a superior can supervise effectively. It is closely related to the hierarchical structure and to departmentalization. Implicit in the span of control concept is the necessity for the coordination of the activities of the subordinates by the superior. It emphasizes superior-subordinate relationships which allow for the systematic integration of activities. Traditional theory advocates a narrow span to enable the executive to provide adequate integration of all the activities of subordinates. It does not recognize the possibility of other means for coordination.

Line and Staff

As organizations grew more complex, it was necessary to integrate personnel with specialized knowledge and functions into the managerial system. This required modifications in the concepts of the scalar structure, unity of command, authority, and responsibility. In many ways, the line and staff concept can be viewed as a necessary compromise in terms of the other classical principles. The line organization is vested with the primary source of authority and performs the major functions of the organization; the staff supports and advises the line. The staff is an aid to the executive, an extension of his personality. Through the use of specialized staffs. reporting directly to the executive, it is possible to use their knowledge without sacrificing the executive's coordinating function. This view maintains the integrity of the line organization as central in the scalar chain and as the source of authority.

Many modern management writers are critical of the application of these traditional principles. However, they do have a place if they are applied with discrimination. They are useful at a certain stage in the development of an organization. They provide a basis for the initial formalizing of relationships as an organization grows from a small, informal operation. They are also appropriate where the organization is dealing with programmed and routine activities and has a stable environment and technology.

However, we would agree with the critics that absolute adherence to these principles is unrealistic. While they may serve as useful guidelines, organizations in a dynamic environment will generally need to have more fluid relationships. These principles were quite useful at the time of their formulation, during the early part of the twentieth century; however, with accelerating technology and new organizational requirements, they need to be modified.

These principles dealt with the two fundamentals of organizing—the differentiation and integration of activities. Differentiation and integration are related to the broader scientific concepts of *analysis*—the separation of a whole into its constituent elements—and *synthesis*—the combination of parts or elements into a complex whole. Structure is concerned with both analysis and synthesis. However, these two forces are often working at cross purposes. One of the problems in establishing an appropriate organization structure is to provide the optimum balance between these forces.

DIFFERENTIATION OF ORGANIZATIONAL ACTIVITIES

Complex organizations are characterized by a high degree of task specialization. Even the simplest enterprise, with just a few employees, has some division of labor among participants. In larger organizations this differentiation is carried much further. For example, a large university can have more specialization in course offerings and faculty personnel than the small liberal arts college which must concentrate on more general, less specialized subject matter. The total task of the organization is differentiated so that particular departments and units are responsible for the performance of specialized activities. "*Differentiation* is defined as the state of segmentation of the organizational system into subsystems, each of which tends to develop particular attributes in relation to the requirements posed by its relevant external environment." [8]

In the organization, this differentiation occurs in two directions: the vertical specialization of activities, represented by the organizational hierarchy, and the horizontal differentiation of activities, called departmentalization. Figure 9.1 illustrates these two bases of separation of activities. The vertical differentiation is represented by the hierarchy moving from the president to the vice-presidents, plant managers, and supervisors, and finally to the operative level. The vertical differentiation establishes the managerial structure, whereas the horizontal differentiation defines the basic departmentalization. Taken together, they set the formal structure of the organization. [9]

Vertical Differentiation: Hierarchy

The vertical division of labor establishes the hierarchy and the number of levels in the organization. Although organizations differ in the degree of their vertical divisions of labor and the extent to which it is made explicit and formalized, they all exhibit this characteristic. In the more formal organizations, such as the military, the vertical specialization is established by specific definitions of roles for the various positions, and there are significant status differences between levels. There is, for example, a basic separation between officers and enlisted personnel. Within the officer ranks, there is a distinct difference of role, status, and position in the hierarchy from second lieutenant to five-star general. Other organizations may not have such a clear-cut hierarchical differentiation in role and function. In the university there is a hierarchy from instructor to assistant professor to associate professor to full professor in the professorial ranks. However, the beginning instructor may perform a teaching and research role quite similar to that of the full professor.

In the formal organization this hierarchy sets the basic communications and authority structure, the so-called "chain of command." In the business organization there are typically vertical differentiations of positions ranging from hourly employees to

---

[8] Paul R. Lawrence and Jay W, Lorsch, "Differentiation and Integration in Complex Organizations," *Administrative Science Quarterly*, June 1967, pp. 3–4.
[9] Peter M. Blau, "A Formal Theory of Differentiation in Organizations," *American Sociological Review*, April 1970, pp. 201–218.

first-line supervisors, middle managers, and top executives. These levels are fairly well defined, with major differences in functions and status for the various positions.

There are substantial rewards for moving upward in the hierarchy. Position in the vertical dimension frequently determines the authority and influence, privilege, status, and rewards enjoyed by the incumbent. Theoretically, the further up the vertical hierarchy, the broader the considerations and the more strategic the decisions. Thus, the president should be concerned with broad strategic decisions, whereas his subordinates would be concerned with more narrowly confined decisions, and so forth down to the lower levels, where the concern is with technical operations. This vertical differentiation of activities also has the effect of creating the organizational pyramid. Inasmuch as each superior has more than one subordinate reporting to him, the organization tends to broaden out (see Figure 9.1).

Horizontal Differentiation: Departmentalization

Organizations typically have some basis for horizontal differentiation of activities. Even in a small retail store operation one partner often performs certain functions such as purchasing and inventory control, with the other in charge of advertising and sales promotion. In a small organization, this differentiation may be informal and may arise out of the natural interests and skills of the individuals involved. In a more complex organization, this horizontal specialization of activities is a necessity because of the need to perform particular functions effectively and efficiently.

The appropriate division of organizational activities into departments for purposes of administration was one of the fundamental concerns of traditional management theorists. Although there have been many criticisms of their emphasis on departmentalization and related prescriptions, the necessity for differentiation of activities is inherent in organizations. [10]

The three primary bases of departmentalization are (1) function, (2) product, and (3) location. [11] Departmentalization by *function* is shown in Figure 9.1, wherein the activities of the organization are divided into the primary functions to be performed— manufacturing, marketing, engineering, research and development, employee relations, and finance. This arrangement has the advantage of the specialization and concentration of similar activities within a departmental unit. It is the most prevalent form of departmentalization and is seen not only in business enterprises but in hospitals,

---

[10] For a discussion and criticism of the traditional management theorists' emphasis upon departmentalization, see March and Simon, op. cit., pp. 23-24. Their primary criticism was the lack of consideration of the problems of integration of activities between the various departments. They say: "One peculiar characteristic of the assignment problem, and of all the formalizations of the departmentalization problem in classical organization theory, is that, if taken literally, problems of coordination are eliminated. Since the whole set of activities to be performed is specified in advance, once these are allocated to organization units and individuals the organization problem posed by these formal theories is solved." March and Simon, op. cit., pp. 25-26.

[11] Material in this section relies on Ernest Dale, *Planning and Developing the Company Organization Structure,* American Management Association, New York, 1952, pp. 28-49; and William H. Newman, Charles E. Summer, and E. Kirby Warren, *The Process of Management,* 3d ed., Prentice-Hall, Inc., Englewood Cliffs, N.J., 1972, pp. 21-39.

governmental agencies, and many other kinds of organizations. The major problem associated with this form is the coordination of the specialized activities.

Product departmentalization has become increasingly important, especially for large, complex organizations. For example, companies such as General Electric, General Motors, and DuPont have major product divisions with substantial autonomy. This form has been used increasingly, particularly in the post-World War II period during which there has been a trend toward heterogeneous diversification.

A third primary basis of departmentalization is *location.* All the organizational activities performed in a particular geographic area are brought together and integrated into a single unit. This has been the pattern adopted by chain stores in establishing regional offices. The geographic basis of departmentalization also has become an important form for multinational business corporations. Thus, many large-scale international companies such as IBM, Nestlé Corporation, and Unilever utilize this form.

In addition to these primary bases of departmentalization, there are several others. Some organizations may departmentalize on a basis of *customers,* with separate units for retail and wholesale or for government and commercial sales. In many manufacturing organizations, departmentalization may relate to the *processes* or *equipment* utilized.

In the large organization, there is no one basis of departmentalization which is carried out uniformly throughout the entire enterprise. For example, at one level in the organization there may be the product divisions. At the next level, there may be functional specialization, and at the third level, departmentalization based upon geographic location or customer.

Role of Specialists

A traditional basis of differentiation of managerial activities has been in terms of line and staff functions. The line has direct command authority over the activities of the organization and is concerned with the primary functions. In contrast, the staff performs an advisory role and is concerned with supportive or adjutant activities. The development of the line-staff concept was necessary to provide some means of integrating the activities of numerous highly trained specialists who contribute important knowledge and skills.

The role of staff has changed substantially with greater specialization and complexities of many organizations. Staffs have come to play much more important roles. With the expansion of this role the clear delineation between line and staff activities is no longer possible. The view of line as having command authority and staff as only having an advisory role does not always hold true. The staff expert, because of knowledge and technical competence in a particular area of specialization, is frequently viewed as a source of authority and influence in the organization.[12] This is particularly

---

[12] Pfiffner and Sherwood make an interesting distinction between line and staff. The line is *substantive* (direct) in its contribution to the organization's overall objectives, and the staff is *adjective* (indirect) in its contribution. Staff activities are frequently intellectual processes. "The staff person has his time freed to gather data, study, reflect, and come up with solutions arrived at through intellectual processes. He is the thinking and planning arm of the organization. He must inevitably wield power." Pfiffner and Sherwood, op. cit., p. 173.

true where the staff has functional authority. Functional authority resides within a specialized staff which exercises control over other operational units. Quite frequently, for example, the industrial relations department has functional authority over many personnel practices in all departments throughout the organization. Functional authority represents a substantial variation from the traditional emphasis upon the line structure and unity of command.

Etzioni suggests that in certain types of organizations, such as research laboratories, hospitals, and universities, the roles of staff and line are reversed.

> In full-fledged professional organizations the staff-professional line-administrator correlation, insofar as such distinctions apply at all, is reversed. Although administrative authority is suitable for the major goal activities in private business, in professional organizations administrators are in charge of secondary activities; they administer *means* to the major activity carried out by professionals. In other words, to the extent that there is a staff-line relationship at all, professionals should hold the major authority and administrators the secondary staff authority. [13]

Although many organizations, particularly business and the military, attempt to differentiate between the line and staff activities, it is our view that this distinction is becoming increasingly difficult to justify. Newer organizational forms, specifically developed to ensure the integration of activities, both on a vertical and horizontal basis, may be replacing the traditional line-staff form. While organizations with a uniform technology and operating in a stable environment may still find the differentiation of activities in terms of line and staff meaningful, organizations with dynamic technology and changing environment are finding this concept obsolete.

We have looked at some of the ways in which organizations differentiate activities. It appears that in all forms of complex organizations there has been a continual *trend toward the differentiation of activities into specialized subsystems*. Part of this has been a consequence of increased size, but even more significant has been the growing need for more specialization within organizations.

NASA Organization Structure

The National Aeronautics and Space Administration (NASA) provides an excellent example of the vertical and horizontal differentiation of organizational activities. NASA was established in 1958 as a civilian agency of the federal government to plan and conduct space exploration for peaceful purposes. In early 1961 the national space program was changed dramatically with the announcement of the objective of a manned moon landing and return by 1970, the Apollo program. This major policy

---

[13] Amitai Etzioni, *Modern Organizations,* © 1964, p. 81. Reprinted by permission of Prentice-Hall, Inc., Englewood Cliffs, N.J.

National Aeronautics and Space Administration

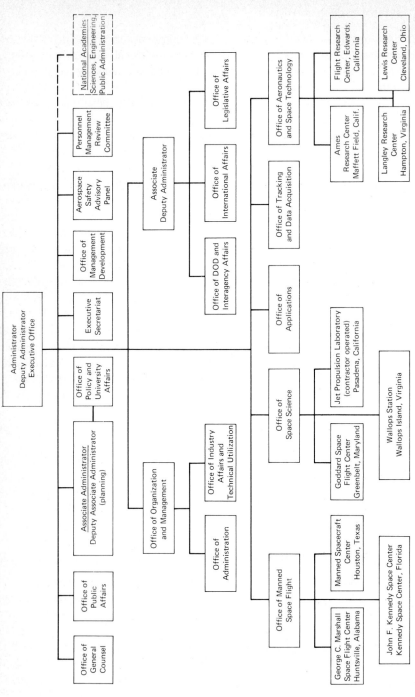

FIGURE 9.2 ORGANIZATION OF THE NATIONAL AERONAUTICS AND SPACE ADMINISTRATION (*NASA Authorization for Fiscal Year 1973*, Hearings before the Committee on Aeronautical and Space Sciences, U.S. Senate, 92d Cong., 2d Sess., 1972, p. 134)

decision affected NASA's entire operation. During the 1960s NASA's yearly budget was in excess of $5 billion, and the number of direct employees was over 34,000. In addition, approximately 300,000 people employed by industry, universities, and research organizations were working on NASA projects.

Since the successful landing of Apollo 11 on the moon and the safe return of the astronauts to Earth in August 1969, NASA's activities have been gradually scaled down to an estimated expenditure level of $3 billion in fiscal year 1973. However, this still represents a major national commitment of resources.

The NASA organization structure was adapted to the requirements of rapidly changing technology and many diverse programs. NASA's overall program structure includes five major areas: manned space flight, space science, applications, tracking and data acquisition, and aeronautics and space technology (see Figure 9.2). These program areas are supported by a complex of functional activities reporting to the office of the administrator on the strategic level (relating NASA to its external environmental system—including the Department of Defense, Congress, universities, industry, and society).

Figure 9.3 shows a more detailed organization of the Office of Manned Space Flight. This is the program level within the NASA organization. The Apollo program (manned lunar landing) represented the major effort of this office for a number of years. With the completion of Apollo 17, the last manned lunar landing, this program was phased out. Skylab, the country's first manned orbital space station, and the more sophisticated Space Shuttle and Space Station represent a major part of current and

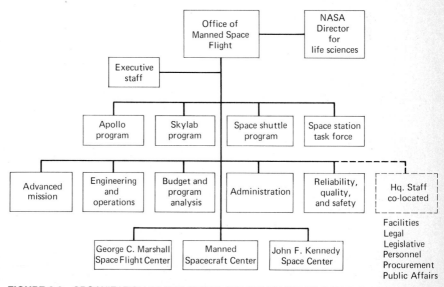

FIGURE 9.3   ORGANIZATION OF THE OFFICE OF MANNED SPACE FLIGHT (*NASA Authorization for Fiscal Year 1973,* Hearings before the Committee on Aeronautical and Space Sciences, U.S. Senate, 92d Cong., 2d Sess., 1972, p. 135)

National Aeronautics and Space Administration, George C. Marshall Space Flight Center

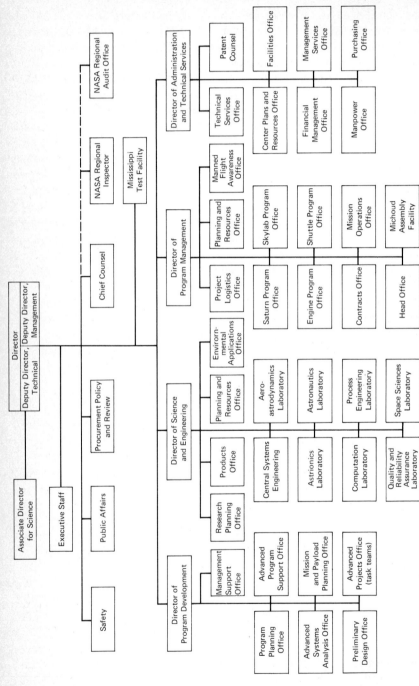

F!GURE 9.4 ORGANIZATION OF THE GEORGE C. MARSHALL SPACE FLIGHT CENTER (*1973 NASA Authorization*, Part 4, Hearings before the Committee on Science and Astronautics, U.S. House, 92d Cong., 2d Sess., 1972, p. 288)

future effort. In addition to these program activities there are a number of functional specialists reporting to the administrator of the Office of Manned Space Flight who develop broad policies and evaluate the effectiveness of the functional efforts on all programs. The technical task performance is carried out in the three space centers.

Figure 9.4 provides a detailed chart for one of these space centers, the George C. Marshall Space Flight Center in Huntsville, Alabama. This center is responsible for the management of all activities leading to the design, development, production, test, and delivery of four major operating elements: program development, science and engineering, program management, and administrative and technical services. The various activities are also supported by industrial contractors. Therefore, in addition to the organization structure represented by these three charts, hundreds of industrial firms are integrated into the various NASA programs.

These charts indicate the three major vertical levels in the NASA organization—the office of the administrator, the five program areas, and the field centers. However, the extent of the horizontal differentiation is not indicated. For example, each of the other four major program areas in the NASA structure has a lower-level organization structure similar to that of the Office of Manned Space Flight. It would have required many more pages to illustrate the total organization structure for NASA. However, the charts do illustrate the substantial differentiation—both vertical and horizontal—for a complex organization. This increased differentiation of activities has magnified the problems of coordination.

INTEGRATION OF ORGANIZATIONAL ACTIVITIES

The second overall consideration in the design of organization structures is that of coordination of activities. "*Integration* is defined as the process of achieving unity of effort among the various subsystems in the accomplishment of the organization's task."[14] Through the processes of vertical and horizontal differentiation the activities required for organizational performance are separated. They then have to be integrated. The requirements of the environment and the technical system often determine the degree of coordination required. In some organizations, it is possible to separate activities in such a way as to minimize these requirements. This is typically true of chain store operations where each individual store unit has substantial autonomy. In other organizations, particularly those departmentalized functionally, integration is more important.

It is important to recognize the interaction between the need to specialize activities and the requirements for integration. The more differentiation of activities and specialization of labor, the more difficult the problems of coordination.

> Both horizontal and vertical differentiation present organizations with control, communication, and coordination problems. Subunits along either axis are

---

[14] Lawrence and Lorsch, op. cit., p. 4.

nuclei that are differentiated from adjacent units and the total organization according to horizontal or vertical factors. The greater the differentiation, the greater the potentiality for difficulties in control, coordination, and communications. [15]

Bases of Coordination

Organizations typically establish several different mechanisms for achieving coordination. Litterer suggests three primary means: through the hierarchy, the administrative system, and voluntary activities. [16] In *hierarchical* coordination, the various activities are linked together by placing them under a central authority. In Figure 9.1, the major functions are coordinated by the president. In the simple organization, this form of coordination might be sufficient. However, in the complex organizations such as NASA with many levels and numerous specialized departments, hierarchical coordination becomes more difficult. Although the typical pyramidal chart indicates that there is one central position which is a focal point for coordination of all the activities, this is impossible for the larger organization. It would be difficult for a top-level executive to cope with all the coordinating problems that might come up through the hierarchy. There are also major problems of communication up and down the hierarchy which make it difficult for the individual at the top to have the information required for the coordination of activities at lower levels. This is particularly true when there are many layers in the organization. Thus, coordination through the hierarchical structure must be supplemented by other means.

The *administrative* system provides a second mechanism for coordination of activities. "A great deal of coordinative effort in organization is concerned with a horizontal flow of work of a routine nature. *Administrative systems* are formal procedures designed to carry out much of this routine coordinative work automatically." [17] Many work procedures such as memos with routing slips help coordinate efforts of different operating units. To the extent that these procedures can be programmed or routinized, it is not necessary to establish specific structural means for coordination. For nonroutine and nonprogrammable events, specific units such as committees may be required to provide integration.

A third type of coordination is through *voluntary means*. "The individual or group of individuals sees a need, finds a program, and applies it when deemed necessary." [18] Much of the coordination may depend upon the willingness and ability of individuals or groups to voluntarily find means to integrate their activities with other organizational participants. Achieving voluntary coordination is one of the most important yet difficult problems of the manager. Voluntary coordination requires that the individual have

---

[15] Richard H. Hall, *Organizations: Structure and Process*, Prentice-Hall, Inc., Englewood Cliffs, N.J., 1972, p. 146.
[16] Joseph A. Litterer, *The Analysis of Organizations*, John Wiley & Sons, Inc., New York, 1965, pp. 223–232.
[17] Ibid., p. 230.
[18] Ibid., p. 223.

sufficient knowledge of organizational goals, adequate information concerning the specific problem of coordination, and the motivation to do something on his own.

The problems of integration for the organization with a stable environment, a constant technology, and routine activities are substantially different from those for the organization facing rapidly changing environmental and technological forces. The stable organization can rely upon the hierarchical structure and established procedures to ensure coordination. The organization facing change must develop different mechanisms for integration.

Development of Means of Integration

Problems of integrating diverse activities in complex organizations have stimulated the development of many coordinative mechanisms. One approach to integrating activities is the committee. Committees typically are made up of members from a number of different departments or functional areas and are concerned with problems requiring coordination. Many business organizations have established executive committees at the corporate level to provide integration. [19] The use of committees for purposes of coordination is a well-established approach in other institutions such as universities and hospitals. Committees can be viewed as a means for the organization to achieve coordination between diverse groups.

Additional means for integration have developed in many organizations. Lawrence and Lorsch studied six organizations operating in the chemical processing industry to determine how they achieved integration. These organizations used a technology that required highly differentiated and specialized activities but also a major degree of integration among them. [20] The study was concerned with how organizations achieve both substantial differentiation and tight integration when these forces seem paradoxical. They found that successful companies used task forces, teams, and project offices to achieve coordination. There was a tendency to formalize coordinative activities which had developed informally and voluntarily.

In the most successful organizations, the influence of the integrators stemmed from their professional competence rather than from their formal position. They were successful as integrators because of their specialized knowledge and because they represented a central source of information in the operation. These results suggest that it is possible for the complex organization to achieve both differentiation of activities and effective integration but that new organizational arrangements are required to do so.

Others have recommended new structural forms to help with the problems of

---

[19] For a discussion of different types of committees in business organizations, see Ernest Dale, *Organization,* American Management Association, New York, 1967, chap. 10, "Coordination Through Committee," pp. 163–178.

[20] Lawrence and Lorsch, op. cit., pp. 1–47. For a detailed look at the relationship between differentiation and integration in a number of other organizations, see Paul R. Lawrence and Jay W. Lorsch, *Organization and Environment,* Division of Research, Graduate School of Business Administration, Harvard University, Boston, 1967.

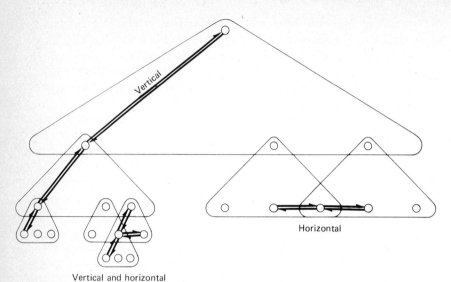

Vertical and horizontal

FIGURE 9.5 LINKING-PIN PATTERNS

integration. Likert says, "Increases in functionalization, in turn, make effective coordination both more necessary and even more difficult."[21] He suggests that one mechanism for achieving integration is by having people serve as "linking pins" between the various units in the organization (see Figure 9.5). Horizontally, there are certain organizational participants who are members of two separate groups and serve as coordinating agents between them. On the vertical basis, individuals serve as linking pins between their own level and those above and below. Thus, through this system of linking pins, the "voluntary coordination" necessary to make the dynamic system operate effectively is achieved. This constitutes a multiple, overlapping group structure in the organization. Likert says,

> To perform the intended coordination well a fundamental requirement must be met. The entire organization must consist of a multiple, overlapping group structure with *every* work group using group decision-making processes skillfully. This requirement applies to the functional, product, and service departments. An organization meeting this requirement will have an effective interaction-influence system through which the relevant communications flow readily, the required influence is exerted laterally, upward, and downward, and the motivational forces needed for coordination are created.[22]

---

[21] Rensis Likert, *The Human Organization,* McGraw-Hill Book Company, New York, 1967, p. 156.
[22] Ibid., p. 167.

ELABORATION OF STRUCTURE

One characteristic of large-scale organizations in every field of endeavor has been the increased elaboration and complexity of structure. This is true for business enterprises as well as hospitals, universities, and local, state, and federal governmental (including military) organizations. Although size may be a contributing factor to this elaboration, other forces are also significant.

Impact of Sociocultural Environment

A number of writers have investigated the relationship between the sociocultural environment and organization structure. For example, Stinchcombe suggests that firms founded during the nineteenth century have a different structure than do automotive plants and other companies founded during the twentieth century. He says, "Extensive 'staff' departments made up of professionals trained in colleges and universities do not appear in industries founded before the twentieth century, while practically all industries whose organizational forms were developed within this century have extensive staff departments." [23] The specific structural form depends upon the social, cultural, environmental forces prevailing at the time the organization is established. Even though modifications are made over time, organizations seem to retain a strong flavor of their original form. He also suggests that organization structure cannot precede developments in the sociocultural environment which makes the particular forms possible.

> The organizational inventions that can be made at a particular time in history depend on the social technology available at the time. Organizations which have purposes that can be efficiently reached with the socially possible organizational forms tend to be founded during the period in which they become possible. Then, both because they can function effectively with those organizational forms, and because the forms tend to become institutionalized, the basic structure of the organization tends to remain relatively stable. [24]

There is substantial evidence to verify Stinchcombe's thesis. For example, the organization structure for NASA is significantly different from that of older governmental agencies. It has substantially more differentiation and specialization of activities and also has developed different means for achieving integration, such as program orientation. NASA's organization is very dependent upon forces in the sociocultural environment. It would have been impossible to adopt the current structure without having highly trained technical specialists available in large numbers from our universities.

Forces in the task environment are likely to have the greatest impact on structure at the strategic level in the organization. This level is in direct interaction with external

---

[23] Arthur L. Stinchcombe, "Social Structure and Organizations," in James G. March (ed.), *Handbook of Organizations,* Rand McNally & Company, Chicago, 1965, pp. 143-144.
[24] Ibid., p. 153.

influences and is affected more than the coordinative and operating subsystems. For example, organizations typically establish separate departments to deal with relevant components of their task environment—sales, purchasing, public relations, and personnel recruitment.

The basic structural design of multinational corporations is strongly influenced by the differing cultures in which the organization operates. [25] It cannot simply transplant its domestic operations to a foreign country, but must adapt its goals, structure, and managerial approach to the different culture.

Structural Evolution in Industrial Organizations

For large-scale industrial organizations, certain patterns are evident in the structural changes that have occurred over periods of time. Chandler states that as firms developed new strategies in response to the changing social and economic environment, basic changes in structure have been required. [26] In an intensive study of four large corporations, E. I. du Pont de Nemours & Co., General Motors Corporation, Standard Oil Company of New Jersey, and Sears, Roebuck and Company, supported by a survey of seventy other large industrial firms, he found certain evolutionary patterns of structure. Changing population, income, technology, and other forces in the environment have led to the expansion of these firms into new fields. This strategy of diversification and expansion has required major modifications in structure. ''A new strategy required a new or at least refashioned structure if the enlarged enterprise was to operate efficiently. . . . Unless new structures are developed to meet new administrative needs which result from an expansion of a firm's activities into new areas, functions, or product lines, the technological, financial, and personnel economies of growth and size cannot be realized.'' [27]

The pattern of development of large industrial enterprises led to the adoption of a multidivisional structure where the central corporate office plans and coordinates the activities of a number of operating divisions and makes allocations of personnel, facilities, funds, and other resources. The actual operations of the organization are decentralized to the operating divisions, which have a substantial degree of autonomy. This structural form has been the typical pattern adopted in the past several decades. This evolution is illustrated later in the chapter with a discussion of the Boeing Company.

The development of large-scale conglomerates in recent years has resulted in further structural modifications. Organizations such as International Telephone and Telegraph (ITT), Gulf and Western Industries, Litton Industries, and Textron have grown tremendously by encompassing within their structures a number of previously unrelated businesses in different industries. They have accumulated vast financial resources and have spread their risks through expansion into many diverse fields.

---

[25] Lawrence E. Fouraker and John M. Stopford, ''Organizational Structure and Multinational Strategy,'' *Administrative Science Quarterly,* June 1968, pp. 47–64; and Hans Schollhammer, ''Organization Structures of Multinational Corporations,'' *Academy of Management Journal,* September 1971, pp. 345–366.
[26] Alfred D. Chandler, Jr., *Strategy and Structure,* The M.I.T. Press, Cambridge, Mass., © 1962.
[27] Ibid., pp. 15–16.

The structural forms of these conglomerates are usually quite different from the older diversified organizations such as General Motors and Du Pont. They have grown through acquisition and merger rather than through internal expansion. Typically they have much smaller corporate headquarters staffs and do not attempt to tightly control the operating units or to coordinate activities among them. [28] Allen suggests the following characteristics for conglomerates:

> Conglomerates have several organizational characteristics which make them a unique corporate form: diversity, comparatively simple integrative devices, pooled interdependence, major subunits which are both self-contained and autonomous to a considerable degree, and interunit coordinative requirements that center mainly around corporate-divisional relationships. [29]

The conglomerates have carried differentiation of activities to an extreme. However, they have generally adopted a loose structure which does not require substantial coordination between the different operating units. Integration is achieved primarily through corporate-divisional interactions with minimum division-to-division integration. The basic strategy is to achieve integration over broad financial and other policies at the strategic level but with very limited attempts to achieve integration between the coordinative and operating subsystems of the different divisions. [30]

Growth of Administrative Structure

There has been substantial research to determine the primary causal factors determining organization structure. We have suggested earlier that the nature of the technical subsystem has a primary impact upon structure at the operating level whereas environmental influences are more important in determining the structure at the strategic level. Two other important factors influencing structure are *size* of the organization and *complexity* of operations. [31]

The research findings relating structure to organizational size are not conclusive. Some have concluded that size is one of the major determinants of the structure of organizations. [32] Others have argued that size is not a critical factor in determining structural form. [33] Almost all researchers do agree that larger organizations have more

---

[28] Norman A. Berg, "What's Different about Conglomerate Management?" *Harvard Business Review,* November–December 1969, pp. 112–120.

[29] Stephen A. Allen, III, "Corporate-Divisional Relationships in Highly Diversified Firms," in Jay W. Lorsch and Paul R. Lawrence (eds.), *Studies in Organization Design,* Richard D. Irwin, Inc., and the Dorsey Press, Homewood, Ill., 1970, p. 22.

[30] Ibid., pp. 31–33.

[31] Hall, op. cit., pp. 109–171.

[32] Peter M. Blau and Richard A. Schoenherr, *The Structure of Organizations,* Basic Books, Inc., Publishers, New York, 1971, pp. 56–62, and D. S. Pugh, D. J. Hickson, C. R. Hinings, and C. Turner, "The Context of Organization Structures," *Administrative Science Quarterly,* March 1969, pp. 91–114.

[33] Richard H. Hall, J. Eugene Haas, and Norman J. Johnson, "Organizational Size, Complexity, and Formalization," *American Sociological Review,* December 1967, pp. 903–912.

complex and elaborated structures. However, there may be other intervening variables, such as technology and complexity, that are also characteristics of large organizations. For example, NASA has a very complex structure, but this may be due more to the nature of the technology and environmental forces than to size alone.

The research on complexity appears to be more conclusive. There is substantial evidence suggesting that the more differentiated and diverse the activities of the organization and the more integration required, the more complex the structure. "There is a strong tendency for organizations to become more complex as their own activities and the environment around them becomes more complex." [34]

There is a general view that as organizations increase in size, the number of administrative personnel increases more than proportionately. However, research findings suggest that, if anything, the ratio of administrative personnel to operative personnel decreases. [35] However, there is a relationship between the number of administrative personnel and the complexity of operations. In a survey of forty-one industries, Rushing found that the factor of size alone did not lead to an increase in the proportion of administrative personnel; however, the factor of complexity was directly related to the relative size of the administrative force. [36] These findings are consistent with the view that as an organization increases in specialization and complexity, the scope of the managerial coordination problems increases. Therefore, it seems logical that the number of people engaged in administrative tasks would also increase.

Within the administrative group there are three primary subgroups: management, clerical, and professional personnel. Management provides coordination through the managerial hierarchy. For professional personnel, the primary coordinative mechanism is expertise and knowledge. Clerical personnel are concerned with coordination of work flow and procedural communications. As complexity increases in the organization, the relative number of people in the professional and clerical subgroups increases more than that in the managerial group.

> With increases in the division of labor, managerial activities may be increasingly supplemented with the activities of clerical and professional personnel. Thus, relative to managerial authority and supervision, formal communication and professional authority may become increasingly important in coordination as industries become increasingly complex. Decisions may be made and coordination may be effected less and less on the basis of direct observation of the work process by the managerial hierarchy and more and more indirectly on the basis of information processed by professional and clerical personnel. [37]

---

[34] Hall, *Organizations: Structure and Process,* op. cit., p. 163.
[35] For a discussion of the research on this relationship, see William A. Rushing, "The Effects of Industry Size and Division of Labor on Administration," *Administrative Science Quarterly,* September 1967, pp. 273–295.
[36] Ibid., p. 273.
[37] Ibid., p. 292. Also see William A. Rushing, "Two Patterns of Industrial Administration," *Human Organization,* Spring–Summer 1967, p. 37.

These findings suggest that with the growing complexity and elaboration of organizations, different forms of integration may be utilized. Increasingly, coordination through professional authority and standard operating procedures maintained by clerical personnel may serve as substitutes for coordination through the managerial hierarchy.

HORIZONTAL AND DIAGONAL RELATIONSHIPS

Most organization charts are drawn to emphasize the vertical hierarchy and superior-subordinate relationships. Very few indicate horizontal interactions, those integrative activities which flow between departments, units, or individuals at approximately the same level.

> Horizontal relationships are those whose functions are not primarily the passing down of orders or the passing up of information and whose nature and characteristics are not primarily determined by the fact that one actor is superior to the other in the organization's hierarchy. The function of horizontal relationships is to facilitate the solution of problems arising from division of labor, and their nature and characteristics are determined by the participants having different organizational subgoals but interdependent activities that need to intermesh. [38]

As organizations have become more complex, it has been impossible to provide the necessary coordination through the vertical hierarchy. For example, in the modern hospital, a great many horizontal interactions are required. Patient treatment may involve a number of departments and specialized units, many of which are highly technical. It would be impossible for any single superior to coordinate all the activities required. As Sayles and Strauss say, "The modern organization depends on lateral relationships precisely because there are so many specialized points of view and so many required contacts that no single manager could handle the communication flow alone." [39]

In the industrial organization, the need for establishing effective horizontal relationships is also important. For example, the required interaction between product research and manufacturing, between sales and inventory control, and between advertising and finance is evident. Increasingly, new organizational units such as operations research groups and data processing centers have been established. They can succeed only if they are able to establish effective horizontal relationships with numerous other units in the organization.

---

[38] Henry A. Landsberger, "The Horizontal Dimension in Bureaucracy," *Administrative Science Quarterly,* December 1961, p. 300.
[39] Leonard R. Sayles and George Strauss, *Human Behavior in Organizations,* Prentice-Hall, Inc., Englewood Cliffs, N.J., 1966, p. 424.

In a study of 142 purchasing agents in different firms, Strauss found that the relationships between purchasing and other departments could not be understood in terms of traditional superior-subordinate or line-staff concepts. The purchasing agents' internal relationships were almost entirely lateral. "They are with other functional departments of about the same rank in the organizational hierarchy—departments such as production scheduling, quality control, engineering, and the like. Most agents receive relatively little attention from their superiors; they must act on their own, with support being given by higher management only in exceptional cases." [40] While technically the purchasing department is classified as a staff department, it is much more involved than merely advising and for all practical purposes has authority over many of the work-flow processes. Many conflicts developed between purchasing and other departments, and purchasing agents developed mechanisms for their resolution. Conflicts were rarely referred up the hierarchy to be resolved by a common superior. The purchasing agents used other means, primarily based upon their own expertise and personal influence, for coordinating activities with other departments.

Developing Communication Networks

Establishing effective means for dealing with the problems of horizontal integration in complex organizations is perhaps the single most important structural problem. Traditionally, lateral communication has been left to the informal structure. However, with increasing differentiation and the growing need for integration, more consideration has to be given to these issues. As a result of their research on the relationship between organization structure and communication, Hage, Aiken, and Marrett made the following conclusion.

> Together these findings suggest that, as organizational structure becomes more diversified and, in particular, as personal specialization increases, the volume of communication increases because of the necessity of co-ordinating the diverse occupational specialists. The major direction of this increased flow of information is horizontal, especially cross-departmental communications at the same status level. . . . These findings suggest that as organizations become more diversified, and more specialized (personal specialization, not task specialization) and more differentiated, they have to rely less on a system of programmed interactions to achieve the necessary linkages between parts of the organization and more on a system of reciprocal information flows to achieve co-ordination. We have also suggested that such organizations would more likely rely on socialization rather than use of sanctions as a key mecha-

---

[40] George Strauss, "Tactics of Lateral Relationship: The Purchasing Agent," *Administrative Science Quarterly,* September 1962, p. 162.
[41] Jerald Hage, Michael Aiken, and Cora Bagley Marrett, "Organization Structure and Communications," *American Sociological Review,* October 1971, pp. 869–870.

In recent years many new structural mechanisms have developed to help provide better communication networks not only vertically but horizontally and diagonally as well. Committees, linking-pin arrangements, and others have been utilized. We cannot cover all of the forms in detail but can illustrate such structural arrangements with a more detailed discussion of program management.

PROGRAM MANAGEMENT

The program management approach is geared to changing managerial requirements in the research, development, procurement, and utilization of large-scale military, space, and civilian projects. With the advent of newer, more complex programs, the military services as well as other government agencies and private companies have had to adapt their organizational structures away from traditional functional arrangements. The pressures of accelerating technology and short lead times have made it necessary to establish some formalized managerial agency to provide overall integration of the many diverse functional activities.

Various terms have been used to designate these integrated management functions such as *systems management, program management, weapon system management, product management,* and *project management.* Although there are some differences among these terms and their meanings, they have a thread of commonality—the integrated management of a specific program on a systems basis. ''The project manager acts as a focal point for the concentration of attention on the major problems of the project. This concentration forces the channeling of major program considerations through an individual who has the proper perspective to integrate relative matters of cost, time, technology, and total product compatibility.'' [42] This approach has been used in many major weapon systems and space programs. [43] For example, the Air Force sets up a system program office wherein the Air Force manager has the major responsibilities for integration of activities. The Navy established a program management type of organization in the form of the Special Projects Office for the Polaris system. The National Aeronautics and Space Administration has also used this approach in its more complicated projects, including the manned space flight program (see Figures 9.2, 9.3, and 9.4). This approach is being used throughout industry as well. [44]

Functions of Program Manager

A program manager is responsible for organizing and controlling all activities involved in achieving the ultimate objective. He is usually superimposed upon the functional organization, creating new and complex relationships. This structural approach re-

---

[42] David I. Cleland, ''Why Project Management?'' *Business Horizons,* Winter 1964, p. 83.
[43] For a discussion of the evolution of the program management concept, see Fremont E. Kast and James E. Rosenzweig, ''Organization and Management of Space Programs,'' in Frederick I. Ordway, III (ed.), *Advances in Space Science and Technology,* Academic Press, Inc., New York, 1965, pp. 273-364; and Richard A. Johnson, Fremont E. Kast, and James E. Rosenzweig, *The Theory and Management of Systems,* 3d ed., McGraw-Hill Book Company, 1973, chap. 13, ''Program Management,'' pp. 388-425.
[44] For an extensive report on project management in the aerospace industry, see George A. Steiner and William G. Ryan, *Industrial Project Management,* The Macmillan Company, New York, 1968.

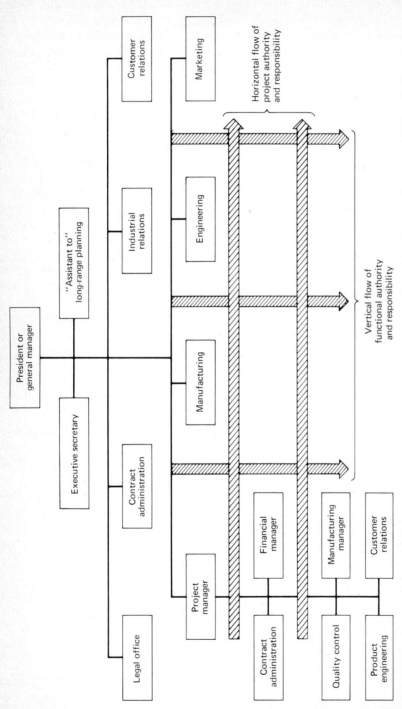

FIGURE 9.6 FUNCTIONAL ORGANIZATION WITH PROJECT MANAGER IN A LINE CAPACITY (David I. Cleland and William R. King, *Systems Analysis and Project Management*, McGraw-Hill Book Company, New York, 1968, p. 177)

quires organizational modifications, emphasizes the integrative aspects, and requires the development of effective horizontal and diagonal information-decision networks.

There are various organizational approaches to program management. In the "staff" form the program manager is an adviser to the chief executive or general manager—he has little authority on his own. The functional managers retain the primary authority. At the other end of the spectrum, the program manager is granted complete authority over all the activities necessary to carry out the program. This is the approach used in many major military or space projects. Figure 9.3 shows that all the operational activities report directly to the Office of Manned Space Flight.

The matrix form is a compromise between these two extremes (see Figure 9.6). The functional managers such as manufacturing, engineering, and marketing are responsible to the general manager for their special activities. The project manager reports directly to the general manager on a line basis. He may have personnel assigned to his project from the various functional departments. Under the matrix form there are two primary flows of authority—the vertical flow of authority from the various functional managers and the horizontal flow of project authority.

Authority Relationships

The essence of program management is that it is interfunctional and is often in conflict with the normal organization structure. Thus, where the program management approach is used, there is a natural conflict system. [45] Instead of an organization operating under the traditional view with a well-defined hierarchical structure, a unity of command, and clear-cut authority and responsibility relationships, the system is much more dynamic and less structured.

The program manager cannot operate effectively if he relies solely on the formal authority of his position. Success is more likely to depend on his ability to influence other organizational members. Because he is a focal point in the operation, he does have informational and communications inputs which provide him with a strong basis of influence. "One of the project manager's greatest sources of authority involves the manner in which he builds alliances in his environment—with his peers, associates, superiors, subordinates, and other interested parties. The building of alliances supplements his legal authority; it is the process through which the project manager can translate disagreement and conflict into authority (or influence power) to make his decisions stand." [46]

The program manager's authority and influence flow in different directions from hierarchical authority. They flow horizontally across vertical superior-subordinate relationships existing within the functional organization. Throughout the program, person-

---

[45] For an interesting discussion of some of the human problems created by program management see Clayton Reeser, "Some Potential Human Problems of the Project Form of Organization," *Academy of Management Journal,* December 1969, pp. 459–467.
[46] David I. Cleland and William R. King, *Systems Analysis and Project Management,* McGraw-Hill Book Company, New York, 1968, p. 239.

nel at various levels and in many functions must contribute their efforts. For each new program, lateral information-decision networks must be established which differ significantly from the existing networks based upon the established structure. The organization should be sufficiently flexible to allow for evolving relationships and networks as program requirements change.

Other Characteristics

The program manager's task is finite. He takes a project from the beginning and works it through to completion. Once completed, his task is over, and the program management group can be reassigned to new activities. Thus, by its very nature the function is temporary. The organizational structure is dynamic, and people must be prepared to accept change. The emphasis upon flexibility rather than permanency of relationships strongly affects the psychosocial and managerial systems.

The program manager and his staff usually serve in an important boundary-spanning capacity. Many activities, particularly in military and space programs, require interorganizational coordination. The program manager is the central point of the information-decision system regarding program activities, and he is the natural focal point for interorganizational coordination. "Rarely does the project manager find that the project activities are limited to his own organization; he usually must work with participants (or contributors) outside the company. He therefore has superior knowledge of the relative roles and functions of the individual parts of the project which makes him a logical person to take part in major interorganizational decisions affecting the project." [47]

Frequently the introduction of the program approach creates additional organizational units and more management positions as well. In several companies which adopted program management, Middleton found a significant increase in the number of departments, the number of vice presidents and directors, and the number of second-level supervisors. [48]

Although program management has been used primarily in the defense and aerospace sectors, it has found increasing application in many other areas. Steiner and Ryan suggest forces that will influence this trend: "Our projection of greater use in the commercial world is predicated on several bases: increased sophistication of customer needs, increased complexity and size of business, increased pace of technological change, increased involvement of the Government as a customer in nondefense areas, and the changing needs of people in organizations." [49] Program management will be used increasingly in noncommercial sectors for dealing with problems such as transportation, urban renewal, and pollution control. It is one of the most important innovations in the structure of organizations.

---

[47] Ibid., p. 165.
[48] C. J. Middleton, "How to Set up a Project Organization," *Harvard Business Review,* March-April 1967, pp. 81–82.
[49] Steiner and Ryan, op. cit., pp. 158–159.

AN EXAMPLE OF ORGANIZATION STRUCTURE

Because of the great diversity among industrial organizations it would be impossible to set forth a single structure to represent American industry. For purposes of illustration we are showing the structure represented by organization charts for a large company in the aerospace industry, the Boeing Company.

This company is one of the largest industrial corporations in the United States, ranking among the upper twenty-five. [50] In 1972 the company had sales of over $3 billion, more than $2.4 billion in assets, and over 60,000 employees. It is one of the major firms in the aerospace industry and has been the contractor for many of the nation's major defense and space programs, such as the B-52 airplanes, the Minuteman missile system, the Saturn booster program, and the Lunar Rover. It is the world's largest producer of commercial aircraft, including the 707, 727, 737, and 747 series.

Over the past several decades the organization structure has become increasingly complex through continual differentiation and elaboration. This resulted from the expansion of the company into a number of new fields and program efforts and from the increasingly complex technology which requires greater specialization. One of the basic trends has been the vertical elaboration of the structure through the establishment of major groups which are composed of several product divisions. Figure 9.7 shows the overall corporate structure and the major groups and divisions.

The corporate headquarters, through the management council, establishes major policies and plans, coordinates the activities of the operating groups and divisions, and allocates personnel, facilities, funds, and other resources. The actual operations of the company are decentralized. The headquarters staff is composed of a number of functional vice-presidents who establish broad policies and coordinate the group and divisional efforts relating to their functions. They carry on many activities which are important to the corporation as a whole.

The organization structure for the Commercial Airplane Group is shown in Figure 9.8. This is the largest group, with over 25,000 employees, and is engaged in the production of commercial and military aircraft and support systems. It is divided into three divisions.

Figure 9.9 shows in more detail the structure of the largest division in this group, the 707/727/737 Division. This division has all of the resources and facilities necessary to carry out its three major program efforts.

These charts indicate the vertical levels in the organization. They do not, however, show all of the program activities in the total structure. There are six other groups and divisions in the corporation which are involved in many different programs. For example, the company is designing and building a spacecraft for a dual mission to Venus and Mercury as part of the Mariner series sponsored by NASA. It has programs in water purification and desalination, solid waste disposal, urban rapid transit systems, automated personal rapid transit systems, and commercial hydrofoils. Boeing Computer

---

[50] "The 500 Largest U.S. Industrial Corporations," *Fortune*, May 1972, p. 190.

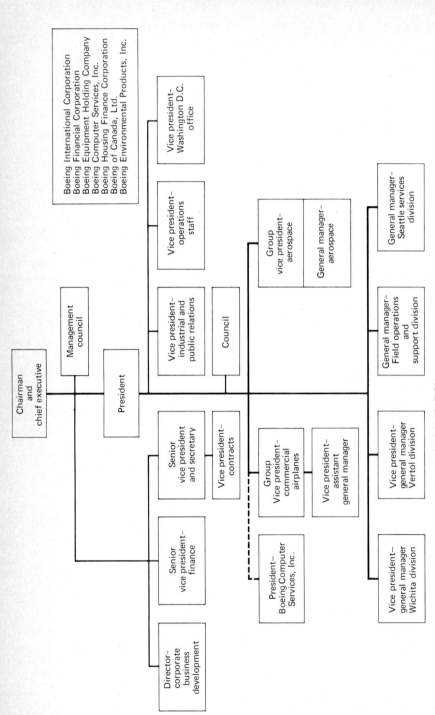

FIGURE 9.7 THE BOEING COMPANY, CORPORATE ORGANIZATION

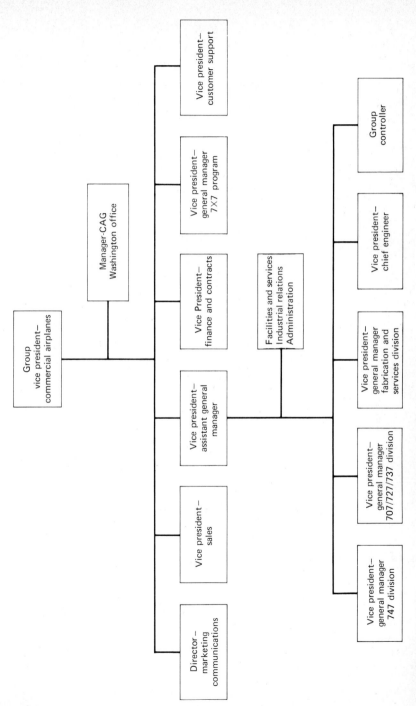

FIGURE 9.8 THE BOEING COMPANY, COMMERCIAL AIRPLANE GROUP

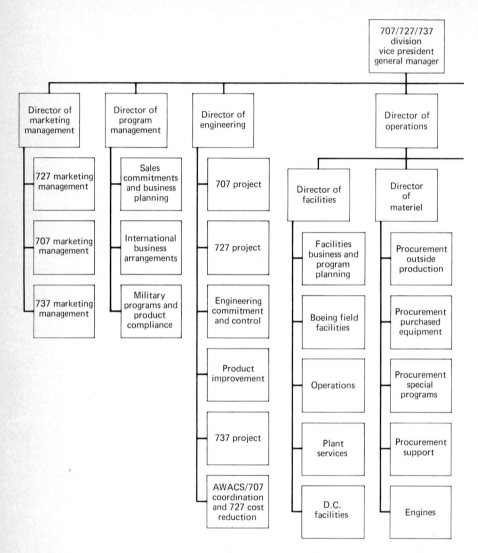

FIGURE 9.9 THE BOEING COMPANY, COMMERCIAL AIRPLANE GROUP, 707/727/737 DIVISION

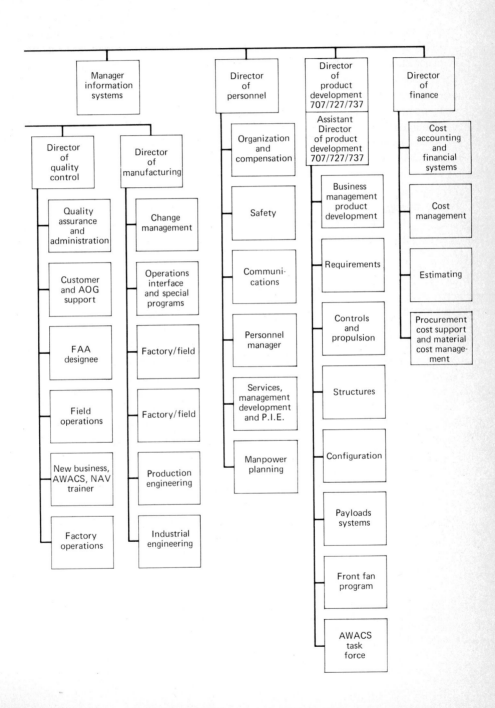

Services, Inc., is one of the nation's largest suppliers of computer services to outside users.

These charts present a general picture of the structure at one point in time. In reality, the structure is continually evolving and changing to meet new program require-ments, changing technologies, and environmental influences. There have been scores of major changes in structure over the past twenty years and hundreds of changes throughout lower levels in the organization. An important new program effort, such as the short-takeoff-and-landing (STOL) transport aircraft, requires the reassignment of many personnel and a restructuring of the organization. The organization must remain flexible in order to meet dynamic changes.

This multigroup structure with program efforts in the divisions provides for both maintenance and adaptability in the organization. The corporate headquarters operates at the strategic level and deals with environmental uncertainties. The groups and divisions are primarily concerned with specific programs. They have broad autonomy for the development of new program efforts. When the company undertakes a new program, it is possible to make the changes at the group and divisional levels without upsetting the entire structure. This approach provides for the adaptability which is vital in the dynamic aerospace industry.

DYNAMICS OF ORGANIZATION STRUCTURE

As a result of many forces most organizations undergo relatively frequent structural changes. A look at the organization of a modern metropolitan hospital will show that dramatic changes have occurred over the past two decades. Most universities are currently undergoing structural changes in order to meet the requirements of advancing knowledge.[51] In business organizations, the changes are equally dramatic. Daniel reported that in a three-year period at least two-thirds of the nation's top 100 industrial companies reported major organizational realignments.[52] He estimated that on the average, the larger industrial corporations have at least one major restructuring every two years. Increasingly, industrial organizations are accepting the necessity for chang-ing their structure as a fact of life and are establishing permanent departments charged with the responsibility for organizational analysis and planning.

The movement toward dynamic, flexible structures and away from the rigid bu-reaucratic form seems to be a trend in modern organizations. Figure 9.10 summarizes the characteristics of adaptive-organic and bureaucratic-mechanistic systems. Instead of providing for permanent, structured positions, as characteristic of the mechanistic system, the adaptive-organic system has less structuring, more frequent change of positions and roles, and more dynamic interplay among the various functions. The organic system requires more time and effort toward integration of diverse activities. The

---

[51] Francis E. Rourke and Glenn E. Brooks, *The Managerial Revolution in Higher Education,* The Johns Hopkins Press, Baltimore, 1966.
[52] D. Ronald Daniel, ''Reorganizing for Results,'' *Harvard Business Review,* November–December 1966, p. 96.

FIGURE 9.10 ORGANIZATIONAL CHARACTERISTICS OF ORGANIC AND MECHANISTIC STRUCTURES

	TYPES OF ORGANIZATION STRUCTURE	
ORGANIZATIONAL CHARACTERISTICS INDEX	ORGANIC	MECHANISTIC
Span of control	Wide	Narrow
Number of levels of authority	Few	Many
Ratio of administrative to production personnel	High	Low
Range of time span over which an employee can commit resources	Long	Short
Degree of centralization in decision making	Low	High
Proportion of persons in one unit having opportunity to interact with persons in other units	High	Low
Quantity of formal rules	Low	High
Specificity of job goals	Low	High
Specificity of required activities	Low	High
Content of communications	Advice and information	Instructions and decisions
Range of compensation	Narrow	Wide
Range of skill levels	Narrow	Wide
Knowledge-based authority	High	Low
Position-based authority	Low	High

SOURCE: Ralph M. Hower and Jay W. Lorsch, "Organizational Inputs," in John A. Seiler, *Systems Analysis in Organizational Behavior*, Richard D. Irwin, Inc., and The Dorsey Press, Homewood, Ill., 1967, p. 168.

bureaucratic-mechanistic form provides for coordination through the hierarchical structure. In the adaptive-organic form, mechanisms for horizontal and diagonal integration are established. "The function of the 'executive' thus becomes *coordinator,* or 'linking pin' between various project groups. He must be a man who can speak the diverse languages of research and who can relay information and mediate among the groups. *People will be differentiated not vertically according to rank and role but flexibly according to skill and professional training.*"[53]

Obviously, the organic form, requiring a dynamic, changing structure, will not be feasible for all organizations. Many organizations can perform most effectively with a more mechanistic structure. These two organizational forms represent polar points on a continuum. In many organizations it will be necessary to operate certain sections such as research and development by utilizing the organic system, and other sections (production operations) with a more mechanistic system. This subject will be discussed in more detail in Part 7, Comparative Analysis and Contingency Views.

A number of the organizational characteristics shown in Figure 9.10 for organic and mechanistic systems are more closely related to the psychosocial and managerial systems than to structure. These are discussed in Parts 5 and 6.

[53] Warren G. Bennis, *Changing Organizations,* McGraw-Hill Book Company, New York, 1966, p. 12.

SUMMARY

Structure may be considered as the established pattern of relationships between the components or parts of the organization. Unlike mechanical or biological systems, the structure of the social organization is not visible; it is inferred from operations.

Organizations have both formal and informal structure. The formal structure is the result of explicit decision making concerning organizational patterns and is typically expressed in charts, manuals, and position descriptions. Organization charts are usually highly simplified, abstract models of the structure and deal with a limited number of relationships.

Traditional management theorists were vitally concerned with the design of efficient organization structures. Many principles were based on experiences with stable organizations such as the military, church, and established public bureaucracies. Some of the most important of these principles were: organization specialization and the division of labor; the scalar principle; concepts of authority, responsibility, and accountability; span of control; and line and staff relationships. Many modern writers are critical of these principles; however, they are still applicable in some organizations and in parts of others.

Complex organizations are characterized by a high degree of task specialization or division of labor. This differentiation occurs in two directions—the vertical, represented by the hierarchy; and the horizontal, represented by departmentalization. Increased differentiation has magnified the problems associated with integration. Organizations have developed many mechanisms for achieving coordination, such as the formal hierarchy, the administrative system, and voluntary means. Organizations facing a changing environment and accelerating technology have found it necessary to adopt new means for ensuring integration, such as committees, task forces, coordinating teams, and program managers.

Program management has been used effectively to provide the necessary integration of activities on a total systems basis. However, it creates many problems of organizational conflict, particularly between the program and functional managers.

Most modern organizations undergo frequent changes in structure. Instead of providing for permanent, highly structured relations as characteristic of the bureaucratic-mechanistic system, the adaptive-organic organization has less structuring, more frequent change of positions and roles, and a more dynamic interplay between the various functions. Obviously, however, the organic form is not feasible for all organizations. Many organizations, operating in a stable environment and with a uniform technology, can perform more effectively by utilizing a mechanistic structure.

QUESTIONS AND PROBLEMS

1 What is the structure of an organization? How does this differ from the structure of a physical or biological system?

2 What are advantages and disadvantages of using charts to illustrate organization structure?

3 What is the distinction between the formal and informal organization?

4 Evaluate the contributions of the traditional management theorists to the concept of structure.

5 Why have large organizations increasingly differentiated their activities?

6 Why is integration becoming more important in complex organizations? Discuss alternative means for achieving integration.

7 How is it possible for an organization to achieve both greater differentiation and more effective integration?

8 Investigate a specific organization to determine how it has developed both vertical and horizontal differentiation. Evaluate the means by which this organization achieves integration.

9 Why have horizontal and diagonal relationships become so important in the modern organization?

10 What is program management, and why has it evolved? How does the ''authority'' of the program manager differ from traditional line authority?

If you dig very deeply into any problem you will get to "people."

J. Watson Wilson

Every man is in certain respects like all other men, like some other man, like no other man.

Clyde Kluckhohn and Henry A. Murray

We are not only gregarious animals, liking to be in sight of our fellows, but we have an innate propensity to get ourselves noticed, and noticed favorably, by our kind. No more fiendish punishment could be devised, were such a thing physically possible, than that one should be turned loose in a society and remain absolutely unnoticed by all the members thereof.

William James

The modern organization . . . is a medium for recouping psychological losses in a rapidly changing society.

Harry Levinson

I believe the greatest assets of a business are its human assets, and the improvement of their value is a matter of both material advantage and moral obligation.

Clarence Francis

Physical resources unused—lie inert. Coal left alone for a million years is still coal. Human resources left unutilized deteriorate.

Rupert Vance

THE PSYCHOSOCIAL SYSTEM

Individuals in social relationships constitute the psychosocial system in organizations. The general "atmosphere" is affected by many variables, some integral, others peripheral. Societal culture sets an overall framework; industry mores and practices have an impact; and many variables are peculiar to specific organizations. Technology and structure affect organizational climate, as do employee attitudes and morale. The behavioral sciences—anthropology, psychology, and sociology—have contributed significantly to our basic knowledge and understanding of organizational psychosocial systems.

In Chapter 8 we consider behavior and motivation, recognizing that the basic unit for analysis in organizations is the individual. Understanding what motivates individual behavior toward productivity is a fundamental requirement for managerial success. The need-hierarchy concept and other related models are discussed, with emphasis on self-actualization and its role in the psychosocial system of organizations.

Status and role systems are considered in Chapter 9. Here we are concerned with how individuals relate to one another in systematic ways within organizations. Societal status systems provide a framework for this analysis which can be carried to the organization level. Each status position has a related role—an expected behavior pattern for any incumbent.

In Chapter 10, we turn to the consideration of group dynamics. Understanding individual behavior is complex enough. However, the organizational atmosphere becomes even more complex when the dynamics of interpersonal relations in small groups is considered. Small groups mediate between organizations and individuals. While formal status and role systems provide relatively definite relationships for organizational participants, many informal relationships are apparent, inevitable, and necessary.

Given the complexity of the psychosocial system in organizations, management is nevertheless charged with coordinating activity toward objective accomplishment. In Chapter 11 influence systems and leadership, important for achieving such coordination, are discussed. A "means of influence" spectrum is identified—ranging from emulation, suggestion, and persuasion to coercion. Power and authority underlie influence systems and affect the appropriateness and/or effectiveness of various leadership styles.

INDIVIDUAL BEHAVIOR
AND MOTIVATION

Organizations are comprised of individuals. As the atom is basic to physics, the individual is the fundamental unit of analysis in organization theory. The behavioral sciences—anthropology, psychology, and sociology—provide much of the foundation for our understanding of individual behavior in organizations. Various psychological processes—perception, cognition, and motivation—provide the means through which people develop as personalities. The ''whole man'' concept reflects the integration of inherent and acquired characteristics. People act and react in environmental settings—cultural and organizational. Individual behavior patterns are the result of many complex factors and represent an integral and important part of the psychosocial system. In this chapter individual behavior and motivation will be discussed in terms of the following topics:

> The Individual and the Psychosocial System
> Behavior Patterns
> Personality Theory
> Individual Similarities
> Individual Differences
> Motivation and Productivity
> Hierarchy of Needs
> Two Views of People
> Motivation-Hygiene Concept
> Expectations and Performance
> Achievement Motivation
> Opportunity for Self-actualization

THE INDIVIDUAL AND THE PSYCHOSOCIAL SYSTEM

The psychosocial system in any organization is a mixture of many ingredients. The individual is the basic unit of analysis, and even by himself, a person is an extremely complex entity. Interpersonal relationships, between two or among many people, add complications. The more environmental complications introduced into the analysis, the more complex the system becomes. Simplicity may be achieved by ignoring many confounding variables; however, such a simplistic approach is not of much use to managers in understanding and predicting organizational behavior.

The psychosocial system—the individual in social relationships—can be understood in terms of motivation and behavior occurring in an environment which includes:

> Status and role systems
> Group dynamics
> Influence systems
> Leadership

Status systems serve to structure social relationships and provide a framework within which group endeavor can be coordinated toward objectives. Role systems are integrally related with status systems. Status concerns the relative prestige of a position in a structural relationship within organizations; role relates to the behavioral patterns identified or expected for a given position.

Small groups typically provide a mediating mechanism between individuals and organizations. Group dynamics—activities, interactions, and sentiments—play an important part in organizational behavior. An individual's higher-level needs (social esteem and self-actualization) are satisfied via his position in a small group or large organization.

Status and role systems, along with group dynamics, provide the setting within which motivation operates to affect individual behavior. Recognizing the complexity of the psychosocial system, managers are interested in effective ways to influence behavior and hence provide leadership to the organization.

Leadership styles are related to influence systems; they should reflect the situation, the leader and the led. The determination of an appropriate leadership style involves consideration of all elements in the psychosocial system of organizations and appraisal of the most effective ways to influence behavior.

Each of the key elements in the psychosocial system will be discussed in detail in Part 5. These human aspects, along with values, technology, and structure, provide the internal framework within which the managerial system (Part 6) functions. Our analysis turns first to individual behavior—the basic unit of organization theory.

BEHAVIOR PATTERNS

Behavior is a manner of acting; it refers to a person's conduct. Behavioral patterns are modes of conduct used by an individual in carrying out his activities. Three relatively distinct divisions in the study of human systems are apparent: the study of *anatomy* provides a view of the organization of the body; the study of *physiology* provides information with regard to the physical processes involved; and the study of *behavior* refers to the overt action patterns of individuals. [1] These various parts of the human system can be studied individually in order to gain more detailed knowledge. However, physiology cannot be understood completely apart from anatomy. The desire to behave in a certain way cannot be fulfilled if anatomical and physiological capabilities are not present. Similarly, the anatomical and physiological capacity for a particular activity does not ensure its occurrence. For example, the barriers to improved performance in activities such as athletics are often considered more psychological than physical. Given the determination to push for a "record," the body can respond more nearly to its ultimate capacity. When Roger Bannister became the first human being to run a mile in less than four minutes, his behavior was the result of the combination of anatomical, physiological, and psychological development.

Inherent or Acquired?

Are behavior patterns inherited or learned? Obviously, this question cannot be answered with a yes or no. There is a gradation of relative impact of inheritance or learning, depending on the particular facet of behavior being considered. Anatomy and physiology are relatively more inherited than psychological aspects. We inherit a range of capabilities, but the specific level of performance within that range is acquired through learning.

> The developmental range, which always does have limits, is inherited, but the point within that range is acquired. That is why the strict statement that something is *either* inherited *or* acquired becomes meaningless. Human speech is a striking and familiar example. The specifically human capacity for true speech is completely determined by genetic control of development. The particular language spoken by any one man is acquired; it is learned. [2]

Individual life experiences play an important role in modifying the psychological system.

Two parallel and interacting "evolutions," one biological and one cultural, are fundamental to behavior. Biological evolution has provided the capacity for development and a broad framework which limits or constrains the cultural evolution. However, there are wide latitudes, as evidenced by the great variety of cultures and the significant differences in degree of development. [3]

Psychologists have approached the study of individual behavior through the concept of personality—a combination of inherited characteristics and acquired behavior patterns.

---

[1] George Gaylord Simpson and Anne Rowe, "The Evolution of Behavior," in Bernard Berelson (ed.), *The Behavioral Sciences Today*, Basic Books, Inc., Publishers, New York, 1963, p. 90.

[2] Ibid., p. 95.

[3] Dwight E. Robinson, "The Evolutionary Heritage of Corporation Man: Introducing the Organizational Theory of Antony Jay," *Academy of Management Journal*, September 1972, pp. 345-353.

PERSONALITY THEORY

Personality theory has its foundations in the writings of classical scholars such as Hippocrates, Plato, and Aristotle. Philosophers over the centuries have devoted considerable attention to the nature of man and why he behaves the way he does. Psychology also has deep roots in physiology and medicine.

Personality theory has occupied a special role in the development of general psychology. It is concerned with the whole man in his total environment and it is of particular importance for organization theory and management practice. However, there is no clear-cut, well-defined body of knowledge to draw upon. A number of alternative (and sometimes conflicting) concepts have been suggested by various researchers as fundamental for personality theory. [4]

Personality Defined

Like many other terms, there are many connotations of personality. For example, we often talk in terms of the presence or absence of personality: "He has no personality." Or, "She is not much to look at, but she has a lot of personality." These usages imply that personality is equivalent to social skill or adroitness. Other common usage stresses a particular aspect, such as aggressiveness or joviality.

More technical definitions stress different views of personality:

1 The adjustment of the individual to his environment
2 The unique aspects of individual behavior
3 The "social stimulus value" of the individual
4 The specific organic characteristics which can be described and measured

Actually, all of these are important in understanding individual behavior.

An integrative approach fits with the concept of a psychosocial system. We are interested in personality and behavior as one way to integrate many complex elements into a total system for an individual. Physical, physiological, and psychological functions are fundamental. Both self-perception and the perception of others are important considerations. In short, personality represents a total, complex individual system; it is a key element in the social system; theories of personality are important inputs for organization theory; and understanding and predicting individual behavior according to personality theory is a crucial problem for practicing managers.

INDIVIDUAL SIMILARITIES

Anatomically and physiologically, human beings are quite similar. People with more or less than five fingers or toes (on one hand or foot) are rare. To be sure, structural differences are apparent between Caucasian, Oriental, and Negro races. However,

---

[4] Calvin S. Hall and Gardner Lindzey, *Theories of Personality,* John Wiley & Sons, Inc., New York, 1957.

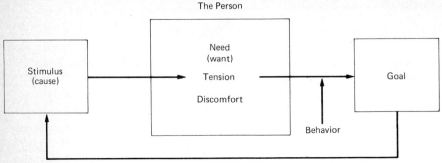

FIGURE 10.1   A BASIC MODEL OF BEHAVIOR (Harold J. Leavitt, *Managerial Psychology*, 2d ed., The University of Chicago Press, Chicago, 1964, p. 9)

even these apparent differences are slight in comparison to the basic similarities involved. Regardless of the superficial physical appearances, physiological processes are similar for all Homo sapiens.

The anatomical and physiological nature of human beings has evolved slowly over time, so slowly that change is imperceptible to any living being. Yet some long-run evolution is apparent; for example, average height has increased significantly over several generations. More individual differences are evident in psychological processes. The "generation gap" is much more apparent for overt behavior patterns than for physiological differences.

On the other hand, the process of behavior is similar for all individuals. That is, while behavior patterns may vary significantly, the process by which they occur is fundamental to all individuals. Three interrelated assumptions can be made about human behavior: [5]

1 Behavior is caused.
2 Behavior is motivated.
3 Behavior is goal-directed.

These three elements are linked together in the basic model of behavior in Figure 10.1. This model can be applied to all people, of all ages, in all cultures, and at all times.

If these three assumptions are valid, then behavior cannot be spontaneous and aimless. There must be a goal, whether explicit or implicit. Behavior toward goals is generated in reaction to a stimulus—all behavior is caused. A stimulus is filtered through a system of wants or needs which may take many forms. A lack of water causes thirst and results in behavior such as obtaining a drink of water. Feedback from the goal to the stimulus indicates the sequential nature of this process. If the goal is achieved,

---

[5] Harold J. Leavitt, *Managerial Psychology*, 2d ed., The University of Chicago Press, 1964, p. 12.

the current behavior is terminated, and the individual's attention turns to some other activity. If the goal is not achieved, the individual may partake of a second glass of water and so on until a particular need is satisfied.

This basic model of the behavior process is the same for all individuals. However, it is easy to see that actual behavior can vary significantly. Differential perception could alter the stimulus phase, for example. Needs or wants vary by individuals, and such differences can be culturally determined or learned. Variations in perception, cognition, and motivation, for example, can lead to different behavior patterns from the same or similar stimuli.

INDIVIDUAL DIFFERENCES

Many factors lead toward individual differences in behavior. Figure 10.2 shows some of the influences on individual behavior in a work situation. The actual working conditions, including physical conditions, psychological processes, and formal organizational relationships, have considerable impact on behavior. Of special interest is the effect of technology on the work situation and on behavior. Cultural norms or mores also influence general attitudes and behavior on specific tasks. Group relationships have an impact on behavior directly as well as indirectly through the managerial system. Economic incentives also affect most work situations, but their importance varies considerably, depending upon the individual involved.

Potential influences filter through personal attitudes via perception, cognition, and motivation. The effect of various events on behavior depends on how they are perceived

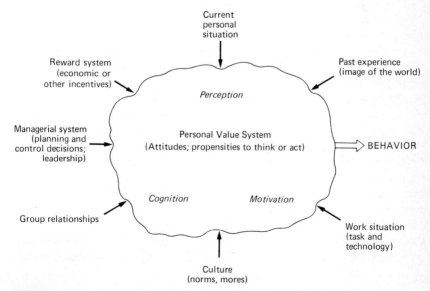

FIGURE 10.2 SOME INFLUENCES ON BEHAVIOR IN A WORK SITUATION

by the individual. Similarly, if behavior results after a period which allows thinking or problem solving, personal attitudes play an important part in fashioning the specific response. Value systems are affected significantly by total past experience and current personal situations.

This diagram of influences on behavior in a work situation could be reproduced, that is, a similar model could be developed, for other situations in which the individual is involved—family, educational, recreational, or other situations.

Perception

Perception is basic to understanding behavior because it is the means by which stimuli affect an organism or individual. A stimulus that is not perceived has no effect on behavior. Another key is that people behave on the basis of "what is perceived" rather than "what is." A direct line to "truth" is often assumed, but each person really has only one point of view based on individualistic perceptions of the real world. Some considerations can be verified in order that several or many individuals can agree on a consistent set of facts. However, in most real-life situations many conditions are not verifiable and are heavily value laden. Even when facts are established, their meaning or significance may vary considerably for different individuals.

Figure 10.3 is a model of the way perceptions are formed and hence influence individual behavior. Numerous external forces such as the stress of the situation, group pressure, and reward systems are involved. Past experience has a direct influence on interpretation of stimuli. Several basic processes (mechanisms) of perception formation can be identified—selectivity, closure, and interpretation.

The concept of *selective* perception is important because voluminous information is received and processed. Individuals select information which is supportive and satisfying. [6] They tend to ignore information which might be disturbing. For example, after purchasing a new automobile, the buyer typically will pay more attention to ads for the brand purchased and tend to ignore ads for other models. In this way, he is more likely to be satisfied with his decision. Having chosen a family physician, we tend to pay attention to any feedback in the community which indicates that our doctor is outstanding and probably number one in his graduating class. We tend to miss, ignore, or discount any information which would indicate that he was seventy-fifth in a class of seventy-five and that he might be relatively incompetent.

The same stimulus can be interpreted differently by several individuals. *Interpretation* depends on past experience and the value system of each particular person. An attitudinal set or propensity to think or act in a certain way provides a framework for interpreting various stimuli. Not only does the individual perceive selectively, he interprets the situation in ways which will be supportive.

The process of *closure* in perception formation relates to the tendency of individuals to have a complete picture of any given situation. Thus a person may perceive more

---

[6] Ibid., p. 32.

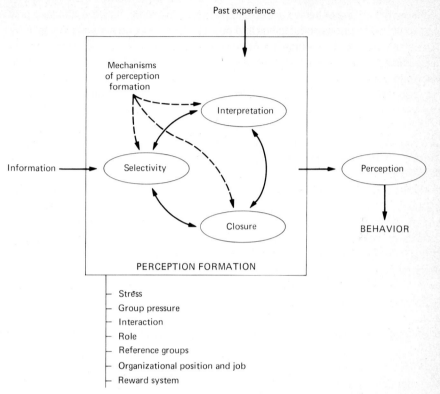

FIGURE 10.3 PERCEPTION FORMATION AND ITS EFFECT ON BEHAVIOR (Adapted from Joseph A. Litterer, *The Analysis of Organizations,* John Wiley & Sons, Inc., New York, 1965, p. 64)

than the information seems to indicate. He adds to the information input whatever seems appropiate in order to close the system and make it meaningful and supportive. Closure and interpretation have a feedback to selectivity and hence affect the functioning of this mechanism in subsequent information processing.

While there is a tendency to perceive supportive information and ignore disturbing information, it is obvious that threatening, bad, or frightening information does "come through." We cannot ignore the real world indefinitely, assuming that we are within the "normal" range in terms of sanity.

Cognition

The term *cognition* can be used in two ways. Individuals have cognitive *systems* which represent what they know about themselves and the world about them. These systems are developed through cognitive *processes* which include perceiving, imagining, thinking, reasoning, and decision making. The more we understand about an individual's cognitive system, the better we are able to predict his behavior. "If we understand how man comes by the ideas about things and people which make up his world image, if we understand the principles which govern the growth and development and interaction of these ideas, we will have taken the first step toward understanding man's behavior in this world of his own making." [7]

Cognition implies a conscious or deliberate process toward acquiring knowledge. The term *rational* is often used in conjunction with cognitive processes in order to differentiate irrational acts. Yet rational should be viewed in the context of the individual involved. "However bizarre the behavior of men, tribes, or nations may appear to an outsider, to the men, to the tribes, to the nations their behavior makes sense in terms of their own world views." [8]

The cognitive or personal value system is affected by an individual's physical and social environment, his physiological structure, his physiological processes, his wants and goals, and his past experiences. Wants and goals refer particularly to motivational aspects of the value system. This is a central issue in personality theory and is of particular importance in understanding and predicting differences in individual behavior.

Motivation

A *motive* is what prompts a person to act in a certain way or at least develop a propensity for specific behavior. This urge to action can be touched off by an external stimulus, or it can be internally generated in individual thought processes. Differences in motivation are undoubtedly the most important consideration in understanding and predicting individual differences and behavior.

Unfortunately, motivation is not a simple concept. "One of the most difficult tasks for psychologists is to describe the urge behind behavior. The motivation of any organism, even the simplest one, is at present only partly understood." [9] It involves needs, wants, tensions, and discomfort. Underlying behavior, there is a push or drive toward action. This implies that there is some imbalance or dissatisfaction in the individual's relationship to his environment. He identifies goals and feels obligated to engage in some behavior which will lead toward achieving those goals.

Motivation is related to the cognitive system.

Man's actions are guided by his cognitions—by what he thinks, believes, and anticipates. But when we ask *why* he acts at all, we are asking the question of motivation. And the motivational answer is given in terms of active, driving forces represented by such words as "wanting" and "fearing"; the individual

---

[7] David Krech, Richard S. Crutchfield, and Egerton L. Ballachey, *Individual in Society,* McGraw-Hill Book Company, New York, 1962, p. 17.
[8] Ibid.
[9] James Deese, *Principles of Psychology,* Allyn and Bacon, Inc., Boston, 1964, p. 54.

wants power, he wants status, he fears social ostracism, he fears threats to his self-esteem. In addition, a motivational analysis specifies a goal for the achievement of which man spends his energies. Wanting power, he commits his effort, time, and substance to become governor of his state; wanting status, he tries to buy his way into the "proper" country club; fearing social ostracism, he shies away from acquaintances and friends who would engage him in the support of an unpopular social cause; fearing threats to self-esteem, he avoids situations in which his intellectual competence might be challenged. [10]

It is apparent that needs vary with the individual and hence lead to differential behavior patterns. To confound the matter even further, an individual's needs vary over time. His value system evolves continually, and an integral part of that evolution is the motivational process. As some needs are satisfied, they become less important in the scheme of things. Others develop through experience. Conflict and frustration are good examples of forces which modify individual wants. While dissatisfaction can be a motivator toward concerted effort, continual dissatisfaction or complete frustration may lead to a cessation in a particular mode of behavior. Feedback concerning achievements or the relative appropriateness of a particular behavior pattern can modify aspiration levels with regard to objectives. Thus understanding individual motivation requires continual updating in order to reflect the most current mix of goals. An identical stimulus used at two different points in time may evoke entirely different responses because the value system has been changed.

MOTIVATION AND PRODUCTIVITY

Productivity is of central importance in organization theory. Managers are interested in efficient utilization of resources in achieving objectives. Human capability is a critical resource, one which is extremely variable. In fact, latent human capability may very well be the greatest untapped resource. If so, we need to understand individual behavior as it relates to the work situation.

Figure 10.4 illustrates the complexity of the work environment by indicating the numerous factors which directly and indirectly affect productivity. The relative size of the various segments does not necessarily reflect their relative importance in the overall system.

In general, productivity depends upon two major variables—employees' job performance and the resources utilized. The resources illustrated here are raw materials and technology. Obviously, improvement in technology—plant and equipment plus knowledge concerning the process—can make a significant difference in the productivity of the system. Similarly, changes in the raw material to be processed can affect efficiency. The relative importance of technology in productivity depends on the particu-

[10] Krech, Crutchfield, and Ballachey, op. cit., p. 68.

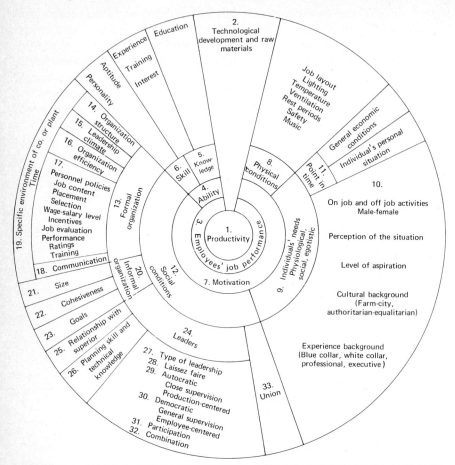

FIGURE 10.4 MAJOR FACTORS AFFECTING EMPLOYEE JOB PERFORMANCE AND PRODUCTIVITY (Robert A. Sutermeister, *People and Productivity,* 2d ed., McGraw-Hill Book Company, New York, 1969, p. ii)

lar situation. In automated systems, the human element is not very important. However, in most organizations the performance of employees is relatively more important than equipment and raw materials. Even in automated operations, productivity in strategic and coordinative subsystems is largely dependent on human performance.

Disregarding technological considerations, the productivity of an individual depends primarily on ability and motivation to perform. Ability depends upon both skill and knowledge. Physical and physiological attributes are involved in determining the ultimate capacity for an individual. His level of attainment within that range will depend upon experience, training, and interest. Similarly, the capacity for knowledge is relatively fixed hereditarily within a given range. However, the particular fund of knowledge achieved within a cognitive system depends upon education, experience, training, and interest. It is apparent that the ability an individual brings to a particular task is fairly complex and affected by many forces.

The motivational variable of the individual productivity equation is an even more complex issue. Physical conditions such as safety and lighting play an important role. Social conditions are also of vital concern and will be considered in more detail in subsequent chapters in this section—status and role systems, group dynamics, influence systems, and leadership. Of particular interest in this chapter is the individual's own approach to the task. Why does he behave the way he does? Why does one individual work at 110 percent of capacity while another one "pegs" his output at considerably less than capacity?

Many factors are involved in the development of an individual's value system, which in turn affects his perception of the situation surrounding a particular task. General economic conditions and his own personal situation at a particular point in time can have significant impact on an individual's behavior on the job. Work experience, cultural background, aspiration level, leisure-time activities—all affect his perception of the situation and help determine his inclination to perform a task in an organization. These various influences are filtered through an individual's needs, which lead to motivation to perform at some degree of capacity.

HIERARCHY OF NEEDS

The need-hierarchy concept was developed by Abraham Maslow as an alternative to viewing motivation in terms of a series of relatively separate and distinct drives. His concept stressed a hierarchy, with certain "higher" needs becoming activated to the extent that certain "lower" needs become satisfied. [11] Five basic needs are identified as physiological, safety, love, esteem, and self-actualization.

1 The physiological needs such as hunger, thirst, the activity-sleep cycle, sex, and evacuation
2 The safety needs for protection against danger, threat, and deprivation
3 The love needs for satisfactory associations with others, for belonging to groups, and for giving and receiving friendship and affection
4 The esteem needs for self-respect and for the respect of others, often referred to as the ego or status needs
5 The self-actualization or self-fulfillment needs to achieve the potential within himself, for maximum self-development, and for creativity and self-expression

These needs are related to each other and arranged in a hierarchy of prepotency. This means that the most prepotent goal will monopolize consciousness and will tend to evoke behavior in response to it.

---

[11] A. H. Maslow, "A Theory of Human Motivation," *Psychological Review*, July 1943, pp. 370-396.

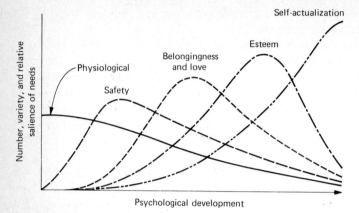

FIGURE 10.5 RELATIVE IMPORTANCE OF VARIOUS NEEDS AS MOTIVATORS OVER THE COURSE OF PSYCHOLOGICAL DEVELOPMENT (David Krech, Richard S. Crutchfield, and Egerton L. Ballachey, *Individual in Society,* McGraw-Hill Book Company, New York, 1962, p. 77)

While these levels in the need hierarchy can be separated for analysis and understanding, they are probably all active in actual behavior patterns. The lower-level needs are never completely satisfied—they recur periodically—and if their satisfaction is deprived for any period of time, they become extremely potent as motivators. On the other hand, a completely satisfied need is not an effective motivator of behavior. Esteem and self-actualization needs are rarely satisfied; man seeks indefinitely for more satisfaction of them once they become important to him. Yet they are usually not significant until physiological, safety, and love needs are reasonably well satisfied. The deprivation most people experience with respect to lower-level needs diverts their energies into the struggle to satisfy them, and the need for self-actualization remains dormant. [12]

Maslow was concerned about the false impression that a need must be 100 percent satisfied before the next level becomes potent.

In actual fact, most members of our society who are normal are partially satisfied in all their basic needs and partially unsatisfied in all their basic needs at the same time. A more realistic description of the hierarchy would be in terms of decreasing percentages of satisfaction as we go up the hierarchy of prepotency. For instance, if I may assign prepotency . . . it is as if the average citizen is satisfied 85 per cent in his physiological needs, 70 per cent in his safety needs, 50 per cent in his love needs, 40 per cent in his self-esteem needs, and 10 per cent in his self-actualization needs. [13]

[12] Douglas M. McGregor, "The Human Side of Enterprise," as condensed in *Management Review,* November 1957, pp. 26, 27.
[13] Maslow, op. cit., pp. 388–389.

The relative mix of needs or wants at various times during an individual's psychological development can be seen in Figure 10.5. It shows progressive changes in relative saliency, number, and variety of needs. It indicates that the peak of an earlier main class of needs must be passed before the next "higher" need can begin to assume a dominant role. It also shows that as psychological development takes place, the number and variety of needs increase.

TWO VIEWS OF PEOPLE

Assumptions about the basic nature of man are important in organization theory and management practice. According to Knowles and Saxberg:

> It makes a great deal of difference in systems of social control whether those involved tend to view man, in general, as good or evil. If we assume that man is good, we can believe that misbehavior is a reactive response rather than a manifestation of character. This will lead to a search for causes in his experience rather than in his nature. If we are to find a cause for behavioral failure, we are more apt to look outside the offender than inside and thus consider a whole new range of variables as contributory circumstances.
>
> If, on the other hand, we assume that man himself is bad, a priori, then we are prone to assume that misbehavior is caused by something within him which we cannot alter directly. Accordingly, our attention will focus on limiting his freedom to choose and to act through external curbs or controls. In limiting the causes of behavior, we exclude ourselves from powerful internal sources of control. [14]

These summary statements reflect polar oppositions which, admittedly, are unrealistic. Man is neither completely good nor completely evil. [15] There are obvious spectra for behavior in terms of cooperation-competition, love-hate, friendship-enmity, or harmony-discord. Given a particular issue, an individual's behavior will reflect a position on one or more of these continua. However, the basic assumption one makes can have a significant impact on organization and management. Relationships are structured in certain ways; compensation systems are designed; communication patterns are established; authority-responsibility relationships are identified; planning and control processes are established; and many other pertinent organizational considerations are affected by management's basic assumption with regard to the nature of man.

---

[14] Henry P. Knowles and Borje O. Saxberg, "Human Relations and the Nature of Man," *Harvard Business Review,* March–April 1967, p. 178.
[15] Knowles and Saxberg cite Occidental philosophers in developing the polar views. For a parallel discussion of Oriental views see Chan K. Hahn and Warren C. Waterhouse, "Confucian Theories of Man and Organization," *Academy of Management Journal,* September 1972, pp. 355-363.

The different orientations of traditional management theorists and human relationists resulted, in part, from different assumptions about the nature of man. McGregor set forth two alternative views of people which he termed "Theory X" and "Theory Y." [16]

Theory X

1 Management is responsible for organizing the elements of productive enterprise—money, materials, equipment, people—in the interest of economic ends.

2 With respect to people, this is a process of directing their efforts, motivating them, controlling their actions, modifying their behavior to fit the needs of the organization.

3 Without this active intervention by management, people would be passive—even resistant—to organizational needs. They must therefore be persuaded, rewarded, punished, controlled—their activities must be directed. This is management's task. We often sum it up by saying that management consists of getting things done through other people.

Behind this conventional theory there are several additional beliefs—less explicit, but widespread:

4 The average man is by nature indolent—he works as little as possible.

5 He lacks ambition, dislikes responsibility, prefers to be led.

6 He is inherently self-centered, indifferent to organizational needs.

7 He is by nature resistant to change.

8 He is gullible, not very bright, the ready dupe of the charlatan and the demagogue.

Theory Y

1 Management is responsible for organizing the elements of productive enterprise—money, materials, equipment, people—in the interest of economic ends.

2 People are *not* by nature passive or resistant to organizational needs. They have become so as a result of experience in organizations.

3 The motivation, the potential for development, the capacity for assuming responsibility, the readiness to direct behavior toward organizational goals are all present in people. Management does not put them there. It is a responsibility of management to make it possible for people to recognize and develop these human characteristics for themselves.

[16] McGregor, op. cit., pp. 23, 88-89.

4 The essential task of management is to arrange organizational conditions and methods of operation so that people can achieve their own goals *best* by directing *their own* efforts toward organizational objectives.

These theories can be related to the need hierarchy in the sense that the traditional view of direction and control relies on the assumption that lower-level needs are dominant in motivating people to perform organizational tasks. It assumes that the average human being has an inherent dislike of work and will avoid it if he can. He works to satisfy physiological and safety needs primarily through financial gain. He may be motivated through the threat of punishment and must be coerced and controlled in order to ensure performance. It does not take into account the motivation generated within the individual for achievement in order to enhance self-respect and move toward self-actualization.

Theory Y, on the other hand, assumes that people will exercise self-correction and self-control in working toward objectives to which they are committed. It assumes that individuals have potential for development, will seek responsibility, and will be motivated by esteem and self-actualization needs which, if met, will satisfy both individual and organizational objectives.

Effect on Performance

Good theory should lead to good practice. How do Theory X and Theory Y work out in actual organizations? It seems obvious that the assumptions and approaches identified in Theory X are widespread in ongoing organizations in the United States and throughout the world. And these approaches seem to work. Organizational endeavor is effective; it does accomplish objectives. However, questions can be raised concerning the efficiency of this approach, particularly with reference to the use of human resources. Is the human element as productive as it might be, given other assumptions and managerial practices?

Based on extensive research in contemporary organizations, Likert has concluded that a managerial system paralleling Theory Y makes significantly better use of human resources and enhances both effectiveness and efficiency of organizational endeavor. Over the years, he has evolved several models of management systems, which he designates by number, one through four. System Four incorporates the basic assumptions and approaches of Theory Y and seems to lead to significant improvement in organizational performance. [17] The conclusions may not be completely generalizable, but they apply to many industries, companies, and subunits within organizations. Moving toward such a managerial system is often a slow process which requires reeducation and reorientation of all organizational participants. However, there does seem to be a trend in this direction.

---

[17] Rensis Likert, *The Human Organization,* McGraw-Hill Book Company, New York, 1967.

The role of motivation in an approach emphasizing Theory Y assumptions and System Four approaches is described by Likert as follows:

> This highly motivated, cooperative orientation toward the organization and its objectives is achieved by harnessing effectively all the major motivational forces which can exercise significant influence in an organizational setting and which, potentially, can be accompanied by cooperative and favorable attitudes. Reliance is not placed solely or fundamentally on the economic motive of buying a man's time and using control and authority as the organizing and coordinating principle of the organization. [18]

It is evident that economic motives, which relate directly to physiological and safety needs, are not ignored. However, it is also obvious that higher-level esteem and self-fulfillment needs are emphasized. The importance of an integrated program which recognizes the necessity of considering the whole man (the entire need hierarchy) will provide a synergistic effect and make economic incentives even more effective than they might otherwise be. The problem of opposing forces—motivation in opposite directions—brings up another important issue. Is satisfaction a single dimension, or are there several distinct variables (or groups of variables) which must be considered separately?

MOTIVATION-HYGIENE CONCEPT

In 1959, Herzberg and his associates published a research report concerning the attitudes of people toward their work. [19] The research was designed to test the concept that man has two sets of needs: (1) his need as an animal to avoid physical pain and deprivation and (2) his need as a human being to grow psychologically. The original study involved interviews with 200 engineers and accountants, representing a cross section of Pittsburgh industry. They were asked about events they had experienced at work which either had resulted in (1) a marked improvement or (2) a significant reduction in job satisfaction. [20]

The results of this study and similar ones with other subjects seem to point to two rather distinct sets of factors—one relating primarily to job satisfaction and the other relating primarily to job dissatisfaction.

> Five factors stand out as strong determiners of job satisfaction—*achievement, recognition, work itself, responsibility,* and *advancement*—the last three being of greater importance for lasting change of attitudes. These five factors appeared very infrequently when the respondents described events that paralleled job dissatisfaction feelings. . . .

---

[18] Rensis Likert, *New Patterns of Management,* McGraw-Hill Book Company, New York, 1961, p. 98.

[19] Frederick Herzberg, Bernard Mausner, and Barbara Snyderman, *The Motivation to Work,* 2d ed., John Wiley & Sons, Inc., New York, 1959.

[20] Frederick Herzberg, *Work and the Nature of Man,* The World Publishing Company, Cleveland, 1966, p. 72.

When the factors involved in the job dissatisfaction events were coded, an entirely different set of factors evolved. These factors were similar to the satisfiers in their unidimensional effect. This time, however, they served only to bring about job dissatisfaction and were rarely involved in events that led to positive job attitudes. Also, unlike the ''satisfiers,'' the ''dissatisfiers'' consistently produced short-term changes in job attitudes. The major dissatisfiers were *company policy and administration, supervision, salary, interpersonal relations and working conditions.* [21]

The two clusters of factors can be distinguished in terms of (1) what a person does and (2) the situation in which he does it. The satisfiers relate to job content, achievement of a task, recognition for task achievement, the nature of the task, responsibility for a task, and professional advancement or growth in task capability. The context or environment of a person's job involves factors such as the kind of administration and supervision received in doing the job, the nature of interpersonal relationships involved, the working conditions, and the salary or compensation system.

The environmental variables were labeled *hygiene* factors, indicating an analogy to the concept of preventive maintenance. The satisfier factors were labeled *motivators*, implying their effectiveness in evoking individual behavior toward superior performance.

Relationship to Need Hierarchy

How does all this fit with the need-hierarchy concept described previously? The dissatisfiers or hygiene factors can be related to physiological and safety needs. In modern industry the environmental nature of most jobs has been basically ''satisfactory'' with regard to these lower-level needs. That is, working conditions (safety, lighting, ventilation, etc.) and salaries have generally been acceptable. Thus in Maslow's terms these satisfied needs are not effective motivators. On the other hand, if these conditions are not ''reasonably'' satisfactory, workers can become disenchanted and not even approach ''normal'' performance. However, it is unlikely that concentration on improving these facets of the job environment will lead to extraordinary performance—individual effort ''above and beyond the call of duty.''

Assuming reasonably good environmental conditions, how can superior performance be generated? Concentration on motivators involves recognition of higher-level needs such as esteem and self-actualization. Psychological growth comes from working at a task that is inherently interesting, achieving goals, and receiving recognition for such achievement. The system must provide opportunity for individuals to assume responsibility and to be innovative or creative in their work.

Concentration on lower-level needs or hygiene factors may be essential to provide the proper environment. However, it is a necessary but not sufficient condition. ''The hygiene factors are not a valid contributor to psychological growth. The substance of

---

[21] Ibid., pp. 72-74.

a task is required to achieve growth goals. Similarly, you cannot love an engineer into creativity, although by this approach you can avoid his dissatisfaction with the way you treat him. Creativity will require a potentially creative task to do." [22]

The relative importance of higher-level needs in motivating individual behavior increases with psychological development (see Figure 10.5). As a person matures, esteem and self-actualization needs become more important as motivators. Obviously, not all individuals will develop psychologically to the same extent. Retarded children often do quite well at routine, repetitive tasks. While more normal individuals might abhor such tasks, they represent a real challenge to those persons with less capability. Other individuals seem perfectly satisfied to avoid pain and physical deprivation. They probably have not grown enough psychologically to reach the threshold of higher-level needs. "These happiness seekers, who are motivated to seek only release of satisfaction, have not reached the stage of personal development in which the need for self-realization is active. In other words, hygiene-seekers seek happiness by avoidance behavior and are fixated at a low level of maturity." [23]

One popular approach to the problem of motivation is to assume that hygiene factors or physiological and safety needs are enough to motivate "workers," while motivators such as esteem or self-actualization needs should be considered when dealing with "managers." Theory X applies to workers; Theory Y applies to managers. This dichotomy is unfortunate because it perpetuates a chasm between subsystems of organizations which really should be integrated for effective and efficient performance. All are managers; all are workers. There is really no way to draw a meaningful line of demarcation. The research findings indicate that the hygiene-motivator concept applies to people in all walks of life and at all levels in organizations. "Contrary to prevailing belief, the studies show the basic needs of the blue-collar worker or the assembly-line worker are no different from those of the white-collar worker. The primary sources of job satisfaction for both groups are achievement and recognition." [24]

The relationship of motivation to individual performance is summarized in Figure 10.6. Performance is calibrated as a percentage of individual capacity. If related to physical productivity, it could be readily measurable. However, if it refers to artistic or creative output, evaluation would be much more difficult. In either case, we might consider that "normal" output averages somewhat less than 100 percent of capacity. For the sake of illustration, let us assume (rather generously) that individuals normally produce at about 75 percent of capacity over the long run. For short periods of time, performance at 115 percent (maybe even more) is not uncommon. Sustained effort at such levels is not likely. What factors are involved in moving from 75 to 90 percent performance over the long run? How can we get the subpar (50-percenters) individuals up to "normal" performance?

To the left of the thermometer are indicated various factors which affect performance. Ignoring technology, two basic systems are involved: (1) physical systems,

[22] Ibid., p. 75.
[23] Frederick Herzberg, "Motivation, Morale, & Money," *Psychology Today*, March 1968, p. 66.
[24] Ibid., p. 66.

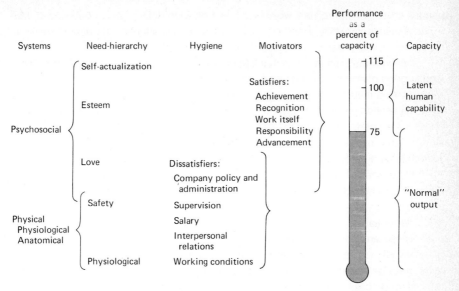

FIGURE 10.6 RELATIONSHIP OF MOTIVATION TO INDIVIDUAL PERFORMANCE

which include physiological and anatomical functions, and (2) psychosocial systems, the individual in organizational endeavor. Relating these systems to the need hierarchy, we find that physiological needs are directly related to physical systems. Safety needs likewise relate to physical systems, but they also relate to psychosocial systems. Of particular importance in the psychosocial system are love, esteem, and self-actualization needs.

As indicated, the hygiene and motivator factors can be related to the need hierarchy. The two systems overlap somewhat; dissatisfiers include love, safety, and physiological needs, while satisfiers reflect self-actualization, esteem, and love needs. In relating these to individual performance, we see that both satisfiers and dissatisfiers are involved in motivating the individual to "normal" performance. However, the dissatisfiers are relatively more important at this long-run average level of output. In tapping latent human capability and moving beyond the normal range of output, the satisfiers become relatively more important.

EXPECTATIONS AND PERFORMANCE

The subject of motivation has been approached on two dimensions which are relatively distinct but not mutually exclusive—*what* motivates people (content) and *how* behavior is produced (process). [25] Much of our discussion so far has related to content—specific

---

[25] John P. Campbell, et al., *Managerial Behavior, Performance, and Effectiveness*, McGraw-Hill Book Company, New York, 1970, pp. 340–384.

needs, drives, or energizers which lead to behavior. Although we have dealt with process issues implicitly, it will be useful to focus our attention on how behavior is produced. In this regard, expectations play an important role. [26]

It seems intuitively obvious that a person will work hard if he believes his effort will lead to good performance and that good performance, in turn, will result in appropriate rewards. And there is an increasing amount of research evidence to support this view of the motivation process. [27] Several key questions are involved in understanding what causes good performance on the part of employees in organizations. Does satisfaction lead to performance? Does performance lead to satisfaction? Are both satisfaction and performance a function of rewards?

Moreover, two basic psychological considerations are involved. Should we assume that man has certain inherent drives and habits which, if tapped, will lead to desired behavior? Or should we rely on a conditioning approach which recognizes good performance and rewards it appropriately?

These are not easy questions and there is evidence to support a number of alternative hypotheses; therefore, it seems reasonably clear that managers should take all of these factors into account. It is important to recognize the complex nature of the motivation process and the possible cause/effect links to good performance. Of particular significance is the reward system used in practice. Are rewards significant (monetary or nonmonetary), to be really appreciated by the recipient? If not, they are probably not very effective. Do rewards come reasonably close upon identification of good performance? If not, it is difficult for employees to believe that more effort will lead to significant rewards, and, hence, they are not likely to increase their efforts. (This is a typical problem in most organizations where annual merit review sessions are standard.) The result is dependence on nonmonetary rewards such as recognition, praise, and increased job scope. On the other hand, if rewards are significant and timely and the employee perceives that a reasonable amount of effort will result in good outcomes, he will be inclined to expend the necessary effort. Whether or not that effort leads to "good" performance depends upon factors such as ability and direction and obstacles that may preclude improved performance. [28]

The essence of the satisfaction-performance-rewards "controversy" is not the theoretical cause-and-effect relationship. Rather, for the practicing manager, it is a question of how to operationalize these concepts in order to design a system within which both the individual and the organization can benefit.

> The use of differential rewards may require courage on the part of the manager, but failure to use them will have far more negative consequences. A

---

[26] V. H. Vroom, *Work and Motivation,* John Wiley & Sons, Inc., New York, 1964.
[27] Lyman Porter and Edward E. Lawler, III, *Managerial Attitudes and Performance,* Richard D. Irwin, Inc., and The Dorsey Press, Homewood, Ill., 1964; and Vance F. Mitchell, "Expectancy Theories of Managerial Motivation," *Academy of Management Proceedings,* 1971, pp. 210–220.
[28] Charles M. Green, "The Satisfaction-Performance Controversy," *Business Horizons,* October 1972, pp. 31–41.

subordinate will repeat that behavior which was rewarded, regardless of whether it resulted in high or low performance. A rewarded low performer, for example, will continue to perform poorly. With knowledge of this inequity, the high performer, in return, will eventually reduce his own level of performance or seek employment elsewhere. [29]

The content and process dimensions of motivation are continually intermeshed. If process is emphasized, managers can practice applied behavior analysis (a form of operant conditioning) by positively reinforcing good performance. [30] This approach has been used successfully in industrial settings by letting individual employees regularly learn how well they are meeting specific company goals and rewarding performance improvement—chiefly through frequent recognition and praise. [31] Although considered simplistic and idealistic by some, organizations such as Emery Air Freight Corporation say it works—citing improved customer service, profits, and employee satisfaction. In short, Emery believes that it has found a way "to link such theoretical ideas as work measurement, management by objective, job enrichment, productivity and profit improvement, and participative management into a practical program that pays off." [32]

In emphasizing positive reinforcement for good performance the exact stimulus or drive or energizer may be unknown or little understood. Multiple causation is likely in most situations. For example, much attention has been focused on three of a long list of needs first conceptualized by H. A. Murray—need for achievement (n Ach), need for affiliation (n Aff), and need for power (n Pow). While all three may be functioning in any situation, the need for achievement seems most directly related to work performance.

ACHIEVEMENT MOTIVATION

The need for achievement, while not set forth explicitly in Maslow's need hierarchy, underlies esteem and self-actualization. Similarly, McGregor's Theory Y has undertones of achievement motivation. [33] Herzberg's motivators emphasize achievement, particularly the recognition of achievement as critical for long-run job satisfaction.

Like any other physical or psychological attribute, the degree of achievement motivation varies by individual. Some individuals rate very high, others very low; groups, organizations, or societies could be rated according to the degree of achievement motivation evident in the total system. McClelland emphasizes the achievement motive in the propensity for economic growth in various countries. [34] In Western culture, the

---

[29] Ibid., p. 41.

[30] Kenneth Goodall, "Shapers at Work," *Psychology Today,* November 1972, pp. 53ff.; and William F. Whyte, "Pigeons, Persons and Piece Rates," *Psychology Today,* April 1972, pp. 66ff. See also B. F. Skinner, *Beyond Freedom and Dignity,* Alfred A. Knopf, Inc., New York, 1971.

[31] "New Tool: Reinforcement for Good Work," *Business Week,* Dec. 18, 1971, pp. 76 and 77.

[32] Ibid., p. 77.

[33] David C. McClelland, John W. Atkinson, Russell A. Clark, and Edgar L. Lowell, *The Achievement Motive,* Appleton-Century-Crofts, Inc., New York, 1953.

[34] David C. McClelland, *The Achieving Society,* D. Van Nostrand Company, Inc., Princeton, N.J., 1961.

Protestant ethic and Social Darwinism undoubtedly have fostered high achievement motivation. The free enterprise system has provided an environment within which such an approach could survive and grow. However, the same phenomenon is evident in other economic systems. Economic growth, corporate profits and individual remuneration are seen as indicators of achievement and are not always sought in themselves. They merely provide an indication to the individual, organization, or society that performance has been good, recognized as such, and rewarded accordingly.

Achievement can be sought in many noneconomic facets of life—amateur athletics, painting, or gardening. However, monetary rewards continue to play an important role in many of these endeavors. The tennis player becomes a professional, and his bonus for signing is an indication of his current prowess as an amateur. The 4-H Club member raises a prize-winning steer, and the excellence of his work is measured by the amount of money obtained at the auction. The race to place a man on the moon and return him safely before 1970 was an example of achievement motivation at work in our society. The rewards in this case were our own self-esteem, plus the status and prestige gained in the world at large.

McClelland found that businessmen, particularly entrepreneur-managers, have relatively more achievement motivation than other identifiable groups in society. Scientists and professionals of all types seem to rate above average, but there is considerable variation within this subgroup of society. Scientists, for example, did not rate particularly high. Although they obviously are striving for accomplishments, they are attuned to more long-run goals and hence are not as mentally geared to concrete achievements as the entrepreneur-manager might be. McClelland suggests several key characteristics of the achiever:

1 He likes situations in which he takes personal responsibility for finding solutions to problems.
2 He has a tendency to set moderate achievement goals and to take "calculated risks."
3 He wants concrete feedback as to how well he is doing. [35]

Without responsibility, the individual would have no personal sense of accomplishment. Without feedback, he would not know where he stood. As indicated previously, this feedback can come in many forms. He may "know" in his own mind that he has done a good job. More important in organizations, typically, is praise from subordinates, peers, and superiors. According to McClelland, individuals with high achievement motivation are inclined to take moderate risks rather than gamble on situations with high potential payoff *and* high potential failure. This seems to make sense intuitively. The achiever will be interested in a consistent string of successes and not want to spoil his record with a complete flop.

---

[35] David C. McClelland, "Business Drive and National Achievement," *Harvard Business Review*, July–August 1962, pp. 99–112.

OPPORTUNITY FOR SELF-ACTUALIZATION

Throughout the discussion of individual behavior and motivation, self-actualization as the ultimate goal has been a recurring theme. The central nature of this concept is illustrated by the following excerpts:

> *The supreme goal of man is to fulfill himself as a creative, unique individual according to his own innate potentialities and within the limits of reality.*
>
> Carl Jung

> *The healthy man is primarily motivated by his needs to develop and actualize his fullest potentialities and capacities. . . . What man can be, he must be.*
>
> Abraham Maslow

> *Productiveness is man's ability to use his powers and to realize the potentialities inherent in him.*
>
> Erich Fromm

> *The primary determinant of motivation is the degree of opportunity offered to people for* self-actualization *and realization both in doing the productive work, in their relations with other people with whom they are associated in the doing, and in receipt of other rewards which they consider consistent with effort expended.*
>
> E. Wight Bakke

> *Unless there are opportunities at work to satisfy these higher-level needs (self-fulfillment), people will be deprived; and their behavior will reflect this deprivation.*
>
> Douglas McGregor

> *If people are able to accomplish and achieve (self-realization), they will like their work. This will accomplish a long-sought social goal.*
>
> Keith Davis

> *The primary functions of any organization, whether religious, political or industrial, should be to implement the needs for man to enjoy a meaningful existence.*
>
> Frederick Herzberg

These comments are illustrative of increasing concern for the individual in an organizational society. Moreover, the same underlying philosophy is apparent on the world scene as many new nations proclaim their independence and desire to shape their own destinies. In many cases, they have thrown off domineering or paternalistic colonial powers and are seeking esteem and self-actualization in their own right. Achievement motivation is evident in this trend.

Underlying these statements of concern for individual self-actualization is an assumption that the work environment and organizational life must play a vital role in the process.

The Work Environment

Business, government, and other employing organizations are pervasive institutions in society. Man spends a great deal of his time in such environments. Therefore, it is only natural to be concerned about the opportunity for self-actualization in employment.

On the other hand, organizations are designed to accomplish objectives effectively and efficiently. Managers are charged with performing in a manner which will satisfy stockholders and other external interests. Large, complex organizations have adopted the bureaucratic principles of specialization, well-designed jobs, and standard operating procedures. Within such an environment individual initiative often is dampened or stifled.

Considerable effort has been spent in an attempt to ameliorate such conditions and provide an environment wherein both individual and organizational achievement can result. Argyris stresses the need for psychological growth and maturation of individuals in the work environment, while at the same time recognizing that organizations strive to achieve their objectives, maintain themselves internally, and adapt to their external environment.[36] Bakke urges that all employees have maximum opportunity to participate and express themselves at work, suggesting that it is inherently possible in *all* positions within an organization.[37] The term *fusion* is used by both Argyris and Bakke to describe a condition where the organization *and* its employees achieve self-actualization. This term implies an ideal mix of company and individual objectives, where they become indistinguishable from each other—literally fused.

Movement away from bureaucratic-mechanistic structure and toward adaptive-organic systems provides greater opportunity for self-actualization. These goals may be attainable in some parts of all organizations or in all of some organizations. On the other hand, they might not be attainable; in fact, they may be somewhat utopian. If integration or fusion of individual and organizational achievements cannot be attained in the work environment, what is the outlook for man in society?

Society as a Whole

Many opportunities exist for self-actualization outside of the work environment. Individuals are members of numerous organizations—family, church, service, leisure, and others. The Little League coach, the Cub Scout pack master, the Exalted Ruler of the

---

[36] Chris Argyris, *Personality and Organization*, Harper & Row, Publishers, Incorporated, New York, 1957.
[37] E. Wight Bakke, "The Function of Management," in E. M. Hugh-Jones (ed.), *Human Relations and Modern Management*, North Holland Publishing Company, Amsterdam, 1958, p. 224.

Elks, the bridge Master, all find ways of fulfilling esteem and self-actualization needs in organizations. From a societal point of view, an individual's work career is only a part of the total system; it provides the means to partake in many leisure-time activities which allow for achievement and psychological growth. Saxberg and Grubb suggest that for some people "the job is not as much of an end in itself, but rather has become more a means to other ends in order to satisfy the 'whole man': enjoyment of leisure and other activities frequently [are] regarded as more enjoyable and more rewarding than work." [38]

It seems to us that since self-actualization relates to the whole man, the process should relate to his entire system. His job is only one part of it. Self-actualization certainly should be of concern, but the work environment obviously cannot carry the entire burden. Managers should seek the most appropriate motivational methods, but we may be asking the impossible to suggest that any organization primarily geared to economic objectives can or should be the vehicle for total need satisfaction. In fact, a society where the individual has freedom in the selection of his organizational relationships—in his work, religious, political, and social life—is the essence of democracy. To ask a business organization to fulfill all these needs might seriously interfere with the broader opportunities for democratic participation in many organizational relationships.

Membership in several or many organizations besides his employing firm does not ensure self-actualization for the individual. Religious, fraternal, recreational, and civic groups are often large-scale, complex organizations with bureaucratic characteristics. Those "in command" may manage via traditional (Theory X) approaches and minimize the extent of democratic-participative decision making and creativity. Thus it is important for *all* organizations in society to embrace "industrial humanism" and develop the kind of atmosphere in which individual self-actualization can be achieved.

SUMMARY

Individual behavior and motivation are a fundamental part of the psychosocial system of organizations. Behavior depends on anatomical, physiological, and psychological conditions. Changes in the first two have evolved slowly over time, whereas psychological elements change relatively more rapidly and hence seem to affect behavior more directly.

Personality theory is an important subdiscipline in general psychology which emphasizes the whole man in his environment and current interpersonal relationships. Motivation is of central concern in personality theory.

Individuals are similar in that all behavior is (1) caused, (2) motivated, and (3) goal-oriented. The particular goals may vary for individuals and between societies, as do the needs underlying motivation. However, the behavioral process outlined by these three ingredients remains the same for all people, in all places, and at all times.

Individual variations in behavior occur primarily because of differences in percep-

[38] Borje O. Saxberg and Edward L. Grubb, "Self-actualization through Work or Leisure?" *The Business Quarterly,* Spring 1967, p. 32.

tion, cognition, and motivation. People "select" information which tends to enhance their satisfaction and ignore information which is disturbing. The cognitive processes of thinking and problem solving are important in learning and acquiring knowledge. These processes facilitate the evolution of a system of knowledge which is important in mediating between stimulus and response. Needs are key elements in personal value systems and are important in the motivation process.

For many goal-oriented organizations, productivity is important; performance must be both effective and efficient. Productivity is a function of technology and individual performance. Individual performance, in turn, is affected by ability and motivation to produce. Because of the tremendous reservoir of latent human capabilities, motivation is critical for productivity, particularly in strategic and coordinative subsystems in organizations.

The need-hierarchy concept is central to motivation and individual behavior. This model includes levels of prepotent needs such as physiological, safety, love, esteem, and self-actualization. Only those needs which are not satisfied are considered motivators. Rather than a mutually exclusive system of needs, there is usually a complex mixture with relative satisfaction of various needs in the hierarchy. Therefore, at various times different needs become active as motivators of individual behavior.

Many writers have suggested concentration on higher-level need satisfaction in order for man to realize his full potential. McGregor stresses Theory Y (as contrasted to Theory X). Likert has evolved System Four with the same goal in mind. Herzberg stresses motivating factors such as achievement, recognition, responsibility, and the task itself, rather than the hygiene functions such as working conditions, salary, and administrative climate. McClelland describes the achievement motive as related to esteem and self-actualization needs and stresses its importance for many individuals in society, particularly entrepreneur-managers.

Of particular concern in the discussion of individual behavior and motivation is the opportunity for self-actualization—at work or in society as a whole.

QUESTIONS AND PROBLEMS

1 What basic disciplines contribute to the understanding of psychosocial systems? How?
2 Relate anatomy, physiology, and psychology to behavior.
3 Are behavior patterns inherited or acquired?
4 Using the basic model in Figure 10.1, trace several examples of behavior—eating, kissing, obtaining a master's degree, or running for president. Why is this model applicable to all people, of all ages, in all cultures, at all times?
5 Summarize the impact of perception, cognition, and motivation on individual differences in behavior.
6 Explain the following relationship:
   Productivity $= f$ (technology, ability, motivation)
   What does it mean for managers?

7 Trace your own psychological development in terms of the hierarchy of needs in Figure 10.5. How does the mix of needs affect behavior?

8 Describe two polar views of people. What is your assumption concerning the basic nature of man? Why?

9 What is the motivation-hygiene concept? How is it related to the need-hierarchy concept?

10 What impact does achievement motivation have on individual behavior? On societal behavior?

11 What should be the role of the work environment in providing opportunity for individual self-actualization?

11

STATUS AND ROLE SYSTEMS

Understanding individual behavior through concepts such as personality and motivation is a necessary but not sufficient condition for coordinating human endeavor in organizations. Managing requires considerable knowledge concerning the organizational environment—the structure and processes which influence individual behavior in many direct and indirect ways. Status and role systems represent two important concepts in this regard. An individual's socially defined status and his individually perceived role have a significant effect on how he acts and how others react to him. Discussion of these aspects of the organizational psychosocial system will be focused around the following topics:

> Status and Role Defined
> Status Systems
> Classless Society?
> Occupational Prestige
> Status Symbols
> Role Systems
> Role Episode
> Role Conflict
> Bureaucratic Man?

STATUS AND ROLE DEFINED

Status refers to the ranking or stratification of people in a social system. It involves degrees of prestige and, unfortunately, implications of good-bad or superiority-inferiority. While "all men are created equal," some are more equal than others. Status hierarchies seem to be an inevitable phenomenon in social systems. An ordering, stratification, or ranking develops among individuals in any group. Status depends upon the censensus of group members. Pfiffner and Sherwood describe status as "the comparative esteem which members of the various social systems accord to the positions in them." [1]

It is useful to distinguish social status and organizational status, although the two certainly interact. Social status refers to ranking in a community or society, and an individual's relative position is often based on a number of factors—age, strength, size, wisdom, family relationships, occupation, and personality, for example. These criteria could be expanded or subdivided to provide a list of numerous status characteristics. The composite impact of ranking on various factors results in an individual's general status within a social system such as the community, state, or country.

Organizational status may also rely on the composite of several characteristics but is usually more narrowly defined than societal status. It typically refers to a specific hierarchical position within a particular organization. Barnard defines such status as follows:

> By "status" of an individual in an organization we mean . . . that condition of the individual that is defined by a statement of his rights, privileges, immunities, duties, and obligations in the organization and, obversely, by a statement of the restrictions, limitations, and prohibitions governing his behavior, both determining the expectations of others in reference thereto. Status becomes systematic in an organization when appropriate recognition of assigned status becomes the duty and the practice of all participating, and when the conditions of the status of all individuals are published by means of differentiating designation, titles, appellations, insignia, or overt patterns of behavior. [2]

This definition of status implies its integral relationship to behavior; certain things can be done, and others cannot be done.

The concept of *role* relates to the activities of an individual in a particular position. It describes the behavior he is expected to exhibit when occupying a given position in the societal or organizational system. The relationship of role to individual behavior is apparent. For example, "a role is commonly defined as a set of behaviors which is expected of everyone in a particular position, regardless of who he is. These behaviors are of course socially ordained; and the role therefore sets a kind of limit on the types of personality expression possible in any given situation." [3]

The integration of concepts such as status and role, which are social, and *person-*

---

[1] John M. Pfiffner and Frank P. Sherwood, *Administrative Organization,* Prentice-Hall, Inc., Englewood Cliffs, N.J., 1960, p. 274.
[2] Chester I. Barnard, "The Functions of Status Systems," in Robert K. Merton et al. (eds.), *Reader in Bureaucracy,* The Free Press of Glencoe, New York, 1952, p. 242.
[3] Pfiffner and Sherwood, op. cit., p. 39.

ality, which is individual, is important for understanding and predicting individual behavior in organizations. The interaction of these basic ingredients can result in a multiplicity of behavior patterns. Although these concepts are inseparable in real situations, it will be helpful to consider them in detail separately and then to integrate them with the psychosocial system.

STATUS SYSTEMS

Status is derived from a multiplicity of characteristics. However, certain basic elements compose most societal status systems. Actually, these basic elements are categories which represent numerous specific characteristics which affect status in particular situations.

Basic Categories

Parsons cites five basic factors which underlie societal status systems: birth, personal qualities, achievements, possessions, and authority. [4]

Heredity still plays an important part in most status systems. While the "divine right of kings" has lost much of its attraction throughout the world, it still holds sway in some cultures. Of course, heredity combines with another basic element—money or possessions—to perpetuate the status of a particular family line. While the status of birth into an aristocratic stratum of society may wane over the years, the perpetuation of wealth through inheritance has continuing impact.

Achievements include education and occupation, which are often integrally related. Formal education is required for professional occupations such as medicine or law. These are often necessary but not sufficient attributes for high status in a particular social system. In many cultures, age, sex, or other physical attributes such as strength or beauty still play an important part in determining status.

Authority attached to positions in an organizational hierarchy provides another basis for status differentiation. A formal chart designates the various relationships among people. The chart can be amplified by job descriptions which define the system of relationships in more detail.

The relative importance of these basic characteristics depends on the particular culture and the point in time. In April 1968, *Seattle* magazine published an article entitled "The Establishment," which indicated that it takes money plus position and gregariousness to play "king of the castle" in the city of Seattle. (If you're not on the list, you're a dirty rascal.) [5] Three basic power centers were identified on the basis of numerous

---

[4] Talcott Parsons, *Essays in Sociological Theory: Pure and Applied*, The Free Press of Glencoe, New York, 1949, pp. 171–172. Parsons also mentions a sixth category of status—that which is achieved by illegitimate means.

[5] "The Establishment," *Seattle*, April 1968, pp. 19–25.

committee lists and interviews with residents. Separate lists were identified for establishments in social, cultural, and business circles. "Of the three principal power-centers, the Social one is the least significant. The Cultural power-center, on the other hand, has greatest impact, but only in terms of the city's artistic life. The greatest influence by far is exerted by the sprawling Business power-center, whose members make up the bulk of civic committees." [6]

Kinds of Status

Several dichotomies have been identified which facilitate understanding the concept of status. In this section we will discuss the following pairs: ascribed-achieved, functional-scalar, positional-personal, and active-latent.

Ascribed status is that which a person is born into. The individual's family has a certain position in society, and, at least initially, all members of that family are ascribed with that status. The caste system in India and other cultures is an example of such a system. Regardless of personal attributes, an individual is often locked into a particular status from birth. While some mobility has developed, caste status systems are still relatively rigid and upward movement is nominal at best.

More import for the study of organization and management is *achieved* status. Here, education and/or skill provide the means for achieving a specific position in the social system, particularly the work environment. The story of the "self-made man" is common in Western society, particularly the United States. The individual who was "born on the wrong side of the tracks" can achieve high status primarily through occupational prestige. Several routes are open, including politics, education, and entrepreneurial success.

In the United States, education has been the most expedient means of improving status. Thus, many first-generation immigrant families, finding themselves in a low status position in society, have stressed education for their offspring. Most modern large-scale organizations provide opportunity for achieving increased status as one moves up the hierarchical ladder. Here again, however, although an individual might achieve the Presidency after starting on the assembly line with an eighth-grade education, it is very unlikely. A college education is becoming minimal; moreover, the probability of success and increased status improves considerably if the individual has a master's degree.

In organizations the distinction between *scalar* and *functional* status is important. [7] Scalar relates to a position in the vertical hierarchy; functional relates to the particular task or function which an individual performs. In an aerospace firm, for example, design engineering typically has more functional status than manufacturing or accounting. However, the controller or manufacturing manager has much more scalar status than

---

[6] Ibid., p. 19.
[7] Barnard, op. cit., pp. 242–243.

many design engineers. While scalar status is often quite explicit and set forth formally in the organization charts, functional status is more implicit and dependent upon the value system and perception of a particular evaluator. Accountants may perceive their own functional status as much higher than that accorded them by design engineers, and vice versa.

In universities, as in many organizations, a certain general status attaches to particular functions even though theoretically (according to the structural model) they are all equal. There is a "pecking order" of academic disciplines which implies relative superiority or inferiority rather than merely difference in function. Mathematicians may accord electrical engineers and political scientists less status than other mathematicians. Such status differentials depend upon individual perception, and there is no official, formal published list of functional status. However, it does exist and has an impact upon organizational behavior. Scalar status, on the other hand, is explicit and published in chart form. The relative status of the various positions in the system can be readily ascertained, and the privileges and limitations of each position are relatively well known.

Another useful dichotomy in understanding status systems relates to *personal* and *positional* status. A certain amount of status is attached to a particular position in the social system without regard to its occupant. Thus, the position of lawyer or teacher may connote more status than clerk or hobo. On the other hand, Cliff Hangar may be a lousy lawyer and Pete Moss may be an excellent clerk. In these instances, status is attached to the personal performance of an individual in a particular position. Other characteristics such as attractiveness and gregariousness affect personal status, which may vary significantly for a given individual in several different groups. In organizations it is helpful if personal and positional status are congruent. If other members hold an individual in low esteem but he has a relatively high position organizationally, the atmosphere may not be conducive to effective and efficient operation.

The concepts of *active* and *latent* status are also important. Because an individual occupies many positions (plays many roles) in various organizations in society, status attaches to him in many ways. He has both ascribed and achieved status; he has both functional and scalar status; and he has both positional and personal status—separately and together. However, all these factors do not necessarily operate at once. At work, status attaches to a particular position the individual occupies in an organization. His status as a Little League coach or amateur bowler does not have as much impact. His status in these realms would be latent, for the most part, during working hours. His active status would vary depending upon organizational setting and timing—family, work, lodge, church, or other. Latent status may be relevant to active status in varying degrees. For example, an individual's status as a lawyer may affect his status in a community action organization more than his status as a ping-pong player. The concepts of active and latent status can be used to refine the notion of multiplicity of variables in assessing composite status for individuals in social systems.

Equality versus Status

If equalitarianism is one of the cornerstones of our cultural heritage, it would seem that status systems are basically dysfunctional. They certainly emphasize inequality based on various key characteristics. However, status systems are natural and inevitable. In social groups cooperative action requires some division of work, both horizontally (by function) and vertically (scalar concepts). The animal kingdom provides many examples of status systems which require the identification of a leader (or leaders) and followers. Superior-subordinate relationships are evident. There are leaders and followers in elephant herds, lion prides, and chimpanzee bands. Similarly, in human groups, functional specialization and superior-subordinate relationships develop quite naturally. Thus, status serves as a means of organizing endeavor by providing a system within which individuals can relate to one another. It facilitates communication and the implementation of systems of authority and responsibility. [8]

On the other hand, status systems create many problems. Overemphasis upon status for its own sake, without recognizing its role in facilitating coordinated group effort, can be detrimental. Individuals can spend great amounts of time, effort, and money in trying to achieve status within a social system. Status differentials can be useful in motivating some people toward superior performance, but others may "break down" in an atmosphere of continual striving. In most large-scale organizations, the hierarchy is pyramidal and narrows quite rapidly toward the top. Thus, many are called, but only a few are chosen. If scalar status is overemphasized, those who do not make it may cease to function at par. Disappointments may be overwhelming and extremely dysfunctional to future organizational endeavor. Yet regardless of the disadvantages, social status systems are inevitable. "Social status in America is somewhat like man's alimentary canal; he may not like the way it works and he may want to forget that certain parts of it are part of him, but he knows it is necessary for his very existence. So a status system, often an object of our disapproval, is present and necessary in our complex social world." [9]

CLASSLESS SOCIETY?

Many studies of social class have revolved around a classification scheme somewhat as follows: upper upper, lower upper, upper middle, lower middle, upper lower, lower lower. By and large, on the basis of income, the four middle categories represent an increasing portion of society. Other status characteristics reflect this as well—education, for example. Class is a psychosocial phenomenon, reflected in attitudes and propensities for decision making. "Those in this country who speak of the 'middle class'

---

[8] Robert K. Merton, *Social Theory and Social Structure,* The Free Press of Glencoe, New York, 1957, p. 370.
[9] W. Lloyd Warner, Marchia Meeker, and Kenneth Eells, *Social Classes in America,* Science Research Associates, Inc., Chicago, 1949, p. 10.

as our largest cohesive social group apparently have in mind this conception: they refer to those millions of Americans who share, in general, common values, attitudes, and aspirations." [10]

The increasing proportion of our population in the economic middle class has resulted in increasing use of the term "classless society." Packard describes this trend as follows:

> The rank-and-file citizens of the nation have generally accepted this view of progress toward equality because it fits with what we would like to believe about ourselves. It coincides with the American Creed and the American Dream, and is deeply imbedded in our folklore.
>
> Such a notion, unfortunately, rests upon a noticeable lack of perception of the true situation that is developing. Class lines in several areas of our national life appear to be hardening. And status straining has intensified. [11]

Thus there are evident disagreements with regard to the reality of a classless society. Has it become more homogeneous or more heterogeneous and stratified? Some of the more obvious indicators have disappeared. It is difficult to distinguish a vice-president from a clerk in many organizations on the basis of appearance. The extremes are still quite visible—the opulent can be distinguished from the indigent. However, it is difficult to distinguish the various strata in the vast middle class. On the other hand, while status differentials may be more subtle, they are nevertheless real. Much effort—advertising, for example—goes into distinguishing gradations of status based on material things and activities engaged in.

Mobility

Recognizing the inevitability of stratification and the class system, the concept of social mobility has been stressed in the United States. While other cultures have been characterized as rigid (caste systems, for example), we have emphasized opportunities for upward mobility. The importance of education and entrepreneurial prowess has been stressed.

Of course, this emphasis has led to an environment which almost requires striving for improvement—a reflection of the Protestant ethic and achievement motivation. While opportunities for upward social mobility do exist, there are formidable barriers. Those without entrepreneurial prowess or the capacity to take advantage of educational opportunities find it extremely difficult to better their position. Many current efforts

---

[10] Charles H. Page, "Social Class in American Sociology," in Reinhard Bendix and Seymour Martin Lipset (eds.), *Class, Status and Power*, The Free Press of Glencoe, New York, 1953, p. 48.
[11] Vance Packard, *The Status Seekers*, David McKay Company, Inc., New York, 1959, pp. 4-5.

spotlight the tremendous difficulty for the minority groups in lower-income brackets (or the hard-core unemployed) to break out of their position in society. The riots in the ghettos of many large cities reflect the frustration encountered as people strive without success to better their position within the framework of our society.

Similar problems arise at all levels, but they are not quite so evident. Thus, social mobility has both advantages and disadvantages. It provides opportunity for improved status within our class system, but it also results in an atmosphere where failure can lead to frustration. There are no easy answers. Status systems seem inevitable and useful in structuring organized endeavor, but we must be aware of the dysfunctional aspects and strive for optimal balance.

OCCUPATIONAL PRESTIGE

In modern societies, the hierarchy of occupational prestige is one of the most basic systems of stratification. Extensive empirical studies have shown striking similarities in a variety of nations—socialist and capitalist, developed and developing. "It appears that occupational-prestige hierarchies are similar from country to country and from subgroup to subgroup within a country. This stability reflects the fundamental but gross similarities among the occupational systems of modern nations. Furthermore, knowledge about occupations and relatively strong consensus on the relative positions of occupations are widely diffused throughout the populations involved." [12]

Occupational prestige is important in the social system because it affects the power and influence of occupants of certain positions, as well as the amount of resources which society places at their disposal. In this section we will look at occupational prestige in both the United States and Russia.

United States

Between 1947 and 1963 "scientific occupations were increasing in prestige, culturally oriented occupations were falling, and artisans were enjoying a mild upward trend. Nevertheless, the overriding conclusion must be that the structure of occupational prestige is remarkably stable through time as well as space." [13]

Scientific occupations received a tremendous boost in prestige in the post-*Sputnik I* era. The national goal of putting a man on the moon and returning him safely to earth focused considerable attention on scientific endeavor. The international competition involved has generated repercussions throughout society—government, business, and education. The results of these developments are indicated in the upward movements in prestige of nuclear physicists, scientists, and government scientists. Meanwhile, the physician has remained close to the top of the prestige ladder, second only to Supreme

[12] Robert W. Hodge, Paul M. Siegel, and Peter H. Rossi, "Occupational Prestige in the United States, 1925-63," *The American Journal of Sociology,* November 1964, pp. 286-287.
[13] Ibid., p. 286.

Court justices. Lawyers have moved up significantly from eighteenth to eleventh in the rankings. At the same time, diplomats slipped from fourth to eleventh.

Many individual changes of varying degrees can be cited. However, the general stability in the system is evident. Shoeshiners, streetsweepers, garbage collectors, and sharecroppers remain at the bottom of the ladder. The traditional professions rank relatively high. In general, income is probably correlated with the prestige hierarchy. However, there are obvious examples which distort the picture. Businessmen, either managers or members of corporate boards of directors, probably enjoy significantly larger incomes than many in occupations ranked above them. Salesmen or nightclub singers are often extremely well-paid and yet do not rank very high in occupational prestige as seen by society in general.

Even though occupational prestige is fundamental in social status systems, it is not overriding. It relates primarily to achieved, functional status. In organizations, scalar status may take precedence. The corporate president enjoys a measure of status and prestige over that of the company physician or lawyer. Personal attributes also play an important part, and there is tremendous variation within categories. Some Supreme Court justices acquire more status and prestige than others. The same is true for nuclear physicists, state governors, senators, plumbers, or bartenders. Nevertheless, without detailed knowledge of individual prestige, status is accorded to occupations based on our general impressions of their relative position in the prestige hierarchy. This phenomenon holds true in other cultures as well.

Union of Soviet Socialist Republics

The triumph of the proletariat is supposed to yield a classless society. Russian communism was designed to produce a pure equalitarian social system. Stalin often emphasized that Soviet population was divided into two major classes: the working class and the peasantry, plus a third group, the intelligentsia. Within Soviet society, the members of all three groups were defined as "equal in rights." In the 1930s, Stalin asserted that the amount of social distance and the political and economic contradictions between the groups were diminishing and, indeed, were being obliterated. [14]

While these goals might be achieved in a very simple society, they appear to be unachievable in complex, technological societies. Indeed, the Soviet Union has recognized the need to differentiate on the basis of many characteristics in order to maintain a viable system. Incentive systems have been developed, and differential rewards have been accorded to relative contributions to various societal endeavors. The result has been an elaborately and precisely stratified status system which includes the intelligentsia, divided into several subunits; the working class, also markedly differentiated; and the peasantry, relatively homogeneous but also divided into two distinguishable groups.

An interesting sidelight is the identification of a residual group which has been

---

[14] Alex Inkeles, "Social Stratification and Mobility in the Soviet Union," in Bendix and Lipset (eds.), *Class, Status and Power*, p. 609.

banished to forced-labor camps and is really outside the formal societal structure. There are indications that within these exile societies a status system has been maintained which is parallel to that outlined for society as a whole. In other words, an individual's status in a forced-labor camp correlates quite closely with his former or potential position in society at large. [15] The whole system can be ranked as follows:

CATEGORY	RANK
Ruling elite	1
Superior intelligentsia	2
General intelligentsia	3
Working class aristocracy	4
White-collar workers	5.5
Well-to-do peasants	5.5
Average workers	7
Average peasants	8.5
Disadvantaged workers	8.5
Forced-labor workers	10

This ranking hardly suggests a classless society. The ruling elite refers to the official Communist Party members. On balance, however, the ranking of categories correlates closely with the general occupational categories in the United States. The professional occupations in the United States parallel the relative status of the intelligentsia in Russia. Farm workers and unskilled labor rank very low in both societies. Just as in the United States, many factors are involved in determining an individual's overall status in society. However, the main determinants are occupation and income, plus education and technical expertise, which allow one to exert power and authority in certain phases of societal life.

These similarities in occupational prestige in two major world cultures are illustrative of the pervasiveness of status systems throughout the world and over time. Of particular interest in this regard are the various symbols used to identify position in a status hierarchy.

STATUS SYMBOLS

Numerous symbols can be used to designate status. The most obvious, of course, are those related to physical appearance. The king wears a crown; the indian chief has his headdress; the judge has his robe; and the nun has her habit. The military services probably have the most elaborate system of uniform differentials to identify gradations in status. The visibility of these leaves no doubt with regard to superior-subordinate relationships and facilitates command and control.

---

[15] Ibid., p. 611.

Another prevalent system of status symbols is that of titles. In the military, titles accompany the visible symbols. In other phases of society, however, there are no physical appurtenances. For example, individuals might be indistinguishable in their "Sunday" suits. However, status differentials would be apparent if they were addressed as president, governor, mayor, or mister, respectively. Titles often reflect both functional and scalar status. For example, in an aerospace company, there might be as many as six vice-presidents. Therefore, in order to pinpoint his job more accurately, an individual might use the term Vice-president, Research and Development, on his door and/or stationery. In the aerospace environment, it is likely that this title would carry slightly more prestige than Vice-president, Finance, or Vice-president, Manufacturing. The relative status of functional titles would vary according to the industry and the specific company.

In educational institutions it is often difficult to decipher the titular system. The chairman of a department may use that title only if he assumes it has sufficient prestige. On the other hand, he may sign his letters as "Professor and Chairman" if the former title seems more prestigious. In a medical school, the term Professor may not "carry much weight" because it ranks eighth on the occupational-prestige hierarchy whereas physicians rank number two.

One of our colleagues was introduced to King Olaf of Norway during a 1968 visit to the University of Washington, Seattle, Washington. When asked if he were awed by the experience, he replied, "No, I once shook hands with the Governor of Texas." This illustrates individual perception of the relative ranking of titles.

Many other examples of status symbols could be cited, most of which relate in some way to quantity or quality of material goods, which in turn depend upon the amount of money an individual has. Houses, automobiles, furs, jewelry, and extensive travel, for example, can be used to measure relative status of individuals or families in society. It is common to explain purchasing habits in terms of the search for status. This is obviously the case for many individuals who wittingly or unwittingly are caught up in status seeking. On the other hand, there are many who consciously shy away from this approach. For example, the parking concessionaire at one of Seattle's best restaurants suggests that the status seekers drive the Cadillacs and Continentals, while the members of the upper-upper class drive old station wagons. And Jeremy Main suggests that:

> The kind of car that the well-to-do buy suggests that comfort rather than status is the goal. . . .What is evident is a desire for comfort, plain old middle-class comfort, especially in the home.
>
> Perhaps it is through the houses that the affluent display their status, but that is opulence in private. [16]

---

[16] Main, op. cit., p. 160.

Status symbols in society in general have received considerable attention. Even more attention, however, has been devoted to the "signs of office" within large-scale organizations, both public and private.

Signs of Office

Figure 11.1 illustrates the various paraphernalia that go with rank in the corporate environment. At the lowest level are many employees in a single room, with plain wood or metal desks, an asphalt tile floor, and access to the steno pool, some distance away. At a slightly higher level is a supervisor in a glass-enclosed alcove. Junior executives find themselves with slightly larger desks, two to an office, and sharing a secretary. The general manager or vice-president has an even fancier desk, a work table, bookshelf, and has one secretary all to himself. The president has a "made-to-order" desk, one-inch pile rugs, a private library, imported furniture, and two secretaries plus an administrative assistant.

Many companies have an elaborate scheme established for differentiating by various levels within the corporate hierarchy. As an individual moves from job to job his status is quite evident according to the various physical appurtenances related to his office. Desks, tables, carpeting, air conditioning, view—all play a role in identifying the status of employees in large-scale organizations.

While some organizations have attempted to establish a "classless society" by maintaining uniform signs of office throughout the system, this approach is rare.[17] As in our general culture, a status system seems natural and inevitable. The signs of office accompany a ranking rather than establish it. Most observers stress the functional nature of the system of differentiated physical appurtenances. They provide an incentive for organizational participants who strive for higher levels and the rewards attendant thereto.

ROLE SYSTEMS

The twin concepts of status and role were stressed by Linton as fundamental to the description and analysis of social structure.[18] Status relates to positions in a social system occupied by designated individuals; role relates to the expected behavior patterns attributed to that position. "Status and role, in these terms, are concepts serving to connect the culturally defined expectations with the patterned behavior and relationships which comprise social structure."[19]

---

[17] The office building of the School of Business Administration (University of Washington) was designed so that all offices and furnishings would be identical, except for several corner ones which were assigned to senior professors. However, certain locations (differential views) quickly became preferable. Rugs, upholstered chairs, paintings, and other "signs of office" were also added by occupants. Thus a status system developed informally even though the basic space and furnishings were identical.

[18] Ralph Linton, *The Study of Man,* Appleton-Century-Crofts, Inc., New York, 1936.

[19] Merton, op. cit., p. 368.

FIGURE 11.1 THE PARAPHERNALIA THAT GO WITH RANK

The term *role* is used to designate the composite of culture patterns associated with a particular status position. It includes attitudes, values, and behavior ascribed by the society to any and all persons occupying a specific position. It includes the legitimate expectations of incumbents with respect to the behavior of other persons toward them. "Insofar as it represents overt behavior, a role is the dynamic aspect of status: what the individual has to do in order to validate his occupation of the status." [20] The term *sergeant* has definite status implications because of its position in the military hierarchy. The behavior expected of sergeants is also reasonably well defined. Some aspects of the role are described in detail in a position description; others are part of the folklore handed down via face-to-face contacts, novels, movies, or other media. A typical stereotype is the seasoned, battle-hardened sergeant who has great difficulty in relating to the new, inexperienced second lieutenant.

---

[20] Ralph Linton, "Concepts of Role and Status," in Theodore E. Newcomb and Eugene L. Hartley (eds.), *Readings in Social Psychology*, Holt, Rinehart and Winston, Inc., New York, 1947, p. 368.

Human organizations can be defined as role systems. "In defining human organizations as open systems of roles, we emphasized two cardinal facts: The *contrived nature* of human organizations, and the unique properties of a *structure consisting of acts or events* rather than unchanging physical components." [21] Organizations are much more than aggregates of men, machines, material, time, and space. Predicting organizational behavior requires emphasis on actions and events. What happens in organizations? How does it happen? These questions are more important than the question, What is it?

Certain activities are ascribed to particular positions in organizations. A complete set of activities for a particular position is its role. Formal documents such as position descriptions spell out the activities of a particular position or office, including how it relates to other similar positions in the organization. In many cases roles are not set forth explicitly, and yet they seem to be understood by organizational members. Whether

---

[21] Daniel Katz and Robert L. Kahn, *The Social Psychology of Organizations*, John Wiley & Sons, Inc., New York, 1966, p. 172.

formally or informally established, status and role systems are integral parts of any organization—from two-person groups to society as a whole.

Multiple Roles

However, role systems are not clear-cut; there are several complications which make it difficult to define particular roles and often lead to role conflict. The concept of multiple roles is one such phenomenon. Individuals play many roles simultaneously. Usually, however, only one role is active at a particular time while others are in relative degrees of latency. Multiple roles relate to multiple positions which an individual holds, often in various institutional settings—home, church, service organization, fraternal order, or work environment. Within each organization of which he is a member, he occupies a particular position and performs certain activities associated with that role. An individual's existence obviously varies in complexity according to the number of roles played in the organizations of which he is a part. Varying degrees of consistency in role playing may also affect the complexity of the situation.

Role Sets

For any particular position or status there is a variable number of orientations. Some roles are more complex than others.

> A particular social status involves, not a single associated role, but an array of associated roles. This is a basic characteristic of social structure. This fact of structure can be registered by a distinctive term, *role-set,* by which I mean that *complement of role relationships which persons have by virture of occupying a particular social status.* As one example: The single status of medical student entails not only the role of the student in relation to his teachers, but also an array of other roles relating the occupant of that status to other students, nurses, physicians, social workers, medical technicians, etc. Again: the status of public school teachers has its distinctive role-set, relating the teacher to his pupils, to colleagues, the school principal and superintendent, the Board of Education, and, on frequent occasions, to local patriotic organizations, to professional organizations of teachers, parent-teacher associations, and the like. [22]

It is important to understand the difference between the concept of multiple roles and that of role set. The former refers to different roles in different organizational settings. Role sets, on the other hand, relate to the various orientations which a specific position in a particular organization may require. The ultimate in complexity for individ-

---

[22] Merton, op. cit., p. 369.

ual behavior can be seen in the case of someone involved in many different institutional roles, all of which have complex role sets. At the other extreme (the pastoral life of the shepherd, perhaps) is the individual who is involved in very few organizations and whose roles—those he does play—are extremely simple and have very narrow role sets.

Role Perception

Accuracy in role perception has a definite impact on effectiveness and efficiency in organizations. Individuals have certain abilities and are motivated in varying degrees to perform designated tasks. However, if a task is incorrectly perceived, the result may be quite ineffective from the organizational point of view. On the other hand, an activity or role associated with a particular position could be perceived quite accurately and yet inefficient performance could result because of deficiencies in ability and/or motivation. These various elements are present in any organizational situation and must be considered together. The numerous factors affecting role perception can be considered in terms of the concept of role episode.

ROLE EPISODE [23]

Figure 11.2 illustrates the basic elements of role playing and the numerous confounding variables which influence this process and which illustrate the complexity of the organizational role-taking process. Personality and motivation affect individual behavior within an environment of technology, organization structure, and status systems. Group dynamics and interpersonal relationships (to be discussed in Chapter 12) also affect the role-taking process. In other words, the role episode takes place within the context of organizational technology and structure, the psychosocial system, and the managerial system.

A Model

The concept of a role episode is an oversimplification. It implies a beginning, an event or process, and an end. The core part of Figure 11.2 suggests a total sequence: role expectations (I) lead to role sending (II), which leads to a received role (III) with the episode culminating in a behavioral response to the role as received (IV). In reality, it is difficult to establish a beginning and ending point for role episodes. The process actually is never-ending, and there are many simultaneous processes going on at any given moment in time. Moreover, the model does not illustrate the conflict that is inevitable in the process. It is also an oversimplification to treat the role episode in a vacuum. Its context involves "confounding variables" which have an important impact upon the process itself.

---

[23] This section follows the discussion of "The Role Episode" by Katz and Kahn, op. cit., pp. 182–197.

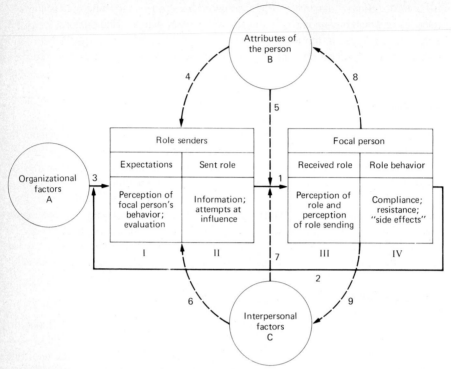

FIGURE 11.2 A THEORETICAL MODEL OF THE ROLE EPISODE AND FACTORS AFFECTING THE ORGANIZATIONAL ROLE-TAKING PROCESS (Adapted from Daniel Katz and Robert L. Kahn, *The Social Psychology of Organizations,* John Wiley & Sons, Inc., New York, 1966, pp. 182 and 187)

Four basic concepts are involved in the role episode model:

Role expectations are evaluative standards applied to the behavior of any person who occupies a given organizational office or position.

Sent role consists of communications stemming from role expectations and sent by members of the role set as attempts to influence the focal person.

Received role is the focal person's perception of the role sendings addressed to him, including those he "sends" to himself.

Role behavior is the response of the focal person to the complex of information and influence he has received. [24]

---

[24] Ibid., p. 182.

A baseball manager is expected to behave in certain ways in carrying out the activities of his office. He gets much advice from owners, fans, sportswriters, coaches, and players about how he should behave in certain situations. He filters this advice via selective perception and uses the residue, along with his own idea of the way the job should be done, to develop a behavior pattern which guides his actions. His actual role behavior is the result of his own propensity to act in certain ways as modified by the influence of those persons in his role set.

This same process or role episode can be detailed for any position—president, department head, or janitor.

Confounding Variables

The role episode takes place in the context of confounding variables such as the attributes of the person, as well as organizational and interpersonal influences. These three major confounding variables are indicated as circles in Figure 11.2. They represent the context of typical organizations regardless of the specific individuals occupying positions therein.

Organizational factors (A) have a direct causal relationship with role expectations. There are various prescriptions and proscriptions associated with particular positions in organizations. These make up the role expectations usually held by members of a role set and are determined, in part, by the broader organizational context, which includes technology, formal structure, job descriptions, policies and procedures, and reward systems. Many of these are spelled out formally in organizations, regardless of the personalities involved. Certainly, individuals adapt the system somewhat to their own idiosyncratic behavior patterns. However, many properties of organizations can be treated as independent of the particular persons occupying the various positions and "playing" the attendant roles.

Similar to organization factors, there are enduring personality traits (B) which describe the propensity of an individual to behave in certain ways. He has an overall value system and is motivated according to a particular hierarchy of needs. Role senders often modify their expectations with regard to particular positions based on their knowledge of the personalities involved. The enduring organizational factors are often adjusted in order to compensate slightly for idiosyncratic behavior on the part of a particular role taker.

The most obvious impact of personal attributes is in mediating between the sent role and the received role. Individual selective perception is at work; individuals are much more likely to receive information and be influenced by "sendings" which reinforce their own expectations with regard to a given role. Role senders may perceive considerable distortion between their expectations and the direction of their influence and the resultant behavior of the focal person. Meanwhile, the individual may sincerely believe he is acting as "directed."

Interpersonal factors (C) operate parallel to personal attributes in affecting the role episode process. The way in which the sent role is received will depend in great measure upon the interpersonal relationships between the focal person and the role senders. For example, influence varies directly with the degree of confidence an individual has in those who would seek to influence him. If he has no confidence or if an antagonistic atmosphere has developed, effective influence may be quite limited. On the other hand, if the sender or senders are respected and a congenial atmosphere prevails, the resultant behavior is quite likely to be influenced significantly by role senders.

As indicated previously, this model is an abstraction and simplification of the impact of role sending and role taking on individual behavior. The processes involved are complex, and they occur simultaneously rather than sequentially. Intuitively, however, these relationships do seem logical and can be observed in ongoing organizations. Moreover, the various phenomena involved have been tested to some extent with empirical research; many findings support the theoretical model as outlined in Figure 11.2. [25]

ROLE CONFLICT

As complex as the process illustrated in Figure 11.2 is, it does not reflect adequately the concept of role conflict. Some is implied in the selective perception or outright rejection of sent role by the focal person. However, many other types of role conflict can be identified. Conflict in this sense does not mean overt antagonism or violence. Rather, it involves the simultaneous occurrence of two or more role sendings for which the compliance with one precludes compliance with the others.

The foreman typically has been cited as a prime example of role conflict. On the one hand, management's expectations and related ''sendings'' stress his role in the managerial system and the need for decisiveness in planning and controlling operations. On the other hand, as a first-line supervisor he often has close ties with the people in his work group—his former peers in many cases. Their expectations and sendings may not coincide exactly with those coming from the top down. Similarly, he has many inputs from other foremen and his own perception of the role to be played. All these work together to provide an extremely complex environment for individual behavior. Let us look at several specific types of role conflict.

Types of Conflict

Four major types of role conflict can be identified: (1) person-role, (2) interrole, (3) intersender, and (4) intrasender. As indicated previously, the concept of *person-role* conflict is implied in Figure 11.2, where personal attributes mediate between the sent

---

[25] See the results of research cited in ibid., pp. 188–197.

role and that which is received by the focal person. Conflict occurs when the requirements of the role violate the needs, values, or capacities of the focal person. For example, Catholic priests have resigned in order to marry or because they could not espouse the doctrine prescribed by the Church on other issues. Or, a sheriff may have great difficulty in carrying out the eviction of an aged widow. This type of role conflict relates to the internal cognitive and motivational aspects of behavior. The other primary sources originate externally and provide part of the complex context for individual behavior in organizations.

Interrole conflict relates to the phenomenon of multiple goals for individuals simultaneously acting in several or many organizations. A person may find himself faced with sent expectations for a role in one organization which conflict with those for another role. An employee who is also an officer in the union could experience considerable role conflict. Similarly, an individual's family role may conflict with what is expected of him on the job. The focal person must somehow develop order out of chaos, rank the various demands on his behavior, and develop a system of trade-offs which allows him to decide that "on balance" he should behave in a certain way at a particular time.

Intersender conflict results when various members of the role set have different expectations for a particular role person and hence transmit sendings which are conflicting. In this case, there are pressures on an individual from many directions as the various senders attempt to influence his behavior. Any office providing service (maintenance perhaps) to many other organizational units experiences such conflict. Everyone presents his project under the guise of highest priority. Obviously, this is impossible, and some system must be invoked. The matrix organization which has resulted from the imposition of project management on top of traditional functional structure has resulted in intersender role conflict. The project manager expects certain behavior from his manufacturing manager. However, the vice-president of manufacturing has certain expectations with regard to the behavior of anyone in manufacturing, regardless of the particular program on which they function. In universities, department chairmen are appointed by deans and are expected to function as an extension of the administrative hierarchy from the board of regents through the president, dean, and to the faculty. On the other hand, the chairman is primarily a faculty member and often seeks to maintain collegial relationships with his former peers, who have definite expectations with regard to the role of the chairman. Intersender role conflict creates a complex environment for the focal person.

Intrasender conflict develops when one sender transmits conflicting instructions or expects behavior which is impossible in the light of earlier directives. A typical example is the supervisor's expectation that the incumbent in a particular position should improve efficiency while at the same time he explicitly denies his subordinate the authority to fire people or even cut costs in other, less dramatic ways. Intrasender conflict can occur with the transmission of messages which have conflicting parts. It is more common, however, for the conflict to arise from messages sent at different time periods.

Conflict by Organizational Level

Role conflict is evident in all organizations. The degree of conflict can vary significantly and can be related to the levels set forth in Figure 5.4. The more complex the job, the more likely the role conflict. For example, task specialization provides the means for developing a narrowly oriented job description with explicit instructions for anyone who occupies a given position. Therefore, in the operating subsystem, it is possible to forestall role conflict by developing explicit, detailed instructions for a particular task. At other levels—coordinative and strategic—there is much more opportunity for inter- and intrasender conflict to occur.The manager in the coordinative subsystem is typically a mediator and compromiser and hence receives much conflicting information designed to influence the decisions he makes and the role he plays. At the strategic level, the manager is operating at the boundary of his organization and hence is subject to much interrole conflict. As a member of the chamber of commerce, he is interested in pollution control. As president of a pulp and paper company, he is acutely aware of the cost of pollution control to his own company. This obviously leads to role conflict.

At any level, person-role conflict can occur. However, as one goes upward from operating through coordinative to strategic levels, the manager's job becomes increasingly complex, and the opportunity for person-role conflict increases. In other words, at higher levels there are many more opportunities for expectations with regard to the particular position to be at odds with the individual's own value system with regard to how he should behave.

One other type of role conflict should be mentioned—that of overload. In many organizations, the expectations of various senders with regard to a particular position may not necessarily conflict. However, there may be so many of them that it is impossible for one individual to fulfill the requirements. [26] In a sense, this creates a conflict between the expectations for the role and an individual's capacity to perform. Unless the focal person can establish a priority system or ignore some demands, he may "fall apart at the seams" or become ineffective in all his actions. Overload role conflict may be temporary if the various pressures are reduced over time. On the other hand, they may persist for an indefinite length of time and hence require more than ad hoc adjustments on the part of the focal person.

Coupled with the question of overload as a source of role conflict is the general aura surrounding the executive role. What behavior patterns must be exhibited in order to move ahead in today's organizations? Much of the folklore which has developed lauds the aggressive competitiveness of entrepreneurs and laments the unaggressive cooperativeness exhibited in most large-scale, complex organizations. In many organizations, these two general strains of folklore lead to role conflict. "The ambitious, zestful

---

[26] The role of the President of the United States has been described as "impossible" because of the multitude of agenices reporting to him. The response has been an increase in the White House staff so that the "office," rather than the President himself, responds to many of the day-to-day pressures. The presidents of many of today's conglomerates face similar problems. As the number and diversity of subsidiaries increase, role overload becomes a real concern.

young manager who is eager to make a mark may at first find pyramid-climbing an exasperating experience. For one thing, he will find himself working in a conflicting value system. He must appear a hot competitor, in keeping with the folklore, yet at the same time—and more important—he must prove himself a hot cooperator.''[27]

BUREAUCRATIC MAN?

''Prior to the 1950's it was part of American folklore that the way to succeed in American business was to follow in the footsteps of great individualists like Henry Ford or John D. Rockefeller. These men were known for their forcefulness and imagination and they were seldom accused of being tactful or cautious.''[28] This statement reflects the Protestant ethic and Social Darwinism as described in the discussion of the evolving managerial ideologies in Chapter 2. The general societal value system emphasized imagination and independence as dominant in business success or life in general. The concept of bureaucracy has been a countertrend. It deemphasizes the human element, particularly capriciousness, and stresses the formal structure of positions and established procedures.

One of the major questions in organization theory in the mid-twentieth century has been the role conflict generated by these two opposing concepts. Many ''viewers with alarm'' have written of the demise of individualism and the triumph of conformism and mediocrity in society in general and business and government organizations in particular.[29] Two of the most widely read works are *The Lonely Crowd,* by Riesman, and *The Organization Man,* by Whyte. The latter introduces the concept of the social ethic which is exemplified by the bureaucratic man who sacrifices individualism for extreme organizational loyalty.[30]

Much subsequent discussion of organizational life has centered around the two concepts of ''inner-directed'' and ''other-directed'' behavior, as set forth by Riesman. In terms of the model of role sending and role taking, inner-directedness emphasizes the internal value system of the focal person and gives greatest weight to his own perceptions and expectations with regard to a particular role. It emphasizes creative individualism in identifying and carrying out a particular organizational role.[31]

Other-directedness stresses the dominance of the expectations of others and role playing based on the external influence of other role senders. The extremes of this approach imply conformity and subservient behavior. The focal person keeps foremost in his mind the expectations of others as he performs his tasks. He must ''look good'' in the eyes of his superiors in order to get ahead. Cooperativeness is critical.

---

[27] Vance Packard, *Pyramid Climbers,* McGraw-Hill Book Company, New York, 1962, p. 21.
[28] Lyman W. Porter and Edward Lawler, III, *Managerial Attitudes and Performance,* Richard D. Irwin, Inc., Homewood, Ill., 1968, p. 99.
[29] See, for example, Alan Harrington, *Life in the Crystal Palace,* Alfred A. Knopf, Inc., New York, 1959; C. Wright Mills, *White Collar,* Oxford University Press, Fair Lawn, N.J., 1956; and Robert Heller, *The Great Executive Dream,* Delacorte Press, New York, 1972.
[30] William H. Whyte, Jr., *The Organization Man,* Simon and Schuster, Inc., New York, 1956.
[31] Robert Townsend, *Up the Organization,* Alfred A. Knopf, Inc., New York, 1970.

Because executives are prone to promote subordinates with characteristics and value systems similar to their own, this type of behavior seems appropriate and useful to ensure progress. A person is likely to emphasize the traits in others which he himself possesses. However, this does not necessarily support a case for other-directedness. He may perceive himself as individualistic and inner-directed and hence look for similar traits in subordinates.

Large-scale, complex organizations do require cooperative effort. Individualistic (particularly idiosyncratic) behavior patterns may be dysfunctional at low and middle levels. The phenomena described by Riesman, Whyte, and many others do seem apparent in organizations and society. It has become popular to decry the trends as a triumph of conformity and go-along-with-the-crowd behavior. The "bureaucratic man" is supposedly noncontroversial, adaptable, and incompetent. [32] The conclusions drawn from the writings of the "viewers with alarm" might well be that the "adaptable, socially attuned individual is going to succeed in business, while the creative, independent individual is in for trouble." [33] However, research has not substantiated such implications. In fact, the research that has been done seems to refute them.

Research on Bureaucratic Man

Porter and Lawler summarize their own research and the results of several other studies by stating, "All of these findings point to the conclusion that organizations not only tolerate but even *reward* inner-directed thinking and behavior." [34] Several kinds of research were involved, including tracing the promotions of lower and middle managers in large-scale organizations and measuring attitudes of managers toward traits which could be identified as relating to either inner- or other-directedness. One study indicated that inner-directedness was tolerated more in large organizations than in small ones. Managers with more inner-directed role perceptions, and presumably behavior, were rated highly both by themselves *and* by their superiors. [35]

Inner-directed behavior was rated higher by top-level managers than by those at lower levels. Presumably, those who have evidenced forceful, individualistic creativity have "fought" their way to the top. Such executives are more likely to prize the traits which they perceive as the keys to success in their own careers.

Other empirical research indicates that,

> There is a small but consistent tendency for men who work in bureaucratic organizations to be more intellectually flexible, more open to new experience, and more self-directed in their values than are men who work in nonbureaucratic organizations. This may in part result from bureaucracies' drawing on a more educated work force. In larger part, though, it appears to be a conse-

---

[32] "In a hierarchy, every employee tends to rise to his level of incompetence." Lawrence J. Peter and Raymond Hull, *The Peter Principle: Why Things Always Go ɓuoɹM*, Bantam Books, Inc., New York, 1969, p. 7.
[33] Porter and Lawler, op. cit., p. 100.
[34] Ibid., p. 117.
[35] Ibid.

quence of occupational conditions attendant on bureaucratization—notably, far greater job protections, somewhat higher income, and substantively more complex work. [36]

These findings seem to indicate that the "viewers with alarm" such as Riesman and Whyte were somewhat premature in their conclusions. Their writings were unsupported by empirical research and were probably based upon small samples of unsystematic observations. The current scene in most organizations certainly includes diverse examples of dress and hair styles that are as surprising as they are refreshing. Activism on many dimensions is also apparent. Values—individual and organizational—do change. [37]

It is also true that modern, large-scale organizations probably do not tolerate extremely deviant behavior, particularly at lower levels. Such individuals probably are not hired, but if so, they do not last very long. At the top levels, we have an entirely different atmosphere. Howard Hughes or J. Paul Getty, our society's two billionaires, can extoll the virtues of individualism and, indeed, can "get away with" eccentric behavior. Entrepreneurs in organizations of many sizes can do likewise as long as they are owner-managers.

The most appropriate behavior pattern for progress toward the top of modern, large-scale organizations seems to be forceful, creative individualism, which is *not too far out of line.* However, this picture certainly does not fit the dismal picture painted by Riesman, Whyte, and others.

Appropriate Managerial Behavior

The folklore concerning conformity and the supposed demise of individualism in our society has resulted in several trends. Many organizations have scrutinized their own atmosphere and reoriented their thinking with regard to role expectations concerning various positions and the behavior patterns which they want to encourage. The new look has been something like "unity without uniformity." While recognizing that organizational endeavor requires cooperative effort, organizations have made concerted attempts to preserve an opportunity for individual expression and different points of view.

Decentralization of decision making and functional professionalization foster individualism in organizations. At the same time, however, they spotlight the need for understanding human behavior and coordinating organizational endeavor. [38]

Job enlargement has become a focal point in many organizations. Rather than specializing tasks and reducing the amount of individual participation and decision

---

[36] Melvin L. Kohn, "Bureaucratic Man: A Portrait and an Interpretation," *American Sociological Review,* June 1971, p. 461.

[37] George E. Berkley, *The Administrative Revolution: Notes on the Passing of Organization Man,* Prentice-Hall, Inc., Englewood Cliffs, N.J., 1971.

[38] George Strauss, "Organization Man: Prospect for the Future," *California Management Review,* Spring 1964, pp. 5–16.

making, jobs have been delegated to employees in larger chunks, allowing them to exercise individual initiative in planning and controlling their own effort. As indicated earlier, this approach fosters role conflict of various types. However, the atmosphere created often improves enough that both effectiveness and efficiency increase. Self-actualization can be realized more readily, and achievement motivation is increasingly important in organizational behavior. These trends are likely to continue in the future.

The complexity in modern large-scale organizations is evident. The need for imaginative, innovative individualism is well recognized. However, the coordination of diverse resources toward objective accomplishment requires great skill in human relations as well. As Sayles says:

> It is strange indeed that the contemporary manager is now being maligned for what is his greatest challenge and potential accomplishment. The mainte-nance of effective human relationships in large-scale organizations is one of the marvels of our age. The skills of administration required to direct and control tens of thousands of people with differing backgrounds and interests, in order to produce coordinated effort directed toward predetermined objec-tives, tower above the achievements of the business buccaneers of an earlier age. They dealt with a few, simple variables primarily in the market place. Their apparent bravery and daring were more a product of the simplicity of their problem than of extraordinary skills or brute native courage. The diverse and complex responsibilities of the modern business offer a challenge many times more exciting to human abilities than an uncomplicated "inner-directed" ob-jective of maximum personal profits. [39]

SUMMARY

Status and role systems are basic to the psychosocial system of organizations. They provide frameworks within which perception, cognition, and motivation operate to influence individual behavior. Status refers to the prestige ranking of an individual in groups—small, informal groups, large, formal organizations, and society as a whole. With each status position is a related role or behavior pattern expected of the incumbent.

Heredity, money, education, and occupation are society's typical prestige-mea-suring characteristics. Overall status in a society may depend upon the composite of a multiplicity of such characteristics. Several kinds of status can be identified: (1) as-cribed or achieved, (2) functional or scalar, (3) positional or personal, and (4) active or latent.

Social classes have been identifiable throughout history. The goal of equality is a utopian concept because for each status characteristic some people are "more equal" than others. In many societies, there has been a typical pattern of a small super-rich

---

[39] Leonard R. Sayles, *Individualism and Big Business*, McGraw-Hill Book Company, New York, 1963, p. 184.

aristocracy and a vast number of very poor people. The increasing middle class in the United States and other countries can be identified on the basis of status characteristics such as income or education.

Occupational prestige is one of the most obvious and persistent systems of status. Moreover, the relative position of various occupations is quite similar for many cultures throughout the world.

Many symbols are used to indicate status. Uniforms, titles, and visible material goods (automobiles or houses, for example) are used to formalize relative positions of individuals in various groups. Desk size, carpet thickness, and view are several of the many "signs of office" in organizations.

Roles refer to ongoing behavior or the action related to a particular position in the organizational structure. Multiple roles are evident for individuals who are members of several or many groups. Moreover, each particular position has a role set—the organizational interfaces which call for specific behavior patterns. It is obvious that multiple roles and diverse role sets can lead to an extremely complex environment for the individual.

The *role episode* concept provides a useful framework for understanding the impact of roles on individual behavior. Role senders have expectations which are transmitted to the focal person who is a role taker. The sent role is received by the focal person, who behaves according to his own propensities as modified by the influence of the role senders. This basic role episode operates in the context of organizational and interpersonal variables together with the personal attributes of the focal person.

Person-role conflict occurs when an individual's value system is incongruent with the expectations he perceives for his behavior. *Interrole* conflict occurs when the expectations for one or more of the multiple roles precludes the performance of another. *Intersender* conflict occurs when inconsistent expectations are transmitted from several sources of pressure. The focal person cannot carry out both behavior patterns simultaneously. *Intrasender* conflict occurs when two incompatible sets of expectations are transmitted from one influence source.

A major source of concern in the mid-twentieth century is the overall role conflict which is evident. Should an individual be inner-directed or other-directed? Should he internalize the Protestant ethic or the social ethic? Should he conform or be individualistic? While much of the popular literature seems to suggest that the social ethic, other-directedness, and conformity prevail and are undermining the very foundations of American society, empirical research seems to indicate that the Protestant ethic, inner-directedness, and individualism are still widespread and rewarded in most organizations.

QUESTIONS AND PROBLEMS

1 Define and compare status and role.
2 Compare and contrast societal and organizational status.
3 Briefly describe the several kinds of status. Illustrate each kind with an example from your own experience.

4 "Status systems are inevitable and inherently useful." Do you agree? Why or why not?

5 What are the functional and dysfunctional aspects of social mobility?

6 Why have occupational prestige rankings been so stable over time? How do United States rankings compare with those in other cultures?

7 Make a list of various status symbols or "signs of office" which are apparent in your social, school, or work environment.

8 Compare and contrast multiple roles and role sets. How can these concepts be applied in your own situation?

9 Illustrate the concept of role episode (see Figure 11.2) with examples such as a bank vice-president, a traveling salesman, and a new employee with M.B.A. degree in hand.

10 Define the four major types of role conflict. Relate them to the examples in question 9.

11 Does empirical research support or refute the contentions of "viewers with alarm" that individualism and entrepreneurship are waning and that other-directedness is the best characteristic for success in organizations? What is your view of the "appropriate" behavior pattern for success in organizations? For success in general?

GROUP DYNAMICS

The human group is a pervasive phenomenon in modern society. As individuals we are members of families, neighborhood gangs, school cliques, athletic teams, fraternal orders, committees, and work groups. Small groups play an important role in establishing the psychosocial system of large organizations. Without social groups, concepts such as status and role would be meaningless. Social needs such as belongingness and esteem are powerful motivators which emanate from group relationships. Dynamic forces operate in small groups to facilitate the integration of individual activity toward collective achievement. Our discussion of group dynamics will be structured around the following topics:

> Group Defined
> Groups and Organizations
> Small Groups
> Performance of Work Groups
> Committees
> Communication
> Group Conflict
> Organization Improvement via Group Dynamics

GROUP DEFINED

A group is an assemblage, cluster, or aggregation of persons considered as being related in some way or united by common ties or interests—class, race, or occupation, for example. In psychology and sociology the emphasis is on interrelationships among members; the connotation of aggregation is not stressed. For example, Schein describes a psychological group as "any number of people who (1) interact with one another, (2) are psychologically aware of one another, and (3) perceive themselves to be a group." [1] The criteria of mutual awareness and interaction suggest that a casual crowd, a planeload of travelers, or a nationwide organization are not psychological groups.

Churchman says, "a group is any manifold of persons, identifiable over a period of time, and sufficiently integrated so that its actions and objectives are identifiable." [2] This adds the concept of identifiability from outside as well as inside the group.

In order to emphasize the significant difference between a large aggregation and a group, the concept of "small" groups has been used extensively. It is this connotation which we will emphasize in this chapter.

> By this term is meant an aggregate of people, from two up to an unspecified but not too large number, who associate together in face-to-face relationships over an extended period of time, who differentiate themselves in some regard from others around them, who are mutually aware of their membership in the group, and whose personal relations are taken as an end in itself. It is impossible to specify a strict upper limit on the size of the informal group, except for the limitation imposed by the requirement that all the members be able to engage in direct personal relations at one time—which means, roughly, an upper limit of around fifteen to twenty. If the aggregate gets much larger than that, it begins to lose some of the quality of a small group or, indeed, begins to break up into small subgroups. [3]

This definition covers families, neighborhood gangs, athletic teams, school cliques, committees, subparts of departments in large organizations, and many other similar groups.

Interaction and Dynamics

The definition of a group, particularly a small group, stresses face-to-face relationships and interaction among individuals. Interaction can be broadly construed as any type of communication—written or oral as well as gestures or facial expressions. "Usually interaction is direct communication—mainly talking and listening, often writing and reading—but it can also include gestures, glances, nods, or shakes of the head, pats on the back, frowns, caresses, or slaps, or any other way in which meaning can be

---

[1] Edgar H. Schein, *Organizational Psychology*, 2d ed., Prentice-Hall, Inc., Englewood Cliffs, N.J., 1970, p. 81.

[2] C. West Churchman, *Prediction and Optimal Decision*, Prentice-Hall, Inc., Englewood Cliffs, N.J., 1961, p. 299.

[3] Bernard Berelson and Gary A. Steiner, *Human Behavior*, Harcourt, Brace & World, Inc., New York, 1964, p. 325.

transmitted from one person to another and back again.''[4] Without these kinds of interactions a group would be quite static in nature. It would be a collection of individuals. The term *dynamic* in ''group dynamics'' implies the kinds of interactions indicated above. It also implies continuously *changing* and *adjusting* relationships among group members. This aspect of group behavior is a key ingredient in the overall psychosocial system of organizations.

GROUPS AND ORGANIZATIONS

The small group performs a mediating function by linking the individual and the organization. Each individual is a member of various formal and informal small groups within a given organization. He is formally assigned to a work group which may develop informal subgroups in the process of carrying out the assigned task. He may serve on several or many permanent or temporary committees. While he may contribute individually—as a salesman or researcher—the small group is a more typical mechanism through which individuals contribute to organizational endeavor.

An *organized group* is a particular variety of social group. ''It is based on the repetition of interaction among members, and the resulting relationships have some degree of permanence. The organized group is a continuous group. It can disperse, reassemble with the same membership, and repeat the relationships established between pairs of positions.''[5] The important aspect of this statement is the concept of repetitive relationships. Moreover, there is reference to pairs of ''positions'' rather than people. This implies the structural nature of organized groups.

An organization structure is an abstract entity which is comprised of several positions rather than people. Formal organizations are defined by diagrams relating positions or documents describing the duties and responsibilities of various roles. As an organized group persists and develops a unique character, it becomes formalized and structured. Technology often dictates organizational arrangements as well as the type and degree of interaction in work groups. A noisy assembly line often precludes communication between workers; scientific research may call for isolated individual effort or a team approach; and a planning committee involves considerable group effort by design.

An organization can be thought of as the merger of two concepts: (1) the group as a set of persons and (2) the structure as a set of positions. Obviously, groups change with the addition or subtraction of members. The structure, however, does not change with changes in personnel. The positions remain the same until formal adjustments are made in the set of positions involved. An organization, being a combination of these two phenomena, does adjust with changes in personnel. However, the amount of such change varies by organization. Rigid, bureaucratic-mechanistic organizations may be relatively institutionalized and immune to changes in personnel. Adaptive-organic orga-

---

[4] Ibid., p. 326.
[5] Theodore Caplow, *Principles of Organization*, Harcourt, Brace & World, Inc., New York, 1964, p. 12.

nizations may be less rigidly defined and show a tendency to adjust continually to the personalities occupying the various positions. Obviously each organization, or subpart of a particular organization, varies with respect to this phenomenon. The particular institutional environment affects the organization structure, and this in turn affects the group dynamics taking place in various subparts of the overall system.

Various kinds of relationships are evident between groups and organizations. In some cases the organization may be coterminous with a small group—less than twenty members interacting daily on a face-to-face basis, for example. In most cases, however, the group of persons comprising an organization will be divided into many subsystems. Depending upon the overall size, the subdivision process may progress through many vertical levels and/or across horizontal departmentation. Many informal, unauthorized subgroups develop spontaneously because of a felt need of the individuals involved.

Peer groups are probably the most common of such relationships. However, informal groups can and do span vertical levels in many organizations. The "tie that binds" may be external in origin, such as ethnic background or common recreational pursuits. It may be related to the organization—a car pool, for example. Or, such groups may be based on the development of an interest in a particular idea or project within the scope of the formal endeavor.

While groups of all sizes are important in understanding organizational behavior, the small group is of particular interest because of its integral role in mediating the relationship between the individual and the organization. Much of the research and writing on group dynamics has emphasized small groups in general and small work groups in particular.

SMALL GROUPS

Small-group theory has developed as a separate area of study in the behavioral sciences. In this section we will concentrate on a general framework as background for a specific type of small group—the work group. Shull describes the importance of small-group theory in organization and management as follows:

> The theoretical relevance of this body of knowledge is evident from a number of standpoints, since the small group: (1) is an ubiquitous and inevitable element of complex social systems; (2) plays an important part in the development and elaboration of personality; (3) is a major factor in processes of socialization and control; (4) bears many resemblances—as a social system—to large-scale social systems; and (5) can be mobilized as a powerful motivational force. [6]

---

[6] Fremont A. Shull, Jr. (with André L. Delbecq), *Selected Readings in Management* (second series), Richard D. Irwin, Inc., Homewood, Ill., 1962, p. 313.

Several of these points have been stressed previously. Individuals are inevitably involved in numerous small groups which affect overall personality development and specific behavior. Social needs are powerful motivators which are often implemented via small groups. Individual behavior patterns evolve, in large part, through the processes of socialization and control which are evident in the various small groups within which a person maintains membership.

Conceptual Schemes

Homans suggests three concepts for understanding individual behavior in social groups: *activity, interaction,* and *sentiment.*[7] This framework makes explicit some commonsense notions about social groups. The more the people share activities, the more likely they are to interact with one another. The reciprocal is also true; interaction in one sphere of activity often leads to shared activity in unrelated spheres. Individuals with shared sentiments are more likely to interact with one another and to engage in joint activities. And as activities are shared and interactions increase over a period of time, the degree of shared sentiments is also likely to increase. In other words, individuals in social groups, particularly small groups, are likely to evolve similar value systems. This is particularly true concerning the basic activity of the specific group. However, continued interactions of an intimate, face-to-face nature may result in shared sentiments over a wide range of subjects beyond the legitimate interests of the group itself.

Sentiments evolving from interactions and activities in the total system are carried by individuals into the internal environment of the small group, providing an overall "atmosphere" for its activities and interactions. However, this is a two-way street whereby sentiments evolving out of activities and interactions in the small group have an impact on the external environment and hence the total social system.

Using a technique called *sociometry,* researchers have analyzed small groups in order to establish patterns of interactions among members. The results of such analysis provide a picture of the way the participants relate to each other when engaged in various activities, both formal tasks and informal activities such as eating lunch or riding to work. A typical set of relationships developed via sociometric analysis is shown in Figure 12.1. According to Scott, "there are three status categories: the primary group, the fringe status, and the out status. The primary group, which corresponds to the concept of 'small group' as we have been using it, is the focal point of this organization's orbit. It is made up of people who have reached consensus. The primary group establishes and maintains a value system comprising behavioral norms."[8]

The informal leader is A. Other individuals are grouped around him in various degrees of "inness." K and L are completely "out of it." G, H, I, and J have fringe status with respect to the primary group. Such status may be temporary in that an individual

---

[7] George C. Homans, *The Human Group,* Harcourt, Brace & World, Inc., New York, 1950, p. 43.
[8] William G. Scott, *Organization Theory,* Richard D. Irwin, Inc., Homewood, Ill., 1967, p. 93.

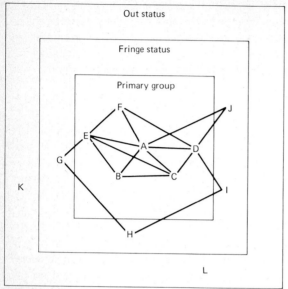

FIGURE 12.1 THE ORBIT OF SMALL-GROUP RELATIONSHIPS (William G. Scott, *Organization Theory*, Richard D. Irwin, Inc., Homewood, Ill., 1967, p. 93)

may be in the process of working himself into or out of the primary group. Or, such status may be relatively permanent in the case where a "fringy" shares only a limited number of the interests of the small group.

The individuals with "out" status in this model appear to be isolates. That is, they have no common interests or ties but are alike only in that they are not a part of the group depicted. Such isolation may be of no consequence to the individual if he has little or no interest in belonging to the primary group. If he has a strong desire to join, however, his recognition of his excluded condition could have significant impact upon his personality and behavior. If several individuals recognize such a condition, they may band together and form a primary group whose main tie is the degree of isolation from some other primary group.

Other Characteristics

Relatively permanent, primary, spontaneous, informal small groups have a high degree of *naturalness*. Spontaneity leads to the presence of this characteristic. Contrived groups may develop it over a period of time if the natural or informal interactions coincide with the formally designated ones.

Members of small groups typically have the ability to *empathize* to a high degree with other group members. Constant interaction over a relatively long period of time provides the opportunity to gain insight into the value system of other members of the group. This allows the "putting yourself in another's shoes" frame of reference which is important for empathizing.

Small, informal groups often give evidence of considerable *pressure to conform* to established standards. Constant face-to-face interaction makes most individual behavior an "open book." Thus maintenance of a position in any primary group typically requires behavior patterns which are acceptable, in large measure, by the group.

While many small groups do not guide the behavior of members explicitly, *unity of purpose* is a necessity. Group objectives must be internalized by individual members. Similarly, a *cohesive* relationship is to be expected in small, informal groups.

Social distance is at a *minimum* in small, informal groups. One can deal "at arm's length" with other members of large social groups or organizations. This approach is also possible in dealing with "positions" in bureaucratic institutions. In small, informal groups, however, such formality is impossible; members must interact with other unique and relatively well-defined personalities.

PERFORMANCE OF WORK GROUPS

Many variables affect individual performance in any activity, particularly work. Physical working conditions are important, as are individually oriented elements such as safety or monetary rewards. Many of the factors which motivate individuals to perform are social in nature—prestige or recognition, for example. "Our brief analysis of the role of motivation in productivity reiterates and confirms what the greater bulk of research on motivation in industry has borne out: Motivation is not wholly—nor even primarily—an individual variable. Certainly its force and direction are functions of the social situation in which it arises and is exercised."[9]

Another influence on performance is competition between one individual and another or many others. Allport cites several research studies which compare an individual's normal solitary performance with his performance when other people are present. The results indicate that group situations produce a greater output of energy and achievement.[10] He elaborates on this conclusion by distinguishing two probable factors: "emotional competitiveness on the one hand, and simple dynamogenic effect resulting from the sights and sounds of co-workers on the other."[11] These are generalizations, of course. In some cases individuals do worse in competitive situations—quantitatively and/or qualitatively.

The dynamics of work-group performance is concerned particularly with face-to-face or cooperative groups. While some attention is devoted to the sum of individual output in group situations, more attention has been devoted to the output of the group as a collective entity. In many cases output can be summed for the various individuals

---

[9] Hubert Bonner, *Group Dynamics: Principles and Applications,* The Ronald Press Company, New York, 1959, pp. 289–290.
[10] Gordon W. Allport, "Historical Background of Modern Social Psychology," in Gardner Lindzey (ed.), *Handbook of Social Psychology,* Addison-Wesley Publishing Company, Inc., Reading, Mass., 1954, p. 46.
[11] Ibid.

because their efforts are independent. In many other cases, however, productivity is dependent on the efficiency of the complete system of interdependent parts. Total performance is only as good as the weakest link.

The dynamic complexity of work-group performance came to light originally as the result of the now legendary experiments at Western Electric's Hawthorne Works in Chicago. The studies, summarized in Chapter 4, were conducted during the late 1920s and early 1930s and focused on sources of employee satisfaction or dissatisfaction at work. The impact of experimental conditions fostered changes in the relationships among operators and between operators and supervisors. It became apparent that group processes were important in facilitating or inhibiting change. [12]

Thus social interrelationships and many other aspects of group dynamics moved from tangential interest into the spotlight of organization theorists and management practitioners. A great deal of attention has been focused on the problem of work groups restricting output, that is, "pegging" production at some level below the actual capacity of the group and hence suboptimal from the standpoint of the overall organization. There are a number of causes of this tendency, one of the most important of which is cohesiveness.

Cohesiveness and Internalization of Organizational Goals

The joint or compound impact of cohesiveness and internalization of organizational goals on group effectiveness and efficiency is illustrated in Figure 12.2. The degree of cohesiveness in a group is a complex phenomenon which results from combining the

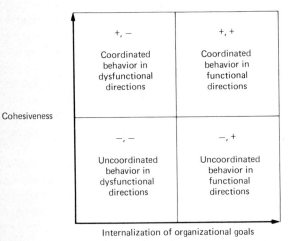

Cohesiveness

+, − Coordinated behavior in dysfunctional directions	+, + Coordinated behavior in functional directions
−, − Uncoordinated behavior in dysfunctional directions	−, + Uncoordinated behavior in functional directions

Internalization of organizational goals

FIGURE 12.2   THE JOINT IMPACT OF COHESIVENESS AND INTERNALIZATION OF ORGANIZA-TIONAL GOALS ON GROUP EFFECTIVENESS AND EFFICIENCY

---

[12] Fritz J. Roethlisberger and William J. Dickson, *Management and the Worker*, Harvard University Press, Cambridge, Mass., 1939.

net attraction (or repulsion) for each member. Many forces are at work on each individual which either attract or repel him. Some members may "go through the motions" as far as group activities are concerned. They may interact perfunctorily and only when absolutely necessary. It is unlikely that such a situation would result in shared sentiments. Hence the group would not be very cohesive.

Obviously, in any group there is a gradation of attraction for individual members. Some will identify more strongly with group values than others. Similarly, the composite of individual attitudes will vary widely. Some groups will be extremely cohesive and integrated; others will be uncohesive and diffuse. Figure 12.2 shows only two distinct categories. However, the left axis indicates a continuum of cohesiveness with a dichotomy identified as uncoordinated versus coordinated behavior. The second dimension, "internalization of organizational goals," is related to direction of effort. This concept, much like cohesiveness, can be viewed as a complex phenomenon which is a composite of individual propensities to internalize organizational goals. Again, there are degrees for each individual and for the group composite.

The joint impact of these two phenomena can be illustrated via the simplified dichotomy in Figure 12.2. The degree of cohesiveness in a work group can lead toward uncoordinated or coordinated behavior. If the group, through its individual members, accepts and internalizes the objectives of the organization, behavior will very likely be functional from the overall system point of view. However, subgroup goals may vary as much as 180 degrees from those of the organization. In such cases subgroup behavior will probably be dysfunctional from the overall system point of view. If the individuals in a subgroup have not internalized the organizational goals *and* are not well integrated, the results are unpredictable but probably dysfunctional.

Highly cohesive groups with goals which differ from those of the organization can be quite successful in disrupting the system. If unintegrated individuals just happen to have goals which coincide with those of the organization, the result is likely to be functional from the organization point of view, but haphazard, uncoordinated behavior is to be expected.

The optimal condition is described as "coordinated behavior in functional directions." In this case the group is cohesive and motivated in directions which are in line with organizational goals. This is the condition which organization theory seeks to understand. The evolving body of knowledge is of utmost interest to managers as they strive to develop work groups with characteristics which lead toward organizational effectiveness and efficiency, as well as participant satisfaction.

Productivity

Accelerating technology has had a significant impact upon organization structure and psychosocial systems. Since the industrial revolution, there has been a relentless trend toward mechanization, automation, and specialization of worker effort. A major thrust of scientific management was the division of tasks into elemental parts which could be mastered by workers with specialized skills. Mass production has been facilitated by breaking manufacturing tasks into subparts, a task that can be accomplished through specialization of mechanical equipment and/or personal skills. Coordinating such complex systems becomes increasingly important as specialization is carried to the extreme.

In the pre-mass-production era an individual could manufacture a pair of shoes or a wheelbarrow by himself. There was no need to coordinate or manage his activities in any other way than through his own internal decision-making processes. At the other extreme are large-scale, complex organizations involved in producing goods and services. Men, machines, materials, money, time, and space must be managed astutely in order to ensure effective and efficient operations. A great deal of planning is required in order to design an effective system—one which accomplishes the task as defined.

Obviously, specialization has an important place in organizational endeavor. It facilitates increased productivity in many cases. Moreover, in many situations the jobs are too large and/or complex for any one individual to carry out. The scientific and technological requirements for the Apollo project illustrate this condition. No one individual can be expected to have the knowledge and skills required to accomplish such a task. Breaking the overall job into specialized subsystems is absolutely essential. The increasing importance of management as the integrative and coordinative function is evident.

Another question concerns the efficiency or productivity of the system. As long as people are involved, individual, small-group, and organizational motivation becomes important for performance. The psychosocial system provides the overall atmosphere within which work groups operate. Extremely specialized mass-production systems often preclude the use of "groups" on the job. Individuals are relatively isolated because of the physical separation of the jobs on an assembly line and/or because the noise level in many operations precludes much communication among workers. However, small groups do develop during lunch breaks or before and after work. Such groups, while not interacting during the actual work period, can, nevertheless, have a significant impact on the productivity of the system.

Considerable attention has been focused in recent years on reversing the trend toward specialization. Job enrichment has been stressed as a means of providing a greater worker satisfaction from the task itself. In many cases this approach has involved letting work groups decide on the breakdown of tasks and the assignment of jobs to individuals. Often some system of rotation is developed in order to enlarge the scope of each individual's skill.

Trist and Bamforth describe the impact of increased mechanization in English coal mining. [13] Traditionally the work was organized in such a way that small teams of two to four men performed the entire operation of mining coal. Over a period of time these small face-to-face working groups became extremely cohesive and well-integrated. The introduction of the new, more mechanized longwall method completely disrupted the established system. It specialized the operation with a separate phase

---

[13] E. L. Trist and K. W. Bamforth, "Some Social and Psychological Consequences of the Longwall Method of Coal-getting," *Human Relations*, February 1951, pp. 3–38.

being carried out on each of three shifts during a twenty-four-hour period. Groups of ten or twenty "specialists" worked on each shift.

The abolition of small face-to-face work groups in the mechanization and reorganization led to serious problems of absenteeism, turnover, and sickness among miners, including psychosomatic disorders. Productivity dropped off considerably under the physically improved, mechanized longwall method. The aftermath of these developments has been a gradual, spontaneous, and informal drift back toward the previous system. Trist and Bamforth suggest that these various readjustments focused on restoring small face-to-face work groups with responsible autonomy, greater work-group cohesiveness, and greater satisfaction. They conclude that "it is difficult to see how these problems can be solved effectively without restoring responsible autonomy to primary groups throughout the system and insuring that each of these groups has the satisfying sub-whole as its work task, and some scope of flexibility in work pace." [14]

These developments parallel similar trends in United States industry. Job enrichment for the individual as well as for primary work groups is an integral part of an overall movement toward power equalization and industrial humanism. [15]

The Hawthorne experiments originally were not designed to study group dynamics. They focused on the impact of physiological factors such as fatigue and the physical environment. However, "the conclusion finally arrived at was that increased productivity was a function of improved human relations. The entire social situation had been altered in ways that fostered friendly relations among workers. In addition, the supervision of workers had been taken over by the researchers, who, in the interest of maintaining worker cooperation in the experiments, were very informal and non-directive in their approach." [16]

A complex system of forces was at work—group dynamics. In these studies, and others carried out since, observers have identified many informal relationships which can either facilitate or hinder productivity. Norms are often established for a "fair day's" work. Those that fall significantly below are pressured by the group to "shape up." At the other extreme, an individual who sets too fast a pace may be cautioned (or even coerced) to "get back in line." In a small-work-group environment which includes "fixed" productivity, modal producers enjoy the highest informal status among peers. "Because of these conditions the over-producers as well as the under-producers are penalized by loss of respect or even rejection." [17]

While work restrictions have probably been the most publicized facet of small-group dynamics, other more positive aspects should be recognized. As indicated above, the subpar producer is encouraged and often helped to improve his productivity.

---

[14] Ibid., p. 38.
[15] Richard E. Walton, "How to Counter Alienation in the Plant," *Harvard Business Review*, November–December 1972, pp. 70–81.
[16] Peter M. Blau and W. Richard Scott, *Formal Organizations*, Chandler Publishing Company, San Francisco, 1962, p. 90.
[17] Abraham Zaleznik et al., *The Motivation, Productivity, and Satisfaction of Workers*, Harvard Graduate School of Business Administration, Boston, 1958, pp. 231–232.

In many cases individuals learn from peers within the primary group. In some cases the better workers help others to attain more and better-quality output.

One study indicated that salesmen cooperated informally to balance their production even though management placed great stress on competition between salesmen through the use of commission systems, contests, and other similar incentives. [18] Whether or not such an informal system is dysfunctional to overall organizational endeavor is difficult to determine. A competitive system may have resulted in larger total sales. However, it is not clear that efforts to balance sales among the members of the group resulted in a reduced total output. Less emphasis on strictly "selling" activity allows time for using individual skills and developing customer relations on a broader scale. Such "nonsales" activity could lead to more well-rounded individuals and more effective and efficient performance of the work group as a whole.

The importance of work-group solidarity has been recognized by the armed forces. Because of the intimate face-to-face contacts of combat units over a period of time, extreme personal loyalties and group cohesion are often developed. An individual replacement in such a unit is often extremely disruptive. Thus, in World War II it became the practice, wherever possible, to substitute entire units, which had been molded through a training period, rather than individuals.

Likert cites a number of researches, both in this country and abroad, which result in similar findings with regard to the effect of work-group dynamics on performance. He concludes:

> As the importance of group influence has been recognized and as more precise measurements have been obtained, there is increasing evidence which points to the power of group influences upon the functioning of organizations. In those situations where the management has recognized the power of group motivational forces and has used the kind of leadership required to develop and focus these motivational forces on achieving the organization's objectives, the performance of the organization tends to be appreciably above the average achieved by other methods of leadership and management. Membership of groups which have common goals to which they are strongly committed, high peer-group loyalty, favorable attitudes between superiors and subordinates, and a high level of skill in interaction clearly can achieve far more than the same people acting as a mere assemblage. [19]

This statement stresses the potential for group work performance and the role of management in creating an appropriate environment. The role of leadership will be discussed in more detail in the following chapter. Also, we must recognize that the potential envisioned may or may not be achieved, depending upon whether the group goals and those of the overall organization are "in tune."

---

[18] Nicholas Babchuck and William J. Goode, "Work Incentives in a Self-determined Group," *American Sociological Review*, October 1951, pp. 679–687.
[19] Rensis Likert, *New Patterns of Management*, McGraw-Hill Book Company, New York, 1961, p. 36.

COMMITTEES

Committees have probably had as much "bad press" as any phenomenon in modern Western civilization. They are described as both ineffective and inefficient. Typical quips are "A camel is a horse designed by a committee" and "The purpose of a committee is to: (1) reduce tranquility, (2) increase dissatisfaction, (3) divide responsibility, and (4) stave off action." We all seem hypersensitive to the seemingly endless committee meetings which are a part of organizational activity. Committees function at all levels in organizations from the board of directors to the shop grievance committee.

Why are committees so ubiquitous? Part of the reason lies in man's basic nature as a social animal. He seeks cooperative relationships in all phases of his life. He typically enjoys face-to-face relationships in groups of all types, including committees.

The dynamic, self-made, entrepreneur type of individual may espouse an abhorrence for committees. He may advocate that an individual can and must have the authority and responsibility for decision making and that committees only cloud the issue and make the system both less effective and less efficient. Obviously there are situations where an individual approach is both necessary and appropriate. However, there are many other situations where it is inappropriate if not impossible.

A democratic society is based on collective wisdom for planning and controlling activities. We shy away from totalitarian approaches and the fiats of dictators. We use twelve-man juries to decide many legal questions, and a nine-man Supreme Court provides the ultimate interpretation for many complex societal issues. We assume that the collective wisdom of the elected congressional officials is superior in important ways to a "one-man show." At times the process seems tedious and inefficient because of the seemingly endless fact finding of subcommittees and the long time spans between the introduction of proposed measures and their enactment.

Similar processes are evident in all large-scale organizations—business, government, and other. For many business problems one man simply does not have all the required knowledge and/or skill. Therefore, he must call on others for support. Extended committee deliberation is typical among doctors, all of whom may be specialists in different subparts of the medical field, as they attempt to diagnose and prescribe treatments for specific cases.

Often the committee approach is useful in planning the implementation of changes in organization structure and/or processes. Involving several people in the decision-making phase may seem inefficient; however, if the support of these persons is critical in order to ensure wholehearted cooperation of employees during the implementation phase, such time may be an investment which pays off manifoldly over the long run.

Making Committees More Effective

In modern organizations committees are seen as not only necessary but functional. The key question is how to make them more effective. By making sure that only relevant people are involved on a particular issue we can avoid wasting the time of committee members. By involving members in building agendas we can encourage participation on topics of interest to the group. By paying attention to the process by which the committee functions, as well as to the task it is engaged in, we can improve performance and increase participant satisfaction. For example, it may be useful to encourage the normally quiet members in order to ensure wider participation.

The frustration level of committees can often be reduced by having written information items distributed rather than read and by separating issues into (1) action items and (2) exploratory discussions. In this way the group has a better sense of what it is trying to accomplish during a particular meeting.

The pervasiveness of committee approaches to decision making in all organizations in society fits our general contention that many activities are carried out on a group basis. Hence, understanding group dynamics in any setting is important for understanding committee processes. Committees are only one specific example of the countless small groups in society. For committees or task-performing groups, several aspects of group dynamics (communications and conflict) are important enough to warrant specific detailed treatment.

COMMUNICATION

The core of group dynamics is interaction among members. Interaction, in the broad sense, is any means of communication between people. Thus communication plays an extremely important role in group dynamics.

Most of the research on communication in small groups has emphasized informal relationships which seem to develop spontaneously. However, certain kinds of communication patterns can be established formally—when a chairman is appointed to an ad hoc committee or when the physical arrangements of a particular room dictate relationships. Even in these kinds of situations communication patterns can evolve which support or transcend and subvert the supposedly established pattern. The analysis of communication processes in groups often reveals a communication ''center'' which was not planned.

While countless variations could be identified for small groups, certain basic communication patterns have emerged from numerous research studies. Four typical arrangements of five-member groups are illustrated in Figure 12.3. The numbers refer to how many times that particular individual was recognized as a leader. The data indicate that a leader seems to emerge at the position of highest centrality—the hub of the wheel, the fork of the Y, and the midpoint of the chain. For the circle, forces other than the communications network obviously become more important in the evolution of the leader in the small group.

These communication patterns could be elaborated in many ways. For example, the ties between any two of the individual group members could be either one-way or two-way communication. Also, in the wheel pattern, communication might flow only outward to peripheral members. Or there might be differential patterns for various pairs within the same basic network. A particular individual may communicate on a two-way

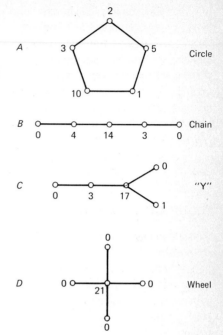

FIGURE 12.3 BASIC COMMUNICATION NETWORKS IN TASK-ORIENTED SMALL GROUPS. The numbers refer to the frequency of occurrence of recognized leaders at different positions in the various patterns. (Adapted from Bernard Berelson and Gary A. Steiner, *Human Behavior,* Harcourt, Brace & World, Inc., New York, 1964, p. 356.)

basis with one member and on a one-way basis with another. This kind of analysis could superimpose a combination of several patterns—some elements of a wheel and some of a circle, for example—within the primary group identified by sociometric analysis.

The question of one-way versus two-way communication can be related to the discussion of committees. An individual may make a decision and communicate it to group members with the expectation that a particular action will be carried out. However, the probability that what the listener heard coincides with what the speaker or writer said or wrote is quite small. The technical problems of communication are quite severe. Of even more concern are semantic difficulties. Redundancy and feedback (through mutual communication) go a long way to offset the hazards of one-way communication. By sitting down to discuss an issue or plan there can be enough interaction to ensure a reasonable amount of understanding.

Mr. B can reply by saying, "This is what I understand you to mean, right?" Mr. A can then nod in agreement or elaborate further if, in his impression, B has not received the message accurately. This sort of mutual give-and-take can proceed as long as necessary in order to achieve mutual understanding. Obviously, not all issues require such a process. Simple directives might well be issued outward and/or downward from a central source on a one-way channel. However, many other issues should be given more thorough "airing" in order to forestall misunderstandings and long-run dysfunctional consequences.

Two-way communication and ''checking for meaning'' are typically a time-consuming process compared to one-way communication. However, research indicates that the accuracy of transmitted messages as well as the confidence of receivers increases when a two-way process is used. There is a need, therefore, to couple a cost/benefit analysis with a sense of the situation. Emphasis on a one-way communication process in order to save time may be shortsighted because the illusion of communication may lead to dysfunctional organizational consequences. We recently noticed a sign in a steno pool which seems apropos:

> Why is it that there is never enough time to do it right in the first place, but there is always enough time to do it over again?

GROUP CONFLICT

Conflict can have functional as well as dysfunctional effects on persons, groups, and organizations. It has been an important subject in behavioral science and has been studied from many points of view. However, Coser suggests that ''the majority of sociologists who dominate contemporary sociology . . . center attention predominately upon problems of adjustment rather than upon conflict; upon social statics rather than upon dynamics. Of key problematic importance to them has been the maintenance of existing structures and the ways and means of ensuring their smooth functioning. They have focused upon maladjustments and tensions which interfere with consensus.'' [20] As an example, he suggests that Parsons' general orientation has led him to view conflict as dysfunctional and disruptive and to disregard its positive functions. Conflict is described as a partly avoidable, partly inevitable and endemic form of sickness in the body social. [21]

In contrast to these views there is the notion of conflict not only as inevitable but as an important, positive phenomenon in society. In a decision-making framework, there is always conflict whenever alternatives are apparent. Individuals, groups, and organizations must make choices and ''resolve'' such conflict. This is a recurring phenomenon with continuing cycles of conflict and resolution.

Coser uses Simmel's basic treatise as a framework for his own analysis and concludes that conflict is a form of socialization. [22]

> This means essentially that, to paraphrase the opening pages of Simmel's essay, no group can be entirely harmonious, for it would then be devoid of process and structure. Groups require disharmony as well as harmony, dissociation as well as association; and conflicts within them are by no means altogether disruptive factors. Group formation is the result of both types of

---

[20] Lewis Coser, *The Functions of Social Conflict,* The Free Press of Glencoe, New York, 1956, p. 20.
[21] Ibid., p. 23.
[22] Georg Simmel, *Conflict,* trans. by Kurt H. Wolff, The Free Press of Glencoe, New York, 1955.

processes. The belief that one process tears down what the other builds up, so that what finally remains is the result of subtracting the one from the other, is based on a misconception. On the contrary, both "positive" and "negative" factors build group relations. Conflict as well as cooperation has social functions. Far from being necessarily dysfunctional, a certain degree of conflict is an essential element in group formation and the persistence of group life. [23]

Dimensions of Conflict

Conflict can take many forms—from ideological differences to personality clashes and from competition between companies to war between nations. Pondy describes a variety of interpretations:

> The term conflict has been used at one time or another in literature to describe: (1) *antecedent conditions* (for example, scarcity of resources, policy differences) of conflictful behavior, (2) *affective states* (e.g., stress, tension, hostility, anxiety, etc.) of the individuals involved, (3) *cognitive states* of individuals, i.e.; their perception or awareness of conflictful situations, and (4) *conflictful behavior,* ranging from passive resistance to overt aggression. [24]

Rather than trying to determine which use is "correct," they all should be considered part of the dynamic processes of social groups. Conditions, attitudes, cognitions, and behavior can be considered parts of a recurring process such as that illustrated in Figure 12.4. Five stages of a conflict episode are identified and related to the various connotations set forth above. They are (1) latent conflict (conditions), (2) perceived conflict (cognition), (3) felt conflict (affect), (4) manifest conflict (behavior), and (5) conflict aftermath (conditions). This general model describes typical conflict situations. However, it should not be assumed that every conflict episode results in overt aggression. Or that latent conflict is always perceived and felt.

As indicated in Figure 12.4 the conflict episode is an open system with inputs from the environment which can conceivably alter latent conflict. Similarly, both organizational and external forces affect the individual personality, leading to differential degrees of felt conflict. Suppression mechanisms are also an integral part of the individual personality and hence affect the degree to which latent conflict is perceived and felt. While some individuals are insensitive to signals which may indicate latent conflict, others have sharply focused perceptive mechanisms and in a sense are "always looking for trouble."

If conflict reaches the manifest stage, overt behavior depends upon the individual, the environment, and his perception of strategic considerations as well as upon the availability of conflict resolution mechanisms. Conflicts may be resolved in a number of

---

[23] Coser, op. cit., p. 31.
[24] Louis R. Pondy, "Organizational Conflict: Concepts and Models," *Administrative Science Quarterly,* September 1967, p. 298.

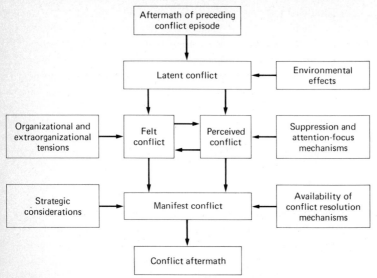

FIGURE 12.4 THE DYNAMICS OF A CONFLICT EPISODE (Louis R. Pondy, "Organizational Conflict: Concepts and Models," *Administrative Science Quarterly,* September 1967, p. 306)

ways, and each result provides a different aftermath or "atmosphere" for future conflict episodes.

This general framework provides an umbrella for many specific conflict situations in groups. Latent conflict situations abound. The degree to which they are perceived, felt, and become manifest will vary considerably because of the multitude of complex forces affecting individual behavior in small groups and organizations.

Many writers have stressed the difficulty of integrating individual and organizational goals as one of the most critical problems of modern industrial civilization.[25] It is an important part of the psychosocial system of organizations. An individual who is dissatisfied with his situation in a specific small group is not likely to engage wholeheartedly in the group's activities. Thus his level of interaction will be curtailed and the likelihood that he will develop sentiments "in line" with other organizational members is decreased. Such a condition very likely will lead to conflict among members of the group, decrease cohesiveness, and hence have a significant impact on the group's performance.

However, the constructive and positive role of conflict in fostering creativity and innovation should not be ignored. Some friction should exist between members in the small group as a condition for the generation of fresh ideas. A conflict-free group may be static and operate at considerably less than capacity.

[25] See, for example, Chris Argyris, *Personality and Organization: The Conflict between the System and the Individual,* Harper & Row, Publishers, Incorporated, New York, 1957.

Intergroup Conflict

Conflict within a small group depends to a considerable extent on the external environment in general and intergroup conflict in particular. Manifest conflicts with another small group, or with the large-scale organization of which it is a part, may foster an increased degree of loyalty and cohesiveness (often suppressing latent conflict) which would not be the case if its external relationships were conflict-free.

One type of intergroup conflict is competition between subgroups within the organization. Just as conflict is inevitable in social relationships, it is inevitable between subgroups of organizations. The sources of latent conflict are always present and provide seeds for clashes of many types. Such conflicts can develop between groups on the same horizontal level in an organization or between groups on different levels.

Some interdepartmental conflicts seem to gain much publicity—that between the production and distribution phases of manufacturing enterprises, for example. The production group is interested in optimizing its operation and sees the interface in a particular way. The marketing department, on the other hand, may stress salability rather than producibility, and the obvious result is a conflict situation. This can be resolved in a number of ways. One department may dominate the other; there may be a compromise solution which neither really likes; or they may achieve an integration of goals by recognizing their roles in an overall system. This latter approach to conflict resolution would appear to be the most fruitful. [26]

Conflicts are often cited between engineering and manufacturing, with the crux being that the designs are not producible. Similarly, there can be considerable conflict between research organizations and the operating groups which must relate to them. A typical comment goes as follows: "One of the members of research mentioned that he thought of the industrial engineers as just dumb, stupid, and no good. There was no meeting ground on a value which the two groups could bring to a common project." [27] These kinds of attitudes are difficult to overcome until mutual understanding prevails. Such conflict is likely to be dysfunctional to a degree. Until we begin to think of the activities of others as just "different" rather than "inferior" or less useful, we will continue to waste valuable energy in conflict situations.

However, interdepartmental conflict can be functional in overall organizational endeavor. The managerial system should function to generate conflict which will have a positive impact on creativity, innovation, and progress. A conflict-free organization is likely to be static and sterile and without much challenge for group members.

ORGANIZATION IMPROVEMENT VIA GROUP DYNAMICS

The term *organization improvement* covers a wide spectrum of formal and informal processes. It includes operational analysis, strategic and comprehensive planning, organization development, and management development. In this section we are con-

---

[26] For a discussion of the consequences of intergroup competition and possible steps toward integration, see Schein, op. cit., pp. 96–103.

[27] John A. Seiler, "Diagnosing Interdepartmental Conflict," *Harvard Business Review*, September–October 1963, p. 127.

cerned with those approaches where the body of knowledge about group dynamics is used to make organizations more effective and/or efficient, as well as more satisfying for participants. Our coverage will be illustrative rather than exhaustive and focuses on sensitivity training, team building, and intergroup relations. The managerial grid approach to organizational development will be described as an example of these concepts in practice.

Sensitivity Training: T Groups

Sensitivity training has several broad objectives: self-insight, better understanding of other persons and awareness of one's impact on them, better understanding of group processes and increased skill in achieving group effectiveness, increased recognition of the characteristics of larger social systems, and greater awareness of the dynamics of change. These objectives are elaborated by the National Training Laboratories as follows:

SELF	INTERPERSONAL AND GROUP RELATIONS	ORGANIZATION
Becoming aware of own feelings and motivations	Establishing meaningful interpersonal relationships	Understanding organizational complexities
Correctly perceiving effects of own behavior on others	Finding a satisfying place in the group	Developing and inventing appropriate new patterns and procedures
Correctly understanding effect of others' behavior on self	Understanding dynamic complexities in group behavior	Helping to diagnose and solve problems between units of the organization
Hearing others and accepting helpful criticism	Developing diagnostic skills to understand group problems and processes	Working as a member and as a leader
Appropriately interacting with others	Acquiring skills of helping the group on task and maintenance problems	

T groups concentrate on understanding individual behavior as it happens in the group (approximately twelve people) itself. The activities, interactions, and sentiments of the small group are the focal point of attention, Organization improvement is seen as a long-run goal achieved through individuals who have had T-group experience working together in more effective relationships. If such experience is garnered externally to an individual's own organization, he may return with new insights and find himself isolated and unable to effect change. This has been a common frustrating experience for many who have been exposed to sensitivity training.

Organizational change is more likely if a T group is drawn from an existing organization, particularly if all members are involved. However, it is difficult to develop enough openness and candor (when all the members are well acquainted) to facilitate T-group training.

By understanding the "driving forces" and "restraining forces" which maintain

People who learn in T-groups seem to possess at least three attributes:

1 A relatively strong ego that is not overwhelmed by internal conflicts.
2 Defenses which are sufficiently low to allow the individual to hear what others say to him (accurately and with minimal threat to his self), without the aid of a professional scanning and filtering system (that is, the therapist, the educator).
3 The ability to communicate thoughts and feelings with minimal distortion. In other words, the operational criterion of minimal threat is that the individual does not tend to distort greatly what he or others say, nor does he tend to condemn others or himself.

This last criterion can be used in helping to select individuals for the T-group experience. *If the individual must distort or condemn himself or others to the point that he is unable to do anything but to continue to distort the feedback that he gives and receives, then he ought not to be admitted to a T-group.*

To put this another way, T-groups, compared to therapy groups, assume a higher degree of health—not illness—that is, a higher degree of self-awareness and acceptance. This is an important point. *Individuals should not be sent to the laboratory if they are highly defensive.* Rather, the relatively healthy individuals capable of learning from others to enhance their degree of effectiveness are the kinds of individuals to be selected to attend.

FIGURE 12.5   WHO LEARNS FROM T-GROUP EXPERIENCES? (Chris Argyris, "T-Groups for Organizational Effectiveness," *Harvard Business Review*, March–April 1964, p. 67).

fixed attitudes, adjustments can be made which foster unfreezing, change, and refreezing of new value systems and behavior patterns. T-group sessions are often uncomfortable for participants because of their unstructured nature. Those with a low tolerance for ambiguity are likely to be extremely frustrated. As the group progresses, however, it begins to recognize and develop its own group dynamics. Most individuals become increasingly comfortable even though conflict and its resolution are an inherent part of this system.

Part of the approach can be described as "confrontation and support." This relates to the feedback which a group provides to individuals with regard to the image projected in general or on specific issues. Such feedback may be painful in some cases, but it is really the only way an individual can gain valuable insights into his impact on others. The propensities an individual should have in order to benefit most from T-group training are set forth in Figure 12.5. Like most educational experiences, you get out of it what you put into it. If a person will not or cannot meet the criteria, the experience is not likely to be of much benefit.

The costs and benefits of such training have been the subject of much debate. [28] Cost effectiveness is not only an economic consideration in this case. Also of concern are the psychological costs and the lasting effects of such training on individuals and organizational development. Critics suggest that benefits have not really been demonstrated rigorously and that the cost for participants is high, including nervous breakdowns in some cases. [29] Proponents suggest that mental breakdowns have occurred at the rate of only 4 in 10,000 and that in most of these cases there was a prior history of psychological problems. [30] The T group is stressed as a vehicle for healthy individuals to strengthen their mental condition. Some confusion is evident from the standpoint of the layman, however, because the setting for T groups is similar to that for group therapy among mentally disturbed patients.

On the effectiveness question, no real answers are available. Typically such questions are answered in terms of the responses of trainees after the sessions. In most cases they are positive and stress the tremendous value to the individual. Little has been done to test the lasting value of such training or the degree to which it is damped out when an individual returns to his basic organization.

Will more authentic interpersonal relationships lead to improvements in small-group and overall organizational performance? Is there some optimal level of openness beyond which individuals should not go? Should some façade be maintained in order to achieve optimal effectiveness for the individual, the small group, and the organization as a whole? Much empirical research is needed to answer these questions. [31]

Team Building

Team-building efforts concentrate on existing work groups and solving real problems. Prior T-group experience may facilitate progress in team building, but it is certainly not necessary. Interpersonal issues such as communication skill (listening effectively, for example) may be a focus of attention. However, it is equally likely that more formal tasks, such as role clarification, will be addressed in team-building sessions. Other issues, such as leadership styles, organization structure, mutual expectations, and meeting effectiveness, typically receive attention.

Team-building sessions also involve solving problems related to the specific task of the group. The process includes problem sensing, diagnosis, evaluation of alternative solutions, planning action steps, and developing means for follow-up and evaluation.

The effectiveness of team-building efforts depends in large measure on the process of consensus formation and the development of group norms for subsequent behavior. It involves everyone in the problem-solving process and enhances the prob-

---

[28] John P. Campbell and Marvin D. Dunnette, "Effectiveness of T-Group Experiences in Managerial Training and Development," *Psychological Bulletin,* August 1968, pp. 73-104.

[29] George S. Odiorne, "The Trouble with Sensitivity Training," *Training Directions,* October 1963.

[30] Chris Argyris, "A Comment on George Odiorne's Paper," *Training Directions,* October 1963.

[31] For a discussion of these questions from the point of view of the practicing manager see: Robert J. House, "T-Group Training: Good or Bad?" *Business Horizons,* December 1969, pp. 69-77.

ability of group cohesiveness and the internalization of group and organizational goals. By taking time to focus on group processes as well as tasks, team building facilitates unfreezing, changing, and refreezing new patterns of behavior.

Intergroup Relations

More sensitive individuals and more cohesive groups may or may not lead to organization improvement. Another dimension that needs attention is intergroup relationships. As indicated previously, conflicts do develop between groups in organizations, and the results can be dysfunctional from an overall point of view. Several means are available to prevent or ameliorate such conflict: (1) avoiding win/lose situations, (2) rotating people among groups in order to facilitate mutual understanding, (3) emphasis on total organizational effectiveness, and (4) increased communication and interaction between groups. [32] Obviously, group dynamics is heavily involved in number (4).

If both groups recognize intergroup problems and are willing to invest time in solving them, several approaches can be beneficial. A simple means of facilitating mutual understanding is to have each group generate a list of positive and negative impressions of the other group—things they like about the other group and things they don't like. It is also helpful to generate a list of predictions of how the other group will respond. The lists then serve as a means to stimulate discussion, understanding, and problem solving.

If the group is interested in how it interacts with a number of other units in an organization, it may not be feasible to get all of the relevant people together. Therefore, it is sometimes useful to get representatives from each unit to sit down with the group seeking help (focal group) and provide feedback concerning how it "comes across." A process similar to the one described above could be used. Representatives could provide feedback concerning what they like and dislike about the focal group's behavior. An important ingredient in either of these approaches is concentration on listening to what others have to say. Questions of clarification are appropriate, but arguing each point as it arises is not likely to be beneficial. After all of the feedback has been generated, it is then appropriate to engage in a problem-solving process which identifies potential new behavior patterns and specific action steps for the future.

The Managerial Grid

The managerial grid has been used extensively as a framework for organization improvement programs based on group dynamics. [33] Team learning forms a link between individual growth and total organization improvement.

---

[32] Schein, op. cit., p. 120.
[33] One such program is described in Robert R. Blake and Jane S. Mouton; Louis P. Barnes and Larry E. Greiner, "Breakthrough in Organizational Development," *Harvard Business Review*, November-December 1964, pp. 135-155.

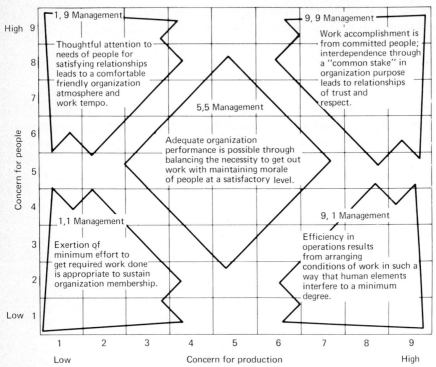

FIGURE 12.6 THE MANAGERIAL GRID (Robert R. Blake and Jane S. Mouton, *The Managerial Grid*, Gulf Publishing Company, Houston, 1964, p. 10)

The underlying framework for the program is the managerial grid (see Figure 12.6). It represents an underlying philosophy of management based on two principal dimensions: (1) the concern for production and (2) the concern for people. Each individual can identify his own particular philosophy in terms of degrees on these two basic dimensions. The middle-of-the-road approach is identified along with four extreme positions. The goal is to bring about a "9,9" managerial philosophy which will influence organization improvement.

The relationship between this approach and the basic concepts of group dynamics is evident. Work is accomplished by committed people; interdependence through a "common stake" in organization purpose leads to relationships of trust and respect. This can be related directly to the concept of a joint impact of group cohesiveness and internalization of organizational goals. It can also be related to Homans' basic framework of group activities, interactions, and sentiments.

The organization development program involves two parts and six phases.

Part I Management development within an organization
    1 Managerial grid laboratory-seminar training
    2 Team development

Part II Organization

    3 Horizontal and vertical intergroup linking

    4 Setting organizational improvement goals

    5 Implementing planned change by attaining established goals

    6 Stabilization

"The first two phases involve *management* development so that the other four phases can help managers work toward the 9,9 goals of *organization* development."[34] Teams of small groups are formed using a diagonal slice of the organization chart. Thus different levels are represented, but no one is included with his immediate superior. There are approximately fifty hours of intensive problem solving, evaluation of individual and team results, and critiques of team performance. Extensive use is made of simulation of organizational situations in which interpersonal behavior affects the task performance. Teams regularly evaluate their own behavior and problem-solving abilities, and they provide feedback concerning managerial styles. Emphasis is placed on helping the manager understand his own attitudes and sentiments and on developing open and effective group interactions.

In phases 3, 4, 5, and 6 these skills and attitudes are extended throughout the organization. Intergroup development concentrates on new approaches to conflict resolution which play down domination and compromise and focus on integration through joint problem-solving efforts which stress total system values. The setting and attainment of overall goals in conjunction with those for various subsystems provide a useful mechanism for integrating activities, interactions, and sentiments.

Considerable attention is devoted to stabilizing the changes which have occurred in managerial philosophies and in the organizational atmosphere. Unless the new approaches become ingrained, much of the program's effort will go for naught as the organization reverts to its original status.

Group dynamics plays an important part in the managerial grid approach because of the central role of small groups in both the training and implementation phases. The small-group setting provides an important facilitating mechanism for unfreezing old individual managerial philosophies, inducing new ones, and stabilizing or refreezing them so that long-lasting change results.

SUMMARY

Group dynamics is a fundamental aspect of psychosocial systems. Man's inclination toward sociability is demonstrated by the number of small groups to which he belongs.

Group dynamics stresses face-to-face relationships and interaction among individuals. It involves many modes of communication and implies continually changing and adjusting relationships among members. Groups vary in terms of degree of permanence, openness, and formality.

---

[34] Ibid., p. 137.

The small group performs a mediating function by linking the individual and the organization. Each individual is a member of formal and informal small groups within larger organizations. An organized group has a degree of permanence based on the repetition of interaction among its members.

Many conceptual schemes are useful for analyzing small groups as micro systems. One approach stresses activities, interactions, and sentiments. Another approach is sociometry, which focuses on the degree of interaction among participants during various activities.

The output of individuals depends upon their ability and inclination to produce. Productivity of work groups can be analyzed in terms of two key variables: (1) cohesiveness and (2) the degree to which members have internalized organizational objectives. A cohesive group with goals congruent to those of the overall organization is the most desirable situation. Overall effectiveness and efficiency depend upon the coordinated efforts of individuals working together in small groups within a larger organizational system.

Committees have been given much bad publicity as being ineffective and inefficient. They are, nevertheless, a ubiquitous phenomenon. Moreover, research indicates that modern executives view committees in a positive way and stress their usefulness in organizational endeavor.

Communication is the basis of group dynamics, allowing the interactions which are necessary in carrying out the group's activity. Several basic communication patterns have been identified for small groups—circle, chain, "Y," and wheel. Research data indicate that a leader seems to emerge at the position of highest centrality—the hub of the wheel, the fork of the "Y," and the mid-point of the chain.

Conflict has typically been thought of as "bad" for organizations. It is unlikely, however, that any human group can attain a completely conflict-free situation. Intragroup and intergroup conflict appear to be inevitable. Therefore, its dysfunctional aspects need to be recognized and guarded against, and its functional aspects should be encouraged by managers.

One approach to organization improvement is concentration on individual growth and small-group effectiveness. T groups, team-building sessions, and intergroup problem-solving exercises are typical means of using group dynamics to facilitate organization improvement. The managerial grid approach uses these elements in a comprehensive, long-range program.

QUESTIONS AND PROBLEMS

1 Compare and contrast a group and an assemblage. What key criteria distinguish a "small" group?
2 What is meant by the term *dynamics* in the phrase "group dynamics"? How is it related to such factors as degree of permanence or openness?
3 In what ways do small groups link individuals and organizations?
4 Describe the interrelationships among activities, interactions, and sentiments in small groups.

5 Illustrate sociometric concepts such as primary group, fringe status, and out status with several examples from your own experience.

6 How do cohesiveness and internalization of organizational goals affect the performance of work groups? Why are positive "readings" on one dimension of Figure 12.2 not sufficient for good performance from the organizational point of view?

7 How can managers "use" small-group dynamics to improve organizational productivity?

8 What is your view of the role of committees in organizational affairs?

9 How do communication patterns affect the development of leaders in small groups?

10 "Man is basically conflictive. He cooperates just enough to get from one conflict situation to the next." Do you agree? Why or why not?

11 Illustrate intergroup conflict with your own experience in an organization.

12 What is organization improvement? What role does group dynamics play in this process?

INFLUENCE SYSTEMS
AND LEADERSHIP

Management involves coordinating men, machines, material, money, time, and space. The external environment as well as internal factors, such as goals and values, technology, and structure provide a framework for this effort. The psychosocial system pervades the atmosphere, affecting the most critical aspect of the managerial task—the integration of individual efforts toward organizational objectives. This aspect of the managerial role is leadership—a term which means many things to many people. In this chapter, we will discuss ways of influencing the behavior of individuals, groups, and organizations. These various means comprise the influence system which, as part of the psychosocial system, provides a framework within which leadership takes place. We will explore the following topics:

> Influence Systems
> Power
> Authority
> Leadership Defined
> Traits and the "Great Man"
> Leadership Styles
> Organizational Climate
> Leadership and Productivity
> Facilitating Effective Leadership

INFLUENCE SYSTEMS

An integral part of the psychosocial system in organizations concerns attempts to influence behavior. Influence is exerted in many directions—up and down the hierarchy and laterally in peer-group relationships. Before discussing various specific ways to influence behavior, we need a more explicit definition. The term *influence* seems to pick up a variety of connotations depending upon the particular field of study and the specific context.

Influence Defined

Influence denotes any "changes in behavior of a person or group due to anticipation of the responses of others." [1] An influence system involves people taking the roles of influencer and influencee. Behavior changes can be "caused" by ideas or some other inanimate factor. For example, a change in the weather may influence someone to abandon picnic or golf plans. Typically, however, influence systems refer to situations wherein behavioral changes occur as a result of relationships among people. These relationships may involve interaction which is direct or indirect (through the medium of ideas).

The term *influence* is often used in conjunction with other terms such as *power* and/or *authority*. In some cases, they are considered as mutually exclusive concepts, with influence covering those ways of influencing behavior which cannot be termed power or authority. In other cases, they appear to be synonymous or at least overlapping in connotation. Our approach is to consider influence as the all-inclusive concept which covers *any and all* modes by which behavioral change is induced in individuals or groups. [2] Katz and Kahn summarize this position as follows:

> *Influence* includes virtually any interpersonal transaction which has psychological or behavioral effects. Control includes those influence attempts which are successful, that is, which have the effects intended by the influencing agent. Power is the potential for influence characteristically backed by the means to coerce compliance. Finally, authority is legitimate power; it is power which accrues to a person by virtue of his role, his position in an organized social structure. [3]

We shall return to a more detailed discussion of concepts such as power and authority in subsequent sections.

Ways to Influence Behavior

A spectrum of ways to influence behavior is indicated in Figure 13.1. Several distinct means are identified—emulation, suggestion, persuasion, and coercion—ranging from indirect and invisible approaches to very evident, direct, and forceful methods.

---

[1] Julius Gould and William L. Kolb (eds.), *A Dictionary of the Social Sciences*, The Free Press of Glencoe, New York, 1964, p. 332.

[2] Both covert and overt behavior are included. Influence is both an alteration of behavior and a maintenance of behavior as it was, but other than what would have been without the intervention of the influence. Herbert Goldhammer and Edward A. Shils, "Types of Power and Status," *American Journal of Sociology*, September 1939, p. 171.

[3] Daniel Katz and Robert L. Kahn, *The Social Psychology of Organizations*, John Wiley & Sons, Inc., New York, 1966, p. 220.

FIGURE 13.1 SPECTRUM OF MEANS FOR INFLUENCING BEHAVIOR

INFLUENCE SPECTRUM

Emulation: striving to equal or excel; imitating with effort to equal or surpass; approaching or attaining equality	*Suggestion:* placing or bringing (an idea, proposition, plan, etc.) before a person's mind for consideration or possible action	*Persuasion:* prevailing on a person by advice, urging, reason, or inducements to do something (rather than force)	*Coercion:* forcing constraint; compulsion; physical pressure or compression

Emulation requires no direct contact between individuals; yet it is a powerful influence on behavior. Public figures (famous athletes or elected officials, for example) are usually aware of the degree to which young people imitate their behavior. Some professional athletes have refused lucrative contracts to endorse cigarettes because of an image they wish to portray to teenagers. Books (particularly biographies), movies, and television provide tremendous exposure for ideas and life styles. People often pick out certain behavior patterns and strive to equal or surpass them.

Emulation is a much more subtle phenomenon than is indicated by our reference to celebrities. In organizations, participants are aware of the behavioral patterns of fellow workers and various executives. Certain individuals become ''models,'' and their behavior patterns are adopted by others who hope to attain similar success. Others ''play'' certain roles in organizations. Many behavior patterns are perpetuated in organizations primarily on the basis of emulation—with neither formal position descriptions nor direct interaction in the form of persuasion or suggestion needed.

Suggestion involves direct and conscious interaction between individuals or between an individual and a group. It is an explicit attempt to influence behavior by presenting an idea or advocating a particular course of action. A suggestion may relate to relatively immediate behavior or be directed at a more long-range adjustment. If the suggestion is not implemented, the influence attempt has failed. However, typically this mode is used when several alternative behavior patterns for individuals or groups are acceptable and the influencer is merely suggesting a preferred pattern. Normally he will not get too excited if his preference is ignored because other behavior patterns are also deemed acceptable.

If this tolerance for different behavior in a particular role were not present, the influencer would use some other mode such as persuasion or even coercion. *Persuasion* implies urging and the use of some inducement in order to evoke the desired response. It involves more pressure than a mere suggestion but falls short of the type of force implied by the term coercion. Applied behavior analysis (a means of behavior modification stemming from Skinnerian operant conditioning) can be viewed as a subtle form of persuasion. Positive reinforcement for desired (from the point of view of the influencer or "shaper") behavior tends to induce the influencee to continue that behavior. Reward systems that may include only recognition and praise have proved successful in modifying individual behavior—reduced absenteeism, for example—in a number of organizational settings. [4]

Coercion involves forcible constraint, including physical pressure. "We will have to do some arm-twisting" is a typical phrase which figuratively describes a method of persuasion based on physical pressure. Literally, a hammerlock could coerce an individual into a particular bit of behavior ("say uncle," for example). A person wielding a gun, knife, or other similar weapon can forcibly evoke specific behavior from another individual or a group, the typical skyjacking episode.

Many forms of coercion, other than physical force, are evident. In organizations, salaries and/or promotions can be used to constrain or influence behavior. In many cases the threat of dismissal is also a powerful influencer.

Interaction-Influence Systems

The concept of an *influence system* is critical. The process of influencing behavior is not necessarily attached to an organizational hierarchy. Any interaction between individuals results in a transaction which has psychological and/or behavioral effects. Thus, by definition, influence "happens" in such situations. Taken together, these numerous pairs of relationships in groups or organizations can be termed an *interaction-influence system.*

Power, the ability to influence behavior, underlies the entire spectrum of means shown in Figure 13.1. The more power an individual has in a given situation, the more effective his influence attempts will be. *Authority,* as institutionalized power or the right to influence behavior, also underlies the entire spectrum of ways to influence behavior in organizations. Typically, positions high in the hierarchy will have more influence than those at lower levels. However, this is not necessarily the case; it depends upon the issues involved and the participants in the interaction-influence system.

The old adage "knowledge is power" is appropriate to this discussion. Quite often the flow of influence is lateral or upward as hierarchical relationships are transcended because an individual has specific knowledge concerning a particular question. A corporate president is likely to be influenced by the advice of tax and/or legal advisors who point out pitfalls in his proposal. If the chief test pilot says the airplane is not ready, the first flight will be postponed even though several hundred dignitaries and high-level corporate officials have gathered for the occasion.

In these examples it is clear that a person in a formal position may be quite dependent on others at the same level or below him. He needs various kinds of support in order to carry out his job. This dependence increases the power of others in the

---

[4] Kenneth Goodall, "Shapers at Work," *Psychology Today,* November 1972, pp. 53ff. See also B. F. Skinner, *Beyond Freedom and Dignity,* Alfred A. Knopf, Inc., New York, 1971.

organization relative to him (and increases their ability to influence his behavior). Mechanic describes this process as follows:

> Within organizations one makes others dependent upon him by controlling access to information, persons, and instrumentalities, which I shall define as follows:
>
> **a** *Information* includes knowledge of the organization, knowledge about persons, knowledge of the norms, procedures, techniques, and so forth.
> **b** *Persons* include anyone within the organization or anyone outside the organization upon whom the organization is in some way dependent.
> **c** *Instrumentalities* include any aspect of the physical plant of the organization or its resources (equipment, machines, money, and so on).
>
> Power is a function not only of the extent to which a person controls information, persons, and instrumentalities, but also of the importance of the various attributes he controls. [5]

Within this general model, individuals influence the behavior of others in many ways. Subordinates can influence their superiors if they have technical expertise concerning a particular subject. This form of power is often termed the "authority" of knowledge. [6] The term *functional authority* refers to the degree of dependence on a particular activity or function. Individuals in staff positions theoretically have little formal authority in organizations. However, they influence behavior effectively because of the dependence of other organizational members on them for information concerning procedures or techniques.

Location can have bearing on the ability to influence behavior. An "assistant to," although he or she is low on the status ladder, has considerable power because of his or her close proximity to a high-level executive. With little formal authority a person in such a position finds others in the organization dependent upon him for information about his boss and how he is likely to react to various proposals. Also, he is in a position to screen and/or filter messages in both directions—to the boss from other members of the organization and vice versa.

Many organizational relationships involve peer groups. In such cases the interaction-influence system has no relationship to the hierarchy. Thus, power that underlies influence attempts must come from some source other than authority. The potential effectiveness of persuasion and suggestion depends on knowledge, concern for continued social relationships, and other similar factors.

---

[5] David Mechanic, "Sources of Power of Lower Participants in Complex Organizations," *Administrative Science Quarterly*, December 1962, p. 352.
[6] This widely used concept is actually a misnomer because, by definition, authority is institutional rather than personal.

At all points on the spectrum of ways to influence behavior illustrated in Figure 13.1, the degree to which a particular means is effective depends upon the degree of power and/or authority held by the influencer relative to the influencee. Power and authority are not separate and distinct or mutually exclusive ways of influencing behavior. Rather, they underlie all means and are both related to the concept of potential force. They have a definite impact upon the success of influence attempts. A suggestion from someone with great power and/or authority would be expected to have more influence than one coming from someone without it. People at the top or those with substantial charisma are much more likely to be emulated as well.

POWER

Power is the capability of doing or affecting something. [7] It implies the ability to influence others. In its most general sense, power denotes (1) the ability (exercised or not) to produce a certain occurrence or (2) the influence exerted by a man or group, through whatever means, over the conduct of others in intended ways. [8] This relates to the spectrum of ways to influence behavior as indicated in Figure 13.1 and suggests that power is involved along the entire spectrum as long as there is an ability to produce a certain occurrence.

While power underlies the entire spectrum of ways to influence behavior, its everyday connotation leans toward the persuasive-coercive end of the spectrum. Although power is the *general* ability to produce a certain occurrence, it implies the force, if necessary, to control or command others. [9]

Power is the capacity to affect behavior in predetermined ways. ''Only groups which have power can threaten to use force and the threat itself is power. Power is the ability to employ force, not its actual employment, the ability to apply sanctions, not the actual application.'' [10] If coercion or the application of force is ineffective, there is no power. Power exists only when it is effective; it is the capability to influence behavior by limiting the alternatives available in social situations.

Power is evident in informal organizations and informal groups. It may be based on position, knowledge, physical ability, or money. In formal organizations, institutionalized power is referred to as authority. In other situations, however, there are many types of power which can be distinguished to facilitate the understanding of this concept.

The concept of power as latent force can be illustrated by international relationships in the nuclear age. For many years the so-called ''nuclear powers''—the United States, Russia, and Great Britain—had a tremendous latent force in nuclear warheads

---

[7] Bertrand Russell, *Power*, W. W. Norton & Company, Inc., New York, 1938. Russell contends that power is a fundamental concept in social science in the same sense that energy is fundamental in physics. He defines power as the ability to produce intended effects (p. 35). This is certainly a broad connotation which does not relate to methods used—only the results. For our study of organization and management we are more interested in ''intended effects'' as they relate to social interaction.

[8] Gould and Kolb, op. cit., p. 524.

[9] Robert Bierstedt, ''An Analysis of Social Power,'' *American Sociological Review*, December 1950, p. 733.

[10] Ibid.

and the means to deliver them. The addition of France and China as nuclear powers upset the balance of power.

Types of Power

The power underlying the various means of influencing behavior in organizations has been classified into three categories: physical, material, and symbolic. [11] These categories are related to the coercive, utilitarian, and normative (normative-social or social) approaches, respectively. In some organizations a gun, whip, or actual physical force may be required to influence and control behavior—prisons or custodial mental institutions, for example. In most cases the application of physical force is not necessary. However, the threat of its use underlies coercive power in organizations.

Material rewards or sanctions come primarily in the form of money (or lack of it) which can be used to buy goods and services. Monetary incentive systems, including promotions and layoffs, are examples of utilitarian power which can be used in organizations to influence the behavior of participants.

Symbolic means of influencing behavior are those which are not physical or material. They relate primarily to prestige and esteem (normative symbols) or love and acceptance (social symbols). [12] When an organizational participant is encouraged to improve his performance, normative power is being used. The appeal is based upon what he "ought" to do as a "good" employee. If the behavior of an individual is influenced through the medium of his small group, normative-social power is the base. A boss may suggest that other participants in a work group apply pressure on a particular member in order to get him to "shape up." Social power underlies the effort of a group to influence the behavior of individual members. The social power—love and acceptance—which peers exercise over one another is an important and integral part of the influence system in groups and organizations.

For a football team, normative power underlies the coach's attempt to get a player to improve his performance. The coach may appeal to achievement motivation and suggest that the player has not been performing up to capacity and ought to play much better. Influence attempts may include the focal person's teammates, who are encouraged by the coach to apply a little pressure from the standpoint of the team. The argument is that as a team member he "should" do better in order that the team might be successful. Without any direction from the coach, the team may use its social power to help influence the behavior of particular members. Ignoring the curfew or not "putting out" on the field may lead to sanctions from his teammates—from barbed comments to the silent treatment. If none of these influence attempts is successful, utilitarian power can be invoked, and the player can be fined for violating regulations or making repeated "bonehead" plays on the field. And, coaches have been known to use physical force in attempting to influence the behavior of a player who makes repeated mistakes or does not seem to "get the picture."

---

[11] Amitai Etzioni, *Modern Organizations*, Prentice-Hall, Inc., Englewood Cliffs, N.J., 1964, p. 59.
[12] Ibid.

It is evident that an organization's influence attempts are varied and flow in all directions continually. However, certain approaches seem appropriate and typical for specific types of organizations.

> Ordering organizations from high to low according to the degree to which coercion is stressed, we find concentration camps, prisons, traditional correctional institutions, custodial mental hospitals, and prisoner-of-war camps. Ordering organizations from high to low according to the degree to which utilitarian power is predominant, we find blue-collar organizations such as factories, white-collar organizations such as insurance companies, banks, and the civil service, and peacetime military organizations. Normative power is predominant in religious organizations, ideological-political organizations, colleges and universities, voluntary associations, schools, and therapeutic mental hospitals. [13]

This framework suggests what is predominant or probable in the various organizations identified. Typically all types of power are used to back up influence attempts in a particular organization depending upon the time and situation. Yet participants come to expect certain kinds of influence attempts as normal. In general the trend in organizations has been away from the use of coercive and utilitarian power bases. Normative power, including normative-social and social, tends to be involved in an increasing proportion of influence attempts in organizations.

Power Equalization

"The general trend of twentieth-century society, particularly in the U.S., is toward a wider distribution of power, a broadening of participation by individuals in controlling their own lives and work." [14] Leavitt describes numerous trends which can be described as power equalization in organizations. [15] We have discussed the trends toward industrial humanism—the primary concern being the individual rather than the work itself or an organization per se. A focal point has been self-actualization and the theory that individuals cannot grow and develop in an atmosphere of overwhelming position power (authority) underlying predominantly downward attempts to influence behavior. There has been a plea for more balance in the distribution of power so that influence can flow in many directions in organizations.

For example, Theory X implies an emphasis on the hierarchy and the use of coercive and/or utilitarian power to back influence attempts in the organization. Theory Y, on the other hand, assumes a balance of power and relatively more use of normative-social power.

---

[13] Ibid., p. 60.
[14] Max Ways, "More Power to Everybody," *Fortune*, May 1970, p. 174.
[15] Harold J. Leavitt, "Applied Organizational Change in Industry: Structural, Technological, and Humanistic Approaches," in James G. March (ed.), *Handbook of Organizations*, Rand McNally & Company, Chicago, 1965, pp. 1144–1170.

Obviously, power equalization and the related types of appropriate power bases cannot be generalized too far. A particular time and situation must be identified in order to ascertain which approach may be better. For repetitive (programmed) work, well-defined procedures and a utilitarian power base may be the most appropriate. For creative and innovative (nonprogrammed) tasks, however, influence attempts should probably be based more on normative-social power.

If power equalization is a recognized objective, several measures can be taken. [16] Decision making can be made more participative, decentralized, and independent. This is particularly true in determining the goals of subgroups and/or the organization as a whole. But it also applies to the means of implementing strategic decisions. Power equalization can be considered explicitly in assessing cohesiveness and conformity in subgroups. Specific attention can be focused on group pressure, recognizing that decentralized, participative decision making can lead to complex and ambiguous overall situations. Two-way communication and multiple channels can also be helpful in facilitating power equalization organizations.

The concept of power as both *unilateral* and *bilateral* is quite important. In any social system the power relationships are quite complex and do not flow on a one-way street. While superiors typically wield more power than subordinates, the latter do have the ability to influence the behavior of their superiors. On a one-to-one basis the power of the subordinate is not always very evident. However, if his contributions are critical for the organization and important to the superior, any threat to withhold them provides a power base. Thus, individuals with key skills may often wield considerable power even though they are not established high in the organizational hierarchy. The power of subordinates increases significantly when they act as a group. This is the rationale behind collective bargaining.

The balance of power between the individual and the organization, as represented by a superior, is decidedly in favor of the organization. It can apply sanctions without regarding too seriously the repercussions which might stem from one individual. However, the group as a whole can wield considerable power, including the ultimate withdrawal of contributions in the form of a strike. This alternative often is extremely unpalatable to the organization, and hence the balance of power swings in favor of the subordinate group.

AUTHORITY

We have defined authority several times in the discussion of influence systems and power. To repeat, authority is institutionalized power, an extremely important concept in the study of formal organizations. "Authority is the institutionalized right to limit choice. In other words, it is the institutionalized right to employ power. In a sense authority represents an artificial structuring of power." [17] The notion of artificiality is

---

[16] Ibid., pp. 1161–1165.
[17] Dale Henning, "Authority: Concepts, Conflicts, and Synthesis," in Harry R. Knudson, Jr. (ed.), *Human Elements of Administration*, Holt, Rinehart & Winston, Inc., New York, 1963, p. 130.

important. Groups typically would develop power relationships based on characteristics such as physical prowess, knowledge or wisdom, or some other means of identifying status relationships and positions or roles. Tradition and charisma also help identify a power structure within groups. If the organization is a legal entity, relationships are formalized and positions established somewhat artificially. As we shall see later, the spontaneous system may not necessarily coincide with that which is established legally to achieve the objectives of a formal organization.

Authority and Individualism

Natural social groups develop in the form of families, clans, tribes, states, and nations. Within these groups superior-subordinate relationships develop in the form of status and role systems. Based on any of a number of characteristics, power structures evolve naturally, and they in turn are perpetuated via tradition. [18]

It is hard to imagine that the human community could proceed in its endeavors without an institutionalized power structure which we call authority. Anarchy is inconceivable; but so is the other extreme, authoritarianism. As in so many similar conceptual frameworks, we are interested in a workable compromise. We need enough authority to ensure cooperative action and progress toward group goals. However, we also want to encourage individuality, creativity, and innovation.

Authoritarianism results from an obsession with hierarchical relationships to the degree that superiors eschew consultation with subordinates. At the same time, subordinates are disposed toward zealous obedience to hierarchic superiors and often tend toward obsequiousness and sycophancy. Superiors are overbearing and scornful in their demeanor toward anyone in their sphere of power. [19]

Progress depends upon the uncommon man and his unwillingness to perpetuate a given system. Often, his struggle is against the societal power structure and the specific authority systems in formal organizations. Benne sums up this perennial struggle as follows:

> Authority is a necessity of all stable community life. Today, under the impact of growing collective interdependence men are forced to rethink and reconstruct the operating bases of community authority. The widespread attempt under the historic liberal ideology to deny the principle of authority in human relations has helped to blur the recognition of operating bases of authority necessary to stable and responsible individual and group life, thus paradoxically contributing to the restoration of extreme authoritarianism in human affairs. [20]

---

[18] Anthony Jay, *Corporation Man,* Random House, Inc., New York, 1971.
[19] Gould and Kolb, op. cit., p. 42.
[20] Kenneth D. Benne, *The Conception of Authority,* Bureau of Publications, Teachers College, Columbia University, New York, 1943, p. 27.

Given the inevitability of informal and formal organizations, there is a need for some means to ensure that efforts are directed toward appropriate objectives. "Every organization faces the task of somehow reducing the variability, instability, and spontaneity of individual human acts." [21] Authority, coupled with status and role systems, supplies this necessary element. These key ingredients result in reasonably well-defined roles to be performed by organizational participants. In many cases behavior of organizational members is identical—starting at eight and quitting at five, for example. They may wear certain styles of attire (even uniforms) which distinguish them from other organizations; or, they may develop special behavior patterns which are essential to the work of the organization.

Most complex organizations have some examples of identical jobs for large groups of people. However, there are many other examples of tasks broken down into significantly different types of effort, which must be coordinated in order to keep the complete system in control. In such cases, *uniformity* of behavior is not the goal. But there must be enough *unity* so that role performance is not entirely "spontaneous and unrehearsed." Individual creativity and innovation are desirable within limits, that is, as long as they are functional rather than dysfunctional for the system as a whole.

Types of Authority

According to Weber three basic types of legitimate authority can be identified—rational-legal, traditional, and charismatic. [22] *Charismatic* "authority" depends upon the magical qualities of individual leaders. No rules or regulations are involved. Charisma is more a concept of power than of authority because it depends on personal characteristics rather than position.

Charismatic authority often evolves into *traditional* authority as informal status and role systems become stabilized over time. It is exemplified by the phrase, "it has always been this way." Policies, procedures, and rules are developed by those traditionally "in command." Over a period of time the system evolves to the point where directives are carried out by subordinates without question. Changes or adjustments in the system result when traditional leaders deem it necessary and/or desirable. The traditions in the system may be handed down explicitly in written form or implicitly in a manner similar to the transmission of folklore.

Just as charismatic authority often evolves into traditional authority, so traditional authority can evolve into *rational-legal* authority if the system is legitimized formally. Common law has become codified into an elaborate body of offical criteria for administering justice in society. Legal authority in organizations is also established by means of specific legislation. Governmental agencies are designated responsibility for a

---

[21] Katz and Kahn, op. cit., p. 199.
[22] Max Weber, *The Theory of Social and Economic Organizations*, trans. by A. M. Henderson and Talcott Parsons, Oxford University Press, Fair Lawn, N.J., 1947, p. 328.

sphere of activity and are accorded commensurate authority in order to carry out their specific tasks. This framework provides the means to structure a hierarchy through which authority is delegated to positions in the system.

Most large-scale business organizations are legal entities called corporations which derive their authority from the various states. Their charters designate what they can and cannot do, depending upon the particular sphere of activity engaged in. Insurance companies have special rules and regulations, as do airlines or drug manufacturers. The authority system in a corporation is based upon institutional rights granted to it by the state. This authority is delegated throughout the system on the basis of typical hierarchical patterns. Organizational participants recognize the legitimate authority based on ownership. It may be used by an owner-manager or delegated to a group of "professional" managers, as is the case in many large-scale, complex organizations in society.

Most organizations have a mixture of rational-legal, traditional, and charismatic authority underlying the influence system used to secure coordinated effort on the part of participants. Some may be influenced to extraordinary efforts based on the charismatic character of key employees. Others are influenced by traditional relationships which have evolved over a period of time. While these forms of authority are effective in many situations, rational-legal authority can be invoked to elicit desired behavior on the part of participants who are not inclined to contribute willingly. In other words, it is the latent force which underlies formal sanctions that the organization can bring to bear in order to ensure compliance with rules and regulations and guide behavior toward organizational objectives.

But it does not always work as smoothly as it would appear. This approach stresses the flow of authority from the top down and the concept that behavior can be made to conform to the expectations of the influencer. However, there has always been the notion that effective authority depends on the "consent of the governed."

Acceptance Theory of Authority

The institutionalized right to influence behavior may or may not be effective depending on the consent of organizational participants. Simon suggests that the crux of the authority relationship is that a subordinate "holds in abeyance" his own critical faculties for choosing between alternatives and uses the receipt of a command as his basis for choice. [23] This line of reasoning leads to a zone of acceptance from the point of view of the subordinate. He has a certain tolerance level or range within which he will accept directives without analyzing the merits of the behavior as related to the problem at hand. Barnard expressed a similar idea and termed it the zone of indifference. [24]

The concept of "zone of acceptance" is important in understanding effective authority. Unless a directive falls within this range, it will not be effective, and the

[23] Herbert A. Simon, *Administrative Behavior*, The Macmillan Company, New York, 1959, p. 126.
[24] Chester I. Barnard, *The Functions of the Executive*, Harvard University Press, Cambridge, Mass., 1938, p. 167.

influence attempt fails. In such cases, repeated attempts to influence behavior can be made with the same means, or a different approach can be used. If it still is not effective, the various sanctions underlying the authority system can be imposed, including dismissal. But if the objective is to coordinate group effort and the result is loss of organizational participants, the overall system has failed. Formal authority is limited by the zone of acceptance.

Individuals typically undergo a socialization process from infancy to adulthood which stresses the acceptance of authority—family, church, school, and work relationships. However, in modern, large-scale organizations a countertrend seems apparent in that the zone of acceptance for participants has narrowed over the years. Employees are likely to exercise their own judgment more often and accept uncritically the directives of others in fewer situations. The educational process has fostered a long-run trend in this direction. As employees at all levels become better educated, they are less likely to defer evaluational and decision-making activities to superiors over wide ranges of activities. More and more people want to know *why* a particular course of action is the desired one.

Student unrest and the attendant demands for an increased role in decision making in universities are an example in point. In our society many years ago, students did not dare question either faculty members or the administration. Charisma, tradition, and the rational-legal system of authority was evident and accepted. And the professor was "always" right. Yet there have been dissent and agitation throughout history. It seems today, however, that such activities are accelerating; the zone of acceptance for students has decreased significantly and will continue to do so. Similar trends are evident in most large-scale, complex organizations—businesses, hospitals, and governmental agencies, for example.

Synthesis of Authority Concepts

A great deal has been written about the apparent conflict in the nature of authority.[25] Specifically, does authority flow downward in organizations based on an institutionalized right to employ power? That is, is the authority system based on a legitimate right (property rights, for example) granted by society and delegated throughout the organizational hierarchy? Or does authority stem from the bottom up, based on the zone of acceptance which participants maintain with respect to the directives of superiors?

A synthesis is possible if we recognize that the rational-legal authority framework is accepted as legitimate by most participants. And, when it is coupled with traditional and charismatic sources of authority, the zone of acceptance is widened significantly. The zone of acceptance should relate to specific influence attempts by particular people. An appeal based on utilitarian aspects may evoke no response; the same appeal based on normative-social or peer-group power may elicit the desired behavior.

---

25 See, for example, Merton J. Mandeville, "The Nature of Authority," *Academy of Management Journal*, August 1960, pp. 107–118; or Henning, op. cit., pp. 129–136.

When positional and personal authority reinforce each other, we have added evidence of the synthesis of the acceptance theory with the right-to-command theory.

Formal authority does give position power, a basis for influencing organizational behavior. However, it is not enough to ensure effective cooperation. When greater reliance must be placed on other means of influencing behavior, leadership becomes a vital factor.

LEADERSHIP DEFINED

Leadership is (1) a process and (2) a status grouping. Directors, executives, administrators, managers, bosses, and chiefs would typically be included in the category called leadership. Identification of those "in" the group has been important in studying the phenomenon of leadership in the past.

However, we are more concerned with a process than a status grouping. The leadership process has been defined in many ways—from "that which leaders do" to long, complex paragraphs including several or many elements. Fiedler cites nearly a dozen different definitions with varying connotations and degrees of emphasis on subparts. He concludes that a leader is "the individual in the group given the task of directing and coordinating task-relevant group activities or who, in the absence of a designated leader, carries the primary responsibility for performing these functions in the group." [26] Emphasis on coordinating task-oriented group activities seems to indicate that leading is synonymous with managing. Typically, however, management is considered to be a more broadly based function including activities other than leading.

> Leadership is a part of management, but not all of it. A manager is required to plan and organize, for example, but all we ask of the leader is that he get others to follow. . . . Leadership is the ability to persuade others to seek defined objectives enthusiastically. It is the human factor which binds a group together and motivates it toward goals. Management activities such as planning, organizing, and decision making are dormant cocoons until the leader triggers the power of motivation in people and guides them toward goals. [27]

This connotation stresses the role of leadership in eliciting behavioral responses which are more than routine. It suggests the "tapping" of latent human capability in achieving group objectives. And it relates to our concept of an influence system by stressing the role of persuasion.

The differential exertion of influence is one way to define leadership. [28] This approach recognizes that in social groups there are typically bilateral processes of

---

[26] Fred E. Fiedler, *A Theory of Leadership Effectiveness,* McGraw-Hill Book Company, New York, 1967, p. 8.
[27] Keith Davis, *Human Relations at Work,* 3d ed., McGraw-Hill Book Company, New York, 1967, pp. 96–97.
[28] Katz and Kahn, op. cit., p. 301.

interpersonal influence. Those with a positive balance—a net outflow of influence—would be designated as leaders; those with a minus balance would be followers. Obviously, the process of identifying leaders would have to be repeated for each group because the balance in any one group would shift according to the situation. For example, the 98-pound weakling may have been a forgotten man at the senior picnic, where the emphasis was upon appearance, physical skill, and strength. On the way home, however, his first-aid training may thrust him into the leadership role during the aftermath of an automobile accident.

Differential influence is apparent in informal social relationships and in formal organizations. Typically, designated position holders do have a positive balance in the influence system. However, this may not always be the case. The positional authority of a ''leader'' may not be enough to persuade subordinates to engage in appropriate activities. Influence attempts fail, and leadership is ineffective.

Tannenbaum and Massarik summarize the relationship between leadership and influence systems by stating that leadership is ''*interpersonal influence, exercised in situations and directed, through the communication process, toward the attainment of a specified goal or goals.* Leadership always involves attempts on the part of a *leader* (influencer) to affect (influence) the behavior of a *follower* (influencee) or followers in situation.'' [29]

We are interested in what makes followers and what leadership style is appropriate for a given psychosocial system. Often, the person who best satisfies the needs of the individuals in a group will emerge as leader.

TRAITS AND THE ''GREAT MAN''

For centuries, philosophers have argued the ''great man'' theory. Was *history made by men* such as Alexander the Great, Napoleon, Lenin, or Churchill? Or, on the other hand, were such *men made by history?* Is there something about the personality of such individuals that enables them to have a significant effect on the course of human events? Or do such men become leaders because they just happen to be in the right place at the right time? Based on most current research, we would answer: some of both. The situation is important in determining the kind of leadership style which will be most appropriate. Given the particular environment, there will be one individual whose personality and leadership style fit the situation best. Moreover, he happens to be in the right place at the right time.

Debates over the great-man theory brought considerable attention to the so-called ''trait'' approach. It emphasized the personality characteristics, value system, and life style of leaders. The typical approach to such research consisted in identifying characteristics of established leaders. The list of traits could be endless but typically includes such things as size, energy (both nervous and physical), intelligence, sense

---

[29] Robert Tannenbaum and Fred Massarik, ''Leadership: A Frame of Reference,'' *Management Science,* October 1957, p. 3.

of direction and purpose, enthusiasm, friendliness, integrity, morality, technical expertise, decisiveness, perceptual skills, knowledge, wisdom, imagination, determination, persistence, endurance, good looks (physical and sartorial splendor), and courage. One obvious problem is that there is little agreement with regard to which traits should be included and which should be excluded. Moreover, there is disagreement with regard to which of those included are the more important. [30]

There have been many attempts to distill out of these long lists of characteristics some key attributes which subsume many of the positive traits indicated. The reduced list includes both traits and behavioral characteristics. Their presence does not ensure leadership success; nor does their absence preclude it. However, an individual possessing these basic ingredients has a higher probability of becoming a successful leader (regardless of the led and the situation) than someone without them. Davis illustrates this approach by stating:

> Measurement of a trait usually occurs after a person becomes a leader, and does not necessarily prove a cause-and-effect relationship. Recognizing these limitations, we can now mention four traits which appear to be related to successful organizational leadership.
>
> *Intelligence.* Leaders tend to have somewhat higher intelligence than the average of their followers.
>
> *Social maturity and breadth.* Leaders tend to have broad interests and activities. They are emotionally mature so that they are neither crushed by defeat nor overelated by victory. They have high frustration tolerance.
>
> *Inner motivation and achievement drives.* Leaders have a strong personal motivation to keep accomplishing something. As they reach one goal, their level of aspiration rises to other goals; so one success becomes a challenge for more success.
>
> *Human relations attitudes.* Successful leaders realize that they get their job done through people and therefore try to develop social understanding and appropriate skills. They develop a healthy respect for people, if for no other reason than that their success as leaders depends on cooperation of people. [31]

This seems to be a reasonable distillation of traits which we might find in "successful" leaders. And if good leadership is defined according to some consensual

---

[30] For summaries of early research, see Cecil E. Goode, "Significant Research on Leadership," *Personnel,* March 1951, pp. 342-350; and Ralph M. Stogdill, "Personal Factors Associated with Leadership: A Survey of the Literature," *The Journal of Psychology,* January 1948, pp. 35-71. An integrating theory is presented in Warren G. Bennis, "Leadership Theory and Administrative Behavior," *Administrative Science Quarterly,* December 1959, pp. 259-301.

[31] Davis, op. cit., pp. 99-100.

yardstick, these attributes are important. Not only must behavior be coordinated and influenced toward group objectives, but those objectives must be "good" in the eyes of the evaluators.

The danger of the trait approach is illustrated by Solomon, who suggests that these qualities are obviously desirable in a leader but that none of them seems to be essential.

> The world has seen numerous great leaders who could hardly lay claim to any kind of formal education. History is replete with non-trained, non-academic Fords, Edisons, and Carnegies who couldn't even claim a grammar school education yet managed to become leaders whose influence was felt around the globe.
>
> As for appearance or robust health, need we mention more than the delicate Gandhi, or George Washington Carver, the frail, shriveled, insignificant little Negro who was one of America's greatest scientists? And so many more like them? As for high ideals, fine character, etc., where would Hitler, Capone or Attila the Hun rate here? [32]

J. A. C. Brown suggests that such individuals are examples of situations where a particular personality defect seemed to be called for in the environmental context. A sick society may choose a sick leader. [33]

The differential between the leader and the follower cannot be too great for a pertinent trait. On key characteristics the leader must be relatively close to the rest of the group in order to maintain rapport. He cannot be *too* intelligent; otherwise, he might lose contact with others in the group.

LEADERSHIP STYLES

The trait approach refers to what a leader is. Another approach to understanding leadership success concentrates on what the leader does—his *style*. A number of terms, such as autocratic, democratic, bureaucratic, neurocratic, and laissez faire, have been used to describe the general approach used by leaders in human situations. To research the effectiveness of various styles, it is necessary to hold the situation constant. Thus, any findings have to be interpreted in the light of the environmental situation used in an experiment or observed in real organizations. A study by White and Lippitt concentrated on the impact of three leadership styles in task-oriented groups of ten-year-old boys. [34] The three relatively distinct styles are described in Figure 13.2.

---

[32] Ben Solomon, *Leadership of Youth*, Youth Services, New York, 1950, p. 15.
[33] J. A. C. Brown, *The Social Psychology of Industry*, Penguin Books, Inc., Baltimore, 1954, pp. 222.
[34] Ralph White and Ronald Lippitt, "Leader Behavior and Member Reaction in Three 'Social Climates,'" in Dorwin Cartwright and Alvin Zander (eds.), *Group Dynamics: Research and Theory*, Harper & Row, Publishers, Incorporated, New York, 1953, pp. 385–611.

FIGURE 13.2 THREE LEADERSHIP STYLES

AUTHORITARIAN	DEMOCRATIC	LAISSEZ-FAIRE
1. All determination of policy by the leader	1. All policies a matter of group discussion and decision, encouraged and assisted by the leader	1. Complete freedom for group or individual decision, with a minimum of leader participation
2. Techniques and activity steps dictated by the authority, one at a time, so that future steps were always uncertain to a large degree	2. Activity perspective gained during discussion period. General steps to group goal sketched, and when technical advice was needed, the leader suggested two or more alternative procedures from which choice could be made	2. Various materials supplied by the leader, who made it clear that he would supply information when asked. He took no other part in work discussion
3. The leader usually dictated the particular work task and work companion of each member	3. The members were free to work with whomever they chose, and the division of tasks was left up to the group	3. Complete nonparticipation of the leader
4. The dominator tended to be "personal" in his praise and criticism of the work of each member; remained aloof from active group participation except when demonstrating	4. The leader was "objective" or "fact-minded" in his praise and criticism, and tried to be a regular group member in spirit without doing too much of the work	4. Infrequent spontaneous comments on member activities unless questioned, and no attempt to appraise or regulate the course of events

SOURCE: Ralph White and Ronald Lippitt, *Autocracy and Democracy,* Harper & Row, Publishers, Incorporated, 1960, pp. 26–27 (our title). By permission of Harper & Row, Publishers.

In the White-Lippitt experiments, the leaders "played" the designated roles over an extended period. With all other aspects of the groups held as constant as possible, the difference in leadership styles allows some conclusions with regard to their impact on individual participants and group behavior.

Although the quantity of work in autocratic groups was slightly more, the quality in democratic groups was consistently better. When the leader left the room, the autocratic groups collapsed completely, whereas the performance in democratic groups decreased only slightly.

In general, the findings seem to indicate that a laissez faire approach, or complete permissiveness, was not effective in terms of group performance. Moreover, it did not seem to produce any other benefits, such as improved morale or satisfaction of individual group members. On the contrary, these dimensions were improved, along with performance, in democratic groups. While the quantity of output in autocratic work groups was slightly better than under a democratic approach, there were important negative side effects which cast doubt on the long-run usefulness of such a leadership style. Given the situation as described, it would seem that a democratic-participative approach, on balance, was the most effective and efficient. These findings have been corroborated by other similar experiments and in actual industrial situations.

Jennings cites bureaucracy as a special variation of autocracy. "Autocracy is one-man rule, bureaucracy is rule by rules. The one aims at making things happen, the other at making things orderly. The man of action becomes the man of logic. Productivity is replaced by efficiency. The system rather than the executive becomes indispensable. Bureaucracy is subtle autocracy." [35] This leadership style is related to rational-legal systems of authority and an explicit set of procedures, rules, and regulations. The system has a high degree of formality and uniformity. Problems are solved by referring to "the book" and/or standard operating procedures.

A leadership style based upon bureaucracy is depersonalized. The system of rules and regulations is designed to cover all exigencies. Hence the role of the leader is one of monitoring routine activity within the guidelines established by the system itself. The bureaucratic style stresses administrative tidiness, regularity, and accuracy. This style is evident in many of today's large-scale, complex organizations.

The Need for Flexibility

A discussion of leadership styles should not leave us with the impression that an individual can or should maintain a consistent style in all his activities. On the contrary, he should be as flexible as possible, gearing his style to the specific situation and the individuals involved. This takes us back to the key elements of the leadership system— the leader, the led, and the situation.

Figure 13.3 shows a continuum of leadership behavior with the basic ingredient being the degree of authority used by a manager vis-à-vis the amount of freedom left for subordinates. Different styles can be identified across this continuum from boss-centered leadership to subordinate-centered leadership.

Here again, we should not get the implication that some managers always make a decision and announce it and that others always define limits and then ask the group to take a vote. On the contrary, it seems obvious that different styles will be appropriate in different situations. In a military combat situation, subordinates must rely on the decision making of their group leader. The crew of a ship hit by a torpedo would not be inclined to discuss the alternatives and then vote. If the captain announces, "Abandon ship," the order would be carried out immediately. On the other hand, in situations where time permits, it may be extremely useful to include subordinates in the decision-making process. This does not necessarily mean that a vote will be taken and that the majority rules. A manager may be very explicit to the effect that he is interested in the various points of view and an exhaustive study of the question. However, he may state emphatically, in the beginning, that he will make the decision at the end of the discussion. The authority to make some decisions may be decentralized completely with only broad guidelines established by the manager.

In other situations, a bureaucratic style may be more effective and efficient. For

---

[35] Eugene E. Jennings, *The Executive*, Harper & Row, Publishers, Incorporated, New York, 1962, p. 165.

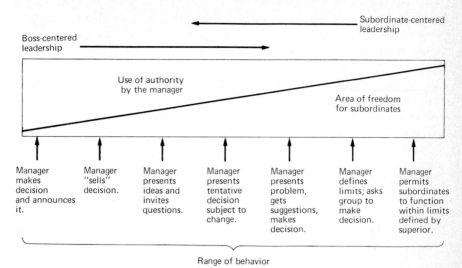

Boss-centered leadership

Subordinate-centered leadership

Use of authority by the manager

Area of freedom for subordinates

| Manager makes decision and announces it. | Manager "sells" decision. | Manager presents ideas and invites questions. | Manager presents tentative decision subject to change. | Manager presents problem, gets suggestions, makes decision. | Manager defines limits; asks group to make decision. | Manager permits subordinates to function within limits defined by superior. |

Range of behavior

FIGURE 13.3 CONTINUUM OF LEADERSHIP BEHAVIOR (Robert Tannenbaum and Warren H. Schmidt, "How to Choose a Leadership Pattern," *Harvard Business Review*, March–April 1958, p. 96)

relatively routine decisions, standard operating procedures might be entirely appropriate. On the other hand, referring to the "rules" when in fact there is an extraordinary set of circumstances might be dysfunctional for the organization.

The important thing is for the leader or manager to perceive situations accurately in order that an appropriate leadership style might be employed. Similarly, he must be able to empathize with other group members in order to understand the human element in each particular situation. Only when he can perceive these facets of the situation accurately is he able to use an appropriate leadership style. A word of caution is needed here. The leader can really "get in hot water" if he is out of phase—employing an autocratic style where a democratic-participative approach would be more appropriate, and vice versa. Moreover, leadership style must come relatively naturally. It can be developed over time if attention is given to it. However, if a particular style is used ineptly or insincerely, the result might be disastrous.

The manager should begin by assessing his own value system and determining the general leadership style with which he is most comfortable. Next, he should determine where that style is most appropriate and where it would need modification in order to be more effective. Once he accomplishes this, he needs practice to perfect a flexible approach.

ORGANIZATIONAL CLIMATE

Several key factors are involved in assessing the environmental setting within which leadership styles are employed. Assuming that a person has the appropriate traits and flexibility of style to lead, what is there in the organizational environment which affects his ability to motivate individual members and coordinate their effort toward group goals? Fiedler postulates three factors of major importance: (1) the leader's position power, (2) the structure of the task, and (3) the interpersonal relationships between leader and members. [36]

Position power relates to the formal authority which is identified with a specific position in the organization. A person occupying that role typically would expect compliance with directives issued to subordinates in the organization. While this is usually the case, it is not necessarily so. Positional authority may or may not be commensurate with personal ''authority'' or power. Given both positional authority and leadership ability, the individual should be expected to be more effective in his influence attempts than if he has only one or none of these two attributes.

The *task* to be performed provides an important ingredient in the leadership situation. A task-oriented group's performance is a measure of leadership effectiveness. However, the task itself may have an important impact on the degree to which leadership can affect performance. Well-structured, routine operations allow little margin for creativity in leadership. Unstructured, ambiguous situations allow considerable leeway but make the job of the leader much more difficult. ''The structured task is, in effect, one way of influencing member behavior by means of the organizational sanctions which can be imposed, and it reinforces position power. Alternatively, we may say that a group which is engaged in a highly structured task does not need a leader with as much position power because the leader's influence is implied by the instructions inherent in the task.'' [37]

Both position power and task structure are determined by the formal organization. *Interpersonal relationships* between the leader and other members of the group are affected by these two attributes as well as the personalities involved—the leader and the led. In most organizations, it appears that this dimension of the leadership system is the most crucial. While position power and task structure may seemingly provide a framework within which a leader can operate effectively, poor interpersonal relationships can negate the entire system. A small group may subvert the system by ''pegging'' output or by complete noncompliance.

Moreover, a leader who enjoys excellent interpersonal relationships in a system with a loose task structure and no formally designated power position may be extremely effective. His personal power enhances his ability to motivate individuals to capacity and to coordinate their efforts.

In this connection, it is important to define ''effective'' leadership. Influence attempts may be successful or unsuccessful. If the successful attempts result in behavior toward organization goals, we can say that leadership has been effective. It is obvious that influence attempts could be successful and the results off target in terms of the organization's goals. Good leader-member interpersonal relationships should lead to a high proportion of successful influence attempts. However, this does not ensure that they will all be effective. ''The *effectiveness* of the leadership act is not dependent on the

---

[36] Fiedler, op. cit., p. 22.
[37] Ibid., pp. 27–28.

leader-member relations. Rather, it depends upon the appropriateness and wisdom of the suggestion or order which the leader has given. There is no reason to believe that the well-liked leader will give better or wiser orders and directions than the less-liked leader.'' [38]

Good interpersonal relationships are necessary but not sufficient for long-run leadership effectiveness. The manager must plan his course of action carefully in order to coordinate effort toward objectives. He must devote his attention to the achievement of specific goals as well as to the maintenance or strengthening of relationships among group members and between himself and subordinates. Accurate perception and understanding of position power, task structure, and leader-member relationships will provide the framework which the manager can use in choosing an appropriate leadership style.

LEADERSHIP AND PRODUCTIVITY

Organization theory and management practice relate to task-oriented groups. Therefore, productivity is an important measure of managerial performance, which depends in large measure on leadership effectiveness. Thus, the basic question concerns the impact of various leadership styles on group productivity. For example, is an autocratic approach ''better'' than a democratic-participative one? Or, do we get better results from a laissez faire or ''hands off'' approach? Should the system be structured with rules and regulations so that it can run itself? Obviously, the answer to these questions is, ''It all depends.'' It depends upon the situation—the nature of the task, the position power of the leader, and the interpersonal relationships among group members. All of these are part of the overall psychosocial system within which a leader must operate.

Nevertheless, this question of productivity has been posed rather sharply as a dichotomy between production-centered leadership and employee-centered leadership. Much research has been done in an effort to support the position that, over the long run, employee-centered leadership will be more productive. As in the White-Lippett study cited earlier, there are indications that an autocratic, production-centered approach may lead to higher productivity in some cases. Typically, however, there are side effects with regard to employee morale and satisfaction which may be dysfunctional over the long run.

> Research in organizations is yielding increasing evidence that the superior's skill in supervising his subordinates *as a group* is an important variable affecting his success: the greater his skill in using group methods of supervision, the greater are the productivity and job satisfactions of his subordinates. . . . Supervisors with the best records of performance focus their primary attention on the human aspects of their subordinates' problems and on endeavoring to build effective work groups with high performance goals. [39]

---

[38] Ibid., p. 31.
[39] Rensis Likert, *New Patterns of Management*, McGraw-Hill Book Company, New York, 1961, pp. 26 and 7.

This describes the concept of employee-centered leadership as contrasted with a job-centered approach which concentrates on the task and uses various pressures to keep subordinates busily engaged in a prescribed way.

This controversy can be traced back to the evolution of management thought. Scientific management emphasized "the one best way" to do a job. The human relations movement concentrated on people—their individual needs and group dynamics. There seems to be increasing evidence that we are not confined to an either-or approach. By concentrating on the satisfaction of the employee's needs, we do not necessarily sacrifice productivity. Nor, on the other hand, does emphasis on effective and efficient performance necessarily mean that the human element must be ignored. Democratic-participative approaches give promise of increased individual satisfaction and group morale while at the same time facilitating improved productivity for the organization as a whole.

FACILITATING EFFECTIVE LEADERSHIP

French summarizes the complex nature of the leadership system and cites three factors which should be considered simultaneously.[40] We can try to foster the *organizational climate* which facilitates effective leadership. Similarly, we can continue to attempt to identify basic personal *characteristics*. While recognizing that their presence does not ensure success, individuals possessing them have a higher probability or potential for leadership success than those without the key characteristics. The appropriate *behavior* patterns can be encouraged through training programs of many types—on-the-job training or coaching and formal intraorganizational educational programs which include lecture-discussions, case analysis, role playing, sensitivity training, and team building.

Similarly, training can be carried on outside the organization via professional groups, trade associations, or universities. All of these methods are aimed at developing the overall environment and individual leaders to the point where they are flexible enough to cope effectively with varied and complex situations.

Another approach to more effective leadership is to match particular skills with specific situations. Based on Fiedler's dimensions of position power, task structure, and leader-member relations, individuals could be reassigned to fit the proper niche, and/or groups could be restructured in order to facilitate better leader-member relations. This approach can be summarized as follows:[41]

1 *We can change the leader's position power.*
2 *We can change the task structure.*
3 *We can change the leader-member relations.*

We can change an individual's title and/or adjust the degree of authority delegated to him. For example, his position power would be reduced if his signature had to be

---

[40] Wendell French, *The Personnel Management Process*, 2d ed., Houghton Mifflin Company, Boston, 1970, pp. 124-126.
[41] Fred E. Fiedler, "Engineer the Job to Fit the Manager," *Harvard Business Review*, September-October 1965, p. 122.

countersigned by another executive. Detailed instructions concerning the task reduce the leadership ability needed. Adding a subgroup of experienced, well-qualified employees to the work group would very likely affect the leader-member relationships significantly.

This matching approach, coupled with training, provides the means with which to develop leadership talent while at the same time using available skills more effectively. Concerted attention in both directions will result in long-run benefits for the system as a whole.

SUMMARY

Influence is an all-inclusive concept which covers any means by which behavioral change is induced in individuals or groups. An influence system involves a spectrum of ways to affect behavior—emulation, suggestion, persuasion, and coercion. The concept of interaction-influence systems stresses the multidirectional nature of influence processes—laterally as well as up and down the organizational hierarchy.

Power and/or authority underlie the entire spectrum of ways to influence behavior. Power is the *ability* to induce psychological or behavioral change. Power is a latent force which may never be manifest but, nevertheless, backs up all means of influencing behavior. Types of power include the coercive, utilitarian, and normative-social approaches. Power equalization in organizations is an evident trend toward offsetting coercive and utilitarian position power with normative-social power as a basis for influence attempts.

Authority is a special subclass of power; it is an institutionalized *right* to induce psychological or behavioral change. Throughout human history there has been conflict between individualism and the need for authority as a cohesive agent in cooperative social relationships.

Authority can be described in terms of three basic categories—charismatic, traditional, and rational-legal. Charismatic "authority" depends upon the magical qualities of individual leaders. Charismatic authority often evolves into traditional authority as informal status and role systems become stabilized over time. Traditional authority can evolve into rational-legal authority if the system is legitimatized formally.

The effectiveness of authority depends upon the "consent of the governed." Unless subordinates "accept" a positon holder as legitimate, he may not have much influence on their behavior. The "zone of acceptance" for employees in most organizations appears to be narrowing as people become better educated and more inclined to think for themselves. When positional and personal authority reinforce each other, we have a fusion of the acceptance theory with the right-to-command theory based on a rational-legal framework.

Influence systems provide the broad setting within which leadership occurs. Leadership has two basic connotations: (1) a status and (2) active performance of a role. Leadership is only part of management, not all of it. It often connotes the idea of eliciting behavioral responses which are more than routine; it takes *leadership* to evoke responses which are "above and beyond the call of duty."

According to the bilateral nature of interaction-influence systems, there is a net balance for each individual in any group. A leader is the one who has the largest net positive balance. The leadership system involves three basic elements—the leader, the led, and the situation.

The presence of certain basic personality traits and behavioral characteristics is helpful but neither necessary nor sufficient for success as a leader. A person with traits such as intelligence, social maturity and breadth, inner motivation and achievement drives, and appropriate human relations attitudes has a higher probability of success as a leader than someone without them. But the entire system must be considered in any analysis of leadership effectiveness.

Effectiveness of various leadership styles has also been the subject of intense research. To date, there are no clear-cut conclusions concerning the merit of autocratic, democratic, or laissez faire styles. It depends on the objectives established as well as the followers and the situation.

Of utmost importance is the concept of flexibility in leadership style. Managers must understand individual personality, group dynamics, and the total organizational psychosocial system.

QUESTIONS AND PROBLEMS

1 Define influence. Illustrate the four means of influencing behavior shown in Figure 13.1.

2 What is an interaction-influence system? Give examples of influence flowing horizontally and upward in organizations.

3 Compare and contrast power and authority. How do these concepts relate to influence systems?

4 Illustrate the use of (a) coercive, (b) utilitarian, and (c) normative-social power in influencing organizational behavior. Which approach is best? Why?

5 Explain the concept of power equalization. What trends have been apparent? What do you foresee for the future?

6 Compare and contrast anarchy and authoritarianism. How much is "enough" authority to *ensure* cooperative action and progress toward group goals?

7 Explain rational-legal, traditional, and charismatic authority. Compare personal and positional authority.

8 Discuss the zone of acceptance. What affects its scope? In general, will it widen or narrow in the future?

9 Define leadership and relate it to influence systems and management.

10 Identify several leaders in organizations in which you are a member. Check them against the sample list of traits (at least the four summary items) in the chapter. How do they compare? Do your findings tend to support or refute trait theory?

11 Compare and contrast autocratic, democratic, and laissez faire leadership styles. Should a leader pick a style and "stay with it" regardless? Why or why not?

12 How do variables such as position power, task structure, and leader-member relationships affect the appropriateness of various leadership styles?

*A management system is a process of
people interacting to apply resources
to achieve goals.*
M. Scott Myers

*Under any social order from now to Utopia, manage-
ment is indispensable and all-enduring. . . . The
question is not: "Will there be a management elite?"
but "What sort of elite will it be?"*
Sidney Webb

*If we could first know where we are and whither we
are tending, we could then better judge what to do
and how to do it.*
Abraham Lincoln

*Utimately all policies are made . . . on the basis of
judgments. There is no other way, and there never
will be. The question is whether those judgments have
to be made in the fog of inadequate and inaccurate
data, unclear and undefined issues, and a welter of
conflicting personal opinions, or whether they can be
made on the basis of adequate, reliable information,
relevant experience, and clearly drawn issues. In the
end, analysis is but an aid to judgment. . . . Judgment
is supreme.*
Alain C. Enthoven

*Keeping the wheels turning in a direction already set
is a relatively simple task, compared to that of
directing the introduction of a continuing flow of
changes and innovations, and preventing the
organization from flying apart under the pressure.*
H. Edward Wrapp

THE MANAGERIAL SYSTEM

The managerial system is primarily concerned with decision making for planning and controlling organizational endeavor. Other organizational considerations, both structure and process, are contextual for the more substantive function of coordinating diverse enterprise activities toward objective accomplishment. Up to this point we have considered in detail the organizational constraints which constitute the complex internal and external context of managerial decision making.

The central theme for Part 6 is set forth in Chapter 14, Managerial Information-Decision Systems. One approach to the study of organizations is to concentrate on decision-making processes. This can lead to the study of organization structure based on decision points and information flow. Similarly, management can be approached through the study of decision making, particularly if it is broadly construed and includes implementation and a continuous flow of various types of decisions.

Concepts such as open and closed systems plus a programmability continuum provide useful frameworks for discussing managerial decision making. Chapter 15 is concerned with computational decision making, which assumes certainty in relatively closed systems. The concept of rationality is considered in detail, as are quantification and symbolic model building. Several illustrative examples of quantitative techniques useful in managerial decision making are also discussed.

Chapter 16 is concerned with judgmental decision making in relatively open systems with uncertain conditions. Emphasis in this chapter is on the behavioral aspects of managerial decision making. It focuses on the human being as a decision maker and on the complexities that arise because of the impact of the value systems which each individual brings to the decision-making process. Attention is devoted to group decision making and the impact of groups on individual decision makers.

Another way of viewing the managerial system would be to think of (1) mobilizing to accomplish a task or achieve an objective, (2) doing the job, and (3) checking the results. The mobilizing process is analogous to organizing and includes all the effort involved in getting ready to do something. The doing or executing function involves planning some action and implementing it. The checking activity is analogous to the control function, which is concerned with maintaining a dynamic equilibrium. This frame of reference provides a means of separating planning and controlling activities from other organizational considerations. In Part 6 planning and controlling are discussed in terms of the overall framework of decision-making processes. Chapter 17 is concerned with managerial planning, and Chapter 18 with organizational control.

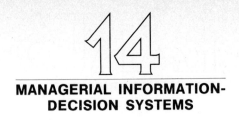

MANAGERIAL INFORMATION-DECISION SYSTEMS

Thinking, problem solving, and decision making are fundamental to man's behavior. Managerial decision making receives considerable attention from researchers and practitioners. It is a useful way of viewing what managers actually do in the process of coordinating organizational endeavor. Information is a vital ingredient for decision making. Information-decision systems pertain to both individual and organizational decision making and the attendant information flow relevant to the process. In this chapter we will explore managerial information-decision systems in terms of the following topics:

> The Managerial System
> Decision Making Defined
> Pervasiveness of Decision Making
> Possible Foci of Attention
> The Decision-making Process
> Information Defined
> Information and Decision Making
> Management Information-Decision Systems
> Future Promise and Problems

THE MANAGERIAL SYSTEM

Everyone is a manager, if only of his personal affairs. Our primary concern, however, is management in organizational settings—the coordination of group effort toward an established purpose. This coordination is effected primarily (1) through people, (2) via techniques, (3) in an organization, and (4) toward objectives. Essentially, management is the process of integrating human and material resources into a total system for objective accomplishment.

The managerial system is the means of linking other primary subsystems of organizations. The environmental suprasystem provides the setting within which organizations function. The technology is important and is often directly related to organizational structure, both formal and informal. The psychosocial system provides an internal atmosphere for day-to-day operations. The managerial system's primary role is that of integrating activities toward the achievement of explicit or implicit goals.

Alternative Views of Managerial Systems

One approach to studying managerial systems would be to analyze the role of the manager in various institutional settings. The focal point would be a comparison of the managerial function in business enterprises, government agencies, educational institutions or other fairly distinct kinds of organizations such as prisons, churches, or the military. The role of the managerial system would be developed by comparing and contrasting the activities required to coordinate organizational efforts in the various institutions studied. This comparison would provide meaningful information with regard to the pervasiveness and universality of the managerial system. This particular subject—comparative analysis—is discussed in more detail in Part 7.

Another approach to understanding the managerial system would be a detailed analysis of the process involved. This approach has been an integral part of the management literature, stemming from the traditionalists. A typical framework is that of planning, assembling resources, organizing, motivating, and controlling. While it is recognized that arbitrary categorization of this sort has proved unrealistic, these phases of the management process seem fairly distinct and can be studied individually. This approach is often coupled with the development of principles based on empirical research and deductive reasoning on the part of practitioners. Thus, we have "principles of organization" or "principles of leadership." Some writers subdivide these categories to obtain an even longer list of steps in the management process. A more common approach, however, is to reduce the number to a basic core which is usually planning-organizing-controlling.

Planning and controlling are the primary activities involved in integrating purposeful organizational activity. The organizing process provides the setting within which planning and controlling occur. Organizing takes into consideration the external environmental system as well as the internal technical and psychosocial systems. Given an organization reflecting the constraints of these various systems, the managerial system functions by planning and controlling short-, medium-, and long-range endeavor toward objective accomplishment. A slightly different approach views management as a continual cycle of planning and implementation. This suggests that organizing, assembling resources, motivating, and controlling are subsumed under "implementation."

Decision making, another means of viewing the managerial system, is a fundamental process which relates to man's basic unit of behavior. Behavior is goal-oriented, and human beings move toward goals by making choices (decisions) from among alternative courses of action. All behavior results from a sequence of decision-making steps which culminate in choice.

Organizational decision making can be described in the same way because individuals are involved in the process. Managers decide on organizational objectives. Planning involves numerous decisions concerning how goals should be pursued. Decisions are made with regard to the organizational arrangements required to implement strategic and tactical plans. Control decisions are made in order to maintain organizational endeavor within acceptable limits according to policies or standards which have been established (decided previously).

Organizational Subsystems and Decision Making

Three organizational subsystems or levels can be described as operating, coordinative, and strategic (see Figure 5.4). The *operating* subsystem relates to the substantive activity of any organization. What does the organization do as its primary *raison d'être?* In a manufacturing organization this involves the input of raw materials and components, processing them, and outputting finished goods. Management of this activity on a day-to-day basis requires many decisions. Given a relatively short-run time horizon and an engineering point of view, computational techniques can be employed in managerial decision making.

Strategic considerations relate to the boundary between the organization and its environment. Here the time horizon is more long-run and uncertain, thus requiring more cogitative and judgmental decison making on the part of management. *Coordinative* management is primarily concerned with integrating the other two subsystems. Both short-run and long-run time horizons must be kept in mind as managers attempt to integrate the technical or substantive activity of the organization with its environment. Compromise and mediation describe the approaches used in this endeavor.

A wide spectrum of decision-making methods are relevant to the managerial system. Within the operating subsystem there is relative certainty; hence, well-defined problems can be solved via straightforward computational techniques. For long-range strategy, the board of directors and top management are faced with considerable uncertainty and novel, ill-structured problems. Computational approaches are less appropriate for decision making at the strategic level except for subparts of some problems.

DECISON MAKING DEFINED

To decide means to pass judgment or make up one's mind. It implies two or more alternatives under consideration with the decision maker making a choice to end his deliberation. Many connotations are evident for the term decide; there are many synonyms with shades of meaning involved. For example:

> *Decide* implies the bringing to an end of vacillation, doubt, dispute, etc., by making up one's mind as to an action, course, or judgment; *determine* in

addition suggests that the form, character, functions, scope, etc., of something are precisely fixed (the club decided on a lecture series and appointed a committee to determine the speakers, the dates, etc.); *settle* stresses finality in a decision, often one arrived at by arbitration, and implies the termination of all doubt or controversy; *to conclude* is to decide after careful investigation or reasoning; *resolve* implies firmness of intention to carry through a decision (he resolved to go to bed early every night.) [1]

Synonyms such as "settle" or "conclude" connote a finality which may be misleading, particularly in an organizational context. Managerial decision making is usually a sequential process, with subsequent decisions based on developments that have accumulated over a period of time.

"Resolve" connotes continuing action involved in carrying out a decision. The action may be overt or explicit in terms of carrying out a decision to buy new equipment or take a new job. Or, it may involve only the intent to behave accordingly at some future time. For example, a person may decide that he is a Democrat or that the Ajax Company is a poor credit risk. These latter decisions result in a propensity on the part of individuals and organizations to decide in a certain way if the particular issue should arise in the future.

In task-oriented organizations problem-solving activities are often termed decision making. In this context it is sometimes considered synonymous with managing— particularly if decision making is broadly construed to include searching out and recognizing problem situations. It involves inventing, developing, and analyzing alternative courses of action. Analysis leads to the choice of a particular course of action and the decision is implemented.

PERVASIVENESS OF DECISION MAKING

Decision making is fundamental to organism and organization behavior. It provides the means for control and allows coherence in systems.

The living systems are a special subset of the set of all possible concrete systems, composed of the plants and the animals. They all have the following characteristics (among others):

They are open systems. . . .

They contain a decider, the essential critical subsystem which controls the entire system, causing its subsystems and components to coact, without which there is no system. [2]

From the moment we decide to (1) turn off the alarm, (2) roll over, and (3) go back to sleep, until we reset it again (optimistically!) late that night, we are making decisions.

---

[1] *Webster's New World Dictionary of the American Language*, College Edition, The World Publishing Company, Cleveland, 1966, p. 380.
[2] James G. Miller, "Living Systems: Basic Concepts," *Behavioral Science*, July 1965, pp. 203–204.

Which tie should I wear? How should I respond to the customer complaint? Where shall we eat lunch? Shall we invest more money in developing a "cloud nine" product idea? And so on throughout the day. We make personal and organizational decisions endlessly.

All managerial activity might be considered decision making. For example, Simon states, "What part does decision making play in managing? I shall find it convenient to take mild liberties with the English language by using 'decision making' as though it were synonymous with 'managing.'"[3] If *all* behavior results from decision making and if managing is a particular kind of behavior, then managing is decision making. Obviously, there are other useful ways to view management—concentration on processes or functions, for example. But decision making is one of the most important tasks of managers. It pervades the performance of all managerial functions.[4] In this context management can be studied in terms of decisions made in planning, organizing, or controlling enterprise activities. In short, decision making is a pervasive activity and provides a useful approach for studying managerial systems.

Conscious or Unconscious

The examples cited above refer to conscious or deliberate choices from among alternatives. However, even within this set of examples we have a gradation of consciousness from the relatively automatic shutting off of the alarm to the relatively contemplative approach invoked when deciding upon additional investments in new product development.

It seems to us unnecessarily restrictive to require conscious behavior for decision making. It is useful to consider all behavior in the framework of decision making and recognize that there is a gradation of consciousness involved. Such a framework allows the use of terms such as *programmed* and *nonprogrammed decisions*. Relatively automatic (programmed) decisions such as reflex actions appear to be completely unconscious. However, even this type of behavior, according to evolutionists, has been learned over millions of years. For instinctive or impulsive reactions, decisions and behavior are relatively unconscious. Habits are a form of relatively programmed decisions. At some point in time, deliberate consideration was required. Through repetitive processes, however, a choice becomes more and more automatic, given similar stimuli. Organizations develop habits in the form of standard operating procedures and computer programs for coping with repetitive situations. Programmed decisions reduce the amount of rethinking necessary in repetitive situations. This conserves time and energy which management can devote to nonprogrammable problems. However, habits can stifle innovation—programmed activity can increase to absorb available time.

---

[3] Herbert A. Simon, *The New Science of Management Decision,* Harper & Row, Publishers, Incorporated, New York, 1960, p. 1.
[4] This approach is emphasized in the following framework: *"Model-building, model-solving,* and ultimately *model use* are . . . the strongest means by which to consider *decision-making,* which in turn can be viewed as the gateway to the more complex management functions." Martin K. Starr, *Management: A Modern Approach,* Harcourt Brace Jovanovich, Inc., New York, 1971, p. viii.

Within the range of nonprogrammed decision making, there is considerable variation. There is a continuum from one-time decisions such as the Cuban missile crisis or the SST (supersonic transport) controversy to problems which may occur periodically but may call for modified approaches because of changing internal conditions or external environmental factors.

A Basic Unit of Behavior

The question of whether or not unconscious behavior involves decision making has deeper roots in psychological theory. Behaviorists contend that the physiological pattern of the reflex arc explains the stimulus-response relationship. This school of thought explains behavior in terms of learning new conditioned responses through experience.

Cognitive theorists, on the other hand, support the idea that there is some mediating force between stimulus and response which is much more complex than a simple reflex arc. The "image" or sum total of past experience is often cited as the mediating force. [5]

The difference between the two positions is illustrated by the following statement:

> [The brain] is far more like a map control room than it is like an old-fashioned telephone exchange. The stimuli, which are allowed in, are not connected by just simple one-to-one switches to the outgoing responses. Rather, the incoming impulses are usually worked over and elaborated in the central control room into a tentative, cognitivelike map of the environment. And it is this tentative map, indicating routes and paths and environmental relationships, which finally determines what responses, if any, the animal will finally release. [6]

Miller, Galanter, and Pribram support the cognitive theorists and offer the TOTE (Test-Operate-Test-Exit) unit of behavior (see Figure 14.1) as an alternative to the reflex arc. [7] This unit incorporates the notion of feedback control and suggests that actions are guided constantly by the outcomes of various tests. An organism continually tests the situation for congruity or incongruity. If congruity exists, i.e., if the situation is consonant with some plan or expectation, no further action is called for. However, if the test indicates incongruity, some operation is invoked. Tests are made repeatedly in order to indicate whether or not the operation should continue.

For example, when parking an automobile parallel to the curb, the driver continually *tests* the situation to ascertain how close he has come to achieving the goal.

---

[5] Kenneth E. Boulding, *The Image,* The University of Michigan Press, Ann Arbor, Mich., 1966.
[6] Edward C. Tolman, "Cognitive Maps in Rats and Man," *Psychological Review,* July 1948, pp. 189-208.
[7] "It seems obvious to us that a great deal more goes on between the stimulus and the response than can be accounted for by a simple statement about associative strengths. . . . Our theoretical preferences are all on the side of the cognitive theorists. Life is complicated." George A. Miller, Eugene Galanter, and Karl H. Pribram, *Plans and the Structure of Behavior,* Holt, Rinehart and Winston, Inc., New York, 1960, p. 9.

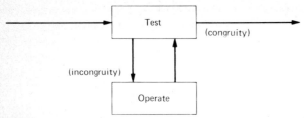

FIGURE 14.1 THE TOTE UNIT (George A. Miller, Eugene Galanter, and Karl H. Pribram, *Plans and the Structure of Behavior,* Holt, Rinehart and Winston, Inc., New York, 1960, p. 26)

Information concerning distance from the curb and/or other automobiles is processed and checked against the plan. If the current position fits the plan *(congruity),* the driver proceeds to turn off the ignition, set the brake, and get out. If there is *incongruity,* he will continue to maneuver *(operate)* the car toward the goal (parking).

The TOTE unit is purposely quite similar to the basic feedback loop in computer programming. Organism behavior is considered analogous to the hierarchical approach used in developing computer programs. Large feedback loops for complete tasks are comprised of many nested subloops, all the way down to the basic instruction step.

In this scheme it appears that decisions are made at all levels, conscious or not. Reflex actions are highly programmed behavior patterns but still involve rapid use of TOTE units to execute the behavior in question. Conscious, deliberate, and cogitative decision processes could also be described under the general model of the TOTE unit. The overall scheme, of which the TOTE unit is the basic unit of analysis, includes the following concepts:

> *Image.* All the accumulated, organized knowledge that a person has about himself and his environment.
>
> *Plan.* A rough sketch of some course of action (strategy) as well as more detailed operating procedures (tactics).
>
> *Execution.* Carrying out a plan step by step, completing one part and then moving to the next. It may involve overt action or only the collection and/or transformation of information. [8]

The image provides the environment for planning which results in strategy, tactics, and execution. Decision making is involved at all levels. This schema is presented for organism behavior, but it could refer to organizations as well. Organizations have images or "character," which is the sum total of their past experience. They have master plans or strategies, and they operate via sequential steps which are tactical in nature.

---

[8] Ibid., pp. 16–18.

Feedback control is used to check actual results against plans, thus initiating corrective action if needed. We will return to this framework in Chapters 17 and 18, "Managerial Planning" and "Organizational Control." The purpose here is to illustrate the pervasiveness of decision making and how a basic feedback or decision unit can be used to describe all behavior on a continuum of programmability or unconsciousness-consciousness.

POSSIBLE FOCI OF ATTENTION

The voluminous literature on decision making seems to stem from two basic points of view, descriptive and prescriptive, and to congregate at three levels of interest. The simplified model in Figure 14.2 refers to the decision itself, the decision maker, and the process used. The various disciplines engaged in research on decision making concentrate on whichever focus of attention is most meaningful to them. Management science techniques have emphasized maximization principles in the choice among alternatives. Some psychologists have concentrated on the individual as the decision maker, and others have been concerned with the impact of reference groups on decision making. Considerable attention has been devoted to the decision-making process, both normatively and descriptively. Much has been written on "how to make optimal decisions," or at least better decisions than before. A body of knowledge has developed from describing decision processes in real organizations. Such research is concerned primarily with understanding more about how decision makers actually behave, rather than with prescribing better ways to make decisions.

Several dimensions of importance to managerial decision making are shown in Figure 14.3. The context of the decision maker varies from relatively closed to relatively open systems. If the decision maker is continually interacting with the "environment,"

FIGURE 14.2 LEVELS AT WHICH DECISION MAKING HAS BEEN STUDIED, WITH ILLUSTRATIVE RESEARCH QUESTIONS

	DESCRIPTIONS OF BEHAVIOR (WHAT IS HAPPENING OR WHAT HAS HAPPENED)	PRESCRIPTIVE OR NORMATIVE MODEL BUILDING (WHAT OUGHT TO HAPPEN)
The decision	What decisions are made in an organization?	What is an optimal decision?
	How do these decisions "turn out"?	How can decisions be improved?
The decision maker	What are the characteristics of the decision makers in the organization?	How should a rational decision maker behave?
	What factors influence the behavior of decision makers?	
The decision process	How are decisions actually made in the organization?	How should decisions be made in an organization?

SOURCE: Albert H. Rubenstein and Chadwick J. Haberstroh (eds.), *Some Theories of Organization,* rev. ed., Richard D. Irwin, Inc., and The Dorsey Press, Homewood, Ill., 1966, p. 578.

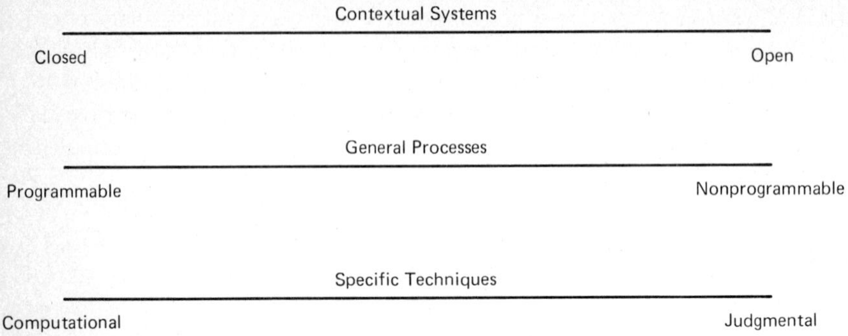

Contextual Systems
_____

Closed   Open

General Processes
_____

Programmable   Nonprogrammable

Specific Techniques
_____

Computational   Judgmental

FIGURE 14.3 SEVERAL DIMENSIONS OF DECISION MAKING

the system is relatively open. Informational inputs are gathered from diverse sources and become a part of the process. However, if the decison maker does not seek additional information, he tends to close the system and routinize the process. Alexis and Wilson describe this phenomenon as follows:

> In closed models a few dimensions of the decision environment are selected and admitted into the decision process: action-outcome relations, utility, and so on. The decision maker is assumed to be a logical, methodical maximizer. In contrast, the open decision model parallels an "open system." Like the open system, it is continually influenced by its total environment, and, of course, it also influences the environment. Decisions shape as well as mirror the environment. Contrary to the assumptions of closed decision models, the open model does not assume that the decision maker can recognize all goals and feasible alternatives. A more realistic view of his capabilities is emphasized. He is viewed as a complex mixture of many elements, including his culture, his personality, and his aspirations. [9]

With human beings in the decision process, the system can vary from relatively open to relatively closed, depending upon the individual's propensity and the given situation. In many cases the human element has been eliminated; then the system becomes even more closed. In such cases, computer programs have been developed to handle routine, repetitive decisions.

The dimension of programmability parallels the open-closed continuum of the contextual system. In those cases where the contextual complexity is included, the process becomes relatively nonprogrammable. That is, it becomes exceedingly difficult to develop a program which eliminates the human element from the decision-making process.

Another dimension relates to specific techniques which may be used. Computa-

[9] Marcus Alexis and Charles Z. Wilson, *Organizational Decision Making,* © 1967, p. 158. Reprinted by permission of Prentice-Hall, Inc., Englewood Cliffs, N.J.

tional techniques can be programmed to supplant human decision makers when the contextual system is relatively closed. In open systems more judgment is involved, and hence the process cannot be programmed explicitly. In general, these three dimensions parallel each other and provide a meaningful framework for understanding managerial decision making.

In Chapter 15, we will be concerned with computational techniques which can be used by managers in relatively closed systems. In Chapter 16 we will stress the human element—judgmental decision making in open-system contexts. It is recognized that there is no evident demarcation between the open and the closed, the programmable and the nonprogrammable, and the computational and the judgmental dimensions. Rather, there is a gradation along each of these continua. Recognizing the artificial dichotomy, we will discuss the polar positions in the two following chapters.

Regardless of the assumptions concerning the dimensions described above, there is a general model which can facilitate understanding the decision-making process. This general model can be applied computationally or judgmentally. And it can refer to open or closed systems which may determine its degree of programmability.

THE DECISION-MAKING PROCESS

Just as there are many connotations for the term *decision making,* there are many paradigms or schema setting forth the *elements* involved. For example, "As a by-product of attempts to define and outline a 'complete' model, we have come to recognize at least six elements common to all decisions: (1) the state of nature; (2) the decision maker; (3) the goals or ends to be served; (4) the relevant alternatives and the set of actions from which a choice will be made; (5) a relation that produces a preference ordering of alternatives; and (6) the choice itself, the selection of one or some combination of alternatives." [10]

These elements provide the basic ingredients for the *steps* in the decision-making process.

> The first phase of the decision making process—searching the environment for conditions calling for a decision—I shall call *intelligence* activity (borrowing the military meaning of intelligence).
>
> The second phase—inventing, developing, and analyzing possible courses of action—I shall call *design* activity.
>
> The third phase—selecting a particular course of action from those available—I shall call *choice* activity. [11]

These are elaborations of the general, three-step process outlined by Dewey long ago. [12]

---

[10] Ibid., p. 149.
[11] Simon, op. cit., p. 2.
[12] What is the problem? What are the alternatives? Which alternative is best? John Dewey, *How We Think,* D. C. Heath and Company, Boston, 1910, pp. 101-105.

Other models include more steps in an attempt to understand the process in more detail. Even elaborate multistep models are oversimplifications, however. For example, the steps normally are not as discrete as a list would indicate. Much of the decision-making activity goes on simultaneously. That is, evaluation of alternatives can point up another problem to be solved. Usually there are a number of problems "in the wind." Thus the manager is involved simultaneously in intelligence, design, and choice activity. Attempts at designing alternative courses of action may turn up additional problems, thus setting off new intelligence activities. A continuing problem-solving cycle or decision process might contain a series of subcycles. As the system becomes more complex, it is obvious that refined systems of information flow and tools of analysis must be developed in order to facilitate the decision process.

Figure 14.4 shows a flow chart of the decision-making process. As indicated, there are a number of factors which make up the context for the problem and the decision maker. This could also be termed the state of nature. Some of the factors are external and some are internal to the decision maker. His "image" or value system will have an effect on the decision-making process at several stages. Theoretically, the number of alternative solutions could be infinite. However, for all practical purposes only a finite number can be verbalized and isolated.

The next step involves the assessment of the probable future effects of the various alternatives specified. This phase involves a predicting system which may tend toward objectivity or subjectivity, depending on the degree of uncertainty involved. If recorded past experience is available, the probabilities of various outcomes may be ascertained quite readily. With less information, especially for new or unique problems, prediction becomes more speculative and subjective. However, the decision maker does assess the future in some manner—consciously or unconsciously, objectively or subjectively.

Once the effects have been anticipated and an estimate made of the probability of each occurrence, the decision maker then assesses the importance of a particular outcome to him. If it is inconsequential, it may be discarded from further consideration. If, however, a particular outcome is extremely consequential (even with only a slight chance of occurrence), it may weigh heavily in the decision process. An example is the problem of live virus in vaccine where there might be only a slight (even remote) possibility of actual disease. Yet if the disease is fatal, it becomes an extremely critical factor in the decision process, and steps must be taken to ensure that it does not occur. Manned space flight presents a similar example where 95 percent reliability is not good enough.

After the alternatives have been scrutinized and importance attached to the various outcomes, the decision maker evalutes the relevant information and chooses. Each decision then feeds back into the environment of subsequent decisions.

Obviously, managers do not approach all decisions explicitly via a framework such as shown in Figure 14.4. Many routine or programmed activities are evident in individual and organizational behavior. For nonroutine or nonprogrammed situations, a process such as the one outlined (or something similar) is often followed. Such a

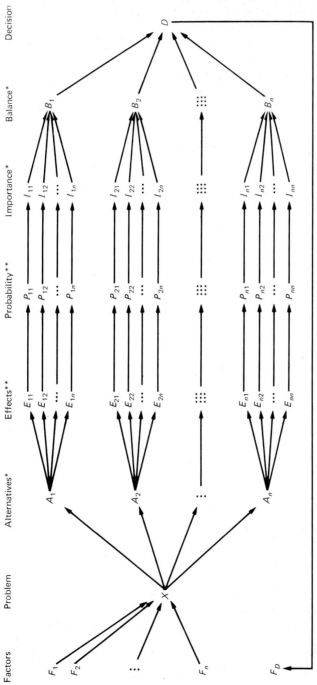

FIGURE 14.4 FLOW CHART OF THE DECISION-MAKING PROCESS. Some value framework is invoked when identifying "appropriate" alternatives, attaching importance to the effects anticipated, and balancing the alternatives in the final evaluation. (Refer to items with single asterisk in the figure.) The prediction system is involved in the stages indicated by the double asterisk. Probability of occurrence ranges between 0 and 1 — along the continuum of certainty and uncertainty (including risk). Much subjective probability is utilized in the typical decision-making process. A system of information flow is vital to the decision-making process — in the intelligence activity involved in pinpointing problems, in the search activity involved in identifying alternatives, and in the evaluation process leading to a choice.

diagram is a simplification of the decision-making process; yet it is useful to identify the process explicitly in order to understand it better.

Considerably more detail could be developed for a particular phase of the decision process. For example, in developing alternatives, the complex question of creativity arises. How can innovation be fostered? Descriptive research suggests that most decisions are incremental in nature. That is, they move only a slight way from the approach previously used, particularly if it was successful. In a sense this is satisficing behavior— accepting a workable alternative without being overly concerned that it is "the best."

A system of information flow is vital to the decision-making process. Information is the raw material of intelligence activity which touches off the recognition that a decision is to be made. Information is vital in evaluating alternative courses of action. A decision maker can be viewed as an information processing organism. Similarly, an organization can be viewed as an information processing system. These two points of view might be termed the micro and macro aspects of information-decision systems.

INFORMATION DEFINED

Information is another word which means many things to many people. In the context of decision making, it implies additional knowledge relevant to the particular decision problem in question. Other concepts related to the term are as follows:

> *Information* applies to facts that are gathered in any way, as by reading, observation, hearsay, etc., and does not necessarily connote validity (inaccurate information); *knowledge* applies to any body of facts gathered by study, observation, etc., and to the ideas inferred from these facts, and connotes an understanding of what is known (man's knowledge of the universe); *learning* is knowledge acquired by study, especially in languages, literature, philosophy, etc.; *erudition* implies profound or abstruse learning beyond the comprehension of most people; *wisdom* implies superior judgment and understanding based on broad knowledge. [13]

Facts, data, and first impressions provide the raw material for processing systems which result in information. The most obvious examples are computerized systems, which reduce voluminous data into meaningful information for particular decisions.

Communication is intercourse by words, letters, or similar means, and it involves interchange of thoughts or opinions. It also presents the concept of communication systems, for example, telephone, telegraph, or television. Communication implies information; the terms are part of the same family. In the broadest sense information has been defined as "that which is communicated."

Information is often evaluated in terms of its pertinence for decision making. Facts,

---

[13] *Webster's New World Dictionary of the American Language*, pp. 749–750.

numbers, and data are processed to provide meaningful information—an increment of knowledge which alters the degree of uncertainty in a particular situation. [14] For example, miscellaneous accounting data provide information when arrayed in balance sheets and income statements. Ratio analysis and graphic displays of pertinent relationships provide even more meaningful information. But if the problem is one of evaluating the effectiveness of a new advertising campaign, traditional accounting data, however elaborately processed, may be meaningless. Thus, what constitutes "information" depends on the problem at hand and the decision maker's frame of reference.

Information can be conveyed in many ways, both formally and informally. Periodic reports with a standard format provide formal feedback on the operating system. The grapevine illustrates how informal, interpersonal relationships provide channels of communication. Information is the substance of communications systems. In its various forms—electronic impulses, written or spoken words, informal or formal reports—information is a basic ingredient for decision making.

INFORMATION AND DECISION MAKING

Information facilitates carrying out the managerial functions of planning, organizing, and controlling operations. Information is the raw material for the managerial decision-making process. According to Forrester, "Management is the process of converting information into action. The conversion process we call decision making. . . . An information feedback system exists whenever the environment leads to a decision that results in action which affects the environment." [15]

For many problem-solving tasks, the individual has stored knowledge which he brings to bear in the decision-making process. This knowledge or "experience" may be sufficient (at least as he sees it) to handle the problem. On the other hand, he may seek additional information and hence require service from formal or informal communication systems.

Some psychologists have suggested that mental illness results from information overload in individuals. If individuals can remain in equilibrium with their environment, they are healthy. In a sense they are able to cope with external conditions and maintain a "normal" role in society. If they are unable to process information—both internal and external flows—efficiently, however, a condition of information overload occurs and there is a breakdown in the individual system. The overload may develop because of the inability to sceen out irrelevant data for the individual's decision-making tasks. When a person loses touch with reality, he is described as mentally ill.

Organizational health has many dimensions, one of which is the effectiveness and efficiency of the managerial system. Its role in linking other systems—values, technical,

---

[14] Robert H. Hayes, "Qualitative Insights from Quantitative Methods," *Harvard Business Review,* July-August 1969, p. 114.
[15] Jay W. Forrester, "Managerial Decision Making," in Martin Greenberger (ed.), *Management and the Computer of the Future,* The M.I.T. Press, Cambridge, Mass., and John Wiley & Sons, Inc., New York, 1962, pp. 37 and 39.

structural, and psychosocial—is vital for organizational well-being. Managerial decisions are necessary to integrate activity toward objectives and to maintain a viable organization in a dynamic equilibrium. Information is a key ingredient in decision-making processes, and it is important for organizations to devote attention to designing appropriate systems of information flow.

Information Flow/The Communication Process

The general model of the communication process set forth in Figure 14.5 can be applied to individual as well as organizational information flow. When interpersonal communication is involved, the problems of the content and meaning of messages become important. Semantics has long been recognized as a vital problem in interpersonal communications.

In communication systems the goal is *understanding*—getting the sender and receiver "tuned" together for a particular message. Although repetition (redundancy) can be helpful, there is no direct correlation between the amount of communication or information transmission and the degree of understanding. Several basic problems are apparent according to Guetzkow, "When the symbols fail to carry the full contents of the messages, their semantic properties are transformed as they are handled within a communication flow—either by omission of aspects of the contents, or by the introduction of distortions." [16] Some of the sender's meaning is lost in the process of encoding and transmitting a message. A memo may not reflect accurately the manager's feeling about a situation. Direct conversation with his staff may help clarify the issue, but even in this case his tone of voice or facial expression can alter the message significantly. The use of graphic display adds another dimension—"a picture is worth a thousand words."

Another basic problem in achieving understanding in communication systems is that of decoding. Even if a message were coded and transmitted accurately, it is unlikely that it would be decoded in the same way by everyone receiving it. People read, see, and hear what they want to read, see, and hear. Memos, statistics, and diagrams are

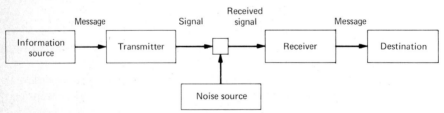

FIGURE 14.5 SYMBOLIC REPRESENTATION OF THE COMMUNICATION PROCESS (Claude E. Shannon and Warren Weaver, *The Mathematical Theory of Communication,* University of Illinois Press, Urbana, Ill., 1949, p. 98)

[16] Harold Guetzkow, "Communication in Organizations," in James G. March (ed.), *Handbook of Organizations,* Rand McNally & Company, Chicago, 1965, p. 551.

interpreted in terms of value systems which are as unique to individuals as fingerprints. A person's perception or "image" of the environment depends on his total past experience; messages are distorted as receivers "read in" meanings not intended by the sender. A report from headquarters to several branches might be interpreted several ways with each receiver quite satisfied that he "got *the* message." Zalkind and Costello summarize their findings on the problem of managerial perception as follows:

> Without vigilance to perceive accurately and to minimize as far as possible the subjective approach in perceiving others, effective administration is handicapped. . . . Research would not support the conclusion that perceptual distortions will not occur simply because the administrator says he will try to be objective. The administrator or manager will have to work hard to avoid seeing only what he wants to see and to guard against fitting everything into what he is set to see. [17]

Understanding is facilitated if there are the means and time for feedback and verification. If the issue can be "talked out," there is a chance that people can empathize and understand. However, time pressure works against this process; if the flow of information on complex issues is accelerated, the probability of complete understanding decreases. Distance and communication media also affect the process significantly.

Understanding on the part of organization members is critical in implementing plans appropriately, and it is basic to the control function as well. For example, the central theme in cybernetics is that of communication and control. Unless there is effective control, the communication process has not been complete. [18]

Information Flow and Organization

Organizations have been faced with dynamic world conditions, rapidly changing technology, changing markets, and other similar phenomena which have required adaptation on their part. Adjustments have been made, but without recognition, in many cases, of the impact of organizational changes on communication systems. Thus much information that was appropriate under older arrangements has now become obsolete. Furthermore, additional types of information are urgently needed in order to plan and control current operations. According to Daniel, "Management often loses sight of the seemingly obvious and simple relationship between organization structure and information needs. Companies very seldom follow up on reorganizations with penetrating reappraisals of their information systems, and managers given new responsibilities and decision-making authority often do not receive all the information they require." [19]

---

[17] Sheldon S. Zalkind and Timothy W. Costello, "Perception: Some Recent Research and Implications for Administration," *Administrative Science Quarterly,* September 1962, p. 235.
[18] Norbert Wiener, *The Human Use of Human Beings,* rev. ed., Houghton Mifflin Company, Boston, 1954, p. 16.
[19] D. Ronald Daniel, "Management Information Crisis," *Harvard Business Review,* September–October 1961, pp. 112–113.

Information geared to managing functions such as engineering, production, and distribution may be irrelevant if a company is reorganized along product lines. Schedule and cost data (among others) per product are essential in order to manage material and energy flow through the total system. Thus information flow should be adjusted to reflect decision-making needs in the revised organization.

MANAGEMENT INFORMATION-DECISION SYSTEMS

Figure 14.6 shows a skeletal model of an organization with the basic flow of information necessary for the managerial system. Management considers internal and environmental information in the process of establishing objectives (strategic level). Premises with regard to governmental relations, political conditions, the competitive situation, customer needs and desires, internal capabilities, and many other factors, evolve over a period of time and form a frame of reference for strategic and comprehensive planning. Plans for repetitive and nonrepetitive activities are transmitted to the operating system and to storage in the coordination and control systems for later comparison with oper-

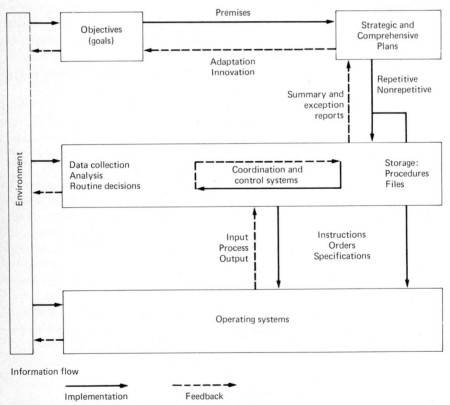

FIGURE 14.6 INFORMATION FLOW IN AN ORGANIZATION

ating results (coordinative and operating levels). Detailed orders, instructions, and specifications flow to the operating system.

Feedback is obtained on the output of the system in terms of quality, quantity, cost, etc. The operating system is monitored in order to maintain process control, and input inspection provides feedback at the earliest stage in the operating system. Information flow is an integral part of the control system because it provides the means of comparing results with plans. Feedback data from various phases of the operating system are collected and analyzed. The analysis involves processing data, developing information, and comparing the results with plans. Decisions are also made within the control system itself because routine adjustments can be preprogrammed in the set of procedures or instructions. Within the control system there is a flow of information to implement changes to the program based on feedback from the operating system. Thus procedures are changed and files updated simultaneously with routine decision making and adjustments to the operating system.

Summary and exception reports are generated by the control system and become a part of a higher-level process of review and evaluation which may lead to adaptation or innovation of goals. Subsequent planning activity reflects such feedback, and the entire process is repeated. Over time, an organization "learns" through the process of planning, implementation, and feedback. [20] Approaches to decision making and the propensity to select certain ends and means change as organizational value systems evolve. This basic or simplified model of information flow can be applied to any organization; it shows the necessary flow of information, regardless of the sophistication of the data processing technology involved.

Although some information exchange with the environment is evident at each level, the boundary is more permeable where top management is concerned. The strategic subsystem is primarily responsible for interacting with the environment and maintaining the organization in a dynamic equilibrium. Nevertheless, some interchange of information occurs between the environment and managers in the operating and coordinative subsystems. Such information is mixed with internal flows to provide the total "picture" for managers at all levels.

The differential nature of the management information-decison system by levels or subsystems is emphasized in Figure 14.7, which shows the relationship of data and information bases. Data processing systems have been developed to facilitate many organizational functions or transactions—payroll, inventory control, accounting (accounts payable or accounts receivable, e.g.), et al. Such data processing systems provide the raw material for management information-decision systems.

While all data could be considered part of an organizational information base, it is obvious that for any fairly large and complex organization such an approach would be impossible. Therefore, most systems include exception reporting wherein pertinent information from the various internal data processing activities becomes part of the

---

[20] Richard M. Cyert and James G. March, *A Behavioral Theory of the Firm,* Prentice-Hall, Inc., Englewood Cliffs, N.J., 1963, p. 123.

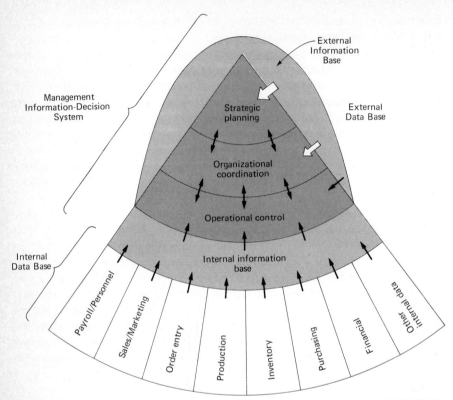

FIGURE 14.7 RELATIONSHIP OF DATA AND MANAGEMENT INFORMATION-DECISION SYSTEMS

overall information base when it is brought to the attention of appropriate decision makers. As indicated in Figure 14.7, a considerable amount of such information is used in controlling the operating subsystem of the organization. Some of the internal information is useful for strategic planning. Such information is coupled with that gathered from external sources in order to provide appropriate information for decision making at the top level. Most of the relevant external information flows into the organization through the strategic subsystem.[21] However, some of it comes in via the coordinative and operating subsystems as well. Information used in the coordinative subsystem comes from both operations and strategic planning activities.

In an age of increasingly sophisticated computerization, it may be possible to include all data from all subsystems in a management information-decision system. But, even if it were possible, it is not clear that it would be an efficient use of resources. The

---

[21] Judson Gooding, "It's No Easy Trick to Be the Well-informed Executive," *Fortune*, January 1973, pp. 85–89.

system should be evaluated on the basis of cost/benefit analysis. A balance should be maintained between the cost of the system and the value of the information generated.

Much attention has been focused on computerized management information systems (MIS). [22] However, it is important to recognize that managerial decision making typically requires input of much information—opinions, e.g.—that cannot be computerized. Thus overall management information-decision systems should be designed to include explicit attention to nonquantifiable inputs as well as those which result from computerized data processing applications.

Organizations typically develop information systems which are more suitable for controlling than for planning. "We hear more and more these days about new techniques for inventory, cost, and other types of control, but information systems for business planning still represent a relatively unexplored horizon." [23]

Several kinds of information are required for planning: environmental information, competitive information, and internal information. While most companies have some systematic approach to development of internal information for planning purposes, few have formal systems at the strategic level for developing information concerning competitors' plans, programs, and past performance. Nor do they deal in a systematic fashion with the social, political, and economic environment of the industry or industries within which they operate. Formal recognition of the decisions which must be made at various points and of the type of information required to do an optimal job in that decision process should point the way toward development of information flows which will be helpful.

The differences between information appropriate for planning purposes and that appropriate for control purposes indicate the importance of carefully designing information-decision systems. Blind adherence to organizational patterns for the flow of information often will hamper the development of an optimal system. Particularly where there have been organizational adjustments and there is a mixture of functional organization and program or product organization, the development of an information-decision system becomes critical.

Designing Information Systems

Much of the literature on design emphasizes the development of mechanized systems. Electronic computers have fostered the design of sophisticated systems of information flow. But the analysis involved is applicable to information-decision systems of all kinds—computerized or not. Indeed, designing with reference to existing equipment may result in perpetuating the processing of data which is irrelevant to management.

Another hazard in designing information systems is that of attempting to develop

---

[22] "Management Information System: The combination of human and computer-based resources that results in the collection, storage, retrieval, communication, and use of data for the purpose of efficient management of operations and for business planning." Joseph F. Kelly, *Computerized Management Information Systems*, The Macmillan Company, New York, 1970, p. 5.
[23] Daniel, op. cit., p. 113.

as much data as possible for use in the system. Voluminous data of many types might be collected and stored in case they are needed at some point in time. It is easy to see that massive amounts of useless data might result.

The best approach is oriented to decision making. It minimizes the development of useless information because only data likely to be meaningful in decision making at various points are collected. This approach emphasizes the problem involved rather than techniques of analysis. The objective is not optimization of data processing systems; rather, the objective is development of better information-decision systems for management.

By establishing criteria for management information needs, the decision system can be set forth explicitly. A picture of the current information flow can be obtained by use of graphic flow charts. This key technique in systems design helps in visualizing the interrelationships among activities involved in the operation.

Preliminary designs spell out in rough form the requirements of the system under study. Considerable detail must be included, such as the timing of information needs, alternative routings, and types of equipment that might be utilized in implementing the system. At this stage, benefits ordinarily will accrue from the process of analysis, even if new, more elaborate equipment is not installed.

In order to install the revised system or to adjust the existing system in some manner, it is necessary to specify the changes explicitly. Haphazard or loose instructions with regard to implementation often negate excellent work on the part of the designer. He must be able to specify the required changes and communicate them to the organization in a manner that enhances acceptance.

Upon installation, the system must be debugged and modified in order to fit the situation. Revised systems do not resemble interchangeable parts. The approach is more like fine watchmaking, where individual parts often must be filed and fitted in order to complement the other parts of the system. This process is vital and requires great skill. Once installed, debugged, and modified, the subsystem under study becomes a part of the total system. The analyst can then look toward other parts of the overall system, possibly those systems which are interconnected with the one most recently under scrutiny. The systems-review function requires periodic checking to ensure that all subsystems maintain their complementary nature and are integrated toward efficient accomplishment of the goals of the system as a whole.

Responsibility for Information Systems Design

Implementation is implicit in the connotation of systems design; otherwise it would be an empty exercise. Therefore, the interface between managers and information system designers is critical, and mutual understanding should be fostered in order to maximize returns from design efforts. The information-decision system should be tailored to the needs of the organization and adapted continually as circumstances change. Management should play a large and active role in design projects in order to ensure the development of useful systems.

In a general sense managers engage in systems design work on a day-to-day basis. They plan activities and organize systems to accomplish objectives. However, staff groups have evolved for tasks such as long-range planning, organization studies, and systems design. Special effort should be made to make such activities an extension of the manager's role rather than a separate function.

In discussing the design of information systems, Thurston cites four factors which play a major role in determining success:

1 Understanding of the objectives of an operation and knowledge of the existing operating patterns, coupled with ability to relate the information system to operating needs.
2 Ability and organizational position to work with operating people to effect change.
3 Competence in the designing of information systems.
4 Motivation to make systems changes. [24]

Operating managers fulfill the requirements in points 1 and 2; they understand the organizational decision-making requirements and the information needed to support the system. Probability of success in implementation is enhanced considerably if management is vitally interested in the project. On the other hand, technical expertise and motivation for change are more likely to be found in staff groups.

The answer would seem to be a team approach, with specialists supporting operating managers who would be responsible for the project's success. A manager might work part time on such an effort or full time on a temporary basis if the task requires it. Thurston says, "I want to emphasize, however, that where I have seen operating men who, being motivated to do the job, did take control, the record of successful completion of projects was better than where staff men directed operations." [25]

Many systems do not get beyond the design phase because of unanticipated resistance of people essential to the implementation phase. The following remarks concerning a long-delayed project are typical: "Well, we have good systems. We have them on the drawing board. The hardware and software are okay, but the people are lousing up our system." [26] This condition can be avoided or ameliorated by involving the affected employees in (or at least keeping them aware of) the design process. The most elegant system imaginable will be useless if people are not motivated to implement it.

Three stages in a continuous process of design and implementation for computerized information systems can be described as follows:

Stage 1: *Systems Specification* . . . includes the design of all of the aspects of a management information system that are important to *the users*. It includes

[24] Philip H. Thurston, "Who Should Control Information Systems?" *Harvard Business Review,* November–December 1962, p. 138.
[25] Ibid., p. 138.
[26] M. Scott Myers, "The Human Factor in Management Systems," *Journal of Systems Management,* November 1971, p. 13.

principally the basic decisions as to what information should be provided by the system.

Stage 2: *Data-Processing Implementation* . . . is concerned with those things that are important *to the processing of the data.* The purpose in this stage is to design a data-processing system that will most efficiently implement the systems specified in Stage 1.

Stage 3: *Programming* . . . starts with the systems flow charts and ends when the program is running on the computer. [27]

Specification work should be delegated to operating people who will use the system. If decisions and information flow form the basis for the system, operating decision makers will be in a better position to identify current and future needs. Specialists can "get in the act" in the second phase, when the feasibility of implementing the specified system is investigated.

For electronic data processing, implementation can and should be centralized because knowledge of equipment and techniques is essential to sound selection decisions. If a companywide data base is to be established, compatibility throughout the system is an important consideration. Integration of information systems provides economies, and staff specialists can contribute their expertise to the various subsystems without detailed understanding of the specifications.

Computer programming also can and should be centralized for reasons of economy and because it requires special knowledge of equipment and programming languages. These skills can be applied effectively to various subsystems with significantly different specifications.

Staff groups with equipment and programming expertise can be considered facilitative because resources are allocated to various system design projects as needed to implement the system specifications. In actual practice the stages overlap somewhat because operating managers, as designers, will want to enlist the advice and counsel of staff specialists. Moreover, if the systems design and implementation project is a major one, it is likely to last for months and even years. In such cases there will be redesigning and reprogramming work along the way because of changes in the environment and/or internal capabilities of the organization. This requires the integration of managers and specialists to achieve the best possible design.

If the project involves an integrated system for the entire company, it may well require years to complete. If operating people are delegated responsibility and authority for the project, particularly systems specification, they should maintain enough contact with day-to-day operations to retain their expertise on decision making and attendant information flow. If the environment is dynamic and/or internal capabilities undergo changes, it might be wise to rotate people from operations to systems design work

---

27 John Dearden, "How to Organize Information Systems," *Harvard Business Review*, March–April 1965, pp. 66–67.

periodically so that operating expertise is updated continually. Similarly, programmers and data processing specialists should maintain their expertise so that an optimal skill mix can be brought to bear on systems design problems at all times.

FUTURE PROMISE AND PROBLEMS

The accelerating technological developments in computer-oriented hardware and software systems will allow increasing sophistication of information-decision systems in the future. [28] Most discussions of future systems focus on the development of a complete data base pertinent to an organization's activity. Data can be processed to various degrees and be available when needed in decision-making processes. The information thus developed can be utilized in the entire spectrum of programmed-nonprogrammed decisions. Many organizational activities can be handled relatively automatically within the internal information-decision system.

Of particular emphasis in some current and more future systems is the concept of fast response. That is, the system provides information to decision makers in a matter of seconds or minutes. The ultimate in this approach involves real-time systems where the data base is updated simultaneously with organizational activities and pertinent changes in the environment. Decision makers have immediate access to such real-time information via many kinds of input-output devices including visual consoles. Pertinent statistics or graphic information could be obtained in response to a managerial inquiry.

For data-processing systems in general, the least progress has come in input-output phases. The processing phase has become extremely sophisticated and fast enough to handle most needs. However, problems of source recording and high-speed transmission have not been solved adequately. For management information systems an important link will be transmission of pertinent information to the point of decision on a timely basis.

> For senior management, however, the mechanism of communication with the processing system must be far more capable of doing what the telephone does for him now. It must permit him to interact with the processor without having to learn a new language or code, without having to know how to type, without having to wait until the processor noisily hammers out its message to him one printed character after another. The typewriters, teletypes, and even the vast arrays of push-buttons that so often accompany current and popular impressions of direct access management systems are still of much value, but only in the hands of the skilled technicians whose jobs require their special capabilities. [29]

---

[28] Robert G. Murdick and Joel E. Ross, "Future Management Information Systems," *Journal of Systems Management,* April and May 1972.
[29] Joseph Spiegel, John K. Summers, and Edward M. Bennett, "AESOP: A General-purpose Approach to Real-time Direct Access Management Information Systems," *Systems & Procedures Journal,* July–August 1967, p. 39.

The system described in this article is a laboratory-based prototype of a general-purpose, on-line, visually oriented information system. It has been used to investigate ways of handling many different types and levels of command and management problems, covering organizational levels from the executive suite down through the staff and operations analyst to the actual systems designers and programmers. It describes some sophisticated information-decision systems with emphasis on fast response for managerial decision making. While the concepts may seem somewhat ''cloud nine'' in character, they are based on actual technology now being used in some military and other organizations. [30] The magnitude of the design task and the costs involved may make such systems out of reach for many organizations. However, technological developments may change this picture in time. Therefore, it is useful for managers in all organizations to be aware of the possibilities of fast-response information-decision systems which utilize a real-time data base.

The Browsing Era

''A partnership or conversational mode, or browsing technique between man and computer is still in the early formative stages. However, just enough evidence has already appeared to document the beginning of the browsing era.'' [31]

Time-sharing computing centers provide engineers, scientists, professors, students, and managers with a new kind of analytical capability. The decision maker actually evolves a problem-solving technique as he goes along. There is no necessity for him to be a programmer or to know anything about the detailed language of the machine. Several specific examples can be described as follows:

> The designer can browse through selections of design shapes, sizes, and techniques. The partnership of the relatively large memory capacity and computing capability of the computer with the ingenuity and inventiveness of man produces a new level of creativity.
>
> Students using terminals connected on-line to a computer can study and learn using automated teaching or programmed learning techniques. Trial-and-error browsing with reinforcements by the computer for correct learning patterns produces faster learning curves on the part of the student.
>
> Library research using browsing methods will revolutionize the library itself as well as the way in which researchers use library facilities.
>
> Doctors and medical researchers are using time-shared concepts to aid in diagnosis and laboratory analysis. Two-way partnership communication and browsing are important in this situation.

---

[30] J. H. Winbrown, ''A Large-scale Interactive Administrative System,'' *IBM Systems Journal,* vol. 10, no. 4, 1971, pp. 260-282.
[31] Richard E. Sprague, ''The New Era in Information Systems,'' *Systems & Procedures Journal,* July-August 1967, pp. 26-27.

One final technique which will evolve in the Browsing Era is a form of browsing by executives which might be labelled "what if." Managers, either individually or in groups, will ask "what if" types of questions and browse through many alternatives in direct management language communication with the system. Again, the conversational mode is the important capability in doing this, and the currency of the information dealt with is not nearly so important as the fast response. [32]

While there is a great deal of optimism with regard to the potential for automated information-decision systems, there is also a note of caution in the wind. Pessimistic points of view suggest that it will "never work." However, in an era of accelerating technology such as our society has witnessed over the past several decades, this would seem to be a dangerous position. While we may remain skeptical, we should recall our attitude toward Buck Rogers and his space ships of the 1930s.

A better approach is to evaluate such systems in terms of the kinds of decisions managers make and the kinds of activities management engages in. For example, Dearden divides top management's functions into six general categories: management control, strategic planning, personal planning, coordination, operating control, and personal appearances. [33] He concludes that real-time methods can be useful in certain types of operating systems, particularly logistic systems. And, depending on the amount of time the executive spends in direct controlling of organizational activities, a fast-response system may also be useful in this regard. For the other functions, however, it is evident that real-time, fast-response systems would not be particularly beneficial.

It is important to assess the total incremental cost of equipment and programming as well as the continuing expense of system development. Such costs should be analyzed in terms of potential benefits from improved managerial decision making. [34] This type of analysis should be made for any information system. We should be concerned with both effectiveness and efficiency. It is important to gear the system to the needs of the decision makers in the organization and to have it work. However, there are also constraints of efficiency that must be recognized. It is not enough that the system be technologically feasible.

It will be important to distinguish types of decisions and design the system accordingly. For example, the browsing concept relies heavily on fast-response systems. However, this does not necessarily require that all information provided by the system has to be on a real-time basis. Some information might be inserted into the data base as events take place. Other information might be fed in daily, weekly, monthly, or annually. A decision maker may want real-time information but be willing to wait several days or weeks for the information to be developed. Figure 14.8 shows a matrix of

---

[32] Ibid., pp. 27–28.

[33] John Dearden, "Myth of Real-time Management Information," *Harvard Business Review,* May–June 1966, p. 125.

[34] Ibid., p. 131.

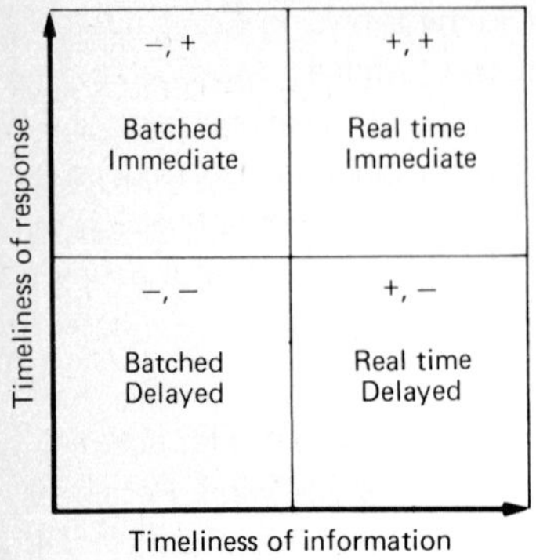

FIGURE 14.8 TIMELINESS OF RESPONSE VER-
SUS TIMELINESS OF INFORMATION IN MANAGE-
MENT INFORMATION-DECISION SYSTEMS

timeliness of information versus timeliness of response. Obviously, the most difficult task for an information-decision system is to provide real-time information on a fast-response basis. It is important for managers and systems designers to identify the needs of the organization and employ available technology to satisfy those needs.

SUMMARY

The managerial system functions in organizations by means of information-decision systems. Decision making is a pervasive activity and is fundamental to organism or organization behavior. Whether consciously or unconsciously, individuals make decisions continuously in a contextual system which can be relatively open or closed. Types of decisions can be arrayed on a spectrum of programmability, and techniques used range from computational to judgmental. For individuals, instinctive behavior and habits would fall toward the highly programmed end of the spectrum, as would standard operating procedures for organizations. For both individuals and organizations, conscious, deliberate, cogitative decision-making behavior would fall at the other end of the spectrum—nonprogrammable.

The decision-making process involves recognition of a problem, identification of alternative courses of action, evaluation of potential outcomes, and a choice. Information is the raw material for the decision-making process. It may be entirely internal information flow for an individual or an organization. On the other hand, it very likely involves inputs from the environment. Such information may flow to the decision point routinely, or it may be required for a specific problem. Information is data which are processed and meaningful for a particular decision problem.

An information-decision system is the means by which management carries out its day-to-day functions at all levels—strategic, coordinative, and operating. It involves decision makers (individuals or organizational units) and the attendant information flow. The information-decision system serves all levels and subsystems throughout the organization.

Much attention has been devoted to designing information-decision systems. This approach provides a useful vehicle for studying ongoing organizations and is a framework for designing new systems. Because the essential ingredient is managerial decision making, operating executives should be involved in designing information-decision systems. This ensures that all aspects important to operating management are included in the system. Key decisions can be identified, as can the required information service. The use of technicians is important to infuse the needed expertise into the system design effort. The best approach is a team effort with specialists supporting operating managers who are responsible for the system design project.

Accelerating technological developments in computer-oriented hardware and software systems will allow increasing sophistication of information-decision systems in the future. Prognostications focus on a data base for organizations which can be queried at any time by decision makers. The data can be processed to various degrees and be available when a particular need arises. For real-time systems the data base is updated simultaneously with organizational activities. Some current and more future systems emphasize the concept of fast response to inquiries. The most sophisticated system of the future will couple fast response with a real-time data base.

QUESTIONS AND PROBLEMS

1 Define decision making, and discuss three possible foci of attention in studying it.
2 Relate the dimensions of decision making (closed-open context, programmable-nonprogrammable process, and computational-judgmental techniques) to organizational levels (operating, coordinative, and strategic).
3 Do you agree that "managing is decision making"? Why or why not?
4 Relate the TOTE concept of organism behavior to organizations in general.
5 Using the model in Figure 14.4, trace the flow process for several decisions with varying degrees of programmability.
6 Define information, and relate it to communication. Relate information flow to organization.
7 Discuss the concept of an information-decision system and its relationship to organization and management. What key concepts are involved?
8 What role should technicians play in the design of information-decision systems? What role should managers play?
9 What has been the impact of electronic computers on information-decision systems? What do you predict for the future?
10 Define the concepts "timeliness of information" and "timeliness of response." Which is more important for managerial decision making?

15

COMPUTATIONAL DECISION-MAKING TECHNIQUES

When faced with a difficult problem-solving task, man typically seeks ways to simplify the environment. One approach to simplification is that of assuming away some of the complexity of the real world in order to achieve a tidier, more well-defined problem. This process of closing the system to confounding variables is a pervasive behavior pattern. We do it unconsciously by assuming simple, straightforward relationships rather than by considering "all" the factors involved. On the other hand, we do it consciously when faced with specific problem-solving tasks which, by definition, are complex and require a cogitative approach. The system is deliberately simplified or closed in order to bring to bear applicable analytical techniques. The real test is knowing exactly how much simplification is appropriate without destroying the essence of the problem. In this chapter we will consider computational decision making in relatively closed systems in terms of the following topics:

Problem-solving Methods
Rationality
Model Building
Quantification
Specific Techniques
Statistical Decision Theory

PROBLEM-SOLVING METHODS

Throughout history man has approached problem solving in a number of ways. At least six reasonably distinct methods can be identified:

1 Appeal to the supernatural
2 Appeal to worldly authority—the older the better
3 Intuition
4 Common sense
5 Pure logic
6 The scientific method [1]

No chronology is implied by the list because all these approaches are being employed currently in problem-solving situations throughout the world. However, the list does imply a gradation leading toward more careful, searching, and logical approaches. Combinations of several of these are involved in many problem-solving efforts. Intuition can be helpful in the laboratory, as can common sense and logic. Disciplined imagination, a vital ingredient for researchers and decision makers, may depend on both intuition and common sense. The scientific method can be compared to the steps in the decision-making process as set forth in Chapter 14.

Certain fundamentals are implied by the term *scientific method*. It suggests the use of generally recognized procedures and techniques. Another important ingredient is the attitude of the researcher or decision maker. A relatively formal, systematic, and thorough approach to problem solving suggests objectivity and reasoning rather than emotion. It implies logical solutions to problems with as little bias as possible. Using the scientific method, either explicitly or implicitly, one reserves judgment until all the pertinent information is available. For many centuries man sought final, definitive answers to problems; more recent approaches have pointed toward a spectrum of possibilities and show a tendency to express knowledge in terms of probability rather than certainty. The scientific method suggests a mind which is constantly challenging, weighing, and explaining—one which is continually diagnosing and asking, "Why?"

In organizations, managers are confronted with complex situations at all levels—strategic, coordinative, and operating. When problems concern only the inanimate economic and technical aspects of the operating system, the application of specific techniques can be relatively straightforward and computational. When the problem deals with the human aspects, the task becomes more difficult and judgmental. [2] And

---

[1] Stuart Chase, *The Proper Study of Mankind,* Harper & Row, Publishers, Incorporated, New York, 1956, p. 3.
[2] For example, see: James R. Emshoff, *Analysis of Behavioral Systems,* The Macmillan Company, New York, 1971, and John M. Dutton and William H. Starbuck (eds.), *Computer Simulation of Human Behavior,* John Wiley & Sons, Inc., New York, 1971.

when the analysis includes large-scale, sociotechnical systems, the problem becomes even more complex.

Management science can be defined as the use of the scientific method to answer questions of concern to managers. In this sense it has an extremely broad connotation. However, as indicated in Chapter 4, current common usage suggests a much more restricted sense. It implies a closed system, quantifiable models, and mathematical problem-solving techniques. The term *rationality* is often involved—referring to both the method and the decision maker.

RATIONALITY

The management science literature emphasizes recognized procedures and techniques which are relatively formal, systematic, and thorough and used by decision makers who are objective rather than subjective. A rational process is considered to be one "based on reasoning," one which is objective rather than subjective, one which is logical and sensible. However, the use of terms like "sensible" and "reasonable" implies a consensual yardstick. That is, *most of us* would agree with regard to what is a sound or logical approach to problem solving or decision making. Certainly intuition or common sense may suffice in isolated incidents. However, better long-run average results are obtained by the use of more objective methods.

In many problem-solving situations an assumption is made that the objective of the decision maker can be assessed in quantitative terms, most often with money as the common denominator. Rationality in this sense is concerned with the choice that a decision maker makes with reference to clear-cut alternatives. Here again, rationality is measured in terms of a consensual yardstick—what would a "prudent economic man" do under these given circumstances? In this chapter we will utilize, for the time being, the assumptions for rational behavior as developed in classical economics:

1 Complete knowledge of relevant environmental factors
2 Ability to order preferences according to some yardstick of utility (usually money)
3 Ability to choose the alternative which maximizes the decision maker's utility

These assumptions provide the framework for the techniques which are applicable under relatively closed-system conditions. According to Miller and Starr: "The objective of the individual is held to be the maximization of the total utility he can achieve with his limited resources of time, effort, and money. The rationality of the individual is defined in terms of the utilization he makes of his scarce resources to achieve this end of maximum utility."[3] The management science techniques described in this chapter

---

[3] David W. Miller and Martin K. Starr, *The Structure of Human Decisions,* © 1967, p. 24. Reprinted by permission of Prentice-Hall, Inc., Englewood Cliffs, N.J.

are often prefaced with the adjective "rational," implying both a reasonable, exhaustive, and objective process and an appropriate choice in the light of a well-defined goal. A basic assumption is that of a relatively closed system.

> The most commonly used and accepted analytical framework for choice behavior or decision making in organizations is the *closed* decision model. . . .
> Many of the widely accepted decision models in management science assume a kind of administrative rationality similar to that prescribed for the ideal rational man. These models are structured in closed frameworks. They are closed because they give little weight to the environment of the decision maker and to the complexity of the act of choice as such. [4]

Individual Rationality

Rather than appraising rationality on the basis of a consensus of what is an appropriate decision-making process or choice, it is important that we look at the problem from the point of view of the decision maker himself. By not imputing a certain value system which will determine the utility of particular outcomes, the variability of individual value systems is recognized, and hence the system becomes much more open. With such a framework a rational decision would be one which moved the individual decision maker toward his own goal(s). His consideration of what is "good" might differ considerably from some other individual's or group's. This view suggests that what is rational for Smith may not be rational for Jones. Philosophers have been concerned about this problem for centuries. The current state of this search can be summed up as follows: "Goodness remained a philosophical, theological, and personal matter. Individual truth came to be viewed as a property of cerebral-sensory systems; universal truth was approachable but openly unknowable. And so an operational philosophy of decisions developed, wherein the goodness of a decision would be measured by the extent to which its results satisfied the decision maker's objectives." [5]

What satisfies one decision maker may not satisfy another. Thus, the question of rationality must be approached with certain preliminary ground rules. If we speak of a choice from the point of view of the decision maker, it must always be rational. A decision to jump from the Golden Gate Bridge is perfectly rational if it satisfies the objective of suicide. From an outsider's point of view—or the consensus of society— the rationality of such a choice is questioned. In this case there may be a question of irrationality (insanity) in a medical or legal sense. In most ongoing organizations, however, we assume that decision makers are all within the "normal" range on the sanity continuum. This presumes an acceptable degree of rationality from a medical-legal point of view. Within this "normal" range, however, we typically make judgments

---

[4] Marcus Alexis and Charles Z. Wilson, *Organizational Decision Making,* © 1967, pp. 149–150. Reprinted by permission of Prentice-Hall, Inc., Englewood Cliffs, N.J.
[5] Miller and Starr, op. cit., p. 23.

regarding the rationality of both problem-solving processes and particular choices. In an organizational context it may be better to use a continuum of rational-nonrational, leaving irrationality to the medical-legal definition.

Other Dimensions of Rationality

It is also useful to consider individual versus organizational rationality.[6] A decision might be rational from the individual's point of view but not from the standpoint of the organization (as determined by some consensus or some other individual). Organizations involve cooperative effort; hence it is unlikely that each individual can maximize his own individual objectives at all times. The rationality of organizational behavior should be determined in the light of *group* objectives, not according to "what *I* would do in that situation."

Bounded rationality is the concept that a decision maker does not have complete knowledge of the situation and hence must deal with a limited picture of any given problem. In such a case he makes a choice which moves him toward his objectives to the best of his knowledge. An outside agency, with more complete knowledge, may wonder about the rationality of such a decision. The individual himself may question his sanity at some later point in time. ("What a crazy thing to do!") In both cases, however, the appraisal is made with the benefit of more complete knowledge concerning the problem in question.

The most important aspect of rationality involves the recognition of differing value systems which are affected by many forces (psychological and sociological, as well as economic). This obviously confounds the situation and makes it difficult to determine the rationality of individual or organizational choices.

> The effect of these psychological and sociological factors leads individuals to make decisions and to take actions without recourse to maximization of utility in the classical economic sense. Alternatively phrased, it can be said that these factors cause people to act irrationally—but it should be noted that this is simply a matter of definition, rationality having been defined as maximization of economic utility.[7]

If the system is closed and related only to economic utility, the valuation of rationality is relatively straightforward. But if the system is opened to include variable value systems, then utility is much more difficult to pin down.

---

[6] Actually there are a number of ways to view rationality. For example:
>A decision may be called "objectively" rational if *in fact* it is the correct behavior for maximizing given values in a given situation. It is "subjectively" rational if it maximizes attainment relative to the actual knowledge of the subject. It is "consciously" rational to the degree that the adjustment of means to ends is a conscious process. It is "deliberately" rational to the degree that the adjustment of means to ends has been deliberately brought about (by the individual or by the organization). A decision is "organizationally" rational if it is oriented to the organization's goals; it is "personally" rational if it is oriented to the individual's goals.

Herbert Simon, *Administrative Behavior*, 2d ed., The Macmillan Company, New York, 1959, pp. 76–77.

[7] Ibid., p. 25.

The most typical approach assumes an ideal decision maker much like the prudent-man concept used in a legal sense. Here again, we are implying a societal consensus with regard to what is logical, sensible, and reasonable. Obviously, if society has a clear-cut and identifiable value system, the valuation process is fairly simple. However, given a dynamic environment and pluralistic value systems, a consensus with regard to the ideal rational man may be hard to establish.

It is also useful to distinguish between a rational choice and a rational process. There may be much more agreement with regard to what is a careful, exhaustive, searching, reasoned approach to problem solving. The scientific method has come to be accepted in all research and problem-solving endeavors as a rational approach. On the other hand, there may be steps in the process which require valuational assumptions. If so, the process may be deemed rational and the choice considered not so rational. In other words, we may evaluate an individual or an organizational decision process in the following manner: "He seemed to go about it in a careful, diligent, and thoughtful manner, but he made a lousy choice."

In the remainder of this chapter we will be concerned with problem-solving techniques which, under the general umbrella of scientific method or management science, make the decision *process* relatively more rational than intuitive, rule-of-thumb, or seat-of-the-pants methods. This assumes that we are discussing relatively closed systems which emphasize economic utility and that the decision maker is intendedly rational in his *choice* within this framework. In the following chapter we will relax these assumptions and consider decision making in more open systems.

MODEL BUILDING

Model building and model use provide a framework for managing. "Models are the crux of rational management." [8] They provide a means for analyzing and synthesizing complex situations or systems.

A typical step in the management science approach to problem solving is that of constructing a mathematical model to represent the system under study. It involves the quantification of variables. While the development of a mathematical model is an essential step in solving problems under closed-system assumptions, this approach represents only a minute part of the overall endeavor. Indeed, model building is one of man's most pervasive activities. In general, models provide a means of abstraction which aids communication. Language itself is a process of abstraction and mathematics is a particular kind of symbolic language. Model building is the crux of conceptualization; models are developed to describe, explain, or predict pertinent phenomena in the real world.

Models vary over many dimensions, one of the most important of which is the degree of abstractness involved. A life-size mannikin would be a realistic model of a human being. A photograph would be more abstract, and several pages of prose description would be even more abstract. However, in these examples we would be

---

[8] Martin K. Starr, *Management: A Modern Approach*, Harcourt Brace Jovanovich, Inc., New York, 1971, p. 26.

modeling only the physical characteristics of an individual. The mannikin, photograph, or description would not provide much insight with regard to an individual's value system or behavior. A "picture" of this aspect might be obtained via biographical or autobiographical prose.

Similarly, balance sheets and profit and loss statements provide a model of an organization. However, these bare statistics are quite abstract. A better image of the organization is obtained if we have pictures or other descriptive material such as are typically found in annual reports. The more information added to the modeling process, the more difficult the conceptualization. If an investor is satisfied with the price/earnings ratio as a model of a particular firm for purposes of deciding whether or not he will invest, the choice may be relatively straightforward. However, many investors are interested in a more detailed analysis which may include less tangible factors such as the astuteness of the management team. The more variables added to the model-building process, the more realistic the picture becomes. However, realism is often nebulous and cumbersome, if not impossible, to deal with. Hence, more simplified, abstract versions of the real world are sought.

This brings up the problem of narrow, stereotyped thinking based on limited information for model building. The process of enriching models is a fundamental part of the educational process. Each successive stage—preschool, grade school, secondary school, and beyond—involves relearning or at least elaborating on models developed in previous stages. Simple, straightforward models are presented early because more complex descriptions would be incomprehensible. However, as a person picks up more and more information and develops intellectual powers, he can comprehend more complex systems. Yet an appropriate balance must be maintained in terms of degree of abstractness, depending upon the objectives. If description and understanding are the primary concern, then more elaborate and comprehensive models should be developed. On the other hand, if quantitative analysis and prediction are of prime importance, it is necessary to develop simplified, more abstract models which can be dealt with explicitly. Symbolic or mathematical models are usually more appropriate for this purpose.

The problem of model building can be related to the polar admonitions—"paralysis by analysis" or "extinction by instinct." Continuing to research a problem situation may develop a more and more realistic model of the phenomena in question. In so doing, however, a decision may not result until it is too late. In this case, an elaborate, sophisticated, realistic model would be of little use. In addition to the time dimension, costs are also important. The cost of gathering additional information in order to refine a model may be prohibitive in a particular situation. Thus, the cost of model refinement or enrichment should be balanced against the benefits to be derived therefrom.

At the other end of the spectrum, many decisions are based on oversimplified models of the real world. A decision maker may be very comfortable with his particular model of the phenomena involved and make little or no attempt to expand his knowledge of the situation. Bigotry and dogmatism often result from simplified models of the real world. Quite often we find that those with the least knowledge of a particular situation are the most certain about how to solve the problem. Individuals may be quite sure that their straightforward models of the world are realistic and appropriate for problem solving. They are perfectly happy to rely on their instinct or "common" sense and are often quite surprised and irritated if someone expresses doubt concerning their view of the situation.

This attempt to simplify is a necessary and typical human endeavor. We must do it in order to deal symbolically with the complexity of our environment. However, the process can be carried too far. Boulding describes this closure process as follows:

> There seems to be a fundamental disposition in mankind to limit agenda, often quite arbitrarily, perhaps because of our fears of information overload. We all suffer in some degree from agoraphobia, that is, the fear of open spaces, especially open spaces in the mind. As a result, we all tend to retreat into the cosy closed spaces of limited agendas and responsibilities, into tribalism, nationalism, and religious and political sectarianism and dogmatism. [9]

Closure can develop in two ways. As an unconscious process, and carried to extremes, it can be dysfunctional as far as decision making is concerned. It is much like blinders on a race horse; part of the real world is screened off or shut out. In this way individuals unknowingly have a distorted or partial model of reality.

On the other hand, closure can be deliberate in an attempt to develop models which can be used in analytical work. In this case, simplifying assumptions are made consciously in order to make the analysis amenable to available techniques. If after solutions are obtained by using simplified models, the restrictions are relaxed and the result interpreted accordingly, there is no particular problem. But, if managers or management scientists become enamored with the model and forget the simplifying assumptions made in its development, the results may not be applicable to the real situation. In this way, model building is a useful process but one which must be monitored closely during conception, analysis, and application. Let us turn to model building as a particular phase in applying management science techniques to organizational problem solving.

Management Science Models

Constructing a model is a common technique of abstraction and simplification for studying the characteristics or behavioral aspects of objects or systems under varying conditions. The model itself is usually a representation of objects, events, processes, or systems (a clay mockup of a new automobile design, for example). Manipulation of the model is used to test the impact which proposed changes (in one or more components) will have on the system as a whole. In this way tests can be carried out without

---

[9] Kenneth Boulding, "The Ethics of Rational Decision," *Management Science,* February 1966, p. B-167.

disturbing the subject of the model. The various types of models have been classified into three general groups.

1 An *iconic* model pictorially or visually represents certain aspects of a system (as does a photograph or model airplane).
2 An *analogue* model employs one set of properties to represent some other set of properties which the system being studied possesses (e.g., for certain purposes, the flow of water through pipes may be taken as an analogue of the "flow" of electricity in wires).
3 A *symbolic* model uses symbols to designate properties of the system under study (by means of a mathematical equation or set of such equations). [10]

Scale-model airplanes in wind tunnels are iconic models used to simulate actual flight conditions. In operations research, the word "model" usually means a mathematical description of an activity which expresses the relationships among various elements with sufficient accuracy so that it can be used to predict the actual outcome under any expected set of circumstances. Mathematical models are of many types, depending upon the real-life situations they are designed to represent. They have both advantages and disadvantages as analytical tools. The model, rather than the system it represents, can be manipulated in a variety of ways until a relatively good solution is found. On the basis of such experimentation, the actual system can be adjusted with a minimum of disruption. Obviously, duplicating reality completely is impossible. Also the process, while beneficial, can be time-consuming and costly.

Model building provides a tool for extending the decision maker's judgment in handling large-scale, complex systems. The use of a model allows creative manipulation in order to test new ideas concerning system components and/or relationships. Any set of equations designed to represent a particular problem area, no matter how narrow, can be thought of as a model. Various assumptions are made about the number of factors which must be included in order to represent the situation accurately. Then numerical values can be assigned to the variables in the problem in order to develop a workable model. Once the system has been described and numerical values have been assigned, the problem can be solved with whatever technique seems appropriate.

Computers and Models

Electronic computers have fostered much of the advance in management science over the past several decades. Trivial problems, often used as textbook examples, can be solved quite readily with hand calculations or, at most, the use of a desk calculator. However, real-life problems in complex industrial settings often are not amenable to

---

[10] C. West Churchman, Russell L. Ackoff, and E. Leonard Arnoff, *Introduction to Operations Research,* John Wiley & Sons, Inc., New York, 1957, p. 158.

such approaches. Numerical solutions to such problems may require thousands of individual steps involving endless hours of clerical work. A computer allows the solution of typical problems in a matter of minutes rather than weeks or months. In fact, real-time problem solving is possible with the system performing computations immediately upon receipt of a query from an input station. The result can be displayed graphically or communicated in any one of several standard media. Moreover, the computer is not subject to fatigue and hence is more likely to provide error-free solutions than the typical statistical clerk. While the programming of solutions to typical problems can be both challenging and time-consuming, the results of such effort can be applied over and over again to similar problems as they arise. The trend toward modular programs, which can be put together in a variety of forms, facilitates the solution of new problems with existing computer programs. [11]

It is dangerous to assume that all management science work involves the use of electronic computers. The problems in question must be analyzed in the light of the most likely techniques and the most efficient processing of data required for solution. As techniques are developed for automating management decisions in areas such as inventory, quality, and production control, the mathematical analysis involved can be integrated into general data processing systems. In such cases the mathematical analysis required for automatic decisions is imbedded in an overall information-decision system programmed to handle all but the exceptional situations involved in day-to-day operations. Larger-scale mathematical analysis may be required for management decisions in areas such as long-range planning. In this case a computer serves primarily as a calculator in the solution phase rather than as a data processor in the information-decision system.

The symbol processing and logic capabilities of computers have led to much research in artificial intelligence. Although they have been called "giant brains," computers have not been considered "thinking" machines. The term often is used facetiously because everyone "knows" that thinking is a *human* activity. Nevertheless research has progressed on simulating "thinking-like behavior" where the goal is ". . . to construct computer programs which exhibit behavior that we call 'intelligent behavior' when we observe it in human beings." [12]

The Art of Modeling

Problems may fall into classic categories and be solvable by well-defined, specific models. For example, we might have a standard inventory, queuing theory, or linear programming problem and solve it by applying a ready-made technique. Yet such an approach may stifle imagination, impose artificial constraints, and close the system unnaturally.

---

[11] J. W. Pomeroy, "A Guide to Programming Tools and Techniques," *IBM Systems Journal,* vol. 11, no. 3, 1972, pp. 234–254.
[12] Edward A. Feigenbaum and Julian Feldman (eds.), *Computers and Thought,* McGraw-Hill Book Company, New York, 1963, p. 3. See also Dutton and Starbuck, op. cit., part II, "Individuals," pp. 147–242.

Symbolic World

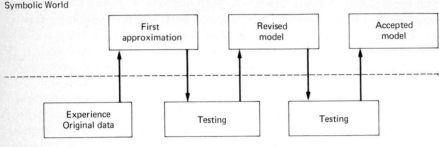

Real World

FIGURE 15.1 THE MODELING PROCESS

Dealing with the problem in all its complexity may lead to inaction because managers and/or analysts cannot "get a handle on it." Therefore it is useful to find ways of simplifying the situation without assuming away the problem. It may be possible to divide the problem into subparts and attack them one at a time. Or, it may be possible to develop a model for a simplified version of the problem and then enrich it progressively once a workable model is developed. Real-world problems seldom fall into the classical models of management science. Variations must be developed which may involve combinations of several models in order to depict the complete system realistically.

> Skill in modeling certainly involves a sensitive and selective perception of management situations. This, in turn, depends on the sort of conceptual structures one has available with which to bring some order out of the perceptual confusion. Models can play the role of giving structure to experience. Yet we seldom encounter a model which is already available in fully satisfactory form for a given management situation, and the need for creative development or modification is almost universally experienced in management science. [13]

A model should be tested against the real world periodically in order to assess its fidelity. Figure 15.1 illustrates the continual looping process, which is fundamental to model building. Actual data and experience provide a starting point for a symbolic model which is referred to the real world in order to determine its fidelity. Test data from the real world are used to evaluate the symbolic model, and adjustments can be made on the basis of such evaluation. The cycle is a continuing one which goes on until a satisfactory representation of the real world is obtained.

Figure 15.1 shows a three-step process. However, the amount of testing and refinement will vary with the situation. An acceptable model may result rather quickly,

---

[13] William T. Morris, "On the Art of Modeling," *Management Science*, August 1967, p. B-708.

or many tests and refinements may be required to capture the essence of the system. This general modeling process can be applied to many problems—work flow, organizational relationships, PERT-type networks, or linear programming, for example. [14]

QUANTIFICATION

Models can be broadly characterized as qualitative or quantitative. Typically there is a transition in the model-building process from qualitative to quantitative concepts. The initial approach in most complex situations is to develop a mental picture of the system. By writing out our description of the system, we attain a simplified (and less realistic) version, but one which can be communicated. However, there are many difficulties in the communication process because of the semantic problems with spoken or written language.

In many cases, real systems are not amenable to modeling. The relationships involved may be too complex to be stated formally in graphic or symbolic terms. Moreover, the pertinent variables may not be well defined, and even if they are, the relationships between them are not clear-cut. Many of the problems faced by managers in today's organizations are of this type. Nonprogrammable decisions arise at all organizational levels but predominate in the environment of middle (coordinative) and top (strategic) management.

On the other hand, there are problems which can be modeled quantitatively. The symbolic language of mathematics provides a means of relating variables precisely to define the system in detail. When this is possible, powerful techniques of analysis become available. For example, Miller and Starr suggest that "the real *tour de force* of scientific decision making emerges at the point where quantification becomes possible." [15]

Our view is that the scientific method—and hence scientific decision making— can be employed without necessarily quantifying the relationships of the system. Yet the connotation that scientific is related to quantification seems overwhelming. Although we do not accept this view, we are cognizant of the power of quantitative techniques in managerial decision making. Many advantages accrue when quantification of models becomes possible. Mathematics is a compact and efficient language which minimizes communication problems such as semantics. Translating models into mathematical symbols forces the decision maker to identify pertinent variables and their relationships explicitly. A system of equations can be manipulated in order to test a model's ability to predict. In large, complex systems this testing process may involve many refinements and voluminous calculations. Mathematical models lend themselves to computerization, a step which facilitates the model-building process.

---

[14] For a discussion of model suitability based on five major criteria (realism, flexibility, capability, ease of use, and cost) see: William E. Souder, "A Scoring Methodology for Assessing the Suitability of Management Science Models," *Management Science,* June 1972, pp. B526–B543.
[15] David W. Miller and Martin K. Starr, *Executive Decisions and Operations Research*, Prentice-Hall, Inc., Englewood Cliffs, N.J., 1960, p. 144.

Quantification forces the use of a common denominator as a criterion for optimizing. Frequently the common denominator is money because an organization is concerned with solving problems which are related to cost or profit. While monetary terms do have broad usefulness and understanding, there are problems. Although money may have an exact meaning numerically—$100 in Seattle equals $100 in Miami—the value of particular amounts may vary considerably among decision makers. For example, it is not obvious that $10 is worth twice as much as $5 to a particular decision maker. The actual value would relate to an individual's particular situation at a specific point in time.

One means to achieve a "more common" denominator is the concept of *utiles*. This approach is an attempt to measure precisely the value of potential outcomes to decision makers. The objective is to provide a system whereby preferences can be ordered cardinally on a scale of utiles. That is, 7 utiles is 1 better than 6 utiles, or 10 utiles is twice as good as 5 utiles. This is an attempt to integrate value systems and to achieve quantification of system variables.

Probability must be considered in the quantification of models. Some systems are deterministic in that the parameters are completely defined and the outcomes related to particular courses of action are certain. In real situations, however, there are many probabilistic aspects which must be reduced to quantitative terms. Outcomes might be described as quite likely or remote. In order to incorporate such concepts into quantitative models, it is necessary to attach more precise descriptions to such phenomena. For example, "quite likely" might equal .85 and "remote" might equal .01.

Figure 15.2 shows the relationship between certainty, uncertainty, and risk. Certainty lies at one end of the spectrum and really should be separated, at least conceptually, from the continuum. Similarly, complete uncertainty might be viewed as a separate condition at the opposite end of the spectrum. In theory there may be a continuum between these two points. However, it seems more realistic to consider two separate states with a continuum in between. Certainty involves complete knowledge, and quantitative models which describe such systems are deterministic and can be solved in straightforward fashion. At the other end of the spectrum is uncertainty or a complete lack of knowledge. In such a state of affairs any identifiable potential outcomes would have to be considered equally likely. The continuum between certainty and complete uncertainty is called risk. In situations of this sort, outcomes are not predictable precisely. However, risk implies some knowledge which can be used to predict the likelihood of anticipated outcomes. Toward the certainty end of the spectrum are objective

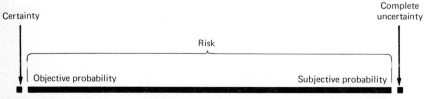

FIGURE 15.2 CERTAINTY-UNCERTAINTY "CONTINUUM"

probabilities which have been obtained through past experience, large samples, or repeated experiments. Such information provides a clue as to the likelihood of various possible results. Toward the other end of the spectrum are subjective probabilities which are based on less concrete information and limited experience with the problem under analysis. The decision maker may have a small sample to refer to, or he may rely on intuition based on similar experience. In any case, he has subjective estimates of the probability of future outcomes. This information must be translated into numerical terms in order that it can become a part of a quantitative model.

Computational Approaches

Once a quantitative model has been developed, any one of several computational approaches may be used. A basic concern is whether or not the system is deterministic or probabilistic. In the former case, each variable takes on a definite quantitative value as given in the problem. In other words, the system is completely determined by the statement of the problem, the equations making up the model of the system, and by the constraints imposed in the particular situation. Deterministic models represent completely closed systems.

Many systems cannot be completely determined because some of the variables are probabilistic. That is, their values cannot be determined precisely for any given set of conditions. In such cases a range of values can be identified, and the probabilities of occurrence can be assigned. As long as probabilities can be identified explicitly, quantitative models can be developed for the system and solved.

Two other terms which relate to computational approaches are algorithmic and heuristic. Algorithmic techniques are step-by-step procedures which lead to a solution in a well-defined, closed system. Such "cookbook" approaches are often sufficient. The manager or a technician needs merely to follow the prescribed steps and a solution automatically results. Heuristic approaches, on the other hand, involve sophisticated trial-and-error and do not lead to the same results invariably. Heuristic problem-solving techniques rely on relatively more human judgment at various junctures in the decision-making process and hence are useful in relatively open systems. A heuristic approach may be effective but not efficient; a satisfactory solution may be found by a very roundabout path. On the other hand, it may be an efficient method but with no assurance of optimality.

Algorithms set forth a definite procedure which will lead to a solution. However, in many cases the number of steps involved may be prohibitive. For example, an algorithm could be developed to consider every possible combination for a safe. Eventually the correct combination would be identified. However, the number of combination locks in use throughout the world attests to the fact that an algorithmic approach for this problem is not feasible. A heuristic approach would start by eliminating some "obviously" inappropriate approaches and would concentrate on several which appear to be likely. This sophisticated trial-and-error might not achieve a solution but would cut down the magnitude of the problem-solving task significantly.

Other terms used in describing management science tools are analytical, numerical, and simulation. *Analytical* techniques obtain a unique answer through a process of formal mathematical deduction. Break-even points, economic lot size, and correlation coefficients are examples of unique answers obtained through analytical approaches. *Numerical* analysis involves successive approximations to obtain a solution. In such situations there is also a unique answer, but the method of obtaining it is not as direct as in a case of analytical approaches. *Simulation* processes are used when a system under study is too complex to be conveniently represented by a complete mathematical statement. [16] Or, the primary interest may be evaluating the impact of policy decisions upon overall system performance. "What if" questions can be asked to test the effect of changes.

"In general, analytical methods are used to solve problems involving relatively simple systems. Numerical solutions can be used in more complex cases, and simulation is usually employed when relationships between variables are too complex for the effective use of either analytical or numerical methods." [17] In order to understand these relationships more clearly, let us turn to some specific examples.

SPECIFIC TECHNIQUES

The list of specific techniques which might be used in closed-system problem solving is lengthy. Examples might be ratio analysis, break-even analysis, inventory models, mathematical programming, queuing theory, game theory, budgetary control, equipment replacement analysis, payoff matrices, decision trees, network analysis, and simulation. In some cases these categories refer to related mathematical techniques. In others the classification is based upon particular types of problems found in the real world. However, it should not be assumed that problems faced by managers fall neatly into such categories. Most decisions require bringing several or many techniques to bear in a particular situation.

Moreover, within these categories there are wide variations in the techniques themselves. For example, linear programming and systems analysis derive their names from generalized models which relate to a broad class of problems. However, the simplified versions or general models probably do not apply in specific instances. Managers and/or technicians should tailor the approach to the particular problem at hand; this involves the art of modeling.

Some of the techniques have proved worthwhile in management decision making over a period of years. Some have not been applied fruitfully in real situations as yet. Still

---

[16] For details on simulation techniques and examples see: Robert C. Meier, William T. Newell, and Harold L. Pazer, *Simulation in Business and Economics,* Prentice-Hall, Inc., Englewood Cliffs, N.J., 1969; Forrest P. Wyman, *Simulation Modeling: A Guide to Using SIMSCRIPT,* John Wiley & Sons, Inc., New York, 1970; and Albert N. Schrieber (ed.), *Corporation Simulation Models,* Graduate School of Business Administration, University of Washington, Seattle, 1970.
[17] W. W. Thompson, Jr., *Operations Research Techniques,* Charles E. Merrill Books, Inc., Columbus, Ohio, 1967, p. 6.

others fall in between these extremes, having had limited application in practical situations. It is important for managers to ascertain the usefulness of specific techniques in planning and implementing programs of action. This means enough understanding to evaluate their applicability in particular situations.

Much has been written about operations research or management science; the reader is advised to follow up his interest in the general subject, as well as specific quantitative techniques, via the many books and/or articles that are available. [18]

In this chapter we will look at one family of techniques as a means of *illustrating* the role of computational methods in decision making under assumptions of relatively closed systems. Statistical decision theory provides a way of looking at a broad spectrum of managerial problems, including strategic issues. The approaches or models discussed—payoff matrices and decision trees—help us define the problem, clarify the factors and relationships involved, and understand the essential elements. We will make no attempt to be exhaustive in coverage, nor will we go into great detail with regard to the specific techniques. However, a general grasp of the method aids in conceptualizing a wide variety of managerial problems. The discipline of model building can be helpful by forcing us to think through the system explicitly.

STATISTICAL DECISION THEORY

The term *statistics* covers a wide range of techniques which are useful for managerial decision making. Descriptive statistics are often important inputs in the decision-making process. Sampling and statistical inference also provide meaningful information in many cases. The term *statistical decision theory* has taken on a particular connotation and relates primarily to the process of evaluating potential outcomes for alternative courses of action in a given situation. The concepts and techniques of statistical decision theory can be related to the general model or flow chart of the decision-making process (Figure 14.4). When the system can be closed enough to allow quantification of all pertinent considerations, statistical decision theory can be utilized. In this section we will consider briefly two concepts—payoff matrices and decision trees—and will outline the fundamentals which are important from the standpoint of managerial decision making.

Payoff Matrices

One way to approach the subject of statistical decision theory is to look at examples of payoff matrices and identify the key concepts involved. Figure 15.3 illustrates the general model. Across the top of the matrix are identifiable and relatively discrete states

---

[18] See articles in *Management Science, Operations Research,* and *Decision Sciences* or books such as:

Howard Raiffa and Robert Schlaifer, *Applied Statistical Decision Theory,* Division of Research, Graduate School of Business Administration, Harvard University, Boston, 1961.

Harvey M. Wagner, *Principles of Management Science,* Prentice-Hall, Inc., Englewood Cliffs, N.J., 1970.

David W. Miller and Martin K. Starr, *Executive Decisions and Operations Research,* 2d ed., Prentice-Hall, Inc., Englewood Cliffs, N.J., 1969.

States of nature

	N_1	N_2	N_3
S_1	P_{11}	P_{12}	P_{13}
S_2	P_{21}	P_{22}	P_{23}
S_3	P_{31}	P_{32}	P_{33}

Strategies

FIGURE 15.3 GENERAL PAYOFF MATRIX MODEL

of nature—N_1, N_2, or N_3. This indicates that the environment of the decision maker includes three mutually exclusive conditions which might prevail at some time in the future. The decision maker may have no idea of the likelihood of each state, or he might have in mind fairly definite probabilities for each of them.

It is assumed that a decision maker has a definite objective in mind such as profit maximization or cost minimization. In order to achieve his goal he can outline several distinct strategies which are indicated along the left-hand side of the matrix as S_1, S_2, or S_3.

The entries in the cells of the matrix indicate the payoffs which will accrue for each strategy coupled with each future state of nature. For example, P_{11} represents the payoff which will accrue if strategy 1 is chosen and state of nature 1 occurs. Similarly $P_{3,2}$ is the payoff for S_3 and N_2.

In general, two conditions prevail in the decision maker's environment. In one case he is completely certain about a future state of nature and hence can assess payoffs directly and choose the one which maximizes his movement toward an objective. For example, the decision maker may know for sure that N_2 will prevail in the future. Given N_2 he has only to pick the best payoff from among $P_{1,2}$, $P_{2,2}$, and $P_{3,2}$. In this context decision making appears as easy as "falling off a log." However, choosing a strategy under conditions of certainty typically is not as easy as it might appear from our simplified payoff matrix. For example, the decision maker may have fifteen identifiable alternative strategies, and hence the analysis relative to the best payoff may be quite complex. In such deterministic situations linear programming might be used to identify an optimal course of action.

A more typical environment for decision makers is one of uncertainty. As shown in Figure 15.2 an environment of uncertainty ranges from complete ignorance to a condition of relative confidence concerning the probabilities of the various states of nature. If a manager can assign probabilities to the states of nature and can assign values, typically in monetary terms, to each outcome in the matrix, he can ultimately determine the expected value of each individual strategy. The expected value in each cell is the product of its certain value to the decision maker and the probability of that outcome occurring. Expected value for a strategy is the sum of the expected values across all potential states of nature. These basic concepts can be illustrated and reinforced by a specific example.

States of nature

States of nature

	Poor (1)	Moderate (2)	Excellent (3)
Same (1)	0	+2	+4
Refit (2)	−4	+4	+8
New (3)	−10	0	+20

(a)

	Poor (1) [0.30]	Moderate (2) [0.50]	Excellent (3) [0.20]
Same (1)	0	+2	+4
Refit (2)	−4	+4	+8
New (3)	−10	0	+20

(b)

Strategies

FIGURE 15.4 PAYOFF MATRIX FOR THE OWNER-CAPTAIN OF A FISHING BOAT

Figure 15.4 (*a*) shows a payoff matrix which the owner-captain of a fishing boat might develop in assessing his approach to a new season. One strategy with regard to equipment may be to maintain his ship in substantially the same condition as previously. A second alternative might be to refit it with more modern gear and hence increase its effectiveness and efficiency. A third strategy might be to trade it in and obtain a new ship for the coming season. The states of nature could be expressed in terms of the expected volume of the salmon run. Obviously, this aspect of the problem would vary on a continuum; the indicated states of nature—poor, moderate, and excellent—are over-simplifications of the situation. On the other hand, they may be sufficiently identifiable to facilitate thinking in terms of relative payoffs for different strategies under these conditions.

The payoffs (net benefits) in the matrix have been translated from monetary terms to the more general utile form. In this version +4 is twice as good as +2. We can illustrate decision making under certainty (although this is obviously an artificial as-sumption in this case) by looking at the columns in the matrix. If the captain knew, for example, that a moderate salmon run was forthcoming, he would decide to refit his ship, because +4 is the best payoff under those conditions. If he had no preconceived notions about the probability of the three states of nature, he would assume them to be equally likely. He could then multiply each certainty payoff by ⅓ and sum across the rows. In this case strategy 1 would yield 2; strategy 2 would yield 2⅔; and strategy 3 would yield 3⅓. Therefore the captain should obtain a new ship because the expected value for this strategy is greater than for the other two.

On the other hand, if the captain could assign probabilities to the various states of nature—perhaps based on historical trend data or intuitive judgment—he could refine the computation of expected values. Let us assume that the probabilities for poor, moderate, and excellent are .30, .50, and .20, respectively, as shown in Figure 15.4 (*b*). In this case strategy 1 has an expected value (*EV*) of 1.8; for strategy 2, *EV*=2.4; and for strategy 3 *EV* = 1.0. Given these assumptions, the appropriate strategy would be that of refitting the ship for the new season.

Of particular importance for managerial decision making is the discipline of identifying the states of nature explicitly and coupling them with alternative strategies. This
approach enhances the probability that the problem will be considered in a careful,
systematic manner.

Decision Trees

Decision trees allow management to assess the consequences of a sequence of decisions with reference to a particular problem. The approach involves linking a number
of event "branches" which, when fully arrayed, resemble a tree. The process starts with
a primary decision which has at least two alternatives to be evaluated. The probability
of each outcome must be ascertained as well as its monetary value.

As an illustration let us take a slightly modified version of our previous fishing boat
example. Assume that the captain has two alternatives facing him at the beginning of
a new season—keeping the same boat or trading it in on the purchase of a new one.
In the previous example there were three states of nature—a poor, moderate, or excellent salmon run—with probabilities attached to each. In this case we will assume either
a good run (.7 probability) or a poor run (.3 probability). Obviously a new boat involves
an increase in the captain's investment. In order to simplify the analysis, however, we
concentrate on the net cash flow which will result from the various outcomes. For
example, as shown in Figure 15.5, the payout or net cash flow would be $90,000 if a

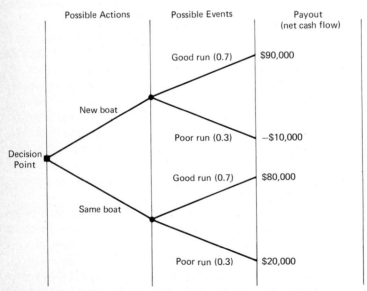

FIGURE 15.5 ONE-YEAR DECISION TREE FOR THE OWNER-CAPTAIN OF A FISHING BOAT
(PROBABILITIES IN PARENTHESES)

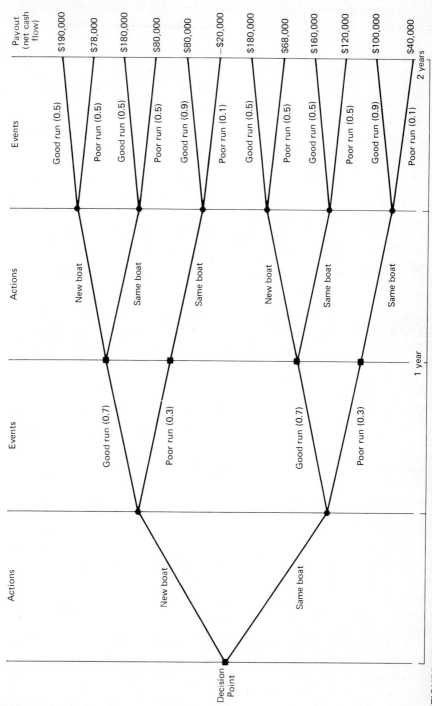

FIGURE 15.6 TWO-YEAR DECISION TREE FOR THE OWNER-CAPTAIN OF A FISHING BOAT

new boat were purchased and a good run were to materialize. However, a new boat and a poor run would result in a loss of $10,000. If the captain were to keep his boat, a good run would result in $80,000 and a poor run would net $20,000.

Both sides of the event fork can be evaluated in terms of expected value. Multiplying the probabilities by the payout and summing them results in an expected value of $60,000 for the new boat and $62,000 for the old boat. This approach allows the decision maker to consider each of the alternatives explicitly in terms of his best estimates of future results. A one-step problem, such as that illustrated in Figure 15.5, is quite similar to the payoff matrix. The real contribution of decision trees comes from the ability to link several decisions (of the type illustrated) together in order to see the impact of a sequence of decisions-events-results over time.

For example, we could expand the present analysis to include a second year and develop a decision tree such as the one illustrated in Figure 15.6. In this case we can trace the impact of decisions made over a period of two fishing seasons. For example, assuming that a new boat were purchased at the beginning of year 1 and that the results as estimated in Figure 15.5 were to accrue, at the beginning of a subsequent season the captain would again be faced with the problem of whether to buy a new boat or keep his old one. Similarly the second season could be described in terms of a good run or a poor run with net cash flows similar to those of the first year.

However, some important differences should be recognized, as illustrated in Figure 15.6. At the beginning of the second year the captain would have had the results of one year's activity and, theoretically, be in a position to adjust the probabilities for the states of nature in the second year. Given some past experience with salmon runs and their cyclical nature, he might be able to adjust the probabilities somewhat. Or even without any extensive past experience with regard to the likelihood of good or bad seasons, the captain may develop some subjective notions as to the probability of a good run or a poor run. Regardless of the foundation for his appraisal, he will develop some implicit concepts of the future. The decision tree merely makes his thinking process more explicit.

In this case past experience might indicate that a good run in year 1 makes a poor run in year 2 somewhat more likely. Also past experience might indicate that a poor run is very seldom followed by another poor run. These conditional probabilities are illustrated in Figure 15.6. The payout or net cash flow is the sum of the two years under consideration. The expected value over the entire period can be computed by working backward in the decision tree from right to left. An expected value for each event fork can be calculated and related to each action. Taking the highest value for the possible actions, the decision tree can be simplified and reduced. The same process can then be applied to the reduced tree, and expected values can be obtained for the two principal branches stemming from the original point of decision. We will leave the computations in this case for the student.

The additional decisions in the sequence might result in a changed picture for the overall system. For example, whereas the one-year analysis indicated that the captain should keep his old boat, analysis over a two- or three-year period might indicate that a new boat should be purchased as soon as possible. In this regard decision trees provide an important tool for short- and medium-range planning. Decision trees for much longer periods become much more cumbersome because of their size and also because estimates for more than two or three years in the future must of necessity be quite speculative. [19]

Opening the System

The use of payoff matrices and decision trees requires simplifying assumptions. To reduce complex problems to a few numbers in a matrix or connected by forked lines may be less than realistic in many cases. However, these approaches do facilitate explicit consideration of the key aspects of many problems.

Theoretically, the states of nature and the various strategies available to a decision maker are infinite. However, for all practical purposes a few reasonably distinct states of nature can be identified, and the strategies often can be reduced to workable proportions, perhaps two to five. Many problems fall into a yes-no situation. The more strategies and states of nature included in the analysis, the more open the system becomes.

Another key assumption in the use of payoff matrices is that of quantification and the development of some system of values for the payoff to a decision maker. The system is often artificially closed by forcing the quantification of outcomes. Figure 15.7 shows an approach which is much less constraining—the use of qualitative payoffs. We are not concerned with the value of any particular outcome; rather, we are interested in their relative values. For example, looking at the future from a decision maker's point of view, if strategy 1 were followed and N_2 were to occur, the outcome would be excellent (e). However, if N_1 were to occur, the outcome would be poor (p). Similarly, if strategy 2 were chosen and N_2 were to occur, the outcome would be fair (f) from the decision maker's point of view.

The use of qualitative payoffs allows the decision maker to consider a wide variety of situations wherein specific numerical values could not be readily ascertained. It may well be that most of the benefits from this type of analysis can be obtained without the constraint of quantification. The concept of states of nature forces the decision maker to anticipate the future environment consciously. Similarly, he must analyze his situation in detail and identify explicit alternative strategies. Then he must systematically relate these strategies to the states of nature and determine the impact or payoff. He will have some objective or subjective opinion concerning the probability of the various states of nature and hence can, in a rough fashion, determine the expected value of various strategies. For example, he might determine that the expected value of strategy 3 is

[19] We have barely scratched the surface with regard to decision trees as a management tool. For additional information see Edward A. McCreary, "How to Grow a Decision Tree," *Think*, March–April 1967, pp. 13–18; John F. Magee, "Decision Trees for Decision Making," *Harvard Business Review*, July–August 1964, pp. 126–138; John S. Hammond, III, "Better Decisions with Preference Theory," *Harvard Business Review*, November–December 1967, pp. 123–141.

States of nature

	N_1	N_2	N_3
S_1	p	e	f
S_2	g	f	g
S_3	p	g	p

Strategies

FIGURE 15.7   QUALITATIVE PAY-OFF MATRIX. p = poor; f = fair; g = good; e = excellent.

somewhere between good and poor, probably less than fair. Thus most of the benefit from the concept of payoff matrices can be obtained even though quantification is impossible or not easily obtained.

Another basic assumption in the case of both payoff matrices and decision trees is that expected values are appropriate for deciding the merits of various strategies. Using expected values assumes that a decision maker is willing to "play" the averages over the long run. In real situations, however, this may be an oversimplification. Individuals vary considerably with regard to their attitude toward risk. In the use of payoff matrices, for example, a pessimistic decision maker may pick the strategy which has the "least-worst" outcome; a large potential gain via some other strategy may be discounted heavily. On the other hand, the optimist selects a strategy which may result in the greatest gain and seemingly ignores the potential substantial losses from unfavorable outcomes. In these cases, the expected values, or long-run averages, do not seem to play an important part in the decision maker's analysis. His inherent attitude toward risk colors his perception and evaluation of the situation.

Regardless of an individual's inherent attitude toward risk, a particular situation may dictate a strategy other than might seem appropriate according to expected values. In an atmosphere where management is having difficulty "meeting the payroll," a choice may be dictated on the basis of other than expected values. For example, Figure 15.8 shows a situation where management is faced with the choice of whether or not to develop a patentable product. To do so would require an investment of $100,000. Consumer acceptance is about 80 percent sure once it is developed. However, there is the possibility that consumers will not accept it or that an innovation will come along almost simultaneously and make the product obsolete. The payoff for success would be $1,000,000. The expected value for this example would be

$$.8\ (\$1,000,000) - .2\ (\$100,000) = \$780,000$$

However, if there is even a remote chance of losing $100,000 and such loss would bankrupt the company, management would be very reluctant to take the risk. A more solvent firm could afford to gamble. "Them that has, gets."

We see such behavior in much of life. The player with the largest bankroll typically has an advantage in a crap game. Strategy seems to vary with the size of the pile of

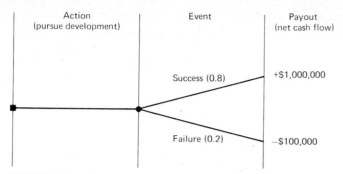

| Action
(pursue development) | Event | Payout
(net cash flow) |

Success (0.8) +$1,000,000

Failure (0.2) −$100,000

FIGURE 15.8 POTENTIAL RESULTS FROM DEVELOPING A PATENTABLE PRODUCT

chips in front of a poker player. Attitudes toward risk vary among individuals, and they vary over time for a given individual. [20]

An interesting phenomenon that seems evident from research concerning individual preference curves is the predominance of conservatism. [21] It appears that the typical organizational decision maker is overly concerned about the potential negative results of a decision. The entire atmosphere seems to stress the dangers of losing money. If an individual's career is at stake, he may forego a 50 percent chance for tremendous gain through innovation and accept a 90 percent chance for a small incremental improvement through a relatively routine approach to a particular problem. Realistically, management should assess decision makers on the basis of the entire decision process rather than on the results only. Tools such as decision trees make this process visible and allow review of the entire process rather than an ex post evaluation of the results. Given a probabilistic world, this would seem to be an important improvement in assessing the merits of managerial decision making. The use of decision trees and preference curves allows visibility in decision making and focuses attention on the value systems of individual decision makers. Organizations can provide a framework for decision making by stating explicitly the attitude which top management considers desirable in assessing risky ventures. An explicit framework would provide considerable consensus among decision makers throughout the organization.

Including preference curves or attitudes toward risk in the decision-making process tends to open up the system considerably. Assuming that all decision makers are "averages" players and hence tuned in to expected values is an oversimplification of the real world. Attitudes vary among individuals, and an individual's attitudes vary over time. All these considerations must be taken into account in applying computational techniques such as payoff matrices and decision trees.

If the system is opened to include nonmonetary aspects, decision making be-

---

[20] Hammond, op. cit.
[21] Ralph O. Swalm, "Utility Theory: Insights into Risk Taking," *Harvard Business Review*, November–December 1966, pp. 123–138.

comes even more complex. For example, the captain in our fishing boat illustration may buy a new vessel even though a two- or three-year analysis shows the net cash flow from the old one to be significantly better. His choice is perfectly rational to *him* because he would "feel better" with a new boat. It may involve safety or prestige; in any case, other factors seem to outweigh the monetary considerations. Other similar examples are evident. Bank presidents may *want* a "showcase" electronic computer facility. Doctors and/or hospital administrators may *want* the latest equipment or processes even though higher "expected values" cannot be demonstrated explicitly. "Potential" lives saved is an extremely forceful argument in some situations.

SUMMARY

The term *computational* suggests a closed system, quantifiable models, and mathematical problem-solving techniques. Management science comes under the general heading of scientific method, which is a relatively formal, systematic, and thorough approach to problem solving and implies objectivity and reasoning rather than emotion.

Management science techniques are typically described as rational approaches to problem solving. The term can apply to both the decision-making process and the choice made. The process may be systematic, logical, and reasoned—hence, rational. If considered from the point of view of the decision maker and at the time of the decision, a choice is *always rational* because it moves the decision maker toward his goal *as he sees it.* Considerations of rationality should be prefaced with guidelines concerning frames of reference—process or choice and from whose point of view.

Mathematical models are a fundamental part of the management science approach to problem solving. Relatively closed systems can be represented by well-defined relationships which can be quantified and expressed as systems of equations. The development of appropriate mathematical models is an art which goes beyond the use of existing classical models for particular types of problems. Real-world problems do not fall in clear-cut categories, and hence the basic models must be enriched to include the unique aspects of any particular problem.

Many examples of computational approaches to managerial decision making could be cited. In this chapter we have used two techniques as illustrations. Statistical decision theory is represented by the basic concept of a payoff matrix which relates possible future states of nature and alternative strategies on the part of the decision maker. Forcing this information into quantitative form in a matrix results in a relatively closed system which can be analyzed from the point of view of the decision maker.

The payoff matrix concept can be extended for several periods of analysis by means of decision trees. The basic framework is the same, however, because it involves assessing the interaction of alternative strategies and a probabilistic environment. The value system of the decision maker, particularly his attitude toward risk, affects the analysis considerably. An optimist will perceive the same data quite differently from a pessimist and decide accordingly.

If the analysis admits nonmonetary considerations, individual attitudes become an even more integral part of the decision-making process. Quantitative models, often in monetary terms, provide a basic framework or point of departure, but the system is opened significantly when behavioral aspects are included. Such considerations tend to open the system and make it much more complex from the standpoint of the managerial decision maker.

QUESTIONS AND PROBLEMS

1 Define management science. How does it relate to decision making?

2 Discuss the use of the term *rational* in describing (1) the process followed and (2) the choice made by a decision maker.

3 ''Model building is one of man's most pervasive activities.'' Do you agree? Why or why not? Is model building functional or dysfunctional for individual decision makers? Why?

4 Describe the modeling process in management science. What has been the role of electronic computers in this endeavor?

5 ''The real *tour de force* of scientific decision making emerges at the point where quantification becomes possible.'' Do you agree? Why or why not?

6 Relate the certainty-uncertainty continuum to the quantification of models.

7 Outline the assumptions necessary to ''close the system'' and allow the use of computational decision making in:

a Statistical decision theory

b Break-even analysis

c Linear programming

d Ratio analysis

e Queuing theory

f Network analysis

Discuss the use of these techniques by managers in relatively open systems.

8 Calculate the expected value for the two-year decision tree shown in Figure 15.6. If the results of one-, two-, and three-year analyses all pointed to keeping the old boat, is there any chance that the captain might purchase a new one anyway? Why or why not?

BEHAVIORAL ASPECTS OF DECISION MAKING

Managerial decision making covers a range of situations much broader than can be programmed under closed-system concepts. Computational techniques apply primarily to a relatively narrow range of well-defined, quantifiable problems at middle- and lower-management levels. Other approaches must be used in making the majority of decisions in organizations. Problem solving in the strategic and coordinative subsystems involves mediation and compromise. Political and philosophical considerations become factors in judgmental decision making. Behavioral aspects—value systems of individuals and groups, for example—become increasingly important as we concentrate on the decision maker rather than on the process or technique used. A broad open-system framework, applicable to managerial decision making in general, facilitates identification of situations wherein more definite, explicit, quantifiable techniques can be applied. We will discuss the behavioral aspects of decision making via the following topics:

> Complexity
> Open-System Decision Model
> Individual Decision Making
> Value Systems
> Groups and Decision Making
> The Interface of Computational and Judgmental Approaches

COMPLEXITY

Management science techniques have concentrated on mechanistic and deterministic applications. Probabilistic aspects have been included in many problem-solving models, but the emphasis has been on relatively objective probability distributions. These constraints dictate that only simple, well-defined systems are amenable to typical computational approaches. For more complex nonprogrammable problems, the human element plays a more prominent role in the process. Realistic situations often call for sequential decision making wherein a manager's interpretation is necessary at each of several stages. Also, many of the critical factors involved in complex systems are nonquantifiable variables which, nevertheless, must be included in the managerial decision-making process.

The increasing complexity of organizations was stressed in Chapter 1 as part of the framework for the body of knowledge related to organization theory and management practice. At this stage we are concerned more specifically with complexity as it relates to the managerial system at all levels. Both the internal organizational atmosphere and the external environment affect managerial decision makers. Increased size, accelerating technology, better-educated employees, specialization, both blue- and white-collar unionism, conflicts between organizational and professional allegiance, and other similar factors add up to an exceedingly complex internal atmosphere. Coincidentally, the external environment of organizations is becoming more and more complex—intra- and interindusty relationships, political considerations, legal and governmental aspects, plus the more evident relationships with stockholders, suppliers, and customers. The felt need for social responsibility is also important. All are inputs to managerial decision making in modern organizations. The scope of these considerations makes it evident that many decisions must be made in relatively open systems. It is impossible to mold all the factors which management must consider into an explicit, well-defined model which can be quantified and solved. The scope and complexity of typical problem-solving situations call for a framework of open-system considerations.

Relatively closed systems imply clear-cut goals toward which the system is focused. The importance of definite, well-defined objectives is emphasized for the managerial functions of planning and control. However, in many instances clarity is not possible. Complex situations often defy explicit statements of goals which can be understood and/or accepted by organization members. In many other cases it is not even desirable to clarify objectives in great detail.

Human beings find it difficult to focus attention on more than a few things at a time. If a particular problem involves a large number of factors in a total system, the objectives of some of the subsystems may of necessity be relatively vague. Concentration on a few aspects allows consideration in depth but also may lead to suboptimization with regard to the overall system. Similarly, if a problem under consideration ultimately covers a long time span, medium- and long-term goals must be relatively more vague than those of immediate concern.

Such an environment is an open system—one which is extremely complex from the standpoint of managerial decision making. The complexities of the real world indicate that traditional concepts of rationality and explicit, computational problem-solving techniques often do not apply. Therefore a more general model is necessary to provide the framework for managerial decision making and to facilitate understanding of the process as it occurs in typical real-life situations. The open-system decision model provides such a framework.

OPEN-SYSTEM DECISION MODEL

The open-system model of decision making is an attempt to describe a more realistic process for individual and organizational decision making. It focuses on human involvement in the various steps of the process and allows for the impact of numerous environmental forces. This view opens the system by eliminating the assumptions of classical rationality. That is, we do not assume that the decision maker has complete knowledge and is a logical, systematic maximizer in economic-technical terms. Concentration on the human element leads to concepts such as learning and adaptation. Continual feedback during the decision process causes adjustments in both ends and means. The system is dynamic rather than static; thus explicit computational techniques must give way to more judgmental approaches.

An open-system decision model is shown in Figure 16.1. It involves a sequence of decisions which may result from the perception of a problem. As indicated in the figure, period 1 is devoted primarily to identifying objectives. However, it is recognized that no explicit, clear-cut, "idealized" goal structure is typically available. Therefore, the decision maker has an approximate level of aspiration toward which he takes causal action.

A decision maker typically identifies a limited number of seemingly feasible alternatives rather than an exhaustive list. [1] Usually he will select those most readily apparent and relatively close to a current solution or approach to the problem. The alternatives are evaluated in many ways—on a continuum from hunch through "guesstimation" to scientific method. Out of this evaluation comes a choice and its implementation.

The decision maker then considers the outcome and its relationship to his original aspirational level. The possible results are readily apparent; the value of the outcome could meet the aspiration level exactly, or it could be higher or lower. If the outcome is close and there is substantial congruity in the system, the decision maker will probably wait for further problematic stimuli to trigger another decision-making process. If the value of the outcome exceeds the aspirational level, the decision maker is apt to increase his level of aspiration in similar situations and also decrease his range of alternative identification. That is, he may be quite satisfied with his approach to the problem and not be inclined to "rock the boat" by searching for alternative solutions. He will be satisfied to solve the same or similar problems with the approach which has "proved" successful in the past. As in the case of congruency, if the outcome is more than the aspiration level, the decision maker will most likely move to the stage of waiting for further stimuli concerning similar or different problems.

On the other hand, if the outcome turns out to be less than the aspiration level, a different chain of events typically is touched off. The decision maker may decrease his

---

[1] In this sense the system is relatively open or closed, depending on the decision maker himself. Although he may close the system by considering few alternatives, the *potential* range of alternatives is quite open. Computational techniques consider all the alternatives as identified in the model. However, the model itself usually represents a relatively closed system as compared with reality. The critical aspect of the open-system decision model is emphasis on the human element and the potential scope of continual interaction between the decision maker and the environment.

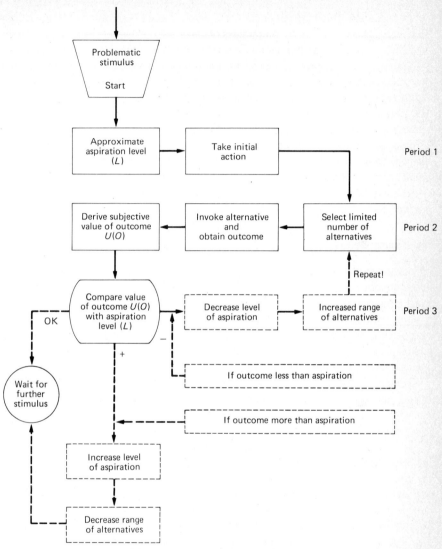

FIGURE 16.1   AN OPEN-SYSTEM DECISION MODEL. *Period 1:* The individual starts out with an idealized goal structure and defines one or more action goals as a first approximation to the "ideal goal" in the structure. The action goals may be considered as representative of the decision maker's *aspiration level. Period 2:* The individual engages in search activity and defines a limited number of outcomes and alternatives. He does not attempt to establish the relations rigorously. His analysis proceeds from loosely defined rules of approximation. The alternatives discovered establish a starting point for further search toward a solution. *Period 3:* Search among the limited alternatives is undertaken to find a satisfactory solution, as contrasted with an optimal one. "Satisfactory" is defined in terms of the aspiration level or action goals. (Adapted from Marcus Alexis and Charles Z. Wilson, *Organizational Decision Making*, Prentice-Hall, Inc., Englewood Cliffs, N.J., 1967, p. 160.)

level of aspiration. This may not occur immediately, but it becomes more likely as the number of "failures" increases. Regardless of the ensuing aspiration level, the decision maker must again assess the alternatives available. If he had several which seemed reasonably close in "appropriateness," he may repeat stage two by selecting one of the other original alternatives to be evaluated. He may move from a relatively routine approach toward adaptation, and ultimately to innovation.

It should be emphasized that this model of the decision-making process is more descriptive than normative. It depicts what *typical* decision makers *usually* do following a problematic stimulus. It obviously does not hold for every decision maker in every situation. One could think of examples where failures might lead to an increased aspiration level. For example, failure to "make" the high school football team may cause an individual to raise his sights and eventually become an All-American in college. However, such examples are relatively rare and can be treated as exceptions.

Satisficing Behavior

The general model emphasizes finding satisfactory rather than optimal solutions. In this framework optimality is a utopian concept because of the lack of complete knowledge and a tendency for the decision maker to test alternative solutions which are readily apparent. He does not attempt an exhaustive search and evaluation program. However, this does not mean that decision makers cannot approach optimality. On the contrary, most studies indicate that even in complex, dynamic situations decision-making processes described by the open-system model will lead *toward* the best solution.

Empirical research involving the observation and description of decision-making processes in real organizations can shed additional light on the various stages of the open-system model. For example, Cyert and March describe four case studies in terms of the model portrayed in Figure 16.1. [2] The studies involved were of organizational rather than individual decision making. However, the model applies to both, and the tentative findings from the case studies can be related to this framework.

In general the researchers found little evidence of explicit objectives. Rather, the very nature of the organization as a coalition of subsystems suggests the presence of multiple objectives. At times the goals are hierarchical in nature and complementary. At other times, conflict among goals is apparent.

The research indicated little conscious comparison of specific alternatives. It seemed that rules of thumb resulted in "reasonably good" solutions to problems. However, there was no way to identify optimality and hence establish a yardstick of goodness. The cases studied involved two crises and two situations which allowed a more cogitative or planning approach. In neither did it appear that an exhaustive list of alternatives was organized and/or evaluated. "In every case, once an alternative was evoked, it was accepted if it satisfied the general cost and return constraints and enjoyed the support of key people in management. This support in turn came about

---

[2] Richard M. Cyert and James G. March, *A Behavioral Theory of the Firm,* Prentice-Hall, Inc., Englewood Cliffs, N.J., 1963, pp. 44–82.

through a rather complex mixture of personal, suborganizational, and general organizational goals." [3]

Organizational Search

Organizational search appears to be a more complex process than envisioned in closed-system models of decision making. The classical theory indicates that there is a search for alternatives followed by evaluation and choice. The empirical research suggests that the search may continue beyond the point of choice as a means of rationalizing the decisions during the implementation phase. Organizations may engage in elaborate processes to justify a decision that has already been made. "Organizational 'search' consists in large part of evoking from various parts of the organization considerations that are important to the individual subunits; the relevance of such considerations, and the impetus to insist on them, are not manifest until the implications of the decision are made specific through implementation." [4]

If an individual or an organization has an abundance of resources, inefficiencies may be lightly regarded. Effectiveness then becomes of primary concern; a satisfactory solution will be one that works. If resources are limited, then efficiency becomes relatively more important and solutions must be both effective and efficient. In fact there may be trade-offs; less effective solutions may be accepted if substantial savings are made in the use of resources. This, of course, involves the continual adjustment of objectives.

Another facet of the classical theory of decision making suggests that the search for alternatives is a one-way street. That is, the individual or organization seeks to identify alternatives and then to evaluate them. Empirical research indicates that the process is somewhat more complex. "Many of the events in these studies suggest a mating theory of search. Not only are organizations looking for alternatives, alternatives are also looking for organizations." [5] Whether a relatively routine decision or a more adaptive or innovative decision, it seems that alternatives are suggested to decision makers by outside agencies such as salesmen, staff specialists, or other similar organizational units. The presentation of alternatives, therefore, may be a problematic stimulus which touches off the managerial decision-making process.

In the cases studied, computation with regard to the anticipated consequences of alternatives were carried out in rough fashion and tended to be quite simple in nature. Only a few calculations were made and elaborate techniques were rarely employed. Two important steps were checking for feasibility and improvement—was money available, and was the proposed solution better than the existing situation? These questions were often difficult to answer, but much less difficult than trying to determine the expected net return on all alternative investments.

The multiplicity of objectives made evaluation of anticipated outcomes quite difficult. Individuals and organizations face a different mix of results for various alterna-

---

[3] Ibid., p. 79.
[4] Ibid., pp. 79–80.
[5] Ibid., p. 80.

tives. There is no single dimension on which to measure all relevant considerations. Ascertaining the best solution "on balance" is an extremely difficult task. It involves establishing trade-offs for cost, speed, accuracy, safety, quality, and many other factors which may be pertinent according to the specific problem. However, this balancing act *is performed* by operating managers in organizational settings.

Selective Perception

The situation is even more complex because of the role played by selective perception or even bias. An individual may unconsciously anticipate outcomes which are favorable. He may attach a higher than realistic probability to a certain outcome if it is particularly desirable to him. This type of conscious or unconscious bias may have an important effect on the choice of alternatives.

> In each of the cases studied there is some suggestion of unconscious or semiconscious adjustment of perceptions to hope. . . . In addition, there is some evidence of more conscious manipulation of expectations. The classic statement came from a staff member involved in one of the decisions. He told a group of men outside the company, "In the final analysis, if anybody brings up an item of cost that we haven't thought of, we can balance it by making another source of savings tangible." [6]

Where human beings are involved in decision-making processes in dynamic organizations, they are confronted with complex environmental forces. The model shown in Figure 16.1 provides the framework for decision making in relatively open, complex systems. It is a descriptive model developed from observations of decision makers in actual problem-solving situations. And, it provides a flexible framework which can be used for all individual and organizational decision making.

In certain cases where the decision problem can be closed by means of realistic assumptions, a more clear-cut approach can be employed. A mathematical model can be generated and computational techniques used to solve specific problems. However, it is important to understand the open-system model as the general framework for managerial decision making and to fit more precise techniques into the framework when conditions warrant.

INDIVIDUAL DECISION MAKING

In Chapter 14 we identified three possible foci of attention for decision theory—the choice, the process, and the decision maker. Recognizing the place of the individual decision maker in the process calls for consideration of relatively open systems. The individual is subject to many environmental forces, and he has his own cognitive

---

[6] Ibid., p. 81.

processes to contend with. He is a variable in the decision process because each person has a different perception of a problem situation.

An individual's image or value system results from his total past experience and is as unique as his fingerprints. However, values are extremely difficult to "get a handle on." They cannot be seen or felt. They result in a propensity to decide or act in a specific way, given a particular problem. Value systems must be hypothesized by working backward from overt actions or expressions made by individuals in response to various stimuli.

The individual is the focal point of the open-system model of decision making. And there is a continuum of openness depending upon the individual's frame of mind with regard to a particular question. In many instances people maintain a relatively closed mind on an issue because it is easier than investigating unfamiliar or unpalatable points of view. For example, Boulding suggests that:

> There is also a considerable relationship between the capacity of a decision maker to handle large quantities of information and his ability to widen his agenda. People who have narrow agendas, the bigots, the Birchers, the Marxists, the nationalists and the schizophrenics, are by and large people whose information processing capacities are highly limited. They retreat into narrow agendas because they cannot bear the information overload which would seem to result from the wide ones. [7]

Even when considering ill-structured policy issues and using an open-system model such as depicted in Figure 16.1, the decision maker may use an approach that results in a relatively closed decision process. If he does not push beyond well-entrenched beliefs, conclusions may follow relatively automatically, given a problematic stimulus. The more a decision maker is disposed toward seeking new alternatives and additional information, the more open the decision-making process. The process can be described as relatively open or closed, and the decision maker can be described as relatively open-minded or closed-minded. [8]

Apparently a particular degree of open-mindedness does not hold true across all issues. Individuals may be closed-minded with regard to religious issues but relatively open-minded on political questions. Similarly, a person might be relatively closed-minded with regard to financial matters and yet quite open-minded with regard to human rights. Moreover, research findings indicate that we can have open-minded conservatives and closed-minded liberals, contrary to popular misconceptions.

Rokeach cites key criteria for open-mindedness, or the ability to form new belief systems, as follows:

1 The ability to remember or to keep in mind all the new parts to be integrated

---

[7] Kenneth E. Boulding, "The Ethics of Rational Decision," *Management Science,* February 1966, p. B-167.
[8] Milton Rokeach, *The Open and Closed Mind,* Basic Books, Inc., Publishers, New York, 1960, pp. 392–393.

    2 A willingness to "play along" or to entertain new systems

    3 Past experience, which determines whether a particular system is, psycho-
    logically speaking, new or not new. [9]

    The implications of related research findings stress the importance of personality
rather than intelligence in cognitive functioning. And the ability to synthesize seems
much more important for creativity than the ability to analyze. Cognitive and affective
(emotional) functioning are not mutually exclusive; they are different facets of a person's
total behavior. [10]

    These findings and implications are particularly important in the consideration of
the role of the decision maker in open systems. Synthesis is stressed as more important
than analysis. This coincides with descriptions of effective executives (managerial
decision makers). They are typically described as being good conceptualizers with the
facility for grasping a situation and understanding the parts and their relationships in a
total system. A more closed-minded approach might concentrate on analysis and, in
doing so, narrow the problem unrealistically. Some decision makers are very uncomfortable in a relatively open system and make every attempt to close it by the use of
simplifying assumptions leading ultimately to quantifiable models and to analytic solutions. It seems that open-minded decision makers are more comfortable with ambiguity
stemming from complex environmental forces and thrive on the analysis and synthesis
required to cope with the situation.

VALUE SYSTEMS

Value judgments come into play at many stages of the open-system model. Given
different backgrounds and perspectives, one manager may recognize a problem in a
particular situation, while another may not. The identification of relevant and appropriate
alternatives may depend on individual value systems. An alternative suggested by one
individual may be entirely unpalatable to another. Individual hopes or biases have an
important effect on the assessment of the probabilities of outcomes related to various
alternatives.

    The most obvious role for value systems is in attaching importance to various
outcomes (see Figure 14.4). Decision makers may agree on the specific probability
involved, but the "importance" of any particular outcome will vary with the perspectives
of the decision maker. The general model indicates that a choice is made by balancing
the importance of outcomes. "Balancing" is generally laden with value judgments, but
the process is very difficult to identify.

    While the open-system model of decision making is saturated with value judg-
ments, there are factual considerations as well. In any problem-solving situation, the
factual elements are those which can be verified by testing. For example, if the director

---

[9] Ibid., p. 398.
[10] Ibid., pp. 398–399.

of athletics is faced with the decision of whether or not to fire the football coach, he has some factual and many value considerations. It is a fact that the team won two and lost nine games during the season. It is a fact that the coach's contract has two more years to run at $24,000 per year. It is a fact that at least some alumni are unhappy, as evidenced by the letters received. On the other hand, there may be a wide difference of opinion regarding the merits of a 2 and 9 record. Similarly, there may be divergent opinions with regard to the importance of the $48,000 necessary to pay off the coach's contract. Also, there may be differences of opinion with regard to the coach's ability as a tactician, manager, recruiter, or other qualities perceived to be necessary in a good coach. None of these latter considerations can be verified; they are value judgments.

The importance of values cannot be overemphasized, but the concept is difficult to define explicitly. It has many connotations. For example, its economic meaning seems to be the worth of something as measured by the amount of other things for which it can be exchanged (monetary overtones). The term also connotes valuing—to consider excellence, usefulness, or importance. In this latter sense we have the foundation for the development of the concept of value systems. The image, or total past experience, provides a framework (a propensity) by which an individual appraises or evaluates the relative merit, usefulness, or importance of things, ideas, or alternative courses of action. The relevance of this connotation to decision making is obvious. More specifically:

> A value is a conception, explicit or implicit, distinctive of an individual or characteristic of a group, of the desirable which influences the selection of available modes, means and ends of action. . . . Value may be defined, as that aspect of motivation which is referable to standards, personal and cultural, that do not arise solely out of immediate tensions or immediate situations. [11]

Many values that a decision maker holds will be implicit to him. He will rarely, if ever, consciously introspect enough to identify his own value system and its impact on his decision-making process. In some cases, however, where decisions are particularly important and visible, a decision maker may consciously consider the values which he holds to be important. He may assess explicitly the impact of various alternatives on his value system and make a decision accordingly. Value systems develop bit by bit over the life cycle of individuals and hence are intricately interwoven with instinctual and habitual behavior as well as more cogitative decision-making activity.

The development of value systems which are in part learned from other individuals or groups distinguishes humans from other animals. Man transmits such knowledge across generations. "*Homo sapiens* is physiologically capable, unlike other species, of

---

[11] Clyde Kluckhohn et al., "Values and Value-orientations in the Theory of Action," in Talcott Parsons and Edward A. Shils (eds.), *Toward a General Theory of Action*, Harvard University Press, Cambridge, Mass., 1951, pp. 395 and 425.

a wide variety of mutually exclusive responses to given stimuli. This capacity for choice is the essential physio-psychological basis for the development of what we identify as 'values,' namely standards of the desirable which men apply in making choices." [12]

Learned phenomena seem to be more easily changed than innate biological aspects. Communications from generation to generation are seldom precise, and in a dynamic and complex environment, intrageneration changes in norms are readily apparent. Compared with other species, human value systems change relatively rapidly. The individual's perspective is affected by his biological and psychological makeup as well as his social and cultural milieu. Many forces influence a decision maker as he engages in problem-solving activity. Each individual relates to his environment in a unique way, and the impact of his particular value system in decision making must be recognized.

Ethical Pluralism

So far we have not made any normative statements with regard to what values should be paramount for decision making. Yet the prescriptive approach has been the focal point of philosophical thought for many centuries. The emphasis has been on what *ought* to be rather than what is (the realm of science). More importantly for this discussion, philosophers have attempted to force all value considerations under one all-encompassing goal. Many classical philosophers concentrated on developing a moral law or framework which pinpointed a single supreme "good" by which evaluations could be made. Over the years philosophers have attacked the monolithic systems— in some cases advocating an alternative supreme "good" but in many cases offering no substitute system.

The monolithic approach is an example of closed-mindedness in the sense that one yardstick provides the answer in all problematic situations. Given the complexity of modern society, this approach does not seem to offer much to organizational decision makers. Yet the other end of the spectrum does not offer much either. This is the extreme case of situational ethics wherein no framework is available for evaluating the impact of alternative courses of action. Some moderate or middle ground would seem to be appropriate. Leys sets forth this concept as follows:

> The "value framework" that I shall articulate consists of a set of standards, tests, or criteria which are always relevant but none of which is always controlling. I believe that, in the making of a decision, it is possible to consider these values in a somewhat orderly fashion. I believe that administrators who learn how to review these criteria in an orderly manner are the ones that have

---

[12] Philip E. Jacob et al., *Values and Their Function in Decision-Making*, Supplement no. 9 to *The American Behavioral Scientist*, May 1962, p. 13.

1. Happiness—Epicurus, Bentham, Mill
2. Lawfulness—Thomas Aquinas
3. Harmony or Consistency—Plato, Kant
4. Survival—Hobbes
5. Integrity—Epictetus, Spinoza, Santayana
6. Loyalty—Hegel, Marx, Royce

FIGURE 16.2 THE RELATIONSHIP OF VALUES TO DECISION MAKING (Adapted from Wayne A. R. Leys, "The Value Framework of Decision-making," in Sidney M. Mailick and Edward H. Van Ness (eds.), *Concepts and Issues in Administrative Behavior*, Prentice-Hall, Inc., Englewood Cliffs, N.J., 1962, pp. 87–88)

acquired the art of "asking the right questions," and that by practicing this art they improve the quality of their judgment. [13]

It is useful to identify some framework of values explicitly. They may not all apply in a given situation, and the weight of any particular value may change with the situation. But the system should not be infinite because such an approach would not be particularly helpful to a decision maker in practical situations. He should have a framework of contingencies which he can use on a day-to-day basis when he has decisions to make which allow a reflective approach.

A system which is reduced to workable proportions is found in Figure 16.2. The decision maker can look out from the point of action in six relatively distinct directions and apply the types of standards identified according to their relative appropriateness for a particular problem. The list of six basic moral standards includes the names of philosophers who advocated that particular standard as the focal point of a complete ethical system, hence providing a relatively closed-minded approach to evaluation and

[13] Wayne A. R. Leys, "The Value Framework of Decision-making," in Sidney M. Mailick and Edward H. Van Ness (eds.), *Concepts and Issues in Administrative Behavior*, © 1962, p. 81. Reprinted by permission of Prentice-Hall, Inc., Englewood Cliffs, N.J., 1962, p. 81.

decision making. The list indicates controversy over the centuries with regard to which goal should be the keystone of ethical monism. The variety of candidates indicates the probable complexity of the situation and the improbability of a single concept's sufficing for all issues and for all time.

When these standards are apparent to a decision maker, the situation becomes more realistic. However, even this model is an oversimplification in that it segregates these goals completely. Actually there are overlaps at times, and there are obvious conflicts. This model is important because several considerations are made explicit and can be dealt with sequentially as the decision maker considers his problematic situation. For example, survival is a potent value in decision making. However, there are numerous examples in which individuals have given their lives in situations where other values must have predominated, perhaps loyalty. Similarly, individuals give up the potential desirable results of a monetary windfall in order to preserve self-respect and integrity when they return a wallet found bulging with $20 bills.

It seems obvious that ethical pluralism exists in the real world. The model in Figure 16.2, or some similar schema, is a good description of the complex forces involved in any individual problem-solving situation. Moreover, we think it is good normative theory; it is the approach that should be used explicitly when a decision maker is confronted with a difficult choice. In a sense he can talk to himself in terms of various standards or principles. He may have to compromise a particular norm or value in a given situation, but he can be reasonably comfortable if he recognizes that certain other values are enhanced by so doing. He must cope with pressures from individuals and/or groups from inside and outside the organization. Formally and informally, various values are "pushed" at the decision maker, who either discards them or integrates them into his own value system. This is the "balancing act" performed in any judgmental decision process. On balance, what is most important? What tips the scale in this particular situation?

Decision makers in the real world cannot afford the luxury of deciding policy questions in general. This leads to all-encompassing values or standards which do not really apply in specific situations. The decision maker is better advised to develop a sense of the situation and deal with each problem on its own merits. "The philosopher or value-theorist . . . should not try to make the official's decisions. Only the man at the scene of action has access to the factual components of the decision." [14]

It is important to stress the general approach rather than the specific norms or ethical standards identified in a simplified model. Within our culture some consensus may be developed for a model such as the one presented in Figure 16.2. However, even this may be too much to ask. In addition, it is obvious that such a system would not apply across cultural boundaries. The weights given to various objectives or standards of conduct vary considerably. Therefore, a model such as this would have to be developed

---

[14] Ibid., p. 93.

for each culture in order that managerial decision makers would have a useful value framework for making difficult choices.

The relationship of personal values and organizational strategy seems quite evident. [15] While a manager may feel that he is objective in his decision making with regard to setting goals and devising strategy, he should recognize that his value system stems from his total past experience and is a very subtle yet ever-present factor. Identifying this value system through introspection will be helpful if the executive wants to understand why he decides the way he does. Moreover, such an appraisal should be a continuing endeavor because the value profile may change over time. Economic considerations may be paramount at one stage in an individual's career but give way to other values at some later stage. Identifying one's own values is not easy, and it is even more difficult to empathize with someone else. However, even moderate success in such a complex task should pay off many times over.

GROUPS AND DECISION MAKING

We are interested in the role of groups in the open-system decision model for two reasons. First, there is organizational decision making in which groups themselves are the agents of choice. Second, in organizational settings there is the impact which groups have on individual choice behavior. Two basic questions: How do groups make decisions, and how do groups affect individual decision making?

In order to predict the decision-making behavior of groups, it is important to identify their value systems in order to anticipate more easily their propensity to behave in certain ways. Obviously, if a group is made up of individuals with very similar value systems, prediction of group decisions is relatively easy. On the other hand, if a group is comprised of diverse members, prediction may be much more difficult. Moreover, the degree of cohesiveness may vary with respect to different issues.

There is a spectrum of cohesiveness with regard to individual and group goals. If identical, progress toward group aims is likely. At the other end of the spectrum, minimal agreement between individual and group goals may be evident. Such groups would be relatively unstable and not very well "organized." In some cases group values are quite explicit and endure for long periods of time while organizational membership experiences continuing turnover and change. Those who internalize the group goals remain and become part of a cohesive unit. Those that cannot adjust to the group values will become less active and may eventually drop from the fold. Many religious and other similar volunteer organizations could be described in such terms.

---

[15] For a discussion of how individual value profiles (relative strengths of economic, theoretical, political, religious, aesthetic, and social orientations) affect organizational strategy and major policies, see William T. Guth and Renato Tagiuri, "Personal Values and Corporate Strategies," *Harvard Business Review*, September–October 1965, pp. 123–132.

Groups as Decision Makers

A comparison of individuals and groups as decision makers can be useful. A number of issues might be considered—effectiveness, efficiency, open- or closed-mindedness, risk, and rationality.

For example, is a group more effective than an individual decision maker? Often we hear the adage that the best way not to get a decision is to appoint a committee to study the issue. If effectiveness is related only to whether or not a decision is made expeditiously, a committee may be less effective. On the other hand, the evidence on this matter is not clear-cut. Individuals often procrastinate when faced with complex decisions.

A number of specific methods are used by groups to make decisions: (1) *lack of response,* i.e., to a proposed solution by one or a few members; (2) *authority rule,* the leader "announcing" the decision; (3) *minority rule,* a few people with assumed expertise and/or loud voices; (4) *majority rule,* let's take a vote; (5) *consensus,* the most acceptable (not necessarily optimal) solution for all members; and (6) *unanimity,* a possible, but not probable, condition in complex situations. Research has shown that on complex problem-solving tasks where there is a single correct answer, groups using a consensus mode have been more effective than individuals (except in rare cases), averaging techniques, or other group methods cited above. [16] The strength of the consensus approach is that differences of opinion are used creatively; they are assumed to be natural and are expected. Different points of view are sought out, heard, and encouraged. "Disagreements can help the group's decision because with a wide range of information and opinions, there is a greater chance that the group will hit upon more adequate solutions." [17]

Formal status systems can inhibit social interaction and thereby reduce group effectiveness if all resources are not utilized. This is particularly true if the status system is inversely related to expertise. [18] Obviously, the most effective approach would be to match degree of expertise with degree of participation and influence. This is a very difficult objective to achieve because problems are different, group membership changes, and degree of expertise may be impossible to ascertain, at least a priori.

The effectiveness of a group in decision making relates to the particular values which seem most desirable—speed, accuracy, or creativity, e.g. And participation may be important from the standpoint of implementing a decision. In many problematic situations, no decision may be the best solution, at least for the time being. Thus, referring the decision to a group wherein conflicting value systems become evident and no action is taken may be the best approach after all.

With regard to efficiency, it seems obvious that more man-hours are spent in group decision making than if an individual were to tackle the problem himself. Yet, an

---

[16] Jay Hall, "Decisions, Decisions, Decisions," *Psychology Today,* November 1971, pp. 51–54ff.
[17] Ibid., p. 86.
[18] Charles R. Holloman and Hal W. Hendrick, "Effects of Status and Individual Ability on Group Problem Solving," *Decision Sciences,* October 1972, pp. 55–63.

individual could spend more time in analyzing a problem because of the need for gathering diverse information input. From this point of view, concentrated group attention to the problem may be more efficient in terms of man-hours. The efficiency of specialization can also be brought to bear on the problem. While more time might be spent via the group approach, the cost may be less than if a higher-priced executive were to do it himself. Also, efficiency should be viewed from the broader perspective of both deciding and implementing. In this context the group approach may be more efficient in the long run.

A group tends to open the system more than an individual. An individual, on a particular issue, might range on a spectrum from closed-mindedness to open-mindedness. If a group is involved, it seems likely that a more open total value system would prevail. This is not automatic, however. A group may be extremely cohesive, and individual members may have internalized group goals to the extent that they think as one mind. Groups with divergent member opinions are probably more typical. The decision process in such cases involves information inputs from several or many points of view, and hence the value system would tend to be more open. Figure 16.3 illustrates this latter situation. The most likely result from such a group is a decision not to decide. The most hopeless situation would be that of a group composed of closed-minded individuals with diverse value systems. On the other hand, a group of open-minded individuals with diverse value systems might prove to be an effective and efficient problem-solving agent.

Groups are usually considered to be conservative decision makers. The committee, for example, is often accused of recommending solutions which represent ''the lowest common denominator.'' This implies status quo, or at best, moving incrementally not very far from some current practice. On the other hand, in Chapter 15 we indicated how individual decision makers, by and large, tend to be conservative in terms of their risk preferences. Rather than gamble on an extremely large payoff, most individuals are willing to accept a smaller gain which is almost ''sure.'' In organizational settings an individual may be satisfied with relatively small certain improvements in operations rather than risk a loss in an attempt to obtain a bonanza. Organizations typically ''punish'' individuals for losses, seemingly without recognizing that the decision, even though risky, was in the long-run best interest of the organization. In this case ''best interest'' would be evaluated in terms of expected payoff over some time period.

There is some evidence to indicate that groups in similar situations are more risky. [19] In part, this can be explained by the concept of spreading risk. If one individual is solely responsible for a risky venture, he may balk. If a group is involved in making the decision, responsibility is effectively diffused and no one individual feels that he is ''under the gun.'' Therefore groups may, in fact, engage in more risky decision-making behavior than individuals. Of course, in all these instances we are considering averages or tendencies. Some individuals will be much more risky than most groups. Some

---

[19] Yeshayahu Rim, ''Social Attitudes and Risk Taking,'' *Human Relations,* August 1965, pp. 259–265.

FIGURE 16.3 DIVERSE VALUE SYSTEMS AND GROUP DECISION MAKING (Jules Feiffer, *Seattle-Post Intelligencer*, Aug. 27, 1967. Courtesy of Publishers-Hall Syndicate)

groups, because of the composite of individual value systems, may be much more conservative than most individuals.

Group Rationality

How do groups compare with individuals in terms of rationality and decision making? It is important to remember two views of rationality: (1) the choice and (2) the process. To achieve a logical, methodical, exhaustive, systematic decision process, an organized group effort may be the answer. Weber's normative bureaucratic model was designed in part to offset the capriciousness of individual decision makers. His concept was that explicit, well-defined organizational procedures would tend to eliminate, or at least alleviate, the problems stemming from rule-of-thumb methods used by individual decision makers. He was concerned with the individual bias which often resulted in decisions which were "out of line" with organizational objectives.

Groups may use more rational decision-making processes than individuals when the procedure is formalized and the steps, as depicted in Figures 14.4 and 16.1, are followed to the letter. This explicit, visible approach tends to make the process more systematic. Again, these are tendencies; some individuals may follow extremely rational approaches to decision making while some groups may be quite capricious.

In terms of the choice itself there is no clear way to differentiate between groups and individuals. In both cases decisions are intendedly rational. That is, an alternative is chosen which will move the individual or group toward a goal (expressed or implied). The rationality of choice may appear quite different to someone other than the decision-making agent. If rationality is to be measured in terms of a consensus, then maybe a group approach will result in a greater readiness, on the part of all concerned, to term the decision rational. Having participated in the process, most group members will probably engage in less "second guessing" and accept the chosen alternative as the best under the circumstances.

A group may facilitate the development of more information with regard to a problematic situation and hence move the decision closer to "ideal" rationality, where one of the requirements is complete knowledge. However, the inclusion of diverse information inputs often widens the scope of the problem environment, introduces confounding variables, and, in general, makes the situation more complex. As a result, the evaluation of alternatives, particularly predicting the probability and importance of outcomes, becomes much more difficult.

Groups and Individual Decision Makers

It is apparent that social forces influence individual attitudes and behavior. Decisions about individual goals or actions are affected significantly by "group pressure" in a setting of shared norms regarding such goals or actions. [20]

---

[20] Edith B. Pelz, "Some Factors in 'Group Decision,'" in E. E. Maccoby, T. M. Newcomb, and E. L. Hartley, *Readings in Social Psychology,* 3d ed., Henry Holt and Company, New York, 1958, pp. 212–219.

Asch tested the degree to which subjects move toward group responses to unambiguous visual stimuli, once they perceive themselves to be quite divergent. [21] Many variations of the experiment were tried, but the basic framework involved two cards, one of which contained a standard line. The other card had three lines on it, one of which matched the standard line on the other card. Groups of subjects were assembled in a testing room and asked to identify the comparable line on the second card over a long series of examples. Typically, one bona fide subject was included with a group of stooges who responded according to a predetermined pattern. After a few correct responses the stooges would begin to deliberately select alternatives which "obviously" were not correct. The essence of the study was to determine the effect of felt pressure on the bona fide subject to conform to the phony responses of his fellow "subjects." Asch describes the results as follows:

> Of course individuals differed in response. At one extreme, about one quarter of the subjects were completely independent and never agreed with the erroneous judgments of the majority. At the other extreme, some individuals went with the majority nearly all of the time. The performances of individuals in this experiment tend to be highly consistent. Those who strike out on the path of independence do not, as a rule, succumb to the majority even over an extended series of trials, while those who choose the path of compliance are unable to free themselves as the ordeal is prolonged. [22]

Some subjects showed a tendency to conform even when the discrepancy between the correct line and the group's choice was as much as seven inches. When the subject was supported to some degree, either deliberately by one of the stooges or by a second bona fide subject, the probability of his retaining independence was increased significantly. Apparently the feeling of isolation was overwhelming in many cases, and even the slightest indication of support was used as substantiation of his independent judgment.

In spite of these results, subjects, when interviewed, almost without exception maintained that independence was preferable to conformity. Independence may be a normative theory while conformity may be more descriptive of the real world. The tendency to conformity varies with the individual, and for a given individual, it varies according to particular situations. When he is experienced or knowledgeable about a particular issue, he may retain his independent judgment. On other issues he may feel less well informed and hence be willing to adjust his thinking according to the majority of his peers, subordinates, or superiors. There may be some fine lines between traits such as independence and closed-mindedness. A bigot is not likely to adjust his thinking merely because the majority holds a different view. Open-minded independence would be the "golden mean," but such a balance may be hard to achieve.

The reluctance of individuals to voice counterarguments in cohesive groups is a pervasive phenomenon. Janis suggests that "The more amiability and esprit de corps

---

[21] Solomon Asch, "Opinions and Social Pressure," in Harold J. Leavitt and Lewis R. Pondy (eds.), *Readings in Managerial Psychology*, The University of Chicago Press, Chicago, 1964, pp. 304–314.
[22] Ibid., p. 308.

there is among the members of a policy-making ingroup, the greater the danger that independent critical thinking will be replaced by groupthink." [23] The term *groupthink* is used purposely to connote the detrimental aspects of group pressure as decribed by George Orwell in *1984*. [24] After studying a massive amount of material on policy decision-making processes (formal and informal) concerning major issues such as Pearl Harbor, Viet Nam, and the Bay of Pigs, Janis concluded that the groups that committed the fiascos were victims of groupthink. [25]

For example, several key people in strategic groups under Presidents Kennedy and Johnson later reported that they failed to express their doubts about the alternatives chosen because of the seeming unanimity in the group, only to find later that at least one other person had the same doubts. If either had expressed his opinion, and been supported by the other, there is a strong possibility that the group would at least have reconsidered the issue.

President Kennedy took positive steps to offset the groupthink phenomenon, and essentially the same ingroup seemed to be much more effective in the Cuban missile crisis. Effective groups typically have some or all of the following characteristics or features:

1 The leader encourages each member to be a critical evaluator.
2 The leader (and key members) should be impartial in the early stages of deliberations.
3 Same problem is assigned to outside groups who input results.
4 At intervals, before a consensus is reached, each member tests proposals on his own subordinates and reports the results.
5 Outside experts are invited in and encouraged to challenge views of key group members. [26]
6 At every meeting someone is assigned the role of devil's advocate.
7 Explicit empathy with rival (nation or organization) to anticipate consequences of actions.
8 Subgroups are used to get more involvement, then differences are addressed in the total group.
9 After consensus is reached a follow-up meeting should be held (time permitting) in order to allow "second-thoughts" and residual doubts to be aired. [27]

This process can be overdone if diverse points of view are never resolved and inaction results. The leader must maintain an equilibrium in the group's interactive process that encourages critical thinking and involvement but does not preclude consensus when a decision must be made.

---

[23] Irving L. Janis, "Groupthink," *Psychology Today,* November 1971, p. 44.
[24] George Orwell, *1984,* Harcourt, Brace and Company, Inc., New York, 1949.
[25] Janis, op. cit., p. 43.
[26] The importance of truly "outside" and *independent* (maybe even hostile) evaluators cannot be overemphasized. Daniel S. Greenberg, "Don't Ask the Barber Whether You Need a Haircut," *Saturday Review,* Nov. 25, 1972, pp. 58–59.
[27] Janis, op. cit., p. 76.

Cognitive Dissonance

A tendency toward uniformity results from internal cognitive processes on the part of the individual. He recognizes differences in his perception of a situation from those of others or from the group as a whole as he understands it. The mental state resulting from this situation has been termed *cognitive dissonance*.[28] The theory says that two cognitions are dissonant if, considering those two alone, the adverse of one element would follow from the other. The theory further holds that dissonance, being psychologically uncomfortable, will motivate the person to try to reduce dissonance and achieve consonance.

With regard to group pressures on individual decision makers, cognitive dissonance could result if group action were contrary to individual values, beliefs, and perceptions. The individual may play a role in an organization and hence have a need to decide issues in a way which will be organizationally rational. At the same time, his own private value system may not be able to accept the alternatives implemented (person-role conflict). Because this is an uncomfortable mental state, the individual typically will engage in cognitive behavior which will reduce dissonance and result in a more comfortable state of mind. An individual copes with dissonance and/or strives for cognitive consonance in many ways.

1 He can *blame himself;* i.e., come to believe his own judgment is faulty and that the group is correct.
2 He can *blame the group;* i.e., the group judgment is faulty and his is correct.
3 He can try to *reconcile discrepant judgments* and look for reasons that ''explain away'' the differences.
4 He can *accept the fact of individual differences,* particularly when the issues involved are subjective and/or personal.
5 He can *avoid evidence of discrepancy* and maintain independence through ''isolation'' from the group.
6 He can decide that he has been *deceived* (in an experiment or some actual situation) and that no ''real'' discrepancy exists.[29]

Overt pressure to conform does not create as much dissonance as self-determined discrepancies because the individual can ''rationalize'' conforming behavior in terms of being forced into it. More dissonance and more change result from felt pressures which are internalized and not easily attributable to an outside agency. Another subtle form of dissonance results when a person outwardly behaves differently from the way he believes inwardly. This may be a case of ''expedient'' conforming where an individual publicly agrees with a group decision but privately is convinced that they are wrong. The cognitive dissonance resulting from this situation may be resolved via one of the modes described above or by merely concluding that the issue is ''not worth it.''

---

[28] Leon Festinger, *A Theory of Cognitive Dissonance,* Harper & Row, Publishers, Incorporated, New York, 1957.
[29] David Krech, Richard S. Crutchfield, and Egerton L. Ballachey, *Individual in Society,* McGraw-Hill Book Company, New York, 1962, pp. 516 and 517.

Not all group pressure should be viewed as pressure toward conformity or uniformity. Some groups exist to ensure divergent points of view. Discussion groups or legislative bodies may set up elaborate mechanisms so that they can agree to disagree. There is explicit recognition of the need for different opinions and an open-minded approach to decision making.

Because the individual typically belongs to many groups simultaneously, the group pressure he feels on various issues may result in his being relatively open-minded. For example, he could (1) come from a small farming community; (2) have a father who is a relatively conservative merchant; (3) be exposed to liberal teachers; (4) work for a large national company; (5) belong to a rather puritan religious sect; (6) be a registered Democrat; (7) own a Playboy key; (8) have a Republican wife; (9) be an Elk and/or a Shriner; (10) coach a Little League baseball team; and (11) be active in union affairs. Of course, such pressures (some explicit, many implied) make the individual's environment exceedingly dynamic and complex.

THE INTERFACE OF COMPUTATIONAL AND JUDGMENTAL APPROACHES

Managerial decision making—at operating, coordinative, and strategic levels—takes place in systems that can be considered along a continuum from relatively closed to relatively open. Within this framework it is obvious that problems can develop anywhere along the spectrum. In some cases all the assumptions required for closed-system, programmed approaches may be appropriate. Factors can be quantified, and sophisticated computational techniques can be applied.

In other cases these assumptions simply do not hold at all. If they are made, the resulting models are extremely artificial and any solutions derived are probably not applicable in the real world. The important thing is to recognize the particular situation for what it is, be it a relatively closed or relatively open system. Quantification and mathematical techniques have been most useful for computational problem solving where few variables have to be considered and value issues are restricted. As managers face decisions which encompass more territory, involve numerous variables, and include nonquantifiable aspects, such methods lose their usefulness, and judgment plays a more important role. Wise decision makers recognize where different approaches will be appropriate. A problem may be made up of numerous subproblems, all of which can be solved with computational techniques. The overall problem, however, requires integrating the "solutions" from subproblems into a total system. Often the larger system will be relatively open because it includes more environmental inputs and relies on the judgment of managerial decision makers. In this latter case the individual or group value system comes into play, adding more openness and complexity.

Unfortunately, the attention devoted to computational problem-solving techniques has far outstripped that devoted to judgmental considerations. The literature of management science or operations research abounds with techniques for decision making. The inordinate amount of time devoted to clear-cut, quantifiable problems is unfortunate from the standpoint that such situations represent such a small proportion of managerial decision making (primarily economic-technical considerations at the operating level). The number of decisions which can be so construed is much less than the number which cannot be approached in that manner. And, the importance of such decision problems is much less than that of the more complex, comprehensive policy issues which management faces continually in the coordinative and strategic subsystems.

Why the imbalance of treatment? The small-scale, tidy problems can be dealt with in simplified terms. Many complex theories are explained by the use of simplified examples. Unfortunately such examples have little relation to the real world. However, they do serve as a vehicle in the process of explaining and understanding the theory. Hence we tend to concentrate on simple situations, sometimes without using a disclaimer or an admonishment that real situations may be much more complex. The hope is that the simple models will instill a framework or an approach which can be used when the manager or analyst comes face to face with a more complex situation. However, the literature abounds with statements suggesting that the system was simplified "a little bit" in order to make the techniques applicable. The actual situation was not "exactly" this way, but if we make these slight modifications, the technique can be applied.

It seems evident that much of the literature is technique-oriented, dealing with sophisticated refinements of various management science tools. Management scientists have been accused of "talking to themselves" in terms of techniques, with less than desirable orientation to real-world problems. [30] More emphasis on problems rather than techniques has been urged by many writers, particularly practicing managers.

Why has more not been done concerning nonprogrammable problem solving in open systems? The best answer probably relates to the complexity of open systems and the "messy" decisions that are often required. It is not that nothing has been done. On the contrary, much scientific knowledge is available from the behavioral and social sciences which relates to decision making in complex situations. And, the scientific method as an approach to problem solving has been stressed in many disciplines and practical settings. The difficult part is putting the general approach together with the untidy aspects of open-system problems in the context of managerial decision making. Much more work needs to be done in this regard.

Algorithmic (cookbook) approaches proceed according to an explicit, programmed set of computations. Heuristic (sophisticated trial-and-error) approaches, on the other hand, rely more heavily on the wisdom and judgment of the human decision maker at all stages in the decision-making process. Lindblom describes the applicability of these approaches to policy decisions as follows:

> For complex problems, the first of these two approaches [root or algorithmic or computational] is of course impossible. Although such an approach can be described, it cannot be practiced except for relatively simple problems and

---

[30] Donald F. Heany, "Is TIMS Talking to Itself?" *Management Science,* December 1965, pp. B-146–155; and Harry Stern, "Is Information Systems Talking to Itself?" *Interfaces,* August 1972, pp. 54–57.

even then only in a somewhat modified form. It assumes intellectual capacities and sources of information that men simply do not possess, and it is even more absurd as an approach to policy when time and money that can be allocated to a policy problem is limited, as is always the case. Of particular importance to public administrators is the fact that public agencies are in effect usually instructed not to practice the first method. That is to say, their prescribed functions and constraints—the politically or legally possible—restrict their attention to relatively few values and relatively few alternative policies among the countless alternatives that might be imagined. It is the second method [branch or heuristic or judgmental] that is practiced. [31]

Lindblom states that the second method *describes* how most administrators approach complex questions. The first method is not workable for complex policy questions and hence merely *prescribes* how decisions "ought" to be made.

We do not suggest perpetuating existing managerial behavior by teaching what is done in current organizations. Obviously, many approaches could be improved. On the other hand, it is dangerous to pretend that methods dependent upon simplifying assumptions will be applicable in the real world. Naturally, some reasonable middle-ground approach is needed so that normative or prescriptive models are enriched with realism garnered from practical experience. This appears to be a perfectly sound objective, but achieving it is extremely difficult. [32]

The first steps may be the development of mutual understanding on the part of practicing managers and management scientists. Managerial decision making is an art, not a science. Like all arts, however, it is dependent on a body of knowledge stemming from scientific disciplines. There must be mutual respect for the endeavors of both groups. Managers should understand the value systems of management science. Similarly management scientists should understand the value systems of managers and the complexity of real-world problem-solving situations. Then, and only then, will the applicability of various techniques be appraised realistically.

Shakun suggests that mutual understanding can be enhanced via situational normativism, a process which "involves a search by manager and management scientist for a synthesized situational frame of understanding (involving analytic and heuristic knowledge) within which solutions to the . . . problem can be found." [33] Joint diagnosis requires interaction which leads to mutual understanding and unity of science and management. This forms the basis for increased probability of implementing innovative changes because emphasis on situational diagnosis (rather than techniques of analy-

---

[31] Charles E. Lindblom, "The Science of 'Muddling Through,'" in Leavitt and Pondy, op. cit., pp. 62-63. (The words algorithmic, heuristic, computational, and judgmental have been added by the authors.)
[32] James E. Rosenzweig, "Managers and Management Scientists (Two Cultures)," *Business Horizons,* Fall 1967, pp. 79-86.
[33] Melvin F. Shakun, "Management Science and Management: Implementing Management Science via Situational Normativism," *Management Science,* April 1972, p. B-367.

sis) should lead to realism in model building. An ultimate objective is to make the situational-normativism approach an integral part of the organization's problem-solving process.

The complexity of open systems should be recognized. But complexity does not mean chaos. Recognizing the heuristic approaches often used by competent decision makers can lead to descriptive models which incorporate untidy factors and uncontrollable environmental aspects. Managerial decision making in such open systems can be improved significantly, in many cases, by making the process more explicit. Management can become much more effective if managers consciously think through a process which may have been subconscious before.

SUMMARY

Judgmental decision making in relatively open systems recognizes the complexity of the internal organizational atmosphere and the external environment of decision makers. At strategic and coordinative levels particularly, it is impossible to mold all the factors which management must consider into explicit, well-defined models that can be quantified and solved via computational techniques.

The individual is an integral part of the decision-making process and makes the system relatively open or closed according to his mental set. Closed-minded individuals tend to restrict the search for alternatives and then evaluate those that are identified in terms of a narrow set of criteria and limited information. Open-minded individuals, on the other hand, tend to push for a wider horizon in terms of alternatives and encourage the input of as much diverse information as possible.

Value systems or "images" result from an individual's total past experience. Value judgments come into play at many stages of the open-system model of decision making. Ethical pluralism recognizes that the real world is composed of complexities and that all decisions cannot be referred to *one* clear-cut standard. However, pluralism does not imply an infinite number of criteria or that there are *no* guidelines for decision makers in specific situations. On the contrary, it is useful to identify some values explicitly in order to provide a framework for day-to-day decisions which allow a cogitative approach.

The personal values of businessmen and others have been classified as theoretical, economic, aesthetic, social, political, and religious. It has been found that those values which are most important to executives have a definite impact upon their strategic and tactical decisions. In most cases, individuals are not aware of their own values and tend to misjudge the orientation of others.

Groups are important in behavioral aspects of decision making for two reasons: (1) they are agents of choice and (2) they have an impact on individual decision makers. Many experiments have been undertaken to assess the impact of groups on individual decision makers. The research centers around a significant difference in group and individual responses. In many cases there is a tendency for individuals to accept "incorrect" group responses and move toward them (or conform) on subsequent trials.

Individualism versus conformity is not an either-or issue. Individuals are members of groups and hence subject to pressures at all times. There are relative degrees of autonomy and control, but without some group control there would be no organization. Individuals are relatively *free* to make decisions within constraints which may be explicit or implicit at many levels—societal, organizational, or small, informal groups. However, the constraints do *determine* individual behavior to a considerable degree.

Most individual and organizational decision making takes place in relatively open systems. Computational techniques can be applied to managerial decision making at the operating level. However, coordinative and strategic problems are usually too complex for such approaches and the judgment of the decision maker becomes relatively more important. Within the overall management system it is essential to recognize the context of problems and determine the appropriateness of various approaches.

QUESTIONS AND PROBLEMS

1 What trends are evident in the increasing complexity of the internal atmosphere and external environment of organizations? What impact do these trends have on managerial decision making?

2 Using the open-system decision model (Figure 16.1), trace several individual and/ or organizational decisions through the steps identified. Does it seem to fit actual behavior? Why or why not?

3 How does the individual's value system or particular approach in a given situation affect the openness of the environmental system for decision making?

4 Distinguish factual and value considerations in decision making. Which are more important? Why?

5 What role does ethical pluralism play in managerial decision making? Should we seek an all-encompassing value as a frame of reference for all decisions? Why or why not?

6 How do individual value systems affect organizational strategy? Give examples.

7 Compare and contrast group and individual decision making with respect to: (*a*) effectiveness, (*b*) efficiency, (*c*) open- or closed-mindedness, (*d*) risk, and (*e*) rationality.

8 Discuss the impact of groups on individual decision making, particularly (*a*) pressure to conform, (*b*) cognitive dissonance, (*c*) free will vis-à-vis determinism, and (*d*) autonomy vis-à-vis control.

9 "The attention devoted to computational problem-solving techniques has far outstripped that devoted to judgmental considerations." Do you agree? Why or why not?

10 How should open-system, heuristic, judgmental approaches to managerial decision making be integrated with closed-system, algorithmic, computational techniques? What are the prospects?

MANAGERIAL PLANNING

The planning function is an integral part of the managerial information-decision system. It involves setting organizational objectives and designing the means for achieving them. Planning provides a framework for integrated decision making throughout the organization. At the strategic level, long-range, comprehensive plans are developed to achieve overall missions. Short-range plans are used at the operating level and implemented via detailed tactics. In between, at the coordinative level, management is involved in translating strategy into tactics, developing policies and procedures, and coordinating the planning activity. Planning is a key managerial function which provides the means by which individuals and organizations cope with a complex, dynamic, ever-changing environment. Our discussion of planning will involve the following topics:

Planning Defined
The Role of Planning
Setting Goals
Planning Dimensions
Systems Concepts and Planning
Steps in the Planning Process
Who Does the Planning?
Integration of Planning and Control
Examples of Planning

PLANNING DEFINED

A plan is any detailed method, formulated beforehand, for doing or making something. [1] Planning is the process of deciding in advance what is to be done and how. It involves selecting objectives and developing policies, programs, and procedures for achieving them. Planning provides a framework for integrating complex systems of interrelated future decisions. [2] *Comprehensive planning is an integrative activity that seeks to maximize the total effectiveness of an organization as a system in accordance with its objectives.*

Planning has an implication of futurity, and it implies that there is some skill involved in designing plans for objective accomplishment. *In short, a plan is a predetermined course of action.* Essentially, a plan has three characteristics. First, it must involve the future. Second, it must involve action. Third, there is an element of personal or organizational identification or causation; that is, the future course of action will be taken by the planner or someone designated by or for him within the organization. Futurity, action, and personal or organizational causation are necessary elements in every plan. [3]

Long-Range Planning

Obviously, managers have always engaged in some sort of planning, either explicitly or implicitly. However, over the past several decades increased emphasis has been placed upon formal long-range or strategic planning as a means for the organization to adapt to its environment. Warren defines long-range planning as "a process directed toward making today's decisions with tomorrow in mind and a means of preparing for future decisions so that they may be made rapidly, economically, and with as little disruption to the business as possible." [4] Steiner is even more specific: "Long-range planning deals with the futurity of present decisions in terms of (1) setting goals and developing strategies to achieve them, and (2) translating strategies into detailed operational programs and assuring that plans are carried out." [5]

Decision Making and Planning

Decision making and planning are closely related. A decision is basically a resolution of alternative choices. A decision is not a plan in that it need not involve either action or the future. On the other hand, a decision involving merely the acceptance of an idea

---

[1] *Webster's New World Dictionary,* 2d College Edition, The World Publishing Company, Cleveland, 1970, p. 1088.

[2] Russell L. Ackoff, *A Concept of Corporate Planning,* Wiley-Interscience, New York, 1970.

[3] Preston P. LeBreton and Dale A. Henning, *Planning Theory,* Prentice-Hall, Inc., Englewood Cliffs, N.J., 1961, p. 7.

[4] E. Kirby Warren, *Long-range Planning: The Executive Viewpoint,* Prentice-Hall, Inc., Englewood Cliffs, N.J., 1966, p. 18.

[5] George A. Steiner (ed.), *Managerial Long-range Planning,* McGraw-Hill Book Company, New York, 1963, p. 15.

can influence future individual or organizational behavior. Decisions, of course, are necessary at every stage of the planning process and therefore inextricably linked to planning. Koontz and O'Donnell relate the two concepts as follows:

> Planning involves selecting objectives—and the strategies, policies, programs, and procedures for achieving them—either for the entire enterprise or for any organized part thereof. Planning is, of course, decision making, since it involves selecting among alternatives. [6]

Some definitions seem to include the entire management system and stress the integration of planning and control decisions via the feedback mechanism. For example, Drucker says that planning is "the continuous process of making *present entrepreneurial (risk taking) decisions* systematically and with the best possible knowledge of their futurity, organizing systematically *the efforts* needed to carry out these decisions, and measuring the results of these decisions against the expectations through *organized, systematic feed-back.*" [7]

The information-decision system provides an overall framework through which the managerial process is carried out. Planning is one phase of managerial decision making, and plans provide a framework for decision making and planning in subsequent activities, particularly at lower levels in organizations or in subsystems of overall operations.

Forecasting

The futurity implication of planning suggests that forecasting is an important part of the process. Anticipation of the states of nature and/or the results of alternative courses of action is a crucial phase of the decision-making process. Individually and organizationally we act on the basis of estimates of the future. Therefore, forecasting is a fundamental part of planning; it is the foundation upon which rather elaborate frameworks are often established. As the time element is extended, forecasting becomes increasingly hazardous and more subjective but remains an essential ingredient in the planning process. As the foundation for long-range planning, forecasting is an attempt to make the future environment less uncertain. Conscious effort toward anticipating the technological, economic, political, and social climate for the organization helps the manager avoid pitfalls that might possibly be disastrous. Constant surveillance does not necessarily ensure success; the organization must have the capacity to take advantage of recognized opportunities. However, forecasting and long-range planning should re-

---

[6] Harold Koontz and Cyril O'Donnell, *Principles of Management*, 5th ed., McGraw-Hill Book Company, New York, 1972, p. 47.

[7] Peter F. Drucker, "Long-range Planning: Challenge to Management Science," *Management Science*, April 1959, p. 240.

duce the environmental uncertainty for the organization and provide the framework for managerial decisions which make the best of situations as they arise.

> Uncertainty is the complement of knowledge. It is the gap between what is known and what needs to be known to make correct decisions. Dealing sensibly with uncertainty is not a byway on the road to responsible business and governmental decisions. It is central to it. The subject is complex, elusive, and omnipresent. [8]

THE ROLE OF PLANNING

Most organizations operate in an environment of change. They must be prepared to accept change as the inevitable consequence of operating in a dynamic world. The general political, economic, social, and ethical philosophies in our country have promoted an atmosphere of freedom of change for the enterprise. In fact, continued success generally has demanded adaptation and innovation. This is in direct contradiction to many societies—both past and contemporary—in which political, religious, cultural, and other institutions placed major impediments in the path of economic and social progress.

Rapidly advancing technology has also emphasized the need for planning. Companies not abreast of current technology are in trouble over the short run. Moreover, companies unaware of the technical changes likely to occur over the next five to twenty years will be in a disadvantageous position.

On the other hand, the organization faced with a changing environment has often found many obstacles which make planning for optimum adaptation difficult. Even technological advances, which themselves are purveyors of change, can create degrees of inflexibility. For example, automation, while requiring major changes for its establishment, results in some inherent inflexibilities and increased resistance to change. In a typical multiproduct business, for instance, automated operations are predicated on expected variations in volume, product mix, quality, and demand. Since automation establishes a relatively inflexible overall system, it is vitally important that the right decision be made at the outset. Thus it is evident that effective long-term business planning is of critical importance.

Management itself is not free from practices which restrict change and make planning difficult. Current experience with the impact of computers on integrated systems of information flow indicates reluctance on the part of white-collar employees and management personnel with vested interests to accept the required modifications in organizational and status relationships. As business organizations have increased in size and complexity, they have had difficulty in ensuring that the innovations necessary

[8] Ruth P. Mack, *Planning on Uncertainty,* Wiley-Interscience, New York, 1971, p. 1.

to meet new conditions and evolving objectives will be accepted by each department as guidelines to action. These and many other forces tend to make it more difficult for the business organization to sustain adaptiveness in a dynamic environment.

With a stable environment and small, uncomplicated operations, the planning function can be carried out relatively easily with a short-range viewpoint. With a more dynamic environment and large, complex units operating in the face of many forces that restrict flexibility, the planning function becomes critical and must be thought of on a total systems basis. Since the consequence of any decision has such a broad and drastic impact, management, through its planning function, must seek the optimal course of action.

Planning requires consideration of the organization as an integration of numerous decision-making subsystems. The primary function of top-management (strategic-level) planning is one of systems design, which involves (1) the establishment of objectives, policies, procedures, and organizational relationships on a systematic basis for guidance of decision making and planning at various organizational levels and (2) the provision for the flow of information to and from these planning and decision-making centers.

SETTING GOALS

Basically, goals are plans expressed as results to be achieved. In this broad sense, goals include purposes, missions, objectives, targets, quotas, deadlines, etc. Goals represent not only the end point of planning but the end toward which the other managerial activities, such as organizing and controlling, are aimed. Goals are established for subfunctions such as production or marketing, and subgoals are established as planning moves down through the various levels in the organization.

In order to be operational, objectives such as "to make a profit" or "to provide a service" or "to be efficient" should be translated into more specific terms. In other words an operational objective might be to earn 5 percent on sales or 15 percent on net worth. Service objectives would be related to specific clientele and somehow measured in terms of degree of satisfaction achieved.

When goals can be quantified, they can be translated into explicit plans such as budgets or sales quotas. This provides a relatively clear-cut framework around which activities can be organized and performance measured.

Multiple Goals

Individuals and organizations rarely focus on a single purpose. Multiple goals are common and hence cloud the issue of setting objectives. Profitability is usually required for survival of a business enterprise. However, market share objectives may take precedence at a particular point in time. Or, community consciousness may forestall the closing of an unprofitable branch plant. Organizations have objectives with regard to both ends and means. Both quality and quantity of output may suffer in the short run as the organization builds its future capabilities. As the football coach often says, "Just wait 'til next year."

General systems philosophy emphasizes consideration of subsystem goals and their interrelationships. However, simultaneous consideration of performance in all the areas suggested above would be impossible. The relative weight of these various aspects will depend on the value system of individual managers. Some will be oriented toward ends, and others toward means. "It is not whether you win or lose, it is how you play the game," as contrasted to "It is not how you play the game, it is whether you win or lose."

An additional consideration is the time horizon for goal achievement. Is the organization to be measured in terms of short-run or long-run performance? Satisfying stockholders by means of higher dividends in the short run may conflict with long-run viability of the organization, which might require reinvestment of profits in human and physical resources.

Recognizing the Human Element

In stressing the need for clear-cut objectives in order to guide organizational behavior, quantification is probably warranted. Developing explicit quantitative goals enhances clarity and makes objectives operational. On the other hand, management should be cognizant of the multiplicity of organizational performance criteria and be willing to adjust the appraisal of goal achievement in the light of the complexity involved. Recognition that organizations are people systems should also temper management's approach to setting goals and planning activities. According to Gross:

> The first elements in both structure and performance, let it be noted, are human; people and the satisfaction of people's interest. All other elements and their many decisions—both financial and technological—are ways of thinking about people and their behavior. An organization's plans for the future are always plans made by people for people—for their future behavior and for their future relations with resources and other people. Financial and technological planners may easily lose sight of these human elements. Another virtue of general-systems analysis, therefore, is that it helps to bring together the "soft" information of human relations people with the "hard" data of accountants and engineers. [9]

Plans should reflect a realistic marriage of environmental opportunity with organizational capability—both physical and human resources. The human element includes inclination or interest as well as capacity. Employees may be quite capable of carrying out a plan developed by top management, and yet performance may fall far

---

[9] Bertram M. Gross, "What Are Your Organization's Objectives?" *Human Relations*, August 1965, p. 199.

short of expectations. Athletic teams often exemplify this phenomenon—"the coach wasn't able to get the best out of his material," or a team is described as "operating at 110 percent of capacity." That the psychosocial system in organizations plays an important part in implementing plans and achieving objectives should be recognized and understood by planners. Ewing suggests that:

> If business planners could anticipate . . . how different kinds of reporting, budgeting, controlling, and operating procedures would affect behavior, they would then be able to plan with greater skill and sophistication. In other words, planning is a two-sided affair. Planners may think only of the formal, economic, physical resources side when they develop a program, but the other side—the human side—is present just the same. If the human side is not attended to properly, then the chances are that planning will not be successful. [10]

The Virtue of Vagueness

Amid the clamor for clarity in organizational goals, it might be wise to consider the possible virtues of vagueness. Clear-cut goals and mechanistic programs for achieving them may discount the human element and lead to a sterile environment which stifles individual initiative and results in underutilization of human resources. Ultrapurposeful action proceeding according to blueprint and schedule may be unpalatable to organizational participants.

In an environment of multiple objectives it is impossible to focus on more than a few at any one time. When concentrating on one particular objective, other goals in the system must of necessity be relatively vague. The same is true for different periods of time. Short-range goals may be rather explicit, while medium- and long-range goals are more vague. It is impossible and unrealistic to identify long-range goals in clear-cut terms. These two concepts are analogous to the task of focusing the lens of a camera. In order to obtain a clear picture of a particular subject, other background or peripheral objects must be slightly fuzzy. It is impossible to obtain a sharp focus across the entire spectrum of a wide angle or over great distances.

If goals are stated in general terms, there is room for organizational participants to fill in details according to their own perception and to modify the pattern to their own liking. Ultraprecision can destroy flexibility and make it more difficult for individuals and organizations to adapt to changing conditions. Vagueness makes it possible to work toward goals by many different means. The concept of equifinality—achieving the same end via different means—is an important consideration in viable systems. Vagueness may also foster serendipity—the achievement of a particular worthwhile goal by accident. Such results may be an unexpected by-product of organizational activity. The

---

[10] David W. Ewing, "Corporate Planning at a Crossroads," *Harvard Business Review,* July–August, 1967, p. 83.

probability of such a happening is increased when objectives are relatively vague and there is room for initiative with regard to the means used to achieve them.

Unclear objectives facilitate compromise on the part of participants with diverse value systems. As long as people can read into organizational statements their own interpretation of the ends to be achieved, compromise is feasible. Thus tacit agreement is often reached with regard to both ends and means in organizational settings. For example, consider the difficulty of achieving unanimous approval and wholehearted commitment toward a set of objectives for a university or college. Agreement on a definitive set of objectives (ends) coupled with a detailed set of policies, procedures, and requirements (means) would not be very likely. If the organization were to go even further and spell out the content and pedagogical approach for each course, the probability of acceptance would approach zero. By maintaining some degree of vagueness with regard to ends and by not detailing the means, agreement and commitment on the part of organizational members is much more likely.

Within the coordinative subsystem, mediation and compromise are essential ingredients in integrating efforts toward short- and long-range goals. The element of vagueness is important in any compromise situation, and its virtues should be recognized. However, it is hard to advocate this approach explicitly. The best approach may be to continue to strive for clarity as a means to make goal setting operational but to recognize that inability to do so may not be necessarily catastrophic and in fact may be beneficial to the organization. This is another example of the necessity for management to "play it by ear" in a complex and dynamic environment.

PLANNING DIMENSIONS

Understanding the planning function may be enhanced by looking at the process from several points of view which might be called planning dimensions. For example, planning might be discussed in terms of some continuum of *repetitiveness*—planning for novel, one-time projects as against development of procedures to handle activities that will occur repeatedly. This approach may parallel but not necessarily be coincident with a hierarchical dimension. It may be meaningful to discuss planning from the standpoint of the organizational *subsystem or level* involved. Similarly, the scope of planning may vary from functionally oriented activity to total organizational endeavor. Typically, *scope* would increase as the level increases, but this may not necessarily be the case. Another relevant dimension is *time*. Planning may be considered in terms of the day-to-day activities of an organization or in terms of its attempts to achieve goals set five or ten years in the future. Again, it is obvious that the time dimension may be interrelated with others mentioned above. Finally, consideration should be given to the dimension of *flexibility*. Some plans may be highly fixed and respond to anticipated future conditions while others may be flexible, capable of adaptation to a variety of potential circumstances.

It will become apparent from the discussion that there are often patterns of relationships among these various dimensions. For example, long-range, comprehensive plans are the primary concern of top management and frequently deal with complex, multidimensional problems. The resulting strategic plans are usually quite flexible and capable of adapting to changing circumstances. In contrast, short-term, operational plans are more limited in scope, tend to be the responsibility of lower management, and usually are more fixed.

Repetitiveness

Essentially, plans for nonrepetitive problems *(single-use plans)* set forth a course of action to fit a specific situation and may be obsolete when the goal is reached. This is in contrast to standing plans which are designed to have continuing usefulness. There is a hierarchy of single-use plans ranging from (1) major programs, (2) projects, and (3) special tasks to (4) detailed plans.

There are many examples of major programs, such as the design, development, and construction of a rapid transit system. Advancing technology requires long-range planning for large-scale programs. The success of a major program depends upon the establishment of more detailed single-use plans for special projects within the total system. These single-use plans should all be integrated into an overall planning hierarchy.

Plans for repetitive action are often called *standing plans.* They include policies, methods, and standard operating procedures designed to cover the variety of repetitive situations which organizations frequently face. These plans are of importance to any established organization. It can be argued that even informal organizational relationships such as social groups and bowling teams have established plans. For the more formal organization the standing plans are a primary cohesive force connecting its various subsystems. Plans for repetitive action become the habit patterns of the organization, similar to the habit patterns of individuals.

Policies are the broadest of the standing plans and are general guides to organizational behavior. At the strategic level policies generally set broad premises and constraints within which further planning activities take place. A policy is a general plan of action that guides the members of the organization in the conduct of its operation. Every large organization has a wide variety of policies covering its most important functions which frequently are formalized and written in organization or policy manuals. Even in those situations where policies are not written, the organization should have policies which are understood clearly and known, even though not formally established. Quite often these informal policies are established because of the habitual pattern of decisions which results when the organization is confronted with a series of similar problems.

Methods and procedures are also standing plans. Usually they are less general than policies and establish more definite steps for the performance of certain activities in the organization. The basic difference between a policy and standard methods and procedures is a matter of degree, with both providing guidance for integrated decision making.

There are many organizational advantages to the use of plans for repetitive action. Through the use of standing plans and the concept of "management by exception," top management's influence is extended to all organizational levels. Once a policy decision has been reached, the standing plan serves as a guideline for decision making throughout the organization. Another advantage of the standing plan is that it creates a uniformity of operations throughout the organization. Once established, understood, and accepted, it provides similarity of action in meeting certain situations. This is of vital importance to large-scale, complex business or government organizations. Given established policies, a client of the organization is usually assured of a relatively uniform decision regardless of the location of facilities or the level in the organization.

The use of standing plans is typical of the bureaucratic organization regardless of whether it is government, business, labor, or any other type of large-scale, complex organization. Herein, perhaps, lies one of the problems. Standing plans are useful when they provide for a uniformity of decisions and when they meet the requirement of the situation. They are not useful when the situation changes so abruptly that the plan does not fit the new situation. Attempting to force new and dynamic situations under a particular standing plan often can lead to dysfunctional consequences.

Nevertheless, the wise use of the standing plans is essential to systematic planning. They provide the basic means for interweaving the organizational processes throughout the entire system.

Time Span

Much emphasis has been placed upon long-range planning, which is closely associated with the goal-setting responsibilities of management at the strategic level. Generally, strategic planning deals with decisions regarding the broad technological and competitive aspects of the organization, the allocation of resources (human and material) over an extended period, and the long-run integration of the organization within its environment. Some authors make a distinction between long-range planning and programming, which is defined as derivative, functional, or operational planning. [11] In the ideal sense the short- and intermediate-range operational plans are based on and integrated into the strategic planning. [12]

It is our view that strategic or long-range plans are not a separate type of plan. Rather they are an integral part of the total planning process and establish the basic framework upon which more detailed programming and operational planning take

[11] For a discussion of this distinction between long-range planning and programming, see George A. Steiner, op. cit., pp. 6–12.
[12] Ernest C. Miller, *Advanced Techniques for Strategic Planning,* American Management Association, Inc., New York, 1971.

place. Figure 17.1 illustrates the interdependency of plans for various time periods. Long- and medium-range plans provide a framework for short-range plans, which refer primarily to current operations. Feedback from ongoing activity is a part of the information flow which management uses in making decisions. Forward planning is based on past history, the current situation, and estimates of the future.

The designation "long range" varies by organization. For a firm engaged in mail-order merchandising, long range may be the next catalog (six months hence). For a firm engaged in growing timber as a crop, the outlook may approximate 100 years. On this relative basis, long range might vary from a matter of months to a matter of centuries. Typically, however, organizations engage in planning for five-, ten-, or fifteen-year intervals. As companies move the planning horizon further out on the time scale, specificity typically decreases. Rather than emphasize specific achievements, goals are stated in terms of acceptable ranges. These are usually tied to forecasts of societal conditions which also must be expressed in terms such as the expected range. Forecasts of economic activity, for example, can be fairly definite over the short run—several quarters or a year. However, in estimating gross national product for 1990, a fairly broad range would be used.

Most authors writing about long-range planning emphasize that it involves decision making which commits resources over the long-run future and that planning is necessary in dealing with the uncertainty of the future. Herein lies a major dilemma. On the one hand, there is rapidly advancing technology, changing competitive and market situations, increasingly active governmental, labor, and other interests, and many other forces which make forecasting the future environment extremely difficult. [13] Yet organizations must plan their activities over a long-run period and must commit resources in spite of future uncertainties. Witness the problems of planning and decision making for a program such as the SST aircraft, in which the Boeing Company and the federal government were cooperatively joined in its design and development. Both parties made commitments of resources based upon plans which were subject to drastic changes (e.g., the possibility that society, through Congress, would not tolerate sonic booms).

Thus we find the dilemma—the need for long-run commitments of resources and organizational endeavor in the face of an increasingly dynamic environment and future uncertainties. What is the solution to this long-range planning dilemma? More thorough and complete planning at the early stages runs the risk of complete inflexibility in the face of inevitable changes. Extending the planning period runs the risk of even more uncertainty.

Some of the earlier writers on long-range planning exhibited naïveté in expecting that business would be able to establish highly specific and carefully laid out plans which would remain viable for an extended period. This was one of the major reasons for increasing skepticism regarding the appropriateness of long-range planning. Fortu-

---

[13] One speaker introduced his remarks with the statement, "Prediction is hazardous, especially when it relates to the future."

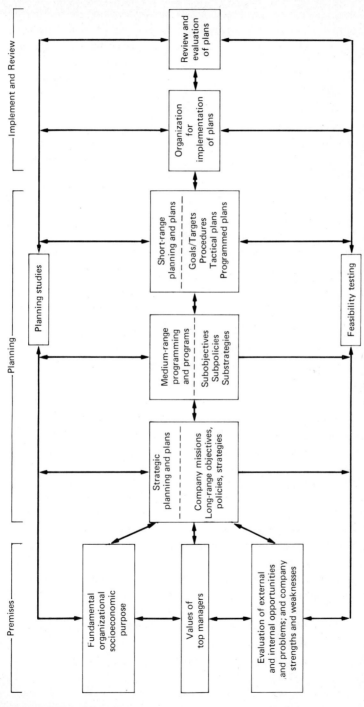

FIGURE 17.1 THE STRUCTURE AND PROCESS OF MANAGERIAL PLANNING (George A. Steiner, *Top Management Planning*, The Macmillan Company, New York, 1969, p. 33)

nately, current authors are more sophisticated and recognize that long-range planning must provide for organizational flexibility in meeting changes. Warren says, ''The major purpose of planning is the development of processes, mechanisms and managerial attitudes which will do two things. First, they will make it possible to make commitment decisions today with a greater awareness of future implications, and second, they will make it possible to make future decisions more rapidly, more economically, and with less disruptions to the ongoing business.'' [14] His second point emphasizes that long-run planning must provide for future flexibility in decision making.

Most successful companies seem to have (1) organized programs to seek and promote new business opportunities, (2) an orientation to growth fields and markets, (3) a proven competitive ability in present lines of business, (4) courageous and energetic management, and (5) luck. While luck may be a factor in organizational success, it is not reliable. Long-run probabilities are enhanced by continuing efforts in long-range planning. Whether this means one individual cogitating about the future for a few minutes periodically or a large-scale, departmentalized effort in this regard, the task is the same—coping with the environment and hopefully acting in a way which will be not only adaptive but innovative.

Scope

Another useful dimension in thinking about planning is that of scope. We often hear the term ''master plan,'' which connotes the idea of a general or overall plan for the organization. Within this framework, other more detailed plans are developed for sub-parts of the total endeavor. Branch describes three types of planning—functional, project, and comprehensive:

> We have developed considerable skills in *functional planning*—planning a component or aspect of a large endeavor. We can perform intricate series of actions which lead to a predetermined result, be it in connection with a chemical process, structural design of a beam, manufacturing a watch, or accounting for the transactions of a large enterprise. . . .
>
> Like functional planning, *project planning* has been developing since early historical times. Road building today is the culmination of experience dating back to before Roman times, and modern systems of urban water supply incorporate principles known on the island of Crete some three thousand years ago. The extent to which we have carried the art and science of project planning is represented in such feats as the construction of a Boulder Dam, aircraft carrier, large manufacturing plant, orbiting communication satellite, or any one of the multitude of physical undertakings comparable in their level of accomplishment.

---

[14] Warren, op. cit., p. 29.

Normally, this form of planning incorporates a greater range of elements than functional planning. It deals with more numerous and diverse parts. . . .

Comprehensive planning is the term describing the ultimate in man's endeavor to perform a major achievement, shape his environment, or affect the future. It includes functional and project planning, but transcends them in scope, magnitude, and complexity. It includes not only three-dimensional accomplishments in space but social mechanisms such as laws, regulations, policies, and forms of organization—for example, planning for a nation or large region, city or metropolitan area, far-flung business enterprise, or an extensive sphere of governmental activity such as agriculture, the military services, and space travel. What we are concerned with in comprehensive planning is the spectrum of human awareness, knowledge, capacity to consider and act. [15]

The complexity of the environment increases rapidly as the scope of the planning function increases. Comprehensive or master plans must, of necessity, deal with broad societal elements. [16] Corporate planning for a large industrial firm would include sociopolitical considerations, legal aspects, and other similar variables which might not be necessary or appropriate at the branch plant level. The necessary information might be provided by headquarters and hence dealt with as "given" in managerial planning at that branch. Planning activity at the subsystem level is complex in a different way because of the increasing amount of detail that must be considered.

While increasing the scope of planning introduces more variables, they often are considered in a somewhat loose fashion. The complexity of broader scope is one of increasing uncertainty. As scope narrows, on the other hand, uncertainty may decrease, but making the elements fit together into a workable pattern is a difficult task. Top management may approve master plans "in principle" without worrying about implementing them in practice. While scope and level appear to be quite similar dimensions, it may be useful to consider the hierarchical nature of planning separately.

Subsystem or Level

As decisions are made with regard to goals and plans are developed to achieve them, the scope of the planning process is constrained for lower levels in the organization, or subsystems. The plan may call for integration of functional efforts in order to achieve a particular objective. Therefore, subgoals are established for the various functions, and plans must be drawn for accomplishing them. Within a particular function, there will be a further breakdown of activity which has to be planned in order that it can fit into the

[15] Melville C. Branch, *Planning: Aspects and Applications*, John Wiley & Sons, Inc., New York, 1966, pp. 10–11.
[16] For example, see Alfred J. Kahn, *Theory and Practice of Social Planning*, Russell Sage Foundation, New York, 1969.

overall system. Goals call for master plans, which in turn foster subplans, and so on down to very detailed operating levels where procedures are spelled out on a step-by-step basis.

Managers at all levels of the organization are engaged in all the basic functions of the management process. As the manager moves up the organizational hierarchy from operating toward strategic levels, however, he is likely to spend relatively more of his time planning than implementing. Moreover, at the top level there is also a gradation of the amount of time spent on planning for varying time periods in the future. The top executive not only devotes most of his time to planning but must recognize the necessity for long-range planning. Management at the strategic level defines the desired role of the organization in the future, relates the organization to its various environmental systems, and perceives the niche which the organization can fulfill.

This does not mean that top executives can plan in a vacuum. Rather, they should develop these long-range plans with the full participation of those organizational members who have information inputs vital to the decision process. Effective planning is not the exclusive domain of a few top managers but requires the integration of inputs from all levels in the organization. Furthermore, there should be an awareness of the motivational impacts of participation, not only in the actual planning process but also in the implementation of plans. With expanded requirements for innovation, creativity, and flexibility within modern organizations and with increased employment of highly educated participants, it is imperative for management to develop effective means of integrating this knowledge into the planning function.

Flexibility

One of the major considerations in planning is the degree of rigidity or flexibility of plans. This dimension was introduced in our discussion of long-range planning (time span). One of the major mistakes in long-range planning is to assume future certainty in the face of a turbulent environment. This leads to great rigidities in plans and limits adaptiveness. This is a *Cook's-tour planning approach*[17] and assumes that the future is sufficiently certain so that we can move in an exact straight line from here to there (see Figure 17.2). Cook's-tour planning requires substantial precision and is most appropriate where the planner is facing a relatively certain environment.

In contrast, the *Lewis-and-Clark planning approach* acknowledges that in the future there will be many decision points and alternative courses of action. [18] From the present viewpoint it is impossible to determine their location or timing. In this approach it is not the function of planning to chart a precise course of action. Rather, it is to prepare the organization to cope with the uncertainties of the future, to note the signs in the environment which indicate that a point of decision has been reached, and to develop a means of responding.

---

[17] Cook's World Travel Service is one of the oldest and largest travel agencies. It was one of the originators of thoroughly planned travel tours with clearly prescribed itineraries and detailed schedules.
[18] These two approaches are discussed in detail in James R. Schlesinger, *Organizational Structure and Planning,* The Rand Corporation, Santa Monica, Calif., 1966.

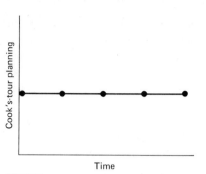
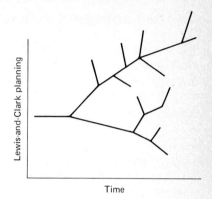

FIGURE 17.2   TWO APPROACHES PLANNING

The Lewis-and-Clark planning approach is similar to that suggested by Colm for governmental planning:

> It is important to recognize that planning means more than merely preparing a plan—it should be understood as a system of decision-making. Government decisions, in part, are always concerned with factors which are outside government control, such as foreign markets, foreign capital, the response of people to government measures, the weather, etc. Estimates can be made concerning these factors, but they are subject to a high degree of error. Consequently, planning is decision-making under conditions of uncertainty which requires a mechanism for adapting the plan to unexpected developments. Under conditions of uncertainty a plan is always tentative and subject to revision in the course of its execution and in the preparation of a subsequent plan. [19]

For the manager it would seem that whenever uncertainties in the internal subsystems and in the environment are substantial, planning should shift toward the Lewis-and-Clark approach. However, it often goes "against the grain" of the more bureaucratic, stable organization because it substitutes flexibility for fixity and false exactness. There are many organizational pressures to establish long-range plans in a highly specific and exact fashion. This gives the appearance of planning perfection but with the high cost of inflexibility and the likelihood of future events completely destroying the established plans.

The organization may have to compromise on the rigidity-versus-flexibility dimension. It will generally accomplish this by developing relatively fixed short-term operational plans under the general umbrella of more flexible, longer-range, strategic plans.

---

[19] Gerhard Colm, *Integration of National Planning and Budgeting,* National Planning Association, Washington, D.C., 1968, p. 3.

SYSTEMS CONCEPTS AND PLANNING

The systems approach stresses the complexity of sociotechnical systems and the importance of planning as a means of coping with the environment. Organizations are changing constantly, with dynamic equilibrium as one goal. They contain many diverse subunits which are themselves complex suprasystems. In addition, there are many overlapping systems which transcend hierarchical relationships. Many components are imperfectly coordinated, partially autonomous, and only partially controllable. There is much uncertainty; some variables probably are not identified; and others that are identified are not clearly defined. Organizations are subject to considerable uncertainty with respect to current information, future environmental conditions, and the consequences of their own action.

Recognition of the complexity surrounding most man-resource systems is a step in the right direction. Systems concepts provide a frame of reference which can be useful in thinking about the job of managing in such an environment. Information-decision systems provide the means for carrying out the management task. Planning is a key phase because it initiates behavior. Management is a continuing and sequential process of planning and implementing plans.

Means for Systems Change

Planning has been defined as "intelligent cooperation with the inevitable." If behavior were to be described along a continuum such as routine-adaptive-innovative, this approach would fall somewhere in the middle of the spectrum. It connotes a dynamic rather than static approach to coping with the environment. Maintaining a dynamic equilibrium, either individually or organizationally, calls for adaptive behavior at the least. Organisms and organizations require means for *both* maintenance and adaptation in order to remain viable systems. Control emphasizes maintenance; planning emphasizes adaptation. Completely routine approaches or static behavior in the dynamic environment of most organizations would be detrimental and maybe suicidal. Hopefully, planning provides a means for moving further toward the innovative end of the spectrum. It allows individuals or organizations to shape their own environment to some extent.

In a dynamic society, the major way in which organizations, as subsystems of the total system, adapt to changing requirements is through planning. The planning process can be considered as a means for accomplishing system change. This distinguishes the social organization from other open systems. In other types of open systems change occurs when environmental forces demand that a new equilibrium be established. In the organization these changes are dependent upon human decision processes. This differentiates social systems such as business organizations from the inanimate, physical open systems, where the equilibrium adjustments can be described as automatic reaction to change. For the social system the only vehicle for change (adaptation or innovation) is the human planning and decision-making process.

Galbraith suggests that planning has become a vital function of business, both as a method of adapting to market forces and as a means of shaping the market and the total environment. "Market behavior must be modified by some measure of planning." [20] No longer can the enterprise merely adapt to the demands of the marketplace; it must anticipate and modify the future environment in order to survive. Other institutions, such as universities and hospitals, also are actively engaged in comprehensive organizational planning. In the past these institutions have adapted primarily to forces in the society rather than engaging in comprehensive planning which would help shape the environment and the institution's responses to it. Many public universities which have grown to tremendous size and complexity are attempting to determine their social objectives more rationally and to plan more comprehensively for efficient utilization of resources.

Creativity in Planning

Innovation and creativity are key elements in effective planning. There has been increasing interest in the study of individual and organizational creativity as this characteristic has become more critical. Creativity is the recognition, development, proposal, and implementation of new and more effective solutions to problems. It is a new, adaptive response of a system in its environment. Creativity in organizations is dependent upon: the creative capacity of individual participants; the environment for creativity structured by the organization; and the interactions between the creative individual and the organizational system.

A great deal of interest and research has centered on the creative individual. [21] Numerous studies suggest that there are certain personal characteristics which correlate with creativity. The creative individual tends to show a preference for symbolic and ideational activities and places a higher value upon intellectual interests than upon social interaction. He is more likely to view authority relationships as flexible rather than absolute, to have a less dogmatic and a more relativistic view of things, to show independent judgment and less conformity, and in general to be less controlled in his activities.

Organizational relationships are also significant for creativity. There is evidence that the highly structured and hierarchical form of the bureaucratic organization is not conducive to creative planning. While the large, modern bureaucratic organization is usually efficient in production, it may limit innovation. "The bureaucratic orientation is conservative. Novel solutions, using resources in a new way, are likely to appear threatening. Those having a bureaucratic orientation are more concerned with the internal distribution of power and status than with organizational goal accomplishment." [22]

---

[20] John Kenneth Galbraith, *The New Industrial State,* Houghton Mifflin Company, Boston, 1967, p. 25.
[21] For a review of current concepts on individual creativity, see Paul E. Meehl, "The Creative Individual: Why It Is Hard to Identify Him," in Gary A. Steiner (ed.), *The Creative Organization,* The University of Chicago Press, Chicago, 1965, pp. 25–34.
[22] Victor A. Thompson, "Bureaucracy and Innovation," *Administrative Science Quarterly,* June 1965, p. 7.

Creativity and innovation are not isolated, individual characteristics that can be purchased in the marketplace; they are dependent upon the organizational environment. There is strong evidence to suggest that creativity and innovation in planning are enhanced by an organizational system which allows for diversity of ideas and inputs and does not attempt to structure human behavior totally. [23] Yet, if organizational planning is to be effective, it must operate within an established system of individual and organizational relationships. Awareness of the total system, including the subsystems of individuals and small groups, will help in providing a creative and innovative organization. [24]

STEPS IN THE PLANNING PROCESS

A plan can be thought of as an inventory of decisions for the future. They may be explicit in terms of particular courses of action which will be taken, given certain conditions in the environment, or in terms of the occurrence of particular events. In contrast, a plan may also involve certain propensities to behave in a particular manner. Plans provide a means for both individuals and organizations to come to grips with the future and establish definite courses of action or at least intentions. A logical approach to business planning would include the following steps:

1 Appraising the future political, economic, competitive, and technological environment
2 Assessing the long-run values, interests, and aspirations of managers and other participants
3 Visualizing the desired socioeconomic role of the organization in its future environment
4 Analyzing the organization's resources and capabilities for fulfilling this desired role
5 Designing a corporate strategy which matches the future environmental opportunity, values and aspirations, desired socioeconomic role, and organizational resources
6 Developing specific objectives and strategic plans which will direct the efforts of the total organization
7 Translating comprehensive plans into functional efforts on a more detailed basis—research, design and development, production, distribution, and service
8 Developing more detailed planning and control of resource utilization within each of these functional areas—always related to the overall planning effort

[23] This view is expressed by Harold Guetzkow, ''The Creative Person in Organization,'' in Gary A. Steiner, op. cit., pp. 36-45.
[24] Ibid., pp. 25-26.

9 Providing a system of communication and information flow whereby organizational members can participate in planning processes

10 Designing an information feedback and control system to determine the progress and problems in the implementation of plans

This approach, developed and understood throughout the organization, provides an integrated decision system. Such a framework can be used to focus the efforts of the entire organization toward a common set of goals. Furthermore, if the underlying expectations and planning premises are set forth explicitly, all departments can carry out their planning functions within the same guidelines. Major decisions can be evaluated in the light of the comprehensive plan to determine whether a particular course of action would carry the organization toward or away from its desired future position. In this way the planning process tends to facilitate the integration of all segments of the organization.

A well-documented example of the steps in the planning process and the integration of diverse efforts is illustrated by the Allied invasion of Europe during World War II. First the overall goal of the invasion was established. This led to a whole series of secondary requirements—for example, weather conditions, the number and type of men needed, and the necessary materials. These were translated into more detailed plans which were further translated throughout the military hierarchy down to the most detailed planning at the lowest operating level. [25] This entire planning process was complicated by the requirement of secrecy for the entire operation.

The same process is evident in a more current national effort, the National Aeronautics and Space Administration (NASA) program leading to man's exploration of the moon. In May, 1961, President Kennedy set forth the broad national objective as follows: ''I believe that this Nation should commit itself to achieving the goal, before this decade is out, of landing a man on the moon and returning him safely to earth.'' [26] With this broad objective as a guideline, the Office of Manned Space Flight was established within NASA with prime responsibility for the manned lunar landing. [27] Three major projects were established under the Manned Space Flight Program—Mercury, Gemini, and Apollo. They constitute a step-by-step approach to develop a broad capacity for manned exploration of space. Given the broad goal, planning for each of these projects was initiated and integrated into the complete program.

Operating under the premise of this broad strategic decision, it was necessary to develop increasingly detailed plans to meet specific requirements. For example, for each launch of an orbiting, manned vehicle, it was necessary to develop numerous detailed plans for launching, tracing, communications, and recovery—the safety of the

---

[25] Dwight D. Eisenhower, *Crusade in Europe,* Doubleday & Company, Inc., Garden City, N.Y., 1948.

[26] *Urgent National Needs,* Address of the President of the United States, H. Doc. 174, 87th Cong., 1st Sess., 1961, p. 11.

[27] For a discussion of this organization and its responsibilities, see D. Brainerd Holmes, ''NASA Programs Leading to Exploration of the Moon,'' in Fremont E. Kast and James E. Rosenzweig (eds.), *Science, Technology, and Management,* McGraw-Hill Book Company, New York, 1963, pp. 238-247.

astronauts being always a prime consideration. This illustrates the importance of effective information flow in a total planning system. The specific and detailed information about how the astronauts perform in space is important feedback which affects planning for the next phases in the program.

The success of the Apollo program—from the first manned lunar landing in August 1969 (No. 11) through the final mission in December 1972 (No. 17)—was a tribute to man's scientific and technological achievements as well as to his ability to plan and implement a tremendously complex program.

WHO DOES THE PLANNING?

In organizations, planning is one of the major functions of line managers. However, with the growing need for investigation, analysis, and evaluation, planning has frequently become a specialized activity. In many cases a specialized staff is set up to aid in the planning function. This is particularly true in the area of long-range planning where devotees have taken on the aura of a cult. Those engaged in long-range planning may tend to overemphasize its importance and the role of their subgroup in overall organizational activity.

If planning specialists emphasize generalized approaches or techniques, the organization's particular (maybe even unique) situation may not be recognized. The manager should be directly involved in order to provide his perception of the environment and the organization's special niche in it. St. Thomas suggests:

> The manager who successfully undertakes his planning work must begin by recognizing that the primary key to his effectiveness lies in his capability to adapt. His fundamental challenge is to learn to adapt the knowledge and methods of business planning to *his* company, *his* markets, and *his* products, and to do this in a way that will enable *his* planning to be effective with *his* people.
>
> To put this another way, it is doubtful that any two managers or any two businesses can ever do their planning in exactly the same manner. There are too many variables to contend with. The effective manager must therefore first identify those variables at play in *his* situation and then undertake his planning responsibilities with these in mind. [28]

All too frequently, a staff group assumes that its role is planning rather than facilitating the planning activities of line management. Left to its own discretion this staff proceeds to set goals and develop plans according to its own conception and premises, often developing elaborate research reports to substantiate its positions.

---

[28] Reprinted by permission of the publisher from *Practical Business Planning,* by Charles E. St. Thomas, pp. 9–10. © 1965 by the American Management Association, Inc., New York.

Meanwhile "back at the ranch," line managers are proceeding to develop their own planning premises, possibly in the executive dining room. Unless there is considerable dialogue and mutual understanding between specialized staff personnel and operating managers, a gap may develop which is dysfunctional for the organization.

The "planning gap" is a divergence in the expectations, premises, objectives, and basic concepts which exists between various units and individuals within organizations, thus preventing the establishment of an effective, well-defined framework for integrated decision making. The gap we are primarily concerned with in this instance is between operating management and a specialized planning staff. This relationship problem is similar to that between managers and management scientists or managers and systems designers. Specialized staff activities must be carried out in relation to the real world as conceived by operating management. Certainly, sophisticated tools and techniques and refined information inputs can lead to adjustments in the manager's perception of the organization and its role in its environment. Staff personnel should push for adaptations and innovations. On the other hand, they should be cognizant of all the factors involved and should be in tune with the value system of operating management. The staff activity should be an extension of operating management. Line managers should be encouraged to participate actively and continually in the planning function. They should be encouraged to consider relatively longer time factors as they move upward in the organizational hierarchy. Similarly they must be concerned with more comprehensive plans and begin to comprehend combinations of subsystems.

In large-scale organizations with many-leveled departmentation, diverse subobjectives, and organizational and human limits on rationality, it is improbable that the planning gap can be completely eliminated. To do so would be to assume complete knowledge, absolute predictability, perfect communication, and full agreement throughout the organization. These assumptions are too much to ask for. However, the gap can be minimized if specialized staff work is conceived as an extension of the manager's planning function. Continuing dialogue can help to establish a common set of premises to be used throughout the organization.

INTEGRATION OF PLANNING AND CONTROL

Planning and control are typically separated for purposes of discussion. Managers, too, often think of these functions as distinct tasks. In both cases this is a useful approach because it allows concentrated attention and/or detailed examination. On the other hand, these phases of managerial task are not completely separable in practice. Therefore, before citing specific examples of planning, we think it will be useful to consider how these two functions are related.

A complete operating cycle for any individual or organization would include the following phases:

1 Objective setting
2 Planning

3 Action
4 Accomplishment
5 Feedback
6 Control

This is a generalized model which can be applied at any level. It does not specify the technology employed in carrying out the designated activities. Feedback may be relatively automatic and computer based, or it may depend on the subjective appraisal of human beings. Planning and control are integral phases of the overall cycle; in a sequential process their interdependence is evident. They can only be separated conceptually.

Anthony presents a meaningful approach which identifies two different types of control activity—management control and operational control. He distinguishes these from strategic planning and uses all three as a framework for planning and control systems. He defines the concepts as follows:

> *Strategic planning* is the process of deciding on objectives of the organization, on changes in these objectives, on the resources used to attain these objectives, and on the policies that are to govern the acquisition, use, and disposition of these resources. . . .

> *Management control* is the process by which managers assure that resources are obtained and used effectively and efficiently in the accomplishment of the organization's objectives. . . .

> *Operational control* is the process of assuring that specific tasks are carried out effectively and efficiently. [29]

In general, these categories coincide with the three subsystems or levels—strategic, coordinative, and operating—which have been cited previously as part of any organization. At the *strategic level* managers engage primarily in *strategic planning*—functioning at the boundary to relate the organization to its environment. There is a relatively long-run outlook, and forecasting is used to reduce uncertainty. Strategic decision making is primarily judgmental as managers attempt to negotiate a niche in the environment and maintain a posture of opportunistic surveillance. At the *operating level* the system requires relatively more control than planning. Managers are concerned with day-to-day *operational control*—meeting short-run objectives in situations where performance can be evaluated in terms of both effectiveness and efficiency. At the *coordinative level* the terms mediation, compromise, and coordination are paramount. *Management control* involves integrating the long and short run by designing the means of

---

[29] Robert N. Anthony, *Planning and Control Systems: A Framework for Analysis,* Division of Research, Harvard Graduate School of Business Administration, Boston, 1965, pp. 16, 17, 18.

FIGURE 17.3 EXAMPLES OF ACTIVITIES IN A BUSINESS ORGANIZATION INCLUDED IN MAJOR FRAMEWORK HEADINGS

STRATEGIC PLANNING	MANAGEMENT CONTROL	OPERATIONAL CONTROL
Choosing company objectives	Formulating budgets	
Planning the organization	Planning staff levels	Controlling hiring
Setting personnel policies	Formulating personnel practices	Implementing policies
Setting financial policies	Working capital planning	Controlling credit extension
Setting marketing policies	Formulating advertising programs	Controlling placement of advertisements
Setting research policies	Deciding on research projects	
Choosing new product lines	Choosing product improvements	
Acquiring a new division	Deciding on plant rearrangement	Scheduling production
Deciding on non-routine capital expenditures	Deciding on routine capital expenditures	
	Formulating decision rules for operational control	Controlling inventory
	Measuring, appraising, and improving management performance	Measuring, appraising, and improving workers' efficiency

SOURCE: Robert N. Anthony, *Planning and Control Systems: A Framework for Analysis,* Division of Research, Harvard Graduate School of Business Administration, Boston, 1965, p. 19.

implementing strategic planning. Decision rules based on objectives and policies are formulated to serve as guidelines for operational control.

As a means of illustrating the main categories in his framework, Anthony sets forth examples of activities in a business organization which might be included under the headings described above. These activities are shown in Figure 17.3. The difficulty in separating planning and controlling is evidenced in the listing. Most of the activities under strategic planning are in fact planning activities. Management control, on the other hand, involves a mixture of both planning and control activities, and those listed under operational control are almost entirely control activities. "In operational control, the focus is on execution; in management control it is on both planning and execution." [30]

This framework is an alternative view to the hierarchy of planning and the identification of control as a separate activity. Strategic planning relates primarily to setting goals and identifying key elements in master or comprehensive plans. Little control is implied. However, as indicated in Figure 17.3, the control process involves some general overall appraisal of organizational performance which is the culmination of specific control activities over a period of time. Therefore some higher-level control, possible quite subjective, would be invoked in evaluating whether or not the organiza-

---

[30] Ibid., p. 18.

tion has "developed" according to plan. Similarly, top management would be evaluating whether or not new product lines, just introduced, were in fact the most appropriate for the market at a particular point in time.

Strategic planning provides a framework within which management control is carried out. Master plans provide a framework for more detailed plans which might take the form of a sales budget. This, in turn, sets up a framework for plans with regard to hiring salesmen, advertising, and sales promotion.

Management control implies some freedom or discretion in setting intermediate objectives and in planning how the work is to be carried out. Operational control, on the other hand, implies given objectives and in many cases standard operating procedures. This sort of framework provides a very definite yardstick for control; the process can be controlled in terms of the detailed steps previously outlined, and performance in terms of units produced or degree of quality can be evaluated quite readily. Both effectiveness and efficiency are of concern at this detailed level.

EXAMPLES OF PLANNING

Managerial planning is carried out in many ways. In this section we will look at several examples in order to better understand the concepts and processes involved. Diversification planning has become a "way of life" for many so-called "conglomerate" companies. Network analysis or critical path method has evolved as an essential planning tool for complex projects of many types. Interactive, online planning via computer simulation provides managers with a powerful means of analysis and synthesis.

Diversification Planning

In a dynamic economy, product-line determination is one of the major planning areas because the successful company must adapt continually to changing product-mission requirements.[31] Examples of this need are seen in a variety of industries—automobile companies in expanding their product lines, or aircraft companies in determining whether or not to move into the fields of propulsion and/or electronics. For some companies the product line may range from atomic submarines to sand and gravel. Extreme diversity puts special strains on the management system; therefore, careful consideration should be given to new lines of endeavor. The opportunities must be attractive enough to outweigh the problems of complexity for managerial planning. Some companies appear to thrive on such complexity; indeed, diversification seems to be a goal in itself.

Diversification planning is not confined to business enterprise. Government agencies—federal, state, and local—should continually reappraise their services in order to ascertain what changes or additions might be in order. The Peace Corps, for example,

---

[31] For a detailed discussion of diversification planning utilizing systems concepts, see George A. Steiner, "Why and How to Diversify," *California Management Review*, Summer 1964, pp. 11–18.

might change its program mix in the light of feedback concerning performance in relation to its identified mission.

Network Analysis

Network analysis is a technique which is particularly useful in planning and controlling large, complex projects. Network analysis can be considered a refinement of earlier approaches (Gantt charts, for example) to identifying the relationship between the subparts of a project via time as the common denominator. The critical path method (CPM) has been used for many years in the construction industry primarily. Another specific example of network analysis is PERT (performance evaluation and review technique), which was first used in complex weapon system planning. Subsequently PERT and its refinements have found widespread use in government and industry.

Network analysis is a useful tool in systems design because it assists the analyst in recognizing and identifying the relationships which exist among the subsystems. First, each separate segment, or link, of the system is described in terms of other components or activities of the system. This makes explicit the total system and the interrelationships among the parts. The network may be illustrated by a flow chart or diagram. The flow of materials and/or information is measured in terms of volume, specifications, or time. The visual representation of the system achieves a comprehensive description and therefore outlines the task to be accomplished. This technique allows the manager to reappraise existing systems and identify examples of duplication and overlap which may detract from the system's efficiency. Further, it helps management evaluate the subsystems and their interconnecting networks continuously, consistent with the overall objectives of the system.

Continuous reevaluation of the system is necessary and feasible through network analysis. The purpose of a system changes; different outputs are specified; and different inputs are required. It is important that subsystems be adjusted to these changes and that the total systems be revised accordingly. Network analysis fosters this type of approach by representing the entire system visually. It also allows an evaluation of the impact of various subsystem changes on other subsystems and/or the total system. A change in type of output or a change in scheduling in a particular subsystem can affect operations in other areas. The effect can be determined in units of time, money, facilities, or other resources.

By laying out the network of jobs the manager can obtain an explicit visual representation of the relationship between all the tasks involved. [32] For example, in the construction of a house, it is evident that the rough wiring, heating, and plumbing must be accomplished before the project can move into the plastering stage. Obviously, for simple projects, the manager, assuming a reasonable amount of experience, could

---

[32] For detailed consideration of the mechanics of network model building, see Richard A. Johnson, Fremont E. Kast, and James E. Rosenzweig, *The Theory and Management of Systems,* 3d ed., McGraw-Hill Book Company, New York, 1973, pp. 244–267.

keep a model tucked away in his mind and probably operate quite successfully. On the other hand, if he were in charge of the Apollo project instead of building a house, the mental model probably would not suffice. For large-scale, complex projects an explicit network is extremely useful, if not absolutely necessary.

Interactive, Online Planning

Computer simulation of large-scale, complex systems has provided managers with a powerful tool for analysis and synthesis. [33] The model development process requires explicit consideration of important variables and their interrelationships. Factors such as the flow of money, raw materials, and personnel, as well as facilities utilization, can be tied together in systems of simplified algebraic equations. Any tangible organizational interrelationship can be modeled and simulated. Working toward a system of equations that represents the system realistically helps the manager increase his understanding of the operation.

Moreover, simulation models provide an opportunity to anticipate the consequences of strategic decisions. They enrich the planning process by allowing the manager to ask "what if" questions and get probabilistic estimates of future conditions before committing resources to a new course of action. The manager is involved in the planning loop; his judgment is required in deciding what alternatives to test, in interpreting the results of the simulation, and in selecting a particular course of action.

Of particular importance in this approach to planning is the integration of the cognitive complexity and flexibility of the human decision maker with the speed and precision of the computer. Instant modeling and time-shared computing facilities provide an opportunity for the manager to interact in a nearly conversational mode with the computer. [34] By using both the manager and the computer according to their respective special capabilities, the planning process can be improved through effective interaction. Fast, accurate computer analysis of detailed operational planning can be used as input to the comprehensive, strategic planning of top management. Many combinations of interesting possibilities can be considered by means of computer simulation.

Freeing top managers from the detailed analysis and calculation involved in operational planning enables them to concentrate their energy on the creation of more innovative strategic alternatives. "Thus, the availability of analyzed information, combined with concentration on the abstract features of the planning and deep interest resulting from the fascination of having an online computer servant may provide the necessary catalysts for creative insights and intuition." [35]

---

[33] For descriptions of a variety of simulation models useful in the planning process see Albert N. Schrieber (ed.), *Corporate Simulation Models,* Graduate School of Business Administration, University of Washington, Seattle, Wash., 1970. See also Jay W. Forrester, *Industrial Dynamics,* John Wiley & Sons, Inc., New York, and The M.I.T. Press, Cambridge, Mass., 1961; *Urban Dynamics,* The M.I.T. Press, Cambridge, Mass., 1969; and *World Dynamics,* Wright-Allen Press, Inc., Cambridge, Mass., 1971.
[34] James B. Bolden, "Instant Modeling," in Albert N. Schrieber (ed.), op. cit., pp. 578–599.
[35] H. Kleine and R. L. Citrenbaum, "Interactive Management Planning," in Harold Sackman and Ronald L. Citrenbaum (eds.), *Online Planning,* Prentice-Hall, Inc., Englewood Cliffs, N.J., 1972, p. 260.

SUMMARY

A plan is a predetermined course of action. Comprehensive plans, established at the strategic level, provide a framework for decision making at lower levels in the organization or in subsystems of overall operations. Managerial planning provides a framework for integrated decision making across a spectrum of diverse activities and over a relatively long period of time. It is a means of coping with the uncertainty of the future; it facilitates adaptation and innovation.

Long-range plans provide the framework within which medium- and short-range plans are established. As an organization moves through time, adjustments are made in order to maintain a dynamic equilibrium with the environment. There is a constant cycle of planning and implementation with continual review of performance which becomes part of the information-decision system for managerial planning.

Plans for nonrepetitive problems (single-use plans) set forth a course of action to fit a specific situation and may be obsolete when the goal is reached. This is in contrast with standing plans, which are designed to have continuing usefulness and provide the basic means for integrating organizational processes throughout the entire system. Comprehensive planning is complex because it involves the consideration of all internal and external environmental variables. Planning at the top level provides guidelines for the next level, and so forth, down through the organization.

Systems concepts provide a framework within which planning activity can be carried out. Planning requires consideration of the enterprise as an integration of numerous decision-making subsystems. The amount of time spent on planning typically increases as a manager moves upward in the organizational hierarchy. At the very top level more time is spent on planning than on any other phase of the managerial process. Because of the magnitude and complexity of the task, specialized staff groups have been established to aid in carrying out the planning function. Line managers must be deeply involved in the planning process, however, in order to keep abreast of dynamic situations.

While planning and control are often separated conceptually for discussion purposes, it is important to recognize that they are inseparable in practice. At the strategic level managers engage primarily in strategic planning—functioning at the boundary to relate the organization to its environment. There is a relatively long-run outlook, and forecasting is used to reduce uncertainty. Strategic decision making is primarily judgmental as managers attempt to negotiate a niche in the environment and maintain a posture of opportunistic surveillance. At the operating level the system requires relatively more control than planning. Managers are concerned with day-to-day operational control—meeting short-run objectives in situations where performance can be evaluated in terms of both effectiveness and efficiency. Management control involves integrating long- and short-run goals by implementing strategic planning. Decision rules, based on objectives and policies, are formulated to serve as guidelines for operational control.

QUESTIONS AND PROBLEMS

1 Define planning. How does it relate to (*a*) forecasting and (*b*) decision making?

2 What factors have increased the importance of planning:

   a In a large business organization

   b In a large community general hospital

   c In a university

   d In the Department of Defense

3 How do multiple goals affect the process of setting objectives? When is vagueness of organizational objectives a virtue?

4 Discuss the various dimensions of planning, and relate them to the plans in an organization with which you are familiar.

5 How can systems concepts facilitate managerial planning?

6 "The planning process is the means of accomplishing system change." Do you agree? Why or why not ?

7 How can management foster creativity and innovation in planning?

8 What recommendations do you have for minimizing the planning gap?

9 How are planning and control related in the overall operational cycle of an organization?

10 Relate Anthony's planning and control system to the three organizational subsystems or levels—strategic, coordinative, and operating.

11 Apply the network analysis concept in planning a project in which you are involved. Identify the critical path.

ORGANIZATIONAL CONTROL

Management involves coordinating men and material resources toward objective accomplishment by means of an information-decision system. The managerial process includes planning, organizing, and controlling. The control function monitors the system, "keeps things in line," and facilitates the integration of activities. Organizational control is inextricably intertwined with planning. Planning provides a framework against which the control process works. On the other hand, feedback from the control phase often identifies the need for new plans or at least adjustments to existing ones. Typically, individual and organizational behavior involves a continuing sequence of planning-implementing-controlling cycles. The following topics will be considered in our discussion of organizational control:

> Control Defined
> Elements of Control
> Control Process
> Closed- and Open-Loop Control
> The Time Dimension
> Social System Control
> Indirect Control
> Examples of Control
> The Economics of Control

CONTROL DEFINED

The concept of control can be quite general and can be used as a focal point for the managerial system. For example, planning can be thought of as a means to allow control of individual or organizational behavior. Similarly, the task of organizing can be construed as providing a means of controlling activities. In short, the theory of control can be quite pervasive. According to Bellman:

> Control theory, like many other broad theories, is more a state of mind than any specific amalgam of mathematical, scientific or technological methods. The term can be defined to include any rational approach used by men to overcome the perversities of either their natural or their technological environment. The broad objective of a control theory is to make a system—any kind of system—operate in a more desirable way: to make it more reliable, more convenient or more economical. [1]

The word "control" has several meanings and, more specifically, several connotations which are meaningful to the discussion in this chapter. For example, it means:

1 to check or verify,
2 to regulate,
3 to compare with a standard,
4 to exercise authority over (direct or command), or
5 to curb or restrain. [2]

At least three relatively distinct lines of thought are apparent in this definition— (1) curbing or restraining, (2) directing or commanding, and (3) checking or verifying. All are significant for organization theory and management practice. However, we are primarily concerned with the third connotation of control.

Checking or verifying implies some means of measurement and some standard which can serve as a frame of reference in the control process. The planning function typically provides the necessary yardstick—hopefully explicitly but, if not, at least implicitly. Litterer describes the checking or measuring approach to control as "matching" behavior.

> We are concerned with control in relation to matching performance with necessary or required conditions to obtain a purpose or objective. The essence here is on directivity and integration of effort, required accomplishment of an end. . . . Control and coordination are closely related. . . .
>
> Control is concerned not only with the events directly related to the accomplishment of major purposes, but also with maintaining the organization in a condition in which it can function adequately to achieve these major purposes. [3]

---

[1] Richard Bellman, "Control Theory," *Scientific American,* September 1964, p. 186.
[2] *Webster's New World Dictionary,* 2d College Edition, The World Publishing Company, Cleveland, 1970, p. 309.
[3] Joseph A. Litterer, *The Analysis of Organizations,* John Wiley & Sons, Inc., New York, 1965, p. 233.

Several ideas are important here. Control is an important means of coordinating diverse activity toward objective accomplishment. The control function regulates system output by measuring actual with expected performance. The control function is also concerned with means as well as ends. Continual feedback concerning how organizational activity is carried out is important for long-run stability. Both effectiveness and efficiency are important. That is, we are concerned with whether the system works at all—output; and with how well resources are employed—input utilization.

The control function can be defined as that phase of the managerial process which maintains organization activity within allowable limits as measured from expectations. These expectations may be implicit or explicitly stated in terms of objectives, plans, procedures, or rules and regulations. Just as there is a hierarchy of plans on a continuum of comprehensiveness, there are comparable control procedures appropriate at different levels.

Homeostasis and Dynamic Equilibrium

The self-regulating or control property of a living process is homeostasis. Provided that the stimulus is not too great, when an organism is disturbed from its "normal" state, it tends to return to it. The organism has built-in control mechanisms which maintain a dynamic equilibrium throughout its life cycle. Many of the self-regulating processes of an organism such as the human being are highly programmed and operate without conscious intervention of the individual. During strenuous exercise, for example, breathing becomes more rapid and pulse quickens in order to deliver more oxygen via the blood stream to muscles throughout the body. Other self-regulating processes require overt decision-making behavior on the part of the individual. In other words, he consciously provides closure in the feedback system which regulates behavior.

For organizations the analogy is not precise; however, the concept of homeostasis is still useful. Organizations have relatively programmed behavior patterns—standard operating procedures—which provide stability over time (maintenance systems). On the other hand, there are processes for making innovative decisions (adaptive systems) which move the organization along its life cycle in response to external and internal stimuli. There is a continuum of programmable control processes, from the relatively mechanistic to those where conscious and deliberate action is required on the part of human decision makers.

Organisms and organizations are not static; they change and adjust over time— while exhibiting goal-oriented behavior. The process can best be described as a dynamic equilibrium.

Cybernetics

Cybernetics is another important concept for the control function. The word stems from the Greek *kybernetes,* or helmsman, and thus relates to the connotation "direction of." Cybernetics involves communication and control. [4] It is concerned with information flow

---

[4] Norbert Wiener, *The Human Use of Human Beings,* rev. ed., Houghton Mifflin Company, Boston, 1954, p. 16.

in complex systems. Although cybernetics has been applied primarily to mechanistic engineering problems, its model of feedback, control, and regulation has significance for biological and social systems as well. The example of the helmsman illustrates the most important and useful connotation of the control function—maintaining a course toward a goal.

Feedback

Feedback is an essential ingredient in any control process. It provides the information for decisions which adjust the system over time. A plan provides the framework for integrated decision making over time. As plans are implemented, the system is tracked or monitored in order to ascertain whether or not performance is on target and whether objectives are being met. Feedback is usually obtained with reference to both the ends sought and the means designed to achieve them. In relatively closed systems, feedback leads to automatic adjustments in the system. In relatively open systems, feedback is received by human beings who process it and decide on appropriate action. Many kinds of feedback systems can be designed to facilitate control. The manager may desire a continual flow of information to monitor the system. Or he may assume that "no news is good news" and hence require information on only the exceptional situations. The type and complexity of feedback required also depend on the interrelatedness of organizational subsystems.

> If the problem of coordination is trivial, control becomes a means of assuring subunit efficiency; if coordination is the overriding concern, control becomes the means for ensuring the collective contribution of organizational subunits. However, and perhaps generally, if neither the separable nor collective aspects of subunit activity can be taken for granted, the control function must be concerned with both and with the conflicts between them. [5]

Organizational control is that phase of the managerial decision system that monitors performance and provides feedback information which can be used in adjusting both ends and means. Given certain objectives and plans for achieving them, the control function involves measuring actual conditions, comparing them to standards, and initiating feedback which can be used to coordinate organizational activity, focus it in the right direction, and facilitate the achievement of a dynamic equilibrium.

ELEMENTS OF CONTROL

Regardless of the specific type of control in question, there are four fundamental elements common to all control systems (see Figure 18.1). These elements are involved in all organism and organization control systems. They hold true regardless of the

---

[5] John V. Baumler, "Defined Criteria of Performance in Organizational Control," *Administrative Science Quarterly*, September 1971, p. 340.

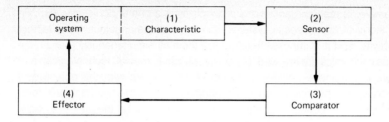

FIGURE 18.1   THE BASIC ELEMENTS OF A CONTROL SYSTEM: (1) a measurable and controllable characteristic for which standards are known; (2) a means (sensory device) of measuring the characteristic; (3) a means of comparing actual results to standards and evaluating differences; (4) a means of effecting changes in the system in order to adjust the pertinent characteristic.

degree of sophistication in the system. That is, they are not a function of mechanization or computerization. There is a continuum of refinement in control, from a simple on-off light switch (with a human decision maker involved) to an elaborate heating-cooling system where a computer program might respond not only to changes in the environment but to feedback on rates of change as well. Most sophisticated mechanical or electronic control systems are designed to simulate a human decision maker.

In general, control is maintained by means of decisions which are made as a part of the ongoing process. As for any decision-making process, information flow is the raw material or key ingredient. For example, knowing standards implies information about the system. Sensing or measuring also involves information which is used in the comparing phase. Information flow is the essence of the feedback which is necessary to change the system if need be. Its role in the control process is illustrated in Figure 14.6, which shows a typical business organization. In that model, the preeminence of planning and control is evident. The internal system involves feedback as a means of controlling current operations. Summary and exception reports provide control information for overall management planning. This type of internally generated information, coupled with that from the environment, provides the raw material for adaptive and innovative decisions which result in adjustments in objectives.

Control in Complex Social Systems

It is important to recognize that control systems typically focus on only one (or at most several) characteristic at a time. A thermostatically controlled home heating system concentrates on temperature and ignores humidity. Automatic street lights are often controlled by time rather than the degree of darkness. In complex social systems it is impossible to control behavior completely. Out of necessity, choosing characteristics to control becomes a sampling process. Considerable managerial skill is required to design a system which provides organizational control effectively and efficiently. Over-control may be both expensive (the time and effort involved) and dysfunctional. Picking the appropriate characteristic to monitor is extremely important because individual behavior and organizational performance will be "directed" accordingly.

For example, in many organizations productivity is a primary objective. As indicated in our study of psychosocial systems, this is a complex subject. Many factors affect productivity, and it is impossible to control them all simultaneously (see Figure 10.4). Two basic variables are involved: (1) ability (physical, mental, technological) and (2) motivation. If a manager installs a system of time clocks with the objective of improving productivity, he may be quite disappointed. Given the two basic variables involved, this approach—controlling the amount of time spent on the job—may have little effect. If the employees are not capable, rigorous adherence to a time schedule probably will not improve performance. Moreover, the installation of time clocks may be dysfunctional if employees resent the change and deliberately slow down.

Even more complex examples of the difficulty in designing control systems occur at the societal level. There has been continuing debate over which characteristic should be emphasized in a societal control system—law and order or justice. It is evident that "enforcing the law" and "ensuring justice" may be significantly different objectives. If so, the control systems designed for them should also differ. Strict enforcement of the law (a logical characteristic to be measured and controlled) often seems dysfunctional if a significant proportion of the population feels that it is unjust—*booze* in the 1920s and *pot* in the 1970s, for example. [6] Complex situations cannot be controlled with simplistic approaches.

Sophisticated systems have to be designed in order to monitor complex organizations effectively and efficiently. The key is in recognizing which characteristics are important and controllable. They should provide the basis for functional control systems.

CONTROL PROCESS

The fundamental elements in any control system become the control process when linked sequentially in a cycle. Figure 18.2 shows a general model of the control cycle. Objectives are established, programs planned, resources allocated, and work is performed. As actual performance is compared with the plan, feedback is generated to adjust work loads and the allocation of resources. This type of comparison relates primarily to the means used to accomplish objectives. Another comparison is made between actual achievements and the program originally planned. At this stage information is fed back to the program planning phase as well as forward to a comparison with the original goals. Finally, this comparison leads to a reaffirmation of existing objectives or adjustments for the future. As indicated in the model, this cycle can take place at any level. There is an interface with higher-level control at the step where objectives are determined. Also, there is an interface with lower-level control at the stage where work is performed by the system itself.

---

[6] The authors of a 623-page report based on a five-year study under the auspices of Consumers Union concluded that prohibition and scare publicity are countereffectual as deterrents and that many current antidrug laws that actually increase the use of drugs should be abandoned. Edward M. Brecher et al., *Licit and Illicit Drugs: The Consumers Union Report on Narcotics, Stimulants, Depressants, Inhalants, Hallucinogens, and Marijuana—Including Caffeine, Nicotine and Alcohol,* Little, Brown, & Co., Inc., Boston, Mass., 1972.

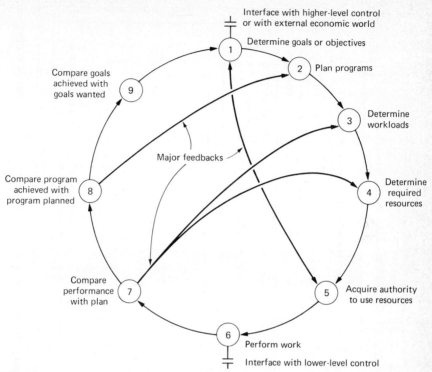

Interface with higher-level control
or with external economic world

Determine goals or objectives

1

2 Plan programs

Compare goals
achieved with
goals wanted
9

3 Determine
workloads

Major feedbacks

Compare program
achieved with
program planned
8

4 Determine
required
resources

Compare
performance
with plan
7

5 Acquire authority
to use resources

6

Perform work

Interface with lower-level control

FIGURE 18.2 THE CYCLE OF CONTROL (Marvin E. Mundel, *A Conceptual Framework for the Management Sciences,* McGraw-Hill Book Company, New York, 1967, p. 162)

Figure 18.3 is a general model of the control process, emphasizing the flow of activity and the interrelationships among the key elements, and is an elaboration of the simplified version set forth in Figure 18.2. The triangular performance center (1) represents some measurable and controllable characteristic in an operating system. It might refer to the quality or quantity of output, the efficiency of input utilization, employee morale, or an agreed upon method of striving for goal achievement. The second step (2) of the control process involves measuring the characteristic(s) in question. This could involve literal measurements with a micrometer or a subjective performance rating of a subordinate by a superior. The next step (3) involves comparing the actual results (as measured) with expected performance. Comparison suggests some explicit or, at least, implicit standards which can be used as a frame of reference. Steps (4), (5), and (6) show an elaboration of the decision-maker (effector) element of the control process. Several alternative courses of action are typically open, based on the results of the appraisal step. If there is no deviation or if performance exceeds expectation, there may be no adjustment to the system and the process loops back to the performance center for a subsequent measurement. Above-standard performance, however, may lead to adjustment in aspiration level and hence call for an upward adjustment in standards.

If a deviation is noted but a characteristic is uncontrollable, there would be no

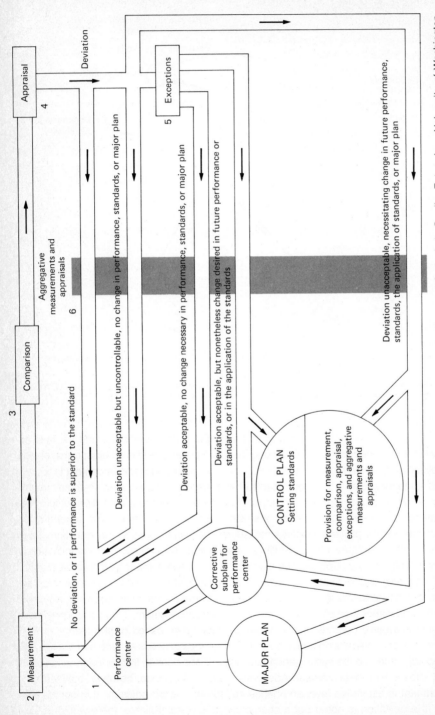

FIGURE 18.3 MODEL OF THE CONTROL PROCESS (Dale A. Henning, *Non-financial Controls in Smaller Enterprises*, University of Washington Bureau of Business Research, Seattle, 1964, p. 22)

change in performance, standards, or plans. Another case might involve recognition of a deviation of difference between actual and expected performance, but one which is not large enough to require a change to be effected.

Another possibility involves an acceptable deviation for the present, but recognition that some adjustment is necessary to keep the system "in control" in the future. Another alternative is a clearly unacceptable deviation which necessitates relatively immediate change in either the standards, procedures, or performance. Feedback in the latter two cases flows into the subsystem for setting standards (control plan) as well as to the major plan and corrective subplan for the performance center. Feedback may affect only the subsystem which includes the particular performance center. Or, on the other hand, it may involve changes which also affect the master or comprehensive plan to which the control process relates.

Item (6) cuts across all the appraisal alternatives and relates to some sort of aggregate or overall control process which relies on cumulative information to be used as raw material for decision making. Certain aspects may have a rather high threshold before the control process evokes significant adjustments in the system.

Just as the elements cited previously refer to any control system, the process described herein applies to any control system regardless of the degree of sophistication in the various steps outlined. The *means* employed to sense, compare, and effect may be highly programmed, mechanistic, and computerized. Or, subjective human beings may be involved in each step of the process. The inclusion of human decision makers in the process tends to make the control system relatively more open.

CLOSED- AND OPEN-LOOP CONTROL

The concept of closed- and open-loop control depends upon the presence or absence of automatic feedback. Closed-loop systems involve a sensor, a comparator, and an effector that allow for changes in the system on the basis of the control process which is operating simultaneously with the performance of the system itself. The classic thermostat example is a closed-loop system because feedback from the environment causes changes in system components to keep the system in balance. The closed loop does not involve information inputs from outside the system. However, the home heating system is closed only in the short run. Human intervention is involved to adjust the thermostat periodically according to a subjective impression of the environment. Thus the overall system is open, but we have closed-loop control once the thermostat is set.

Many organizational systems are of this same nature. They can be considered on a continuum from relatively closed to relatively open. In many cases mechanistic systems with closed loops allow the system to perform automatically over a long time. Many computer-based control systems are of such nature. However, these systems rely on programs designed by human beings, and the programs can be changed if need be. Thus, in the long run, highly automated systems are also open.

The inclusion of human decision makers in control systems as part of the feedback loop moves the systems toward the open end of the spectrum. The individual is subject to many external pressures and sources of information which work their way into his decision-making process. It is true, however, that decision makers can be trained to react on a somewhat programmed basis. Thus habits or standard operating procedures tend to close the system.

THE TIME DIMENSION

The time dimension is important to the control function in several ways. Organizations develop ex ante or precontrol by developing standing plans comprised of policies, procedures, and rules or regulations. The development of relatively uniform value systems among organization members provides valuable precontrol. Emphasis is on preventing the system from deviating too far from preconceived norms. Considerable organizational effort goes into maintaining the system within designated limits—preventing undesirable occurrences. Education of the citizenry with regard to traffic laws and the consequences of operating outside the law is an attempt at precontrol of driving behavior.

However, it is apparent that precontrol is often not sufficient to maintain systems within desirable limits. Therefore, considerable effort must also be devoted to postcontrol—ascertaining the results of behavior, evaluating it, and taking action which hopefully will correct or adjust behavior in future situations. For example, a flashing red light, siren, and $30 fine are a form of postcontrol designed to induce a particular driver to drive within the posted speed limit. In such a case, the precontrol effort of education and a set of rules did not prove effective. Therefore, postcontrol in the form of punitive action is invoked.

There is considerable disagreement concerning the relative weight which should be place on pre- and postcontrol. The most extreme position suggests that if enough effort is given to precontrol, there will be no need for postcontrol. [7] That is, if group value systems were internalized completely, all individual and organization actions would fall within desirable limits and the system would be self-regulating. So far, however, this appears to be a utopian concept, and considerable attention continues to be devoted to postcontrol. Many examples of postcontrol in organizations could be cited: reviewing profit performance as related to established goals, checking the reject or scrap rate at the end of the year, or checking a salesman's expense account at the end of the month. In each case the difference between actual and expected would be ascertained, and a decision would be made concerning the appropriate corrective action which, hopefully, would lead toward improved performance in the future.

If feasible, current or real-time control is more satisfactory from the standpoint of maintaining a dynamic equilibrium in organizations. It is often better to adjust behavior as it is happening rather than waiting until the results are in and then initiating corrective action or postcontrol. It is important to identify critical points for controlling operations.

---

[7] B. F. Skinner, *Beyond Freedom and Dignity*, Alfred A. Knopf, Inc., New York, 1971.

For example, the place to detect a flaw in the main landing-gear support is when the part itself is first cast or forged, not after the landing gear has been assembled and attached to the complete airplane.

Real-time control suggests that immediate feedback is important to the process. This is the theory behind teaching machines or programmed learning, where students are given feedback immediately with regard to the relationship between their response and the correct answer. The same theory has been used in designing incentive systems so that immediate feedback—either reward or punishment—is designed to enhance the probability of an appropriate response on the part of an employee (appropriate from the organization's point of view).

The concept of immediate feedback is important to the objective of maintaining a dynamic equilibrium. Adjusting minor deviations as they occur is usually easier than correcting wider deviations at some later point in time. Thus, the notion of current or real-time control is important in maintaining behavior within desired limits as the system moves through time. As measurements are made and comparisons drawn, a system can be adjusted before it deviates too far from preset standards. Immediate feedback allows the control process to keep abreast of current operations and helps the system "learn" to operate within the desired limits.

SOCIAL SYSTEM CONTROL

Increased pressure for social change during the 1960s and 1970s has focused attention on the performance of the total societal system. Previously, the President's economic report made up the bulk of his annual State of the Union message. This no longer suffices. The nation is interested in the President's social report as well. It is becoming increasingly apparent that economic well-being is not a comprehensive measure of societal progress. The "great society" or the "good life" is a much more complex subject.

Many of the objectives of the Declaration of Independence and the Constitution have not been achieved "in general" in society. Some type of feedback reporting will be necessary if we are to monitor progress in all phases of our complex social system. What kind of a system will provide the necessary information? "Economic information itself cannot fully answer these questions. In addition to economic aspects, every situation has political, social, cultural, and biophysical aspects also. Moreover, qualitative information may be fully as important as quantitative information. Overemphasis upon statistics, because they seem more precise, or upon economic data, because they may be more readily available, often yields a narrow, unbalanced view of the state of a nation." [8]

A more meaningful view could be developed through a system of national social accounting which integrates information with regard to concepts developed by econo-

---

[8] Bertram M. Gross, *The State of the Nation: Social Systems Accounting*, Social Science Paperbacks, London, 1966, pp. 1-2.

mists, political scientists, sociologists, anthropologists, and social psychologists. The task is not an easy one. However, the need is imperative. Managers throughout society, particularly in government positions, need feedback with regard to progress toward identified goals. Also, legislators—federal, state, and local—need some means to appraise the impact of programs which are put into practice. How effective are programs such as Medicare, the Job Corps, or Urban Renewal? What has the Peace Corps really accomplished? Are Equal Opportunity Employment and Affirmative Action Programs achieving stated objectives? Answers to these questions do not come easily in a pluralistic society. However, there may be ways to bring some order out of chaos. [9]

Societal Complexity

Figure 18.4 shows a variety of social systems and indicates the complexity of a society such as the United States. Feedback control for single enterprise units or individual government agencies may be relatively simple to design. But even in such cases, the merit of a program and its progress over time may require more than quantitative, economic information in order to assess whether or not the program is "in control."

For a multiple-unit enterprise or government unit such as a metropolitan area, the evaluation process becomes even more difficult. However, there seems to be evidence of progress in defining complex systems as they relate to particular projects. The key steps are setting goals for the particular program, planning the means of achieving them, and devising a system of feedback information to use in evaluating overall progress.

Systems have two vital aspects: structure and process. [10]

> The structure of any social system consists of (1) people and (2) non-human resources (3) grouped together into subsystems that (4) interrelate among themselves and (5) with the external environment, and are subject to (6) certain values and (7) a central guidance system that may help provide the capacity for future performance. [11]

This model is, of course, a simplification of the real world. Each of the elements is itself multidimensional. The concept of structure can be thought of as a cross-section analysis of the system at a particular point in time. It is much like a corporate "balance sheet" which provides a static model of the financial condition as of a certain date. A comprehensive picture of a social system structure would include human and institutional assets as well as the more obvious physical and financial ones.

---

[9] For a discussion of these issues, see Michael Springer, "Social Indicators, Reports, and Accounts: Toward the Management of Society," *The Annals of the American Academy of Political and Social Science,* March 1970, pp. 1–13.
[10] Alfred J. Kahn, *Theory and Practice of Social Planning,* Russell Sage Foundation, New York, 1969.
[11] Bertram M. Gross, op. cit., p. 39.

FIGURE 18.4 VARIETIES OF SOCIAL SYSTEMS

LEVELS	PEOPLE[1]	GROUPS[1]		FORMAL ORGANIZATIONS[1]			TERRITORIAL ENTITIES[2]	
		INFORMAL GROUPS	FAMILIES	ASSOCIATIONS	ENTERPRISES	GOVERNMENT AGENCIES	GOVERNMENTS	AREAS
1 Micro systems	Individuals	Small groups	Nuclear families	Single associations	Single enterprise units	Single agencies	Local governments	Villages Local communities Neighbourhoods Towns and cities Metropoli
2 System clusters		Mobs Crowds	Extended families	Local, state, and regional federations	Multi-unit enterprises or groups	Agency groups	Inter-governmental bodies; State and regional	Megalopoli Intra-national states and regions
3 System constellations			Tribes	National federations	National multi-unit enterprises or groups	Nation-wide agencies	National states (unitary) or federal	Nations
4 Macrosystems				International federations	International multi-unit enterprises or groups	International agencies	International regions or systems "World-wide" governmental federations	International regions World

[1] These columns include only *simple* systems. *Complex* systems are networks composed of formal organizations (usually different types), groups, and individuals.
[2] As here defined, "territorial entity" includes a variety of other social systems within its spatial boundaries. Almost every territorial entity is a complex system.

SOURCE: Bertram M. Gross, *The State of the Nation: Social Systems Accounting*, Social Science Paperbacks, London, 1966, p. 26.

Performance appraisal relates to how well a process works over time—a dynamic rather than a static picture. Is the system effective; does it accomplish its task? Is it efficient; does output seem satisfactory in terms of the inputs required? This model of structure and process provides a general approach to evaluating complex programs in terms of more than economic factors. The task is not an easy one. However, now that a beginning has been made, society is thinking along the lines indicated and attempting to evaluate programs in rather broad terms.

As an example, in an article concerning the application of systems management techniques to urban redevelopment in San Francisco, Herrmann states that the Community Renewal Program identified two sets of goals to meet the challenge of change, "One is to achieve the largest total income possible; the other is to achieve the finest living environment possible." [12] He goes on to say that the series of proposals had the "ultimate purpose of restoring the city to its position of prosperous trade, diversified commerce, and good living." [13] These comments illustrate widespread thinking in terms of rather nebulous concepts such as "good living." While it may be difficult to measure progress along these lines, some guidelines can be established, and qualitative information can be used to assess the system. In most cases such an appraisal has been carried on implicitly; now the evaluation of these aspects of social systems is being dealt with more formally.

At the corporate level some tentative steps are being taken toward assessing performance in activities that affect the society around them—"measuring the unmeasurable." Bauer and Fenn provide some guidelines for a social audit process that should at least give managers a more explicit "feel" for the costs and benefits involved. [14]

Human Asset Accounting

The complexity of evaluating the structure or process of complex multiunit subsystems in society is evident. The task becomes more manageable if a single unit is involved— a business enterprise or government agency, for example. However, the traditional approaches are still most prevalent—economic-technical variables are used to indicate current status and system performance over time. Financial conditions are monitored via budgets, balance sheets, profit and loss statements, and break-even charts.

Some organizations make periodic attempts to assess human assets by surveying employee morale and/or estimating customer goodwill. Progress is evident in the latter case because many firms designate goodwill as an asset formally and attach a monetary value to it when assessing the financial worth of the firm. In nonbusiness organizations, however, there is no formal way to take into account customer goodwill (or ill will).

---

[12] Cyril C. Herrmann, "Systems Approach to City Planning," *Harvard Business Review*, September-October 1966, p. 77.
[13] Ibid.
[14] Raymond A. Bauer and Dan H. Fenn, Jr., *The Corporate Social Audit*, Russell Sage Foundation, New York, 1972.

Typically we have a "feeling" with regard to how well an organization—a public school system or a general hospital, for example—serves its clientele. In a complex society, unanimity or consensus are probably utopian concepts. However, we may be able to identify major trends with regard to goodwill for a particular organization.

Although business firms and other organizations do attempt to measure employee morale, it is not reflected in the formal accounting statements as an asset or liability. Nevertheless, it certainly affects current performance as well as long-run viability. An organization with a "bad atmosphere" may have difficulty attracting new talent. Therefore, it may gradually decline as a viable organization in spite of significant technological improvements. It is apparent that some organizations "do better" than others with seemingly the "same" resources. That is, they have similar technology, and approximately the same number of people. However, the quality of the human resource may vary significantly and hence result in more output per unit of input. Moreover, the latent human capability may be approximately equal, but the inclination to perform may be significantly greater in one organization than in another and hence result in superior performance. Likert suggests a number of conditions which differentiate the human assets in an organization:

1 Level of intelligence and aptitudes
2 Level of training
3 Level of performance goals and motivation to achieve organizational success
4 Quality of leadership
5 Capacity to use differences for purposes of innovation and improvement, rather than allowing differences to develop into bitter, irreconcilable, interpersonal conflict
6 Quality of communication upward, downward, and laterally
7 Quality of decision making
8 Capacity to achieve cooperative teamwork versus competitive striving for personal success at the expense of the organization
9 Quality of the control processes of the organization and the levels of felt responsibility which exist
10 Capacity to achieve effective coordination
11 Capacity to use experience and measurements to guide decisions, improve operations, and introduce innovations [15]

Each of these could vary on a continuum from poor to excellent. An organization which rated excellent across the board would have a significantly different climate from one which rated poor in all categories. The value of the human organization in the former case would seem to be significantly greater than in the latter case. However, in real

[15] Rensis Likert, *The Human Organization,* McGraw-Hill Book Company, New York, 1967, p. 148.

situations, there are likely to be offsetting factors. An organization may rate high in several of these factors and low in others. The total mix is reflected in the psychosocial system and is often described in such nebulous terms as organizational "atmosphere."

Obtaining feedback from these variables is not always easy. In some cases, measurement is relatively straightforward; in other cases, it is quite difficult. How do we identify "quality" of communication or "capacity" to achieve effective coordination? This phase of the organizational control system requires judgmental decision making by experienced executives. The first step is identifying a current structure and performance level to serve as a yardstick for evaluating future conditions. The performance at any given time should be related to past levels of achievement as well as to any absolute standards imposed by the decision maker. This type of evaluation is difficult but absolutely necessary in order to obtain a composite measure of organizational worth. Human assets are receiving increasing attention and undoubtedly will be included in evaluation processes more and more in the future. [16]

The Value of Management

The role of human assets in evaluating an organization is illustrated by the importance which security analysts place on company management. They spend many hours evaluating industry data and economic potential. They analyze individual companies within an industry and trace past history and future potential in terms of sales, profits, price earnings ratios, and other similar economic-technical factors. Yet the most important element in most cases is managerial potential. "Knowing the statistics of an industry—prices, production, retailing figures, capital spending—is important, of course, but the main thing is assessing management." [17]

The analyst attempts to assess the energy and astuteness of top management in order to predict whether or not the company will be able to take advantage of opportunities which are likely to present themselves in the future. An energetic, knowledgeable top management group is considered to be a critical determinant of the potential success or failure of the organization. This human asset is not reflected in the financial data published for popular consumption. But this is exactly what the analyst is looking for, because in his eyes the organization is significantly undervalued if the figures reflect a poor or mediocre situation which is on the verge of blossoming. The likelihood of superior performance in the future is enhanced by excellence in the managerial system.

It is evident that more and more attention will be placed on social system and human asset accounting in the future. While evaluation in these spheres is not particularly easy, it is essential and will become more important. Evaluation has always included them, if only implicitly. The trend will be to formalize these systems somewhat and to elevate them to a level of prominence now held exclusively by more traditional

---

[16] Eric Flamholtz, "Should Your Organization Attempt to Value Its Human Resources?" *California Management Review,* Winter 1971, pp. 40–45.
[17] "Students of Stocks," *Wall Street Journal,* Jan. 23, 1968, p. 1.

quantitative, economic-technical evaluation systems. As these more humanistic factors are included in the control process, individual and organizational behavior will be "directed" (consciously and unconsciously) along new avenues.

INDIRECT CONTROL

Because control is related so closely to planning, it seems obvious that there should be a hierarchy of types of control similar to the hierarchy in planning activity. Indeed, typically there is some overall institutional control with regard to general statements of organizational goals. A master or comprehensive plan designed to achieve such goals will also have some control mechanism built into the process explicitly, or else control will take place implicitly in the managerial process. As plans move down the scale and toward more detail, the control mechanism becomes more evident. A goal of producing 100,000 cars is quite explicit, and a simple counting procedure will provide the necessary control. However, if the goal is stated in terms of producing a new model which will be more attractive to the consumer, evaluating whether or not the organization achieves this purpose is a much more difficult task. Let us consider several types of indirect control that can be applied in organizations.

Organizational Conditioning

At the strategic level the development of reasonably consistent value systems, at least with regard to pertinent organizational issues, is an important means of control. If all key organizational decision makers "think alike," the managerial system is very likely "in control."

The extreme, of course, is some form of brainwashing wherein individuals come to think in only one extremely narrow way about pertinent issues. The "organization man" concept, when carried to the extreme, is only a step away from the notion of brainwashing. Certainly there are cases where conformity is carried too far. We continue to advocate and respect individual initiative. On the other hand, organizations require group effort; the term itself implies cooperation and compromise on the part of the group members as they attempt to achieve some common purpose. Somewhere along the continuum there is a happy medium—perhaps "unity without uniformity."

Tannenbaum suggests that man derives much from organizational membership but often pays heavily for such benefits and that at the heart of this particular exchange lies the control process. He states:

> Characterizing an organization in terms of its patterns of control is to describe an essential and universal aspect of organization which every member must face and to which he must adjust. Organization implies control. A social organization has an ordered arrangement of individual human interactions. Control processes help circumscribe idiosyncratic behaviors and keep them

conformant with the rational plan of the organization. Organizations require a certain amount of conformity as well as the integration of diverse activities. It is the function of control to bring about conformance to organizational requirements and achievement of the ultimate purposes of the organization. The coordination and order created out of the diverse interests and potentially diffuse behaviors of members is largely a function of control. It is at this point that many of the problems of organizational functioning and of individual adjustment arise. [18]

If managers were so diverse in individual value systems that no agreement on organizational purpose could be achieved, chaos would result. But the other extreme is not very palatable either. If value systems are so consistent that there is absolutely no friction or conflict we might have a completely static and stale organization. The control function refers to maintaining systems within allowable limits (maintaining a dynamic equilibrium) and suggests that change is acceptable and desirable. However, the system must be stable enough to withstand periodic shocks and still maintain its course toward pertinent goals.

Socialization of Managers

Any individual entering a stable social system, such as most organizations, is "socialized" to a degree. The new member "learns the value system, the norms, and the required behavior patterns." [19] The amount of overt attention paid to explicit means of socialization depends on the dynamics of the particular industry or company. Those organizations in relatively stable environments and evidencing little growth may develop indirect control without really trying. Individuals may face a long, step-by-step process in moving to positions of real authority and responsibility. In so doing they gain a value system through long years of experience, almost by osmosis. One of our colleagues spent a summer in a large firm in a rather static industry. Upon his return he said, "I understand now why the _____ industry is so static. It takes 40 years for anyone to reach a position which allows him to make decisions which have any effect. By that time he knows only one way to do it." In contrast, Levitt suggests that:

> The younger a man is when he reaches the top, or the less dependent his accession is on a generation of selected screening and dedicated commitment to a restricted purpose, the more likely he will see that his company's interests lie in supporting changes coming from outside. He will have escaped the disciplining and narrowing process regarding the external environment

---

[18] Arnold S. Tannenbaum, *Control in Organizations*, McGraw-Hill Book Company, New York, 1968, p. 3.
[19] Edgar H. Schein, "Organizational Socialization and the Profession of Management," in David A. Kolb, Irwin M. Rubin, and James M. McIntyre (eds.), *Organizational Psychology: A Book of Readings*, Prentice-Hall, Inc., Englewood Cliffs, N.J., 1971, p. 3.

that tends to distort his vision. He will be more flexible, more tolerant of diversity, more understanding of the necessity and virtue of man-made change. [20]

In the dynamic industries and organizations, there is an influx of people from the outside, and progress may be relatively rapid up through the hierarchy. In this case more overt attention may be paid to developing consistent value systems throughout the organization. Elaborate orientation programs may be put on for new employees. Periodic in-company training programs may be held for supervisors, foremen, lower-middle management, upper-middle management, and top management. These development programs are carried on in addition to training for specific skills or functions within the organization. The emphasis is often on general management philosophy and its application in a particular company. William G. Scott describes this approach:

> Development is not to be confused with other types of instruction used in business. Operative training, supervisory training, technical training, and education have fairly clear, commonly understood objectives. Development is considered here as the planned influence of individual psychological processes. *Its purpose is to gain from an employee an attitudinal commitment to the philosophy, values, and goals of a business organization.* [21]

The concept of indirect control has great significance for the relevance of a managerial philosophy such as decentralization of decision making—the delegation of authority and responsibility downward in the organizational hierarchy. If the managerial group, by and large, has a consistent value system with regard to pertinent organizational issues, members of top management can delegate decision making and be reasonably confident that the results will conform to their expectations. That is, the decisions will be made just as if they were doing it themselves. Without this confidence, management is likely to retain centralized control and reserve the right to make decisions or at least review them at the top level.

It is unlikely that many organization members become completely conditioned or developed in today's complex environment. We are part of a pluralistic society and belong to many organizations simultaneously. Conformity might be induced if the organization were isolated from its environment and if its participants were totally committed to its purpose only. Fortunately, such situations are relatively few in our society. Religious training schools may be the only organizations where both isolation and a total institutional atmosphere can be maintained. Current intrafaith conflicts illustrate the difficulty in maintaining a consistent value system for large, complex organizations. In

---

[20] Theodore Levitt, "Why Business Always Loses," *Harvard Business Review,* March–April 1968, pp. 86–87.
[21] William G. Scott, "Executive Development as an Instrument of Higher Control," *Academy of Management Journal,* September 1963, p. 192.

general, people become less tractable as they become better educated. This trend alone would seem to indicate extreme difficulty in the future in "developing" employees to narrowly construed organizational value systems.

On the other hand, it is important that general agreement be reached on important issues such as organizational purposes or objectives and other pertinent areas of concern to top management. A degree of vagueness may be necessary to foster compromise and commitment. The control function at higher levels must be sophisticated and flexible enough to meet changing conditions. It is designed to keep the organizational endeavors in a dynamic equilibrium while progressing toward operational objectives. Indirect control involves a considerable amount of subjective appraisal on the part of top managers. Decisions require wisdom born of intelligence and experience.

EXAMPLES OF CONTROL

The control function is carried out directly via many specific organizational processes. By considering several of these specific activities in more detail, we will be able to better understand the concept of control. Again, the difficulty in separating planning and control is evident in the examples to follow—the procedures outlined involve both activities.

Budgetary Control

A budget is often described as a plan set forth in financial terms. That is, organizational activity is translated into expected results with dollars as the common denominator. Most writers stress the positive or planning aspects of budgetary control rather than the strictly control phase. Yet the connotation of restriction and constraint is widespread in business and government organizations.

The procedures of budgetary control can be applied to a wide variety of situations. Several basic elements are involved in financial budgeting.

1 *Expressing in dollars the results of plans anticipated in a future period.* These dollar figures are typically set up in the same way as the accounts in a company's accounting system. The budget shows how the accounts should look if present plans are carried out.
2 *Coordinating these estimates into a well-balanced program.* The figures for sales, production, advertising, and other divisions must be matched to be sure that they are mutually consistent; financial feasibility of all plans added together must be assured; and the combined results must be examined in terms of over-all objectives. Some adjustments will probably be necessary to obtain such a balanced program.
3 *Comparing actual results with the program estimates that emerge from step 2.*

Any significant differences point to the need for corrective action. In short, the budget becomes a standard for appraising operating results. [22]

Budgetary control, as described above, nearly parallels the management process. It involves planning, coordinating, and controlling.

In many organizations this does, in fact, happen. The budget becomes the primary tool for managing organizational activities. For business enterprises, objectives are typically expressed in terms of dollar sales. Sales forecasts are developed in the light of both external and internal informational inputs with the results providing a foundation for all organizational activity. An advertising budget is drawn up to fit the sales forecast. The wage and salary budget is designed in view of the manpower requirements for accomplishing the objectives as established. Throughout the organization, future activity is spelled out in dollar terms.

The budgeting process forces management to consider future plans explicitly and attach dollar values to them. By asking organization members at all levels to develop subparts of the budget, a sense of participation and organizational involvement is often achieved. Self-generated plans or budgets often are easier to control than those imposed by others.

Once the various parts of the budget are integrated into a comprehensive financial plan, it becomes a standard against which performance can be measured during the ensuing period. In most cases budgets are flexible enough that adjustments can be made, if need be, according to the way circumstances develop. It is not necessarily a rigid constraining device.

Budgetary control in many organizations involves dollar allocations whereby a total amount of money is divided and earmarked for certain functions over a period of time. In this sense the budget is a constraining device because activities dependent upon available funds must be curtailed if the funds run out. Therefore, the control process is typically one of ascertaining expenditures over time as measured against some planned rate.

A typical problem in organizations of this type is that of running out of funds before the budget period expires. Either funds must be transferred from other endeavors, or activity in this phase of the organization must be curtailed. Another less typical but evident problem is that of coming to the end of a budgetary period with excess funds on hand. At this point there is often a mad scramble to expend the funds in order that the budget officer and/or appropriating agency (legislative body) will not interpret efficient performance as a lack of need and hence cut off the supply of funds in the future. In large, complex organizations, the allocation process is difficult. Matching needs with resources is an important function, and the process should be flexible enough to adjust according to changes in the environment. In most cases, however,

---

[22] William H. Newman, Charles E. Summer, and E. Kirby Warren, *The Process of Management*, 3d ed. © 1972, pp. 602–603. Reprinted by permission of Prentice-Hall, Inc., Englewood Cliffs, N.J.

changes are rather slow in coming, thus resulting in a continuation of expenditures in relatively obsolete activities and undersupporting new and growing areas of need.

Planning-Programming-Budgeting System

The "planning-programming-budgeting" philosophy developed by the Department of Defense is an attempt to give more of the planning connotation to the government budgeting process. [23] In the past the various services typically developed a budget request on an annual basis for their particular needs. This request went to Congress, which reviewed the request and made appropriations. The categories used often had little relationship to strategic military programs over a period of time. For example, certain missions involve subunits of several systems and hence cut across traditional functional boundaries. As more and more emphasis was placed on military missions and programs to accomplish them, it became evident that the funding process needed revision. [24]

The planning-programming-budgeting philosophy requires the identification of weapon-system missions and all associated costs from perception of need through design, production, delivery, and utilization. Budgets developed by functions and service are of little value in assessing the cost effectiveness of a particular weapon system over its projected life span. Each mission fits into the overall scheme for national security and can be evaluated in terms of its contribution as compared to its cost.

This approach requires programs to be identified and planning carried out on a program basis for the immediate future and for medium- and long-range objectives. It emphasizes the planning nature of the budgetary process and facilitates the appropriation of funds on a current basis in the light of anticipated total costs for the program over its life span. Budgetary control is maintained by monitoring actual spending rates compared with anticipated rates on a cumulative basis at any point in the program life cycle.

The new managerial approaches of the Department of Defense proved so successful that in 1965 the President directed that the planning-programming-budgeting system should be introduced into all departments of the federal government. [25] Agencies were encouraged to adopt techniques such as systems analysis and cost/effectiveness studies. These new approaches also have been used at state and local levels for dealing with complex problems. [26]

The Subcommittee on Economy in Government of the Joint Economic Committee studied the planning-programming-budgeting system (PPBS) in some detail and concluded:

---

[23] For a discussion of the possibility of merging the planning and budgeting subsystems, see Gerhard Colm, *Integration of National Planning and Budgeting,* National Planning Association, Washington, D.C., 1968.
[24] Charles J. Hitch, *Decision-Making for Defense,* University of California Press, Berkeley, Calif., 1965.
[25] For example, see Elizabeth B. Drew, "HEW Grapples with PPBS," *The Public Interest,* Summer 1967, pp. 9–29.
[26] For examples of these applications, see *Program Financial Planning,* Office of Program Planning and Fiscal Management, State of Washington, Olympia, Wash., May 1970, and Harold I. Steinberg and Robert A. Nielsen, "PPBS for a School District," *Management Controls,* July 1971, pp. 136–143.

The subcommittee is of the firm opinion that PPBS represents a substantial forward step in budgetary techniques. At the same time, it is our opinion that much more work is needed in the definition of national objectives and the determination of priorities in the allocation of public funds. If the Nation had a little clearer notion of its goals and national priorities (bearing in mind that they are apt to be continuously shifting in a society like ours), it would ease the task of PPBS inasmuch as it would give rise to definable objective programs which could then be subjected to a systems approach. [27]

While progress has been made, much more needs to be done to implement systematic program management at all levels of government. [28] Obviously, PPBS is not a panacea; many decisions involve difficult tradeoffs which must be resolved judgmentally and subjectively. Quantitative analysis of economic-technical factors may not suffice for strategic decision making. As Kahn suggests:

In effect, program budgeting, as does any governmental effort, faces the problem of all planning: it represents an attempt to introduce rationality into a world of interest groups, bureaucratic rigidities, informal organizations, politics, and many uncertainties. If the planner is at all times clear that his mission and capability are not to eliminate all of these, but rather to optimize the rational component in the process, he can work comfortably and usefully. . . .

In short, we have found no nostrums or panaceas, but rather helpful tools and constructive perspectives for the social planner. The analyses projected do not *make* the decisions and never will; they may serve to sharpen intuition and enhance judgment. [29]

It is obvious that PPBS can never become the only system for governmental planning and program implementation. However, it can be a useful part of the overall system which includes many other elements, constraints, and inputs.

Educational Control Systems

Within the general educational system there are many subsystems which involve control. One such system that can be used to illustrate the measurement-feedback-correction process, and which is familiar to all students, is the function of testing in education. A teacher may assume that students comprehend the assigned reading and those materials presented in the classroom. As a precaution the instructor might assign several readings covering the same concept, or the assigned readings might be ex-

---

[27] *The Planning-Programming-Budgeting System: Progress and Potentials*, Report of the Subcommittee on Economy in Government, Joint Economic Committee, 90th Cong., 1st Sess., December 1967, p. 10.
[28] *The Current Status of the Planning-Programming-Budgeting System*, A Compendium of Papers Submitted to the Subcommittee on Economy in Government of the Joint Economic Committee, 91st Cong., 1st Sess., 1969.
[29] Alfred J. Kahn, op. cit., p. 261.

plained in class. In spite of such repetition some students still may not understand, while others may be bored by the unnecessary duplication. The educational process, therefore, may not be successful regardless of reinforcing techniques, and/or it may be inefficient.

Control may be added to an educational system by measuring the student's understanding of the course material through testing. First a test is developed which identifies the learning which has taken place. Educators speak of "test validity," or the correlation between the test and the material to be learned. They also speak of "test reliability," or the consistency with which the test produces the same results. How accurate the test is as an indicator of performance may be a subject of some disagreement between teacher and student. Nevertheless each examination is compared against a standard or key, and assuming that the test has been properly designed, the results should indicate which students are having trouble and whether any part of the material needs further review or explanation. As a corrective input the instructor might adjust his method of presenting the material, add additional work assignments, or take any other action which the feedback information seems to indicate.

Typically, students want very few examinations. Such a procedure reduces the ability of the educational system to adjust, however. A single examination at the end of the term would provide information for subsequent sessions but would be of no value to correct current deficiencies. In contrast, if an examination were given each day, the instructor would have the greatest knowledge of when to review or explain further and when to proceed. Usually a compromise between these two extremes is followed, which allows current feedback without spending a disproportionate amount of the class time for testing. In addition, the instructor may seek current control information through classroom participation in oral or written exercises.

Some students may discredit this example of control on the grounds that examinations are used to identify performance and not as feedback for the learning process. Unfortunately, such claims often are valid.

Quality Control

"Control attempts to insure the quality and quantity of system output according to predetermined plans and standards."[30] It involves the maintenance of dimensions and other product characteristics within the specific plan—a responsibility which is broader than rejecting unsatisfactory parts.

A sound quality control program can make significant savings in both direct and indirect costs. For example, effective control of the quality of raw materials can prevent the processing of defective materials. Production time which has been spent in producing or reworking defective parts now can be used to increase the quantity of production. A good product tends to build customer goodwill and to increase sales volume. More-

[30] Richard A. Johnson, William T. Newell, and Roger C. Vergin, *Operations Management: A Systems Approach*, Houghton Mifflin Company, Boston, 1972, p. 282.

over, most workers take pride in producing quality products or in being associated with a company which cultivates a policy of producing high-quality goods.

Quality is always relative to other considerations: (1) to the manner in which the product will be used (e.g., a lathe might be of good quality for a home workshop but would be inadequate as a production machine); (2) to a measurable and definable characteristic (e.g., size, hardness, content, and viscosity); (3) to the economics of manufacturing (there is a direct relationship between quality demanded and manufacturing costs); and (4) to quantity of output (the higher the quality the more difficult it becomes to achieve quantity output).

In the final analysis the quality standards for a product are established by the customer. The sales department represents consumer demands, and every effort is made to satisfy these demands within the limits set by engineering design and the ability to manufacture the product economically. In certain cases quality standards may even be dictated by the government—pure food and drug or automobile safety standards, for example.

Quality control in the automobile industry has become a major issue, as evidenced by the periodic recall of thousands of cars (perhaps the *entire run* of a particular model) for replacement of defective axles, steering mechanisms, or brakes. There is a continuing controversy between manufacturers and dealers over responsibility for quality assurance, with the customer often left "holding the lemon." Government safety standards are playing an increasing role in particular aspects of quality control. And Nader's Raiders fill an overall societal role in this complex process.

The inspection group (the sensor element) must determine when and what number to inspect. It is seldom feasible to inspect every part after each operation; nor is it good policy to wait until the product has been completed before making an inspection. The economic balance lies somewhere between those two extremes. Usually, inspections are made on purchased materials at the time they are received, on materials in process at strategically selected points, and on finished goods ready for shipment.

The amount to inspect involves consideration of the characteristics to be controlled and the cost. The extremes can be 100 percent or small sample inspection. Acceptance or rejection is only one phase of effective quality control. Records and charts of quality performance are kept, and these records are analyzed so that trends in product characteristics can be detected and the necessary corrections made in the production operation.

The typical quality control unit is involved in all elements of the control process. It has a part in determining the controlled characteristic, measures performance, rejects faulty parts, and initiates corrective action.

Real-Time Control Systems

The military services have created several sophisticated control systems which utilize computers in real-time applications. The computer is used as the centralized nervous system to process and analyze input information, make and communicate appropriate decisions, and develop information output in a form appropriate for human decision makers. [31]

SAGE (semiautomatic ground environment) is a control system which receives input information from a vast interconnected network of stations, processes this information against a schedule of planned air flights, and issues information to activate defense weapons if necessary. The SAGE system may be categorized relative to the four elements of control: the controlled *characteristic* is the prevention of flight over the continental United States and other parts of North America by hostile aircraft. Unauthorized flights are noted by *sensors* such as radar units. This information is forwarded to the *comparator* unit where the computer processes the information. The computer output provides information for military officials, the *effector* unit, to make a decision relative to corrective action. The *operating* units, the interceptor squadrons and missile bases, respond according to the instructions released by the effector unit.

Notice that the effectiveness of this control system depends on rapid feedback of information concerning unscheduled flights, the instant processing of information to determine the need for action, and the prompt and effective allocation of operating weapons to confront the enemy.

The same type of real-time control is evident in NASA's space tracking network and the FAA's air traffic control system.

THE ECONOMICS OF CONTROL

Control can never be complete; variations from expectations are inevitable. The control phase of the managerial process should focus on maintaining a dynamic equilibrium within allowable limits of the plan. It is obvious that organizational resources are consumed in the control function. Therefore attention should be devoted to a cost-benefit analysis of control systems.

Figure 18.5 shows the relationship of perfection in the control system and the cost to attain it. System performance is typically improved by using feedback information to control and adjust it. The difference between the cost of the control subsystem and the improvement in system performance is the net economic benefit. A system can be overcontrolled to the extent that the cost of the control subsystem increases faster than the improvements in performance. Indeed, such cost theoretically can be greater than the total value realized from the operation itself. As shown in Figure 18.5, there is a range within which net benefit is at a maximum.

SUMMARY

The control function is that phase of the managerial system which maintains organization activity within allowable limits as measured from expectations which may be implicit, or explicit in terms of stated objectives, plans, procedures, or rules and regulations.

---

[31] Donald G. Malcolm, "Exploring the Military Analogy: Real-time Management Control," in D. G. Malcolm, A. J. Rowe, and L. F. McConnell (eds.), *Management Control Systems*, John Wiley & Sons, Inc., New York, 1960, pp. 187-208.

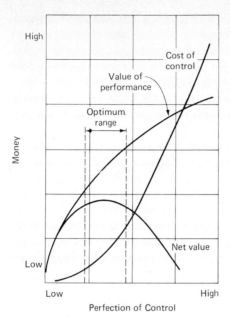

FIGURE 18.5 THE ECONOMICS OF CON-
TROL (Marvin E. Mundel, *A Conceptual
Framework for the Management Sciences,*
McGraw-Hill Book Company, New York,
1967, p. 174)

Planning and controlling are directly related activities, with plans providing the framework for the control phase of the managerial process.

Homeostasis, cybernetics, and feedback are important concepts for control theory. Homeostasis is the tendency for organisms and organizations to return to a stable
equilibrium after being "disturbed" by some external stimulus. Feedback is critical to
control, providing information about past or current performance which is used to
influence future activity or goals. The connotation "direction of" attributed to cybernetics is a key thread for control theory in general.

Four fundamental elements are common to all control systems: (1) a measurable
characteristic, (2) a sensor, (3) a comparator, and (4) an effector.

Closed-loop control systems involve automatic feedback and adjustment of the
system without human intervention. The open-loop system involves a human in the
decision making which is part of the control process. Because human beings are
involved in programming, even the most detailed and automatic closed-loop systems
are open in the ultimate sense.

Timing is an important consideration for control theory. Much effort is devoted to
precontrol—trying to ensure that operations will remain within allowable limits. However, it seems inevitable that operations get out of control in real life. Thus, considerable
attention must also be devoted to postcontrol—adjusting operations after the fact with
the intent of keeping the operation in control in the future. Concurrent or real-time
control is becoming increasingly prevalent; many operations are adjusted continually
and immediately as deviations from expectations occur.

Social system accounting is an attempt to formalize nonquantitative, noneconomic feedback with regard to societal performance. While we often informally evaluate the merit of complex programs such as the Peace Corps or Equal Opportunity Employment, no formal feedback comparable to the President's economic report has been developed. Progress is being made and, in spite of a complex, pluralistic society, more explicit feedback control systems will be forthcoming in the future. At the company or agency level, human asset accounting is being recognized as important feedback concerning organizational well-being.

Indirect or ''higher-level'' control involves considerable precontrol in the form of orientation, in-company management development programs, and job experience. All these activities work together to develop some consensus among executives (organizational conditioning or socialization) with regard to pertinent premises. More specific and detailed control procedures are necessary when referring to technical or operating activities of organizations. In these cases, there are specific techniques which can be used to plan activities and measure performance against expectations. In all cases, an appropriate balance should be maintained between the costs and benefits of control systems.

QUESTIONS AND PROBLEMS

1 Define control. What are its objectives? Illustrate several connotations of control with organizational examples.

2 Relate the following to the concept of control: (a) homeostasis, (b) cybernetics, and (c) feedback.

3 Relate the four basic elements of control to the control cycle.

4 Trace the control process in the following situations: (a) driving to work, (b) coaching a football team, (c) managing an advertising campaign, and (d) administering Medicare.

5 ''Even the most detailed and automatic closed-loop systems are open in the ultimate sense.'' Do you agree? Why or why not?

6 Discuss the relationship between pre-, post-, and current control efforts in organizational control systems.

7 What are the prospects for a President's ''Social Report'' in his annual State of the Union message? Why?

8 How do human ''assets'' affect the value of an organization? What factors are involved? What would you do to increase the value of human assets in your organization?

9 Discuss management ''development'' (or conditioning) as a means to higher-level organizational control.

10 Relate concepts such as inventory control, cost control, and production control to the general models set forth in this chapter.

11 What does the phrase ''economics of control'' mean? Give an example of how costs can exceed benefits.

Knowledge comes from noticing resemblances and recurrences in the events that happen around us.
Wilfred Trotter

We must stop acting as though nature were organized into disciplines in the same way that universities are.
Russell L. Ackoff

What we need are great complexifiers, men who will not only seek to understand what it is they are about, but who will also dare to share that understanding with those for whom they act.
Daniel P. Moynihan

Many seemingly unrelated things follow similar or identical rules of behavior, and . . . knowledge of one therefore provides understanding of another.
Alfred Kuhn

If there is no struggle there is no progress. Those who profess to favor freedom, and yet deprecate agitation, are men who want crops without plowing up the ground. They want rain without thunder and lightning. They want the ocean without the awful roar of its many waters.
Frederick Douglass

PART 7
COMPARATIVE ANALYSIS
AND CONTINGENCY VIEWS

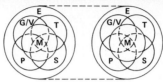

In the six preceding parts of the book we have developed a framework for studying organizations and management. We have looked at the conceptual foundations and the evolution of theory and have analyzed organizations via a systems approach that focuses on the environmental suprasystem and five subsystems—goals and values, technical, structural, psychosocial, and managerial. This framework provides a basis for considering several other issues.

Comparative analysis and contingency views are particularly important in the development of a body of knowledge that is relevant for management practice. Hypotheses and theories need to be tested across a variety of settings or situations in order to develop concepts that reflect the complexity of organizational phenomena.

In Chapter 19 we look at the pervasiveness and importance of comparative organizational analysis and indicate several foci of attention—internally across functions, levels, or subsystems, as well as externally across institutions and cultures. Various ways of classifying organizations are reviewed and evaluated. The systems model is suggested as a framework for comparative analysis. Systems concepts and contingency views are explored in terms of their relevance and potential contributions to organization theory and management practice.

In Chapters 20 and 21 the systems approach is used to describe and analyze two important institutions in society, the community general hospital and the university. The systems model is used as a framework to help understand these specific organizations in terms of characteristics on key dimensions common to all organizations.

COMPARATIVE ANALYSIS
AND CONTINGENCY VIEWS

Two important issues in the study of organization and management are the universality of concepts and the transferability of skills. Does the body of knowledge—organization theory—apply to any and all organizations? Are managerial skills transferable across institutions and cultures? The answers to these questions obviously depend on the scope and direction of organization theory, as well as the connotation of the term managerial skill. If the manager's skill in situational analysis is emphasized, we can enhance the applicability of current knowledge. But much empirical research remains to be done. Comparative analysis using the systems approach can lead to contingency views that facilitate appropriate organization designs and managerial actions. Current efforts in this direction will be discussed via the following topics:

> Comparative Analysis Defined
> Importance of Comparative Analysis
> Classification of Organizations
> Systems Framework for Comparative Analysis
> Systems Concepts and Contingency Views
> Contingency Views and Organization Theory
> Contingency Views and Management Practice

COMPARATIVE ANALYSIS DEFINED

To compare means "to examine in order to observe or discover similarities or differences." We are all continually involved in simplified comparative analysis of organizations. When selecting a college or university to attend, the student will frequently investigate a number of institutions. He or she is likely to look at a limited number of dimensions upon which to compare schools: distance from home, tuition costs, academic reputation, "where friends are going," and other similar criteria. As consumers we are continually making comparisons between organizations. Why do we select one automobile repair shop over another? Because it is closer, cheaper, or more reliable? Why does the housewife shop at A & P, Safeway, or an independent grocer? Prospective employees compare a number of organizations for employment opportunities. Many will look only at the "short-term rewards" such as the salary and fringe benefits. Other, more sophisticated analysts will scrutinize and compare organizations on many dimensions.

These are rather simple examples of comparative analysis of organizations. They are typically limited to only a few dimensions, usually those most directly pertinent to the observer's role as prospective student, customer, or employee.

For organization theorists and practicing managers comparative analysis is much more comprehensive—all relevant dimensions must be considered in order to describe, analyze, or plan effectively. The systems approach—consideration of the environmental suprasystem and the major organizational subsystems—provides an appropriate framework for comparative analysis. But several key questions are involved: What organizations should be compared? What characteristics or dimensions should be used in the analysis? How do we obtain information relevant for comparative purposes?

In general the answer to these questions is, "It all depends on the purpose of the analyst." Thus appropriate analysis includes information (however obtained) on whatever dimensions seem useful in gaining a better understanding of relevant organizations. Comparative analysis can focus on types of organizations or on specific dimensions in terms of their similarities and differences across organizations. In general, analysis has focused on structure and process, with specific emphasis on variables such as authority patterns, decision-making processes, and communication systems. Comparative analysis can take any one of several directions. Two major categories are intra- and interorganizational.

Intraorganizational Analysis

Comparative studies within organizations relate to similarities and differences across functions or other subunits. For example, we have differentiated the managerial task as it relates to organizational subsystems or levels (see Figure 5.4). The managerial task at the operating, coordinative, and strategic levels is compared according to several dimensions—environmental systems, time perspective, viewpoint (optimizing—satisficing), general problem-solving processes, and decision-making techniques. Comparative analysis is also appropriate and useful across functions such as sales, production, engineering, accounting, and personnel. What are the similarities and differences in organizational settings? Should a manager's approach be altered significantly if he moves from one function to another? What are the likely consequences of extending approaches that work in one department to all others?

Interorganizational Analysis

The term comparative analysis has typically been applied to cross-institutional and/or cross-cultural approaches. What can we learn about similarities and differences among several organizations in the same industry or between steel manufacturers and automobile producers, insurance companies and airlines, or hotels and oil refineries? What about comparing and contrasting private enterprises and public agencies, religious organizations and military units, or voluntary associations and correctional institutions?

What are the similarities and differences for organization and management on a cross-cultural basis? What are the variations on key dimensions for organizations in Japan compared to the United States, in India compared to Brazil, or in Sweden compared to Kenya? *Culture* is a difficult term to define precisely; it includes norms, mores, and overall value systems (what is good and desirable behavior). Differences in culture are often obvious when viewed on an international basis. However, the concept of culture ("climate" or "atmosphere") is also relevant within organizations when considering significantly different groups such as line managers and professional staff.

Alternative Approaches

Comparative analysis may be carried out by focusing on one (unidimensional) or several variables (multidimensional). For example, leadership styles might be compared across functions, levels, institutions, or cultures. Such studies provide insight concerning what factors affect a specific variable or dimension.

Typically, however, comparative analysis includes more than one dimension in order to facilitate our understanding of how organizations are similar and different in terms of interrelationships among key variables. The detailed case analysis is a multidimensional approach that concentrates on one organization (or subunit) and analyzes as many facets as time and energy will permit. It provides an opportunity to understand a complex social system in great detail. However, the results of such an analysis cannot be generalized. Findings concerning effective organization design or management practice may or may not be applicable to another organization.

In order to identify patterns of relationships which lead to effective performance, it is important to include many organizations. This is the essence of the comparative method—"systematic comparison of a fairly large number of organizations in order to establish relationships between their characteristics." [1] Obviously, the more organizations that are investigated, the more confidence we have in the findings which emerge consistently. Comparative analysis over a variety of institutions and cultures should reveal patterns of relationships. A body of knowledge presented in this way will allow managers to diagnose situations, anticipate possible consequences of their actions,

---

[1] Peter M. Blau, "The Comparative Study of Organizations," *Industrial and Labor Relations Review,* April 1965, p. 323.

and choose the most appropriate alternative (the one with the highest probability of success). The ultimate body of knowledge will always include a contingency flavor—there are no "absolutes" or guarantees of success. However, better understanding of patterns of relationships should lead to improvement in managerial performance.

IMPORTANCE OF COMPARATIVE ANALYSIS

We have discussed the "what" and "how" of comparative analysis in general terms. At this stage it will be useful to consider the "why" of comparative analysis. What does it contribute to organization theory and management practice? Two central themes stand out: (1) understanding and (2) application. When dealing with complex affairs, to *understand* means to be able to describe and explain what is happening—including how variables are related, what causes what, and the relative importance of the various forces involved.

If two-variable (or multivariate) cause-and-effect relationships can be established in specific situations, we have a good beginning. However, the same phenomena should be investigated in other contexts—levels, institutions, or cultures—in order to determine under what conditions various relationships hold. For example, does participation in decision making lead to greater satisfaction and improved performance in all cases? Do all managers rise to the level of their competence?[2] Or, are there a number of conditions or contingencies which make such conclusions more or less appropriate?

It is only after painstaking, exhaustive research in a number of settings that we can be confident of describing relationships with broad applicability. Moreover, normative conclusions or prescriptions for managerial behavior are always tentative without such a foundation.

A Sign of Maturity

The importance of comparative analysis is underscored by its pervasiveness. Some suggest that "it is formally impossible to study anything without at least implicitly comparing it with something else, or comparing its component parts one with another."[3] Much effort has been devoted to comparative culture, comparative religion, comparative government, and comparative economics.[4] In a sense comparative analysis gives an indication of maturity in a field. It is a shift toward broader perspectives—away from parochialism and a preoccupation with justifying our own particular system or approach. There has been a tendency throughout history for philosophers to establish universal principles based on narrow experience *and* then to extend the "one best

---

[2] "In a hierarchy, every employee tends to rise to his level of incompetence." Lawrence J. Peter and Raymond Hull, *The Peter Principle: Why Things Always Go Буоим*, Bantam Books, Inc., New York, 1969, p. 7.
[3] Stanley H. Udy, Jr., "The Comparative Analysis of Organizations," in James G. March (ed.), *Handbook of Organizations*, Rand McNally & Company, Chicago, 1965, p. 679.
[4] See, for example, William Ebenstein, *Today's ISMS*, 6th ed., Prentice-Hall, Inc., Englewood Cliffs, N.J., 1970.

way'' (often with considerable missionary zeal) to any and all settings. This conversion process has been evident on many dimensions. These dimensions include culture, religion, politics, and economic systems, as well as organization theory and management practice.

Comparative analysis says, in effect, ''Wait a minute; let's see if our approach is really applicable across the board.'' It emphasizes empirical research and recognizes an increasing number of relevant phenomena. It is a shift from concentration on a unique organization, country, or culture toward seeking generalizations about patterns of relationships in a variety of settings. [5]

Comparative analysis recognizes that there are many variables and that interactions among them can present a complex situation for the manager. And research continues to show that there is no one best way to achieve organizational goals. The same ends can be gained via a variety of means (equifinality). For example, Perrow sums up his research experience as follows:

> I have learned as many others have been learning, that there is no one best way to run any organization and that what works for one firm may not work for another. Thus, any theory which does not have built into its body a mechanism for distinguishing types of organizations and predicting from these types rather than an ''other things being equal provision'' or a provision for limiting all generalizations to only those organizations that fit those generalizations, is poor theory indeed. . . . I have learned that the name of the game is operationalization. [6]

Comparative studies provide an important stepping-stone in operationalizing organization theory. By identifying the relationships in different settings there is an opportunity to build a body of knowledge which includes contingent principles or guidelines. Managers are thus provided with relevant information which, coupled with astute diagnosis of specific situations, can lead to appropriate action steps.

Comparative analysis is an essential part of the foundation of organization theory and management practice (see Figure 1.1). It is an explicit part of organization science, the endeavor which underlies organization theory. The comparative approach to management practice is seen in the designation of organizational subsystems as well as in identifying the managerial role in a variety of institutions. Science and practice combine to encourage the development of contingency views—an integral part of principles and propositions that are continually evolving.

---

[5] Dwight Waldo, ''Comparative Public Administration,'' in Preston P. LeBreton (ed.), *Comparative Administrative Theory,* University of Washington Press, Seattle, Wash., 1968, p. 110.
[6] Charles Perrow, ''Some Reflections on Technology and Organizational Analysis,'' in Anant R. Negandhi (ed.), *Modern Organizational Theory: Contextual, Environmental and Socio-cultural Variables,* Kent State University Press, Kent, Ohio, 1973, p. 51.

CLASSIFICATION OF ORGANIZATIONS

Part of the problem in comparative analysis is, ''What should be compared to what?'' *Classification* means ''arrangement according to some systematic division.'' Alfred Kuhn suggests that:

> Things can be classified in numberless ways. Organizations are no exception. Among others, they can be classified as good or bad; profit or nonprofit; public or private; large, medium, or small; producers of commodities or producers of services; centralized or decentralized; primitive or advanced, or as educational, industrial, governmental, religious, philanthropic, or fraternal; and so on and on. No system of classification is ''better'' in any absolute sense, its usefulness depending on the purpose at hand. [7]

Before elaborating on various classification schemes it is important to recognize several key points. *One,* there are no right or wrong ways to classify organizations. The goal is better understanding of organizational phenomena—not perfection in classification. Whatever division is helpful in understanding organizations and facilitating more appropriate managerial action is ''good.'' *Second,* classification often leads to forced compartmentalization. This process can be helpful in describing organizations according to pertinent characteristics. However, it should be recognized that most characteristics are neither wholly present nor absent in organizations. Centralization-decentralization is really a continuum, as are most characteristics used in comparative analysis. *Third,* regardless of the classification used, it is important to specify the particular focus of attention, such as individual behavior, group dynamics, or organizational performance. *Fourth,* for comparative purposes organizational performance should be considered in terms of a multidimensional goal set—effectiveness, efficiency, and participant satisfaction, for example. With these ground rules as background, let us consider various ways that organizations have been classified in order to facilitate comparative analysis. [8]

If organizations are considered open systems with input, transformation, and output, we can classify them on the basis of differences in these three dimensions. Focusing on output (perhaps using the Standard Industrial Classification system) would allow comparison of electrical equipment producers with firms manufacturing electronics. Or petroleum refineries could be compared with insurance companies. However, this approach is often confusing because the same company (organization?) produces automobiles and refrigerators. A conglomerate might include shipyards as well as sand and gravel companies. Ajar Door Company may have fewer than 100 employees and produce no other products. Swinging Door, Inc., may be part of a large, diversified forest products company with 25,000 employees. Comparing these two organizations

---

[7] Alfred Kuhn, *The Study of Society: A Unified Approach,* Richard D. Irwin, Inc., and The Dorsey Press, Homewood, Ill., 1963, p. 431.

[8] For a review of the means for classifying organizations, see Peter M. Blau, op. cit., pp. 323–338, and Stanley H. Udy, Jr., op. cit., pp. 678–709.

may lead to distortions because of differences in key factors other than output. Thus, classification according to output is often not very helpful in understanding organizational phenomena. Aggregating output into goods versus services or human versus material output is not very useful either.

The task and its related technology have provided one of the most useful ways of classifying organizations. [9] This topic was covered in detail in Chapter 8. See Figure 8.1 for examples of classification along a technology continuum from simple to complex and from stable-uniform to dynamic-nonuniform. Craft technology is shown as the most simple, stable, and uniform. Other examples are machine tending, mass-production assembly line, continuous process, and advanced technology (atomic energy, aerospace, and electronics).

Although task and technology have received the most attention in comparative analysis, other approaches have also been useful. Figure 19.1 shows several ways in which organizations can be classified—means of obtaining compliance, social needs orientation, prime beneficiary, and sponsor-recipient relations. As indicated above, there is no overall "best" classification scheme; it depends on the user's purpose. [10] It is good if it facilitates the handling of relevant information about organizations. For example, Udy suggests a multidimensional approach with a social setting, internal administrative system, and a technology as the bases for comparative analysis. [11]

One of the obvious difficulties with classification schemes such as those in Figure 19.1 is overlapping. Many organizations play multiple roles but they are slotted into categories based on their primary functions. A church is mostly cooperative but partly service, profit, and pressure. "A business firm is a profit organization in its normal operations, a service organization in some of its community activities, a pressure organization in its lobbying and some of its institutional advertising, and a cooperative in its nonprofit cafeteria or bowling team." [12]

No classification system can avoid this difficulty of multiple roles and overlapping. If we were to distinguish between business and educational organizations, how would we classify a school owned by a private company for the children of its employees? If we distinguish between public and private organizations, what is a university whose expenses are paid by students, private donors, and taxation? If we distinguish between profit and nonprofit organizations, what is a nationalized railway that turns its profits into the public treasury? "That the same organization falls into several categories simultaneously is not a defect of the classification system, but a reflection of the diversity of organizational phenomena." [13]

If the ultimate goal is understanding organizational similarities and differences, the specific designation is not crucial; it is only a means to an end. Moreover, comparative

---

[9] Charles Perrow, "A Framework for the Comparative Analysis of Organizations," *American Sociological Review,* April 1967, pp. 194-208.
[10] For a comparison of the Blau-Scott and Etzioni typologies, see Richard H. Hall, Eugene Haas, and Norman J. Johnson, "An Examination of the Blau-Scott and Etzioni Typologies," *Administrative Science Quarterly,* June 1967, pp. 118-139.
[11] Udy, op. cit., p. 687.
[12] Alfred Kuhn, op. cit., p. 435.
[13] Ibid., p. 435.

analysis may be more fruitful if it is concentrated at the level of subsystems. If so, we can compare task environments for regulated and nonregulated companies, goals and values for public and private schools, technical subsystems for industrial and governmental research labs, as well as structural, psychosocial, and managerial considerations across a variety of organizations. The emphasis is on describing organizational

FIGURE 19.1 SEVERAL WAYS TO CLASSIFY ORGANIZATIONS

MEANS OF OBTAINING COMPLIANCE*

The compliance structure in organizations is determined by the kinds of power (coercive, remunerative, and normative) applied to lower-level participants.

Three Types of Organizations Based on Kinds of Power Used
1. *Coercive organizations* use force (latent or manifest) as the chief means of control over lower-level participants. These participants are generally alienated from the objectives of the organization. Examples include concentration camps, penal institutions, and custodial mental hospitals.
2. *Utilitarian organizations* use remuneration as the basis of control where lower-level participants contribute to the organization with calculative involvement, based on what benefits they can receive. Examples are businesses and most labor unions.
3. *Normative organizations* use moral control as the main source of influence over participants who have a high motivational and moral involvement. Examples include churches, universities, and hospitals, as well as many political and social organizations.

SOCIAL NEEDS ORIENTATION†

Four Types of Organizations Based on Broad Social Needs to Which They Are Oriented
1. *Organizations oriented to economic production* include business firms that are engaged in the production and distribution of goods and services. Their primary function is economic, although there may be other goals which the organization must achieve in order to maintain itself in the environmental system.
2. *Organizations oriented to political goals* are geared to the attainment of valued goals and to the generation and allocation of power in society. This would include most governmental organizations.
3. *Integrative organizations* are concerned with the adjustment of conflicts and the direction of motivation to fulfill certain social expectations. The court system and legal profession is in this group. It also includes hospitals because they provide the mechanism for meeting the social needs for medical care.
4. *Pattern-maintenance organizations* have primary functions that are cultural, educational, or expressive. Examples are churches and schools.

PRIME BENEFICIARY‡

Four Basic Categories of Organizational Participants
1. The members, or rank-and-file participants
2. The owners or managers of the organization
3. The clients
4. The public at large

Four Types of Organization Based on Prime Beneficiary
1. *Mutual-benefit associations:* the prime beneficiary is the membership; examples are labor unions, trade and professional associations.
2. *Business concerns:* owners are the prime beneficiaries.
3. *Service organizations:* the client group is the prime beneficiary; includes hospitals, universities, religious organizations, and social agencies.
4. *Commonwealth organizations:* the primary beneficiary is the public at large; examples are the military, law enforcement agencies, the post office, and penal institutions.

---

*Amitai Etzioni, *A Comparative Analysis of Complex Organizations*, The Free Press, New York, 1961, pp. 23–67.
†Talcott Parsons, *Structure and Process in Modern Societies*, The Free Press, New York, 1960, pp. 44–47.
‡Copyright © 1962 by Chandler Publishing Company. Reprinted from *Formal Organizations: A Comparative Approach* by Peter M. Blau and W. Richard Scott by permission of Chandler Publishing Company, an Intext publisher.

FIGURE 19.1 SEVERAL WAYS TO CLASSIFY ORGANIZATIONS (CONTINUED)

SPONSOR-RECIPIENT RELATIONS AND TRANSACTIONS§

Roles, or Relationships of Persons to Organizations

    1 *Sponsors:* Those persons whose desires originate and / or continue the organization's existence. Where the terms are appropriate, these will be the persons who control the residual contribution, and who perform the employer function.

    2 *Staff:* The persons who actually produce the commodities or services created by the organization, or who actually perform its main work. In the typical continuing organization these are the employees, who may or may not personally share the goals of the organization.

    3 *Recipients:* The persons who receive the commodities produced, or who are the direct objects of its services. These are the persons at or toward whom the work of the organization is directed.

Four Types of Organizations, by Allocation of Costs and Values

TYPE	COSTS	VALUES	TRANSACTIONAL BASE
Cooperative	Recipients	Recipients	None (Production for Selves)
Profit	Recipients	Sponsors	Selfish
Service	Sponsors	Recipients	Generous
Pressure	Sponsors	Sponsors	Third-Party Strategies

    1 *Cooperative organizations:* group equivalent of producing for oneself; sponsors and recipients are the same group. Examples include the family; legitimate government (run in the interests of its citizens); consumer and producer cooperatives; trade and professional associations; social, fraternal, sports, hobby, and similar organizations; and church congregations.

    2 *Profit organizations:* expression of the selfish transaction; customers are recipients who pay the whole cost of operating, plus the profit. Examples are a wide variety of business firms, as well as rackets and other criminal groups. Other organizations such as churches, government, schools, charities, and cooperatives take on profit characteristics in part and / or periodically.

    3 *Service organizations:* equivalent of generous transactions; sponsors bear the costs and the benefits are directed toward recipients, essentially as gifts. Examples are charities, missionary and charitable aspects of churches, subsidized education, nonprofit research organizations, and other groups who supply legal aid, emergency relief, and the like.

    4 *Pressure organizations:* direct their activities toward recipients who neither receive the benefits of the organization nor pay its costs in any direct sense; purpose is not to gain from transactions with the recipients, as such, but rather to influence the recipients in a roundabout strategy designed to change the power factors in some other transaction of interest to the sponsors, which transaction may be selfish or generous. Examples are lobbies, political parties, labor unions, trade associations (to the extent they are not cooperatives), and propaganda agencies.

---

§Alfred Kuhn, *The Study of Society: A Unified Approach*, Richard D. Irwin, Inc., and The Dorsey Press, Homewood, Ill., 1963, pp. 431–435.

---

phenomena in terms of characteristics that are meaningful for all organizations, regardless of primary orientation or function.

SYSTEMS FRAMEWORK FOR COMPARATIVE ANALYSIS

Our approach to comparative analysis is less concerned with classification per se and more concerned with facilitating understanding organizational phenomena. Thus, we use the systems approach, which has been the framework for the book. Organizations can be compared on the basis of their environmental suprasystem, including the general societal milieu or culture, as well as their more specific task environments. Similarly, organizations can be compared in terms of the various subsystems which are part of any organization—goals and values, technology, structure, psychosocial, and managerial. In order to be meaningful, more detailed dimensions or characteristics for each of the subsystems would have to be identified. The systems framework facilitates the development of organization theory because it focuses attention on meaningful groups of organizational characteristics or relevant dimensions. This fits into the processs described by Blau.

> A theory of organizations, whatever its specific nature, and regardless of how subtle the organizational processes it takes into account, has as its central aim to establish the constellations of characteristics that develop in organizations of various kinds. Comparative studies of many organizations are necessary, not alone to test the hypothesis implied by such a theory, but also to provide a basis for initial exploration and refinement of the theory indicating the conditions on which relationships, originally assumed to hold universally, are contingent. [14]

We will return to the systems framework for comparative analysis in the course of our discussion of contingency views. Contingency views are a natural outgrowth of comparative analysis based on systems concepts.

SYSTEMS CONCEPTS AND CONTINGENCY VIEWS

A system is an organized, unitary whole composed of two or more interdependent parts, components, or subsystems and delineated by identifiable boundaries from its environmental suprasystem. We defined an organization as (1) a subsystem of its broader environment, and (2) goal-oriented; comprised of (3) a technical subsystem, (4) a structural subsystem, and (5) a psychosocial subsystem; and coordinated by (6) a managerial subsystem. Using these ideas we can describe the contingency view as follows:

> The contingency view of organizations and their management suggests that an organization is a system composed of subsystems and delineated by identifiable boundaries from its environmental suprasystem. The contingency view seeks to understand the interrelationships within and among subsystems as well as between the organization and its environment and to define patterns of relationships or configurations of variables. It emphasizes the multivariate nature of organizations and attempts to understand how organizations operate under varying conditions and in specific circumstances. Contingency views are ultimately directed toward suggesting organizational designs and managerial actions most appropriate for specific situations.

The contingency view can serve as a general model or paradigm for the investigation of important organizational and environmental variables and their interactions.

---

[14] Blau, op. cit., p. 332.

Substantial progress has already been made in looking at relationships between the various organizational subsystems. This is the most significant development in modern organization and management theory and it is of relatively recent origin. So far, most of the empirical studies have considered the relationships between only a limited number of organizational variables. For example, there has been substantial research concerning the impact of task/technology on organization structure and/or interpersonal relationships. For example, mechanized assembly lines currently dictate appropriate structural arrangements of people in order for the system to function efficiently. The routinization of the process coupled with the inflexibility of the structure often leads to the dissatisfaction of employees. [15] This seems to indicate that more research and conceptualizing are needed to determine "appropriate" long-run integration of technical, structural, and psychosocial factors.

Modern organization theory reflects a search for patterns of relationships, configurations among subsystems, and a contingency view. Lorsch and Lawrence say:

> During the past few years there has been evident a new trend in the study of organizational phenomena. Underlying this new approach is the idea that the internal functioning of organizations must be consistent with the demands of the organization task, technology, or external environment, and the needs of its members if the organization is to be effective. Rather than searching for the panacea of the one best way to organize under all conditions, investigators have more and more tended to examine the functioning of organizations in relation to the needs of their particular members and the external pressures facing them. Basically, this approach seems to be leading to the development of a "contingency" theory of organization with the appropriate internal states and processes of the organization contingent upon external requirements and member needs. [16]

Numerous others have stressed this same idea. Thompson suggests that the essence of administration lies in understanding the basic patterns which exist between the various subsystems and with the environment. "The basic function of administration appears to be co-alignment, not merely of people (in coalitions) but of institutionalized action—of technology and task environment into a viable domain, and of organizational design and structure appropriate to it." [17]

Organization and management theory has evolved continually. And, as in biological evolution, there has not been a radical transformation which eliminated the old and substituted the new. Rather, the resulting theories at each stage have been mutations

---

[15] There is increasing evidence of employee dissatisfaction in mass-production industries. "Inevitably, the monotony issue will play a bigger part in labor relations in the future. . . . The UAW is talking of making 'alternatives to the assembly line' an issue in 1973 bargaining." "Productivity: Our Biggest Undeveloped Resource," *Business Week*, Sept. 9, 1972, p. 108.

[16] Jay W. Lorsch and Paul R. Lawrence, *Studies in Organization Design*, Richard D. Irwin, Inc., and The Dorsey Press, Homewood, Ill., 1970, p. 1.

[17] James D. Thompson, *Organizations in Action*, McGraw-Hill Book Company, New York, 1967, pp. 157–158.

of the old while retaining many of the more enduring concepts. Furthermore, the most appropriate models are those which best fit the environment of modern organizations (survival of the fittest). Hopefully, we can take the best of the existing theory, develop new insights about organizational relationships via comparative analysis, and refine the body of knowledge accordingly. This process is basic to the development of theory which is applicable to a variety of organizations in specific situations—the essence of a contingency view.

CONTINGENCY VIEWS AND ORGANIZATION THEORY

Systems concepts, comparative analysis, and contingency views have contributed significantly to the evolution of organization theory. The field has moved away from closed-system, simplistic views toward recognition of the rich complexities of modern organizations—systems of interdependent psychological, sociological, technical, and economic variables. General systems theory provides the overall model for the study of social organizations. But it involves a relatively high level of abstraction. Contingency views are based on systems concepts but tend to be more concrete and to emphasize more specific characteristics of social organizations as well as patterns of relationships among the subsystems. [18] This trend toward the more explicit understanding of patterns of relationships among organizational variables is essential if theory is to facilitate improved management practice.

The excerpts in Figure 19.2 suggest the essence of the contingency view as interpreted by several authors. In general, there is a rejection of universal principles appropriate to all situations. There is no "one best way" to organize and manage. Decentralization is not necessarily better than centralization; bureaucracy is not all bad; explicit objectives are not always good; a democratic-participative leadership style may not fit certain situations; and tight control may be appropriate at times. In short, "it all depends" on a number of interrelated external and internal variables. Prescriptive guidelines should be set forth in statements such as, "If the condition is A, then action X is most likely to be effective. However, if the condition is B, then action Y should be used."

A Conceptual Model

Figure 19.3 is an example of the approach needed to develop a comprehensive conceptual model of contingency views for organization theory and management practice. It is a combination of the systems framework utilized throughout this book plus polar descriptions of organization systems or types: closed/stable/mechanistic and open/adaptive/organic.

In developing this terminology, we were influenced by the dichotomization presented by Burns and Stalker—mechanistic versus organic managerial systems. [19] We

---

[18] For more detail on this subject see Fremont E. Kast and James E. Rosenzweig, *Contingency Views of Organization and Management,* Science Research Associates, Inc., Palo Alto, Calif., 1973.
[19] Burns and Stalker, op. cit.

FIGURE 19.2 ESSENCE OF THE CONTINGENCY VIEW

TOM BURNS AND G. M. STALKER *(The Management of Innovation):* We have endeavored to stress the appropriateness of each system to its own specific set of conditions. Equally, we desire to avoid the suggestion that either system (mechanistic or organic) is superior under all circumstances to the other. In particular, nothing in our experience justifies the assumption that mechanistic systems should be superseded by organic in conditions of stability. The beginning of administrative wisdom is the awareness that there is no one optimum type of management system.

HAROLD J. LEAVITT ("Applied Organization Change in Industry: Structural, Technical, and Human Approaches"): If we view organizations as systems of interaction among task, structural, technical and human variables, several different classes of effort to change organizational behavior can be grossly mapped.

Such a view provides several entry points for efforts to effect change. One can try to change aspects of task solution, task definition, or task performance by introducing new tools, new structures, or new or modified people or machines. On occasion we have tried to manipulate only one of these variables and discovered that all the others move in unforeseen and often costly directions.

RICHARD H. HALL *(Organizations: Structure and Process):* A major conclusion from this analysis is that effectiveness is not achieved through following one organizational model. . . . There is no one best way to organize for the purpose of achieving the highly varied goals of organizations within a highly varied environment. Particular kinds of goals coupled with specific kinds of activities within particular kinds of environments do call for particular organizational structures if effectiveness is a major criterion for the organization.

CHARLES PERROW ("A Framework for the Comparative Analysis of Organizations"): Finally, to call for decentralization, representative bureaucracy, collegial authority, or employee-centered, innovative or organic organizations—to mention only a few of the highly normative prescriptions that are being offered by social scientists today—is to call for a type of structure that can be realized only with a certain type of technology, unless we are willing to pay a high cost in terms of output. Given a routine technology, the much maligned Weberian bureaucracy probably constitutes the socially optimum form of organizational structure.

If all this is plausible, then existing varieties of organizational theory must be selectively applied. It is increasingly recognized that there is no "one best" theory (any more than there is "one best" organizational structure, form of leadership, or whatever) unless it be so general as to be of little utility in understanding the variety of organizations.

JAY W. LORSCH ("Introduction to the Structural Design of Organizations"): The structure of an organization is not an immutable given, but rather a set of complex variables about which managers can exercise considerable choice.

. . . Our understanding of organizations as systems is new and it is growing rapidly. The ideas which are presented here will certainly be modified and improved. But as crude as they are, they represent better tools than the principles which have been relied on in the past. These ideas clearly move us in a new and promising direction—that of tailoring the organization to its environment and to the complex needs of its members.

FRED E. FEIDLER ("Style or Circumstance: The Leadership Enigma"): The results show that we cannot talk about simply good leaders or poor leaders. A leader who is effective in one situation may or may not be effective in another. Therefore, we must specify the situations in which a leader performs well or badly.

WILLIAM H. NEWMAN ("Strategy and Management Structure"): The matching of strategy and management design presents a challenging opportunity to scholars of management. It calls for skill in building a viable, integrated system; it draws upon insights on many facets of management; and it plunges us into a highly dynamic set of relationships. Both synthesis and refinement of theory are involved.

. . . A corollary of the proposition that management design should be varied so that it is *(a)* integrated within its parts, and *(b)* matched to specific company strategy is that no single management design is ideal for all circumstances. We cannot say, for example, that management by objectives, decentralization, participative management or tight control are desirable in all situations. Company strategy is one of the important factors determining what managerial arrangement is optimal.

were also influenced by the general systems literature and, in particular, the concept of closed and open systems. [20] While these sources provide the fundamental basis for classification into two system types, many others use similar dimensions or characteristics which fit this classification.

A word of caution. Most authors are clear in emphasizing that any polarization is not characteristic of modern organizations. Total organizations simply cannot be described as closed/stable/mechanistic or open/adaptive/organic. They have characteristics which fit somewhere between these extremes. A production line typically is not completely closed/stable/mechanistic, nor is a research laboratory completely open/adaptive/organic. Conceptually we prefer to think of these characteristics on a dimensional basis rather than as polar positions. Moreover, different departments of a single organization may fall on different points of what we view as a continuum. Sales departments tend to be more open and adaptive than production departments. Practically, however, we have great difficulty in presenting these characteristics as dimensions. We can describe the polar positions, but it is much more difficult to look at each of the possible intermediate positions (theoretically infinite) of certain characteristics—for example, between closed and open systems. Further refinements in contingency views are necessary in order to describe and analyze points along the continuum. We have illustrated this approach by identifying several dimensions for each organizational supra- or subsystem. [21]

The analysis of the key subsystems and their important dimensions provides a pattern of relationships for the relatively closed/stable/mechanistic organizational system which is significantly different from that of the relatively open/adaptive/organic organizational system. Concepts about these relationships have not been "proven" via substantial empirical research. In fact, it is doubtful whether or not they can ever be proven conclusively. Organizations and their environments are much too dynamic to allow us to set forth "laws" about relationships. Rather, we can only expect to identify tentative patterns of relationships among the organizational variables.

However, this initial step of identifying patterns of relationships can be of major importance. We can apply this model in the study of many different types of organizations. For example, the research literature suggests that there are significant differences among correctional institutions which could be better understood by using a contingency view. Those institutions that have *confinement* of inmates as a primary goal tend to exhibit characteristics set forth under "closed/stable/mechanistic" in Figure 19.3. Those organizations which emphasize the goal of *rehabilitation* of participants tend to exhibit characteristics set forth under "open/adaptive/organic." The maximum security prison is very closed, highly structured, and exercises tight control (externally imposed) over inmates. The rehabilitation-oriented correctional institution is more open to society (for example, work-release programs), has a more flexible structure, and tries to develop self-control within each participant.

Even within the military there are differences depending on the nature of specific

---

[20] Thompson, op. cit.
[21] An expanded version can be seen in Kast and Rosenzweig, op. cit., pp. 315-318.

FIGURE 19.3 A CONCEPTUAL MODEL OF CONTINGENCY VIEWS OF ORGANIZATION AND MANAGEMENT

SYSTEMS AND THEIR KEY DIMENSIONS	CHARACTERISTICS OF ORGANIZATIONAL SYSTEMS	
	CLOSED/STABLE/MECHANISTIC	OPEN/ADAPTIVE/ORGANIC
Environmental Suprasystem:		
General nature	Placid	Turbulent
Predictability	Certain, Determinate	Uncertain, Indeterminate
Boundary relationships	Relatively closed. Limited to few participants (sales, purchasing, etc.). Fixed and well defined.	Relatively open. Many participants have external relationships. Varied and not clearly defined.
Overall Organizational System:		
Goal structure	Organization as a single-goal maximizer	Organization as a searching, adapting, learning system which continually adjusts its multiple goals and aspirations
Decision-making processes	Programmable, Computational	Nonprogrammable, Judgmental
Organization emphasis	On performance	On problem solving
Goals and Values:		
Organizational goals in general	Efficient performance, Stability, Maintenance	Effective problem solving, Innovation, Growth
Pervasive values	Efficiency, Predictability, Security, Risk aversion	Effectiveness, Adaptability, Responsiveness, Risk taking
Goal set	Single, Clear-cut	Multiple, determined by necessity to satisfy a variety of constraints
Involvement in goal-setting process	Managerial hierarchy primarily (top down)	Widespread participation (bottom up as well as top down)
Technical System:		
General nature of tasks	Repetitive, Routine	Varied, Nonroutine
Input to transformation process	Homogeneous	Heterogeneous
Output of transformation process	Standardized, Fixed	Nonstandardized, Variable
Methods	Programmed, Algorithmic	Nonprogrammed, Heuristic

Structural System:		
Organizational formalization	High	Low
Procedures and rules	Many and specific. Usually formal and written.	Few and general. Usually informal and unwritten.
Authority structure	Concentrated, Hierarchic	Dispersed, Network
Psychosocial System:		
Status structure	Clearly delineated by formal hierarchy	More diffuse. Based upon expertise and professional norms.
Role definitions	Specific and fixed	General and dynamic. Change with tasks.
Motivational factors	Emphasis on extrinsic rewards, security, and lower-level need satisfaction. Theory X view.	Emphasis on intrinsic rewards, esteem, and self-actualization. Theory Y view.
Leadership style	Autocratic, Task-oriented, Desire for certainty	Democratic, Relationship-oriented, Tolerance for ambiguity
Power system	Power concentration	Power equalization
Managerial System:		
General nature	Hierarchical structure of control, authority, and communications; Combination of independent. static components	A network structure of control, authority, and communications; Co-alignment of interdependent, dynamic components
Decision-making techniques	Autocratic, Programmed, Computational	Participative, Nonprogrammed, Judgmental
Planning process	Repetitive, fixed, and specific	Changing, flexible, and general
Control structure	Hierarchic, specific, short-term. External control of participants	Reciprocal, general, long-term. Self-control of participants
Means of conflict resolution	Resolved by superior (refer to "book")	Resolved by group ("situational ethics")
	Compromise and smoothing	Confrontation
	Keep below the surface	Bring out in open

activities. The organization for basic military training displays characteristics of the closed/stable/mechanistic system. However, in the design, development, and procurement of advanced weapon systems, the military organization can be described as relatively open/adaptive/organic. New approaches, such as program management and matrix organizations, have emerged to meet changing requirements. Other organizations have gone through similar cycles over time. For example, our school systems have had to become more open/adaptive/organic in response to social pressures and the individual participant's needs, particularly in the past two decades.

This model may also be useful in looking at the historical evolution of an organization or even an industry. The airline industry provides an illustration of changing organizational characteristics and patterns of relationships between subsystems over time. In general airlines have been more open/adaptive/organic organizations than railroads, for example. In their early days they were faced with a turbulent environment—accelerating technology, increasing consumer mobility and affluence, growing acceptance of a new mode of travel, and changing government regulations. During this period they could be characterized by the open/adaptive/organic form. However, as the industry became more stable and operations became more routine, they moved toward a more closed/stable/mechanistic form.

Within the total organization the primary task of the airline—the individual flight—became very routine, programmed, and tightly controlled by specific rules and regulations. Individual tasks became much more specific and routinized. (We can remember earlier days when stewardesses were not programmed to greet passengers, check them for guns or bombs, demonstrate oxygen masks, and serve drinks and prepared meals; they even had time to fraternize with passengers.) However, at the coordinative level above that of individual flight—the planning, organizing, and controlling of overall flight operations—the airlines must still operate in a more open/adaptive/organic mode. The system must cope with changes in schedules, high rates of employee turnover, and new mixes of personnel for each flight. And even the routine characteristics of the individual flight may change abruptly when the hijacker suddenly says, "Give me $500,000, three parachutes, and let's fly to Tahiti." The operation moves very rapidly to a more open, adaptive system which cannot utilize procedures programmed for routine flights.

We can use this model to investigate even more subtle differences within organizations. For example, the university is typically thought of as an open/adaptive/organic system. However, within the university various subunits, departments, or programs may have different characteristics. The typical university graduate program (particularly doctoral programs) is more likely to exhibit open/adaptive/organic characteristics than the typical undergraduate program. This hypothesis leads to the suggestion that undergraduate and graduate programs should be organized and administered differently— an approach which is not always carried out in practice.

The history department and the campus police represent two rather distinct organization types. In order to understand them it would be useful to describe them in terms of characteristics or key dimensions within the supra- and subsystems. Until this process of observation and description were completed, it would not be wise to invoke "principles" of organization or management. Situational analysis should precede prescriptions for organization design and management practice.

Much research and conceptualization must be done in order to develop a comprehensive model. Indeed, it is probably an open-ended task. Ideally, empirical research should include multivariate relationships among all of the organizational subsystems or variables. Although this objective is conceptually enticing, it is operationally difficult if not impossible to achieve. The current state of our knowledge about any single variable, such as technology or structure or the psychosocial system, is still very limited. How do we meet this dilemma of needing a more complete understanding of the subsystems and their interrelationships?

Practically, it will be a slow, painstaking process of trying to understand interrelationships and linking the various variables together. After developing a substantial body of knowledge concerning dual relationships, we may be able to introduce additional factors in order to understand the multivariate relationships. Morse, for example, studied the relationship of individual motivation to the general organizational climate as defined by technology, structure, and environmental influences. [22] His research was designed specifically to build on earlier work by Lawrence and Lorsch. Ultimately, through this approach, we will be better able to define certain patterns of relationships among organizational variables and/or subsystems which will facilitate meaningful suggestions for appropriate organization designs and managerial action. This is a major long-run effort on the part of many researchers, investigating a wide variety of organizations and their subsystems. It involves comparative analysis across functions, levels, institutions, and cultures. While we have only really begun this effort, progress seems to be accelerating and we are adding relevant information to the body of knowledge.

CONTINGENCY VIEWS AND MANAGEMENT PRACTICE

Traditional management theory emphasized the development of principles which were appropriate and applicable to all organizations and all managerial tasks. These universal principles were quite prescriptive—there was an appropriate way to design and manage organizations. Although the quantitative and behavioral sciences have introduced new concepts to the study of organizations, they, too, have tended toward prescribing the "one best way." The quantitative sciences have emphasized a normative approach and stressed the logical, rational, algorithmic view of management and decision making. Many behavioral scientists have also emphasized a particular approach to management. For example, it is easy to recognize that McGregor considered his Theory X (man is basically lazy and irresponsible) to be less appropriate, in general, than his Theory Y (man is basically industrious and responsible). [23] Similarly, Likert

---

[22] John J. Morse, "Organizational Characteristics and Individual Motivation," in Jay W. Lorsch and Paul R. Lawrence (eds.), *Studies in Organization Design,* Richard D. Irwin, Inc., and The Dorsey Press, Homewood, Ill., 1970, pp. 84–100.
[23] Douglas McGregor, *The Human Side of Enterprise,* McGraw-Hill Book Company, New York, 1960.

downgraded his highly structured, autocratic System 1 and stressed the functionality and merit of the more democratic, participative System 4 for all organizational situations. [24]

Systems concepts emphasize that organizations are composed of many subsystems whose interrelationships have to be recognized. Once we accept a systems view, it becomes apparent that it is impossible to prescribe principles which are appropriate to all organizations. There are so many relevant variables that it is impossible for a simplistic model to depict reality. A simple view is appropriate only when the system under consideration is stable, mechanistic, and effectively closed to intervening external variables. Once we begin to consider organizations as open systems with interactive components, we can no longer think in simplistic, unidimensional terms.

If the focus is on *describing* and *understanding* why some organizations have been more successful than others, the resulting body of knowledge should be readily translatable into guidelines for action. Prescriptions with a contingency flavor should be applicable more readily than general principles because the manager can relate the theory to his specific situation. The thrust of contingency views in organization theory is to offset the typical response, "The theory may be appropriate in general, but our organization is different."

Do comparative analysis, systems concepts, and contingency views provide a panacea for solving problems in organizations? The answer is an emphatic *no*; this approach does not provide "ten easy steps" to success in management. Such cookbook approaches, while seemingly applicable and easy to grasp, are usually shortsighted, narrow in perspective, and superficial—in short, unrealistic. Fundamental ideas, such as systems concepts and contingency views, are more difficult to comprehend. However, they facilitate more thorough understanding of complex situations and increase the likelihood of appropriate actions. This approach requires a considerable amount of conceptual skill on the part of the manager.

Conceptual skill distinguishes really effective managers at all levels and particularly those who progress to the top. [25] It involves the ability to "see the forest for the trees," to discern key interrelationships, and to attach degrees of importance to the various factors bearing on the problem. "The successful manager must be a good diagnostician and must value a spirit of inquiry. . . . There is no one correct managerial strategy that will work for all men at all times. . . . He may be highly directive at one time and with one employee but very nondirective at another time and with another employee." [26] The manager must be flexible in order to cope with a variety of situations. This approach is obviously more difficult than reliance on general principles and rules. It requires heuristic problem solving rather than indiscriminate application of algorithms. And it requires a pragmatic approach with heavy emphasis on situational analysis. [27]

---

[24] Rensis Likert, *The Human Organization,* McGraw-Hill Book Company, New York, 1967.

[25] George F. Lombard, "Relativism in Organizations," *Harvard Business Review,* March–April 1967, pp. 55–65.

[26] Edgar H. Schein, *Organizational Psychology,* 2d ed., Prentice-Hall, Inc., Englewood Cliffs, N.J., 1970, pp. 70 and 71.

[27] Harvey Sherman, *It All Depends: A Pragmatic Approach to Organization,* University of Alabama Press, University, Ala., 1966.

As we consider contingency views and managerial practice, it is important to recognize that many managers have and will continue to use such an approach implicitly. They have an intuitive "sense of the situation," are flexible diagnosticians, and adjust plans and actions accordingly. Thus, systems concepts and contingency views are not new. However, if this approach to organization theory and management practice can be made more explicit, we can facilitate better management and more effective and efficient organizations. There is nothing as practical as a theory that works.

A Contingency View of the Managerial Task

In order to explore the application of systems concepts and contingency views to management practice, it is helpful to consider that task of the general manager as shown in Figure 19.4. His job involves relating the organization to its environment as well as designing comprehensive systems and plans. Within that role we can identify several distinct spheres of activity, such as strategy formulation, organization design, information-decision systems, influence systems and leadership, and organization improvement. And we can illustrate the application of contingency views in each of these particular functions. The single arrows in Figure 19.4 indicate an appropriate sequence of activities if an organizational endeavor were being established for the first time to achieve an objective. It would also be an appropriate sequence for analyzing and redesigning ongoing organizations. In most situations, however, it is obvious that the various activities will be going on almost simultaneously and that there are crosscurrents among them. The manager functions in the middle of a patterned swirl of events, planning and controlling organizational endeavor in order to maintain a dynamic equilibrium.

A contingency view of strategy formulation is set forth by Learned, et al., as follows: (1) environmental opportunity—what the organization *might do*; (2) competence and resources—what the organization *can do* realistically; (3) managerial interests and desires—what the organization *wants to do*; and (4) responsibility to society— what the organization *should do*.[28] This approach reflects systems concepts and a contingency view because it recognizes the interrelationships between the various components. Assessing the impact of the four components of strategy formulation is a complex and delicate task. While a contingency approach does not make the task any easier, it does facilitate understanding of the complexity and helps the general manager cope with the problem realistically.

Once the objectives and comprehensive strategies for the organization are defined, the next step is determining key operating and coordinating activities. The basic technical system must be identified, as well as structural relationships among people. This typically involves specialization by level and/or function plus coordination of specialized jobs in order to focus activity on organizational goals. Technology and structure (including differentiation and integration of tasks) were discussed in detail in Part 4.

---

[28] Edmund P. Learned, C. Roland Christensen, Kenneth R. Andrews, and William D. Guth, *Business Policy: Text and Cases,* rev. ed., Richard D. Irwin, Inc., Homewood, Ill., 1969, pp. 17-32.

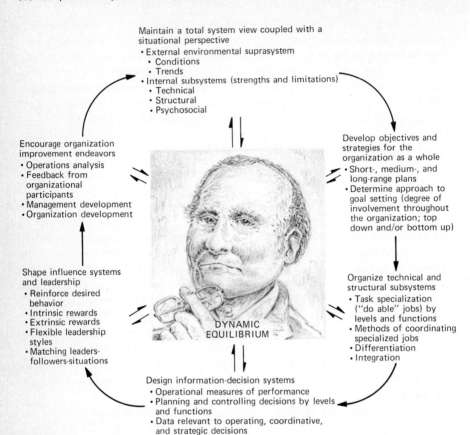

Maintain a total system view coupled with a
situational perspective
- External environmental suprasystem
  - Conditions
  - Trends
- Internal subsystems (strengths and limitations)
  - Technical
  - Structural
  - Psychosocial

Encourage organization
improvement endeavors
- Operations analysis
- Feedback from
  organizational
  participants
- Management development
- Organization development

Develop objectives and
strategies for the
organization as a whole
- Short-, medium-, and
  long-range plans
- Determine approach to
  goal setting (degree of
  involvement throughout
  the organization; top
  down and/or bottom up)

Shape influence systems
and leadership
- Reinforce desired
  behavior
- Intrinsic rewards
- Extrinsic rewards
- Flexible leadership
  styles
- Matching leaders-
  followers-situations

DYNAMIC
EQUILIBRIUM

Organize technical and
structural subsystems
- Task specialization
  ("do able" jobs) by
  levels and functions
- Methods of coordinating
  specialized jobs
- Differentiation
- Integration

Design information-decision systems
- Operational measures of performance
- Planning and controlling decisions by levels
  and functions
- Data relevant to operating, coordinative,
  and strategic decisions

FIGURE 19.4   THE MANAGERIAL TASK

Each situation should be analyzed in order to determine the most appropriate
organization structure. In addition, attention should be given to designing other aspects
of organizational systems, such as planning and control processes, the reward system,
and information-decision systems. Managers should devote explicit attention to both
structure and process (and their interrelationships) in designing organizations.

The term "information-decision system" is in itself a contingency view—information is relevant only as it pertains to managerial decision making. Therefore, it is
important to begin the design process by identifying the types of decisions made in
various parts—functions or levels—of the organization. As indicated in Figure 19.4, the
system should provide data that are meaningful to the planned tasks and measures of
performance. Developing operational measures of performance is crucial because we
tend to "get what we measure" in the way of individual and organizational behavior. If
quantity is the only yardstick, quality may suffer. If only short-run profitability for a unit
is considered, long-run viability may be endangered because of deterioration in physical and/or human resources. For complex systems, sophisticated measures of perfor-

mance should be developed in order for planning and control processes to be functional. More detail on these aspects of the general manager's task can be found in Part 6, particularly Chapters 14 and 18.

Another key function of the general manager is nurturing the psychosocial system. Of particular importance is the development of a reward-penalty system to reinforce desired behavior on the part of organizational participants. Contingency views are quite evident in much of the discussion of the psychosocial system in Part 5. Assumptions about the basic nature of man, balancing extrinsic and intrinsic rewards, and matching leaders and situations all give recognition to the importance of situational analysis and relationships among variables and/or organizational subsystems. For example, in designing a reward system, management should keep the various theories of motivation in mind and apply them where appropriate. Piece rates for individuals may be effective in one department, whereas a group bonus might be better in another situation. Nonmonetary rewards such as positive reinforcement through praise and recognition can be used effectively in many cases. As conditions change—across subunits and/or over time—the reward system should be adapted to fit specific situations.

The task of the general manager also includes encouraging organization improvement endeavors—changing the organization to make it more effective and/or efficient, as well as more satisfying for its participants. This three-part objective has a contingency flavor because a balance must be maintained in order to ensure long-run viability. Effective solutions to organizational problems must be tempered with cost considerations (cost/benefit analysis) in order to be realistic. For example, new equipment might increase output but increase cost per unit simultaneously. Overemphasis on efficiency at the expense of employee satisfaction might result in slowdown tactics, high turnover rates, and an atmosphere of tension and conflict.

A number of specific methods or techniques are available for facilitating organization improvement. The analytical techniques of operations research or management science can be useful in solving many critical problems. Attention can be focused on developing individual managers, as well as groups or organizations. A contingency view is important in order to match an appropriate planned change effort with the existing situation. The general process includes (1) diagnosis, (2) problem solving, (3) action steps, and (4) follow-up (rediagnosis).

A contingency view is emphasized in this sequence of steps. Based on the results of problem diagnosis and the specific focus of attention (individuals, team building, intergroup relations, or total organizational effectiveness), a particular mode of intervention (technique for facilitating change) can be designed. The sequence of the process is critical. Problem diagnosis must come first in order to understand the specific situation. If the process is technique-oriented (applying a "canned" approach to any and all situations), there is considerable danger of dysfunctional consequences—for example, wasting substantial amounts of energy on solving the wrong problem. This is a continuing dilemma in the interface between managers and scientists/consultants/ change agents. Quantitative and behavioral scientists should tailor their analyses and recommendations to the specific needs of the situation. This approach, coupled with systems concepts and contingency views, can result in significant contributions and improved management practice.

The general flavor of the contingency view is somewhere in between simplistic, universal principles and complex, vague notions ("it all depends"). It is a mid-range concept which recognizes the complexity involved in managing modern organizations and uses patterns of relationships and/or configurations of subsystems in order to facilitate improved practice. The art of management depends on a reasonable success rate for actions in a probabilistic environment. It is hoped that contingency views, while continually being refined by scientists/researchers/theorists, will also be made more applicable.

SUMMARY

We are all continually involved in informal comparative analysis of organizations. For example, we attempt (by examining or observing) to discover similarities or differences between schools, employers, or taverns. Formal comparative analysis or research can take any one of several directions—intraorganizational analysis across functions, levels, or subsystems and interorganizational analysis across institutions or cultures.

Comparative analysis goes beyond the case approach (a detailed description of one organization or subunit) in order to make the research results more generally applicable. To identify patterns of relationships which lead to effective performance, it is important to include many organizations.

Comparative analysis is a pervasive activity which helps us understand complex affairs (to describe and explain what is happening—including how variables are related, what causes what, and the relative importance of the various forces involved). When studying anything, we tend to compare it, at least implicitly, with something else. Comparative analysis is a sign of maturity because it opens a system to new information from a variety of situations and reduces the tendency to apply the "one best way" in all circumstances.

Classification is a typical step in comparative analysis. Scientific endeavor involves observation and description which usually lead to categorization in terms of key characteristics. This process has been evident in the development of organization theory. An obvious difficulty with classification schemes is overlapping because of the multiple roles that organizations typically play. This is a reflection of the diversity of organizational phenomena.

If the ultimate goal is understanding organizations, we are not necessarily concerned with perfection in classification systems. It is more important to develop a framework that facilitates understanding complex organizational phenomena in a variety of settings. The systems approach is helpful in this regard. We can compare organizations in terms of their environmental suprasystem and internal subsystems— goals and values, technology, structure, psychosocial, and managerial. The systems framework aids in the development of organization theory because it focuses attention on meaningful groups of organizational characteristics or relevant dimensions.

The essence of the contingency view is set forth in the chapter and a conceptual model is illustrated. This model provides a framework for research and comparative analysis by focusing on supra- and subsystems and their key dimensions and by describing characteristics for organization types—closed/stable/mechanistic and open/adaptive/organic. The application of these concepts to management practice is discussed and illustrated by reviewing various elements of the managerial task from a contingency point of view.

QUESTIONS AND PROBLEMS

1 Define comparative analysis and discuss its pervasiveness. Give examples from your own experience.
2 Outline several approaches to comparative analysis. Which approach is most useful?
3 Why is comparative analysis important in developing a body of knowledge such as organization theory?
4 Why is comparative analysis a "sign of maturity" in organization theory and management practice?
5 Discuss ways of classifying organizations. Which model or framework do you think is the most useful? Why?
6 Using the systems framework in the chapter (and for the book as a whole), sketch out a brief description of a specific organization with which you are familiar.
7 What is the essence of a contingency view of organization and management? Illustrate the concept with several examples.
8 Using the model presented in Figure 19.3, fill in two or three additional dimensions for each of the supra- and subsystems and describe their characteristics for the two polar organization types.

COMPARATIVE ORGANIZATIONAL ANALYSIS: THE HOSPITAL

The general hospital is one of the more complex organizational types. Advancing technology, together with changing medical practices, have created new and evolving goals. Hospitals typically employ a large number of professionals, both physicians and other experts, and have a high degree of specialization of labor. They have developed distinctive structures, psychosocial systems, and management practices in order to accomplish their goals. Because of the increasing need for coordination of specialized activities, managerial systems in hospitals have become more comprehensive. The hospital is becoming the institutional center for dealing with total community health problems. The boundaries of hospital activities have expanded steadily and will probably continue to do so. The following specific topics are considered in this chapter.

> Changing Environment
> Goals and Values
> Technology
> Structure
> Psychosocial System
> Managerial System

CHANGING ENVIRONMENT

In order to understand the current environment of the modern hospital, it is necessary to provide a brief historical perspective. Various social institutions have been established to deal with the problem of the sick, disabled, and dependent. At one time, hospitals were more a refuge for the ill and needy than places for medical treatment. They were established on the routes of medieval crusades and pilgrimages and had their roots deep in religious and altruistic hospitality. From these early beginnings, the hospital continued through the nineteenth century to be a haven for the homeless and impoverished. It was the "charitable last resort of the ill pauper." [1]

The medical technology of the day precluded any real efforts toward treatment, and hospitals were geared to making the ill more comfortable. Because of the unsanitary conditions and high mortality rate among patients, hospitals typically were utilized only by the poor. The more affluent ill received treatment in their own homes by private physicians.

During the eighteenth and nineteenth centuries in the United States, many voluntary hospitals were established as independent institutions managed by their own board of governors or trustees. Funds and support for these hospitals came from a rich benefactor or the local community. Physicians stood substantially apart from the hospitals. Their services were often offered on a gratis basis as a charitable endeavor, and the hospital served as a basis for training through observation of a variety of illnesses. This early detachment of the physician from the hospital was important in establishing the norms of the profession.

During this period when medical practice was becoming a profession, the dominant norm was independent practice and close physician-patient relationships, without the necessity for the intervention of the complex organization. This norm is still inherent to the medical profession, even though today both physician and patient are frequently within the structure of the hospital organization.

The dramatic developments in medical science and technology in the late nineteenth and early twentieth centuries revolutionized the role and functions of the hospital. No longer was it a place for the ill and poor to go to die; it became the primary institution for treatment. Since the beginning of the twentieth century, the hospital has expanded the boundaries of its activity and has taken on a much greater role in providing medical treatment and service to society in general. However, many of the forces affecting the hospital as an organization stem from its earlier, more restricted role. The technology and structure, as well as psychosocial and managerial systems, are also strongly influenced by the historical pattern of development.

Current Scene

Today there are more than 7,000 hospitals in the United States, with approximately 1,600,000 beds. They admit nearly 32,000,000 patients annually and employ over 2,500,000 people, exclusively of physicians. [2] The estimated national expenditure for

---

[1] Robert N. Wilson, "The Social Structure of a General Hospital," *The Annals of the American Academy of Political and Social Science,* March 1963, p. 69.
[2] These figures are from *Statistical Abstract of the United States,* 1972, U.S. Bureau of Census, 1972, pp. 66–73.

hospitals is in excess of $27 billion. This excludes the cost of physicians, other services, and drugs.

There is a wide diversity of types of hospitals. Of the 7,123 hospitals in 1970, 2,665 were operated by federal, state, and local governments; 3,600 were voluntary nonprofit hospitals; and 858 were profit or proprietary hospitals. This discussion is limited to those types classified as voluntary, nonprofit, short-term, and general institutions—representing approximately 3,000 hospitals. These have become known as community, voluntary, or general hospitals. They are typically sponsored by voluntary associations or corporations. They are general in the sense that they admit most but not all short-term patients. The general hospital is familiar to most of us. The other types, such as the government hospital, state mental hospital, and long-term hospital (such as the tuberculosis hospital), have their own characteristics. Obviously even within the definition of the general hospital there are many wide variations which make this a relatively heterogeneous classification. They vary widely by size, ranging from the small, rural general hospital to the metropolitan medical center with thousands of beds and highly specialized treatment facilities. Although general hospitals do differ in degree with respect to various characteristics, there are broad similarities.

GOALS AND VALUES

The general hospital has many diverse objectives. To be sure, the major objective is to satisfy the needs of the patient for care and treatment. But each group of participants— patients, medical staff, nurses, administrative staff, trustees, and others—interpret the means for meeting objectives in terms of their own value systems and requirements. Additional objectives, such as medical and nursing education and research, have to be integrated into the organization. "The major hospital embraces multiple goals, chiefly patient care, teaching, and research. It is at once a hotel, a treatment center, a laboratory, a university. Because the institution's work is so specialized, staffed by a variety of professional and technical personnel, there are very important problems of co-ordination and authority." [3]

Obviously, the general hospital is not isolated from the impact of sociocultural values and norms. The early development of the hospital was closely related to the social norms of charity and treatment of the poor and indigent. Society places a premium on individual welfare and physical health. The hospital has assumed a larger role as the institutional mechanism whereby this social objective is achieved. The very development of the general hospital as a private, voluntary, nonprofit institution is a reflection of community values.

The emphasis upon patient care and treatment permeates the value system and objectives of the hospital, even though there are constraints of technology, economics, and organizational abilities. [4] This value is reflected by the continuing emphasis in the

---

[3] Wilson, op. cit., p. 67.
[4] Basil S. Georgopoulos and Floyd C. Mann, *The Community General Hospital*, The Macmillan Company, New York, 1962, p. 5.

nursing profession upon TLC (tender loving care) and the desire to return to the bedside. Nurses frequently feel a deep sense of frustration and role conflict when their technical and administrative functions interfere with their perceived role of providing direct and intimate patient care.

The educational process for most of the professional participants in the hospital emphasizes patient welfare. The standards of conduct prescribed by the specific professional groups reinforce this value—for example, the Hippocratic Oath of physicians, the Florence Nightingale pledge of nurses, and the Code of Ethics of the American College of Hospital Administrators. Similar codes of other groups operating in hospitals also emphasize patient welfare. This overriding value serves a vital function in unifying the activities of participants in the hospital system and helps explain how it can operate effectively. It causes individual participants to perform their highly professionalized and specialized tasks to a common end, thus providing voluntary coordination of activities. Without this overriding value, the hospital could not function without more formalized control mechanisms. Wren says:

> The fact that a hospital does work under such a system shows clearly that the integrative elements of the system are strong enough to counteract the disruptive forces and, in particular, that the general acceptance of common values and norms of conduct by all those concerned with the hospital, including the physician "outsiders," helps to explain how such a complicated system does work. [5]

The operating goals of hospitals have undergone steady transformation as the boundaries of their activities have expanded. It was suggested that the earlier goal was to provide care for the ill and the poor who did not have the funds to take care of themselves. With advancing technology in the latter part of the nineteenth and early part of the twentieth centuries, there was a major transformation in these goals to give greater emphasis to treatment. Thus, the hospital was changed from a place of last resort for the poor to one where doctors brought their patients for treatment which could not be provided in the home. The hospital became the doctor's workshop where the physician ordered services *à la carte* for his patients. Gradually the hospital has shifted from being a place where the physician could practice his art to include broader objectives. "The hospital began to emerge as a *professional health center,* with institutional responsibility for an identifiable, coordinated program of patient care services, including control of quality, education and research." [6] The objectives and the boundaries of the hospital activities expanded to include emphasis on quality care, on the coordination of the diverse activities of the physician and the hospital staff, and on involvement in educational and research programs. Increasingly, the hospital-practice-

---

[5] George R. Wren, "The Sociology of the General Hospital: A Structural-Functional Consideration," *Hospital Administration,* Fall 1966, pp. 55–56.
[6] Robert M. Sigmond, "Professional Education for Tomorrow's Hospital Administrators: As Viewed by a Hospital Planner," *Hospital Administration,* Summer 1966, p. 27.

oriented physicians (primarily specialists) became more important as compared with the office-practice-oriented physicians (primarily general practitioners). For these physician specialists, the hospital rather than the private office became the primary institution for their activities.

Currently there is an expansion of the boundaries of activity and diversification of goals in many general hospitals. In many areas, particularly in metropolitan centers, there is an increasing concentration of the community's complex health resources in the hospital system. The hospital is taking on as its objective the optimum health service for all people in the community, rather than simply care of individual patients. "The hospital is about to be transformed from a professional health service center to a *community health service center*. As this added goal gradually moves into top priority position in the years ahead, hospital organization, service and administration will undergo dramatic changes." [7]

The passage of the Social Security Amendments in 1965 established the well-known Medicare program for persons aged sixty-five and over and the Medicaid program for low-income people in need of medical care. This step "marked a major legislative milestone in the recognition of the responsibility of the federal government to participate in the financing of health care for its citizens." [8] Currently there is an effort to establish a National Health Insurance program which would interject the federal government even more strongly into providing health care for all citizens. [9] Medicare and Medicaid have had an important effect upon the goals and programs of the hospital. The hospital is the most important existing institution in the health care field and it has had a major role in implementing these programs. In the future under any program of National Health Insurance, the hospital will have an even more vital role. Rather than establishing new institutions to implement these new programs, it will be more effective to utilize the existing hospitals as a focal point for health care.

> A more realistic approach involves identifying the strongest, most comprehensive health care institution already in existence in most communities. This institution should be strengthened still further so that it can effectively assume responsibility for assuring the provisions of comprehensive health care to its entire community. The most cursory examination of the health-care scene indicates that the only institution capable of playing such a role is the hospital. [10]

Thus, the hospital has gradually transformed its objectives, moving from primary concern with individual patient care to the broader problem of total community health service. These changes have influenced the various subsystems of the hospital.

---

[7] Ibid., p. 28.

[8] Howard N. Newman, "Medicare and Medicaid," *The Annals of the American Academy of Political and Social Science*, January 1972, p. 115.

[9] Sylvester E. Berki, "National Health Insurance: An Idea Whose Time Has Come?" *The Annals of the American Academy of Political and Social Science*, January 1972, pp. 125-144.

[10] Anne R. Somers, "The Hospital and the Health Care Delivery System," *Business Horizons*, October 1972, pp. 68-69.

TECHNOLOGY

Throughout the early history of the hospital, the crude technical knowledge severely limited its activities. Medicine was not advanced enough to meet effectively the objectives of treatment and cure of patients—the emphasis was on custodial care. The development of medical technology fundamentally changed the achievable goals of the hospital and consequently the organization structure and other subsystems. The development of the germ theory of disease, x-ray, asepsis, pathological examinations, anesthesiology, and surgical techniques all had a profound influence upon the hospital. The technological revolution brought fundamental changes in structure and goals. [11]

Because doctors were the primary controllers and users of the new technology, the role of the medical staff in the hospital increased appreciably as a result of these technological changes. The hospital became a place where all patients, not just the poor, came for treatment which could not be provided in the home. The physician and the community at large developed a greater interest in the hospital. It became the primary institution within the community that could accumulate the medical technology—knowledge, skills, and specialized equipment—necessary for patient treatment.

In the modern hospital, the medical staff obviously is the primary source of technology. Physicians have the knowledge for task performance based upon intensive training and specialization. Nurses also represent a source of knowledge and carry out many of the technical functions in the hospital. There are also a growing number of specialists who are not part of the medical or nursing staff. The chemist, bacteriologist, physical therapist, recreational director, dietician, social worker, and many other participants are highly trained and are applying their technical knowledge in the hospital setting. The increased number of these specialists has created a more complex organizational structure.

With increased complexities, there has been a growing need for improved techniques of organization and management. In the small, less complicated organization, they were relatively simple. In the modern hospital, more sophisticated approaches for the coordination of activities are necessary.

Not only have the knowledge aspects of technology become more advanced and specialized, but the physical aspects of technology—facilities, machinery, and equipment—also are more costly and complex. The modern hospital is faced with the problem of obtaining and financing newly developed diagnostic and treatment equipment. With unsophisticated technology, the black bag was the physician's equipment. Today, he requires facilities far beyond his own means of acquisition. The hospital has become the central source for the accumulation of the necessary equipment and facilities for patient care and treatment.

STRUCTURE

The organization structure of the typical general hospital differs substantially from the bureaucratic model of other large-scale organizations. The hospital has a unique rela-

---

[11] Charles Perrow, "Hospitals: Technology, Structure, and Goals," in James G. March (ed.), *Handbook of Organizations*, Rand McNally & Company, Chicago, 1965, p. 948.

tionship between the formal authority of position as represented by the administrative hierarchy and the authority of knowledge as represented by the medical practitioners and other professionals. This creates a somewhat diffused and unusual formal structure. [12]

Differentiation of Activities

Extensive differentiation and specialization of activities are evident in the general hospital. "To do its work, the hospital relies on an extensive division of labor among its members, upon a complex organizational structure which encompasses many different departments, staffs, offices, and positions, and upon an elaborate system of coordination of tasks, functions, and social interaction." [13] The tasks of the hospital are carried out by a large number of cooperating participants whose educational background, training, skills, and functions are diverse and heterogeneous. Much of the treatment task is performed by the doctors, who require the collaboration and assistance of many paramedical professional personnel. The medical staff is specialized because of the growing complexities of medical technology. The nursing staff includes graduate professional nurses in various supervisory and nonsupervisory positions, practical nurses, and nurse's aides. In addition, there are the hospital administrator and his staff, which include a number of supervisory personnel heading such departments and services as dietetics, admissions, maintenance, pharmacy, medical records, housekeeping, and laundry. Also, there are medical technicians who work in the laboratories, x-ray departments, and other units. Apart from these direct participants in the hospital system, there is usually a board of trustees that has overall institutional responsibility for the organization.

Administrative Organization and Medical Staff

A major differentiation of activities occurs because of the distinction between the administrative organization and the medical staff. The administrative organization is headed by the board of trustees, which appoints the hospital administrator as the chief executive. Under him are the various departmental directors who are in charge of functional activities such as medical records, laboratories, dietetics, housekeeping, personnel records, public relations, and accounting. These activities are primarily the "care" functions of the hospital—the efficient provision of machinery, laboratory facilities, operating rooms, and so forth.

The other part of the dual differentiation is the medical staff, which is engaged in the treatment or "cure" process. The medical staff is made up of licensed, practicing, self-governing physicians who are engaged in independent practice and are really "guests" of the hospital. The functions and the relationships of the medical staff to other

---

[12] Ray E. Brown, "Strictures and Structures," in Jonathan S. Rakich (ed.), *Hospital Organization and Management,* The Catholic Hospital Association, St. Louis, Mo., 1972, pp. 21–23.
[13] Basil S. Georgopoulos and Floyd C. Mann, "The Hospital as an Organization," *Hospital Administration,* Fall 1962, p. 51.

segments of the hospital are based on the legal position of the doctor. The hospital as an organization cannot practice medicine. Only physicians are legally licensed to practice medicine on patients. The medical staff is largely self-governing and has its primary focus on the therapeutic aspects of patient treatment. The medical staff in most general hospitals is an autonomous structure with a medical director, executive committee, and various functional committees. It is composed of physicians who are engaged in individual practice and who are not really "institutional" members of the hospital. It is fairly independent of the administrative organization.

> The medical staffs in the various hospitals are in almost complete charge of medical policies and medical practice. They have their own organization within the overall hospital organization; have their own constitution, rules, and regulations; and are, in the main, self-disciplining bodies. They do have, however, to abide with certain fundamental hospital policies, such as maintaining adequate patient records up to date, having their membership recommendations formally reviewed by the board of trustees and, generally, operating in a manner that would not jeopardize the accreditation of the hospital. [14]

Typically, medical staffs operate through various committees, such as medical records, education, audit, and credentials. The executive committee represents the staff at large. This executive committee may be appointed by the chief of staff or elected by the staff. The board of trustees and the hospital administrator rely on the committee structure of the medical staff as a link with the administrative organization.

Coordination of Activities

A high degree of differentiation and specialization creates critical problems of coordination in the hospital. Georgopoulos and Mann say:

> Because of this extensive division of labor and accompanying specialization of work, practically every person working in the hospital depends upon some other person or persons for the performance of his own organizational role. Specialists and professionals can perform their functions only when a considerable array of supportive personnel and auxiliary services is put at their disposal at all times. Doctors, nurses, and others in the hospital do not, and cannot, function separately or independently of one another. Their work is mutually supplementary, interlocking, and interdependent. In turn, such a high interdependence requires that the various specialized functions and activities of the many departments, groups, and individual members of the organization

---

[14] Georgopoulos and Mann, *The Community General Hospital,* op. cit., p. 191.

be sufficiently coordinated, if the organization is to function effectively and attain its objectives. Consequently, the hospital has developed a rather intricate and elaborate system of internal coordination. Without coordination, concerted effort on the part of its different members and continuity in organizational operations could not be ensured. [15]

One of the problems in achieving coordination stems from the dual authority system and the high degree of specialization and professionalization. Coordination by means of the organizational hierarchy is difficult. Hospitals do, however, make extensive use of coordination by administrative rules and procedures. These means of coordination are most effective for the programmable, routine events.

However, because of the diverse problems associated with the care and treatment of patients, it is impossible to rely upon administrative procedures exclusively for coordination. Therefore, one of the primary means of integration is voluntary coordination and the willingness of the various participants to work effectively together to deal with unusual and nonroutine events. "The hospital is dependent very greatly upon the motivation and voluntary, informal adjustments of its members for the attainment and maintenance of good coordination. Formal organizational plans, rules, regulations, and controls may ensure some minimum coordination, but of themselves are incapable of producing adequate coordination, for only a fraction of all the coordinative activities required in this organization can be programmed in advance." [16] One of the primary forces ensuring voluntary coordination is the overall value system emphasizing the patient's welfare.

Authority Structure

A primary characteristic of the bureaucratic model is a single authority pyramid. In the general hospital, there is no one line of authority. "Essentially, authority in the hospital is shared (not equally) by the board of trustees, the doctors, and the administrator—the three centers of power in the organization—and, to some extent, also by the director of nursing. In the hospital, authority does not emanate from a single source and does not flow along a single line of command as it does in most formal organizations." [17]

Each of these three groups—the trustees, the medical staff, and the administrator—has a basis for the exercise of legitimate authority. Hennessey points out the basis of this legitimacy:

1 The legally responsible group in the hospital, charged with legislating policy, is the board of trustees; therefore these men must be the policy-makers.
2 The essential activity in the hospital is medical care for the sick, a specialty of physicians; therefore, they should determine the policies of the organization.

---

[15] Ibid., pp. 6-7.
[16] Georgopoulos and Mann, *Hospital Administration*, Fall 1962, pp. 57-58.
[17] Ibid., p. 59.

3 The person most knowledgeable about all phases of life in the hospital, the only full-time professional with wide perspective, is the administrator; therefore, he should decide policy. [18]

Each of these groups has a basis for the exercising of authority; however, they are not clearly delineated and separate. There are many interfaces between these sources of authority which create conflict. It is difficult to select any one of the three as having central authority. [19] Authority is disbursed and shared rather than adhering to the scalar hierarchy.

One way of looking at this relationship is in terms of the three organizational subsystems. The board of trustees has a strategic role, relating the hospital to its social environment and helping it obtain the necessary resources for its operations. The administrator has a coordinative role of negotiating and integrating the various resources and activities of the participants in the organization. The medical staff has the primary technical role in terms of patient treatment. There is no line of authority between these levels. They are three separate sources of authority exercised within the same social organization.

However, there have been transitions in the relative power and influence exerted by these three sources. Perrow suggests that prior to the technological revolution, the primary source of authority and control was the board of trustees. This authority was superseded to a degree by the medical staff because it had the knowledge and skills capable of utilizing the advancing technology. Their professional expertise became the primary source of authority. He suggests that with the growing specialization of activities and the increasing problems of coordination, authority is being progressively transferred to the administrator. "In the future, it seems likely that progressive voluntary hospitals will be controlled by administrators rather than doctors." [20] The authority structure is changing in response to technological changes and the organizational problems which hospitals are facing because of the expansion of their activities and the increasing need for integration. However, in the foreseeable future, there will continue to be a troika at the top which represents a diverse source of authority. [21]

Expanding Boundaries

With the expansion of the hospital toward a community health service center, determining structural relationships and boundaries becomes more difficult. Programs are being developed for regionwide cooperation between various units providing health services.

---

[18] John W. Hennessey, Jr., "The Administrator and Policy Processes," *Hospital Administration*, Fall 1965, p. 66.
[19] Gordon calls this the top management triangle. He says, "The point, therefore, is that, in many hospitals, none of these groups is really 'on top.' The triangle has no single top and no single base. Legally, the board is on top. Professionally, the doctor is on top. In day-to-day affairs, frequently, the administrator is on top—for one thing, because he is there more than anybody else!" Paul J. Gordon, "The Top Management Triangle in Voluntary Hospitals (II)," *Academy of Management Journal*, April 1962, p. 75.
[20] Perrow, "Hospitals: Technology, Structure, and Goals," p. 950.
[21] Wilson, op. cit., p. 72.

The hospital must consider its activities in a broader context. "In the regionalization concept, a greater extension of responsibility of those who plan beyond the immediate interests of the organization or profession of which they are part in the community or region is mandatory." [22] Hospitals are considering means by which they can coordinate their activities with other hospitals and with other community health service agencies. Because of increased specialization and the exceedingly high cost of diagnostic and treatment equipment, there are growing indications that a single hospital, by itself, cannot expect to provide optimum health service—coordination with other institutions is required. "Tomorrow's hospital will be a unit in a multi-hospital network that assumes responsibility for delivering a full range of coordinated health services to a defined population." [23] The development of a regionalized health service system will require increased coordination of the efforts of individual hospital units, independent physicians and their medical societies, public health services, and other state and local agencies. The planning and coordination of medical services on a community basis will require more effective organization and administration.

PSYCHOSOCIAL SYSTEM

The hospital makes use of sophisticated technology and has a complex structure. However, one of its fundamental characteristics is the importance of the psychosocial system. "A hospital is basically, fundamentally, and above all, a man-system. It is a complex, human-social system: Its raw material is human; its product is human; its work is mainly done by human hands; and its objective is human—direct service to people, service that is individualized and personalized." [24]

Hospitals have clearly defined status and role systems. Status symbols are an important part of the social system. Different types of caps, white and colored uniforms, and various titles are used to emphasize status positions. Many of the official and unofficial norms in the hospital are geared to the implementation and maintenance of status identifications.

The roles of the various participants—the physicians, the administrators, the nurses, and the paramedical personnel—are rather well-defined. This role definition stems from professionalization. The long process of education and training emphasizes certain role precepts which delineate the individual's actions. However, many role conflicts occur for individual participants when they are cast in two different roles with incongruent demands. [25] For example, the doctor frequently faces a conflict between his professional role as an independent practitioner and his institutional role as a participating member of the hospital. The nursing supervisor may continually find herself in conflicting roles as a member of the nursing group with an orientation toward her professional colleagues and as a member of the administrative hierarchy. Although

---

[22] Samuel Levey and Alan P. Sheldon, "A New Look at Areawide Planning," *Hospital Administration,* Spring 1965, p. 33.

[23] Sigmond, op. cit., p. 32.

[24] Basil S. Georgopoulos, "Hospital Organization and Administration: Prospects and Perspectives," *Hospital Administration,* Summer 1964, pp. 25–26.

[25] Wren, op. cit., p. 52.

organizational positions are delineated, shaded areas remain, and there are many possibilities for conflict. In this discussion of psychosocial systems, we will look more specifically at each of the human groups in the hospital organization—the patient, as well as the medical, nursing, and administrative staffs.

The Patient

The patient is obviously one of the key individuals in the hospital—he is simultaneously the hospital's client and also its product. He enters the hospital reluctantly at best, with a certain amount of suspicion, awe, and fear. Perhaps his one dominant motivation is to be able to walk out of the hospital under his own power as rapidly as possible. His status external to the organization has little bearing on his status in the hospital. "As he strips off his clothing, so he strips off, too, his favored costume of social roles, his favored style, his customary identity in the world." [26] His new status may be defined by the nature of his illness, the complexities of the medical procedures, his location in the hospital, and the prestige of the attending physicians. The "status" of the first heart transplant patient was significantly different from that of the routine appendectomy patient.

Although we may not have considered it explicitly, our culture does prescribe certain ways of behaving in a "sick" role. Being sick, for example, typically releases us from other obligations such as going to work or school. The sick person is dependent; he cannot care for himself; he must be taken care of. But since being ill is an undesirable state, he has an obligation to want to "get well," and with this goes the obligation to seek technically competent help. [27]

All these role definitions prescribe that the patient act in a very passive and responsive way in the hospital. He is there to get well, and he should cooperate with all the professionals in the hospital—for they, not he, have the technical competence to cure or ameliorate his illness. He tolerates the small incongruities—being drugged to sleep at 10 P.M., rudely awakened for his sponge bath at 5 A.M. in preparation for breakfast at 6, only to lie anxiously wide-eyed for the remainder of the day. (In fairness, it should be indicated that this was more typical of past than of current practice in modern hospitals.) Interestingly enough, there is a growing awareness that there might be therapeutic advantages to having the patient take a more active role in the social structure of the hospital. Greater patient participation is taking place in mental and long-stay hospitals. There are significant barriers to creating a more socially active role for the patient in the general hospital, where his stay is for a relatively short term.

Medical Staff

The medical staff, composed of practicing physicians, has some similarity with patients. Doctors are also "guests" of the hospital, utilizing the facilities provided. They have

---

[26] Wilson, op. cit., p. 70.

[27] Talcott Parsons, *The Social System,* The Free Press of Glencoe, New York, 1964 (paperback edition), pp. 436–437.

both a professional *patient-centered* role and an *institutional* role which they assume as participants in the hospital. [28] Their professional training emphasizes the patient-centered role. The development of the institutional role requires some adaptation. The doctor must make certain adjustments in order to function effectively within the organization. For example, his utilization of the hospital's facilities, such as the operating room, has to be scheduled with consideration of the requirements of other physicians. His motivation in maximizing the care and treatment for his individual patients may have to be modified by the organizational requirements for all patients. These two roles for the medical staff often create substantial conflicts.

However, physicians are making the necessary adjustments to the institutional role. Training in medical schools, with greater emphasis on internship and clinical practice, supports the institutional role. These adjustments to the institutional role are of vital necessity. The physician would be unable to meet requirements for patient care and continue his practice without having the resources and facilities of the hospital available.

The medical staff has a high status position within the hospital organization. Legally, they are the only ones who can prescribe for therapeutic care and treatment. We ascribe a substantial charisma to physicians. This high societal status carries over into the hospital system. It is further reinforced by the degree of specialization of knowledge and technical competence required for practice.

There is a differentiation of status within the medical staff. Interns and residents generally have a status different from independent physicians. The specialist is often ascribed a higher status than the general practitioner, and there are even differences among the various medical specialties.

The group dynamics within the medical staff are very complex. Although each physician engages in independent practice, he must coordinate his hospital activities with other doctors, nurses, various service departments, and paramedical personnel. This requires the development of effective group relationships. Leadership patterns are determined more by the personal characteristics and charisma of the individual physician than by formal organizational position.

Nursing Staff

The nursing staff has the difficult but important function of coordination between the "care" functions of the hospital and the "cure" functions of the physician. There is a long tradition that the doctor has direct and immediate authority over the nurse on the medical aspects of his patient's treatment. This viewpoint implies that the primary role of the nurse is one of "doctor's helper." On the other hand, the nurse is a full-time member of the administrative organization, who reports in the hierarchy through a head nurse, nursing supervisor, and director of nursing to the administrator. To the patient, the nurse is the primary representative of the hospital and is closely associated with his

---

[28] Arthur B. Moss, Wayne G. Broehl, Jr., Robert H. Guest, and John W. Hennessey, Jr., *Hospital Policy Decisions: Process and Action*, G. P. Putnam's Sons, New York, 1966, pp. 221–222.

care and cure. The doctor may see his patient once a day, but nurses are in continual interaction with him.

The official position of the nursing staff depicted in the typical organization chart does not really give recognition to the power and influence it has in the hospital organization. The nursing staff plays a vital role in the group dynamics of the hospital. Because of their full-time association with the hospital, their familiarity with established rules and procedures, their ability to develop informal relationships with other participants, and their close association with both patients and doctors, they become a central force of informal influence and leadership throughout the entire organization. The nurse frequently serves as the go-between for the technical level represented by the physician and the coordinative level represented by the administrator and his staff. In this role she often serves as a negotiator, compromiser, and influencer.

Many forces are changing the status role of the registered nurse in the hospital. There has been a general movement toward the upgrading of the task performed by the registered nurse with the introduction of practical nurses, nurse's aides, and other subordinate participants. This has established a definite status hierarchy within the nursing staff. There is a growing demand for the reduction of time spent on clerical tasks to make more time available for clinical work and direct patient functions. Cries of "return to the bedside" are common. More specialized nursing roles are developing— surgery, orthopedic, cardiac, intensive care, and psychiatric, for example. The nursing role is moving away from the "doctor's helper" toward increased specialized and technical functions. The registered nurse will become a specialized professional in her own right and will be less in the shadow of the physician. The relatively high status differential between doctors and nurses will decrease. A collegial rather than superior-subordinate relationship will become more common in the future.

Administrative Staff

The administrator has an emerging role in the hospital system. Historically, his function was primarily clerical and housekeeping in nature. He provided the facilities for running the "hotel" side of the hospital. His status was low as compared to the medical staff. However, with the growing complexities, the greater need for coordination of the hospital activities, and the increased demands for sophisticated equipment and its effective use, the role of the administrator has expanded. Hennessey discusses the changing role of the hospital administrator:

> The role of the administrator has developed more rapidly than any other in the two decades of recent change in American community hospitals. Every innovation in the medical and surgical treatment of bedded patients has had an effect on the administrator's part in the total drama. New equipment, new practices, and new ways of utilizing resources have altered life in every hospital department, and this fact has made new demands on the administrator. The community now asks more of the hospital, partly as a result of the prolif-

eration of third parties in the health contract. Beyond all these things the administrator is himself part of an emergent profession, one in which graduate education and formal colleague associations are increasingly important. [29]

The suggestion that the hospital administrator's role is an emergent one indicates that his position is less well-defined and does not have the historical precedents of the medical staff or the board of trustees.

Carving out the administrator's role has often created substantial conflict with the other power sources in the organization—particularly the medical staff. The medical staff has a desire for a high degree of autonomy based on their professionalization and a strong orientation to individual patient care. In contrast, the hospital administrator is forced to give consideration to optimal utilization of the resources for all patients and for all interest groups. The desire of the doctors for autonomy frequently conflicts with the need for coordination. As Wilensky suggests, "This fact reflects a common dilemma in organizational life: the simultaneous necessity of giving autonomy to highly-trained specialists and yet giving some occupations the authority to coordinate the specialists." [30] The effective hospital administrator must be prepared to live in a rather ambiguous, uncertain role, one that requires the use of suggestion and persuasion rather than positional authority. The democratic-participative leadership style is generally most effective.

There have been pressures toward professionalization of hospital administration. In some ways, this can be seen as a desire to increase status vis-à-vis the medical practitioners. The move toward professionalization includes specialization of educational requirements through programs at universities, more activities by professional associations, and increasing emphasis upon community service objectives. The hospital administrator is moving toward a professionalized role. However, it will not come easily. In order to achieve the status of a profession there will have to be a redistribution of power within the hospital system. This redistribution will result in a relative decrease of power for the medical staff and board of trustees and an increase in power for the hospital administrators. "It seems clear that hospital administration will arrive at an autonomy befitting professional status only at the expense of control now in the hands of physicians and board members who will not readily yield." [31] Nevertheless, we do see a gradual movement of power equalization between the administrator, board of trustees, and medical staff—one which can be described as a collegial pattern of relationships.

MANAGERIAL SYSTEM

The foregoing discussion of the goals, technology, structure, and psychosocial system of the hospital suggests that the managerial system would also be complex. The

[29] Ibid., p. 84.
[30] Harold L. Wilensky, "The Dynamics of Professionalism: The Case of Hospital Administration," *Hospital Administration,* Spring 1962, p. 20.
[31] Ibid.

diversity of the power base and authority structure creates a dispersal of the planning and control decisions in the organization. The board of trustees has the legal authority and decides on broad financial matters. Traditionally, it was the focal point for long-range planning and interactions with the community and represented the strategic level in the organizational system. The medical staff, on the other hand, has the technical knowledge and authority concerning patient treatment. The administrator and his staff are in charge of the functioning of the hospital and must engage in organizational planning and control. Thus, the managerial system of the hospital is diverse, with all three members of the troika responsible for planning and control decisions in certain spheres of the overall organization.

One of the primary means of control in the hospital is through professionalization and the internalization of values and norms of performance which prescribe certain role behaviors for participants. In addition, each of the various groups has mechanisms for self-control. For example, in the medical staff the review procedures for the selection of members of the staff, for tissue examinations, and for medical audits provide some degree of control over the individual doctor. The board of trustees and the administrative staff establish many control procedures, particularly in such areas as accounting, record keeping, and maintenance. These controls are similar to those utilized in many business organizations. The nursing staff is guided by many normative standards, developed through the process of nursing education. These standards regarding role performance serve as a primary means of internalized control.

In addition, various segments establish "hospital procedures," which range all the way from the surgical procedures established by the medical staff to business methods established by the administrator. These hospital procedures provide the basis for control over relatively programmed activities. However, it should be emphasized that many of the functions in the hospital are nonroutine, and it is difficult to establish well-defined controls for such activities. In certain areas, however, it must rely primarily upon voluntary coordination and control by the participants themselves.

The planning function in the hospital is carried out in many ways. The medical staff has a vital role in planning related to patient treatment. The administrator is engaged in broader strategic and community planning. He is concerned with the financing and procurement of facilities, and planning for their effective utilization. Obviously, the administrator must rely upon the medical staff for technical inputs regarding his plans. However, strategic planning for the hospital system is becoming one of his more important functions. He will also have an expanding role in interhospital planning and coordination.

The foregoing discussion of the general hospital suggests that it is a rather special organization, different from other types of institutions. We have considered only one type, the community general hospital. There would be significant differences in the goals and other subsystems for governmental hospitals or for other types. This discussion of the general hospital, however, has emphasized that it has management and organizational problems which make fitting it into a purely bureaucratic model difficult. To demand that the general hospital be "businesslike" in all its endeavors seems unrealistic in view of its particular role in society, its primary emphasis upon human factors, the high level of professionalization and specialization of knowledge, and the need for an adaptive, innovative organization.

SUMMARY

The general hospital is characterized by a substantial division of labor and application of advanced technology. It embraces many goals and values and has a large number of specialized participants. Historically, the hospital was primarily a place for the care of the sick and dependent. Only after the rapid advances in medical science and technology did it become the primary therapeutic center for patients.

The general hospital has diverse goals. Although the primary goal is the patient's welfare, there are many additional objectives such as medical and nursing education, research, and economic viability. However, the overall value, which emphasizes patient care and treatment, permeates the hospital and provides the basis for motivation and self-control.

The early limitations of medical technology severely restricted the ability of the hospital to accomplish any treatment goals. However, advancements in medical knowledge changed the role of the hospital. It became a place where patients could come for treatment which could not be provided in their homes by private physicians. The hospital became the central source of the most advanced technology within the community.

There is a unique relationship between the formal authority of position, as represented by the administrative hierarchy, and the authority of knowledge as represented by the medical practitioners and other professionals. This creates a diffused and distinctive structure. The administrative organization is headed by the board of trustees, which appoints the hospital administrator as the chief executive. The medical staff is made up of licensed physicians, who are engaged in independent practice. The medical staff is basically self-governing and does not come under the administrative structure.

The hospital has a complex psychosocial system. Although the roles of the various participants—the physicians, the administrative staff, the nurses, and paramedical personnel—are rather well-defined, there are substantial conflicts. The psychosocial system is strongly influenced by the norms and values of professionalism, which are internalized by the various participants.

The managerial system is difficult to define. The diversity of the authority structure creates a dispersal of the planning and control functions. The board of trustees has the legal authority and decides on broad financial and other organizational matters. The medical staff has the technical knowledge and decides on matters of patient care and treatment. The administrative staff is in charge of the functioning of the hospital and must engage in managerial planning and organizational control.

QUESTIONS AND PROBLEMS

1 Evaluate the view that advancing technology, together with changing medical practices, has created new and evolving goals for the general hospital.

2 How does the historical development of the hospital affect current structure?

3 How does the overriding value of patient welfare provide a basis for voluntary coordination of activities in the hospital?

4 Does the organization structure of the hospital fit the traditional bureaucratic model? Why or why not?

5 What is the relationship between the medical staff and the administrative staff in the hospital?

6 How is coordination accomplished in the hospital?

7 Discuss the status and roles of the various participants in the psychosocial system of hospitals.

8 In what ways is the managerial system of a hospital different from that in the business organization? In what ways are they similar?

9 What are the implications for the hospital in becoming a total *community health service center*? What impact would this have on the structure and the managerial system?

21

COMPARATIVE ORGANIZATIONAL ANALYSIS: THE UNIVERSITY

Institutions of higher education have grown significantly in number and in size. An increasing proportion of the relevant age-group population is attending these institutions. The primary product of colleges and universities is knowledge—its creation and dissemination. With the acceleration of science and technology, they have assumed a greater role in society. The traditional "ivory tower" barriers to interaction with the wider community are being removed. These changes have created some fundamental problems for defining the mission of the university and its goals. Its technology and structure as well as psychosocial and managerial systems are significantly different from those of other organizations. Furthermore, these subsystems are not stable but are undergoing changes. We will discuss these and other aspects of universities in terms of the following framework:

Changing Environment
Goals and Values
Technology
Structure
Psychosocial System
Managerial System

CHANGING ENVIRONMENT

Today's institutions of higher education are descendants of the university of the medieval period. Medieval universities had a religious beginning and were associated with cathedral schools and monasteries.[1] There was a continual struggle between the faculties and the church officials over their governance. The concept gradually evolved that the faculties were autonomous bodies with substantial self-government. The Reformation fostered separation of the universities from church control.

Higher education in the American colonies began with Harvard in 1636, and by the time of the Revolution there were nine colleges: "nine home-grown variations on a theme known in the mother country as Oxford and Cambridge."[2] These colleges had a religious orientation, strongly affected by the puritan ethic of the times. However, they did receive state support and encouragement. They were shaped by the aristocratic traditions transmitted from Oxford and Cambridge and cherished the humanistic ideal of classical scholarship, with emphasis upon Greek and Latin, logic, rhetoric, ethics, metaphysics, physics, and mathematics.

During colonial times, the American colleges began to take a shape of their own, which differed from their English origins. They moved away from the classical tradition and adopted a curriculum which was more in line with their sociocultural setting. After the Revolution, there was a substantial increase in the number of colleges. Between 1782 and 1802, nineteen colleges were chartered, with support from the new state legislatures. During the early part of the nineteenth century many new colleges were founded by the various religious denominations, who seemed to be competing to ensure that their views would be perpetuated through institutions of higher learning. There was a democratization of higher education in America, reinforced by the development of a public educational system during the Jacksonian period. "The institutions of the college movement in America intended to be, to the best of their ability and knowledge, democratic institutions for a democratic society."[3]

These institutions were collegiate. They were residential colleges, typically in a quiet rural setting, with close interpersonal relationships between faculty and student. It was a total way of life, encompassing the whole of the individual participant's social relationship and to a major degree, purposely isolated from the broader community. This collegiate pattern became the standard for American higher education during this period. However, there were gradual transformations in curricula to give greater recognition to science and the applied arts. Developments in the natural and physical sciences profoundly affected the colleges of the time and created disruptions in the traditional classical course of studies. There was a continual conflict during the early part of the nineteenth century between the desire to retain the classical tradition and the overwhelming social necessity for adapting to the requirements of the developing and industrializing nation. The American colleges began to lose their traditional unity of purpose and identity which had been prescribed within rather narrow limits since their earlier foundations.

---

[1] Hastings Rashdall, *The Universities of Europe in the Middle Ages,* ed. by F. M. Powicke and A. B. Emden, Oxford University Press, Fair Lawn, N.J., 1936, 3 vols.
[2] Frederick Rudolph, *The American College and University,* © Alfred A. Knopf, Inc., New York, 1962, p. 3.
[3] Ibid., p. 67.

Rise of the University

During the second half of the nineteenth century there were major transformations in American higher education—the development of the land-grant colleges and the rise of the true university. In 1862, the Morrill Federal Land Grant Act, giving new impetus to the development of colleges emphasizing agricultural and technical subjects, was passed. This act provided for the support in every state of at least one college, "where the leading objective shall be, without excluding other scientific or classical studies, to teach such branches of learning as are related to agriculture and the mechanical arts." Each state was given public lands equivalent to 30,000 acres for each senator and representative under the apportionment of 1860. This act and its subsequent supporting legislation led to the development of sixty-eight American land-grant colleges in a variety of forms.

The development of the land-grant colleges paved the way for the evolution of the university which was a fundamental change from the traditional collegiate pattern. The American university took its form from the German universities, rather than from the English colleges. The German universities placed a strong emphasis upon scholarship, creation of knowledge, and training for the learned professions.

> The essence of the German university system, which gave it intellectual leadership in the nineteenth century, was the concept that an institution of true higher learning should be, above all, "the workshop of free scientific research." This emphasis on the disinterested pursuit of truth through original investigation led, on the one hand, to the development of the concept that a true university must maintain freedom of teaching and freedom of learning within certain carefully defined limits. On the other, it led ultimately to a stress on the various services which higher learning could render to the state. [4]

The development of American universities came from a number of directions. Cornell and Johns Hopkins were among the first private institutions to adopt the university pattern. Michigan, Wisconsin, and Minnesota were among the first public institutions to become universities. The earlier colonial colleges such as Harvard, Yale, Princeton, and Columbia superimposed the university system on their collegiate structure. Many variations of the university pattern evolved during the latter part of the nineteenth and early twentieth centuries.

> Variations on these many themes would give to the United States a remarkable flowering of the university idea in the late nineteenth and early twentieth centuries, but they would not give any one answer to the question: What is an

---

[4] John S. Brubacher and Willis Rudy, *Higher Education in Transition: An American History: 1636-1956,* Harper & Row, Publishers, Incorporated, New York, 1958, p. 171.

American university? For as in its people, its geography, its churches, its economic institutions, the United States in its unversities was to reveal a remarkable diversity, and unwillingness to be categorized, a variety that would encompass differences in wealth, leadership, public influence, regional needs. [5]

Universities frequently encompassed as part of their institution the collegial pattern in the form of an undergraduate liberal arts college. However, they also included the scientific and technical areas and developed programs in engineering, law, medicine, business administration, and other professional fields. They provided graduate as well as undergraduate education—emphasizing that the university was a primary creator of knowledge with a responsibility for research and investigation into a wide spectrum of subjects.

There developed a new spirit of vocationalism with the incorporation of professional schools within the university. [6] In fact, the universities helped redefine the concept of professions. These traditionally had included only medicine, law, and divinity, but with the growing need for specialized education in many fields, the distinction between vocationalism and professionalism became blurred. Universities recognized the need for professionalized training in a wide variety of fields such as engineering and other applied sciences, teaching at the elementary and secondary levels, dentistry, business administration, and librarianship. "In assuming responsibility for providing formal professional education, the universities revealed the degree to which American higher education had now broadly entered into the life of the people." [7] The American university system, more than any other in the world, has provided professionally trained people for a wide variety of activities necessary in an advanced industrial society.

Current Scene

Higher education in the United States is characterized by a multiplicity of organizations, functions, and roles. In size, the institutions range all the way from the small liberal arts colleges to the large private and state universities, some with over 100,000 students. They range in level from the two-year community colleges through universities offering doctoral and post-doctoral work. They range in location from large metropolitan areas to rural, pastoral settings. The student bodies are also heterogeneous, ranging from beginning undergraduates to doctoral and postdoctoral students—all with differing interests and objectives. There are both privately endowed and state- and community-supported institutions. The role which they play in society is complex and is undergoing dynamic change. This great diversity makes it impossible to select one single institution as typical.

[5] Rudolph, op. cit., pp. 331–332.
[6] William W. Brickman, "American Higher Education in Historical Perspective," *The Annals of the American Academy of Political and Social Science,* November 1972, pp. 39–41.
[7] Rudolph, op. cit., p. 340.

Statistics on the current status of higher education in the United States give an indication of this diversity. In 1970 there were 8,649,400 students enrolled in higher education in the United States, of which 6,476,100 were enrolled in public and 2,713,300 in private institutions. [8] The enrollment has increased each year since the early 1950s, rising from 2,102,000 in 1951 to over 8 million in 1970. In 1951, there were 24 college students for each 100 persons eighteen to twenty-one years of age in the population. By 1970, there were over 50 college students per l00 persons in the same age group. There were a total of 2,565 institutions of higher education, of which 160 were classified as universities, 1,513 as four-year colleges, and 892 as two-year colleges. Universities were classified as those institutions which gave considerable stress to graduate instruction, which confer advanced degrees as well as bachelor's degrees in a variety of liberal arts fields, and which have at least two professional schools that are not exclusively technological.

In the 1971-1972 academic year there were over 620,000 faculty, a major increase from the 191,396 in the 1949–1950 academic year. [9] The growing role of the federal government in higher education is seen by the contributions of funds for basic research, facilities, fellowships, student assistants, and other support, which increased from $992 million in 1962 to $5,200 million in 1971–1972. The total expenditures on higher education for 1971–1972 were estimated at $31 billion.

Two other trends have had a significant influence on higher education. First, in the post-WW II period public universities have grown more rapidly than private universities, both absolutely and proportionally. Second, there has been an increase in the proportion of graduate to undergraduate students. This is particularly true for the universities, which have taken the role of training at the postbaccalaureate level. Universities had an enrollment in Fall, 1970, of 3,077,000, of which 768,000, or nearly 25 percent, were in postbaccalaureate degree programs.

Many of the public and private universities are very complex and have large student enrollments. The university of 30,000 to 50,000 students with a faculty of several thousand and offering a wide range of teaching and research programs is typical. Many of the universities have established branch campuses in various locations throughout their states.

Higher education in the United States has been responsive to changes in its environmental suprasystem. New institutional types and forms have developed in response to the needs of society. The basic democratic principle holds that every individual regardless of prior background or status should have an opportunity for higher education. This, perhaps, has been the one greatest difference as compared with Western Europe and England. As a consequence of this basic Jacksonian-democratic

---

[8] *Opening Fall Enrollment in Higher Education, 1970,* U.S. Department of Health, Education, and Welfare, Office of Education, Washington, D.C., 1970.
[9] *Digest of Educational Statistics,* U.S. Office of Education, 1971.

view of higher education, the college degree has become one of the primary means for upward mobility in our society. Children of low-income groups have looked to the university as a means of increasing their social positions. [10]

Another distinguishing characteristic is the interest in making higher learning functional and closely related to the needs of society. Again this is part of the democratizing influence and has led to a multiplicity of educational opportunities. The university system has not fostered an intellectual elite but provides a broad segment of the population with educational opportunities. In return, society has come to expect much of institutions of higher education—they should provide a worthwhile and useful service.

A final consideration relates to the diversity of control. There is no one central source of higher authority over these institutions. Control is decentralized down to a state, local, or private level. There is no single integrating force working toward a master plan for higher education.

Our discussion will concentrate upon universities, both private and public, and will not attempt to discuss the other forms of higher education such as colleges, technical institutes, and two-year institutions. However, many of the characteristics of universities will also be true of these other institutions.

GOALS AND VALUES

The social role of the university is the creation and dissemination of knowledge. "Higher education has made its province the realm of knowledge. This knowledge may be inherently valuable for its own sake, for the satisfaction it brings to the individual who seeks to escape ignorance and superstition. This knowledge may be useful in solving human problems from health to production, from justice to unemployment. Knowledge for its own sake and for use—knowledge is what higher education would impart." [11] This sets the broad role of the university but does not indicate more specific goals and values. Actually, the role of institutions of higher education has undergone significant changes.

In the colonial colleges the primary function was that of education for the ministry. "The desire of important religious denominations (such as the Anglican and Calvinist) for a literate, college-trained clergy was probably the most important single factor explaining the founding of the colonial colleges." [12] The dominant views of Christianity set the values, and the majority of the faculty members were clergymen. Gradually, however, these institutions and the colleges which followed moved away from their

---

[10] For a discussion of the relationship between social stratification and higher education, see Christopher Jencks and David Riesman, *The Academic Revolution,* Doubleday & Company, Inc., Garden City, N.Y., 1968, pp. 61–154.
[11] John D. Millett, *The Academic Community: An Essay on Organization,* McGraw-Hill Book Company, New York, 1962, p. 34.
[12] Brubacher and Rudy, op. cit., p. 6.

religious orientation toward broader intellectual pursuits. However, they continued to provide education for an elite group of cultured gentlemen. Their goals and values were taken from the upper class. They followed the English universities with a primary role of preserving and transmitting the Western intellectual heritage to the next generation. They were not concerned with making original contributions to knowledge and did not emphasize scholarly and scientific research.

However, because of the pragmatic nature of the American society, the colleges did move toward a goal of service. The emerging goals for higher education indicated that knowledge should have application in the professions, government, business, and other social institutions. Education could only be useful if it resulted in change and improvement.

In the latter part of the nineteenth century, universities began to emphasize scholarship, research, and professional training. A primary goal of the institution became the creation of new knowledge through research.

Current Institutional Goals

Three predominant institutional goals for universities are:

1 The dissemination of knowledge to students. This is primarily done through the teaching function.
2 The creation and advancement of knowledge. This is accomplished through the research activities of the faculty and specialized staffs.
3 Service to society. This role is related to the first two goals. It establishes the norm that knowledge creation and dissemination should be useful.

It seems apparent that all three goals of the university are not fully recognized either by the general public or, more importantly, by major participants in the university system itself. In class discussions concerning the role of the university, students recognize the importance of teaching but frequently have little appreciation for the goal of creation and advancement of knowledge through research. A university does have the function of transmitting the cultural heritage and disseminating current knowledge to the student, but this is a role which is also fulfilled by other institutions in our society. However, the university has the special function of creating new knowledge through research.

Academic Freedom

If the university is to accomplish its goals, it must maintain an environment of intellectual freedom. It is necessary for the dissemination of knowledge which may not have a popular consensus. There also must be freedom for the pursuit of new knowledge.

Historically universities have always been centers of dissent. Conflict is often between different internal groups but also occurs with the external environment. In pursuing the basic goals of knowledge creation and dissemination, conflicts with the established sociocultural norms and values of society are often inevitable.

> Education is a dangerous business. It is committed to change. It expects first of all to change individuals by augmenting their store of knowledge and by developing their ability to reason. Beyond this, the educated person may become an instrument of social change. . . .
>
> The whole concern in the United States and in the Western world with academic freedom is an effort to acknowledge the unique relationship between higher education and society. Higher education is dangerous. It carries with it at all times the possibility that it may upset an existing power structure in society. It carries with it at all times the possibility that individuals and institutions in society may have to accept new ideas and new ways of behavior. The truth which higher education perpetuates and expands is never final but only tentative. [13]

In the United States the concern with academic freedom did not become important until the emergence of the university. Graduate programs, research orientation, and emphasis upon creation of new knowledge increased the possibility of conflict with the established society. The fight for academic freedom gained gradual acceptance and was enhanced by the establishment of the American Association of University Professors in 1915.

Academic freedom has been under continual stress in the post-World War II period. The loyalty oath legislation of many states in the 1940s and 1950s created much controversy regarding academic freedom and brought about prolonged struggles. However, there was a gradual abatement of these pressures, and the basic concept of academic freedom appeared to have survived.

However, in the 1960s and 1970s the whole concept of academic freedom has been questioned anew. As many groups on university campuses became more concerned and outspoken as social critics, the issue of intellectual freedom reappeared. For example, certain groups within the university community took strong stands for political and social change concerning the Vietnam War and civil rights. Increasingly, there is concern that the traditional views of academic freedom relating to knowledge creation and dissemination might be diverted because of emphasis on direct social and political intervention and change. Academic freedom requires boundaries between the university and society. With increased activity on campuses directed toward social and political change, these boundaries are becoming fuzzy.

---

[13] Millett, op. cit., pp. 55–56.

> The enormous expansion of American higher education, both in its numbers and its range of activities is putting great strains on these insulating mechanisms and thus is threatening the autonomous functions of the university. The expansion of the university is involving it more directly in controversial issues and is therefore increasing the number and range of significant publics in the larger society that are attentive to what goes on in the university. [14]

Universities face the problem of assimilating activist values into the traditional concepts of academic freedom. This resolution will not come easily but is another indication of the continual evolution of the goals, values, and role of the university in society.

Another source of concern relating to intellectual freedom is the increasing influence of the federal government. Statistics from the Office of Education indicate that public and private institutions of higher education received $5.2 billion in federal funds in the academic year 1971–1972. A large part of these funds were for research activities. These expenditures of federal funds raise questions of university autonomy with regard to the way in which these funds are allocated. It has been suggested that the search for funds has caused the professor or research team to seek support from federal research-granting agencies and to lose allegiance to the institution. As the financial problems of universities become greater and with more federal support likely, the whole question of autonomy and the pursuit of the institution's goals will be a pressing problem.

Extracurricular Activities

The role of extracurricular activities such as athletic programs, student associations, fraternities, and social clubs in meeting the goals of universities has been a continuing point of debate. Many people, including some professors, feel strongly that these activities are basically adverse to the primary goals and values of the university. However, the university is a complex social system, and one of the necessary ingredients is to provide for cohesive relationships. These extracurricular activities perform an important role in sustaining and integrating these institutions as social systems.

> During all the years of university growth, the extracurriculum played a major role in sustaining collegiate values. The athletic teams, fraternities and social clubs, theater groups, newspapers, and magazines, all of these various enterprises not only allowed young undergraduates to emulate and prepare for life, but also provided them with experiences that they knew to be profoundly human. Just as the extracurriculum in the collegiate era was a response to the sterility of the curriculum, in the university era it became a compensation for

---

[14] Martin Trow, "Reflections on the Transition from Mass to Universal Higher Education," *Daedalus,* Winter 1970, p. 6.

the one-sided intellectuality and the overwhelming impersonality of the official scheme of things. [15]

Through extracurricular activities, the university has been able to assimilate and accommodate to some degree the traditional collegiate values of fellowship, community of interest, and social relationships. They are an important means for the satisfaction of the primary social needs of the student participants in the organization. The student is within the institution for a period of at least four years, and it would be unrealistic to expect abstinence in the satisfaction of social and fellowship needs in favor of purely intellectual pursuits. One of the student's problems in the large university is the loss of identity and failure to establish satisfactory interpersonal relationships. The university would be a very sterile institution if the only expected interactions occurred in the classroom and centered on intellectual pursuits.

TECHNOLOGY

We have referred to technology as *knowledge* about the performance of certain tasks or activities. By "organizational technology" we mean the techniques used in the transformation of inputs into outputs in the accomplishment of goals. We will discuss the technology of the university under two headings, academic and administrative.

Academic Technology

Teaching and scholarly research are the primary technical tasks of the system. The academic staff—professors, instructors, and teaching assistants—performs these tasks and is the operating subsystem in the university organization.

The academic staff is specialized in its task performance. The university is departmentalized, and professors within each department have individual expertise. They transmit knowledge to students in specialized disciplines. The second major role, knowledge creation through scholarly and scientific research, is also carried on by the academic staff.

The techniques of teaching have not undergone profound changes. The classroom, with its interpersonal relationships, remains the primary vehicle for the dissemination of knowledge. It is supplemented by the use of textbooks and library resources. There have been modifications in teaching techniques, such as closed-circuit television and teaching machines, but these have not made major inroads into the more traditional methods. While faculties are dedicated to the expansion of knowledge in their discipline fields, they have been resistant to experimentation with new teaching techniques. The professor typically adheres to the traditional approach and prefers close interpersonal contact with students in a classroom situation. Although he may reluctantly accept the

---

[15] Rudolph, op. cit., p. 464.

economic necessity for large-scale lectures, it is not a ready acceptance. In most universities, the faculties desire a collegial environment. This is particularly true for advanced undergraduate students and even more so at the graduate level. Consequently, there is a general pattern of decreasing class size and closer interpersonal relationships in the teaching situation as the student advances through his academic career.

Techniques employed in accomplishing the second major goal, that of creation of knowledge through research, have been more subject to change. This is particularly true in the physical sciences, which require research laboratories, cyclotrons, and other equipment, and in such areas as medicine, which must have large research facilities and hospitals. Universities have provided the physical manifestations of technology to enable the staff to perform this role.

At the graduate level, in particular, there is a merging of the technical tasks of knowledge creation and dissemination. Frequently, graduate students are engaged as research assistants in support of the academic staff. The graduate assistant has the dual role of recipient of current knowledge and partner in creating new knowledge.

The diversity of task performance activities in the university suggests the wide differences in technologies in the various disciplines. Each of the academic fields typically has developed techniques which are specialized to its field of endeavor.

Administrative Technology

But a university is more than a professor and a student sitting at opposite ends of a log. Who provides the log? How do we ensure that the student and professor meet at the appropriate time? How are the library resources necessary for an intellectual dialogue accumulated? Who feeds and houses the student and takes care of his medical needs? Who provides the parking facilities for the automobiles each of them wants to drive as close as possible to the log? Who records the number of sessions and the professor's evaluation of the student? How is the professor *paid*? These are a few of the functions necessary to support the primary technical tasks of teaching and research. With a university of 30,000 or 40,000 students and an academic staff in excess of 2,000, the administrative functions required for servicing the primary technical tasks are essential and complex. [16]

Administrative technology in universities can be classified in four principal areas: [17] (1) *academic administration,* which is the primary concern of the academic staff; (2) *administration of student personnel services,* which includes the selection, admission, and supervision of students, and the recording of their academic achievements; (3) *business administration,* which includes such activities as accounting, auditing, reporting, and budgetary control; receipt, custody, and disbursement of monies; investment

[16] Clark Kerr, "Governance and Functions," *Daedalus,* Winter 1970, pp. 108-121.
[17] Thomas Edward Blackwell, *College and University Administration,* The Center for Applied Research in Education, Inc., New York, 1966, pp. 14-15.

of funds; purchasing; management of auxiliary and service activities; operation and maintenance of the institutional plant; selection and promotion of nonacademic personnel; and administration of staff benefits programs; and (4) *public relations,* which includes the relationship with the press, radio, and television stations, alumni, solicitation of funds, and maintenance of contact with possible donors and legislatures. Administrative technology is involved with the latter three areas. Universities are adopting management concepts from business organizations for these functions. In most modern American universities there has been a significant increase in the number of people on the administrative staff to perform these activities.

Computer technology has already revolutionized the maintenance of student records, the grading process, and many other administrative techniques. It is being applied to library systems in order to aid in information storage and retrieval. [18] Such techniques as systems and procedures analysis and cost-effective analysis are being used for more efficient utilization of resources. Administrative offices are being established for long-range planning and organizational analysis. These offices use the same type of planning and administrative technologies as in business and government. Many universities have adopted new planning-programming-budgeting systems (PPBS) to help in the allocation of resources. [19]

There is not a complete separation between academic and administrative technologies. Certainly they are interacting and may be in conflict. The developing administrative techniques have an important effect upon the entire academic community. While we share some of the concern over possible conflicts between academe and "the administration," the application of more effective managerial techniques is vital. It is no longer possible to think of a university with primary responsibility for all administrative matters centered with the faculty. Parsons suggests this need for administration:

> Modern universities have become complex organizations and especially in the research function have come to require an advanced and complex technology. This technology and the imperatives of sheer size have led to a marked growth of administrative organization which is more or less of a bureaucratic character. This has grown up parallel to, rather than displacing, the basic faculty structure which retains its collegial character. [20]

However, the new directions and techniques in management should be designed to facilitate the primary academic endeavors of teaching and research as well as the internal administrative functions of the university.

---

[18] Francis E. Rourke and Glenn E. Brooks, *The Managerial Revolution in Higher Education,* The Johns Hopkins Press, Baltimore, 1966, pp. 20–21.
[19] Paul W. Hamelman, "Missions, Matrices and University Management," *Academy of Management Journal,* March 1970, pp. 35–47.
[20] Talcott Parsons, "Components and Types of Formal Organization," in Preston P. LeBreton (ed.), *Comparative Administrative Theory,* University of Washington Press, Seattle, 1968, p. 18.

STRUCTURE

The structure and authority patterns of universities have changed significantly from their medieval form. The early universities appear to have started as scholastic guilds, a combination of teachers and students somewhat similar to trade guilds. In the early Italian universities, the student had substantial authority over administrative and academic affairs. However, this student control broke down, and the church became the primary source of authority. There was continual conflict between the church and the universities' faculties. One of the most significant changes in this relationship occurred in 1231, when Gregory IX recognized the rights of the several faculties of the University of Paris to administer their own activities. This has been called the Magna Charta of the university. The pattern of the University of Paris became the model for the universities in Central Europe and in England. Oxford and Cambridge were organized around faculty authority.

A later development changed this form. The University of Leyden, founded in 1575, had an external board of "curators," who appointed professors and administered the affairs of the university. This pattern was adopted by the University of Edinburgh, founded in 1582, where the charter gave the town council the right to provide for the teaching of all subjects usual at a university. [21] Two colonial colleges, Yale and Princeton, were modeled after the University of Edinburgh organization and incorporated the principle of an external board of trustees. This set the precedent for the structure of most American colleges and universities.

Increased Differentiation

The colonial colleges had a simple structure. They had a strict and prescribed curriculum, small size, and special purpose. With the development of true universities in the latter part of the nineteenth century, the problems of structure became more acute. The university model brought greater complexities due to increased specialization and the emphasis upon research and knowledge creation. There was also greater diversity of objectives. This process of specialization continued as universities expanded into the various disciplinary fields and added new subject matter.

It became necessary to develop a more complex and elaborate structure. Separate colleges or schools based upon academic disciplines were established. These were further divided into departments with even more academic specialization.

Need for Integration

The university has undergone the same process and faces the same structural problems as the general hospital—providing for the integration of activities. The primary concern is the integration of the specialized disciplines through new means of coordination. The

---

21 Blackwell, op. cit., p. 35.

traditional faculty committee structure and the direct democratic participation in institutional matters are useful devices. However, with increasing size, diversity, and specialization, this system for providing coordination has broken down. It is unrealistic to expect that a full faculty meeting of over 2,000 members could provide integration. Consequently, it has been necessary to develop new means for coordinating specialized activities.

Authority Patterns

The authority structure within the university is not similar to that of the bureaucratic model. There is no way of clearly defining scalar authority from top to bottom of the hierarchy. One university president has likened the university to a collegial partnership between himself and 2,000 faculty members.

In the university there is a wide dispersal of power. A major source of power resides with the holders of knowledge and pursuers of research—the academic staff. The authority of knowledge is a fundamental part of the system and does not rest exclusively in the scalar hierarchy.

One of the primary sources of power for the academic man is the status which he holds in his profession and among his colleagues at other institutions. Therefore, power is not something that can be delegated from the top down in the academic institution. This frequently results in a loosely defined and dynamic authority structure. Caplow and McGee say, "The system works, then, by distributing power in such a way that anyone who is able to exercise it may do so if he chooses. The product of this system is the university 'strong man'—dean, chairman, or professor—who converts his prestige, either disciplinary or local, into authority by enlisting the support of the men around him." [22]

Formal Structure

Despite the diffused nature of power, colleges and universities do have a formal structure. It starts with a board of trustees, governors, or regents—an external body at the top of the hierarchy which is traditional with American universities. Perhaps this pattern developed because of the feeling that the academic community was incapable of governing itself and that it was necessary to have men of practical experience to oversee their activities.

The board delegates authority to the president for the administration of the university. Actually, a university president has a dual function. He is administrative representative of the board but also the leader of the faculty. The president has reporting to him an administrative staff consisting of a provost, a number of vice-presidents, the deans of the various colleges or schools, and other administrative personnel.

---

[22] Theodore Caplow and Reece J. McGee, *The Academic Marketplace,* Basic Books, Inc., Publishers, New York, 1958, p. 207.

In most universities, the president authorizes the faculty to share with him the academic duties and responsibilities for the formulation of policies and rules for the government of the institution. The faculty traditionally has primary responsibility over matters of curriculum and a strong voice in the selection and promotion of faculty colleagues.

This pattern of shared authority which permeates the university is distinct from that existing in most other complex organizations. Instead of utilizing the principle of a hierarchy of authority, universities are organized with a community of authority.

> Basically, the organizational concept which is antithetical to the bureaucratic and which is commonly deemed applicable to colleges and universities is that of *community*. This concept is not as easily defined or described as "organization" as is that of bureaucracy.
>
> Community seems to preclude extensive or complex hierarchical structure. The roles of the members are seldom articulated, although they may be well defined, and special competence which might confer authority on any member is only indirectly acknowledged. Leadership in community organization is often diffused and transient. [23]

Other Structures

There are other structural aspects which should be considered. Students frequently are in control of many activities. They are formally organized in an overall association of students. Within these associations there are formal structures to carry out specific functions. Students may be organized in fraternities and sororities, dormitory living groups, religious groups, service clubs, professional groups, and a host of other activities. It would be impossible to describe all the structural relationships for student activities in a large university. While the emphasis here has been with the authority of the administration and faculty, the power of the student body should not be underestimated. Any university recognizes that the quality of the students is a prime requisite for first-class status.

Another formal structure existing in most universities is a representative faculty organization such as the university senate or council. There may also be formal college or school councils. These bodies can play a strong academic and administrative role.

This diffused authority structure leads to substantial conflict and uncertainty. "The new university is a conflict-prone organization. Its many purposes push and pull in different directions. Its multiple principles of authority and pluralistic power structure make coordination difficult." [24] However, for the institutions whose basic role is one of

---

[23] G. Lester Anderson, "The Organizational Character of American Colleges and Universities," *The Study of Academic Administration,* Western Interstate Commission for Higher Education, Boulder, Colo., October 1963, p. 14.
[24] Burton R. Clark, "The New University," *American Behavioral Scientist,* May–June 1968, p. 4.

creation and dissemination of knowledge, collegial authority appears to be the most appropriate form. It provides for the free expression of ideas, a high level of commitment of the individual to his disciplinary area, a strong sense of participation, and an environment conducive to change.

Example of Structure

The organization of the University of Washington serves as an example of structural relationships. This is a large state-supported university located in a metropolitan area, Seattle. In Fall 1972, it had an enrollment of 34,125 students, of which 7,661, or nearly 23 percent, were graduate. The growth in student enrollment has been substantial, more than doubling since 1959. This is typical of other large state universities. It had over 2,200 regular faculty members and a staff of nearly 800 teaching assistants. The nonacademic staff exceeded 7,900. Taken together, the students, faculty, and supporting staff represented a university community of over 47,000 people. Figure 21.1 shows the administrative organization of the University of Washington. It should be emphasized that this chart shows only part of the structure. It does not show the separate faculty structure, which includes the universitywide faculty senate or councils within the various colleges and schools. It does not show the student organizations, such as the Associated Students of the University of Washington, and its Board of Control. In effect, this organization chart shows just one aspect of the formal structure.

There are eight vice-presidents in charge of functional activities reporting through the executive vice-president to the president. They function primarily in an advisory role to the various academic departments. There are eighteen colleges and schools which represent the academic structure; many of these are divided into departments. For example, the College of Arts and Sciences has thirty-five departments or schools and many other separate units. Many specialized activities are associated with these various schools and colleges. For example, the Graduate School of Public Affairs has an Institute for Governmental Research and the School of Social Work has a Center for Social Welfare Research. There are a number of activities which are administered jointly by two departments. The Center for Bioengineering is a joint endeavor between the School of Medicine and the College of Engineering. The Center for Quantitative Science in Forestry, Fisheries and Wildlife is administered jointly by the College of Fisheries and the College of Forest Resources. In addition, many organizational units are under the direction of the various vice-presidents—planning and budgeting, minority affairs, and research, for example. Typically, these activities have a universitywide function.

While some of the activities presented on this chart are unique to the University of Washington, the overall concept of the administrative organization is similar to that of other public and private universities. It has a multilevel structure on the academic side moving from the president through the schools and colleges down to the departmental level. In addition, it has an administrative staff to deal with universitywide functions such as business and finance, student affairs, and university relations. These administrative units can be considered as staff activities in support of the primary academic functions.

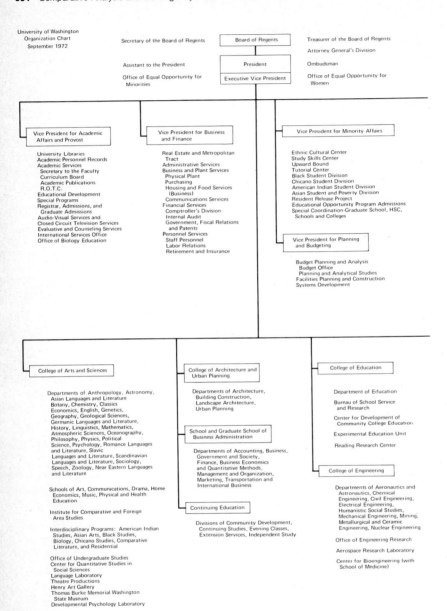

FIGURE 21.1   UNIVERSITY OF WASHINGTON ORGANIZATION CHART (September 1972)

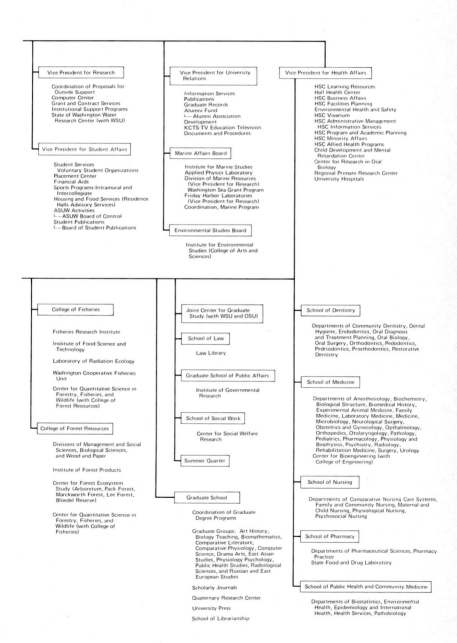

Vice President for Research

Coordination of Proposals for
  Outside Support
Computer Center
Grant and Contract Services
Institutional Support Programs
State of Washington Water
  Research Center (with WSU)

Vice President for Student Affairs

Student Services
  Voluntary Student Organizations
Placement Center
Financial Aids
Sports Programs-Intramural and
  Intercollegiate
Housing and Food Services (Residence
  Halls Advisory Services)
ASUW Activities
  └—ASUW Board of Control
Student Publications
  └—Board of Student Publications

Vice President for University
Relations

Information Services
Publications
Graduate Records
Alumni Fund
  └—Alumni Association
Development
KCTS-TV Education Television
Documents and Procedures

Marine Affairs Board

Institute for Marine Studies
Applied Physics Laboratory
Division of Marine Resources
  (Vice President for Research)
  Washington Sea Grant Program
Friday Harbor Laboratories
  (Vice President for Research)
Coordination, Marine Program

Environmental Studies Board

Institute for Environmental
Studies (College of Arts and
Sciences)

Vice President for Health Affairs

HSC Learning Resources
Hall Health Center
HSC Business Affairs
HSC Facilities Planning
Environmental Health and Safety
HSC Vivarium
HSC Administrative Management
  HSC Information Services
HSC Program and Academic Planning
HSC Minority Affairs
HSC Allied Health Programs
Child Development and Mental
  Retardation Center
Center for Research in Oral
  Biology
Regional Primate Research Center
University Hospitals

College of Fisheries

Fisheries Research Institute

Institute of Food Science and
Technology

Laboratory of Radiation Ecology

Washington Cooperative Fisheries
Unit

Center for Quantitative Science in
Forestry, Fisheries, and
Wildlife (with College of
Forest Resources)

College of Forest Resources

Divisions of Management and Social
Sciences, Biological Sciences,
and Wood and Paper

Institute of Forest Products

Center for Forest Ecosystem
Study (Arboretum, Pack Forest,
Marckworth Forest, Lee Forest,
Bloedel Reserve)

Center for Quantitative Science in
Forestry, Fisheries, and
Wildlife (with College of
Fisheries)

Joint Center for Graduate
Study (with WSU and OSU)

School of Law

Law Library

Graduate School of Public Affairs

Institute of Governmental
Research

School of Social Work

Center for Social Welfare
Research

Summer Quarter

Graduate School

Coordination of Graduate
Degree Programs

Graduate Groups: Art History,
Biology Teaching, Biomathematics,
Comparative Literature,
Comparative Physiology, Computer
Science, Drama Arts, East Asian
Studies, Physiology Psychology,
Public Health Studies, Radiological
Sciences, and Russian and East
European Studies

Scholarly Journals

Quaternary Research Center

University Press

School of Librarianship

School of Dentistry

Departments of Community Dentistry, Dental
Hygiene, Endodontics, Oral Diagnosis
and Treatment Planning, Oral Biology,
Oral Surgery, Orthodontics, Pedodontics,
Pedriodontics, Prosthodontics, Restorative
Dentistry

School of Medicine

Departments of Anesthesiology, Biochemistry,
Biological Structure, Biomedical History,
Experimental Animal Medicine, Family
Medicine, Laboratory Medicine, Medicine,
Microbiology, Neurological Surgery,
Obstetrics and Gynecology, Opthalmology,
Orthopedics, Otolaryngology, Pathology,
Pediatrics, Pharmacology, Physiology and
Biophysics, Psychiatry, Radiology,
Rehabilitation Medicine, Surgery, Urology
Center for Bioengineering (with
College of Engineering)

School of Nursing

Departments of Comparative Nursing Care Systems,
Family and Community Nursing, Maternal and
Child Nursing, Physiological Nursing,
Psychosocial Nursing

School of Pharmacy

Departments of Pharmaceutical Sciences, Pharmacy
Practice
State Food and Drug Laboratory

School of Public Health and Community Medicine

Departments of Biostatistics, Environmental
Health, Epidemiology and International
Health, Health Services, Pathobiology

PSYCHOSOCIAL SYSTEMS

Many diverse participants play various roles in the psychosocial system of a university. These participants have different goals and motivations. One of the predominant characteristics is that most of the participants, faculty and students, have a substantial degree of autonomy, and they operate as individuals within the system. Students, for example, have autonomy in the selection of their areas of specialization and interest. Although their classroom participation is on a group basis, their outside preparation is individualized. The same characteristic is also true of the faculty. The professor is primarily responsible for conducting his class and has full control of the evaluational and grading process. Thus, a university community represents a very diffuse and complex psychosocial system, one that is loosely tied together. In the following discussion, we will look at the three predominant participant groups: student, faculty, and the administrative staff.

Students

Students obviously have a vital role in the academic process. They complete the process of knowledge transmission. Their goals and aspirations, values, motivations, and interests have an impact upon the academic and social life of every university.

With the evolutionary process from college to university, the basic role and position of students changed dramatically. In the early days the student's total life revolved around his college. The curriculum was prescribed, he lived in residence, and he was isolated from the broader community. He lived in a cloistered environment in which the basis of need satisfaction centered in the college itself.

The movement toward the university system changed this pattern significantly. The student has been placed on his own in a strange environment. He has substantial autonomy in the selection of a curriculum of studies, and the opportunities available to him are varied. His responsibilities are centered around meeting class obligations which typically take only twelve to fifteen hours per week. Otherwise he is substantially on his own. Kerr suggests this new role for the student.

> The multiversity is a confusing place for the student. He has problems of establishing his identity and sense of security within it. But it offers him a vast range of choices, enough literally to stagger the mind. In this range of choices he encounters the opportunities and the dilemmas of freedom. The casualty rate is high. The walking wounded are many. *Lernfreiheit*—the freedom of the student to pick and choose, to stay or move on—is triumphant. [25]

Traditionally, colleges and universities accepted the role of *in loco parentis*, in which the institution adopted a paternalistic attitude toward students. This concept of

---

[25] Clark Kerr, *The Uses of the University*, Harvard University Press, Cambridge, Mass. 1963, p. 42.

the university as a second parent to the student is breaking down. The student body is being left to its own devices for the satisfaction of social needs. Obviously, many students respond favorably to this new-found freedom, but for others it creates difficulties of anomie and identification. Many have suggested, for example, that this loss of identity and problems of redefining a new social role have contributed to student unrest in recent years.

Certainly one of the characteristics of university students is their great diversity. A wide variety of programs and curricula exist. Frequently, the value systems which influence students are substantially different between the humanities, physical sciences, and professional schools. There is a substantial age range of students from beginning freshmen to master's and doctoral candidates as well as those in the professional schools of medicine and law. There is a diversity in their domiciles. In metropolitan universities, many students are commuters, living at home. Others live in university-provided dormitories, others in the sororities and the fraternities, and many live in apartments and other quarters not associated with the university.

Students entering the university come with substantially different goals and expectations of the role they will play in the system. Basically, they are not as committed to the existing norms and values as are the faculty and administration. There have been many forces which have contributed to the feeling of alienation on the part of students—the size of classes, the inability to have close faculty-student contacts, particularly at the undergraduate level, the use of teaching assistants in undergraduate classes, the increased computerization of students' records, and the establishment of bureaucratic procedures in other activities associated with the university. [26] The very transientness of students, typically being in the institution for a few years at most, makes it difficult to find effective means for the assimilation of their interests and influence into the university community.

The diversity of the university system has allowed various student cultures to exist. These cultures often are quite different in their goals, reference groups, status, and roles. Searle has defined five student cultures:

1 The *fraternity-sorority culture.* This culture is traditional with undergraduate life in universities, although it has created certain conflicts and problems. Through long experience, the university has come to accommodate and accept this student culture. However, there are strong indications throughout the country that this culture, once dominant, is on the decline.

2 The *professional culture.* This is the student culture which is primarily dedicated to obtaining an education for the pursuit of professional careers. It is practically oriented, and represents many students in engineering, business administration, and medical and dental schools. This student culture is easy assimilated into the university system.

3 The *intellectual culture.* This is composed of students who are interested in

---

[26] William H. Sewell, "Students and the University," *The American Sociologist,* May 1971, pp. 111-117.

knowledge itself and look to the university for intellectual development. Again, this culture is relatively easily assimilated into the university system.

4 The *political culture.* This culture views the university as providing the means whereby they can effect change in the total social-political environment. This is the group which is interested primarily in immediate problems and is frequently engaged in confrontation with the broader society and with other segments of the university itself. Although the political culture of students has been traditional with many foreign universities, it is a relatively new and major phenomenon in United States universities. It is this culture which is most difficult to assimilate within the established university community and has created the great dissension in recent times.

5 The *bohemian culture.* This culture features the nonconformist and experimentalist in matters of dress and social behavior. This may be characterized as the culture which is alienated from the broad mainstream of American life and is often in search of a new sense of identity and cohesiveness. [27]

In the large university, there is an increasing number of students who are subject to a substantial degree of role conflict—graduate teaching and research assistants. In many institutions teaching assistants have control of classes and sections of undergraduate students. Dubin and Beisse suggest that this development is one of the primary causes for concern. [28]

The teaching assistant is treated by his departmental professors as a student even though he performs the central academic function of dissemination of knowledge in the classroom. This suggests a major role conflict for the graduate teaching assistant. On the one hand, he is viewed as a student learning his apprenticeship as a teacher. On the other, he performs the professorial role. One of the problems of the university is to provide some means for establishing the position of the graduate teaching assistant to minimize the role conflict and also to provide greater legitimacy in the minds of the undergraduate students whom he teaches. The position of the teaching assistant is somewhat similar to that of the first-line supervisor in industry and the nurse in the hospital. He is the "man in the middle" and caught between conflicting role requirements.

Faculty

The role of the university faculty in our society has undergone rather dramatic transformation. The traditional concept of the "ivory tower" professor pursuing his academic interests in isolation and dealing with the nonpractical has changed. Increasingly, the community looks to the campus for knowledge and expertise in solving real-world

---

[27] John R. Searle, in Samuel Gorovitz (ed.), *Freedom and Order in the University,* The Press of Case Western Reserve University, Cleveland, Ohio. 1967. pp. 94–103.
[28] Robert Dubin and Fredric Beisse, "The Assistant: Academic Subaltern," *Administrative Science Quarterly,* March 1967, p. 522.

problems. This initially occurred in the physical sciences and engineering as exemplified by the developments in atomic energy. Other academic disciplines are having a strong influence upon practical affairs. Witness the growing role of the economist and other social scientists. This increased reliance on knowledge provided by the universities has created a new role for the academician. "Life has changed also for the faculty member. The multiversity is in the main stream of events. To the teacher and the researcher have been added the consultant and the administrator. Teaching is less central than it once was for most faculty members; research has become more important." [29]

The faculty represents a heterogeneous psychosocial system. This diversity stems from the basic differences in the disciplines. Each discipline has established a certain prescribed value system, "ways of thinking" and "methods of research," which sets it apart from other academic specialties.

In the university there is a formal rank structure for the faculty, beginning with the instructor, assistant professor, associate professor, professor, and, in some cases, a distinguished professorial chair. However, this distinction does not affect the role fundamentally. In the United States universities, as differentiated from many European institutions, the instructor and assistant and associate professor perform essentially the same role of teaching and research as the full professor. They have the same degree of autonomy in conducting their classes and research.

Every member of the faculty has a dual role—as an individual and as a member of the community of scholars. As an individual he has various duties to carry out in the performance of his profession. In addition, each member of the faculty has certain functions in his collegial role at three levels, the department, the college or school, and the university. This role is usually performed by services on various academic and administrative committees.

There has been much discussion of the faculty member's role conflict as a teacher (dispenser of knowledge) and as a scholarly researcher (creator of knowledge). [30] Many suggest that this conflict is absolute—he must choose one of these two roles. He can be either a good teacher or a good researcher but, by inference, not both. "For most members of the profession, the real strain in the academic role arises from the fact that they are, in essence, paid to do one job, whereas the worth of their services is evaluated on the basis of how well they do another." [31] This popularized dichotomy between "publish or perish" is misleading. Part of the confusion centers on the definition of scholarly research. It might be assumed that scholarly research and a publication record are synonymous, but there may be differences. Many professors engage in research which does not result directly in publications but does contribute to the body of knowledge. Conversely, many publications are not based on scholarly research.

The university professor has a dual role of teaching and research, and he cannot

---

[29] Kerr, *The Uses of the University,* p. 42.
[30] Robert S. Morrison, "Some Aspects of Policy-Making in the American University," *Daedalus,* Summer 1970, pp. 609-644.
[31] Caplow and McGee, op. cit., p. 82.

adequately fulfill his responsibilities without giving attention to both. This role conflict is not as real as it may appear. It may serve as a rationalization for those who can neither teach nor perform scholarly research effectively. In the university system, both activities are vital to the basic goals of the institution.

Another possible conflict relates to whether or not the professor is primarily oriented to his role within the university (*local*) or to his professional discipline (*cosmopolitan*). [32] This is typical of the conflicting roles for the professional in all types of organizations. To what extent does he look to the organization for his status, prestige, and motivation (a local) as compared to looking to his external professional colleagues (a cosmopolitan)? In the early history of American colleges, the primary source of status and prestige was within the college community. When the university came on the scene, with its greater emphasis upon scholarly research, there was an increasing trend for faculty to look to professional colleagues for status and prestige.

This move toward greater cosmopolitanism has some primary implications for the faculty role. It makes more difficult the basic view of the university as a community in which there is a sharing of the administrative responsibility with the faculty. The faculty member is often caught between his desire for full participation in his university as a member of the community of scholars and his desire to maintain his externally determined status.

There is a growing interest among faculties in many institutions of higher education for developing some form of collective bargaining. Traditionally, each faculty member has negotiated individually with the institution concerning the terms of his employment. However, there have existed a number of means for joint participation by faculty in university affairs. The tradition of collegiality and sharing of matters of governance between the board of regents, administration, and faculty has created a different role from that of a typical employee in other organizations. However, true collective bargaining as exists for workers in industry, for many governmental employees, and for certain professionals (e.g., nurses and public school teachers) has not been evident on campuses until recently.

Faculties in most universities and colleges have "reluctantly and with skepticism" looked cautiously at collective bargaining. There is substantial fear that active collective bargaining will result in an "adversary relationship" between faculty and administration with a major sacrifice of the concept of collegiality and joint governance of the institution. At the same time, there is a growing concern that the only way for faculty to get a "fair shake" and to maintain their relative position in a period of inflation and limited financial resources is through some form of collective bargaining. In many ways collective bargaining is not compatible with the "professional" norms of the academician. However, the hard realities of life in a large institution where the individual faculty member has a limited individual bargaining position have caused an increasing number of faculty to seek some accommodation between these professional norms and the

---

[32] This distinction was first applied by Alvin W. Gouldner, "Cosmopolitans and Locals: Toward an Analysis of Latent Social Roles—I," *Administrative Science Quarterly*, December 1957, pp. 281–306.

advantages of collective activity. The movement toward full-scale collective bargaining can have a major impact upon the psychosocial system of the faculty:

> There is the likelihood of an extensive alteration in the psychological milieu of the university under collective bargaining. Whether the change will be for the better or not is, again, a matter of wide difference of opinion. The changed psychological atmosphere will be due in part to the strict constructionist view of faculty as "employees." The traditional self-image of university faculty has been that they are not employees in the sense of business enterprise, much less in the sense of industry, but are professionals, with a status, a degree of independence, and a role in governance not usually vouchsafed to employees. This self-image has, on occasion, been upheld by the courts. But the image often no longer coincides with the reality, and to the extent that it does it is the result of the happenstance of the character of a particular administration. [33]

Administrative Staff

Members of a university administrative staff—the president, provost, most vice-presidents, deans, and department heads—are also members of the faculty. Most frequently they have moved from the faculty to an administrative post. Often their assignments as administrators are part time or temporary, and they ultimately return to their faculty positions. Thus they hold many of the same basic values as the faculty. However, of necessity they are more local in their orientation and are concerned primarily with internal and external institutional matters rather than their professional disciplines.

The president, deans, and department heads have a dual role in the university system. Formally, the president is selected by the board of trustees and is responsible to them for the administration of the university. Quite frequently, both faculty members within the institution and prominent faculty and administrators in other universities are consulted in the selection. There is a trend toward more input from students. For example, at the University of Washington two students were on the selection committee to make recommendations to the board of regents for a new president—one representing undergraduates and another representing graduate and professional students. Once selected, the president is the chief administrative officer of the university. However, he has a second role—he is the presiding member of the faculty, first among equals, and is therefore the educational leader. This duality of function holds for deans and department heads. However, it is increasingly more difficult for the academic administrator to fulfill these two roles. The high degree of specialization and the rapid advancements in knowledge make it difficult for him to keep up with his discipline.

---

[33] *Report of the Ad Hoc University Committee on Collective Bargaining,* Michigan State University, East Lansing, Mich., Jan. 31, 1972, p. 4.

Furthermore, the complexities of the administrative function take up much of his time and energy. More and more academic administrators are being excluded from the direct, goal-oriented activities of the university—teaching and research.

The conflict between the administrative and faculty roles is apparent for the departmental chairman. In most universities, the chairman's position is a temporary one, perhaps a three- to five-year tenure. In some cases, he is elected directly by the departmental faculty; in others he is appointed by the dean. However, in all cases, because of the importance of effective collegial relationships, it is considered essential to have a near consensus concerning the selection. From the start he is caught in the middle between the necessity for his performance as an administrator under the president and dean and his desire to maintain relationships with discipline colleagues. The effective departmental chairman is one who recognizes the importance of this collegial relationship and does not think of his position solely in terms of hierarchical authority.

For higher administrative officials the maintenance of a "community of scholars" relationship with the faculty may be even more difficult because of differences between the administrative and faculty functions and the lack of social interactions.

> University executives and faculty members are increasingly isolated from each other in their daily lives, while each is encouraged toward contacts mainly with his own "kind." The administrator, especially a "high-level" executive of a prestigious and fast growing institution, is a chronically busy man. The sheer volume of the demands upon him, and the number of faculty members on his campus, make it effectively impossible for a vice-president or "executive dean" to meet regularly with any significant portion of the institution's faculty. [34]

A critical factor for the academic administrator's own status and prestige needs is the general disdain which many faculty members have for the administrative role. "Administration or management" does not have the long-established tradition of professionalism associated with an academic discipline. The faculty view frequently is that the administration is only there to serve the needs of the professors, who perform the "important" functions of the university. This viewpoint was frequently expressed by one professor as "The dean needs me more than I need him." (However, this was only expressed to colleagues, never to the dean.) This withholding of status and prestige for the academic administrator by his faculty colleagues may lead him to orient his role to other reference groups—typically other administrators—thus creating additional problems in maintaining an effective "community of scholars." [35]

---

[34] Terry F. Lunsford, "Authority and Ideology in the Administered University," *American Behavioral Scientist*, May–June 1968, p. 7.

[35] Lunsford says, "A major effect of these changes has been to erode the informal relationships between administrators and faculty members, relationships which engendered and sustained the trust necessary for an easy exercise of administrative authority, and which muted the potential conflict between administrators and academics in the university of an earlier day. Radical shrinkage of informal contacts has also reduced the actual knowledge that administrators have of faculty and students—and *vice versa*." Ibid., p. 8.

The psychosocial system of academic administrators has many inherent role conflicts and problems of identification with particular reference groups. And, all too frequently, the administrative role has more status and prestige as viewed from the external world than from within the university community.

MANAGERIAL SYSTEM

Planning and control decisions are diffused throughout the entire university system. These functions are shared by many participant groups—students, faculty, administrators, and board of trustees. There is no single managerial system based on a distinct and unified scalar hierarchy. Much of the decision making is in the hands of the individual professor and student. The success of the university system depends on the degree to which the individual internalized objectives mesh with the organization as a whole. We will look briefly at the managerial functions at the departmental, college or school, and university levels.

Departmental Level

The individual faculty member represents the basic operating unit in the university system. In order to accomplish his tasks, he has traditionally been granted a great deal of autonomy. Because of his professional training and the discipline specialization, he is considered the one most appropriate to make decisions concerning the specific conduct of his teaching and research. He determines the course content, texts, instructional methods and procedures, and the means of measuring student performance. However, control is exerted over the faculty member's performance of these tasks. There are formal and informal mechanisms for feedback of information from students about his performance in the classroom, and professional performance is continually being evaluated by his colleagues.

The department is the basic organizational unit in the university. It has the primary function of coordinating the activities of the individual faculty member around a body of knowledge or discipline. Departments have a substantial role in decision making concerning educational matters. For example, they have a major voice in recruitment of new faculty and in evaluating the performance of their own members. Decisions in these matters are subject to the approval of the dean, president, and board of trustees, but there are strong pressures to confirm departmental decisions unless there are exceptional problems. [36]

The departmental chairman serves as a coordinator between the department and the college. [37] Because the chairman is a faculty member, and in most cases will return to his faculty position after a tenure as chairman, his value orientation is to his departmental colleagues and the discipline area. However, he must also be responsive to his relationships with the dean of the school or college.

---

[36] For a discussion of departmental practices, see Eugene Haas and Linda Collen, "Administrative Practices in University Departments," *Administrative Science Quarterly,* June 1963, pp. 44–60.
[37] For a discussion of the role of department chairman, see Winston W. Hill and Wendell L. French, "Perceptions of Power of Department Chairmen by Professors," *Administrative Science Quarterly,* March 1967, pp 548–574.

College or School Level

The college or school is a combination of departments. It provides for a further integration of academic planning and control decisions. Basic decisions are made concerning the broad scope of the curriculum, required courses for majors within the college, and the nature of the various degree programs. In this process, numerous collegewide committees are involved, and the ultimate decisions usually represent a compromise of the viewpoints of the various departmental units. Thus, the decision-making process continues to be one of obtaining consensus rather than one of centralized direction by the dean. However, the dean does have an important role in the use of his power to obtain a consensus.

In most universities, the college or school is the primary level at which the budgetary process is initiated. Thus, the dean has substantial influence in his role as the fiscal officer. The dean is also a "man in the middle." He is a representative of the various departments and faculty members within his college to the higher administration. On the other hand, he serves as the spokesman for the administration to the faculty. Millett suggests that one of the most important functions of the dean is to serve the integrative role for his faculty.

> The dean reviews the personnel practices of departments. He formulates the budget for his college or school and participates in its administration.
>
> Usually the dean is more than this. He does not issue orders to departments or faculty members, but he stands as a symbol of their collegial responsibility. He is a reminder to all the faculty members of a college or school of their common purpose and common interest. To the extent that he can articulate this common purpose and can win adherents to it, the dean has fulfilled an essential role in the academic process. [38]

The University Level

This level includes the board of trustees, the president, the vice-presidents, and other administrative staff. Much of the decision making relating the university to its external environment takes place at this level. It is concerned with financial matters and relationships with legislators, alumni, and many other groups. The president and his administrative staff have two primary decision-making roles. The first is in the overall governance of the university as delegated by the board of trustees. Many activities at this level are concerned with the maintenance of the organization, such as classroom and student facilities, business and financial aspects, and the physical plant. Many of these functions are similar to those in business organizations. The same techniques and approaches for decision making are appropriate. For example, the problems of comput-

---

[38] Millett, op. cit., pp. 92–93.

erizing and programming the decision-making process in such areas as inventory controls, the payroll, and student records are similar to those faced by business.

The second and more complex decision-making role is that concerned with the president as leader of the faculty. The president reviews and approves the academic offerings of the departments and colleges and establishes broad policy for such activities as faculty selection and promotion. He has the help and guidance of a number of groups. For example, there may be a board of deans from the various schools and colleges. It serves as a communications link with the faculty. There are many faculty committees which report to the president and provide him with information on academic affairs.

There has been a growth in the concept of cabinet government in large universities where the president utilizes his administrative staff for consultation and advice. In some cases this cabinet is formalized as an administrative council or committee. More frequently, however, it is an informal "kitchen cabinet" which advises the president on current problems. [39]

Problems in Decision Making

The discussion on planning and control decisions at the various levels in the university indicates that it is a unique managerial system, significantly different from that found in bureaucratic organizations. The concept of shared authority and decision making permeates the university. This raises some important questions on how the various groups within the system can effectively participate in the decision-making processes.

As universities have increased in size and complexity and with greater academic specialization, fundamental questions have been raised about how the faculty can exercise its shared decision-making authority. [40] Traditionally, faculty decision making has been based upon obtaining a consensus of opinion through democratic processes. Growing size and increased specialization have made the "town meeting" process of decision making ineffective. It is necessary to shift to a more representative form of faculty government. This transformation has not come easily. As Rourke and Brooks say, "College and university faculties must come to terms with this trend by creating and delegating authority to committees and individuals empowered to represent the faculty point of view in the on-going business of a university. If a faculty is to be influential in the affairs of a university it must be able to decide as well as to deliberate. And faculties today are not as well organized for decision and action as they are for deliberation." [41]

Student participation in the university's decision-making processes has become a major issue. If the students' desire for greater participation and involvement in the activities of the university is to become real and effective, some means must be developed for true representation. In recent years dissident student groups with particular

---

[39] Rourke and Brooks, op. cit., p. 109.
[40] Dennis F. Thompson, "Democracy and the Governing of the University," *The Annals of the American Academy of Political and Social Science,* November 1972, pp. 157–168.
[41] Rourke and Brooks, op. cit., p. 129.

interests have used pressures to achieve their goals. These pressures often take a disruptive and, as viewed by society and most administrators, illegitimate form. However, a fundamental question must be asked: What are the provisions for true student participation in university affairs? Have students been disenfranchised—perhaps not overtly but because they neither understand nor have a legitimate role in the system? Trow says:

> The chief political processes of the multiversity are through informed negotiations and mediations between and among administrators and faculty. This form of politics is accepted by those participants who have had access to that machinery and who exercise their power within it (with due regard, of course, to the claims of other parties). It is not accepted by those, chiefly student activists, who feel excluded and want to have influence but do not have access to the machinery of decision-making. [42]

Frequently university administrators and faculty are hard-pressed to deal with students because they do not know which groups they represent nor their source of legitimization. [43] One of the major problems facing the university is providing for more effective student participation. Some means must be found for legitimizing the power and voice of various student groups. It is evident that students are demanding full rights of university citizenship with academic freedom and provisions for due process. These goals are legitimate (and are similar to those of other groups in our society such as the employee unions), and the universities will need to accommodate themselves to these interests.

SUMMARY

There have been major transformations in the functions of institutions of higher education in our society. The advent of the modern university in the latter part of the nineteenth century was a fundamental change from the earlier colleges. The primary goals of the university are the creation and dissemination of knowledge. Because of the emphasis upon knowledge creation, it often runs in conflict with established values of the society and is a focal point of change.

The academic staff performs the primary technical tasks of the university—teaching and scholarly research. There is a growing administrative technology associated with the provision of facilities and resources necessary for accomplishing the academic task.

The organization structure of the university cannot be clearly delineated. There have been trends toward greater differentiation of activities because of the high degree of specialization of the various academic disciplines. The process has increased the

---

[42] Martin Trow, "Conceptions of the University," *American Behavioral Scientist*, May–June 1968, p. 18.
[43] Joseph R. Gusfield, "Student Protest and University Response," *The Annals of the American Academy of Political and Social Science*, May 1971, pp. 26–38.

problems of integration. Traditionally, coordination was achieved through the "community of scholars" concept with direct participation in institutional matters by the faculty.

There are many diverse participants with various roles in the psychosocial system of the university. These participants have different motivations and goals. Students obviously have a vital role in the academic process; they are the recipients of the knowledge. In the modern university the student is placed on his own in a complex and strange environment. The student population is by no means homogeneous. A wide variety of programs and curricula foster different value systems. Many student cultures exist which are quite different in their goals, reference groups, identification, status, and roles. One of the major problems facing the university is to find means for the integration of these differing student cultures.

The role of the university faculty has undergone transformation. The traditional concept of the ivory tower professor is no longer a reality. Increasingly, the community looks to the campus for knowledge and expertise in solving real-world problems. Each faculty member has a dual role—individual and collegial. He has substantial autonomy in conducting his classes and in research activities. However, he also is involved in various academic and administrative processes which require his interaction with colleagues and administrators.

Members of the administrative staff have a dual role as administrators and as members of the faculty. This duality frequently creates role conflicts. Increasingly, there appears to be a separation between the administration and the academic faculty in large universities. This process of separation has made the ideal of a "community of scholars" more difficult to achieve.

The functions of planning and control are diffused throughout the entire university system. They are shared by many participating groups—students, faculty, administrators, and the board of trustees. There is no single managerial system based on a distinct and unified scalar hierarchy.

Developing means for effective participation by the students, faculty, and administrators on a collegial basis has become increasingly difficult. The faculty must accommodate to some form of representative rather than full democratic participation. The question of student participation in unversity activities has become a major issue. New means must be found for legitimizing the power of the various student groups within the institution. This remains one of the most important problems facing the modern university.

QUESTIONS AND PROBLEMS

1 How has the role of institutions of higher education changed in our society? What forces contributed to this transformation?
2 What are the primary goals of universities? Do you see any conflict between these goals?
3 Why is intellectual freedom vital to the university? What are some of the major challenges to this concept?
4 Why is an "administrative technology" of growing importance in higher education?

5 How does the concept of collegial or shared authority differ from bureaucratic authority?

6 Examine the structure of your own college or university. How is it similar or different from that of the University of Washington (see Figure 21.1)? How is integration of activities achieved in your institution?

7 According to your own experiences, do you agree that there are various student subcultures? Would your classification be similar to that discussed on pp. 557–558?

8 How is the role of the student changing in universities? What means might be developed to provide students with legitimate opportunities for greater participation in internal affairs?

9 How has the role of the faculty been transformed? What are the types of role conflict which the professor faces?

10 What is the role of the administrative staff in the university? What types of conflict face the administrator?

11 What are the major problems in decision making which the university faces? What suggestion do you have for meeting these problems?

*Self examination, if it is thorough enough,
is nearly always the first step toward change.
No one who learns to know himself remains just
what he was before.*

Thomas Mann

*It is an unfinished society that we offer the world—
a society that is forever committed to change, to
improvement and to growth, that will never stagnate
in the certitude of ideology or the finalities of dogma.*

John F. Kennedy

*Creative organizations or societies are rarely tidy.
Some tolerance for inconsistencies, for profusion of
purpose and strategies, and for conflict is the price of
freedom and vitality.*

John Gardner

*The world is cluttered up with unfinished business in
the form of projects that might have been successful,
if only at the tide point someone's patience had
turned to active impatience.*

Robert Updegraff

*I submit that it is only by trial and error, by insistent
scrutiny and by readiness to re-examine presently
accredited conclusions that we have risen, so far as we
have risen, from our brutish ancestors; and I believe
that in our loyalty to these habits lies our only chance
not merely of progress but even of survival.*

Judge Learned Hand

*Future shock is a time phenomenon, a product of the
greatly accelerated rate of change in society. It
arises from the superimposition of a new culture on
an old one. It is culture shock in one's own society.*

Alvin Toffler

PART 8
ORGANIZATIONAL CHANGE AND THE FUTURE

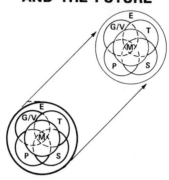

Many organizations have an indefinite life span. Others are more temporal in nature. In any case, organizations must adjust to changing conditions. They must also maintain a system viable enough to accomplish their primary tasks. In short, they need stability and continuity as well as adaptation and innovation.

Organizational change is the topic of Chapter 22. We trace the impetus for change (various external and internal forces) and discuss the typical sources of resistance to change. An important consideration is the development of a process of change that is an integral part of the managerial system. Particular attention is focused on implementing change through a planned-change process that includes problem sensing, diagnosis, action planning, implementation, and follow-up. Issues such as coping with differences and managing conflict creatively are also discussed.

Finally, in Chapter 23, we look at management and organization in the future. We "crystal ball," making use of what is known about existing trends as well as our speculations concerning the future. It is a good probability that uncertainty (turbulent environment, changing value systems, accelerating technology, and other factors) will cause our forecast to be only partially right, at best. However, it is relatively safe to risk being wrong because it will take several decades before our errors can be proved, and by then we should have sufficient skill to rationalize our predictions.

ORGANIZATIONAL CHANGE

Organizations inevitably change because they are open systems in constant interaction with their environment through input and output of material, energy, and information. These boundary-spanning flow processes provide the means for continuing awareness of changing conditions. Although the impetus for change can be attributed to external and/or internal stimuli, the underlying force is the openness of system boundaries that allows new demands, technologies, skills, and values to affect the system. The concept of organizational change will be discussed in terms of the following topics:

> Stability and Continuity *as well as* Adaptation and Innovation
> Sources of Impetus for Change
> Focus of Planned Change Efforts
> Resistance to Change
> Implementing Planned Change
> Dealing with Differences
> Approaches to Conflict ''Resolution''

STABILITY AND CONTINUITY *AS WELL AS* ADAPTATION AND INNOVATION

Considerable attention has been focused on the need for organizations to adapt to changing conditions. It is popular to emphasize the importance of change without recognizing the need for system maintenance and stability. Any organization must maintain enough stability to function satisfactorily, and yet not allow itself to become static, ultraconservative, or oblivious to the need to adapt to changing conditions. A realistic view of organizational change recognizes that both stability and adaptation are essential to survival and growth.

> There is, therefore, a clearly recognized need to learn how to construct, how to adapt, how to change organization in a manner better matched to human aspiration. How to organize human effort effectively into complex, specialized structures within a rapidly changing environment, while maintaining the integrity of the system, is a major concern of our time. [1]

In large measure, changes in individuals and organizations are not readily discernible by those who interact with them on a day-to-day basis. For example, an increase of 20 pounds or gray hair around the temples would be much more noticeable to a friend whom you had not seen for ten years than to a member of the household or a working companion.

Similarly, organizations appear more stable to participants than to clients or observers who interact only intermittently with them. A series of small incremental changes can compound into a significant difference over a long period of time.

Stability and continuity are important attributes to the basic functions of organisms or organizations. An individual's cardiovascular system is essentially the same from birth to death, while increasing in capacity to match body growth. Its overall performance can be modified to meet changed demands—those of a distance runner or swimmer, for example. And short-run increases in capacity can be accommodated to meet the needs of strenuous exercise or a violent struggle for survival. However, the system quickly reverts to normal functioning when the emergency situation no longer exists.

Although organizations are not necessarily destined for a life cycle of birth, growth, maturity, decline, and death, many aspects of such a cycle are apparent. Creation, rapid growth, and bankruptcy are obvious examples. They are traumatic times in the life of an organization when adaptation and innovation are often critical for survival. For organizations that do reach maturity, stability and continuity (maintaining the system) become relatively more important. While changes do occur, the basic functions or operating systems necessary to carry out the transformation process—producing goods or services—remain essentially the same.

Ends and Means

Individuals and organizations undergo changes in both ends and means—the goals they strive for and the methods used. Goals such as survival, profitability, share of the market, service to clients, and growth seem to be quite stable over time. The means of

---

[1] Alexander B. Trowbridge in Wilbur M. McFeely, *Organization Change: Perceptions and Realities,* The Conference Board, Inc., New York, 1972, p. vii.

achieving these goals, however, vary because of factors such as competitive conditions, government regulations, and technological progress. The product range for automobile manufacturers has widened significantly over the years in order to make increasingly diverse demands of consumers. Football teams have pursued the same objective through the use of a wide variety of means—single wing, double wing, basic T, split T, pro set, I formation, and wishbone.

In rare cases the opposite is true; means stay the same while ends are adjusted. When polio vaccine became a reality, the March of Dimes organization changed its focus of attention to birth defects. The basic means for obtaining and channeling funds remained essentially the same. Other examples of this phenomenon are apparent—Nader's Raiders and Common Cause, for example. The same investigatory approach is used to increase public awareness and indignation—whether the goal is improved auto safety, better-quality meat, congressional reform, or more information about campaign contributions.

It is also important to recognize that there can be simultaneous adjustments to both ends and means. A goal of racial balance in schools may require new means—redistricting and/or bussing (voluntary or mandatory), for example. Acceptance of corporate responsibility for pollution control may require a significantly different production process.

Structure and Process

The concepts of stability/continuity and adaptation/innovation can be applied separately to the structure and processes of organizations. Changes in one do not necessarily mean significant changes in the other. The basic transformation process of producing goods and services can continue relatively unchanged while the organization structure is made more centralized or decentralized. The process can be changed significantly (automated, for example) while the basic hierarchical structure remains intact. However, it is also quite likely that both structure and process are adjusted in the course of organizational change to meet new external and/or internal conditions. For example, the introduction of a computer-based management information system usually requires modification in organization structure and decision-making processes. [2]

Dynamic Equilibrium

Management is charged with the responsibility for maintaining a dynamic equilibrium by diagnosing situations and designing adjustments that are most appropriate for coping with current conditions. A dynamic equilibrium for an organization would include the following dimensions:

---

[2] John A. Beckett, *Management Dynamics*, McGraw-Hill Book Company, New York, 1971, pp. 123-133.

1 Enough stability to facilitate achievement of current goals.
2 Enough continuity to ensure orderly change in either ends or means.
3 Enough adaptability to react appropriately to external opportunities and demands as well as changing internal conditions.
4 Enough innovativeness to allow the organization to be proactive (initiate changes) when conditions warrant.

This process is obviously a delicate balancing act which gets more difficult with the accelerating nature of change, both internally and externally.

SOURCES OF IMPETUS FOR CHANGE

The impetus for organizational change comes from many sources. We will discuss this process in terms of the model set forth previously—the environmental suprasystem as well as organizational subsystems (goals and values, technical, structural, psychosocial, and managerial). We are using the systems framework as a means to illustrate the various sources of impetus for change in organizations.

Environment

Organization change is often stimulated by changes in its environment. The *general* environment for any organization in society includes technological, economic, legal, political, demographic, ecological, and cultural factors. Change in these spheres seems to be occurring at an accelerating rate—the pace of change is increasing. Within the general environment, each organization has a more specific set of factors (its *task* environment) that are relevant to its decision-making processes. For example, aerospace technology is likely to be more relevant for an airplane manufacturer than for a food processor. The federal government is a part of the general environment for all organizations but the Civil Aeronautics Board is a part of the specific environment of every airline. A decision on the general rate structure might affect all airlines while a decision about who is authorized to fly on specific routes involves only those having expressed an interest in participating.

Competition is obviously a source of impetus for change. Companies adjust their strategies and/or tactics because of new products or services provided by direct competitors. Indirect influences are also felt. Growth in the use of mobile homes has an impact on those engaged in providing permanent housing. Increased expenditures for water skis and sailboats probably detracts from the demand for spectator sports such as baseball.

The strategic subsystem in an organization has a boundary-spanning function; it maintains an interface with its task environment and tries to maintain surveillance of the general environment as well. Organizations typically try to anticipate changes and adjust accordingly. However, some changes occur that are unanticipated and typically result in a flurry of activity to adjust or forestall the impact until the organization is in a better position to react. Economic and technological forecasting and market research are examples of boundary-spanning activities designed to keep the organization in touch with its environment and allow it to adapt and innovate appropriately.

Goals and Values

Another impetus for change comes from modifications of the goals of the organization. Changes in values (what is good and desirable) are also important because they lead to changes in goals. Or, if the goals remain constant, changes in values can lead to changes in what is considered "appropriate" behavior. For example, several years ago a large Western brewery was counseled to advertise in *Playboy*. Top management rejected the recommendation because there was a consensus that it was an inappropriate medium. Several years later, after a competitor had begun to advertise in *Playboy* and simultaneously increase its share of the market, management reconsidered its decision and accepted the original recommendation. Thus the goal of market share remained the same and the concept of appropriate advertising strategy was adjusted.

New goals can be imposed from external sources—government regulations concerning product safety features, for example—or they can be developed internally as the organization redefines its overall mission. Organizational strategy is a function of factors such as environmental opportunity, internal competence and resources, managerial interest and desires, and social responsibility.

Technical

The technical system is an obvious source of organizational change. New methods for processing material and/or information have provided dramatic examples. Mechanization, automation, and computerization have had widespread influence in organizations. Such changes have had considerable impact on other subsystems—structural and psychosocial, for example—within organizations. Technical changes include the form and/or function of a product (product design) or service as well as the transformation process used by the organization.

Methods used in analyzing the system (or conducting research) are also considered part of the technical subsystem. Technological forecasting has received increasing attention as organizations attempt to cope with an uncertain and dynamic environment. The Delphi method has been used extensively as a means of systematizing the response of "experts" to questionnaires about future scientific and technological progress. [3] Improvements in analysis and research increase the probability of accelerating

---

[3] See, for example, Harper Q. North and Donald L. Pyke, " 'Probes' of the Technological Future," *Harvard Business Review*, May–June 1969, pp. 68–82, and Alan R. Fusfeld and Richard N. Foster, "The Delphi Technique: Survey and Comment," *Business Horizons*, June 1971, pp. 63–74.

changes in the technical subsystem of organizations. On the other hand, the process may be slowed because of problems in translating knowledge and/or technology into action. [4]

Structural

Another source of organizational change is the structural subsystem. Obviously such changes are related to changes in other subsystems. However, adjustments in structure may be appropriate when all other aspects are relatively stable. Different ways of dividing up the work and/or new means of coordination can be designed in order to make an existing organization more effective and efficient. Typical changes might include subdividing an existing department or consolidating three separate units into one department. Such adjustments to the formal ("permanent") organization will have ramifications throughout the total system.

The creation of new structural forms such as conglomerates, multinational corporations, regionwide transportation systems, and consolidated school districts usually leads to many other adjustments. Internal changes such as ad hoc committees, task forces, and program management provide an impetus for change in the organization as a whole. The informal organization—cliques and peer groups, for example—also is a source of ideas for change.

Psychosocial

The impetus for change in organizations often comes from the psychosocial system. Success in achieving organizational goals depends to a great extent upon human factors. The degree to which latent human capability is "tapped" can often make the difference in whether or not organizational endeavors are accomplished. Therefore, changes in the morale and motivation of individuals and/or groups can have a significant impact. Group dynamics can enhance organizational performance or detract from it. Management's ability to lead and influence behavior is also a critical factor. Changes in any or all of these variables can lead to discernible changes in organizational performance.

The role of the psychosocial system is crucial in its relationship to implementing change stemming from other sources. If the change requires behavior modification on the part of individuals or work groups, such factors must be considered in the overall analysis. If support is required and it is not forthcoming, the impact of a technical change can approach zero (or even be negative). We will discuss resistance to change in more detail in a later section.

---

[4] Ronald G. Havelock and Kenneth D. Benne, "An Exploratory Study of Knowledge Utilization," in Warren G. Bennis, Kenneth D. Benne, and Robert Chin (eds.), *The Planning of Change*, 2d ed., Holt, Rinehart and Winston, Inc., New York, 1969, pp. 124–142.

Managerial

The managerial system is involved in planning and controlling organizational activities by means of an information-decision system. The managerial role involves maintaining a dynamic equilibrium between the need for organizational stability and continuity and the need for adaptation and innovation. In most organizations the manager is faced with accelerating change in both the external environmental suprasystem and the other internal organizational subsystems which affect the managerial process.

Accelerating change leads to increasing complexity. In short, the job of the manager is not getting any easier. In general, he needs a tolerance for ambiguity and a coping style. He is continually involved in diagnosing situations and assessing contingencies as he plans and controls organizational activity.

The manager is a central figure in organizational change. As a decision maker he is the ultimate change agent, whether he is centrally involved or merely guiding or coordinating activities. Obviously, change can stem from adjustments in managerial behavior per se—leadership style, approaches to planning and controlling, or degree of participation in decision making. He may respond to suggestions from others or actively instigate changes where the focus is more technical, structural, or psychosocial. He may use internal and/or external consultants to facilitate organizational change. Specialists in economic and market research, operations analysis, industrial relations, and organization development are examples of change agents or facilitators. However, it is useful to view their activities as an extension of the manager, who has ultimate responsibility for organization improvement endeavors.

FOCUS OF PLANNED CHANGE EFFORTS

The concept of planned change assumes that the organization in general and the manager in particular can identify gaps between current conditions and desired conditions on a variety of dimensions. This overall activity can be termed "organization improvement" (see Figure 19.4). At least three dimensions are relevant to this issue: (1) effectiveness, (2) efficiency, and (3) participant satisfaction. In other words, planned change efforts should be related to the question: "How can this organization be more effective, more efficient, and a more satisfying place to work?"

Short- and long-range considerations should be included in order that appropriate attention may be given to stability and continuity. Expedient changes for the sake of effectiveness (achieving goals) or for the sake of efficiency (better utilization of resources) may have dysfunctional consequences for participant satisfaction and long-run viability of the organization. Whenever the organization can identify differences between where it is and where it would like to be on any dimension, it can engage in a process of planned change—organization improvement. The focus of attention might be product appearance, unwieldy organization structure, low morale, inadequate communication processes, or inefficient computer programs. Depending on the type of problem identified, an appropriate change effort can be designed.

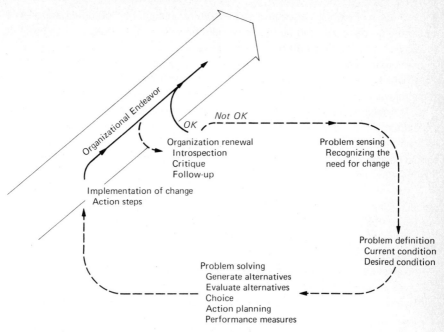

FIGURE 22.1   THE PROCESS OF PLANNED CHANGE

Over and above specific change efforts there is the question of the organization's overall ability to engage in organization improvement endeavors—to look at itself critically. In this case the focus of attention should be on the *process of planned change* rather than particular problems. An improved process of planned change should pay dividends because it facilitates continuing review and identification of appropriate problems to be worked on.

Typical steps in a process of planned change are illustrated in Figure 22.1. Problem sensing involves recognizing the need for a change. Awareness may stem from a variety of sources, the most important of which is a formal organizational process of introspection, critique, and follow-up.

> The organization that will remain viable, creative, and relevant must engage in the process of search that the renewal effort involves. Such renewal will not take place by chance. It must be a purposive effort that embodies more than good intention. An organization renewal process takes time, energy, money, and skill. [5]

---

[5] Gordon L. Lippitt, *Organization Renewal,* Appleton-Century-Crofts, New York, 1969, p. vii.

If the process of planned change is to become an integral part of the organization's "culture," provisions should be made for self-criticism on a relatively routine basis. It should become a natural part of the managerial style.

In order to facilitate a process of planned change, problems should be defined in a way which identifies a gap between a current condition and a desired condition on some relevant dimension. A problem well defined is half solved.

The solution phase involves generating alternatives, evaluating them, and choosing a future course of action. Tentative action steps should be identified and checked for feasibility (requisite skills and/or resources, for example). Performance measures should be established (quantitative and/or qualitative) so that the results of the planned change effort can be evaluated at a later date.

After the change has been implemented there should be a follow-up appraisal of actual results against the plan. This process may lead to no action if the system is "On target" or to a new cycle of planned change if a problem is sensed. The connotation of "problem" (a gap between a current and a desired condition) is important because any organization has room for improvement even if things are going along satisfactorily for the most part. If the general process of planned change (as outlined in Figure 22.1) becomes an integral part of the managerial system, many specific types of organization improvement efforts can be included in the solution phase, depending on the particular problems identified.

Operations Analysis

Taken literally, the term *operations analysis* could cover a broad spectrum of organization improvement activities. The connotation developed from current usage, however, leans toward symbolic model building, quantification, analytical problem solving, and simulation techniques. Terms such as industrial engineering, work simplification, and operations research are also related. Harrison classifies organization improvement efforts in terms of the depth of emotional involvement and suggests that operations analysis requires the least amount of emotional involvement on the part of organizational participants. [6]

While the human element is often involved in the implementation of results of operation analysis, it can be designed out of the analytical process in order to make quantification and computational solutions possible. An example of operations analysis might be designing a computer program for payroll processing so that it takes 25 percent less machine time. The implementation of such a change should have little effect on the people in the system. Defining the optimum number of tellers for various time periods in a branch bank is another example. Implementation of such recommendations might or might not involve significant changes in interpersonal relations of the work group. Recommendations for changes in production processes or the flow of

---

[6] Roger Harrison, "Choosing the Depth of Organizational Intervention," *Journal of Applied Behavioral Science,* April/May/June 1970, pp. 181–202.

information might or might not require significant changes in social systems. [7] In any case, operations analysis tends to be less personalized than other planned change efforts which focus on individual, group, or organizational behavior.

Individual

Planned change efforts which focus on the individual range from informal orientation for new employees to elaborate management development programs for potential top executives. Whether implicitly or explicitly most employees are given an overview of organizational activities (mission, scope, and objectives) along with specific instructions regarding their particular job. On-the-job training may include coaching by peers as well as superiors, with the objective being increased technical skill (and maybe interpersonal skill) for the employee. The assumption is that more skillful individuals will somehow lead to overall organization improvement.

Training programs for first-line supervisors, middle managers, and top executives tend to focus on broader organizational issues, interrelationships among functions, and leadership skills. Here again there is an assumption that better leaders will result in organization improvement. In many cases organizations rely on external training programs (conducted by universities, e.g.) for development of individual managers. Personal growth is enhanced by exposure to heterogeneous groups of managers from diverse organizations, both public and private.

Groups

Focusing planned change efforts on teams or work groups is another way to improve organizations. This is the approach covered by the term *organization development* (OD), which is typically defined as ''a long-range effort to improve an organization's problem-solving and renewal processes, particularly through a more effective and collaborative management of organization culture—with special emphasis on the culture of formal work teams—with the assistance of a change agent, or catalyst, and the use of the theory and technology of applied behavioral science, including action research.'' [8]

In this definition there is an emphasis on improving problem-solving and renewal processes while working on specific issues which are relevant to work groups. A typical feature of organization development activities is inclusion of all participants in the analysis of problems which affect them. The basic steps involved are (1) problem sensing via interviews, questionnaires, or group meetings, (2) prioritizing the issues in terms of factors such as importance/urgency/solvability, (3) refinement of problem statements and further diagnosis, (4) generation and evaluation of alternative solutions or tentative courses of action, (5) refinement of action steps in terms of feasibility, (6) implementation, and (7) follow-up to check actual progress against anticipated results.

---

[7] James R. Emshoff, *Analysis of Behavioral Systems,* The Macmillan Company, New York, 1971, p. 2.
[8] Wendell L. French and Cecil H. Bell, Jr., *Organization Development,* Prentice-Hall, Inc., Englewood Cliffs, N.J., 1973, p. 15.

Within this general approach, a number of problems might be identified which are relevant to group effectiveness—communication, role ambiguity, leadership, and morale, for example. Once a specific issue is identified, an appropriate technique (termed "intervention") can be designed to facilitate the members solving their own problem. [9]

If the focus of attention shifts from intragroup to intergroup issues, the same general approach can be followed. However, the methods used to facilitate intergroup problem solving would be tailored for that specific purpose. For example, people who are in boundary-spanning roles between two groups or departments (engineering and production) may interact in a structured meeting designed to clarify their perceptions of each other and increase mutual understanding. Or, one controversial group within an organization may ask for feedback concerning its image as perceived by other units. While improved effectiveness, efficiency, and participant satisfaction cannot be guaranteed as a result of such problem-solving efforts, clarification of perceptions and expectations typically leads to organizational improvement.

Organization

A focus for planned change efforts can be the organization as a whole. OD practitioners typically emphasize that the endeavor includes the total system and is managed from the top. [10] The total organization can be involved by using surveys which solicit responses from all employees. [11] Planned change efforts are then designed according to the needs expressed by the participants. The data are made available to everyone in the system and periodic follow-up surveys are taken in order to assess the impact of change efforts over relatively long periods of time. Another approach to organizationwide change efforts involves sequential attention to team building by starting with top management and then branching out by focusing successively on appropriate work groups throughout the system.

Management by objectives (MBO) can be focused on individuals and/or teams. The ultimate objective, however, is systemwide change and hence organization improvement. The basic elements in an MBO program include establishment of objectives by a subordinate, modification in a meeting between superior and subordinate, establishing mutual expectations of appropriate behavior, and subsequent follow-up to check results. The objectives established can relate to individual and/or work-group performance. The culmination of this systemwide program should result in overall objectives for the organization as a whole.

A planned change effort which focuses on the organization as a whole can, and probably should, involve efforts focused at a variety of target areas—personal growth, team building, intergroup relations, and total organization issues. Depending on the

---

[9] Ibid., pp. 97–146.
[10] Richard Beckhard, *Organization Development: Strategies and Models*, Addison-Wesley Publishing Co., Boston, Mass., 1969, p. 9; and Chris Argyris, *Management and Organizational Development*, McGraw-Hill Book Co., New York, 1971.
[11] Rensis Likert, *The Human Organization*, McGraw-Hill Book Co., 1967.

resources available for planned change efforts (managerial skills, consultation skills, money, and time), the various problem areas can be addressed simultaneously or sequentially. The ultimate goal in any case is overall organization improvement.

RESISTANCE TO CHANGE

Given the multiple goals of stability and continuity as well as adaptation and innovation while maintaining a dynamic equilibrium in organizations, some resistance to change is not only natural but desirable. However, because of the widespread evidence of change (at an increasing rate), people apparently accept adaptation and innovation. Bennis and Slater suggest that "change has now become a permanent and accelerating factor in American life." [12] Technological changes with obvious benefits and few discernible negative consequences are readily accepted. Changes affecting social relationships take longer to implement.

> Resistance to change has sometimes been interpreted as simple inertia in human nature. It is said that people are "in a rut" or "set in their ways." Actually almost everyone is eager for some kind of change in his life and situation. He would like better health, more money, and more freedom to satisfy his desires. Excitement is more attractive than humdrum existence. If people in organizations do not change, it must be because natural drives toward innovation are being stifled or held in check by countervailing forces. [13]

What are the countervailing forces to natural drives for individual and organizational innovation? Obviously, there are a number of specific forces relevant to particular situations. However, most of them can be grouped under several major headings: sunk costs (including vested interests), misunderstandings (of purpose, mechanics, or consequences of change), group norms, balance of power, and diversity. [14]

Sunk Costs

If the term "sunk costs" is broadly interpreted to include time and energy as well as money, it describes a powerful force in resisting change. Regardless of the merits of a proposal, it is difficult to "put out of mind" the blood, sweat, and tears that have gone into an existing system. A football coach who has invested a great deal of time and energy in developing individuals who can play both offense and defense (one-platoon era) is likely to resist rule changes which allow a two-platoon approach (specialists for offense and defense). An experienced manager is likely to resist suggestions for

---

[12] Warren G. Bennis and Philip E. Slater, *The Temporary Society,* Harper Colophon Books, New York, 1969, p. 9.
[13] This excerpt of "Resistance to Change," by Goodwin Watson is reprinted from *American Behavioral Scientist,* vol. 14, no. 5, pp. 745–766, May–June 1971, by permission of the publisher, Sage Publications, Inc.
[14] Stephen Kerr and Elaine B. Kerr, "Why Your Employees Resist Perfectly Rational Changes," *Hospital Financial Management,* January 1972, pp. 4–6.

changes from internal or external consultants. This may explain why curriculum changes come so slowly and why professors use texts and lecture notes over a long period of time.

The sunk cost concept may also help explain the different propensities to change for various age groups. Older people obviously have a longer history of sunk costs and hence have "more to lose" than younger people. It also helps to explain why staff people (specialists) are more likely to be change agents in organizations. They have less at stake than line managers who have invested time and energy in making the existing system work.

Misunderstandings

When organizational participants are asked to identify those "things" which are keeping the organization from being effective, efficient, and a satisfying place to work, poor communication typically heads the list. This has been our experience and it is substantiated by consultants with experience in many organizations in the United States and abroad. [15] Moreover, we find that the essence of the problem is the *illusion* of communication. The manager's assumption that his subordinates "got the message" is often unfounded. Employees' assumption that management knows how they feel is also often unwarranted. When a person says, "Yes, I understand," he may (1) really understand, (2) have a fair idea, or (3) not understand at all. He may not admit he does not understand because he thinks he would appear stupid or call attention to the manager's inability to communicate clearly. In any event the problems of transferring meaning from one mind to another are a difficult process. We often do not say exactly what we intended to say; others may hear a slightly different message or even a grossly distorted version because they filter the flow of words and delete as well as add to meaning.

How does this affect resistance to change? Whenever individuals do not clearly understand the purpose, mechanics, or potential consequences of a change, they are likely to resist it. If a person is involved in the implementation process, it is important for him to understand why the change is being made. When the mechanics of a change are not clearly understood, they cannot be carried out even if the implementer is willing.

Of crucial importance is uncertainty about the consequences of a change. Speculation and rumor about negative consequences are typically part of the change process. Given little explicit information, an environment of uncertainty will lead people to assume the worst. The obvious result is vigorous resistance to proposed changes.

Group Norms

Established rules and procedures, both formal and informal, are powerful forces for resisting change. If a group or an organization has been successful while following an

---

[15] Robert R. Blake and Jane S. Mouton, *Grid Organization Development*, Gulf Publishing Company, Houston, Texas, 1968, p. 4.

established practice, it is likely to resist adjustments in that behavior. Modes of dress, codes of conduct, levels of output, and other kinds of behavior are all subject to group norms. Managerial exhortations to individuals to produce 25 widgets per day are likely to fall on deaf ears if the "normal" output has been established informally by the group at 22. Because group norms are such powerful forces in the change process, we will want to consider (in a subsequent section) some creative ways to use them in facilitating adaptation and innovation on the part of individuals, groups, and organizations.

Balance of Power

One kind of equilibrium in organizations is a balance of power among individuals, groups, departments, or divisions. Any change which threatens the autonomy of a division or product group may be resisted because the group perceives a decrease in control over its own affairs. Addition of an executive vice-president between the top executive and existing vice-presidents may be resisted for the same reason. Assigning a new product to Division A may cause Division B to resist because of a relative decrease in stature within the total organization. The addition of a new, centralized staff group (such as operations research or computer services) may be resisted because it reduces the autonomy of existing departments.

Diversity

If organizations depend on consensus formation in order to enable significant change to occur, different values and diverse goals among the participants will affect the change process. Some empirical research results to date lead to the following hypotheses:

1 The greater the diversity of the organization, the greater the probability that members will conceive of major innovation.
2 The greater the diversity of the organization, the greater the probability that major innovations will be proposed.
3 The greater the diversity of the organization, the more difficult it will be to get proposals adopted. [16]

Change usually affects members differently, depending on their role in the organization. If the task is complex and human resources are diverse, a change can be resisted for a wide variety of reasons—representing many different points of view. Coping with such situations is a managerial challenge.

On the other hand, diversity and complexity can lead to creativity in organiza-

---

[16] James Q. Wilson, "Innovation in Organizations: Notes toward a Theory," in James D. Thompson (ed.), *Approaches to Organizational Design,* University of Pittsburgh Press, Pittsburgh, Pa., 1966, pp. 193–218.

tions. [17] Characteristics typically cited as enhancing organizational creativity include: (1) heterogeneous personnel, (2) eccentricity allowed, (3) more decentralized, (4) more diversified, and (5) different objectives. [18] It seems to us that a balance must be maintained in order to facilitate planned change. Having no diversity could lead to stagnation; too much diversity could lead to inaction because of the inability to agree on a new course of action.

After a year as President of the University of Cincinnati, Warren Bennis described the multiversity as "society's closest realization of the pure model of anarchy; i.e., the locus of decision making is the individual." [19] High hopes for significant changes and, indeed, the acceptance and use of a process of planned change were eventually dashed against the rocks of apathy and inaction.

> Vast splintering and fragmentation arises from the new populism of those who felt denied in the past and who, rightly, want to be consulted in those decisions that affect them. All this is supposed to add up to "participatory democracy" but adds up, instead, to a cave of the winds where the most that can usually be agreed upon is to do nothing (like the bumper sticker "My Vote Cancels Yours"). [20]

This is obviously an extreme case because universities may be the most diverse and complex organizations in existence. The point remains, however, that diversity can inhibit change by impeding consensus formation in group decision making (see Figure 16.3). In order to manage the process of planned change creatively, a balance must be maintained so that the organization has enough—but not too much—diversity.

IMPLEMENTING PLANNED CHANGE

Implementing planned change requires understanding the forces involved in resistance to change and designing appropriate means to overcome them. Situational analysis coupled with a contingency view is extremely important. For example, it would be important to understand (1) the historical perspective with regard to past change efforts, (2) the general climate for innovation in the organization, and (3) the specific planned change (purpose, mechanics, and consequences, e.g.). A thorough situational analysis should provide the opportunity to design a means of implementation that has the highest probability of success. The specific means used in the planned change effort would be contingent on a number of factors, including organizational climate, type of problem, and focus of attention.

---

[17] "*Creativity* has to do with the development, proposal, and implementation of *new* and *better* solutions; *productivity,* with the efficient application of *current* 'solutions.'" Gary A. Steiner (ed.), *The Creative Organization,* The University of Chicago Press, Chicago, Ill., 1965, p. 4.
[18] Ibid., pp. 16–18.
[19] Warren G. Bennis, "The University Leader," *Saturday Review,* Dec. 9, 1972, p. 49.
[20] Ibid., p. 44.

Climate for Change

The *general* climate for organizational change includes all of the external environment plus internal factors which we have categorized into subsystems—goals and values, technical, structural, and psychosocial. The *specific* climate for planned change depends on a number of factors which are more directly related to the process of adaptation or innovation. A long list of dimensions could be cited, all of which affect the implementability of innovation. [21] However, we will consider only a few of them in order to illustrate the variables involved in the climate for change.

Corwin cites a large number of research studies which point to several conclusions about conditions for success in planned change efforts. For example, it has been postulated that an organization can be changed more easily:

> If it is invaded by liberal, creative, and unconventional outsiders with fresh perspectives.
>
> If those outsiders are exposed to creative, competent, and flexible socialization agents.
>
> If it is staffed by young, flexible, supportive, and competent boundary personnel, or "gatekeepers."
>
> If it is structurally complex and decentralized.
>
> If it has outside funds to provide the "organizational" slack necessary to lessen the cost of innovation.
>
> If its members have positions that are sufficiently secure and protected from status risks involved in change.
>
> If it is located in a changing, modern, urbanized setting where it is in close cooperation with a coalition of other cosmopolitan organizations that can supplement its skills and resources. [22]

These tentative conclusions obviously need more research in a variety of settings, as well as careful interpretation, before straightforward guidelines can be developed. In some cases, they "feel" right intuitively, and the findings to date do point in these directions. For example, adaptation seems to be facilitated when an outside person (or other impetus) is reinforced by at least some receptive change agents within the organization. In other cases, counter arguments are credible. For example, the issue of whether centralization or decentralization provides a more favorable climate for change

[21] Gerald Zaltman and Nan Lin, "On the Nature of Innovations," *American Behavioral Scientist*, May/June 1971, pp. 651–673.
[22] Ronald G. Corwin, "Strategies for Organizational Intervention: An Empirical Comparison," *American Sociological Review*, August 1972, pp. 441–442.

is not completely clear. Autonomy in decentralized units might or might not enhance innovation. If the propensity to innovate is at the top, then a centralized decision-making process would increase the probability of change.

On balance, the research seems to indicate that "the conditions under which any given strategy is applied, that is, the situation into which an innovation is introduced, seems to be as critical as the strategy itself." [23]

Diagnosis and Action

Figure 22.2 provides a way of looking at problem solving which enhances the probability of implementing recommended action steps. This model is a subpart of the general process of planned change as shown in Figure 22.1. The internal circle emphasizes diagnosis and the external band emphasizes action. There must be an appropriate balance between the two. Overdiagnosis results in "paralysis by analysis"; that is, we never reach the action stage. Underdiagnosis—leaping immediately to action—may result in "extinction by instinct." Of course, we are concerned here with relatively complex issues which warrant detailed analysis and considered judgment.

The first step is problem sensing, which may occur in a variety of ways, such as reviewing operating results, obtaining feedback from participants, soliciting customer complaints, or receiving a question from the boss. The second step involves refining the problem to make sure that relevant organizational members agree on the definition. It also involves dimensions such as:

Who is involved—an individual, a group or groups, the total organization?

Who is causing it—a few people, a specific department or function, top management?

What kind of problem is it—lack of skills, unclear goals, intergroup conflict?

What is the goal for improvement?

How can we evaluate results?

The latter question suggests having an accurate picture of the current condition as well as a clear picture of the desired condition.

The third step in problem diagnosis is the generation of alternative solutions. It is important to note the separation of generation and evaluation. This follows the concept of "brainstorming" where evaluation is forestalled in order to facilitate the generation of as many alternatives (including "far-out" suggestions) as possible before beginning to evaluate them. The evaluation process includes identifying tentative action steps, anticipating their possible impact, refining them, and, finally, designing an action plan.

Action steps are followed up at some future point in time in order to check the

---

[23] Ibid., p. 452.

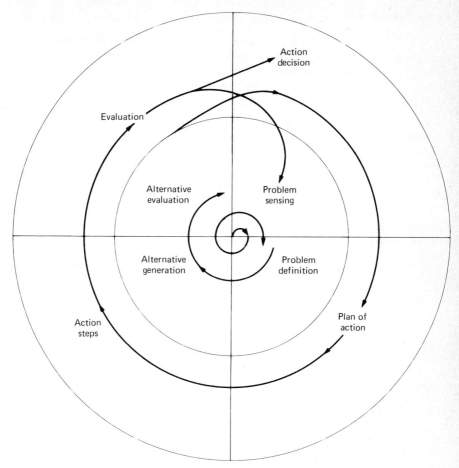

FIGURE 22.2 PROBLEM SOLVING—DIAGNOSIS AND ACTION

actual situation against the plan. The results of this follow-up might be reaffirmation of the action plan or reactivation of the problem-solving process if a discrepancy is identified.

Resistance to change is reduced if those involved in implementation of action steps are also involved in the problem-solving process. The inner and outer circles (Figure 22.2) should not be treated as separate functions. That is, problem solvers, analysts, and planners cannot specialize in the activities of the internal circle in relative isolation and then expect others to implement the findings. Continuing interaction between managers and specialists during the problem-solving process should lead to mutual understanding and higher probabilities for success of planned change efforts.

Force Field Analysis

Force field analysis, as illustrated in Figure 22.3, is a general-purpose diagnostic and problem-solving technique. In any situation there are forces that push for change (driving) as well as forces that hinder change (restraining). If the forces offset completely, we have equilibrium and status quo. Change can occur by increasing the driving forces or by reducing the restraining forces. The latter approach is often more fruitful because to increase driving forces without attention to restraining forces may increase pressure and tension in the system to the point where creative problem solving becomes impossible. This approach facilitates inclusion of a wide variety of factors—technological, structural, and psychosocial (values and feelings, for example). It is particularly important to anticipate antagonism that is likely to be aroused in the imple-

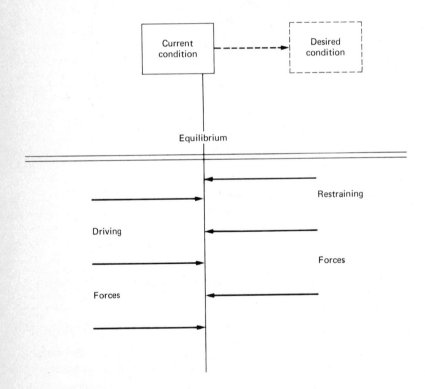

Assumptions:

1. Most problems or situations have multiple causes.

2. Most problems or situations are held in equilibrium between driving and restraining forces.

3. We are more likely to accomplish changes if we identify these forces.

4. It is frequently easier to make changes by reducing restraining forces.

FIGURE 22.3 FORCE FIELD ANALYSIS

mentation of planned change. Accurate assessment will allow creative leadership to cope with hang-ups at the feeling level.

To illustrate the use of force field analysis, let us pick a common individual and/or organizational problem—lack of time. This is a pervasive problem for harried executives. In order to work on the problem effectively we need to clarify it and state it in terms of current and desired conditions. For example, the real issue may be "lack of time to work on important tasks such as developing a comprehensive process for planned change."

Current condition = no time spent on planned change; always react to crisis conditions

Desired condition = large blocks of time for critiquing the organization periodically; a comprehensive and creative process of planned change is an integral part of the managerial system

In order to understand the situation in more detail we can identify those offsetting forces that keep us in equilibrium—no change from the current condition.

Driving forces (pushing us toward the desired condition)

1 Knowledge of theory that says it would be "better."
2 Feeling (conviction) that it would be "better."
3 Success stories from current literature (increased productivity, e.g.).
4 Success stories from acquaintances in similar organizations.
5 Consultants (internal or external) "selling" the virtues of a new approach.

Restraining forces (keeping us in the current condition)

1 Programmed activity increases to absorb available time.
2 Current deadlines preclude taking time to analyze the problem of "lack of time."
3 We seem to be doing satisfactory work—individually and organizationally (we have survived). No sense of urgency.
4 Reluctance of participants to "rock the boat" by analyzing group processes.
5 Assumption that there is no slack in time resources, i.e., time is not wasted currently.

These lists are obviously not exhaustive; the reader can easily add to and/or modify them. However, they do illustrate the approach and lead us to the next step, which is picking one or more of the forces (starting with restraining forces) and generating ideas for increasing or decreasing them. After alternatives have been evaluated, action plans can be designed and implemented.

The analysis can be carried out in as much detail as seems warranted by the problem. For complex issues with likely difficulties in implementation, it may be worthwhile to pursue force field analysis in great depth, with widespread participation. In other cases, it may be sufficient to merely outline the problem in the basic framework and move quickly to the tentative solution phase.

Building Group Consensus

The effectiveness of using group norms and consensus decision making to change individual and organizational behavior has been demonstrated in a number of research studies as well as in highly publicized programs such as Alcoholics Anonymous and Weight Watchers. Lewin's early studies of the effectiveness of lectures versus group discussion and commitment in changing eating habits have been replicated many times. [24] The key findings were that behavior change is more likely to occur and persist when commitment is on a group, rather than individual, basis. The basic process includes unfreezing existing habits or standard operating procedures, changing to new patterns of behavior, and refreezing in order to ensure lasting effects. The key ingredients involved are changing group norms and making the new norms explicit and visible, as well as encouraging public and explicit commitment to abide by them. As indicated in our discussion of resistance to change, group norms represent a powerful force. Therefore, if those norms can be changed, they will enhance the probability of success for planned change efforts.

Reinforcing Innovative Behavior

Another important step in implementing planned change is to concentrate on and enlist the support of influential members of work groups. Energy focused in this direction will often have widespread payoff through the establishment of new norms for behavior. Also, in this same vein, it is important to positively reinforce those who exhibit new behavior in the implementation phase. Positive reinforcement will help perpetuate that behavior and improve the organization's ability to respond to changing conditions by adapting and innovating when appropriate. Promotion and/or monetary rewards (bonus or salary increase) may be used if feasible. For many organizations, however, recognition and praise may be the only means of reinforcement. Fortunately, there is increasing evidence that this rather simple, straightforward approach can be quite successful. [25]

DEALING WITH DIFFERENCES

One of the questions in organizational change is what to do with the maverick, the person who is "far out." Given the organization's legitimate need for stability and

---

[24] Kurt Lewin, "Group Decision and Social Change," in Eleanor E. Maccoby, Theodore M. Newcomb, and Eugene L. Hartley, *Readings in Social Psychology*, Holt, Rinehart and Winston, Inc., New York, 1958, pp. 197–211.

[25] "Where Skinner's Theories Work," *Business Week*, Dec. 2, 1972, pp. 64–65.

FIGURE 22.4 SLOGANS, ISSUES, AND DEMANDS OF ACTIVISM, AND THE INNOVATIONS THEY IMPLY

SLOGANS	ISSUES	DEMANDS	ILLUSTRATIVE INNOVATIONS
1 "Strike!"	How to influence those in power?	"I want to directly influence those in power in my corporation."	An Action Forum where employee-initiated topics are researched and debated, with recommendations for corporate and societal change.
2 "Revolution!"	How to ensure change that improves the fit between needs and resources?	"I want to work for a company that adapts to the changing needs of its people."	Acceptance of multiple roles in corporate operations; criteria for matching talent to projects expanded to include interest, involvement, and commitment; consumers to have a voice within the corporation.
3 "Liberation!"	How to open up things to the possibility of change?	"I want a job that allows me to do *my thing*, and discover what is uniquely mine."	Individual differences emphasized rather than suppressed; corporations expected to build from individual uniqueness.
4 "Commune!"	What kinds of relationships should connect people in organizations?	"I want to work with others in a way that emphasizes my human qualities."	Informal support groups, which cut across organizational levels, designed to help people improve the quality of their lives on the job and at home.
5 "Power to the people!"	At what level should policy be determined?	"I want a voice in regulating my activities. Also, I want others to respect my autonomy."	Decentralized responsibility; scheduled time periods (sabbaticals) when employees are released from formal task responsibilities to engage in creative endeavors.
6 "Relevance!"	How to integrate new, creative, youthful views and values in existing social institutions?	"I want to work for a company that is relevant to pressing needs."	Social action unit that involves each person in focusing corporate resources on pressing issues of the day.

SOURCE: Samuel A. Culbert and James M. Elden, "An Anatomy of Activism for Executives," *Harvard Business Review*, November–December 1970, p. 136.

continuity, can extreme individualism be accepted? By definition, organization means cooperation and, hence, the sacrifice of individualism to some extent. But how much? George Bernard Shaw once said, "The reasonable man conforms to the world. The unreasonable man expects the world to conform to him. Therefore, all progress depends on the unreasonable man."

Organizations seem to be accepting a more diverse group of participants than in the past. Moreover, the individual's zone of acceptance (that is, conformity to "established" organizational norms) is decreasing. In an article urging executives to activism (obviously leading to organizational change), Culbert and Elden cite a number of changing values, as summarized in Figure 22.4. How likely are such changes?

Organizations typically have three general approaches to "differences" in participants: (1) disallow and mold (submerge), (2) accept and tolerate, and (3) understand and value. Over time, organizations in general have moved toward the third approach. Understanding and valuing differences are an important step in keeping the organization tuned to current conditions.

However, it is easy to see a spectrum of all three approaches in modern organizations. Some organizations still maintain rigid codes of dress and hair style, consider the term "woman executive" a paradox, and avoid employees who are racially and/or ethnically different from current managers. For some organizations where there are no legal sanctions—particularly small- to medium-sized, closely held corporations which do not sell to the federal government—these conditions might prevail for years to come. However, many organizations will be forced to change because of legal and economic sanctions. Although they may do so reluctantly, they may discover that an initial approach of "accept and tolerate" will gradually change to "understand and value."

Unquestionably, managing participants with widely diverse value systems is more difficult than coordinating a group of people selected in the manager's own image. And we may be surprised to see a process of mutual accommodation as participants recognize the need to submerge individual values and goals to a degree in order to facilitate the accomplishment of organizational objectives. Massarik suggests that:

> The day will come when the distinction between "Establishment" and "Anti-Establishment" will become trivial. If, in this context we may quote a line from "Hair," more and more the large and formerly bureaucratic organization "will let the sunshine in." It will become more open, though surely it will not flow randomly into an archaic sea of inchoate and unrelated individuals.
>
> *Perhaps the most dramatic change will be management's accelerating willingness to be responsive to value change.* [26]

APPROACHES TO CONFLICT "RESOLUTION"

A likely result of increasingly diverse organizational participants is increased interpersonal and intergroup conflict within organizations. Understanding and valuing differ-

---

[26] Fred Massarik, "Changing Social Values and Their Impact on Future Management Organization and Practice," *Academy of Management Proceedings,* August 1970, p. 75.

ences probably rules out unanimity and makes consensus formation much more diffi- cult. The managerial task of coordination will require increasing adroitness. Management will need to become skilled in the creative use of conflicts and tensions that can be potentially beneficial in generating alternative solutions in the problem- solving process. However, conflicts have to be "resolved enough" to allow the coordi- nation necessary to implement a desired course of action.

Typical approaches to conflict resolution in organizations include (1) withdrawal, (2) smoothing, (3) compromise, (4) confrontation, and (5) forcing. The approaches at either end of the spectrum—withdrawal and forcing—describe a considerable amount of managerial behavior. Henry Ford decided, against the advice of most of his manag- ers, that the consumer could have any color car, as long as he wanted black. A cartoon shows the chairman calling for a vote by stating "All in favor say 'aye'; all opposed say 'I resign.'" Withdrawal may be an appropriate temporary strategy, but it cannot be pursued forever and in all cases. A smoothing approach involves slightly more "working the problem" than withdrawal. However, it still has the connotation of "glossing over" real problems by getting agreement on minor surface issues. Smoothing may be a useful temporary strategy if a more basic approach is followed at a more opportune time.

Compromise and confrontation suggest active attempts to work the problem. Compromise has a slightly negative tone because it assumes that the parties involved have given up something and, therefore, that neither is completely happy. However, compromise is a fact of life and it will be relevant to organizations as long as there are differences, factions, and power struggles. Political negotiation is an evident part of organizational life. For example, it describes the budgetary process in most large, complex organizations such as a university. The resource allocation process typically involves a series of bids and responses until a final figure is reached which is acceptable to the managers involved.

The aim of creative conflict resolution is integration that allows both parties to achieve their objectives. The basic goal is a win-win approach rather than a win-lose approach. However, the latter is much more common in our competitive society and it does indeed take creative conflict management to find integrative solutions. A confron- tation mode might or might not facilitate achieving integrative results. It can mean getting all the cards on the table, good will in empathizing with alternative viewpoints, and actively seeking solutions which satisfy both (or all) protagonists. With increasingly diverse value systems in organizations this is obviously a difficult assignment. (See Chapter 12, "Group Dynamics"—particularly "Intergroup Relations.")

On the other hand, open confrontation of unresolved issues can be therapeutic even if the temporary or long-run solution is to decide not to agree. Smoldering, under the surface tensions and antagonisms drain off untold amounts of physical and psychic energy. If conflict and confrontation are managed creatively, they can be beneficial in releasing resources to concentrate on the primary organizational task.

Withdrawal and smoothing tend to perpetuate a status quo. Forcing obviously leads to organizational change but may overemphasize expediency while not giving due consideration to medium- and long-run results. Compromise and confrontation provide opportunity for creative conflict resolution leading to substantive change or, at least, therapeutic results which facilitate a healthier organization.

SUMMARY

Organizations must maintain a dynamic equilibrium between stability/continuity and adaptation/innovation. Small, incremental changes occur continually, often imperceptibly to participants and observers. Crises such as questions of survival and major new programs are obviously more visible.

We have used our systems model to identify the sources of impetus for change. The environmental suprasystem has an obvious impact on organizations through technological, economic, legal, political, demographic, ecological, and cultural forces. Within these general categories each organization has a more specific environment which impacts it directly. Organizational change also stems from forces within organizational subsystems. The managerial system is in the middle of a patterned swirl of external and internal events and is charged with managing the change process, a coping-type behavior.

Planned change efforts (specific changes as well as improved change processes) concentrate on questions of effectiveness, efficiency, and participant satisfaction. The focus of planned change efforts toward organization improvement can be operations analysis, individuals, groups (team building and intergroup relations), and overall organizational issues.

Because people normally seek new and different experiences, resistance to change in organizations must stem from countervailing forces such as sunk costs (money, time, and energy), as well as misunderstandings about the purpose, mechanics, and consequences (uncertainty) of planned changes. Established group norms, the balance of power, and extremely diverse value systems inhibit change.

The ability to implement planned change requires explicit steps to overcome resistance to change. In general, a problem-solving approach which recognizes the interaction and balance of diagnosis and action is important. A technique such as force field analysis, which allows identification of driving and restraining forces, can be helpful in understanding the problem and ascertaining the most appropriate action steps. Participation, particularly of those to be called on for implementation, is important at all stages in the process of planned change.

The propensity for organizations to change is affected by the way they deal with differences: (1) disallow and mold (submerge), (2) accept and tolerate, and (3) understand and value. Another important factor is the approach generally used in "resolving" conflict.

QUESTIONS AND PROBLEMS

1 What is meant by the phrase "stability and continuity *as well as* adaptation and innovation"?

2 Give examples of how disequilibrium in these processes can lead to negative consequences in organizations.

3 For a specific organization with which you are familiar illustrate how the impetus for change can come from the following sources:

  a External environment

  b Internal subsystems

     (1) Goals and values

     (2) Technical

     (3) Structural

     (4) Psychosocial

     (5) Managerial

4 Explain the connotation of the word "problem" as used in the process of planned change described in the chapter.

5 Give examples of planned change efforts in the following categories:

  a Operations analysis

  b Individual

  c Group

  d Organization

6 For a specific organization with which you are familiar describe instances of resistance to change based on:

  a Sunk costs (vested interests)

  b Misunderstanding and/or uncertainty

  c Group norms

  d Balance of power

  e Diversity

7 Use the force field analysis technique to diagnose the following problems:

  a Current condition = 250 lbs.

     Desired condition = 200 lbs.

  b Current condition = 2.0 g.p.a.

     Desired condition = 3.0 g.p.a.

  c Current condition = Downward, one-way communication; much misunderstanding

     Desired condition = Upward and downward, two-way communication; mutual understanding

  d Any personal or organizational problem that is real for you.

8 Give several examples from your own experience where your participation in a group commitment has been effective in changing your individual behavior.

9 Do you think organizations are tending toward "understanding and valuing" differences? Give examples.

10 What is the connotation of "confrontation" as used in the chapter? What are its advantages and disadvantages as a means of conflict "resolution"?

ORGANIZATION AND MANAGEMENT IN THE FUTURE

The twentieth century has been a period of growth in size and complexity for organizations in all fields—business, government, military, educational, religious, and medical. We have become an "organizational society" in which an increasing proportion of all activities occur within the boundaries of these complex social structures. The practice of management has responded to these and other influences. Managerial concepts have accommodated to the changing sociocultural environment and internal organizational requirements. In this chapter we set forth a framework for looking at the future of organizations and management and consider some of the primary forces involved. The following topics are discussed:

> The Past Is Prologue
> A Rapidly Changing Environment
> Expansion of Organizational Activities
> Response to Technological Change
> Response to Social Change
> Developing a Democratic-Humanistic System
> Dynamic, Flexible Organizations
> Evolving Managerial Systems

THE PAST IS PROLOGUE

It would be presumptuous and naïve to attempt to forecast the future development of organizations and their management. There are too many unforeseeable forces, both in the external environment and in internal operations, which make any attempt at exact prediction impossible. However, certain factors are paramount in shaping the future of management and organization. Projection of these factors is not as risky as it might seem because there are long-term evolutionary trends. The basic economic and social processes initiated in the nineteenth and twentieth centuries continue to set the stage for the future. Many of the unique characteristics concerning the environment, structure, and national heritage of American society were set forth in the 1830s by Alexis de Tocqueville, a young French nobleman and an astute observer of the social scene. [1]

Many of the characteristics reported by de Tocqueville over a century ago remain fundamental ones and profoundly affect our social structure. He emphasized the impact of democracy upon American society and its institutions and organizations. He saw the pragmatic nature of the people and their abiding faith in the ability of man to shape his environment. He discerned the importance attached to knowledge and education. Above all, he emphasized the abiding American faith in the future and the value of change.

On the other hand, we cannot complacently predict the future on the basis of past trends alone. During the 1960s and 1970s strong "counterculture" movements have been evident, rejecting many of the values in our society—the Protestant work ethic, the emphasis on economic growth and material betterment, and the abiding faith in the virtues of scientific and technological achievements. These counter views suggest that we have been guided over the past several centuries by values associated with an industrializing society, and they foresee a transition to a "post-industrial" society in which new social values and goals will emerge. Many popular books reflect these alternative views. For example, Charles Reich, in *The Greening of America,* advocates a moral utopian view in his Consciousness III which rejects many of our traditional values. And Alvin Toffler, in *Future Shock,* suggests the tremendous problems of human adaptation to rapid technological and social change. One of the most difficult problems facing society will be the integration of traditional values geared to economic growth and technological achievement with the emerging values of greater human dignity and social consciousness. "If society is to move toward a generally more liberated life style, the most pressing problem that it faces is how to rectify its economic needs with the more liberated values." [2]

We do not foresee a revolutionary change in social values. There is evidence that the majority of Americans reject the more extreme views of the counterculture. However, many of the more moderate, humanistic values will be integrated into the mainstream of American life. It is unlikely that the "establishment" will be destroyed. But it is likely that it will be modified significantly as a result of these emerging views.

We have become an "organizational society" and increasingly depend upon

---

[1] Alexis de Tocqueville, *Democracy in America,* ed. by Phillips Bradley, Alfred A. Knopf, Inc., New York, 1945. For a discussion of the impact of de Tocqueville's concepts upon sociological thinking, see Robert A. Nisbet, *The Sociological Tradition,* Basic Books, Inc., Publishers, New York, 1966.

[2] Herman Kahn and B. Bruce-Briggs, *Things to Come: Thinking about the Seventies and Eighties,* The Macmillan Company, New York, 1972, p. 22.

various forms of complex organizations to accomplish our goals. They cannot be looked at separately from the total social structure. Rather, they are a vital, integral part of this structure. Throughout this book we have emphasized that the organization is an open subsystem of the broader sociocultural environment. But the reverse is also true—the nature of man's organizations—their goals, values, technologies, structures, and psychosocial systems—has a fundamental effect upon the very nature of society. This is particularly true for the business firm. As Davis and Blomstrom say:

> The modern business is a social system in itself, but it is also part of a larger social system represented by society in general. Clearly there is a reciprocal relationship between business and this larger society. Society does affect business through religion, law, custom and a host of other influences. But business is not a mute servant; it speaks with a voice of leadership in the affairs of society. It is a change agent influencing society in many ways. It is an important voice in a pluralism of many voices. [3]

Man's organizations will have an important influence upon society. The basic issues of democratic participation, individualism, self-actualization, and a meaningful life are not just broad theoretical abstractions. They are primary issues involving the day-to-day relationships of individuals and groups in organizations. Organizational life is an integral part of total life.

Man can shape his destiny. Throughout a long evolutionary process, life was predominately shaped by the environment and natural selection. Man alone is capable of shaping his environment and developing new social structures. He is capable of sociological changes and does not need to wait for evolution through biological mutations. The biologist Huxley expresses this view:

> By exploiting the possibilities of mental advance, man became the latest dominate type of life, and initiated a new phase of evolution, the human or *psychosocial* phase, which operates much faster than biological evolution, and produces new kinds of results. Man's capacity for reason and imagination, coupled with this ability to communicate his ideas by means of the verbal symbols of language, provided him with a new mechanism for evolution, in the shape of cumulative tradition. Pre-human life depended only on the transmission of material particles, the genes in the chromosomes, from one generation to the next. But man can also transmit experience and its results. With this, mind as well as matter acquired the capacity for self-reproduction. Natural selection becomes subordinate to psychosocial selection, and the human phase of evolution could begin. [4]

---

[3] Keith Davis and Robert Blomstrom, *Business, Society, and Environment*, 2d ed., McGraw-Hill Book Company, New York, 1971, p. 397.

[4] Julian Huxley, "A Biologist Looks at Man's Past and Future," in Charles R. Walker (ed.), *Technology, Industry, and Man*, McGraw-Hill Book Company, New York, 1968, p. 333.

Man can use natural resources to shape his physical and social environment. His social organizations are the vehicle for further progress. They have played a fundamental role in the social evolution of the past century and will have an even more important role in the future. Managing these organizations not only for economic and productive efficiencies but also to provide for the broader goals of human satisfaction will be one of the most important challenges of the future.

A RAPIDLY CHANGING EVIRONMENT

One of the more interesting recent developments is the movement toward the "scientific study of the future." Man has always been interested in predicting what lies ahead. Every society had its prophets. Leonardo da Vinci and Jules Verne made remarkable predictions which have been fulfilled only recently. But these were the predictions of insightful and gifted individuals. More recently there has been an attempt to institutionalize the study of the future. A great many governmental commissions and congressional subcommittees, as well as state and local agencies, have been created to predict the future. The Hudson Institute, the Rand Corporation, and the Stanford Research Institute are just a few of the private organizations engaged in these endeavors. Informal study groups have been created in many universities to bring together the accumulated knowledge from various disciplines in order to develop programs for future societal problems. The World Future Society, an Association for the Study of Alternative Futures, was established in 1966 and has attracted thousands of members and established local chapters in most major cities. *Futurology* has enjoyed a tremendous growth.

With the number and diversity of people and organizations engaged in futurology, it is difficult to reach a consensus on how to study the future, much less any agreement on what the future holds. Figure 23.1 indicates the basic trends suggested by Herman Kahn and his associates at the Hudson Institute. Our own views of the future are in agreement with most of these trends. Although there are many disagreements about the exact nature of the future, there is almost complete agreement that it will be even more turbulent and dynamic than the past. The accelerated pace of change is emphasized. We cannot begin to comprehend all the specific changes that will affect organizations and their management, but we can reflect on some of the more general effects.

An organization is an open sociotechnical system in interaction with its environment. In the future the boundaries separating the organization from its environment will become more permeable. Evidence from the recent past suggests that society will be anything but certain and placid. Increasingly, organizations will operate in *turbulent* environments "in which there are dynamic processes arising from the field itself which create significant variances for the component systems."[5] The turbulence will be increased by the expansion of science and technology, by emphasis on educational achievement, and above all, by the growing aspirations for people of all nationalities to

---

[5] F. E. Emery, "The Next Thirty Years: Concepts, Methods and Anticipations," *Human Relations,* August 1967, p. 222.

THERE IS A BASIC, LONG-TERM, MULTIFOLD TREND TOWARD:

1 Increasingly sensate (empirical, this-worldly, secular, humanistic, pragmatic, manipulative, explicitly rational, utilitarian, contractual, epicurean, hedonistic, etc.) culture—recently an almost complete decline of the sacred and a relative erosion of "irrational" taboos, totems, and charismas.
2 Bourgeois, bureaucratic, and "meritocratic" elites.
3 Accumulation of scientific and technological knowledge.
4 Institutionalization of technological change, especially research, development, innovation, and diffusion—recently and increasingly a conscious emphasis on synergisms and serendipities.
5 Worldwide industrialization and modernization.
6 Increasing capability for mass destruction.
7 Increasing affluence and (recently) leisure.
8 Population growth—now explosive but tapering off.
9 Urbanization and recently suburbanization and "Urban sprawl"—soon the growth of megalopolises.
10 Recently and increasingly—macroenvironmental issues (e.g., constraints set by finite size of earth and various local and global reservoirs).
11 Decreasing importance of primary and (recently) secondary and tertiary occupations.
12 Increasing literacy and education—recently the "knowledge industry" and increasing numbers and role of intellectuals.
13 Future-oriented thinking, discussion, and planning—recently some improvement in methodologies and tools—also some retrogression.
14 Innovative and manipulative rationality increasingly applied to social, political, cultural, and economic worlds as well as to shaping and exploiting the material world—increasing problem of ritualistic, incomplete, or pseudo-rationality.
15 Increasing universality of the multifold trend.
16 Increasing tempo of change in all the above.

FIGURE 23.1 TRENDS OF THE FUTURE (Herman Kahn, "The 'Emergent United States' . . . Post-Industrial Society," in *The Management of Information and Knowledge,* Committee on Science and Astronautics, U.S. House of Representatives, 1970, p. 26.)

control, rather than be victims of, their surroundings. As Wilbert Moore suggests, "Never in human history have so many people, or has such a large proportion of mankind, been engaged in attempting to remake the environment, to increase our capacity to use the environment for human purposes, and to remodel the rules and social arrangements that govern man's interaction with his fellows." [6]

[6] Wilbert E. Moore, "Utility of Utopias," *American Sociological Review,* December 1966, p. 765.

Even though the organization of the future may strive for stability and certainty, it will be impossible to achieve. "An alternate description of a turbulent field is that the accelerating rate and complexity of interactive effects exceeds the component systems' capacities for prediction and, hence, control of the compounding consequences of their actions."[7] In a turbulent and uncertain environment the organization will have to be adaptive. When the organization cannot achieve and maintain stability because of future uncertainty, it must emphasize dynamic flexibility and responsiveness to change. However, the other side of the issue should be recognized. "In a society in which a wide variety of organizations and organizational forms exist, as in the contemporary United States, social change is also a constant condition."[8] Thus organizations not only must respond to changes imposed by the environment but they also "output" changes which profoundly affect the society.

As society becomes more "organized," the environment of any individual subsystem is composed of other complex organizations. For example, the business corporation has competitors, suppliers, and customers, as well as interactions with labor unions and public agencies. The problems of integration and interface between organizations will be of critical importance in the future.

Growing Concern for Environment

We are coming to recognize the importance and limitations of the natural environment itself. We have already discussed ecological issues and the necessity for the organization to consider all the effects of its activities, both good and bad, upon the natural environment. According to William Ruckelshaus, first administrator of the national Environmental Protection Agency:

> We have ridden the abundance of nature into fantastic prosperity, and we have yet to pay full fare for the ride. Only in recent years did we begin to realize that callous treatment of nature's resources not only diminished our own lives, but mortgaged the future of our children.[9]

In the future all organizations, both public and private, will have to be more concerned with the deleterious effects of their activities and outputs. The organization will be held accountable for its environmental impact.

Expansion of the Environment

Until recently man's natural environment has been considered limited to the land masses on earth (and to only a relatively small proportion of these areas). In the future

---

[7] Shirley Terreberry, "The Evolution of Organizational Environments," *Administrative Science Quarterly*, March 1968, p. 593.

[8] Richard H. Hall, *Organizations: Structure and Process*, Prentice-Hall, Inc., Englewood Cliffs, N.J., 1972, p. 326.

[9] William D. Ruckelshaus, "The Beginning of the New American Revolution," *The Annals of the American Academy of Political and Social Science*, July 1971, p. 14.

we will see an extension of this environment to the oceans and to outer space. Our first ventures into space open the long-term possibility that man may not be earth-bound. Research endeavors suggest that in the future oceans will be developed via farming and mining operations and also serve as underseas habitats for people. Therefore, man's environment may not be quite as limited as we have thought heretofore. Also, we should recognize that wherever man goes he will take his organizations. There will be organizations and managers on space stations, and there will be organizations and managers in underseas cities.

EXPANSION OF ORGANIZATIONAL ACTIVITIES

Over the past century complex organizations have expanded their activities and boundaries. This process will continue and become even more important in the future. Boundary expansion has resulted from a number of forces. Goal elaboration has caused organizations to increase their scope, and new technologies have caused them to encompass additional activities. Organizations frequently respond to environmental uncertainties by expanding their domain and bringing within internal control those forces creating the uncertainty.

We have indicated how hospitals have expanded their boundaries. In the early days they were typically small units with the primary function of care of indigent patients. Over the past century they have expanded their domain to include all types of care and treatment. The hospital has become a community health service center with a wide variety of medical, psychological, and social functions.

Similarly, the university has evolved from the small college of a century ago to the multiversity of today. And the modern prison also has expanded its boundaries to include not only confinement of prisoners but training and rehabilitation activities as well.

In business organizations this process of boundary expansion is quite evident. The development of the corporate form allowed the business to expand its activities beyond that permitted by the resources of the individual owner. The movements in the early part of the twentieth century toward vertical and horizontal integration were an example of boundary expansion by business firms. More recently, the development of large-scale conglomerates with activities in a wide variety of industrial fields has been a primary example of boundary expansion. Conglomerate corporations encompass within their structure a number of unrelated businesses in different industries and operate them on a decentralized basis. Each separate unit has substantial autonomy with only broad central management control over major policy decisions. Since the end of World War II many of these conglomerates have been created through merger as well as internal diversification of product lines. They can accumulate vast financial resources and can spread their risks by expansion into many different fields. However, they frequently have diverse and complicated structures and major problems of planning, control, and coordination. The managerial system of these conglomerates needs to be substantially more flexible and dynamic than for the more simplified one-product or one-service company.

Multinational Corporations

In the post-World War II period, American business corporations have entered a new, important phase of boundary expansion—international operations. Increasingly, large- and medium-sized corporations are operating in other countries. They are not just investing funds in foreign operations or only establishing sales agencies. Rather, they are engaging in full-scale operations abroad. Corporations which have their home in one country but which operate and live under the laws and customs of other countries as well can be defined as *multinational corporations*. These multinational corporations have increased greatly in number and size over the past several decades, and this trend will continue.

The move from national to multinational corporation changes the environmental framework within which the organization operates. As Kolde states:

> The primary distinction between an international and a domestic business lies in their environmental frameworks and in the organizational and behavioral responses that flow from these frameworks. As a company transcends a national setting, its environmental framework changes progressively in countless respects. There arise new ground rules as defined by law, custom, and culture; new values; new contradictions, interactions, and balances among external forces; and new opportunities as well as uncertainties. The wider the company's international scope, the greater the environmental diversities surrounding it. [10]

The multinational corporation has significantly changed the boundaries of its activities and the diversity of its environment. It must operate in new sociocultural systems and must maintain dynamic flexibility. "The multinational corporate firm is an adaptive-learning system" [11] This trend has important ramifications not only for business and economic activities, but for international relationships as well. "Whatever it does, the cosmopolitan corporation should be mindful of the fact that it represents a more successful instance of international cooperation and a closer approach to global thinking than we have thus far encountered among governments. It is the torch-bearer of One World." [12]

---

[10] Endel J. Kolde, *International Business Enterprise*, 2d ed., © 1973, p. 14. Reprinted by permission of Prentice-Hall, Inc., Englewood Cliffs, N.J.
[11] Howard V. Perlmutter, "The Multinational Firm and the Future," *The Annals of the American Academy of Political and Social Science*, September 1972, p. 140.
[12] Hans B. Thorelli, "The Multi-national Corporation as a Change Agent," in Richard N. Farmer, *International Management*, Dickenson Publishing Company, Inc., Belmont, Calif., 1968, p. 73.

The development of the multinational corporation has raised many problems as well as opportunities. Many Europeans, for example, have become greatly concerned over the possible domination of their industrial scene by United States corporations. [13]

A number of questions have been raised about the impact of the multinational corporation on the sovereignty of individual nations—even the United States. "There is an inherent conflict between the multinational firm and nationalism." [14] There is concern that the development of these huge organizations will conflict with the boundaries of the various sovereign nations and that national interests will be sacrificed to the multinational corporate goals. The future may see the development of supranational governmental regulation and control of multinational business enterprises to ensure that they operate within the framework of national sovereignties.

Boundary Expansion in Public Sector

Expansion of the boundaries of organizational activities in the public sector is also inevitable. Many of the problems facing society—urban redevelopment, pollution control, and transportation systems—will require new and different organizational approaches. Traditionally, these problems have been faced on a piecemeal basis with various government agencies each responsible for a single function. It is becoming apparent that these problems cannot be solved fractionally but will have to be approached on a total systems basis. Many of the current federal, state, and local governmental agencies will undergo dramatic transformation, and new organizational forms will be developed which will encompass broader activities within their boundaries. For example, the State of Washington and the Canadian Province of British Columbia have developed means to coordinate pollution control in areas such as oil spills on Puget Sound and contiguous waterways.

These programs will not be restricted to the public sector. The private sector also will cooperate in dealing with problems such as pollution control and transportation systems. This will alter traditional organizational boundaries and will require the development of new supraorganizational units to solve social problems which can encompass different segments from the public sector (federal, state, and local) *and* the private sector.

One of the most dramatic trends in organizations in the future will be the development of systems-oriented approaches which can deal with broad social problems on a total rather than piecemeal basis. In many ways, the development of wide-boundary organizations will be similar to the evolution of the business corporate form, which has been so successful in the production of goods or services. We do have examples from the past which suggest future trends—the Tennessee Valley Authority, the Communi-

---

[13] J. J. Servan-Schreiber, *The American Challenge,* trans. by Ronald Steel, Atheneum House, Inc., New York, 1968, p. 3.
[14] John Fayerweather, "The Internationalization of Business," *The Annals of the American Academy of Political and Social Science,* September 1972, p. 5.

cation Satellite Corporation, and the various large-scale programs in the Department of Defense, the National Aeronautics and Space Administration, and the Atomic Energy Commission.

The expansion of the boundaries of an organization creates many new and different problems for management. The number of interfaces with environmental units increases, and the organization must be more responsive. Boundary expansion increases internal complexities and creates problems of control. As an organization expands its activities, it cannot continue to use the tight bureaucratic form and philosophy but must develop a more dynamic and less structured system.

Interface between Organizations

There will be increasing emphasis in the future on problems related to the interface between organizations—interorganizational analysis. Administrative coordinating processes between organizations have been used as substitutes for or complements to marketplace coordination. This has occurred in relationships between the government and the national defense industries and in the National Aeronautics and Space Administration programs. In the future, even more administrative coordination between complex organizations will be necessary.

> Most environmental and technical interrelationships also involve organizational interrelationships. To be sure, in the past organizations had relationships with one another. However, most were static or impersonal, defined by rather rigid legal agreements (setting forth mutual responsibilities) or governed by the invisible hand of the marketplace or the more visible hand of the government regulator. Only recently have we come to recognize that most of our contemporary "problem" areas require both the close collaboration of many institutions and rapid, dynamic mutual adaptation. [15]

We do foresee a substantial increase in the interface between government and business. The line between the public sector and private sector in our economy is blurred. Even in the so-called "public sector" the funds may come from federal, state, and local governments but be spent on goods and services produced by the private sector.

There are indications of important developments which will help in interorganizational coordination. For example, the program or systems management approach has been used as a means for improving integration within the organization and for better interorganizational coordination. The systems approach will be utilized to deal with many important social and economic problems. Each participating organization will

---

[15] Leonard R. Sayles and Margaret K. Chandler, *Managing Large Systems: Organizations for the Future,* Harper & Row, Publishers, New York, 1971, p. 316.

assign personnel to participate with their counterparts from other organizations on a particular program. In the past, this frequently has been accomplished through informal communication and ad hoc committee arrangements. In the future, these approaches will become more formalized.

Advancements in information technology aided by developments in the electronic computer will help improve communication systems across organizational boundaries. Traditionally, the concern has been with developing intraorganizational communication systems. In the future, development of systems of information flow between organizations will be emphasized. This trend is already emerging in the banking system with the movement toward a "checkless society."

Organizations will expand the use of "boundary agents" whose primary function will be coordinating activities with the environment. One interesting facet will be an increase in the mobility of various managerial and professional personnel between organizations. As individuals develop greater technical and professional expertise, their services will be in greater demand by other organizations in the environment. Professional mobility may be one of the primary forces helping to increase effective interface between organizations.

RESPONSE TO TECHNOLOGICAL CHANGE

Technology will continue to be one of the most vital forces affecting organizations and their management in the future. It should be reemphasized that technology is not just mechanical or electronic hardware but relates to the knowledge required for task performance. Not only will the organization of the future be influenced by advancing knowledge, it will be the primary social vehicle creating change.

Technological Forecasting

With a stable technology it is possible for the organization to plan its activities with a high degree of certainty. With a dynamic technology, many more uncertainties are introduced into the organizational system. It can no longer take technology as given and then concentrate on other aspects of the situation. Business organizations have come to recognize the importance of environmental and competitive forces and have developed elaborate means for forecasting them. However, with dynamic change it is becoming important to engage in technological forecasting. Quinn suggests this need:

> For years technology has been the dominant force creating change in men's lives. Yet only recently have managers in public and private organizations realized the need to forecast technological change and its impact on their activities. Economic forecasts, market forecasts, financial forecasts, even weather forecasts have become standard tools of management. Someday

soon, technological forecasting—now in its infancy—must become as accepted and useful as these other analytical devices. [16]

Precise technological forecasting will be impossible in the future as it has been in the past. Too many uncertain forces exist. Who could have predicted the dramatic breakthrough brought by penicillin or the laser or atomic energy? However, this does not mean that the organization should give up on such forecasting. It does not have to be exact in predicting the form of the new developments. Rather, like economic and market forecasts, it can be developed in terms of probabilities and general trends. [17]

In the future, organizations of all types—businesses, hospitals, universities, and governmental agencies—will be actively involved in technological forecasting. They will be aided by improvements in communication systems which provide information from other organizations and the environment. But, it should be recognized that technological change is not an independent force—it is closely related to other sociocultural factors. "Technological change cannot be well understood, and certainly not anticipated, if one assumes that it behaves as though it had a life of its own. Any instance of technological change can best be understood as an event in a total socio-economic-technical system. We know enough about such systems to understand that they are characterized by large numbers of interdependent variables." [18] Technological forecasting should be part of a system of forecasting the total future environment for the organization.

Computerized Information Systems

The phenomenal development of the electronic computer and automated information-decision systems over the past several decades portends a dramatic impact on organizations of the future. The automation of manufacturing processes has had a major effect upon the factory. Of equal and perhaps greater importance will be the impact of computerized information systems on management. In universities, hospitals, and libraries, as well as business organizations, the effects of this new technology are being felt. This revolution in clerical and managerial functions covers two primary areas of activity: (1) the use of automatic electronic equipment for the collection and processing of data and (2) the direct application of computers in the managerial decision-making process.

The most important effect in the past has been in the first phase, the use of electronic data processing equipment for processing vast quantities of data. However,

[16] James Brian Quinn, "Technological Forecasting," *Harvard Business Review,* March–April 1967, p. 89.
[17] Daniel O. Roman, "Technological Forecasting in the Decision Process," *Academy of Management Journal,* June 1970, pp. 127–138.
[18] Donald A. Schon, "Forecasting and Technological Forecasting," *Daedalus,* Journal of the American Academy of Arts and Sciences, Summer 1967, p. 766.

the second phase, automated information-decision systems, will have the greatest impact in the future. At the operating level many routine decisions will be programmed. The programming of decisions in such areas as production and inventory control has already been accomplished in numerous organizations.

In the future computerized information systems will have an increasing impact at the coordinative and strategic levels. This does not mean that the computer will supplant managerial decision-making functions. Rather, it will provide the means for the accumulation and transmittal of the necessary information to managers for judgmental decision-making processes.

Computerized information systems will have an important impact upon the structural and psychosocial subsystems. In some cases they may lead to greater centralization of decision making by transmitting more information "to the top." However, it appears just as likely that these systems can provide better information to lower operating levels and thus make greater decentralization feasible. People in the organization will have to adjust to interfacing with the computer. While this may provide many benefits by giving the individual more pertinent information, it may also cause a sense of alienation and the feeling of loss of control. Such systems will certainly change many of the interpersonal relationships within organizations.

The development of more sophisticated computerized information systems will affect the relationships between organizations and their environments. Such systems will provide for better exchange of information across organizational boundaries. In the not too distant future we will see the development of mass (or community) information utilities. "These will be massive complexes of computer hardware and software, information banks, and communications equipment designed to provide a wide array of information services to public, private, and individual users who are on-line to the system in their own environments." [19] Through such systems organizations and even individuals (such as consumers and students at home) can be tied together into a direct information network.

Professionals and scientists will be affected by new computerized information systems. Increasingly, the doctor, lawyer, and engineer will have at his disposal information which will help in his professional activities. For example, systems are being developed for the storage and retrieval of information on case histories, diagnosis, and treatment of medical patients to aid practicing physicians. In the "browsing era" the electronic computer will provide the link between man and much useful information for decision making.

The development of sophisticated communication systems based upon the computer may have an even broader impact on mankind. Marshall McLuhan has noted that already the communications revolution has made us into a "global theater." [20] In the past the telegraph, telephone, radio, and television have increased the speed and volume of information flow between people tremendously. In the future, more sophis-

---

[19] Burt Nanus, "Managing the Fifth Information Revolution," *Business Horizons,* April 1972, pp. 5–6.
[20] Marshall McLuhan, *Culture is Our Business,* McGraw-Hill Book Company, New York, 1970, p. 8.

ticated computer-based systems will provide an extensive nervous system for mankind which will link together the whole human race. This network of communications is tending to produce a world superculture which is superimposed on the more traditional national and regional cultures of the past.

Technology and Social Engineering

There are even broader questions of the relationship of technology to society which will have an impact on organizations of the future. Weinberg suggests that many of the problems of a modern society, such as education, urban decay, and poverty, can be dealt with through either technology or social engineering. Technology is directed toward solving problems by the utilization of scientific knowledge. The social engineering approach is directed toward inducing social change. For many social problems this approach is more difficult, but offers the greatest long-term benefits.

> There is a more basic sense in which social problems are much more difficult than technological problems. A social problem exists because many people behave, individually, in a socially unacceptable way. To solve a social problem one must induce social change—one must persuade many people to behave differently than they have behaved in the past. One must persuade many people to have few babies, or to drive more carefully, or to refrain from disliking Negroes. By contrast, resolution of a technological problem involves many fewer individual decisions. [21]

It is frequently difficult to find solutions to problems by social means—that is, by changing the attitudes, motivations, and behavior of people. The technological approach may offer the best short-run solution. An example of these alternatives may be seen in the various programs for urban redevelopment. One approach would be to try to induce people to return to rural areas (or to refrain from coming to the cities). Currently, this approach is part of the national policy of both Japan and Red China. The other alternative is to use technical knowledge to redesign the cities, given the high level of urban population concentration. We can see many other situations which have similar alternatives. For example, the development of tranquilizers and other drugs has reduced the number of patients in mental hospitals and has returned them to society. This "technological solution" partially accomplishes the goal without solving the basic underlying psychological and social problems which create mental illness. Weinberg suggests that the technological approach has both advantages and disadvantages:

> The Technological Fix accepts man's intrinsic shortcomings and circumvents them or capitalizes on them for socially useful ends. The Fix is, therefore,

[21] Alvin M. Weinberg, "Can Technology Replace Social Engineering?" *The American Behavioral Scientist,* May 1967, p. 7.

> eminently practical and, in the short term, relatively effective. One does not wait around trying to change people's minds: if people want more water, one gets them more water rather than requiring them to reduce their use of water; if people insist on driving autos while they are drunk, one provides safer autos that prevent injuries even after a severe accident.
>
> But the technological solutions to social problems tend to be incomplete and metastable, to replace one social problem with another. [22]

Technological solutions to social problems provide expedient ways to achieve certain goals. However, in the long run many of the problems facing modern society must be dealt with through basic changes in the value systems and behavior of people. Both these methods will be utilized in the future as they have been in the past. They are not necessarily in conflict, but can be complementary.

Complex organizations of the future will be directly involved in this process of utilizing both technology and social engineering in accomplishing the goals of society. One of the key problems facing organizations is maintaining appropriate internal relationships between the technical and psychosocial systems to ensure both satisfaction of organizational goals and individual self-actualization. Technology should be considered in humanistic terms. It is created by man and should ultimately serve the needs of man. Taken alone, technology is neither humanistic nor mechanistic. "Modern technology *need not* destroy aesthetic, spiritual and social values, but it will most certainly do so unless the individuals who manage our technology are firmly committed to the preservation of such values." [23] Man himself determines how advancing knowledge is used. Rickover emphasizes the need for a humanistic technology.

> My plea is for a humanistic attitude toward technology. By this I mean that we recognize it as a product of human effort, a product serving no other purpose than to benefit man—man in general, not merely some men: man in the totality of his humanity, encompasing all his manifold interests and needs, not merely some one particular concern of his. Humanistically viewed. technology is not an end in itself but a means to an end, the end being determined by man. [24]

RESPONSE TO SOCIAL CHANGE

In addition to responding to technological change, in the future organizations will have to adapt to many other forces in the environment. Problems of race relations, poverty, changing family relationships, urban blight, health care, adaptations to leisure, and providing opportunities for self-renewal are just a few examples of broader social issues

---

[22] Ibid., p. 9.
[23] John W. Gardner, *Self-renewal: The Individual and the Innovative Society*, Harper & Row, Publishers, Incorporated, New York, 1963, p. 57.
[24] Hyman G. Rickover, "A Humanistic Technology," *The American Behavioral Scientist*, January 1965, p. 3.

which will affect organizations. In many ways these social issues are more complex than economic and technological problems. And their solution is more difficult.

> The problems are thus infinitely complex and interrelated. No quick, easy, cheap, or final solutions are possible. We must make progress quickly and rapidly, but if we expect to finish the job quickly and get back to our usual concerns, we will certainly be disappointed. The answer is not more education, more money, more jobs, or more and better housing for the disadvantaged, but all of these things and much more. It involves our relations with the rest of the world and our rethinking of whole areas of life. Most of all perhaps, it involves our willingness to pay the price. [25]

These social issues in the general environment will move directly into the task environments of organizations. We have seen this pattern developing over the past several decades. Organizations will need to develop techniques for predicting the social changes of the future and to develop programs in response to such forecasts.

Social Forecasting

"In recent years, researchers have developed the art of forecasting technology (what man can do) but have paid relatively little attention to devising ways to forecast social needs (what man wants)." [26] We have developed sophisticated means for economic forecasting and have increasingly emphasized technological forecasting. In the future, these approaches to forecasting will be broadened to include predictions of other social forces.

> Social expectations and changing environment have produced a shift in types of forecasting of most concern to top management. Traditionally, economic forecasting of such environmental factors as gross national product, interest rates, prices, and wage rates has dominated company top-level forecasting efforts. Forecasting of noneconomic factors in the environment is becoming more important as bases for managerial decision making. I would not be surprised to see in ten years that forecasting of various social values and social indicators will stand beside such traditional economic forecasts as GNP as major projections important to management in decision making. In mind, of course, are projections of how people feel about such social values as work and leisure, materialism, esthetics, and so on. The social indicators will concern elements of life quality, such as medical care, health, clean air, clean water, and so on. [27]

---

[25] Ina Corinne Brown, *Understanding Race Relations,* Prentice-Hall, Inc., Englewood Cliffs, N.J., 1973, p. 240.
[26] Clark C. Abt, "Forecasting Future Social Needs," *The Futurist,* February 1971, p. 20.
[27] George A. Steiner, "Changing Managerial Philosophies," *Business Horizons,* June 1971, p. 8.

It is evident that social forecasting is tremendously complex. It is more difficult than either economic or technological forecasting because of the complexities and uncertainties involved in the evolution of value systems.

The techniques for social forecasting are similar to those used in economic and technological forecasting. *Projection* is an extrapolation based on looking at a series of historical data and extending these into the future. *Probability forecasting* is where the analyst decides which events are possible and then assigns probabilities to the various alternatives. *Judgmental* approaches such as the Delphi technique try to bring the combined knowledge of various experts together to arrive at a consensus forecast. *Analysis* uses models based upon historical data and seeks to identify the underlying causes of social change and to develop models of future relationships. One of the more interesting approaches is the so-called *surprise-free projection* in which the analyst attempts to develop a broad forecast of the future scene using several of the above techniques. It results in a forecast which is not surprising to the analyst and is primarily useful as a context for further analysis and discussion. [28] The listing of likely trends of the future in Figure 23.1 represents a surprise-free projection.

Social Indicators

One of the major problems in social forecasting is the lack of good historical and current information on social conditions. Attempts to develop social indicators and to accumulate these into a national balance sheet of social accounts similar to the national income and product accounts reflect the need for more sophisticated information on social conditions. Although there are obviously many more difficulties than in developing economic indicators, it is apparent that we are moving in this direction. In the future it is likely that individual organizations will be directly tied in with a system of social indicators and accounts which will indicate their social as well as economic effects on society. Organizational performance will be evaluated in terms of social effects as well as economic results.

DEVELOPING A DEMOCRATIC-HUMANISTIC SYSTEM

Organizations have proved over the past century that they are effective in accomplishing many goals. Witness the tremendous productive capacity of our industrial system. In the future, other key issues will assume importance. Can organizations make use of advancing technology in accomplishing their goals while satisfying human and social needs? In the traditional bureaucratic model, the organization was designed to achieve technical functions with little consideration given to the psychosocial system. A continuation of this approach would be unfortunate for society. ''Management must constantly be on guard not to design the human participation in total systems completely in terms

---

[28] Kahn and Bruce-Briggs, op. cit., pp. 39–87.

of technical functions. This requires that at every level the total man involved must be considered." [29]

A number of writers feel that organizations have failed to provide a humanistic work environment by precluding opportunities for self-actualization. We do not share this pessimistic view. While it may have been true that the traditional organization theory of bureaucracy and scientific management emphasized the technical and structural aspects to the detriment of the psychosocial system, there has been a definite trend toward industrial humanism.

Power Equalization in the Future

One of the major forces occurring in organizations in society is the desire on the part of all participants to have greater influence. [30] The rise of labor unions in the 1930s, the growing student demands for participation in university affairs, and the collective activities on the part of public school teachers and nurses are examples of this desire for greater involvement. We see a continuing decline in the gap between organizational elites and lower-level participants. In formal organizations, there appears to be a move toward "power equalization," with all members having greater influence on internal affairs. Organizations of the future will place less emphasis upon a hierarchical structure and will move toward a more equalitarian social system. It is even likely in the not too distant future that a major symbol of stratification, the salute to the superior, will be unceremoniously discarded by the military services.

Latent human capability is the most valuable resource of the organization—much more important than physical or financial resources. Increasingly, management will emphasize the importance of human resources and will recognize that maintaining a viable psychosocial system is one of its most vital tasks. Organizations will develop a more adaptive-organic system in place of a bureaucratic-mechanistic structure. This is not a revolutionary change; it is a continuation of the trend which has long been evident. Obviously, the battle for a humanistic organization will never be completely won. The manager will have the continuing problem of balancing the technical tasks with the objectives of the psychosocial system. This delicate task of balance and integration will be of major concern to future managers.

Rise of the Innovative-Creative Man

A popular theme during the 1950s was the growing conformity and lack of initiative on the part of organizational participants. In this view, the organization had so structured the individual's behavior that his performance was typically mediocre and routine—he lacked individuality and initiative. His basic attitude was one of "don't rock the boat," play it safe, and get the organizational rewards without too much effort.

---

[29] Charles R. DeCarlo, "Changes in Management Environment and Their Effect upon Values," in Charles A. Myers (ed.), *The Impact of Computers on Management*, The M.I.T. Press, Cambridge, Mass., 1967, p. 253.
[30] Max Ways, "More Power to Everybody," *Fortune*, May 1970, pp. 173–178.

This view was based upon the premise that the modern organization required a structuring of human behavior which was more rigid than in earlier, preindustrial society. It romanticized the preorganization man's social environment to suggest that he had almost complete autonomy. This view seems far from reality. "Man apparently neither wants nor has experienced this postulated state of complete autonomy. People have always demanded structure in their lives. With few exceptions, men depend on human relationships, some fixity of structure, routine, and habit to survive psychologically." [31] While it is true that the organization does structure human behavior, so do the family, the informal group, and all other types of social interaction. The complete state of human autonomy and individualism which has served as the romantic ideal probably never has existed for man since he emerged as a social creature.

In our view, the "problem" of the "organization man" will diminish in the future. While the decade of the fifties may have been one of conformity and passivity, the decades of the sixties and seventies appear to be just the opposite. There is greater activism and individual initiative on the part of people in organizations.

A number of forces will continue to reduce pressures to conform. There is a growing sense of professionalism among specialized personnel. They develop loyalties to their professional colleagues and are not as subject to the control and conformity requirements of the organization. Often their loyalty is to a discipline, and they can be innovative and creative within their sphere of competence. Another modifying force is the need for organizations to adapt to dynamic change in the turbulent environment and to stress innovation. The organization man was a product of the bureaucratic-mechanistic structure. The "innovative-creative man" will be required and sought in the adaptive-organic systems of the future.

A Mosaic Psychosocial System

In society and in organizations we have generally emphasized the desirability of developing common cultures, values, and even life styles. This has had a homogenizing effect upon participants and the psychosocial subsystem in organizations. Current trends allow for more individual and group diversity.

American society up to now has stressed the idea of a "melting pot" and has sought to create through public education a uniform culture. With increased affluence and increased political skill, this ideal can now be called into question. Can we now invent a "mosaic" society, composed of many small subcultures, each of which gives its participants a sense of community and identity which is so desperately needed in a mass world, and which can at the same

---

31 Leonard R. Sayles, *Individualism and Big Business,* McGraw-Hill Book Company, New York, 1963, p. 179.

time remain at peace with its neighbors and not threaten to pull the society apart? [32]

We see an increasing possibility of allowing more diverse values, views, and life styles among different participants and groups within the confines of organizations. Over the past decade, universities have developed a diversity of programs which do not require all students to conform to a given pattern. Many churches have accommodated to diverse groups in order to keep them within the overall system. Business organizations have shown indications of a growing tolerance for individual and group variations. The maintenance of a mosaic psychosocial system composed of different subcultures is difficult. Integrating the efforts and interests of people and groups with different values and life styles will tax the skills of managers.

DYNAMIC, FLEXIBLE ORGANIZATIONS

The foregoing discussion of organizations and the factors influencing them in the future can be summarized as follows:

1 Organizations will be operating in a turbulent environment which requires continual change and adjustment.
2 They will have to adapt to an increasing diversity of cultural values in the social environment.
3 Greater emphasis will be placed on technological and social forecasting.
4 Organizations will continue to expand their boundaries and domains. They will increase in size and complexity.
5 Organizations will continue to differentiate their activities, causing increased problems of integration and coordination.
6 Organizations will continue to have major problems in the accumulation and utilization of knowledge. Intellectual activities will be stressed.
7 Greater emphasis will be focused on suggestion and persuasion rather than coercion based on authoritarian power as the means for coordinating the activities of the participants and functions within the organization.
8 Participants at all levels in organizations will have more influence. Organizations of the future will adopt a power-equalization rather than power-differentiation model.
9 There will be greater diversity in values and life styles among people and groups in organizations. A mosaic psychosocial system will be normal.

---

[32] Kenneth E. Boulding, "Expecting the Unexpected: The Uncertain Future of Knowledge and Technology," in *Designing Education for the Future,* Colorado Department of Education, Boulder, Colo., 1966, p. 212.

10 Problems of interface between organizations will increase. New means for effective interorganizational coordination will be developed.

11 Computerized information-decision systems will have an increasing impact upon organizations.

12 The number of professionals and scientists and their influence within organizations will increase. There will also be a decline in the proportion of independent professionals with many more salaried professionals.

13 Goals of complex organizations will diversify. Emphasis will be upon satisficing a number of goals rather than maximizing any one.

14 Evaluation of organizational performance will be difficult. Many new administrative techniques will be developed for evaluation of performance in all spheres of activity.

This listing suggests that there will be a movement away from the mechanistic-bureaucratic organization toward a more adaptive-organic system. Bennis predicts that bureaucracy, as a formal structure of organization based upon logical relationships among functions or tasks, will be replaced within the next twenty-five to fifty years by a new type of organization better suited to the needs of twentieth-century industrialism. He says, "Bureaucracy emerged out of the need for more predictability, order, and precision. It was an organization ideally suited to the values and the demands of the Victorian Empire. And just as bureaucracy emerged as a creative response to a radically new age, so today new organizational shapes and forms are surfacing before our eyes." [33] While we agree that there may be a general movement toward the adaptive-organic form, we cannot agree that the bureaucratic-mechanistic organization will disappear. The very essence of the contingency view, as discussed in Chapter 19, suggests that a wide variety of organizational forms will continue to be appropriate, depending on the specific situation. Where the environment and technology are relatively routine and certain and where the emphasis is on programmable output and productivity, the bureaucratic-mechanistic form may be fitting. However, it is also likely that these conditions will not prevail for as many organizations in the future as in the past.

We have discussed the concepts of the adaptive-organic organization. This approach will require fundamental changes in goals and values, as well as in the structural, psychosocial, and managerial systems. In order to ensure the effective coordination of many of the diverse organizational activities, it will be necessary to establish linking departments and individuals such as program or project managers. Emphasis will be placed on horizontal as well as hierarchical relationships. There will be less concern with strict departmentalization of activities and a more free-form fluidity with people assigned to individual programs and projects where their capabilities and knowledge can be utilized. The adaptive-organic organization will be much more dy-

---

[33] Warren G. Bennis, "Organizations of the Future," *Personnel Administration*, September–October 1967, p. 6.

namic and flexible in its internal relationships than the bureaucratic structure and will be able to respond more effectively to environmental changes.

The adaptive-organic form offers the best opportunity for the organization to meet the two basic and often contradictory requirements of maintenance and change. Chamberlain describes the problems of balancing these two forces:

> The fact of the matter is that the business firm is constantly subject to two pressures which must be maintained in some sort of balance. There must always be a tendency toward systematic, coherent, efficient organization if the firm's existing goals are to be achieved and if the complex of relationships is to be held together at the present point in time. There must always be a tendency toward a state of equilibrium. At the same time there must also be a tendency toward a breakup of existing relationships and the formation of new ones, because of the intrusion of unavoidable environmental changes and the firm's purposiveness with respect to them. There must be a tendency toward disturbing present relations, toward introducing an element of disequilibrium. [34]

This forecast is not limited to business; it applies to all organizational types. In particular, many public bureaucracies will undergo rather fundamental changes. These changes are already taking place in a number of governmental agencies.

EVOLVING MANAGERIAL SYSTEMS

With the growth of large-scale organizations and expansion of their activities, management has changed significantly. In medium and large firms there has been a move away from the traditional owner-manager toward the "professional manager." The trend from the bureaucratic-mechanistic to adaptive-organic systems has also created fundamental changes for management.

Expanding Management's Role

As more human activities are taking place within larger organizations, the role of management has expanded. There has been a significant increase in the number of managers, professionals, and technical personnel in the labor force. In the future the managerial role will be of even greater importance. "The essential task of modern management is to deal with change. Management is the agency through which most changes enter our society, and it is the agency that then must cope with the environment it has set in turbulent motion." [35]

---

[34] Neil W. Chamberlain, *Enterprise and Environment: The Firm in Time and Place,* McGraw-Hill Book Company, New York, 1968, pp. 9–10.
[35] Max Ways, "Tomorrow's Management: A More Adventurous Life in a Free-form Corporation," *Fortune,* July 1, 1966, p. 84.

Management must deal with the dynamics of change and provide coordination for the overall system. We do not agree with some writers who suggest that computerized information-decision systems will take over many managerial functions. While this new technology will help in dealing with the routine, programmable decision-making activities, it will not reduce the more important function of management in dealing with the nonprogrammable, innovative, and creative aspects of organizations.

Will Organizations Become Unmanageable?

The managerial role will not become simpler in the future; it will be even more complex. Gross suggests that many of our complex organizations may be approaching unmanageability:

> In the past, all such organizations have faced new managerial (or administrative) difficulties whenever these conditions developed:
>
> —more uncertainties in their environment
> —more structural intricacy, or
> —more performance complexity.
>
> In the future, these conditions will become increasingly prevalent. During the 1970s, new environmental uncertainties will be brought into being by rapid, uneven, and often unpredictable changes in technology, social structure, human aspirations, government policies, coalitions of political power, and international relations in a world society experiencing unpredictable conflicts. New structural intricacies will be created by growth or reorganization, increased specialization and professionalism, new functions and interrelations. With more sophisticated demands on organizations, more varied activities, and more operations requiring coordination over larger expanses of space, time, and psychic or cultural distance, new complexities in performance will multiply. Under these conditions, managers and administrators at all levels will face greater difficulties in decision-making, communicating, planning, and control. Indeed, some organizations—business firms as well as government agencies, hospitals as well as universities, community as well as international bodies—will approach *unmanageability.* [36]

We agree that these growing environmental and internal complexities will make organizations unmanageable if traditional bureaucratic-mechanistic approaches are used. It is unlikely that these complex systems can be managed effectively "from the top" of the hierarchy. Many of the traditional principles of management reinforced a

---

[36] Bertram M. Gross, *Organizations and Their Managing,* The Free Press of Glencoe, New York, 1968, pp. vii–viii.

structured organization well adapted to standardization and productivity. However, with a more dynamic environment and the need for flexibility, new managerial systems have developed which emphasize more effective utilization of expert knowledge at all levels, lateral and diagonal communication networks, reliance upon group decision-making processes, a project or team approach, and the expansion of the power-equalization concept as a basis for self-actualization of participants.

Management's Use of Knowledge

Increasingly, management has become a more intellectual activity and involves more effective uses of knowledge. Bass says this trend will continue in the future:

> Intellectual processes will be of greater importance to the future manager than to his present-day counterpart; he will spend more time on them. The managerial job will have many more intellectual and educational requirements. It will involve more technical scientific and engineering problems, as well as more complex budgeting and financial decisions. The manager will be functioning in a world where his performance will be evaluated even more than it is today on his intellectual skills in bringing about increases in rate of growth, in quality of services and output. [37]

Management systems will require more participants with advanced education. Managers will be knowledge workers of the future.

One of the defects of the bureaucratic structure is that it frequently develops information and knowledge pathologies when faced with dynamic change. [38] As long as the environment is stable and internal operations can be formalized and routinized, the rigid hierarchy can be relatively effective. However, with dynamic external and internal changes, the bureaucratic structure soon fails under the overload of information requirements. In the organization of the future, knowledge will be possessed by many different participants, not just by top management. Managerial systems will be designed to ensure that sufficient information is available to decision centers. The network of information flow will be even more complicated and sophisticated than at present.

The increasing importance of managers as knowledge workers will create some rather fundamental problems of obsolescence in the future. When management skills were learned by experience, the longer the service, the better qualified the manager. However, as management has become more dependent upon new knowledge of operations and techniques which cannot be learned solely by experience, the likelihood

---

[37] Reprinted by permission of the publisher from "Implications of Behavioral Sciences in the Year 2000," by Bernard M. Bass, *Management 2000*, p. 104. © 1968 by the American Foundation for Management Research, New York.
[38] Harold L. Wilensky, *Organizational Intelligence,* Basic Books, Inc., Publishers, New York, 1967.

of obsolescence is greater. It is highly unlikely that any formal program of education can be developed which will carry a manager through his entire career. The time span for obsolescence of the manager's knowledge will become shorter, just as it has for scientists, professionals, and technicians.

Self-renewal through training and motivation for innovativeness has become a dominant need. Societies, organizations, and individuals grow complacent and stale, and rejuvenation is imperative. The best means for offsetting this paralysis is through emphasis on the individual. "Unless we foster versatile, innovative and self-renewing men and women, all the ingenious social arrangements in the world will not help us." [39] It will be necessary to develop more programs for reeducating managers as they move through their careers. More postexperience programs will be developed for training managers in all types of complex organizations. They will be granted educational leaves to renew their knowledge. The adaptive-organic organization can provide opportunities for participants to change functions, pursue new activities, and meet new challenges.

Both a Managerial and a Behavioral Scientist

We have suggested that management concepts have been substantially influenced by developments in the management sciences and the behavioral sciences. So far there has been a relatively wide divergence between these two approaches, with the management sciences emphasizing economic-technical rationality, quantification, and computational techniques, and the behavioral sciences emphasizing psychosocial factors. For the practicing manager this dichotomy is artificial. The manager of the future will have to have substantial knowledge and competence in both areas. In fact, the management role will be one of integrating and coordinating a diversity of techniques and concepts from a number of fields. As Kirkpatrick says:

> Standing squarely between the forces of economic efficiency and technological development and the irresistible psychological and sociological pressures of the human spirit are the representatives of management. The manager must be a technologist and a psychologist, an engineer and a sociologist, a man who is analytical and reflective, and a man of action—but a man who is deliberate before action. The new manager must indeed be a rare and a *balanced* combination of scientist and humanist! [40]

The manager of the future must deal with both aspects—the technical-economic and the psychosocial—and integrate them to accomplish the goals of both technical efficiency and human satisfaction.

---

[39] Gardner, op. cit., p. xiv.
[40] Reprinted by permission of the publisher from "Implications of Behavioral Sciences in the Year 2000," by Forrest H. Kirkpatrick, *Management 2000*, p. 115. © 1968 by the American Foundation for Management Research, New York.

A Flexible Managerial System

In the future, organizations will tend toward a flexible managerial system. Many of the participants in the managerial system will be performing their activities on a wider variety of programs. Positions and functions will not be as clearly described as in the past. Rather, their activities will be dictated by the forces of change and the requirement of specific programs. At the operating level managers will have to be flexible in meeting change. At the coordinative and strategic levels even more adaptability will be required because of the problems of integration of organizational activities and the dynamics of the environment. At all three levels—the operating, the coordinative, and the strategic—the managerial system of most organizations in the future will emphasize innovation and creativity.

Surviving in a Sea of Ambiguity?

The manager's job will become more difficult and confusing in the future than in the past. He will be faced with many psychological and sociological problems of adjustment to the uncertainties of his role. The life of the corporate executive, the president of the university, the hospital administrator, and the heads of various public agencies will become more complex rather than easier. The ambiguities of managerial positions in organizations of the future will create many role conflicts and will severely test the psychological makeup of incumbents. Society will place increasing demands upon managers for effective and efficient performance in a wide variety of fields. It is unlikely that the manager will be able to so structure his work environment as to create substantial certainty. He will face continual problems and will rarely achieve final solutions. He must accept complexity and uncertainty and try to maintain a dynamic equilibrium in the face of many forces. He must learn to live and cope with a turbulent environment. His survival as an individual may well depend upon reaching an accommodation.

In spite of the growing difficulties of the managerial role, it will offer more opportunities for self-actualization than in the past. Future organizations will be vital in meeting the needs of society and managers will have increasingly important functions. The managerial role will offer great challenges and rewards for those with a high tolerance for ambiguity plus the skills and propensity to cope with complex issues in dynamic and uncertain situations.

QUESTIONS AND PROBLEMS

1 How will the turbulent environment affect organizations of the future?
2 Why has there been an expansion of organizational boundaries? Select several organization types and predict the direction of their future boundary expansion.
3 Why will the problems of interorganizational relationships be of increasing importance in the future? What new means might be used to improve interorganizational coordination?

4 What are the major difficulties in technological forecasting? Given these problems, why should management even attempt such forecasting?

5 Develop a list of various organizations which are engaged in "the scientific study of the future." Investigate the various approaches they have used.

6 Contrast problem solution through technology or social engineering. Make a list of social problems which might be dealt with through either technology or social engineering.

7 Compose your own surprise-free projection for the year 2000.

8 What is meant by social forecasting? Study the approaches used by several organizations in their social forecasting.

9 What is meant by a humanistic technology? Do you think it is possible in an industrial society?

10 Do you agree or disagree that organizations will move toward greater power equalization? Give examples to support your arguments.

11 What are some of the major difficulties in maintaining a mosaic psychosocial system?

12 Why will the organization of the future be concerned with establishing new measures for evaluation of performance? What types of measures might they use?

13 What will be the major changes in managerial systems in the future?

EPILOGUE

*Some men see things as they are and say "Why?";
I dream of things which never were and ask "Why
not?"*

Robert F. Kennedy

*Certitude is not the test for certainty. We have been
cocksure of many things that were not so.*

Justice Oliver Wendell Holmes

*New times demand new measures and new men;
The world advances, and in time outgrows
The laws that in our fathers' day were best;
And doubtless, after us, some purer scheme
Will be shaped out by wiser men than we,
Made wiser by the steady growth of truth.*

James Russell Lowell

*We have not succeeded in answering all our questions.
Indeed, we sometimes feel we have not completely
answered any of them. The answers we have found
only serve to raise a whole new set of questions. In
some ways we feel we are as confused as ever. But we
think we are confused on a higher level and about
more important things.*

Anonymous

BIBLIOGRAPHY

Ackoff, Russell L.: *A Concept of Corporate Planning*, Wiley-Interscience, New York, 1970.

―――: "Towards a System of Systems Concepts," *Management Science*, July 1971, pp. 661–671.

Adler, Mortimer J.: *The Conditions of Philosophy*, Dell Publishing Company, Inc., New York, 1965.

Alexis, Marcus, and Charles Z. Wilson: *Organizational Decision Making*, Prentice-Hall, Inc., Englewood Cliffs, N.J., 1967.

Alland, Alexander, Jr.: *The Human Imperative*, Columbia University Press, New York, 1972.

Ansoff, H. Igor: *Corporate Strategy*, McGraw-Hill Book Company, New York, 1965.

Anthony, Robert N.: *Planning and Control Systems: A Framework for Analysis*, Harvard Graduate School of Business Administration, Boston, 1965.

Ardrey, Robert: *African Genesis*, Dale Publishing Company, Inc., New York, 1963.

Argyris, Chris: *Integrating the Individual and the Organization*, John Wiley & Sons, Inc., New York, 1964.

―――: *Management and Organizational Development*, McGraw-Hill Book Company, New York, 1971.

―――: *Organization and Innovation*, Richard D. Irwin, Inc., and The Dorsey Press, Homewood, Ill., 1965.

Barnard, Chester I.: *The Functions of the Executive*, Harvard University Press, Cambridge, Mass., 1938.

Bauer, Raymond A. (ed.): *Social Indicators*, The M. I. T. Press, Cambridge, Mass., 1966.

Bavelas, Alex: "Leadership: Man and Function," *Administrative Science Quarterly*, March 1960, pp. 491–498.

Beckett, John A.: *Management Dynamics: The New Synthesis*, McGraw-Hill Book Company, New York, 1971.

Beckhard, Richard: *Organization Development: Strategies and Models*, Addison-Wesley Publishing Company, Reading, Mass., 1969.

Bellman, Richard: "Control Theory," *Scientific American,* September 1964, pp. 186–200.

Bendix, Reinhard, and Seymour Martin Lipset (eds.): *Class, Status and Power,* The Free Press of Glencoe, New York, 1953.

Bennis, Warren G. (ed.): *American Bureaucracy,* Aldine Publishing Company, Chicago, 1970.

———: *Changing Organizations,* McGraw-Hill Book Company, New York, 1966.

———, **Kenneth D. Benne, and Robert Chin (eds.):** *The Planning of Change,* 2d ed., Holt, Rinehart & Winston, Inc., New York, 1969.

——— **and Philip E. Slater:** *The Temporary Society,* Harper Colophon Books, New York, 1969.

Berelson, Bernard (ed.): *The Behavioral Sciences Today,* Basic Books, Inc., Publishers, New York, 1963.

——— **and Gary A. Steiner:** *Human Behavior: An Inventory of Scientific Findings,* Harcourt, Brace & World, Inc., New York, 1964.

Berkley, George E.: *The Administrative Revolution,* Prentice-Hall, Inc., Englewood Cliffs, N.J., 1971.

Berrien, F. Kenneth: *General and Social Systems,* Rutgers University Press, New Brunswick, N.J., 1968.

Black, Guy: "Systems Analysis in Government Operations," *Management Science,* October 1967, pp. B-41–58.

Blackwell, Thomas Edward: *College and University Administration,* The Center for Applied Research in Education, Inc., New York, 1966.

Blake, Robert R., and Jane S. Mouton: *Corporate Excellence through Grid Organization Development: A Systems Approach,* Gulf Publishing Company, Houston, 1968.

——— **and** ———: *The Managerial Grid,* Gulf Publishing Company, Houston, 1964.

Blau, Peter M.: "The Hierarchy of Authority in Organizations," *The American Journal of Sociology,* January 1968, pp. 453–467.

——— **and Richard A. Schoenherr:** *The Structure of Organizations,* Basic Books, Inc., New York, 1971.

———**and W. Richard Scott:** *Formal Organizations: A Comparative Analysis,* Chandler Publishing Company, San Francisco, 1962.

Blauner, Robert: *Alienation and Freedom,* The University of Chicago Press, Chicago, 1964.

Boulding, Kenneth E.: "The Ethics of Rational Decision," *Management Science,* February 1966, pp. B-161–169.

———: *The Impact of the Social Sciences,* Rutgers University Press, New Brunswick, N.J., 1966.

———: *The Organizational Revolution,* Harper & Row, Publishers, Incorporated, New York, 1953.

Branch, Melville C.: *Planning: Aspects and Applications,* John Wiley & Sons, Inc., New York, 1966.

Brickman, William W.: "American Higher Education in Historical Perspective," *The Annals of the American Academy of Political and Social Science,* November 1972, pp. 31–43.

Brubacher, John S., and Willis Rudy: *Higher Education in Transition: An American History: 1636–1956,* Harper & Row, Publishers, Incorporated, New York, 1958.

Bruner, Jerome S., Jacqueline J. Goodnow, and George A. Austin: *A Study of Thinking,* John Wiley & Sons, Inc., New York, 1956.

Buckley, Walter (ed.): *Modern Systems Research for the Behavioral Scientist,* Aldine Publishing Co., Chicago, 1968.

Burns, Tom, and G. M. Stalker: *The Management of Innovation,* Tavistock Publications, London, 1961.

Campbell, John P., Marvin D. Dunnette, Edward E. Lawler, III, and Karl E. Weich, Jr.: *Managerial Behavior, Performance, and Effectiveness,* McGraw-Hill Book Company, New York, 1970.

Caplow, Theodore, and Reece J. McGee: *The Academic Marketplace,* Basic Books, Inc., Publishers, New York, 1958.

Cartwright, Dorwin, and Alvin Zander (eds.): *Group Dynamics: Research and Theory,* 2d ed., Harper & Row, Publishers, Incorporated, New York, 1960.

Chamberlain, Neil W.: *Enterprise and Environment: The Firm in Time and Place,* McGraw-Hill Book Company, New York, 1968.

Chandler, Alfred D., Jr.: *Strategy and Structure,* The M.I.T. Press, Cambridge, Mass., 1962.

Churchman, C. West: *The Systems Approach,* Dell Publishing Company, Inc., New York, 1968.

————, **Russell L. Ackoff, and E. Leonard Arnoff:** *Introduction to Operations Research,* John Wiley & Sons, Inc., New York, 1957.

Cleland, David I., and William R. King: *Systems Analysis and Project Management,* McGraw-Hill Book Company, New York, 1968.

Commoner, Barry: *The Closing Circle,* Alfred A. Knopf, Inc., New York, 1971.

Cooper, W. W., H. J. Leavitt, and M. W. Shelly, II (eds.): *New Perspectives in Organization Research,* John Wiley & Sons, Inc., New York, 1964.

Corson, John J.: *Governance of Colleges and Universities,* McGraw-Hill Book Company, New York, 1960.

Coser, Lewis A.: *The Functions of Social Conflict,* The Free Press of Glencoe, New York, 1956.

Crozier, Michel: *The Bureaucratic Phenomenon,* The University of Chicago Press, Chicago, 1964.

Cyert, Richard M., and James G. March: *A Behavioral Theory of the Firm,* Prentice-Hall, Inc., Englewood Cliffs, N.J., 1963.

Dale, Ernest: *Organization,* American Management Association, New York, 1967.

Dalton, Gene W., Paul R. Lawrence, and Jay W. Lorsch: *Organizational Structure and Design,* Richard D. Irwin, Inc., and The Dorsey Press, Homewood, Ill., 1970.

Davis, Keith, and Robert L. Blomstrom: *Business, Society, and Environment,* 2d ed., McGraw-Hill Book Company, New York, 1971.

DeGreene, Kenyon B. (ed.): *Systems Psychology,* McGraw-Hill Book Company, New York, 1970.

Diebold, John: *Business Decisions and Technological Change,* Praeger Publishers, New York, 1970.

Drucker, Peter F.: *The Practice of Management,* Harper & Row, Publishers, Incorporated, New York, 1954.

————: *Technology, Management and Society,* Harper & Row, Publishers, Incorporated, New York, 1970.

Dutton, John M., and William H. Starbuck (eds.): *Computer Simulation of Human Behavior,* John Wiley & Sons, Inc., New York, 1971.

Edmunds, Stahrl, and John Letey: *Environmental Administration,* McGraw-Hill Book Company, New York, 1973.

Elbing, Alvar O., Jr., and Carol J. Elbing: *The Value Issue of Business,* McGraw-Hill Book Company, New York, 1967.

Ellul, Jacques: *The Technological Society,* John Wilkinson (trans.), Alfred A. Knopf, Inc., New York, 1964.

Emery, F. E.: "The Next Thirty Years: Concepts, Methods and Anticipations," *Human Relations,* August 1967, pp. 199–237.

———**(ed.):** *Systems Thinking,* Penguin Books Ltd., Harmondsworth, Middlesex, England, 1969.

——— **and E. L. Trist:** "The Causal Texture of Organizational Environments," *Human Relations,* February 1965, pp. 21–31.

Emshoff, James R.: *Analysis of Behavioral Systems,* The Macmillan Company, New York, 1971.

Etzioni, Amitai: *A Comparative Analysis of Complex Organizations,* The Free Press of Glencoe, New York, 1961.

———: *Modern Organizations,* Prentice-Hall, Inc., Englewood Cliffs, N.J., 1964.

Farmer, Richard N.: "The Ethical Dilemma of American Capitalism," *California Management Review,* Summer 1964, pp. 47–58.

Feigenbaum, Edward A., and Julian Feldman (eds.): *Computers and Thought,* McGraw-Hill Book Company, New York, 1963.

Feldman, Julian, and Herschel E. Kanter: "Organizational Decision Making," in James G. March (ed.), *Handbook of Organizations,* Rand McNally & Company, Chicago, 1965, pp. 614–649.

Festinger, Leon: *A Theory of Cognitive Dissonance,* Harper & Row, Publishers, Incorporated, New York, 1957.

Fiedler, Fred E.: "Style or Circumstance: The Leadership Enigma," *Psychology Today,* March 1969, pp. 38–43.

———: *A Theory of Leadership Effectiveness,* McGraw-Hill Book Company, New York, 1967.

Forrester, Jay W.: *Industrial Dynamics,* The M.I.T. Press, Cambridge, Mass., and John Wiley & Sons, Inc., New York, 1961.

———: *Urban Dynamics,* The M.I.T. Press, Cambridge, Mass., 1969.

———: *World Dynamics,* Wright-Allen Press, Inc., Cambridge, Mass., 1971.

French, Wendell: *The Personnel Management Process: Human Resources Administration,* 2d ed., Houghton Mifflin Co., Boston, 1970.

——— **and Cecil H. Bell, Jr.:** *Organization Development,* Prentice-Hall, Inc., Englewood Cliffs, N.J., 1973.

Gagné, Robert M. (ed.): *Psychological Principles in System Development,* Holt, Rinehart and Winston, Inc., New York, 1962.

Galbraith, John Kenneth: *The New Industrial State,* Houghton Mifflin Company, Boston, 1967.

Gardner, John W.: *Self-renewal: The Individual and the Innovative Society,* Harper & Row, Publishers, Incorporated, New York, 1963.

Georgopoulos, Basil S., and Floyd C. Mann: *The Community General Hospital,* The Macmillan Company, New York, 1962.

Gore, William J.: *Administrative Decision-making,* John Wiley & Sons, Inc., New York, 1964.

Grinker, Roy R., Sr. (ed.): *Toward a Unified Theory of Human Behavior,* 2d ed., Basic Books, Inc., Publishers, New York, 1967.

Gross, Bertram M.: *Organizations and Their Managing,* The Free Press of Glencoe, New York, 1968.

————: *The State of the Nation: Social Systems Accounting,* Tavistock Publications, London, 1966.

Grusky, Oscar, and George A. Miller (eds.): *The Sociology of Organizations,* The Free Press, New York, 1970.

Guest, Robert H.: *Organizational Change: The Effect of Successful Leadership,* The Dorsey Press and Richard D. Irwin, Inc., Homewood, Ill., 1962.

Guth, William T., and Renato Tagiuri: "Personal Values and Corporate Strategies," *Harvard Business Review,* September–October 1965, pp. 123–132.

Haberstroh, Chadwick J.: "Control as an Organizational Process," *Management Science,* January 1960, pp. 165–171.

Hage, Jerald, and Michael Aiken: *Social Change in Complex Organizations,* Random House, New York, 1970.

Hall, Richard H.: "The Concept of Bureaucracy: An Empirical Assessment," *American Journal of Sociology,* July 1963, pp. 32–41.

————: *Organizations: Structure and Process,* Prentice-Hall, Inc., Englewood Cliffs, N.J., 1972.

Hare, Van Court, Jr.: *Systems Analysis: A Diagnostic Approach,* Harcourt, Brace & World, Inc., New York, 1967.

Harrison, Roger: "Understanding Your Organization's Character." *Harvard Business Review,* May–June 1972, pp. 119–128.

Harvey, Edward: "Technology and the Structure of Organizations," *American Sociological Review,* April 1968, pp. 247–259.

Heilbroner, Robert L.: *The Limits of American Capitalism,* Harper & Row, Publishers, Incorporated, New York, 1966.

Herzberg, Frederick: *Work and the Nature of Man,* The World Publishing Company, Cleveland, 1966.

————, **Bernard Mausner, and Barbara Snyderman:** *The Motivation to Work,* John Wiley & Sons, Inc., New York, 1959.

Hickson, D. J., D. S. Pugh, and Diana C. Pheysey, "Operations Technology and Organizational Structure: An Empirical Reappraisal," *Administrative Science Quarterly,* September 1969, pp. 378–397.

Hitch, Charles J.: *Decision-making for Defense,* University of California Press, Berkeley, Calif., 1965.

Homans, George C.: *The Human Group,* Harcourt, Brace & World, Inc., New York, 1950.

Hunt, Raymond G.: "Technology and Organization," *Academy of Management Journal,* September 1970, pp. 235–252.

Janowitz, Morris (ed.): *The New Military: Changing Patterns of Organization,* Russell Sage Foundation, New York, 1964.

Jay, Anthony: *Corporation Man,* Random House, New York, 1971.

Jencks, Christopher, and David Riesman: *The Academic Revolution,* Doubleday & Company, Inc., Garden City, N.Y., 1968.

Johnson, Richard A., Fremont E. Kast, and James E. Rosenzweig: *The Theory and Management of Systems,* 3d ed., McGraw-Hill Book Company, New York, 1973.

————, **William T. Newell, and Roger C. Vergin:** *Operations Management—A Systems Concept,* Houghton Mifflin Company, Boston, 1972.

Kahn, Alfred J.: *Theory and Practice of Social Planning,* Russell Sage Foundation, New York, 1969.

Kahn, Herman, and B. Bruce-Briggs: *Things to Come: Thinking about the Seventies and Eighties,* The Macmillan Company, New York, 1972.

Kahn, Robert L., and Elise Boulding (eds.): *Power and Conflict in Organizations,* Basic Books, Inc., Publishers, New York, 1964.

Kast, Fremont E.: ''A Dynamic Planning Model,'' *Business Horizons,* June 1968, pp. 61–68.

———— **and James E. Rosenzweig:** ''General Systems Theory: Applications for Organization and Management,'' *Academy of Management Journal,* December 1972, pp. 447–465.

———— **and** ————: ''Hospital Administration and Systems Concepts,'' *Hospital Administration,* Fall 1966, pp. 17–33.

———— **and** ———— **(eds.):** *Science, Technology, and Management,* McGraw-Hill Book Company, New York, 1963.

Katz, Daniel, and Robert L. Kahn: *The Social Psychology of Organizations,* John Wiley & Sons, Inc., New York, 1966.

Kelly, Joseph F.: *Computerized Management Information Systems,* The Macmillan Company, New York, 1970.

Kerr, Clark: *The Uses of the University,* Harvard University Press, Cambridge, Mass., 1963.

Knowles, Henry P., and Borje O. Saxberg: ''Human Relations and the Nature of Man,'' *Harvard Business Review,* March–April 1967, pp. 22–40ff.

Kohn, Melvin L.: ''Bureaucratic Man: A Portrait and an Interpretation,'' *American Sociological Review,* June 1971, pp. 461–474.

Koontz, Harold (ed.): *Toward a Unified Theory of Management,* McGraw-Hill Book Company, New York, 1964.

Kornhauser, William: *Scientists in Industry: Conflict and Accommodation,* University of California Press, Berkeley, Calif., 1962.

Kuhn, Alfred: *The Study of Society: A Unified Approach,* Richard D. Irwin, Inc., and The Dorsey Press, Homewood, Ill., 1963.

Kuhn, Thomas S.: *The Structure of Scientific Revolutions,* University of Chicago Press, Chicago, 1962.

Lawrence, Paul R., and Jay W. Lorsch: ''Differentiation and Integration in Complex Organizations,'' *Administrative Science Quarterly,* June 1967, pp. 1–47.

———— **and** ————: *Organization and Environment,* Harvard Graduate School of Business Administration, Boston, 1967.

Leavitt, Harold J.: ''Applied Organization Change in Industry: Structural, Technical, and Human Approaches,'' in W. W. Cooper, H. J. Leavitt, and M. W. Shelly, II (eds.), *New Perspectives in Organizational Research,* John Wiley & Sons, Inc., New York, 1964, pp. 55–71.

———— **and Louis R. Pondy (eds.):** *Readings in Managerial Psychology,* The University of Chicago Press, Chicago, 1964.

LeBreton, Preston P. (ed.): *Comparative Administrative Theory,* University of Washington Press, Seattle, 1968.

Levinson, Harry: *The Exceptional Executive: A Psychological Conception,* Harvard University Press, Cambridge, Mass., 1968.

————: *Organizational Diagnosis,* Harvard University Press, Cambridge, Mass., 1972.

Leys, Wayne A. R.: ''The Value Framework of Decision-making,'' in Sidney Mailick and Edward H. Van Ness (eds.), *Concepts and Issues in Administrative Behavior,* Prentice-Hall, Inc., Englewood Cliffs, N.J., 1962, pp. 81–93.

Likert, Rensis: *The Human Organization,* McGraw-Hill Book Company, New York, 1967.

————: *New Patterns of Management,* McGraw-Hill Book Company, New York, 1961.

Lindblom, Charles E.: ''The Science of 'Muddling Through,' '' in Harold J. Leavitt and Louis R. Pondy (eds.), *Readings in Managerial Psychology,* The University of Chicago Press, Chicago, 1964, pp. 61–78.

Lippit, Gordon L.: *Organizational Renewal,* Appleton-Century-Crofts, Inc., New York, 1969.

Litterer, Joseph A.: *The Analysis of Organizations,* John Wiley & Sons, Inc., New York, 1965.

Litwak, Eugene: ''Models of Bureaucracy Which Permit Conflict,'' *American Journal of Sociology,* September 1961, pp. 177-184.

Lorsch, Jay W.: ''Introduction to the Structural Design of Organizations,'' in G. W. Dalton, P. R. Lawrence, and J. W. Lorsch (eds.), *Organizational Structure and Design,* Richard D. Irwin, Inc., and The Dorsey Press, Homewood, Ill., 1970, pp. 1–16.

———— **and Paul R. Lawrence (eds.):** *Studies in Organizational Design,* Richard D. Irwin, Inc., and The Dorsey Press, Homewood, Ill., 1970.

Mack, Ruth P.: *Planning on Uncertainty,* Wiley-Interscience, New York, 1971.

————: *Management 2000,* The American Foundation for Management Research, Inc., New York, 1968.

Mann, Floyd C., and L. Richard Hoffman: *Automation and the Worker,* Holt, Rinehart and Winston, Inc., New York, 1960.

March, James G. (ed.): *Handbook of Organizations,* Rand McNally & Company, Chicago, 1965.

———— **and Herbert A. Simon:** *Organizations,* John Wiley & Sons, Inc., New York, 1958.

Martindale, Don: *Institutions, Organizations, and Mass Society,* Houghton Mifflin Company, Boston, 1966.

Maslow, Abraham H.: *Motivation and Personality,* Harper & Row, Publishers, Incorporated, New York, 1954.

————: ''A Theory of Human Motivation,'' *Psychological Review,* July 1943, pp. 370–396.

Massie, Joseph L.: ''Management Theory,'' in James G. March (ed.), *Handbook of Organizations,* Rand McNally & Company, Chicago, 1965, pp. 387–422.

Maurer, John G.: *Readings in Organization Theory: Open-Systems Approaches,* Random House, Inc., New York, 1971.

McClelland, David C.: *The Achieving Society,* D. Van Nostrand Company, Inc., Princeton, N.J., 1961.

McFeely, Wilbur M.: *Organization Change: Perceptions and Realities,* The Conference Board, Inc., New York, 1972.

McGregor, Douglas: *The Human Side of Enterprise,* McGraw-Hill Book Company, New York, 1960.

————: *The Professional Manager,* ed. by Warren G. Bennis and Caroline McGregor, McGraw-Hill Book Company, New York, 1967.

McGuire, Joseph W.: *Business and Society,* McGraw-Hill Book Company, New York, 1963.

Mechanic, David: "Sources of Power of Lower Participants in Complex Organizations," *Administrative Science Quarterly,* December 1962, pp. 349–364.

Mee, John F.: *Management Thought in a Dynamic Economy,* New York University Press, New York, 1963.

Meier, Robert C., William T. Newell, and Harold L. Pazer: *Simulation in Business and Economics,* Prentice-Hall, Inc., Englewood Cliffs, N.J., 1969.

Merton, Robert K.: *Social Theory and Social Structure,* rev. ed., The Free Press of Glencoe, New York, 1957.

Mesarovic, Mihajlo D. (ed.): *Views on General Systems Theory,* John Wiley & Sons, Inc., New York, 1964.

Mesthene, Emmanuel G.: *Technological Change: Its Impact on Man and Society,* The New American Library, Inc., New York, 1970.

Miller, David W., and Martin K. Starr: *Executive Decisions and Operations Research,* 2d ed., Prentice-Hall, Inc., Englewood Cliffs, N.J., 1969.

———— and————: *The Structure of Human Decisions,* Prentice-Hall, Inc., Englewood Cliffs, N.J., 1967.

Miller, E. J., and A. K. Rice: *Systems of Organization,* Tavistock Publications, London, 1967.

Miller, Ernest C.: *Advanced Techniques for Strategic Planning,* American Management Association, Inc., New York, 1971.

Miller, George A.: "Professionals in Bureaucracy: Alienation among Industrial Scientists and Engineers," *American Sociological Review,* October 1967, pp. 755–768.

Miller, George A., Eugene Galanter, and Karl H. Pribram: *Plans and the Structure of Behavior,* Holt, Rinehart and Winston, Inc., New York, 1960.

Miller, James G.: "Living Systems: The Group," *Behavioral Science,* July 1971, pp. 302–398.

————: "The Nature of Living Systems," *Behavioral Science,* July 1971, pp. 277–301.

Millett, John D.: *The Academic Community: An Essay on Organization,* McGraw-Hill Book Company, New York, 1962.

Mohr, Lawrence B.: "Organizational Technology and Organizational Structure," *Administrative Science Quarterly,* December 1971, pp. 444–459.

Monsen, R. Joseph, Jr.: *Modern American Capitalism: Ideologies and Issues,* Houghton Mifflin Company, Boston, 1963.

Morison, Robert S.: "Some Aspects of Policy-Making in the American University," *Daedalus,* Summer 1970, pp. 609–644.

Morris, William T.: "On the Art of Modeling," *Management Science,* August 1967, pp. B-707–717.

Morse, John J.: "Organizational Characteristics and Individual Motivation," in Jay W. Lorsch and P. R. Lawrence (eds.), *Studies in Organization Design,* Richard D. Irwin, Inc., and The Dorsey Press, Homewood, Ill., 1970, pp. 84–100.

Mouzelis, Nicos P.: *Organization and Bureaucracy,* Aldine Publishing Company, Chicago, 1968.

Mumford, Lewis: *The Myth of the Machine,* Harcourt, Brace & World, Inc., New York, 1967.

Negandhi, Anant R. (ed.): *Environmental Settings in Organizational Functioning,* Comparative Administration Research Institute, Kent State University, Kent, Ohio, 1970.

Newman, William H.: "Strategy and Management Structure," *Journal of Business Policy,* Winter 1971/1972, pp. 56–66.

Nugent, Christopher E., and Thomas E. Vollmann: "A Framework for the System Design Process," *Decision Sciences,* January 1972, pp. 83–109.

Pareto, Vilfredo, *The Mind and Society,* Arthur Livingston (ed.), Harcourt, Brace & World, Inc., New York, 1935.

Parsons, Talcott: *The Social System,* The Free Press of Glencoe, New York, 1951.

———: *Structure and Process in Modern Societies,* The Free Press of Glencoe, New York, 1960.

Perrow, Charles: "A Framework for the Comparative Analysis of Organizations," *American Sociological Review,* April 1967, pp. 194–208.

———: *Organizational Analysis: A Sociological View,* Wadsworth Publishing Company, Inc., Belmont, Calif., 1970.

The Planning-Programming-Budgeting System: Progress and Potentials, Report of the Subcommittee on Economy in Government of the Joint Economic Committee, 90th Cong., 1st Sess., December 1967.

Porter, Lyman W., and Edward E. Lawler, III: *Managerial Attitudes and Performance,* Richard D. Irwin, Inc., Homewood, Ill., 1968.

Presthus, Robert: *The Organizational Society,* Alfred A. Knopf, Inc., New York, 1962.

Price, James L.: *Organizational Effectiveness: An Inventory of Propositions,* Richard D. Irwin, Inc., Homewood, Ill., 1968.

Pugh, Derek S., D. J. Hickson, and C. R. Hinings: "An Empirical Taxonomy of Structure of Work Organizations," *Administrative Science Quarterly,* March 1969, pp. 115–126.

Raiffa, Howard, and Robert Schlaifer: *Applied Statistical Decision Theory,* Division of Research, Graduate School of Business Administration, Harvard University, Boston, 1961.

Rakich, Jonathan S. (ed.): *Hospital Organization and Management,* The Catholic Hospital Association, St. Louis, Mo., 1972.

Rice, A. K.: *The Enterprise and Its Environment,* Tavistock Publications, London, 1963.

Roethlisberger, Fritz J., and William J. Dickson: *Management and the Worker,* Harvard University Press, Cambridge, Mass., 1939.

Roman, Daniel D.: *Research and Development Management: The Economics and Administration of Technology,* Appleton-Century-Crofts, Inc., New York, 1968.

Rosenzweig, James E.: "Managers and Management Scientists: Two Cultures," *Business Horizons,* Fall 1967, pp. 79–86.

Rourke, Francis E., and Glenn E. Brooks: *The Managerial Revolution in Higher Education,* The Johns Hopkins Press, Baltimore, 1966.

Rubenstein, Albert H., and Chadwick J. Haberstroh (eds.): *Some Theories of Organization,* rev. ed., Richard D. Irwin, Inc., and The Dorsey Press, Homewood, Ill., 1966.

Rush, Harold M. F.: *Behavioral Science: Concepts and Managerial Applications,* The Conference Board, Inc., New York, 1969.

————: *Job Design for Motivation,* The Conference Board, Inc., New York, 1971.

Rushing, William A.: "The Effects of Industry Size and Division of Labor on Administration," *Administrative Science Quarterly,* September 1967, pp. 273-295.

Sayles, Leonard R.: *Managerial Behavior,* McGraw-Hill Book Company, New York, 1964.

———— **and Margaret K. Chandler:** *Managing Large Systems,* Harper & Row, Publishers, Inc., New York, 1971.

Schein, Edgar H.: *Organizational Psychology,* 2d ed., Prentice-Hall, Inc., Englewood Cliffs, N.J., 1970.

Schoderbek, Peter P. (ed.): *Management Systems,* 2d ed., John Wiley & Sons, Inc., New York, 1971.

Schrieber, Albert N. (ed.): *Corporation Simulation Models,* Graduate School of Business Administration, University of Washington, Seattle, 1970.

Scott, William G., and Terence R. Mitchell: *Organization Theory,* rev. ed., Richard D. Irwin, Inc., Homewood, Ill., 1972.

Seiler, John A.: *Systems Analysis in Organizational Behavior,* Richard D. Irwin, Inc., and The Dorsey Press, Homewood, Ill., 1967.

Selznick, Philip: *Leadership in Administration,* Harper & Row, Publishers, Incorporated, New York, 1957.

Shepard, Jon M.: *Automation and Alienation—A Study of Office and Factory Workers,* The M.I.T. Press, Cambridge, Mass., 1971.

Silverman, David: *The Theory of Organizations,* Basic Books, Inc., New York, 1971.

Simon, Herbert A.: *Administrative Behavior,* 2d ed., The Macmillan Company, New York, 1959.

————: *The Shape of Automation for Men and Management,* Harper Torchbooks, Harper & Row, Publishers, Incorporated, New York, 1965.

Skinner, B. F.: *Beyond Freedom and Dignity,* Alfred A. Knopf, Inc., New York, 1971.

Social Responsibilities of Business Corporations, A Statement by the Research and Policy Committee, Committee for Economic Development, New York, June 1971.

Starr, Martin K.: *Management: A Modern Approach,* Harcourt Brace Jovanovich, Inc., New York, 1971.

Steiner, Gary A. (ed.): *The Creative Organization,* The University of Chicago Press, Chicago, 1965.

Steiner, George A.: *Business and Society,* Random House, Inc., New York, 1971.

————: *Top Management Planning,* The Macmillan Company, New York, 1969.

———— **and William G. Ryan:** *Industrial Project Management,* The Macmillan Company, New York, 1968.

Stinchcombe, Arthur L.: "Social Structure and Organizations," in James G. March (ed.), *Handbook of Organizations,* Rand McNally & Company, Chicago, 1965, pp. 142-193.

Strauss, George: "Tactics of Lateral Relationship: The Purchasing Agent," *Administrative Science Quarterly,* September 1962, pp. 161-186.

Sutermeister, Robert A.: *People and Productivity,* 2d ed., McGraw-Hill Book Company, New York, 1969.

Tannenbaum, Arnold: *Control in Organizations,* McGraw-Hill Book Company, New York, 1968.

Tannenbaum, Robert, and Warren H. Schmidt: "How to Choose a Leadership Pattern," *Harvard Business Review,* March–April 1958, pp. 95–101.

Tawney, R. H.: *Religion and the Rise of Capitalism,* Harcourt, Brace & World, Inc., New York, 1926.

Terreberry, Shirley: "The Evolution of Organizational Environments," *Administrative Science Quarterly,* March 1968, pp. 590–613.

Thompson, James D. (ed.): *Approaches to Organizational Design,* The University of Pittsburgh Press, Pittsburgh, Pa., 1966.

————: *Organizations in Action,* McGraw-Hill Book Company, New York, 1967.

Thompson, Victor A.: "Bureaucracy and Innovation," *Administrative Science Quarterly,* June 1965, pp. 1–20.

Toffler, Alvin: *Future Shock,* Random House, Inc., New York, 1970.

Trow, Martin: "Reflections on the Transition from Mass to Universal Higher Education," *Daedalus,* Winter 1970, pp. 1–42.

Udy, Stanley H., Jr.: "The Comparative Analysis of Organizations," in James G. March (ed.), *Handbook of Organizations,* Rand McNally & Company, Chicago, 1965, pp. 678–709.

Vollmer, Howard M., and Donald L. Mills (eds.): *Professionalization,* Prentice-Hall, Inc., Englewood Cliffs, N.J., 1966.

von Bertalanffy, Ludwig: *General System Theory,* George Braziller, New York, 1968.

Vroom, V. H.: *Work and Motivation,* John Wiley & Sons, Inc., New York, 1964.

Wagner, Harvey M.: *Principles of Management Science,* Prentice-Hall, Inc., Englewood Cliffs, N.J., 1970.

Walker, Charles R. (ed.): *Technology, Industry, and Man,* McGraw-Hill Book Company, New York, 1968.

Warner, W. Lloyd (ed.): *The Emergent American Society,* Yale University Press, New Haven, Conn., 1967, vol. 1.

Warren, E. Kirby: *Long-range Planning: The Executive Viewpoint,* Prentice-Hall, Inc., Englewood Cliffs, N.J., 1966.

Ways, Max: "More Power to Everybody," *Fortune,* May 1970.

Webb, James E.: *Space Age Management,* McGraw-Hill Book Company, New York, 1969.

Weber, Max: *The Protestant Ethic and the Spirit of Capitalism,* Talcott Parsons (trans.), Charles Scribner's Sons, New York, 1958.

————: *The Theory of Social and Economic Organization,* A. M. Henderson and Talcott Parsons (trans.), The Free Press of Glencoe, New York, 1964.

Whisler, Thomas L.: *Information Technology and Organizational Change,* Wadsworth Publishing Company, Inc., Belmont, Calif., 1970.

Wiener, Norbert: *The Human Use of Human Beings,* rev. ed., Houghton Mifflin Company, Boston, 1954.

Wikstrom, Walter S.: *Managing by—and with—Objectives,* The Conference Board, Inc., New York, 1968.

Wilensky, Harold L.: *Organizational Intelligence,* Basic Books, Inc., Publishers, New York, 1967.

Woodward, Joan: *Industrial Organization: Theory and Practice,* Oxford University Press, Fair Lawn, N.J., 1965.

Wren, George R.: "The Sociology of the General Hospital: A Structural-Functional Consideration," *Hospital Administration,* Fall 1966, pp. 44–59.

Yarmolinsky, Adam: *The Military Establishment,* Harper & Row, Publishers, Inc., New York, 1971.

Yuchtman, Ephraim, and Stanley E. Seashore: "A System Resource Approach to Organizational Effectiveness," *American Sociological Review,* December 1967, pp. 891–903.

NAME INDEX

SUBJECT INDEX